GLEIM®

2021 Q3-Q4 EDITION

CPA REVIEW

REGULATION

by

Irvin N. Gleim, Ph.D., CPA, CIA, CMA, CFM

Gleim Publications, Inc.
PO Box 12848
Gainesville, Florida 32604
(800) 87-GLEIM or (800) 874-5346
(352) 375-0772
www.gleim.com/cpa
CPA@gleim.com

> For updates to this 2021 Q3-Q4 edition of
> **CPA Review: Regulation**
>
> **Go To:** www.gleim.com/CPAupdate
>
> **Or:** Email update@gleim.com with **CPA REG 2021 Q3-Q4** in the subject line. You will receive our current update as a reply.
>
> Updates are available until the next edition is published.

ISSN: 1547-8092

ISBN: 978-1-61854-430-8 *CPA Review: Auditing and Attestation*
ISBN: 978-1-61854-431-5 *CPA Review: Business Environment and Concepts*
ISBN: 978-1-61854-432-2 *CPA Review: Financial Accounting and Reporting*
ISBN: 978-1-61854-433-9 *CPA Review: Regulation*
ISBN: 978-1-61854-394-3 *CPA Exam Guide: A System for Success*

This edition is copyright © 2021 by Gleim Publications, Inc. Portions of this manuscript are taken from previous editions copyright © 1994-2020 by Gleim Publications, Inc.

First Printing: April 2021

ALL RIGHTS RESERVED. No part of this material may be reproduced in any form whatsoever without express written permission from Gleim Publications, Inc. Reward is offered for information exposing violators. Contact copyright@gleim.com.

ACKNOWLEDGMENTS

Material from *Uniform CPA Examination, Selected Questions and Unofficial Answers*, Copyright © 1974-2021 by the American Institute of Certified Public Accountants, Inc., is reprinted and/or adapted with permission. Visit the AICPA's website at www.aicpa.org for more information.

The author is indebted to the Institute of Certified Management Accountants for permission to use problem materials from past CMA Examinations. Questions and unofficial answers from the Certified Management Accountant Examinations, copyright by the Institute of Certified Management Accountants, are reprinted and/or adapted with permission.

> **Environmental Statement** -- This book is printed on recycled paper sourced from suppliers certified using sustainable forestry management processes and is produced either TCF (Totally Chlorine-Free) or ECF (Elementally Chlorine-Free).

The publications and online services of Gleim Publications and Gleim Internet are designed to provide accurate and authoritative information with regard to the subject matter covered. They are sold with the understanding that Gleim Publications and Gleim Internet, and their respective licensors, are not engaged in rendering legal, accounting, tax, or other professional advice or services. If legal advice or other expert assistance is required, the services of a competent professional person should be sought.

You assume all responsibilities and obligations with respect to the selection of the particular publication or online services to achieve your intended results. You assume all responsibilities and obligations with respect to any decisions or advice made or given as a result of the use or application of your selected publication or online services or any content retrieved therefrom, including those to any third party, for the content, accuracy, and review of such results.

The events, persons, and locations depicted in this book are fictional and not intended to portray, resemble, or represent any actual events or places, or persons, living or dead. Any such resemblance or similarity is entirely coincidental.

ABOUT THE AUTHOR

Irvin N. Gleim is Professor Emeritus in the Fisher School of Accounting at the University of Florida and is a member of the American Accounting Association, Academy of Legal Studies in Business, American Institute of Certified Public Accountants, Association of Government Accountants, Florida Institute of Certified Public Accountants, The Institute of Internal Auditors, and the Institute of Management Accountants. He has had articles published in the *Journal of Accountancy*, *The Accounting Review*, and the *American Business Law Journal* and is author/coauthor of numerous accounting books, aviation books, and CPE courses.

A PERSONAL THANKS

This manual would not have been possible without the extraordinary effort and dedication of Jacob Bennett, Julie Cutlip, Ethan Good, Doug Green, Fernanda Martinez, Bree Rodriguez, Veronica Rodriguez, Teresa Soard, Justin Stephenson, Joanne Strong, Elmer Tucker, Candace Van Doren, and Ryan Van Tress, who typed the entire manuscript and all revisions and drafted and laid out the diagrams, illustrations, and cover for this book.

The author also appreciates the production and editorial assistance of Sirene Dagher, Michaela Giampaolo, Jessica Hatker, Sonora Hospital-Medina, Katie Larson, Michael Lupi, Bryce Owen, Shane Rapp, Michael Tamayo, Alyssa Thomas, and Valerie Wendt.

The author also appreciates the critical reading assistance of Ali Band, Corey Connell, Adrianna Cuevas, Kimberly Haft, Nicola Martens, Martin Salazar, and Maris Silvestri.

The author also appreciates the video production expertise of Nancy Boyd, Gary Brook, Philip Brubaker, Matthew Church, Andrew Johnson, and Michaela Wallace, who helped produce and edit our Gleim Instruct Video Series.

Finally, we appreciate the encouragement, support, and tolerance of our families throughout this project.

REVIEWERS AND CONTRIBUTORS

Garrett W. Gleim, CPA, CGMA, leads production of the Gleim CPA, CMA, CIA, and EA exam review systems. He is a member of the American Institute of Certified Public Accountants and the Florida Institute of Certified Public Accountants and holds a Bachelor of Science in Economics with a Concentration in Accounting from The Wharton School, University of Pennsylvania. Mr. Gleim is coauthor of numerous accounting and aviation books and the inventor of multiple patents with educational applications. He is also an avid pilot who holds a commercial pilot rating and is a certified flight instructor. In addition, as an active supporter of the local business community, Mr. Gleim serves as an advisor to several start-ups.

Lorie M. Gleim, B.S., B.A., J.D., graduated from The Wharton School and the College of Arts and Sciences at the University of Pennsylvania. She went on to receive a Juris Doctor with honors from the University of Florida College of Law. Ms. Gleim practiced complex commercial business litigation for over 22 years at Greenberg Traurig. She is the CEO of Gleim Publications and provided significant editorial assistance for the law content in Regulation.

The following experts provided subtantial editorial assistance throughout the project:

Matthew Hutchens, J.D., CPA, EA, is a Lecturer of Accountancy at the University of Illinois Gies College of Business. Prior to joining the University of Illinois, he was a Staff Attorney at a Low Income Taxpayer Clinic and a Senior Staff Accountant in the National Tax Office of Crowe LLP. He received a law degree from the Indiana University Maurer School of Law and a bachelor's degree in Accounting and Finance from the Indiana University Kelley School of Business.

Grady M. Irwin, J.D., is a graduate of the University of Florida College of Law, and he has taught in the University of Florida College of Business.

D. Scott Lawton, B.S., is a graduate of Brigham Young University-Idaho and Utah Valley University. He has worked as an auditor for the Utah State Tax Commission.

Lung-Chih Lin, M.S. Acc., received a Master of Science in Accountancy with a concentration in Data Analytics from the University of Illinois at Urbana-Champaign.

Sabrina Lopez Little, J.D., M.S.Ed., is a graduate of the University of Florida Levin College of Law, where she is currently a Visiting Legal Skills Professor of Legal Writing. She practiced law for 10 years with Greenberg Traurig, specializing in real estate and condominium law. Ms. Little is one of the CPA Gleim Instruct lecturers.

LouAnn M. Lutter, M.S. Acc., CPA, received a Master of Science in Accounting from the University of Colorado, Boulder. Previously, she was an Accounting Manager in Corporate Accounting and Shared Business Services at Caesars Entertainment.

Mark S. Modas, M.S.T., CPA, holds a Bachelor of Arts in Accounting from Florida Atlantic University and a Master of Science in Taxation from Nova Southeastern University. Prior to joining Gleim, he worked in internal auditing, accounting and financial reporting, and corporate tax compliance in the public and private sectors.

Nate Wadlinger, J.D., LL.M., CPA, EA, is a Lecturer of Taxation at Florida State University, where he teaches tax courses in the Bachelor and Master of Accounting programs. Mr. Wadlinger received his Bachelor of Science in Accounting, Master of Accounting, and Juris Doctor from the University of Florida and his LL.M. in Taxation from Boston University. In addition, he is an EA, a CPA licensed by the State of Florida, and a member of the Florida Bar. Mr. Wadlinger is the EA Gleim Instruct lecturer.

Luke Watson, Ph.D., CPA, is an Assistant Professor of Accounting at Drexel University. Dr. Watson is one of the CPA Gleim Instruct lecturers.

Chun Nam Wo, M.S. Acc., CPA, received a Master of Science in Accountancy with a concentration in Data Analytics from the University of Illinois at Urbana-Champaign.

ACCOUNTING TITLES FROM GLEIM PUBLICATIONS

CPA Review:
- Auditing & Attestation (AUD)
- Business Environment & Concepts (BEC)
- Financial Accounting & Reporting (FAR)
- Regulation (REG)

CMA Review:
- Part 1: Financial Planning, Performance, and Analytics
- Part 2: Strategic Financial Management

CIA Review:
- Part 1: Essentials of Internal Auditing
- Part 2: Practice of Internal Auditing
- Part 3: Business Knowledge for Internal Auditing

EA Review:
- Part 1: Individuals
- Part 2: Businesses
- Part 3: Representation, Practices and Procedures

Exam Questions and Explanations (EQE) Series:
- Auditing & Systems
- Business Law & Legal Studies
- Cost/Managerial Accounting
- Federal Tax
- Financial Accounting

Gleim Publications also publishes aviation training materials. Go to www.GleimAviation.com for a complete listing of our aviation titles.

TABLE OF CONTENTS

	Page
Detailed Table of Contents	viii
A Message from Our Author	x
Optimizing Your Regulation Score	1
Study Unit 1. Ethics and Professional Responsibilities	11
Study Unit 2. Liability of CPAs	29
Study Unit 3. Federal Tax Authority, Procedures, and Individual Taxation	47
Study Unit 4. Gross Income and Exclusions	79
Study Unit 5. Accounting Methods and Special Entities	109
Study Unit 6. Self-Employment	133
Study Unit 7. Adjustments and Deductions from AGI	159
Study Unit 8. Credits and Losses	195
Study Unit 9. Property Transactions: Basis and Gains	223
Study Unit 10. Property Transactions: Special Topics	261
Study Unit 11. Corporate Taxable Income	295
Study Unit 12. Corporate Tax Computations	327
Study Unit 13. Corporate Tax Special Topics	357
Study Unit 14. S Corporations	389
Study Unit 15. Partnerships: Formation and Income	415
Study Unit 16. Partnership Transactions and Book-to-Tax Differences	439
Study Unit 17. Business Organizations	467
Study Unit 18. Contracts	499
Study Unit 19. Agency and Regulation	531
Study Unit 20. Secured Transactions and Debtor-Creditor Relationships	561
Appendix A: Optimizing Your Score on the Task-Based Simulations (TBSs)	595
Appendix B: AICPA Uniform CPA Examination REG Blueprint with Gleim Cross-References	623
Index	641

DETAILED TABLE OF CONTENTS

	Page
Study Unit 1. Ethics and Professional Responsibilities	
1.1. Practitioners	11
1.2. Tax Return Preparers	16
Study Unit 2. Liability of CPAs	
2.1. Licensing and Disciplinary Systems	29
2.2. State Law Liability to Clients and Third Parties	31
2.3. Privileged Communication and Confidentiality	35
Study Unit 3. Federal Tax Authority, Procedures, and Individual Taxation	
3.1. Tax Authority	48
3.2. Tax Procedures	52
3.3. Tax Planning	62
3.4. Filing Status	65
3.5. Dependents	68
Study Unit 4. Gross Income and Exclusions	
4.1. Gross Income	80
4.2. Exclusions	94
Study Unit 5. Accounting Methods and Special Entities	
5.1. Accounting Methods	109
5.2. Exempt Organizations	119
5.3. Trusts	122
Study Unit 6. Self-Employment	
6.1. Business Income and Expenses	135
6.2. FICA and FUTA Taxes	144
6.3. Employee Benefits	147
Study Unit 7. Adjustments and Deductions from AGI	
7.1. Above-the-Line Deductions	160
7.2. Standard and Itemized Deductions	166
7.3. Qualified Business Income Deduction (QBID)	179
Study Unit 8. Credits and Losses	
8.1. Tax Credits	195
8.2. Losses and Limits	206
Study Unit 9. Property Transactions: Basis and Gains	
9.1. Basis	224
9.2. Depreciation and Amortization	233
9.3. Capital Gains and Losses	244
Study Unit 10. Property Transactions: Special Topics	
10.1. Related Party Sales	262
10.2. Installment Sales	264
10.3. Nonrecognition Transactions	267
10.4. Business Property Recharacterization	275
10.5. Gift Tax	283
Study Unit 11. Corporate Taxable Income	
11.1. Definition and Accounting	296
11.2. Formation	298
11.3. Gross Income of a Corporation	302
11.4. Deductions of a Corporation	303
11.5. Losses of a Corporation	316

	Page
Study Unit 12. Corporate Tax Computations	
12.1. Regular Income Tax and Credits	328
12.2. Consolidated Returns	330
12.3. Controlled Groups	333
12.4. Estimated Tax	336
12.5. Earnings and Profits	338
12.6. Distributions	339
12.7. Accumulated Earnings Tax (AET)	345
12.8. Personal Holding Company (PHC) Tax	347
Study Unit 13. Corporate Tax Special Topics	
13.1. Redemptions	357
13.2. Complete Liquidation	361
13.3. Partial Liquidation	363
13.4. Subsidiary Liquidation	364
13.5. Reorganizations	365
13.6. Multiple Jurisdictions	368
Study Unit 14. S Corporations	
14.1. Eligibility and Election	390
14.2. Operations	394
14.3. Distributions	402
14.4. Special Taxes	405
Study Unit 15. Partnerships: Formation and Income	
15.1. Partnership Formation and Tax Year	416
15.2. Partner's Taxable Income	421
Study Unit 16. Partnership Transactions and Book-to-Tax Differences	
16.1. Partners Dealing with Own Partnership	440
16.2. Treatment of Partnership Liabilities	443
16.3. Distribution of Partnership Assets	445
16.4. Reconciling Book and Taxable Income	451
Study Unit 17. Business Organizations	
17.1. General Partnerships	467
17.2. Limited Partnerships	474
17.3. Limited Liability Companies (LLCs)	476
17.4. Corporate Formation	479
17.5. Corporate Operation, Financing, and Distributions	481
17.6. Shareholders' Rights	483
17.7. Directors and Officers: Authority, Duties, and Liability	484
17.8. Mergers and Termination	487
17.9. Advantages and Disadvantages of Corporations	488
Study Unit 18. Contracts	
18.1. Nature and Classification of Contracts	499
18.2. Mutual Assent (Offer and Acceptance)	501
18.3. Consideration	504
18.4. Capacity	506
18.5. Legality	507
18.6. Lack of Genuine Assent	508
18.7. Statute of Frauds	510
18.8. Parol Evidence Rule	512
18.9. Performance, Discharge, and Breach	513
18.10. Remedies	516
18.11. Contract Beneficiaries	517
18.12. Assignment and Delegation	518

Detailed Table of Contents

	Page
Study Unit 19. Agency and Regulation	
19.1. Agency Formation	532
19.2. Agent's Authority and Duties	535
19.3. Principal's Duties and Liabilities	539
19.4. Agency Termination	545
19.5. Employment Tax	547
19.6. Qualified Health Plans	549
Study Unit 20. Secured Transactions and Debtor-Creditor Relationships	
20.1. Security Interests and Attachment	561
20.2. Perfection of Security Interests	564
20.3. Priorities	568
20.4. Rights and Duties of Debtors, Creditors, and Third Parties	572
20.5. Bankruptcy Administration	575
20.6. Bankruptcy Liquidations	579
20.7. Reorganizations	583

A MESSAGE FROM OUR AUTHOR

Welcome to the 2021 Q3-Q4 Edition of Gleim CPA Review! The purpose of this book is to facilitate your preparation to pass the Regulation (REG) section of the CPA Exam. It reflects relevant business law, ethical, and federal tax laws through December 2020.

The CPA Exam is continuously changed in order to maintain its relevance and prestige in the world of accounting. As technology develops, accountants and auditors face new and increasingly complex challenges, which are reflected in the AICPA Blueprints. Our team of accounting experts ensures our materials are always up-to-date, so regardless of when you're preparing for the CPA Exam with Gleim, you have everything you need to succeed.

Our goal is to provide a comprehensive, effective, affordable, and easy-to-use study program. Our course

1. Explains how to maximize your score through learning strategies and exam-taking techniques.
2. Outlines all of the content topics described in the AICPA REG Blueprint and tested on the REG section of the exam in 20 easy-to-use study units.
3. Presents multiple-choice questions taken or modeled from CPA Examinations to prepare you for the types of questions you will find on your CPA Exam.
    a. In our book, the answer explanations are presented to the immediate right of each multiple-choice question for your convenience. Use a piece of paper to cover our detailed explanations as you answer the question and then review all answer choices to learn why the correct one is correct and why the other choices are incorrect.
    b. You also should practice answering these questions through our online platform, which mimics Prometric's user interface, so you are comfortable answering questions online like you will do on test day. Our adaptive course will focus and target your weak areas.
4. Contains an appendix explaining the different types of Task-Based Simulations (TBSs) and how to get the most points possible on the TBS testlets.

The outline format, spacing, and question and answer formats in this book are designed to increase readability, learning, understanding, and success on the CPA Exam. Our most successful candidates use the Gleim Premium CPA Review System, which includes Gleim Instruct videos; our Access Until You Pass Guarantee; our innovative SmartAdapt technology; expertly authored books; the largest test bank of multiple-choice questions and simulations; audio lectures; flashcards; and the support of our team of accounting experts.

Since the release of our first CPA Review book in 1974, Gleim has helped candidates pass more than 1 million CPA Exams with our study materials and recommended learning techniques. With our cutting-edge adaptive technology creating personalized learning paths, we will help candidates pass millions more. Candidates' success is based on the Gleim system of teaching not only the topics tested, but also what you can expect on exam day. We want you to feel confident and in control when you sit for the exam.

We want your feedback immediately after you take the exam and receive your exam score. Please go to www.gleim.com/feedbackREG to share suggestions on how we can improve this edition. The CPA Exam is a **nondisclosed** exam, which means you must maintain the confidentiality of the exam by not divulging the nature or content of any CPA question or answer under any circumstances. We ask only for information about our materials and any improvements that can be made regarding topics that need to be added or expanded or need more emphasis. Our approach has AICPA approval.

Good Luck on the Exam,

– *Dr. Irvin N. Gleim*

April 2021

OPTIMIZING YOUR REGULATION SCORE

Uniform CPA Examination	*1*
Gleim Premium CPA Review with SmartAdapt	*2*
Subject Matter for Regulation	*3*
Which Laws, Rules, and Pronouncements Are Tested?	*4*
AICPA's Nondisclosure Agreement	*5*
Gleim CPA Review Essentials	*6*
Time Budgeting and Question-Answering Techniques for REG	*7*
How to Be in Control	*9*
Questions about Gleim Materials	*9*
Feedback	*9*

UNIFORM CPA EXAMINATION

CPA Exam Section	Auditing & Attestation	Business Environment & Concepts	Financial Accounting & Reporting	**Regulation**
Acronym	AUD	BEC	FAR	**REG**
Exam Length	4 hours	4 hours	4 hours	**4 hours**
Testlet 1: Multiple-Choice	36 questions	31 questions	33 questions	**38 questions**
Testlet 2: Multiple-Choice	36 questions	31 questions	33 questions	**38 questions**
Testlet 3: Task-Based Simulations	2 tasks	2 tasks	2 tasks	**2 tasks**
Standardized Break	Clock stops for 15 minutes			
Testlet 4: Task-Based Simulations	3 tasks	2 tasks	3 tasks	**3 tasks**
Testlet 5: Task-Based Simulations or Written Communications	3 tasks	3 written communications	3 tasks	**3 tasks**

Passing the CPA Exam is a serious undertaking. Begin by becoming an expert in the content, formatting, and functionality of the REG exam before you take it. The objective is no surprises on exam day. Also, you will save time and money, decrease frustration, and increase your probability of success by learning all you can about how to prepare for and take REG.

Review *CPA Exam Guide: A System for Success* at www.gleim.com/PassCPA for a complete explanation of how to prepare for and take each section of the CPA Exam. This free guide includes all of the basic information, test-taking techniques, and time management strategies you need.

More exam tactics and information, as well as breaking news and updates from the AICPA and NASBA, are available in our Resource Center at www.gleim.com/CPAresources and on our blog at www.gleim.com/CPAblog. Follow us on all your favorite social media networks for blog updates and other critical information.

CPA Exam Pass Rates

	Percentage of Candidates		
	2018	2019	2020
AUD	52	51	53
BEC	58	60	66
FAR	45	46	50
REG	53	56	62

The implication of these pass rates for you as a CPA candidate is that you have to be, on average, in the top 50% of all candidates to pass. The major difference between CPA candidates who pass and those who do not is their preparation program. You have access to the best CPA review material; it is up to you to use it. Even if you are enrolled in a review course that uses other materials, you will benefit with the Gleim Premium CPA Review System.

GLEIM PREMIUM CPA REVIEW WITH SMARTADAPT

Gleim Premium CPA Review features the most comprehensive coverage of exam content and employs the most efficient learning techniques to help you study smarter and more effectively. The Gleim Premium CPA Review System is powered by SmartAdapt technology, an innovative platform that continually zeros in on areas you should focus on when you move through the following steps for optimized CPA review:

Step 1:

Complete a diagnostic study session. Your results set a baseline that our SmartAdapt technology will use to create a custom learning track.

Step 2:

Solidify your knowledge by studying the suggested Knowledge Transfer Outline(s) or watching the suggested Gleim Instruct video(s).

Step 3:

Focus on weak areas and perfect your question-answering techniques by taking the adaptive quizzes and simulations that SmartAdapt directs you to.

Final Review:

After completing all study units, take the first Exam Rehearsal. Then, SmartAdapt will walk you through a Final Review based on your results. Finally, a few days before your exam date, take the second Exam Rehearsal so you feel confident that you are ready to pass.

To facilitate your studies, the Gleim Premium CPA Review System uses the most comprehensive test bank of exam-quality CPA questions on the market. Our system's content and presentation are the most realistic representation of the whole exam environment so you feel completely at ease on test day.

Learning from Your Mistakes

One of the main building blocks of the Gleim studying system is that learning from questions you answer incorrectly is very important. Each question you answer incorrectly is an **opportunity** to avoid missing actual test questions on your CPA Exam. Thus, you should carefully study the answer explanations provided so you understand why the original answer you chose is wrong as well as why the correct answer indicated is correct. This learning technique is the difference between passing and failing for many CPA candidates.

The Gleim Premium CPA Review System has built-in functionality for this step. After each quiz and simulation you complete, the Gleim system directs you to study why you answered questions incorrectly so you can learn how to avoid making the same errors in the future. Reasons for answering questions incorrectly include

1. Misreading the requirement (stem)
2. Not understanding what is required
3. Making a math error
4. Applying the wrong rule or concept
5. Being distracted by one or more of the answers
6. Incorrectly eliminating answers from consideration
7. Not having any knowledge of the topic tested
8. Using a poor educated-guessing strategy

SUBJECT MATTER FOR REGULATION

Below, we have provided the AICPA's major content areas from the Blueprint for Regulation (REG). The averaged percentage of coverage for each topic is indicated.

I. (15%) Ethics, Professional Responsibilities, and Federal Tax Procedures
II. (15%) Business Law
III. (17%) Federal Taxation of Property Transactions
IV. (20%) Federal Taxation of Individuals
V. (33%) Federal Taxation of Entities

Appendix B contains the Blueprint for REG with cross-references to the study units in our materials where topics are covered. Remember that we have studied and restudied the Blueprint and explain the subject matter thoroughly in our CPA Review. Accordingly, you do not need to spend time with Appendix B. Rather, it should give you confidence that Gleim CPA Review is the best review available to help you PASS the CPA Exam.

Candidates are expected to demonstrate knowledge and skills related to

- Federal taxation,
- Ethics and professional responsibilities related to tax practice, and
- Business law.

The following general topics will be tested:

- Ethics and responsibilities in tax practice
- Licensing and disciplinary systems

- Federal tax procedures
  - Income taxation
    - ☐ Property transactions
    - ☐ Gift taxation
    - ☐ Tax preparation and planning for individuals
    - ☐ Tax preparation and planning for entities, including sole proprietorships, partnerships, limited liability companies, C corporations, S corporations, joint ventures, trusts, and tax-exempt organizations
- Legal duties and responsibilities
- Business law
  - Legal implications of business transactions
  - Agency, contracts, debtor-creditor relationships, government regulation of business, and business structure
  - Federal and widely adopted uniform state laws

WHICH LAWS, RULES, AND PRONOUNCEMENTS ARE TESTED?

The following is the AICPA's pronouncement policy:

Changes in accounting and auditing pronouncements are eligible to be tested on the Uniform CPA Examination in the later of: (1) the first calendar quarter beginning after the pronouncement's earliest mandatory effective date, regardless of entity type* or (2) the first calendar quarter beginning six (6) months after the pronouncement's issuance date.

Changes in the Internal Revenue Code, and federal taxation regulations are eligible to be tested in the calendar quarter beginning six (6) months after the change's effective date or enactment date, whichever is later.

Changes in federal laws outside the area of federal taxation are eligible to be tested in the calendar quarter beginning six (6) months after their effective date.

Changes in uniform acts are eligible to be tested in the calendar quarter beginning one (1) year after their adoption by a simple majority of the jurisdictions.

For all other subjects covered in the Uniform CPA Examination, changes are eligible to be tested in the later of: (1) the first calendar quarter beginning after the earliest mandatory effective date, regardless of entity type* or (2) six (6) months after the issuance date.

Once a change becomes eligible for testing in the Uniform CPA Examination, previous content impacted by the change is removed. [This simply means that once a new pronouncement is testable, you will no longer be tested on the old pronouncement.]

* Note the following example: A pronouncement issued on February 1, 2020, is effective for public business entities for fiscal years beginning after December 15, 2020, and is effective for all other entities for fiscal years beginning after December 15, 2021. For purposes of the Uniform CPA Examination: (1) the pronouncement is eligible for testing on January 1, 2021 for all entity types and (2) the prior pronouncement is deemed superseded and no longer eligible for testing as of January 1, 2021.

AICPA's NONDISCLOSURE AGREEMENT

As part of the AICPA's nondisclosure policy and to prove each candidate's willingness to adhere to this policy, a confidentiality and break policy statement must be accepted by each candidate during the introductory screens at the beginning of each exam. Nonacceptance of this policy means the exam will be terminated and the test fees will be forfeited. This statement from the AICPA's Sample Test is reproduced here to remind all CPA candidates about the AICPA's strict policy of nondisclosure, which Gleim consistently supports and upholds.

> **"Policy Statement and Confidentiality Agreement**
>
> I hereby agree that I will maintain the confidentiality of the Uniform CPA Exam.
> In addition, I agree that I will not:
>
> - Divulge the nature or content of any Uniform CPA Exam question or answer under any circumstances
> - Engage in any unauthorized communication during testing
> - Refer to unauthorized materials or use unauthorized equipment during testing
> - Remove or attempt to remove any Uniform CPA Exam materials, notes, or any other items from the exam room
>
> I understand and agree that liability for test administration activities, including but not limited to the adequacy or accuracy of test materials and equipment, and the accuracy of scoring and score reporting, will be limited to score correction or test retake at no additional fee. I waive any and all right to all other claims. I further agree to report to the AICPA any exam question disclosures, or solicitations for disclosure, of which I become aware.
>
> I affirm that I have had the opportunity to read the Candidate Bulletin and I agree to all of its terms and conditions.
>
> I understand that breaks are only allowed between testlets. I understand that I will be asked to complete any open testlet before leaving the testing room for a break. In addition, I understand that failure to comply with this Policy statement and Confidentiality Agreement could result in the invalidation of my scores, disqualification from future exams, expulsion from the testing facility, and possibly civil or criminal penalties."

GLEIM CPA REVIEW ESSENTIALS

Gleim CPA Review has the following features to make studying easier:

1. **Backgrounds:** In certain instances, we have provided historical background or supplemental information. This information is intended to illuminate the topic under discussion and is set off in bordered boxes with shaded headings. This material does not need to be memorized for the exam.

> **BACKGROUND 9-1   Accelerated Depreciation**
>
> Accelerated depreciation is a tax relief measure highly desired by businesses. Quickly expensing the cost of investment in plant and equipment for tax purposes allows businesses to significantly reduce their tax liability and thus reduce the cost of capital investment. However, it is important to note that the benefit provided by accelerated depreciation is based on the time value of money (i.e., a deduction today is better than a deduction tomorrow).

2. **Examples:** Illustrative examples, both hypothetical and those drawn from actual events, are set off in shaded, bordered boxes.

> **EXAMPLE 4-3   Refund of Amount Reimbursed by Employer**
>
> John submitted reimbursement requests to his employer for $10,500 in airfare. John was later refunded for $500 of the airfare. If John does not remit the funds to his employer, John must include the $500 in gross income.

3. **Gleim Success Tips:** These tips supplement the core exam material by suggesting how certain topics might be presented on the exam or how you should prepare for an issue.

> **SUCCESS TIP**
>
> The accounting rules for income and deduction items under both the cash and accrual methods have often been tested. The AICPA has used questions that have focused on the timing of the inclusions of various income and expense items under each method.

4. **Detailed Table of Contents:** This information at the beginning of the book is a complete listing of all study units and subunits in the Gleim CPA Regulation Review program. Use this list as a study aid to mark off your progress and to provide jumping-off points for review.

5. **Optimizing Your Score on the Task-Based Simulations (TBSs):** Appendix A explains how to approach and allocate your time for the TBS testlets. It also presents several example TBSs for your review.

6. **Blueprint with Gleim Cross-References:** Appendix B contains a reprint of the AICPA Blueprint for REG along with cross-references to the corresponding Gleim study units.

7. **Core Concepts:** We have also provided additional study materials to supplement the Knowledge Transfer Outlines in the digital Gleim CPA Review Course. The Core Concepts, for example, are consolidated documents providing an overview of the key points of each subunit that serve as the foundation for learning. As part of your review, you should make sure that you understand each of them.

TIME BUDGETING AND QUESTION-ANSWERING TECHNIQUES FOR REG

To begin the exam, you will enter your Launch Code on the Welcome screen. If you do not enter the correct code within 5 minutes of the screen appearing, the exam session will end.

Next, you will have an additional 5 minutes to view a brief exam introduction containing two screens: the nondisclosure policy and a section information screen. Accept the policy and then review the information screen, but be sure to click the Begin Exam button on the bottom right of the screen within the allotted 5 minutes. If you fail to do so, the exam will be terminated and you will not have the option to restart your exam.

These 10 minutes, along with the 5 minutes you may spend on a post-exam survey, are not included in the 240 minutes of exam time.

Once you complete the introductory screens and begin your exam, expect two testlets of 38 multiple-choice questions (MCQs) each and three testlets of Task-Based Simulations (TBSs) (one with 2 TBSs and two with 3 TBSs each). You will have 240 minutes to complete the five testlets.

1. **Budget your time so you can finish before time expires.**

    a. Here is our suggested time allocation for Regulation:

	Minutes	Start Time	
Testlet 1 (MCQ)	47*	4 hours	00 minutes
Testlet 2 (MCQ)	47*	3 hours	13 minutes
Testlet 3 (TBS)	36	2 hours	26 minutes
Break	15	Clock stops	
Testlet 4 (TBS)	54	1 hour	50 minutes
Testlet 5 (TBS)	54	0 hours	56 minutes
**Extra time	2	0 hours	02 minutes

    *Rounded down

    b. Before beginning your first MCQ testlet, prepare a Gleim Time Management plan as recommended in *CPA Exam Guide: A System for Success*.

    c. As you work through the individual questions, monitor your time. In Regulation, we suggest 47 minutes (1.25 minutes per question) for each testlet of 38 MCQs. If you answer five items in 6 minutes, you are fine, but if you spend 8 minutes on five items, you need to speed up. In the TBS testlets, spend no more than 18 minutes on each TBS. For more information on TBS time budgets, refer to Appendix A, "Optimizing Your Score on the Task-Based Simulations (TBSs)."

    **Remember to allocate your budgeted extra time, as needed, to each testlet. Your goal is to answer all of the items and achieve the maximum score possible. As you practice answering TBSs in the Gleim Premium CPA Review System, you will be practicing your time management.

2. **Answer the questions in consecutive order.**

    a. Do not agonize over any one question. **Stay within your time budget.**

    b. Never leave an MCQ unanswered. Your score is based on the number of correct responses. You will not be penalized for answering incorrectly. If you are unsure about a question,

       1) Make an educated guess.
       2) Flag it for review by clicking on the flag icon at the bottom of the screen.
       3) Return to it before you submit the testlet as time allows. Remember, once you have selected the Submit Testlet option, you will no longer be able to review or change any answers in the completed testlet.

3. **Read the question carefully to discover exactly what is being asked.**
    a. Ignore the answer choices so they do not affect your precise reading of the question.
    b. Focusing on what is required allows you to
        1) Reject extraneous information
        2) Concentrate on relevant facts
        3) Proceed directly to determining the best answer
    c. **Careful!** The requirement may be an exception that features negative words.
    d. Decide the correct answer before looking at the answer choices.
4. **Read the answer choices, paying attention to small details.**
    a. Even if an answer choice appears to be correct, do not skip the remaining choices. Each choice requires consideration because you are looking for the best answer provided.
    b. **Only one answer option is the best.** In the MCQs, four answer choices are presented, and you know one of them is correct. The remaining choices are distractors and are meant to appear correct at first glance. Eliminate them as quickly as you can.
    c. Treat each answer choice like a true/false question as you analyze it.
    d. In computational MCQs, the distractor answers are carefully calculated to be the result of common mistakes. Be careful, and double-check your computations if time permits.
        1) There will be a mix of conceptual and calculation questions. When you take the exam, it may appear that more of the questions are calculation-type because they take longer and are more difficult.
5. **Click on the best answer.**
    a. You have a 25% chance of answering correctly by guessing blindly, but you can improve your odds with an educated guess.
    b. For many MCQs, you can **eliminate two answer choices with minimal effort** and increase your educated guess to a 50/50 proposition.
        1) Rule out answers that you think are incorrect.
        2) Speculate what the AICPA is looking for and/or why the question is being asked.
        3) Select the best answer or guess between equally appealing answers. Your first guess is usually the most intuitive.
6. **Do not click the Submit Testlet button until you have consulted the question status list at the bottom of each MCQ screen.**
    a. Return to flagged questions to finalize your answer choices if you have time.
    b. Verify that you have answered every question.
    c. Stay on schedule because time management is critical to exam success.

Doing well on the **task-based simulations** requires you to be an expert on how to approach them both from a question-answering and a time-allocation perspective. Refer to Appendix A, "Optimizing Your Score on the Task-Based Simulations (TBSs)," for a complete explanation of task-based simulations and how to optimize your score on each one.

HOW TO BE IN CONTROL

Remember, you must be in control to be successful during exam preparation and execution. Perhaps more importantly, control can also contribute greatly to your personal and other professional goals. Control is the process whereby you

1. Develop expectations, standards, budgets, and plans
2. Undertake activity, production, study, and learning
3. Measure the activity, production, output, and knowledge
4. Compare actual activity with expected and budgeted activity
5. Modify the activity, behavior, or study to better achieve the expected or desired outcome
6. Revise expectations and standards in light of actual experience
7. Continue the process or restart the process in the future

Exercising control will ultimately develop the confidence you need to outperform most other CPA candidates and PASS the CPA Exam!

QUESTIONS ABOUT GLEIM MATERIALS

Gleim has an efficient and effective way for candidates who have purchased the Gleim Premium CPA Review System to submit an inquiry and receive a response regarding Gleim materials **directly through their course**. This system also allows you to view your Q&A session online in your Gleim Personal Classroom.

Questions regarding the information in this **introduction and/or the Gleim *CPA Exam Guide*** (study suggestions, study plans, exam specifics) may be emailed to personalcounselor@gleim.com.

Questions concerning **orders, prices, shipments, or payments** should be sent via email to customerservice@gleim.com and will be promptly handled by our competent and courteous customer service staff.

For **technical support**, you may use our automated technical support service at www.gleim.com/support, email us at support@gleim.com, or call us at (800) 874-5346.

FEEDBACK

Please fill out our online feedback form (www.gleim.com/feedbackREG) IMMEDIATELY after you take the CPA Regulation section so we can adapt our material based on where candidates say we need to increase or decrease coverage. Our approach has been approved by the AICPA.

STUDY UNIT ONE
ETHICS AND PROFESSIONAL RESPONSIBILITIES

(11 pages of outline)

1.1	*Practitioners*	*11*
1.2	*Tax Return Preparers*	*16*

When a dispute or disagreement over tax issues arises, a taxpayer may have to appear before the IRS. CPAs, enrolled agents (EAs), attorneys, and other individuals authorized to practice before the IRS may represent taxpayers. This study unit discusses the various individuals who may practice before the IRS and their standards of conduct.

1.1 PRACTITIONERS

Rules for practice before the IRS are in Treasury Department Circular 230.

1. **Practice before the IRS**

    a. Practice before the **Internal Revenue Service (IRS)** is the presentation to the IRS or any of its officers or employees of any matter relating to a client's rights, privileges, or liabilities under laws or regulations administered by the IRS.

    b. Practicing before the IRS includes

    1) Representing a taxpayer at conferences, hearings, or meetings with the IRS
    2) Preparing necessary documents and filing them with the IRS for a taxpayer
    3) Rendering written advice with respect to any entity, transaction, plan, or arrangement having a potential for tax avoidance or evasion
    4) Corresponding and communicating with the IRS for a taxpayer

    c. The following do **not** constitute practicing before the IRS:

    1) Preparing less than substantially all of a tax return, an amended return, or a claim for refund
    2) Furnishing information upon request to the IRS
    3) Appearing as a witness for a person

    d. A practitioner who for compensation prepares or assists with the preparation of **all or substantially all** of a tax return, an amended return, or claim for refund must comply with the following:

    1) Have a preparer tax identification number.
    2) Be subject to the duties and restrictions relating to practice before the IRS.
    3) Be subject to the sanctions for violation of the regulations of Circular 230.

2. **Persons Authorized to Practice**
    a. The following persons may practice before the IRS:
        1) Attorneys
            a) An attorney who is a member in good standing of the bar of the highest court of any state, possession, territory, commonwealth, or the District of Columbia
        2) CPAs
            a) A CPA is an individual qualified to practice as a CPA in any state, territory, or possession of the U.S.
        3) Enrolled agents (EAs)
            a) An EA is an individual, other than an attorney or a CPA, who is eligible, qualified, and certified as authorized to represent a taxpayer before the IRS.
            b) The EA designation is issued by the IRS to individuals passing the EA exam.
        4) Enrolled actuaries, enrolled retirement plan agents, and **annual filing season program (AFSP)** participants
    b. To practice before the IRS, an attorney or a CPA must
        1) Not be suspended or disbarred
        2) File a **written declaration** for each party (s)he represents that (s)he
            a) Is currently qualified
            b) Has been authorized to represent the party

	Type of Practitioners*	Attorney, CPA, EA	AFSP Participants (Not attorneys, CPAs, or EAs)
Type of Practice Before the IRS	Allowed Practice before the IRS	Unlimited	Limited
	Preparation of return or claim for refund	Sign returns and refunds when completed "all or substantially all" of a return or refund	Sign returns and refunds when completed "all or substantially all" of a return or refund
	Representation	1) Before anyone at the IRS 2) Examination and appeals 3) Any return or refund	1) Before IRS revenue agents, customer service representatives, and employees 2) During examination only 3) Return that tax return preparer signed him or herself for the period under examination 4) Must participate in AFSP or be specifically permitted to practice
	Tax Advice	Unlimited including tax planning	Limited to return or refund preparation

*For brevity, the chart excludes enrolled actuaries and enrolled retirement plan agents because the extent of their practice rights is not likely to be tested on the CPA Exam.

SU 1: Ethics and Professional Responsibilities

3. **Rules of Conduct before the IRS: Nine Elements Tax Preparers Must Adhere To**
   a. **Conflict of Interest**
      1) A conflict of interest exists if
         a) The practitioner's representation of a client will be **directly adverse** to another client or
         b) There is a significant risk that the representation of one or more clients will be **materially limited** by the practitioner's responsibilities to another or former client, a third person, or by the practitioner's personal interest(s).
      2) A practitioner may represent conflicting interests before the IRS only if
         a) All directly affected parties provide informed, written consent once the existence of the conflict is known by the practitioner (written consent must be within 30 days of informed consent);
         b) The representation is not prohibited by law; and
         c) The practitioner reasonably believes that (s)he can provide competent and diligent representation to each client.
      3) A practitioner is not required to disclose the conflict of interest to the IRS.
   b. **Diligence** must be exercised in preparing and in assisting in preparing, approving, and filing returns, documents, and other papers relating to IRS matters.
      1) Diligence is presumed if the practitioner
         a) Relies upon the work product of another person and
         b) Uses reasonable care in engaging, supervising, training, and evaluating the person.
      2) A practitioner may not unreasonably delay the prompt disposition of any matter before the IRS.
   c. **Information or records** properly and lawfully requested by a duly authorized officer or employee of the IRS must be promptly submitted.
      1) However, if reasonable basis exists for a good-faith belief that (a) the information is privileged or (b) the request is not proper and lawful, the practitioner is excused from submitting the requested information.
      2) A practitioner also is required to provide information about the identity of persons that (s)he reasonably believes may have possession or control of the requested information if the practitioner does not.
   d. A practitioner who **knows** about **a client's noncompliance**–which may be that a client (1) has **not complied** with the revenue laws of the U.S. or (2) has made an error or omission–is required promptly to advise the client of noncompliance and the consequences of such noncompliance, error, or omission under the Code and regulations.
      1) Circular 230 does not require the practitioner to notify the IRS.
   e. A practitioner must not negotiate, including by endorsement, any **income tax refund check** issued to a client.
   f. A practitioner may not charge an **unconscionable fee** in connection with any matter before the IRS.
   g. A practitioner may not charge a **contingent fee** in relation to any matter before the IRS except in relation to (1) an IRS examination of an original return, (2) an amended return, (3) a claim for refund or credit, or (4) a judicial proceeding.

h. A practitioner must **return client records** on request, regardless of any fee dispute. However, the practitioner may retain copies of client records. Records deemed returnable for purposes of this requirement are those records necessary for a client to comply with his or her federal tax obligations.

   1) However, documents **prepared by the practitioner** that (s)he is withholding pending payment of a fee, with respect to such documents, are not included (provided state law permits retention of records in a fee dispute).

i. Circular 230 allows **advertising** and **solicitation** with the following conditions:

   1) False, fraudulent, misleading, deceptive, or unfair statements or claims are not allowed. Claims must be subject to factual verification.
   2) Specialized expertise may not be claimed except as authorized by federal or state agencies having jurisdiction over the practitioner.
   3) Each of the following fees may be advertised:
      a) Fixed fees for specific routine services
      b) A range of fees for particular services
      c) The fee for an initial consultation
      d) Hourly rates
      e) Availability of a written fee schedule

4. **Best Practices for Tax Advisors**

   a. Tax advisors should provide clients with the highest quality representation regarding federal tax issues. They should adhere to best practices in providing advice and in preparing or assisting in the preparation of a submission to the IRS.
   b. Best practices include four general elements:
      1) Performing the steps needed to support the facts for a tax filing
         a) Establish the facts, determine which facts are relevant, evaluate the reasonableness of any assumptions or representations, relate applicable law to the relevant facts, and arrive at a conclusion supported by the law and the facts.
      2) Communicating clearly with the client about the terms of the engagement
      3) Advising the client regarding the importance of the conclusions reached, including, for example, whether a taxpayer may avoid accuracy-related penalties under the Internal Revenue Code (IRC) if a taxpayer acts in reliance on the advice
      4) Acting fairly and with integrity in practice before the IRS
   c. Tax advisors with responsibility for overseeing a firm's practice of (1) providing advice about federal tax issues or (2) preparing or assisting in the preparation of submissions to the IRS should take reasonable steps to ensure that the firm's procedures for all members, associates, and employees are consistent with the best practices.

5. **Written Tax Advice**

   a. When providing written advice about any federal tax matter, a practitioner must
      1) Base the advice on reasonable assumptions,
      2) Reasonably consider all relevant facts that are known or should be known, and
      3) Use reasonable efforts to identify and determine the relevant facts.

b. The advice cannot rely upon representations, statements, findings, or agreements that are unreasonable, i.e., are known to be incorrect, inconsistent, or incomplete.
c. The advice must not consider the possibility that either a tax return will not be audited or a matter will not be raised during the audit in evaluating a federal tax matter.
d. When providing written advice, a practitioner may rely in good faith on the advice of another practitioner only if that advice is reasonable given all the facts and circumstances.
e. The practitioner cannot rely on the advice of a person who either the practitioner knows or should know is not competent to provide the advice or has an unresolved conflict of interest.

6. **Sanctions for Violations**
    a. Practitioners may be censured (public reprimand), suspended, or disbarred from practice before the IRS for willful violations of any of the regulations contained in Circular 230.
    b. The Secretary of the Treasury may censure, suspend, or disbar from practice before the IRS any practitioner who
        1) Is shown to be incompetent or disreputable
        2) Refuses to comply with the rules and regulations relating to practice before the IRS
        3) Willfully and knowingly, with intent to defraud, deceives, misleads, or threatens any client
    c. The following is a brief list of conduct that may result in suspension or disbarment:
        1) Being convicted of an offense involving dishonesty or breach of trust
        2) Providing false or misleading information to the Treasury Department, including the IRS
        3) Negotiating a client's refund check or not promptly remitting a refund check
        4) Circulating or publishing matter related to practice before the IRS that is deemed libelous or malicious
        5) Using abusive language
        6) Suspension from practice as a CPA by any state licensing authority, any federal court of record, or any federal agency, body, or board
        7) Conviction of any felony involving conduct that renders the practitioner unfit to practice before the IRS
        8) Attempting to influence the official action of any IRS employee by bestowing a gift, favor, or anything of value
        9) Willfully evading or assisting others to evade any federal tax payments
    d. A notice of disbarment or suspension of a CPA from practice before the IRS is issued to IRS employees, interested departments and agencies of the federal government, and state licensing authorities.

STOP & REVIEW

You have completed the outline for this subunit.
Study multiple-choice questions 1 through 8 beginning on page 22.

1.2 TAX RETURN PREPARERS

1. **Tax Return Preparers**
    a. A tax return preparer is **any person** who prepares **for compensation**, or employs one or more persons to prepare for compensation, **all or a substantial portion** of any return of tax or claim for refund under the Internal Revenue Code (IRC).
        1) A portion of any return or claim for refund is deemed substantial unless a condition for unsubstantiality is satisfied.
        2) An **unsubstantial portion** is either
            a) Less than $10,000 or
            b) Less than $400,000 **and** also less than 20% of the gross income on the return or claim.
        3) If **more than one** schedule, entry, or other portion is involved, all schedules, entries, or other portions **shall be combined** in determining whether a tax return preparer has prepared a substantial portion of any return or claim for refund.
    b. Persons who are tax return preparers (provided they are compensated) include the following:
        1) A person who provides to a taxpayer or other preparer sufficient information and advice so that completion of the return is simply a mechanical matter.
        2) A **nonsigning** tax return preparer who prepares all or a substantial portion of a return or claim for refund. Examples include preparers who provide advice that constitutes a substantial portion of the return.
    c. Persons who are not tax return preparers include the following:
        1) An employee who prepares a return for the employer by whom (s)he is regularly and continuously employed
        2) A fiduciary who prepares a return or refund claim for any person (the trust)
        3) A person who prepares a refund claim in response to a notice of deficiency issued to another
        4) A person who provides typing, reproducing, or other mechanical assistance, i.e., clerical
        5) A person who merely gives an opinion about events that have not happened, i.e., planning

2. **Due Diligence**
    a. Significant aspects of return preparation require
        1) Making factual inquiries to ensure clients' accuracy and truthfulness and
        2) Taking a position relative to tax law. In other words, assessing the scenario and appropriately applying tax law to the facts.
    b. A tax return preparer may rely, if in good faith, on information provided by the taxpayer without having to obtain third-party verification.
        1) However, the preparer may not ignore the implications of the information.
        2) The preparer must make **reasonable inquiries** if the information appears inaccurate or incomplete.
        3) The preparer should make appropriate inquiries of the taxpayer about the existence of documentation for deductions.

c. When a tax return preparer discovers that a taxpayer has made an error in or omission from any document filed with the IRS, (s)he must notify the taxpayer of the error or omission immediately.

  1) The tax return preparer also must advise the taxpayer of the consequences of the error or omission.

3. **Reportable Transactions**

    a. A reportable transaction is a transaction described in one or more of the following categories:

        1) A **listed transaction** is a transaction that is the same as, or substantially similar to, one of the types of transactions the IRS has determined to be a tax avoidance transaction.

            a) These transactions are identified by notice, regulation, or other form of published guidance as a listed transaction. A taxpayer has participated in a listed transaction if any of the following applies:

                i) The taxpayer's tax return reflects tax consequences or a tax strategy described in published guidance that lists the transaction as a tax avoidance transaction.

                ii) The taxpayer knows or has reason to know that tax benefits reflected on the tax return are derived directly or indirectly from such tax consequences or tax strategy.

                iii) The taxpayer is in a type or class of individuals or entities that published guidance treats as participants in a listed transaction.

        2) A **transaction of interest** is a transaction that the IRS and Treasury Department believe has a potential for tax avoidance or evasion, but for which there is not enough information to determine if it should be identified as a tax avoidance transaction.

        3) A **Sec. 165 loss transaction** is a qualifying loss not offset by any insurance proceeds or other similar compensation.

        4) A **transaction with contractual protection** is a transaction for which the taxpayer or a related party has the right to a full or partial refund of fees if all or part of the intended tax consequences from the transaction are not sustained.

            a) It also includes a transaction for which fees are contingent on the taxpayer's realization of tax benefits from the transaction.

        5) A **confidential transaction** is a transaction that is offered to the taxpayer or a related party under conditions of confidentiality and for which a minimum fee was paid to an advisor.

            a) For a corporation (excluding S corporations), partnership, or trust in which all of the owners or beneficiaries are corporations (excluding S corporations), the minimum fee is $250,000 ($50,000 for all others).

4. **Procedural Requirements**
    a. A return preparer is required to sign the return or claim for refund after it has been completed and before it is presented to the taxpayer.
    b. Before a return preparer allows the client to sign the prepared return, the return preparer is required to provide a completed copy of the return or refund claim to the taxpayer.
    c. A return preparer is required to retain a completed copy of each return or claim prepared for 3 years after the close of the return period.
        1) An alternative is to keep a list that includes, for the returns and claims prepared, the following information:
            a) The taxpayers' names
            b) Taxpayer identification numbers
            c) Their tax years
            d) Types of returns or claims prepared
        2) The return period is the 12-month period beginning on July 1 each year.

5. **Penalties**
    a. Tax return preparers are subject to severe penalties for violations. The degree of severity varies among the penalties.
    b. Individuals with overall supervisory responsibility for advice given by a firm are also subject to penalties.
    c. **Unreasonable positions.** Taking an **undisclosed** position **without a reasonable belief** that substantial authority exists that it will be sustained on its merits results in a penalty of an amount equal to the greater of $1,000 or 50% of the income to be derived.
        1) If the position is **disclosed**, its tax treatment must have a **reasonable basis**.
        2) The penalty does not apply if the preparer proves that
            a) (S)he acted in good faith and
            b) Reasonable cause exists for the understatement.
        3) Positions relating to **tax shelters** are unreasonable **unless** reasonable belief exists that such positions would **more likely than not** be sustained on their merits.
    d. **Negligence.** Negligence includes any failure to make a reasonable attempt to either comply with the provisions of the Internal Revenue laws or exercise ordinary and reasonable care in the preparation of a return.
    e. **Willful or reckless conduct.** If the understatement was caused by the preparer's willful or reckless conduct, the penalty is the greater of $5,000 or 75% of the income to be derived.
    f. **Frivolous submission.** Filing a frivolous return is penalized. A return is considered frivolous when it
        1) Omits information necessary to determine the taxpayer's tax liability,
        2) Shows a substantially incorrect tax or willful understatement of tax liability,
        3) Is based on a frivolous position (e.g., that wages are not income), or
        4) Is based on the taxpayer's desire to impede the collection of tax.

SU 1: Ethics and Professional Responsibilities

- g. The tax code provides that any tax return preparer who endorses or otherwise **negotiates** any check issued to a taxpayer with respect to taxes imposed by the IRC is subject to a penalty of $545.
    1) Furthermore, any tax return preparer who operates a check cashing agency that cashes, endorses, or negotiates tax refund checks for returns prepared also is subject to a penalty.
- h. **Aiding or abetting** in preparation of any document is subject to a penalty if using the document would result in an **understatement** of tax liability.
    1) A preparer may be subject to only one aiding or abetting penalty per taxpayer (i.e., client) per taxable period (or event when there is no taxable period). However, other types of penalties may still apply.
    2) The penalty applies to the preparer even when a subordinate has been ordered to understate the tax liability, or the preparer knows but does not attempt to prevent the subordinate from understating the tax liability.
    3) Any act that constitutes a **willful** attempt to evade federal tax liability, even that of another person, is subject to criminal penalties, including imprisonment.
        a) Furthermore, any person who willfully aids or assists in preparation or presentation of a materially false or fraudulent return is guilty of a felony.
    4) Violations of these rules may result in disciplinary action by the director of the IRS, and an injunction may be issued prohibiting the violator from acting as a tax preparer.
- i. **Fraud and false statements.** Fraudulent transactions ordinarily involve a willful or deliberate action with the intent to obtain an unauthorized benefit. For such action, the penalties are a fine not greater than $250,000 for an individual client ($500,000 for a corporate client), imprisonment of not more than 3 years, or both.

6. **Disclosure of Taxpayer Information**
   a. **Penalty**
      1) A penalty is imposed on any tax return preparer who discloses or uses any tax return information without the consent of the taxpayer.
         a) But the penalty is **not** imposed if the disclosure was specifically for preparing, assisting in preparing, or providing services in connection with the preparation of any tax return of the taxpayer.
      2) The penalty is $250 ($1,000 for misappropriation of identity) per disclosure, with a maximum of $10,000 ($50,000 for misappropriation of identity) per year.
      3) If convicted of knowingly or recklessly disclosing the information, a preparer is guilty of a misdemeanor and subject to up to $1,000 in fines and up to a year in prison.

b. **Exceptions**

1) The penalty for disclosure is not imposed if the disclosure was made in the following circumstances:

    a) In accordance with the Internal Revenue Code
    b) To a related taxpayer, provided the taxpayer did not expressly prohibit the disclosure
    c) Under a court order (subpoena) or to the tax return preparer's legal counsel in the event of legal proceedings
    d) To tax return preparers within the same firm
    e) For the purpose of a quality or peer review to the extent necessary to accomplish the review
    f) For use in preparing, assisting in preparing, or providing services in connection with tax return preparation

c. **Consent**

1) The taxpayer's consent must be a written, formal consent authorizing the disclosure for a specific purpose.
2) The taxpayer must authorize a preparer to

    a) Use the taxpayer's information to solicit additional current business from the taxpayer in matters not related to the IRS
    b) Disclose the information to additional third parties
    c) Disclose the information in connection with another person's return

d. **Confidentiality**

1) The confidentiality privilege is extended to certain nonattorneys.

    a) The privilege may **not** be asserted to prevent the disclosure of information to any regulatory body other than the IRS.

2) In noncriminal tax proceedings before the IRS, a taxpayer is entitled to common-law protections of confidentiality with respect to the tax advice given by any **federally authorized tax practitioner**. They are the same protections a taxpayer would have if the advising individual were an attorney.

    a) A federally authorized tax practitioner includes any nonattorney who is authorized to practice before the IRS, such as a CPA.
    b) **Tax advice** is advice given by an individual with respect to matters that are within the scope of the individual's authority to practice before the IRS.

3) The privilege also applies in any noncriminal tax proceeding in federal court brought by or against the United States.

7. The following penalties may be imposed on tax return preparers:

Act	Fine	Imprisonment
Understatement:		
Due to unreasonable positions	Greater of a) $1,000 or b) 50% of income to be derived	N/A
Due to willful or reckless conduct	Greater of a) $5,000 or b) 75% of income to be derived	N/A
Preparing tax returns for other persons:		
Failure to furnish copy to taxpayer	$50 each, limited to $27,000 per year	N/A
Failure to sign return	$50 each, limited to $27,000 per year	N/A
Failure to furnish identifying number	$50 each, limited to $27,000 per year	N/A
Failure to retain copy or list	$50 each, limited to $27,000 per year	N/A
Failure to file correct information returns	$50 each, limited to $27,000 per year	N/A
Endorses or negotiates checks made to taxpayer in respect of taxes imposed	$545 each, unlimited	N/A
Failure to be diligent in determining credits and head of household status (for the best benefit of taxpayer)	$545 each, unlimited	N/A
Others:		
Promoting abusive tax shelters	Lesser of a) $1,000 for each organization or sale of promotion plan b) Income to be derived	N/A
Aiding and abetting understatement of tax liability	$1,000 each year (noncorporate clients) $10,000 each year (corporate clients)	N/A
Disclosure or use of information	$250 per unauthorized disclosure, limited to $10,000 per year	N/A
Convicted of knowingly or recklessly disclosing information (misdemeanor)	$1,000	Up to 1 year
Fraud and false statements	$250,000 (individual clients) $500,000 (corporate clients)	Up to 3 years
Fraudulent returns, statements, or other documents	$10,000 (individual clients) $50,000 (corporate clients)	Up to 1 year

STOP & REVIEW

You have completed the outline for this subunit.
Study multiple-choice questions 9 through 19 beginning on page 25.

QUESTIONS

1.1 Practitioners

1. Frank Maple, CPA, represents his brother Joe Maple and Joe's business partner Bill Smith. Joe Maple and Bill Smith are equal shareholders in the Joe & Bill Corporation. The Internal Revenue Service examined the corporation and determined that one of the shareholders committed fraud, but could not determine which shareholder it was. Frank has made an appointment with the Internal Revenue Service to determine which partner was guilty. Which of the following statements reflects what Frank should do in accordance with Circular 230?

A. Frank should meet with the Internal Revenue Service and try to convince the examiner that each shareholder is equally guilty.

B. Advise Joe & Bill that they should dissolve the corporation, thereby making it difficult for the Internal Revenue Service to pursue the issue.

C. Advise Joe & Bill that he cannot represent them because there is a conflict of interest.

D. Advise Joe & Bill on creating documents that will convince the Internal Revenue Service that neither shareholder is guilty of fraud.

Answer (C) is correct.
  REQUIRED: The appropriate action in accordance with Circular 230.
  DISCUSSION: An agent may represent conflicting interests before the IRS only if all directly interested parties expressly consent in writing after full disclosure. According to Sec. 10.29(a) of Circular 230, a conflict of interest exists if

1. The representation of one client will be directly adverse to another client or
2. There is a significant risk that the representation of one or more clients will be materially limited by the practitioner's responsibilities to another client, a former client or a third person, or by a personal interest of the practitioner.

Frank Maple should determine whether a conflict of interest exists and get all appropriate consents to the representation. Because acquiring the consent of the parties is required to continue representation of both parties, and since that is not given as an option, Frank should advise Joe and Bill that he cannot represent them.

2. Which of the following statements is true with respect to a client's request for records of the client that are necessary for the client to comply with his or her federal tax obligations?

A. The practitioner may never return records of the client to the client even if the client requests prompt return of the records.

B. The existence of a dispute over fees always relieves the practitioner of his or her responsibility to return records of the client to the client.

C. The practitioner must, at the request of the client, promptly return the records of the client to the client unless applicable state law provides otherwise.

D. The practitioner must, at the request of the client, return the records of the client to the client within 3 months of receiving the request.

Answer (C) is correct.
  REQUIRED: The true statement about a client's request for records of the client.
  DISCUSSION: A practitioner must return a client's records on request, regardless of any fee dispute. Records deemed returnable for purposes of this requirement are those records necessary for a client to comply with his or her federal tax obligations. Returns or other documents prepared by the practitioner that the practitioner is withholding pending payment of a fee are not includible unless applicable state law provides otherwise.
  Answer (A) is incorrect. The client's records are required to be returned if the taxpayer makes such a request to comply with federal tax laws. **Answer (B) is incorrect.** A fee dispute does not relieve the practitioner of responsibility to return documents that the taxpayer needs to comply with federal tax laws. **Answer (D) is incorrect.** The practitioner must return the documents to the taxpayer as quickly as is reasonable.

3. Mike is a CPA. Widget, Inc., is an accrual-basis taxpayer. In Year 3, while preparing Widget's Year 2 return, Mike discovered that Widget failed to include income on its Year 1 return that Widget received in Year 2 but that should have been included in income in Year 1 under the accrual method of accounting. What must Mike do?

A. Advise Widget of the error and the consequences of the error.
B. Include the income on the Year 2 return.
C. Refuse to prepare Widget's Year 2 return until Widget agrees to amend its Year 1 return to include the amount of income.
D. Change Widget to the cash method of accounting.

Answer (A) is correct.
REQUIRED: The action required by a CPA who knows that a client has not complied with the revenue laws.
DISCUSSION: An agent who knows that a client has not complied with the revenue laws of the U.S. is required to promptly advise the client of noncompliance as well as the consequences of noncompliance under the Code and Regulations. Under Circular 230, the agent is not required to notify the IRS.
Answer (B) is incorrect. An amended return would need to be filed, and the agent would file an amended return at the request of the taxpayer. **Answer (C) is incorrect.** It is the client's responsibility to request that an amended return be filed for Year 1. **Answer (D) is incorrect.** Widget, Inc., may be required to maintain an accrual method of accounting due to the Code and Regulations. Also, amending the Year 1 return would be the only way to properly correct the understatement of income.

4. The IRS requested client records from a CPA who does not have possession or control of the records. According to Treasury Circular 230, the CPA must

A. Notify the IRS of the identity of any person who, according to the CPA's belief, could have the records.
B. Require the client to submit the records to the IRS or withdraw from the engagement.
C. Obtain the records from the client and submit them to the IRS.
D. Contact all third parties associated with the records, such as banks and employers, to obtain the requested records for submission to the IRS.

Answer (A) is correct.
REQUIRED: The requirements for records requests according to Circular 230.
DISCUSSION: A practitioner is required to provide information regarding the identity of persons that the practitioner reasonably believes may have possession or control of the requested documents if the practitioner does not have possession or control of the documents.
Answer (B) is incorrect. A practitioner may have a good-faith belief that the client is not required to submit the information. Thus, withdrawal would be improper. **Answer (C) is incorrect.** The client may not be obligated to submit the records to the IRS. Therefore, the practitioner is not required to submit them in all circumstances. **Answer (D) is incorrect.** The practitioner contacts the client for records but does not seek records from third parties.

5. Which of the following is **not** an example of disreputable conduct (as described in Sec. 10.51 of Circular 230) for which a CPA may be suspended or disbarred from practice before the IRS?

A. Knowingly giving false or misleading information to the Treasury Department.
B. Willful failure to make a federal tax return in violation of federal revenue laws.
C. Failure to respond to a request by the Director of the Office of Professional Responsibility to provide information.
D. Misappropriation of funds received from a client for the purpose of payment of federal tax.

Answer (C) is correct.
REQUIRED: The action for which a CPA may not be disbarred or suspended from practice.
DISCUSSION: Section 10.51 of Circular 230 lists several examples of disreputable conduct for which a CPA may be disbarred or suspended from practice before the Internal Revenue Service. Failure to respond to a request by the Director of the Office of Professional Responsibility to provide information is not disreputable conduct under Sec. 10.51 of Circular 230.
Answer (A) is incorrect. Knowingly giving false or misleading information to the Treasury Department is prohibited by Circular 230. **Answer (B) is incorrect.** Willful failure to make a federal tax return in violation of federal revenue laws is prohibited by Circular 230. **Answer (D) is incorrect.** Misappropriation of funds received from a client for the purpose of payment of federal tax is prohibited by Circular 230.

6. Identify the appropriate action that a practitioner should take when (s)he becomes aware of an error or omission on a client's return.

A. Amend the return and provide it to the client.
B. Inform the IRS of the noncompliance, error, or omission.
C. Do nothing.
D. Promptly advise the client of such noncompliance, error, or omission and the consequences thereof.

Answer (D) is correct.
REQUIRED: The appropriate action when a practitioner is aware of an error or omission.
DISCUSSION: Section 10.21 of Treasury Department Circular 230 requires an attorney, a certified public accountant, or an enrolled agent who knows that a client has not complied with the revenue laws of the United States to promptly advise the client of the noncompliance, error, or omission and the consequences of the noncompliance, error, or omission as provided in the IRC and regulations.
Answer (A) is incorrect. A practitioner may not amend the return without first informing the client. **Answer (B) is incorrect.** A practitioner is not required to inform the IRS. **Answer (C) is incorrect.** A practitioner must promptly advise the client of the noncompliance, error, or omission.

7. A tax advisor with what responsibility should take reasonable steps to ensure that the firm's procedures for all members, associates, and employees are consistent with the best practices?

A. Overseeing a firm's practice of providing advice concerning federal tax issues.
B. Overseeing a firm's practice of preparing or assisting in the preparation of submissions to the IRS.
C. Overseeing either a firm's practice of (1) providing advice concerning federal tax issues or (2) preparing or assisting in the preparation of submissions to the IRS.
D. Neither overseeing a firm's practice of providing advice concerning federal tax issues nor preparing or assisting in the preparation of submissions to the IRS.

Answer (C) is correct.
REQUIRED: The tax advisor's responsibility.
DISCUSSION: Tax advisors with responsibility for overseeing a firm's practice of (1) providing advice concerning federal tax issues or of (2) preparing or assisting in the preparation of submissions to the Internal Revenue Service should take reasonable steps to ensure that the firm's procedures for all members, associates, and employees are consistent with the best practices.
Answer (A) is incorrect. Overseeing a firm's practice of providing advice concerning federal tax issues is a tax advisor's responsibility. **Answer (B) is incorrect.** Preparing or assisting in the preparation of submissions to the IRS are responsibilities of the tax advisor. **Answer (D) is incorrect.** Both choices are responsibilities of the tax advisor.

8. All of the following are examples of disreputable conduct for which a CPA may be disbarred or suspended from practice before the Internal Revenue Service **except**

A. Advertising the hourly rates of the CPA.
B. Suggesting that (s)he is improperly able to obtain special consideration from an Internal Revenue Service employee.
C. Maintaining a partnership for the practice of tax law and accounting with a person who is under disbarment from practice before the Internal Revenue Service.
D. Failing to properly and promptly remit funds received from a client for the purpose of payment of taxes.

Answer (A) is correct.
REQUIRED: The action for which a CPA may not be disbarred or suspended from practice.
DISCUSSION: Section 10.51 of Circular 230 lists several examples of disreputable conduct for which a CPA may be disbarred or suspended from practice before the Internal Revenue Service. Advertising the hourly rates of the CPA is not prohibited under Sec. 10.30(a)(2) and is not disreputable conduct under Sec. 10.51 of Circular 230.

1.2 Tax Return Preparers

9. A CPA must sign the preparer's declaration on a federal income tax return

A. Only when the CPA prepares a tax return for compensation.
B. Only when the CPA can declare that a tax is based on information of which the CPA has personal knowledge.
C. Whenever the CPA prepares a tax return for others.
D. Only when the return is for an individual or corporation.

Answer (A) is correct.
REQUIRED: The condition for signing the preparer's declaration on a federal income tax return.
DISCUSSION: Treasury Regulations require preparers to sign all the returns they prepare and to include their identification numbers. However, a preparer is defined as a person who prepares (or employs persons to prepare) for compensation any tax return, amended return, or claim for refund of tax imposed by Subtitle A of the Internal Revenue Code (which covers income taxes on all entities).
Answer (B) is incorrect. The CPA may prepare a return based on information provided by the taxpayer. Personal knowledge of the information is not required. **Answer (C) is incorrect.** The CPA must sign only when (s)he receives compensation. **Answer (D) is incorrect.** The signature requirement applies to returns and claims for refund by all income tax-paying entities.

10. Which of the following statements is **false** regarding tax return preparers?

A. Only a person who signs a return as the preparer may be considered the preparer of the return.
B. Unpaid preparers, such as volunteers who assist low-income individuals, are not considered to be preparers for purposes of preparer penalties.
C. An employee who prepares the return of his or her employer does not meet the definition of a tax preparer.
D. The preparation of a substantial portion of a return for compensation is treated as the preparation of that return.

Answer (A) is correct.
REQUIRED: The false statement about tax return preparers.
DISCUSSION: Under Sec. 7701(a)(36), a tax return preparer is any person who prepares for compensation, or employs others to prepare for compensation, any tax return or claim for refund under Title 26. A person who prepares a substantial portion of a return is considered a preparer even though someone else may be required to sign the return.

11. Arnie is a Certified Public Accountant who prepares income tax returns for his clients. One of his clients submitted a list of expenses to be claimed on Schedule C of the tax return. Arnie qualifies as a return preparer and, as such, is required to comply with which one of the following conditions?

A. Arnie is required to independently verify the client's information.
B. Arnie can ignore implications of information known by him.
C. Inquiry is not required if the information appears to be incorrect or incomplete.
D. Appropriate inquiries are required to determine whether the client has substantiation for travel and entertainment expenses.

Answer (D) is correct.
REQUIRED: The conditions with which a return preparer must comply.
DISCUSSION: A practitioner (i.e., a CPA) may rely on information provided by a client without further inquiry or verification. However, if the information so provided appears incorrect, incomplete, or inconsistent, the practitioner must make reasonable inquiries about the information. This requirement includes inquiry about unsubstantiated travel and entertainment expenses (Circular 230).
Answer (A) is incorrect. Arnie may rely in good faith on the client's information. **Answer (B) is incorrect.** Arnie may not ignore implications of information known by him. **Answer (C) is incorrect.** Arnie is required to make reasonable inquiries about information that appears to be incorrect or incomplete.

12. Mike is a CPA. For the past 5 years, the information that Anne provided Mike to prepare her return included a Schedule K-1 from a partnership showing significant income. However, Mike did not see a Schedule K-1 from the partnership among the information Anne provided to him this year. What does due diligence require Mike to do?

A. Without talking to Anne, Mike should estimate the amount that would be reported as income on the Schedule K-1 based on last year's Schedule K-1 and include that amount on Anne's return.

B. Contact the partnership's CPA to obtain Anne's Schedule K-1.

C. Nothing, because Mike is required to rely only on the information provided by his client, even if he has a reason to know the information is not accurate.

D. Ask Anne about the fact that she did not provide him with a Schedule K-1.

Answer (D) is correct.
REQUIRED: The actions required to perform due diligence.
DISCUSSION: A tax return preparer may rely, if in good faith, upon information furnished by the taxpayer without having to obtain third-party verification. However, the preparer may not ignore the implications of the information furnished. The preparer must make reasonable inquiries if the information appears inaccurate or incomplete.
Answer (A) is incorrect. The tax return preparer is not supposed to make up numbers. The tax return preparer is required to use the actual amounts in preparing a tax return. **Answer (B) is incorrect.** The tax return preparer cannot contact Anne's financial advisor without Anne's consent. **Answer (C) is incorrect.** A tax return preparer is required to make reasonable inquiries if information provided by the taxpayer appears inaccurate or incomplete.

13. All of the following are tax return preparers **except**

A. A person who prepares a substantial portion of the return for a fee.

B. A person who prepares a claim for a refund for a fee.

C. A person who gives an opinion about theoretical events that have not occurred.

D. A person who prepares a United States return for a fee outside the United States.

Answer (C) is correct.
REQUIRED: The person who is not a tax return preparer.
DISCUSSION: A tax return preparer is any person who prepares for compensation, or employs others to prepare for compensation, any tax return or claim for refund under Title 26. A person who gives an opinion about events that have not happened is not a tax return preparer.
Answer (A) is incorrect. A person who prepares a substantial portion of the return for a fee represents tax return preparers under the regulations. **Answer (B) is incorrect.** A person who prepares a claim for a refund for a fee represents tax return preparers under the regulations. **Answer (D) is incorrect.** A person who prepares a United States return for a fee outside the United States represents tax return preparers under the regulations.

14. Jane is a Certified Public Accountant who specializes in preparing federal tax returns. Which of the following returns would **not** qualify Jane as a tax return preparer?

A. Estate or gift tax returns.

B. Excise tax returns.

C. Withholding tax returns.

D. None of the answers are correct.

Answer (D) is correct.
REQUIRED: The types of returns that qualify an individual as a tax return preparer.
DISCUSSION: A tax return preparer is any person who prepares for compensation any return of tax or claim for refund under the IRC. Estate returns, gift tax returns, excise tax returns, and withholding returns are covered by the IRC.
Answer (A) is incorrect. Preparation of gift tax returns does qualify Jane as a tax preparer. **Answer (B) is incorrect.** Preparation of excise tax returns does qualify Jane as a tax preparer. **Answer (C) is incorrect.** Preparation of employment tax returns, including withholding tax returns, does qualify Jane as a tax preparer.

15. Jack, a return preparer, did not retain copies of all returns that he prepared but did keep a list that reflected the taxpayer's name, identification number, tax year, and type of return for each of his clients. Which of the following statements best describes this situation?

A. Jack is in compliance with the provisions of the tax code if he retains the list for a period of 1 year after the close of the return period in which the return was signed.
B. Jack is in compliance with the provisions of the tax code, provided he retains the list for a 3-year period after the close of the return period in which the return was signed.
C. Jack is not in compliance with the tax code since he must retain copies of all returns filed.
D. Jack is not in compliance with the tax code since he has not kept all the information required by the Code.

Answer (B) is correct.
REQUIRED: The statement that best describes record retention requirements for tax return preparers.
DISCUSSION: The person who is an income tax return preparer of any return or claim for refund shall "retain a completed copy of the return or claim for refund; or retain a record by list, card file, or otherwise of the name, taxpayer identification number, and taxable year of the taxpayer for whom the return or claim for refund was prepared and the type of return or claim for refund prepared." The material shall be retained and kept available for inspection for the 3-year period following the close of the return period during which the return or claim for refund was presented for signature to the taxpayer.
Answer (A) is incorrect. The list must be retained for a 3-year period. **Answer (C) is incorrect.** Jack is in compliance with the tax code. **Answer (D) is incorrect.** Jack is in compliance with the tax code.

16. Which of the following persons would be subject to the penalty for improperly negotiating a taxpayer's refund check?

A. A tax return preparer who operates a check cashing agency that cashes, endorses, or negotiates tax refund checks for returns he prepared.
B. A tax return preparer who operates a check cashing business and cashes checks for her clients as part of a second business.
C. The firm that prepared the tax return and is authorized by the taxpayer to receive a tax refund but not to endorse or negotiate the check.
D. A business manager who prepares tax returns for clients who maintain special checking accounts against which the business manager is authorized to sign certain checks on their behalf. The clients' federal tax refunds are mailed to the business manager, who has the clients endorse the checks and then deposits them in the special accounts.

Answer (A) is correct.
REQUIRED: The tax return preparer's obligations and penalty for improperly negotiating a refund check.
DISCUSSION: Section 6695(f) provides that any tax return preparer who endorses or otherwise negotiates any check issued to a taxpayer with respect to taxes imposed by the IRC will be subject to a penalty of $545 for each such check. A tax return preparer who operates a check cashing agency that cashes, endorses, or negotiates tax refund checks for returns that (s)he prepared is subject to the penalty.
Answer (B) is incorrect. The preparer's second business meets the definition of a bank. **Answer (C) is incorrect.** A preparer may receive checks provided (s)he does not cash it. **Answer (D) is incorrect.** The clients endorsed the checks.

17. Which of the following acts by a CPA will **not** result in a CPA's incurring an IRS penalty?

A. Failing, without reasonable cause, to provide the client with a copy of an income tax return.
B. Failing, without reasonable cause, to sign a client's tax return as preparer.
C. Understating a client's tax liability as a result of an error in calculation.
D. Negotiating a client's tax refund check when the CPA prepared the tax return.

Answer (C) is correct.
REQUIRED: The act that will not result in a CPA's incurring an IRS penalty.
DISCUSSION: Understating a client's tax liability as a result of an error in calculation will not result in imposition of an IRS penalty unless it is the result of gross negligence or a willful attempt to avoid tax liability.
Answer (A) is incorrect. A CPA is required to provide his or her client with a copy of the tax return. **Answer (B) is incorrect.** A tax preparer is required to sign the return. **Answer (D) is incorrect.** Any tax return preparer who endorses or otherwise negotiates a refund check issued to a taxpayer is liable for a $545 penalty.

18. Which of the following acts, if any, constitute grounds for a tax preparer penalty?

A. Without the taxpayer's consent, the tax preparer disclosed taxpayer income tax return information under an order from a state court.
B. At the taxpayer's suggestion, the tax preparer deducted the expenses of the taxpayer's personal domestic help as a business expense on the taxpayer's individual tax return.
C. Without the taxpayer expressly prohibiting it, the tax preparer used information from the taxpayer's return in a related taxpayer's return.
D. Without the taxpayer's consent, the tax preparer disclosed taxpayer income tax return information to a CPA firm conducting a peer review.

Answer (B) is correct.
REQUIRED: The acts, if any, that constitute grounds for a tax preparer penalty.
DISCUSSION: A $5,000 penalty is imposed on a tax return preparer if any part of an understatement of tax liability resulted from a willful attempt to understate the liability or from an intentional disregard of rules or regulations. A penalty will not be imposed if client information is disclosed under a court order.

19. A CPA who prepares clients' federal income tax returns for a fee must

A. File certain required notices and powers of attorney with the IRS before preparing any returns.
B. Keep a completed copy of each return for a specified period of time or keep a summarized list of specified return information.
C. Receive client documentation supporting all travel and entertainment expenses deducted on the return.
D. Indicate the CPA's federal identification number on a tax return only if the return reflects tax due from the taxpayer.

Answer (B) is correct.
REQUIRED: The duty of a CPA when preparing federal income tax returns.
DISCUSSION: A CPA who prepares clients' federal income tax returns for a fee meets the definition in the federal tax code of an income tax return preparer. An income tax return preparer is subject to penalties for certain types of failures. For example, for each failure to retain a copy of a prepared return, the penalty is $50. The copy must be retained for 3 years.
Answer (A) is incorrect. The IRC does not require such filing. **Answer (C) is incorrect.** The preparer is not required to examine documents to verify independently information provided by the taxpayer. But (s)he must make reasonable inquiry, if the information appears to be incorrect or incomplete, or determine the existence of required facts and circumstances incident to a deduction. **Answer (D) is incorrect.** The preparer is required to indicate his or her federal identification number on each return filed.

STUDY UNIT TWO
LIABILITY OF CPAs

(8 pages of outline)

2.1	Licensing and Disciplinary Systems	29
2.2	State Law Liability to Clients and Third Parties	31
2.3	Privileged Communication and Confidentiality	35

This study unit covers CPAs' legal responsibilities to clients and third parties. For example, CPAs may be liable for breach of contract, negligence, or fraud. The first subunit outlines federal and state disciplinary systems for accountants. The second subunit describes the reasons (1) for CPAs' liability and (2) the parties (client, third-party user of financial statements, etc.) to which they may be liable for errors and omissions, whether intentional or not. The third subunit addresses the rights and duties of accountants under federal law, state law, and AICPA ethics rules to protect confidential client information.

2.1 LICENSING AND DISCIPLINARY SYSTEMS

1. **State Boards of Accountancy**

    a. State boards of accountancy are governmental agencies that license accountants to use the designation **Certified Public Accountant**.

       1) **Requirements for licensure** vary from state to state. In addition to passing the CPA Examination and paying the applicable license fee, a candidate may need to satisfy a state's educational, experience, and residency criteria.

       2) Continuing professional education (CPE), peer review, and ethics standards also may vary by state. Meeting these standards is necessary to remain licensed.

       3) State boards can suspend or revoke licensure through administrative process, for example, in board hearings.

       4) **State CPA societies** are voluntary, private entities that can admonish, suspend, or expel members.

       5) CPA Examination questions do not test specific state disciplinary systems.

2. **AICPA Disciplinary Mechanisms**

    a. **Professional Ethics Division**

       1) The Professional Ethics Division investigates ethics violations by AICPA members.

       2) It imposes sanctions in less serious cases. For example, it may require a member to take additional CPE courses as a remedial measure.

    b. **Joint Ethics Enforcement Program (JEEP)**

       1) The AICPA and most state societies have agreements that permit referral of an ethics complaint either to the AICPA or to a state society.

       2) The AICPA handles matters of national concern, those involving two or more states, and those in litigation.

          a) JEEP also promotes formal cooperation between the ethics committees of the AICPA and of the state societies.

3. **Other Disciplinary Bodies**
    a. The **SEC**
        1) The SEC may seek an **injunction** from a court to prohibit future violations of the securities laws. Moreover, it may conduct **administrative proceedings** that are quasi-judicial.
            a) Such proceedings may result in **suspension** or permanent **revocation** of the right to practice before the SEC, including the right to sign any document filed by an SEC registrant. Sanctions are imposed if the accountant
                i) Does not have the qualifications to represent others
                ii) Lacks character or integrity
                iii) Has engaged in unethical or unprofessional conduct
                iv) Has willfully violated, or willfully aided and abetted the violation of, the federal securities laws or their rules and regulations
        2) Suspension by the SEC also may result from
            a) Conviction of a felony or a misdemeanor involving moral turpitude
            b) Revocation or suspension of a license to practice
            c) Being permanently enjoined from violation of the federal securities acts
        3) Some proceedings have prohibited not only individuals but also **accounting firms** from accepting SEC clients. Furthermore, the SEC can initiate administrative proceedings against accounting firms.
            a) The SEC may, for example, prohibit a firm from appearing before the SEC if it engages in unethical or improper professional conduct. Such misconduct may include negligence.
        4) The SEC may impose civil penalties in administrative proceedings.
            a) Furthermore, the SEC may order a violator to account for and surrender any profits from wrongdoing and may issue cease-and-desist orders for violations.
    b. The **IRS**
        1) The IRS may prohibit a CPA from practicing before the IRS if the person is incompetent or disreputable or does not comply with tax rules and regulations.
        2) The IRS also may impose fines.

STOP & REVIEW

You have completed the outline for this subunit.
Study multiple-choice questions 1 through 4 beginning on page 37.

2.2 STATE LAW LIABILITY TO CLIENTS AND THIRD PARTIES

1. **Contractual Liability to Client (also called Privity of Contract)**

    a. The contract between an accountant and a client is a personal service contract, so it can be litigated like any other type of contract. The usual remedy for **breach** of the contract is compensatory **monetary damages**.

    b. Legal issues in contract disputes and other matters are covered in the contract law outline in Study Unit 18. Legal issues include the following:

    1) Whether the elements of a contract are present,
    2) The duties of the parties,
    3) Who may enforce the contract,
    4) Who is liable for breach of contract,
    5) What remedies are available for breach, and
    6) Whether the accountant may delegate responsibility for an engagement.

2. **Contractual Liability to Third Parties**

    a. An accountant potentially may be liable to third-party beneficiaries of the contract.

3. **Accountant's Duties**

    a. The accountant is implicitly bound by the contract to perform the engagement with **due care** (nonnegligently) and in compliance with **professional standards**.

    1) Moreover, an accountant must comply with the law and is responsible for exercising independent professional judgment.

EXAMPLE 2-1   Accountant's Breach of Contract

An accountant and a client entity contract for the accountant to perform an audit for $2,500. The audit is contracted to be done within 3 months. The audit actually takes 6 months. A breach of contract has occurred.

---

   b. An understanding should be established regarding what services the accountant is to perform for the client. An **engagement letter** puts this contract in writing.

   1) The engagement letter should describe

   a) The services agreed upon by the client and accountant (whether or not required by professional standards),
   b) Fees to be paid, and
   c) Other pertinent details.

EXAMPLE 2-2   Engagement Letter vs. Professional Standards

The engagement letter may provide for positive confirmation of all accounts receivable. Professional standards may, in the circumstances of the specific engagement, permit negative confirmation of a sample of accounts receivable.

4. **Contractual Defenses**

    a. Typical defenses include the absence of one or more elements of a contract, substantial performance, or the impossibility of the other party to perform. For example, suspension or termination of performance may be justified because of the other party's prior breach.

5. **Tort Liability to Client for Negligence**

    a. An accountant may be liable in tort for losses caused by the accountant's negligence.

       1) A **tort** is a private wrong resulting from the breach of a legal duty imposed by society.

          a) The duty is not created by contract or other private relationship.

    b. Types of Negligence

       1) **Ordinary negligence** may result from an accountant's act or failure to act given a duty to act, for example, failing to observe inventory or confirm receivables.

       2) **Negligent misrepresentation** is a false representation of a material fact not known to be false but intended to induce reliance as opposed to intentional misrepresentation (fraud).

          a) The plaintiff must have reasonably relied on the misrepresentation and incurred damages.

       3) **Gross negligence** is failure to use even slight care.

          a) In extreme circumstances, an accountant may be liable for **punitive damages** if (s)he is grossly (not ordinarily) negligent.

    c. An accountant has a duty to exercise **reasonable care and diligence**.

       1) The accountant should have the degree of skill commonly possessed by other accountants in the same or similar circumstances, but an accountant is not a guarantor of the work.

       2) **Compliance with professional standards** demonstrates that the accountant exercised reasonable care and diligence and is therefore a defense against negligence claims.

       3) Accountants may be liable for failure to communicate to the client findings or circumstances that indicate misstatements in the accounting records or fraud.

          a) They also must communicate all significant deficiencies and material weaknesses in internal control.

    d. A client must prove all four of the elements of negligence.

       1) The accountant owed the plaintiff a **duty**.
       2) The accountant **breached** this duty.
       3) The accountant's breach **actually and proximately caused** harm to the plaintiff.

          a) Proximate cause is a chain of causation that is not interrupted by a new, independent cause. Moreover, the harm would not have occurred without the proximate cause. However, actual causation is insufficient. The harm also must have been reasonably foreseeable. Thus, proximate cause is a limit on liability and a possible defense.

       4) The plaintiff incurred **damages**.

6. **Tort Liability to Third Parties for Negligence**
    a. The majority rule is that the accountant is liable to **foreseen** (not necessarily identified in the contract) **third parties** (foreseen users and users within a foreseen class of users).
        1) Foreseen third parties are those to whom the accountant intends to supply the information or knows the client intends to supply the information.
            a) They also include persons who use the information in a way the accountant knows it will be used.

    > **EXAMPLE 2-3   Foreseen Users and Foreseen Class of Users**
    >
    > Smith, CPA, was engaged by Client, Inc., to audit its annual financial statements. Client's president told Smith that the financial statements would be distributed to South Bank in connection with a loan application. Smith was negligent in performing the audit. Subsequently, the financial statements were given to West Bank as well. West Bank lent Client $50,000 in reliance on the financial statements. West Bank suffered a loss on the loan. Smith is liable to West Bank because it is within a foreseen class of users, and the loan is a transaction similar to that for which the financial statements were audited.

    b. In some states, the accountant is liable to all **reasonably foreseeable third parties**. They are all members of the class of persons whose reliance on the financial statements the accountant may reasonably anticipate.

    > **EXAMPLE 2-4   Reasonably Foreseeable Third Parties**
    >
    > Smith, CPA, is engaged to audit the annual financial statements of Client. Smith is not informed of the intended use of the statements. However, Smith knows that they are routinely distributed to lessors, suppliers, trade creditors, and lending institutions. Client uses the statements, which were negligently prepared, to obtain a lease from XYZ, Inc., a reasonably foreseeable party. Smith will be liable to XYZ because it is a member of a class of reasonably foreseeable third parties.

    c. The traditional view was that an accountant was liable for **negligence** only to a plaintiff in **privity of contract** with the accountant or a primary (intended third-party) beneficiary of the engagement.
        1) A third party is a **primary beneficiary** if
            a) The accountant is retained principally to benefit the third party,
            b) The third party is identified, and
            c) The benefit pertains to a specific transaction. Thus, the accountant knows the particular purpose for which the third party will use and rely upon the work.

    > **EXAMPLE 2-5   Primary Beneficiary**
    >
    > Smith, CPA, was engaged by Client, Inc., to audit Client's annual financial statements. Client told Smith that the audited financial statements were required by Bank in connection with a loan application. Bank is a primary beneficiary and may recover damages caused by the CPA's negligence.

7. **Strict Liability in Tort**
    a. Strict liability without fault is not a basis for recovery from an accountant.

8. **Liability for Fraud**

   a. Fraud is an intentional misrepresentation. It is a willful and deceitful act. An accountant is liable for losses that result from his or her commission of fraud. Punitive and compensatory damages are both permitted.

   > **EXAMPLE 2-6   Fraud**
   >
   > An accountant is engaged to audit financial statements. To increase profits from the engagement, the accountant planned to and did omit necessary audit procedures. The accountant committed fraud.

   b. A finding of fraud requires proof of the following five elements:

      1) The accountant made a **misrepresentation**.
      2) The misrepresentation was made with **scienter**, that is, with actual knowledge of fraud.
      3) The misrepresentation was of a **material fact**.
      4) The misrepresentation induced **reliance**.
      5) Another person **justifiably relied** on the misstatement to his or her detriment.

   c. **Constructive fraud** is a fraud claim with the scienter requirement of actual knowledge satisfied by gross negligence.

      1) **Gross negligence** is such a reckless disregard for the truth that fraud is implied.

   d. Auditor-accountants have **no general duty to discover fraud**.

      1) Nevertheless, an auditor is held liable for failure to discover fraud when the auditor's negligence prevented discovery.
      2) An auditor who fails to follow professional standards and therefore does not discover fraud will probably be liable if compliance with professional standards would have detected the fraud.

   > **EXAMPLE 2-7   Duty to Discover Fraud**
   >
   > U.S. GAAS and PCAOB standards require an auditor to plan and perform the audit to provide **reasonable assurance** about whether the financial statements are free of material misstatement, whether caused by error or fraud. An auditor must (1) identify risks of material misstatement due to fraud; (2) assess the identified risks; and (3) respond by changing the nature, timing, and extent of audit procedures.

9. **Liability to Third Parties for Fraud**

   a. Liability is to all **reasonably foreseeable users** of the work product. A foreseeable user is any person that the accountant should have reasonably foreseen would be injured by justifiable reliance on the misrepresentation.

      1) Privity is not required. The accountant can be sued by others who rely on the work product. The plaintiff does not have to be the person or entity that entered into the contract with the accountant.
      2) A foreseeable user has the right to sue.

SU 2: Liability of CPAs

10. **Defenses to Fraud**
    a. A plaintiff must prove each element of fraud with particularity. Credible evidence that disproves one of the elements tends to negate liability.

STOP & REVIEW

You have completed the outline for this subunit. Study multiple-choice questions 5 through 18 beginning on page 38.

2.3 PRIVILEGED COMMUNICATION AND CONFIDENTIALITY

1. **Accountant-Client Privilege – Federal Law**
    a. Federal law does not recognize a broad privilege of confidentiality for accountant-client communications.
        1) However, a confidentiality privilege covers most **tax advice** provided to a current or prospective client by any individual qualified under federal law to practice before the IRS (e.g., CPA, attorney, enrolled agent, or enrolled actuary).
            a) The privilege is available only in matters brought before the IRS or in proceedings in federal court in which the U.S. is a party.
            b) The privilege applies only to advice on legal issues.
            c) The privilege does **not** apply to criminal tax matters, private civil matters, disclosures to other federal regulatory bodies, or state and local tax matters.

2. **Accountant-Client Privilege – State Law**
    a. State law does not recognize a privilege for accountant-client communications **except** in a minority of states.

EXAMPLE 2-8   **Accountant-Client Privilege under State Law**

State law provides for an accountant-client privilege. The IRS, in conducting a proper investigation, requests Accounting Firm to provide it with records on Client. The federal privilege does not apply. Firm complies, and Client sues Firm in state court. Firm asserts that federal law does not recognize the privilege and preempts state law. State court determines that, because the disclosure was without notice to Client and was made in the absence of service of legal process compelling disclosure, Firm is liable to Client for the voluntary disclosure.

---

1) If the privilege exists, it belongs to the client.
2) If any part of the privileged communication is disclosed by either the client or the accountant, the privilege is lost completely.

EXAMPLE 2-9   **Liability to Client Given a State Privilege**

In Example 2-8, disclosure by Firm to a third party (the IRS) negates the privilege with respect to the information. The information is no longer recognized as a protected confidential communication under the law of the state. However, Firm may still be liable to Client. Given the existence of a state privilege, Firm is still liable if, in the specific case, federal law does not preempt state law. Firm has a professional duty under the AICPA *Code of Professional Conduct*. It must not disclose confidential client information without consent except, for example, to comply with an enforceable summons or subpoena.

3. Client communications with accountants retained by attorneys to aid in litigation are protected by the **attorney-client** privilege. This privilege is recognized in federal and state courts.
4. **Working Papers**
    a. Working papers are confidential records of an accountant's performance of an engagement. They document the procedures performed, evidence obtained, and conclusions reached.
    b. Working papers are the **property of the accountant**.
        1) Because they are prepared by the accountant, they provide the best evidence of the accountant's performance.
        2) However, working papers may be subpoenaed by a third party for use in litigation in the many states that do not recognize a privilege for accountant-client communications.
        3) Without a court order or client consent, third parties have no right of **access** to working papers.
        4) Working papers may be disclosed to another CPA partner of the accounting firm without the client's consent because such information has not been communicated to outsiders.
    c. **Confidential Client Information Rule**
        1) A member of the AICPA in public practice must not disclose confidential client information without the client's consent. This rule does **not** affect the following:
            a) Professional obligations under the Compliance with Standards Rule and the Accounting Principles Rule
            b) The duty to comply with a valid subpoena or summons or with applicable laws and regulations
            c) An official review of the member's professional practice
                i) But a member's practice may be reviewed as part of a purchase, sale, or merger of the practice. However, appropriate precautions (e.g., a written agreement) should prevent disclosures by a prospective buyer.
            d) The member's right to initiate a complaint with or respond to any inquiry made by an appropriate investigative or disciplinary body, e.g., the professional ethics division or a trial board of the AICPA or a state CPA society peer review body
    d. At a minimum, an accountant who does **not** audit public companies should **retain** working papers until the state statute of limitations on legal action has lapsed. The limitations period varies by state and according to the type of claim.
    e. Auditors of public companies must retain working papers for at least 7 years.

STOP & REVIEW

You have completed the outline for this subunit.
Study multiple-choice questions 19 through 22 beginning on page 44.

QUESTIONS

2.1 Licensing and Disciplinary Systems

1. Which of the following professional bodies has the authority to revoke a CPA's license to practice public accounting?

A. National Association of State Boards of Accountancy.
B. State board of accountancy.
C. State CPA Society Ethics Committee.
D. Professional Ethics Division of AICPA.

Answer (B) is correct.
REQUIRED: The body with the authority to revoke a CPA's license.
DISCUSSION: A valid license is a prerequisite to the practice of public accounting. State boards of accountancy are the governmental agencies that license CPAs. Revocation or suspension of a CPA's license may be made only by the issuing board.
Answer (A) is incorrect. Only individual boards have the power to revoke licenses. **Answer (C) is incorrect.** State CPA societies and their ethics committees are not authorized to suspend or revoke a CPA's license. Expulsion by a state society does not prohibit the practice of public accounting. **Answer (D) is incorrect.** The AICPA and its committees are not authorized to suspend or revoke a CPA's license. Expulsion by the AICPA does not prohibit the practice of public accounting.

2. The SEC can suspend or revoke the right of an accountant to sign any document filed by an SEC registrant if the accountant

	Lacks Integrity	Engages in Unethical Conduct
A.	No	No
B.	No	Yes
C.	Yes	No
D.	Yes	Yes

Answer (D) is correct.
REQUIRED: The basis for discipline of an accountant by the SEC.
DISCUSSION: The SEC may conduct quasi-judicial proceedings. Pursuant to such proceedings, it may suspend or permanently revoke the right to practice before the SEC, including the right to sign any document filed by an SEC registrant, if the accountant does not have the qualifications to represent others, lacks character or integrity, has engaged in unethical or unprofessional conduct, or has willfully violated the federal securities laws or their rules and regulations.

3. The Securities and Exchange Commission (SEC) may discipline accountants. Under its disciplinary powers, the SEC may suspend an accountant's right to practice before it. What is a basis for suspension?

A. Conviction of any misdemeanor.
B. Intentional or unintentional violation of SEC regulations.
C. Being subject to a temporary restraining order regarding securities practice.
D. Conviction of a felony.

Answer (D) is correct.
REQUIRED: The basis for suspension of the right to practice before the SEC.
DISCUSSION: The SEC may suspend or permanently revoke the right to practice before the SEC, including the right to sign any document filed by a registrant, if the accountant (1) does not have the qualifications to represent others; (2) lacks character or integrity; (3) has engaged in unethical or unprofessional conduct; or (4) has willfully violated, or willfully aided and abetted the violation of, the federal securities laws or their rules and regulations. Suspension by the SEC also may result from (1) conviction of a felony, or a misdemeanor involving moral turpitude; (2) revocation or suspension of a license to practice; or (3) being permanently enjoined from violation of the federal securities acts.
Answer (A) is incorrect. The misdemeanor must involve moral turpitude, i.e., dishonesty of a high degree. An example of a crime of moral turpitude is bribery. **Answer (B) is incorrect.** The violation must be intentional. **Answer (C) is incorrect.** The injunction (an order to do or not do something) must be permanent.

4. If an ethics complaint is filed against a CPA, the matter

A. Must be handled by the professional ethics division of the AICPA.
B. Must be handled by a state CPA society.
C. Must be handled by a joint trial board of the AICPA.
D. May be handled, in most cases, by either the AICPA or a state CPA society.

Answer (D) is correct.
REQUIRED: The body(ies) that handle(s) ethics complaints against CPAs.
DISCUSSION: Under the Joint Ethics Enforcement Program (JEEP), the AICPA and most state societies have agreements that permit referral of an ethics complaint either to the AICPA or to a state society. However, the AICPA handles matters of national concern, those involving two or more states, and those in litigation.

2.2 State Law Liability to Clients and Third Parties

5. A client suing a CPA for negligent preparation of a tax return in a state court must prove each of the following factors **except**

A. Breach of duty of care.
B. Proximate cause.
C. Reliance.
D. Injury.

Answer (C) is correct.
REQUIRED: The factor not required to be proven in a negligence lawsuit.
DISCUSSION: A client suing an accountant for the unintentional tort of negligence must establish the following elements: (1) The accountant owed the client a duty, (2) the accountant breached this duty, (3) the accountant's breach actually and proximately caused the client's injury, and (4) the client suffered damages. Reasonable reliance on a misrepresentation is an element of fraud or of negligent misrepresentation.
Answer (A) is incorrect. Breach of a duty to conform to a specific standard of conduct for the protection of the plaintiff from unreasonable risk of injury is an element of the tort of negligence. **Answer (B) is incorrect.** Proximate cause is an element of the tort of negligence. Thus, liability is imposed not for all consequences of a negligent act but for those with a relatively close connection. **Answer (D) is incorrect.** The plaintiff must prove that damage to the defendant's person or property resulted from the negligent act.

6. Which of the following penalties is usually imposed against an accountant who, in the course of preparing a tax return, breaches common law contract duties owed to a client?

A. Specific performance.
B. Punitive damages.
C. Money damages.
D. Rescission.

Answer (C) is correct.
REQUIRED: The penalty usually imposed on an accountant for breach of contract.
DISCUSSION: The accountant-client contract is a personal service contract. Recovery for breach of contract ordinarily is limited to compensatory damages, and punitive damages are rarely allowed. Thus, an accountant is usually liable for money damages.
Answer (A) is incorrect. Specific performance for a personal service contract is not granted. **Answer (B) is incorrect.** Punitive damages for breach of contract are rarely allowed. **Answer (D) is incorrect.** Rescission returns the parties to the positions they would have occupied if the contract had not been made. It would only be applicable if the breach were material, such as an unjustifiable failure to perform.

7. Under the common law, which of the following statements is generally true regarding the liability of a CPA who negligently prepares a client's tax return?

A. The CPA is liable only to those third parties who are in privity of contract with the CPA.
B. The CPA is liable only to the client.
C. The CPA is liable to anyone in a class of third parties who the CPA knows will rely on the opinion.
D. The CPA is liable to all possible foreseeable users of the CPA's opinion.

Answer (C) is correct.
REQUIRED: The liability of a CPA to third parties for negligence.
DISCUSSION: Nearly all American courts once followed the landmark case of *Ultramares v. Touche*. The *Ultramares* rule limits a CPA's liability to persons in privity of contract with the accountant. Under *Ultramares*, only clients and primary beneficiaries of the engagement are permitted to sue the CPA. Currently, most courts extend a CPA's liability to anyone in a class of foreseen (but not necessarily individually identified) third parties who the CPA knows will use the information.
Answer (A) is incorrect. Lack of privity is not an effective defense against foreseen users that a CPA knows will rely on his or her opinion. **Answer (B) is incorrect.** A CPA incurs liability to certain third parties that are foreseen. **Answer (D) is incorrect.** While a few courts have adopted the broader view of holding the negligent CPA liable to reasonably foreseeable third-party users, none have adopted a rule of liability for all possible users of the CPA's opinion.

8. Which of the following facts must be proven for a lender to prevail in a state-law negligent misrepresentation action against a CPA who prepared a borrower's tax return that was disclosed to the lender?

A. The defendant made the misrepresentations with a reckless disregard for the truth.
B. The plaintiff justifiably relied on the misrepresentations.
C. The misrepresentations were in writing.
D. The misrepresentations concerned opinions.

Answer (B) is correct.
REQUIRED: The fact that must be proven to establish negligent misrepresentation.
DISCUSSION: Negligent misrepresentation occurs when the accountant makes a false representation of a material fact not known to be false but intended to induce reliance. The plaintiff must reasonably have relied on the accountant's misrepresentation and incurred damages.
Answer (A) is incorrect. Reckless disregard for the truth is an element in proving that a misrepresentation was grossly negligent. **Answer (C) is incorrect.** Under the negligence theory, the misrepresentation relied upon may be oral or written. A written misstatement is not necessary to prove negligent misrepresentation. **Answer (D) is incorrect.** Facts, not opinions, form the bases of a negligent misrepresentation case.

9. Under state law, which of the following statements most accurately reflects the liability of a CPA who fraudulently prepares a client's tax return?

A. The CPA is liable only to third parties in privity of contract with the CPA.
B. The CPA is liable only to known users of the financial statements.
C. The CPA probably is liable to any person who suffered a loss as a result of the fraud.
D. The CPA probably is liable to the client even if the client was aware of the fraud and did not rely on the opinion.

Answer (C) is correct.
REQUIRED: The liability of a CPA for fraud.
DISCUSSION: The distinctive feature of fraud is scienter, that is, intentional misrepresentation or reckless disregard for the truth (sometimes found in gross negligence). Because fraud involves intentional wrongdoing, the courts permit all foreseeable users of an accountant's work product to sue for damages proximately caused by the fraud.
Answer (A) is incorrect. Accountant liability can extend to all persons who incur loss resulting from the accountant's fraud regardless of privity. **Answer (B) is incorrect.** Accountant liability can extend to all persons who incur loss resulting from the accountant's fraud, not only those known to the accountant. **Answer (D) is incorrect.** An element of a fraud action is that the plaintiff relied justifiably on the material misstatement.

10. Hark, CPA, failed to follow generally accepted auditing standards in auditing the financial statements of Long Corp., a nonpublic company. Hark also took several tax return positions that were not likely to be sustained on the merits because they were not supported by substantial authority. Long's management had told Hark that the audited statements and tax returns would be submitted to several banks to obtain financing. Relying on these documents, Third Bank gave Long a loan. Long defaulted on the loan. In a jurisdiction applying the traditional common law doctrine, if Third sues Hark, Hark will

A. Win because Hark and Third were not in privity of contract.
B. Lose because Hark knew that banks would be relying on the financial statements.
C. Win because Third was contributorily negligent in granting the loan.
D. Lose because Hark was negligent in performing the audit.

Answer (A) is correct.
REQUIRED: The liability of a CPA to a third party under the traditional doctrine.
DISCUSSION: An accountant is not liable to all persons who are damaged by his or her negligence. Lack of privity is still a defense in some states. For example, under the holding in the *Ultramares* case, an accountant is liable for negligence only if the plaintiff was in privity of contract with the accountant or a primary beneficiary of the engagement. Under the primary benefit test, the accountant must have been aware that (s)he was hired to produce a work product to be used and relied upon by a particular third party. Because Long's management did not specifically name Third Bank to Hark, Hark will not be liable. However, most courts now extend a CPA's liability to anyone in a class of foreseen (but not necessarily individually identified) third parties who the CPA knows will use the information.
Answer (B) is incorrect. The traditional doctrine required that the accountant be engaged principally to benefit the third party and that the third party be identified. **Answer (C) is incorrect.** Although contributory negligence is a complete or partial limit on liability in certain circumstances, under the traditional doctrine, Hark is not liable to Third. **Answer (D) is incorrect.** Hark had not been contracted to perform for Third, and Third was not a primary beneficiary of Hark's contract with Long.

11. Which of the following elements, if present, would support a finding of common law constructive fraud on the part of a CPA who prepared a tax return?

A. Gross negligence.
B. Ordinary negligence.
C. Identified third-party users.
D. Scienter.

Answer (A) is correct.
REQUIRED: The element supporting a finding of constructive fraud on the part of a CPA.
DISCUSSION: Scienter is a prerequisite to liability for fraud. Scienter exists when the defendant makes a false representation with knowledge of its falsity or with reckless disregard as to its truth. For constructive fraud, the scienter requirement is met by proof of gross negligence (reckless disregard for the truth).
Answer (B) is incorrect. A good faith failure to comply with applicable standards is evidence of negligence. To prove fraud, more is required. **Answer (C) is incorrect.** For fraud, a CPA may be liable to all foreseeable users of his or her work. **Answer (D) is incorrect.** Scienter is a necessary element of fraud. For constructive fraud, the scienter element is proven by evidence of gross negligence.

SU 2: Liability of CPAs   41

12. If a shareholder sues a CPA in state court for nonstatutory fraud based on false information contained in a tax return prepared by the CPA, which of the following, if present, would be the CPA's best defense?

A. The shareholder lacks privity to sue.
B. The false information is immaterial.
C. The CPA did not financially benefit from the alleged fraud.
D. The contributory negligence of the client releases the CPA from liability.

Answer (B) is correct.
   REQUIRED: The best defense of a CPA sued for common law fraud by a third party.
   DISCUSSION: The tort of intentional misrepresentation (fraud, deceit) consists of a material misrepresentation made with scienter and an intent to induce reliance. The misstatement also must have proximately caused damage to a plaintiff who justifiably relied upon it. Scienter exists when the defendant makes a false representation with knowledge of its falsity or with reckless disregard as to its truth. The CPA's best defense would be that the false information is immaterial.
   Answer (A) is incorrect. Privity with the injured party is not an element of common law fraud. Any foreseeable user may recover. **Answer (C) is incorrect.** A benefit to the CPA is not an element of common law fraud. **Answer (D) is incorrect.** The negligence of a client does not excuse a CPA from liability for intentional misconduct.

13. Magnus Enterprises engaged a CPA firm to prepare its annual federal income tax return. Which of the following is a true statement with respect to the CPA firm's liability to Magnus for common law negligence?

A. Such liability cannot be varied by agreement of the parties.
B. The CPA firm will be liable for any fraudulent scheme it does not detect.
C. The CPA firm will not be liable if it can show that it exercised the ordinary care and skill of a reasonable person in the conduct of his or her own affairs.
D. The CPA firm must not only exercise reasonable care in what it does but also must possess at least that degree of accounting knowledge and skill expected of a CPA.

Answer (D) is correct.
   REQUIRED: The CPA firm's liability to a client for negligence.
   DISCUSSION: A professional is held to a higher standard of care than the ordinary person and also must possess and exercise the knowledge and skill of a member of that profession. Thus, the CPA firm must exercise both reasonable care and that expected of a CPA.
   Answer (A) is incorrect. A CPA may limit liability by agreement with the client. **Answer (B) is incorrect.** A CPA does not guarantee detection of fraudulent schemes. **Answer (C) is incorrect.** A CPA firm is held to a higher standard than that of an ordinary reasonable person in the conduct of his or her own affairs.

14. Which of the following is most likely to be effective as a defense in a breach of contract suit brought by a client against a CPA?

A. Inadequate consideration.
B. Partial performance.
C. Suspension or termination of performance justified because of the client's breach.
D. Alleged obligation within scope of contract.

Answer (C) is correct.
   REQUIRED: The defense to breach of contract most likely to be effective.
   DISCUSSION: Suspension or termination of the CPA's performance is justified due to a material breach of contract by the client. The nonbreaching party (the CPA) is discharged from any obligation to perform.
   Answer (A) is incorrect. Failure of consideration is a defense in a breach of contract suit. The adequacy of consideration ordinarily is not addressed by a court. **Answer (B) is incorrect.** Full or substantial performance is a defense in a breach of contract suit. **Answer (D) is incorrect.** A defense in a breach of contract suit is that the CPA's alleged obligation is not within the scope of the contract.

15. Ritz Corp. wished to acquire the stock of Stale, Inc. In conjunction with its plan of acquisition, Ritz hired Fein, CPA, to audit the financial statements of Stale and to prepare its state and federal income tax returns. Based on these documents, Ritz acquired Stale. Within 6 months, it was discovered that Stale's revenues and taxable income had been grossly overstated. Ritz commenced an action against Fein. Ritz believes that Fein failed to exercise the knowledge, skill, and judgment commonly possessed by CPAs in the locality but is not able to prove that Fein either intentionally deceived it or showed a reckless disregard for the truth. Ritz also is unable to prove that Fein had any knowledge that revenues and taxable income were overstated. Which of the following two common law causes of action provide Ritz with proper bases upon which Ritz will most likely prevail?

A. Negligence and breach of contract.
B. Negligence and gross negligence.
C. Negligence and fraud.
D. Gross negligence and breach of contract.

Answer (A) is correct.
REQUIRED: The bases upon which a client will most likely prevail when a CPA fails to exercise due care.
DISCUSSION: A CPA's nonstatutory liability to a client can be based upon breach of contract, negligence, or fraud. A breach of contract occurs when an accountant fails to perform duties required under a contract. These duties can either be express or implied. All contracts carry the implied duty to perform in a nonnegligent manner. To prevail in an action for negligence, the client must prove that the CPA did not act with the same degree of skill and judgment possessed by accountants in the locality. In an action for fraud, the client must prove scienter (intent to deceive or a reckless disregard for the truth). Ritz most likely prevails in an action brought for negligence or breach of contract if Fein failed to perform with the knowledge, skill, and judgment commonly possessed by CPAs in the area.
Answer (B) is incorrect. Ritz is unlikely to prevail in an action based upon gross negligence given its inability to prove an intent to deceive, a reckless disregard for the truth, or guilty knowledge. **Answer (C) is incorrect.** Ritz is unlikely to prevail in an action based upon fraud given its inability to prove an intent to deceive, a reckless disregard for the truth, or guilty knowledge. **Answer (D) is incorrect.** Ritz is unlikely to prevail in an action based upon gross negligence given its inability to prove an intent to deceive, a reckless disregard for the truth, or guilty knowledge.

16. The scope and nature of a CPA's contractual obligation to prepare tax returns for a client that is **not** publicly traded ordinarily is set forth in the

A. Management representation letter.
B. Scope paragraph of the auditor's report.
C. Engagement letter.
D. Introductory paragraph of the auditor's report.

Answer (C) is correct.
REQUIRED: The form of the contractual agreement with a client.
DISCUSSION: The CPA should establish an understanding with the client regarding the services to be rendered. The scope of the services, limitations, responsibilities of the parties, and fees for services should be set forth in a contract evidenced by an engagement letter. An engagement letter should be sent by the CPA to the prospective client on each engagement regardless of the services to be performed. If the client agrees to the contractual relationship by signing a copy of the letter and returning it to the CPA, it represents a written contract.
Answer (A) is incorrect. A management representation letter is obtained to confirm representations by management during an audit, to complement other procedures, and to avoid misunderstandings. **Answer (B) is incorrect.** The scope paragraph states (1) that the audit was conducted in accordance with GAAS [or, in the case of an audit of a public company, the standards of the Public Company Accounting Oversight Board (United States)], (2) the requirements of those standards, (3) a description of the nature of an audit, and (4) that the audit provides a reasonable basis for the opinion. **Answer (D) is incorrect.** The introductory paragraph states (1) that the financial statements were audited and (2) the responsibilities of management and the auditor.

17. ABC Construction Company enters into a personal service contract to hire Brown, CPAs, to perform services as an independent contractor. Brown's status as an independent contractor is inconsistent with

A. Signing a contract to perform tax services for Gator Construction, Inc., a construction company in the same market.
B. Outsourcing tax return preparation services to Green, CPAs, a well-respected local firm. Brown did not consult ABC about this decision.
C. Signing a contract to perform consulting services for Gator Construction, Inc., a similar-sized construction company in the same market.
D. Hiring a staff accountant to assist in the completion of the required services.

Answer (B) is correct.
REQUIRED: The action inconsistent with duties under a personal services contract.
DISCUSSION: The CPA must consult the client and obtain the client's permission when delegating responsibility for the engagement. The personal qualities of the CPAs are an inducement to enter the contract. Thus, performance by Green was not bargained for by ABC.
Answer (A) is incorrect. A CPA may perform services for the client's competitors. **Answer (C) is incorrect.** A CPA may perform services for the client's competitors. **Answer (D) is incorrect.** A CPA may hire another as an employee to assist in performing the engagement.

18. Under the common law, which of the following defenses, if used by a CPA, would best avoid liability in an action for negligence brought by a client?

A. The client was contributorily negligent.
B. The client was comparatively negligent.
C. The accuracy of the CPA's work was not guaranteed.
D. The CPA's negligence was not the proximate cause of the client's losses.

Answer (D) is correct.
REQUIRED: The best defense by a CPA against a client's negligence claim.
DISCUSSION: A plaintiff-client must prove all of the following elements of negligence: (1) the CPA owed the client a duty, (2) the CPA breached this duty, (3) the CPA's breach actually and proximately caused the client's injury, and (4) the client suffered damages. Proximate cause is a chain of causation that is not interrupted by a new, independent cause. Moreover, the injury would not have occurred without the proximate cause. However, actual causation is insufficient. The injury also must have been reasonably foreseeable. Thus, the concept of proximate cause limits liability to foreseeable damages. Accordingly, lack of proof of proximate cause precludes any recovery of damages.
Answer (A) is incorrect. Contributory negligence is not recognized as a defense in a substantial majority of states. Most states have adopted a comparative negligence approach that allows a contributorily negligent plaintiff to recover a percentage of the damages. **Answer (B) is incorrect.** The client is liable for his or her percentage of the damages in a state that applies the comparative negligence rule. **Answer (C) is incorrect.** A CPA's report offers reasonable assurance, not a guarantee.

2.3 Privileged Communication and Confidentiality

19. Which of the following statements is true regarding a CPA's working papers related to tax practice? The working papers must be

A. Transferred to another accountant purchasing the CPA's practice even if the client has not given permission.
B. Transferred permanently to the client if demanded.
C. Turned over to any government agency that requests them.
D. Turned over pursuant to a valid federal court subpoena.

Answer (D) is correct.
   REQUIRED: The true statement about working papers.
   DISCUSSION: The AICPA's Confidential Client Information Rule does not affect a CPA's obligation to comply with a validly issued and enforceable subpoena. Because no federal accountant-client privilege exists, a federal court may subpoena working papers.
   Answer (A) is incorrect. A CPA is required to obtain the client's permission before transferring his or her working papers to another CPA. This is true even if the other accountant is purchasing the CPA's firm. **Answer (B) is incorrect.** Working papers are the property of the CPA and ordinarily need not be transferred to the client upon request. **Answer (C) is incorrect.** Unless a summons or subpoena is issued, a governmental request need not be honored. Moreover, some states have provided for an accountant-client privilege.

20. Which of the following statements about disclosure of confidential client data resulting from a CPA's tax practice is generally true?

A. Disclosure may be made to any state agency without subpoena.
B. Disclosure may be made to any party with the consent of the client.
C. Disclosure may be made to comply with an IRS audit request.
D. Disclosure may be made to comply with generally accepted accounting principles.

Answer (B) is correct.
   REQUIRED: The condition allowing disclosure of confidential client data.
   DISCUSSION: Under the Confidential Client Information Rule, an accountant may disclose any confidential client information with the specific consent of the client.
   Answer (A) is incorrect. Disclosure may be made to a state agency only pursuant to a subpoena or summons or with the client's consent. **Answer (C) is incorrect.** Without a client's consent, an accountant may disclose confidential information to the IRS only in response to a subpoena or summons. **Answer (D) is incorrect.** Compliance with GAAP is a responsibility of clients who issue financial statements, not the accountants who advise them on tax matters or prepare their tax returns.

SU 2: Liability of CPAs

21. Thorp, CPA, was engaged to prepare tax returns and provide other tax services to Ivor Co. During the engagement, Thorp discovered that Ivor was selling worthless mortgages to investors. Ivor was indicted and Thorp was subpoenaed to testify at the criminal trial. Ivor claimed accountant-client privilege to prevent Thorp from testifying. Which of the following statements is true regarding Ivor's claim?

A. Ivor can claim an accountant-client privilege only in states that have enacted a statute creating such a privilege.
B. Ivor can claim an accountant-client privilege only in federal courts.
C. The accountant-client privilege can be claimed only in civil suits.
D. The accountant-client privilege can be claimed only to limit testimony to audit subject matter.

Answer (A) is correct.
REQUIRED: The true statement about accountant-client privilege.
DISCUSSION: Although communication between lawyers and clients is privileged, no common-law concept extends this privilege to the accountant-client relationship. A minority of states have enacted statutes recognizing the confidential communication between an accountant and a client as privileged.
Answer (B) is incorrect. Federal law recognizes a limited privilege for accountant-client communications in certain civil tax matters before the IRS or in proceedings in federal court in which the U.S. is a party. **Answer (C) is incorrect.** In states where the privilege exists, it also applies to criminal actions. **Answer (D) is incorrect.** In states where the privilege exists, it is not limited to audit matters.

22. Which of the following statements is true with respect to ownership, possession, or access to a CPA firm's working papers related to its tax practice?

A. Working papers may never be obtained by third parties unless the client consents.
B. Working papers are not transferable to a purchaser of a CPA practice unless the client consents.
C. Working papers are subject to the privileged communication rule, which, in most jurisdictions, prevents any third-party access to the working papers.
D. Working papers are the client's exclusive property.

Answer (B) is correct.
REQUIRED: The true statement about a CPA firm's working papers.
DISCUSSION: Transferring working papers to a purchaser of a practice is communication of the information they contain and violates the AICPA's Confidential Client Information Rule. However, this rule does not prohibit review of the CPA's practice, including a review in conjunction with the purchase, sale, or merger of the practice, if appropriate precautions are taken. One means of protecting the client's information is to enter into a written confidentiality agreement with the prospective purchaser.
Answer (A) is incorrect. A third party may obtain working papers without client consent when they are lawfully subpoenaed. **Answer (C) is incorrect.** The privileged communication rule does not exist except as provided for by statute in a minority of states. **Answer (D) is incorrect.** The working papers are the property of the CPA unless agreed otherwise. However, a CPA must not only return client-provided records upon request but also must make available information in the working papers not reflected in the client's books and records, without which the client's financial information would be incomplete.

Notes

STUDY UNIT THREE
FEDERAL TAX AUTHORITY, PROCEDURES, AND INDIVIDUAL TAXATION

(25 pages of outline)

3.1	Tax Authority	48
3.2	Tax Procedures	52
3.3	Tax Planning	62
3.4	Filing Status	65
3.5	Dependents	68

This study unit provides an understanding of federal tax authority, tax procedures, and tax planning before beginning our coverage of individual taxation.

Federal tax law (and the authority to tax) is composed of legislative, administrative, and judicial tax law. Understanding the hierarchy and intent of each authoritative source is critical for CPAs to conduct effective and efficient tax research.

Tax procedures cover the processes for

1) Determining a need to file a tax return,
2) Collecting tax through estimated payments,
3) Claiming refunds of taxes paid, and
4) Assessing or collecting a deficiency in payment.

Tax planning is a continuous process of analyzing options available for a business or individual that will minimize tax liabilities, but it is done in a way that maintains the overall objective of maximizing after-tax income. Planning options include timing of income, shifting of income, and conversion of income property. A critical aspect of tax planning is distinguishing between tax avoidance and tax evasion.

Filing status determines the amount of the standard deductions, applicable tax rates, and threshold amounts for various deductions and credits. For various tax benefits, taxpayers may be able to claim a dependent. To qualify as a taxpayer's dependent, an individual must be either a qualifying child or a qualifying relative; the criteria for both are heavily tested on the CPA Exam.

Related portions of IRS tax forms for reporting have been reproduced in the Knowledge Transfer Outline as a detailed practical reference to the related text. Some candidates find it helpful to have the entire tax form side-by-side with our Knowledge Transfer Outline when studying. The full versions of the most up-to-date forms are easily accessible at www.gleim.com/taxforms. These forms and the form excerpts used in our outline are periodically updated as the latest versions are released by the IRS.

3.1 TAX AUTHORITY

> **BACKGROUND 3-1   Constitutional Basis of Federal Taxation**
>
> The U.S. Constitution grants Congress the power to lay and collect taxes. The early federal government relied primarily on tariffs to fund its operations. However, when additional revenue was needed as a result of the Civil War, the United States enacted its first federal income tax in 1861. This tax was allowed to expire shortly after the war ended. Later, in 1894, the federal income tax was reintroduced. However, upon a legal challenge, the United States Supreme Court held that this income tax was a direct tax, and because the Constitution requires direct taxes levied by the federal government to be proportional to each state's population based on a census, the tax was unconstitutional.
>
> To remove this constitutional barrier to a federal income tax, the Sixteenth Amendment to the United States Constitution was ratified in 1913. This amendment provides that "Congress shall have the power to lay and collect taxes on incomes, from whatever source derived, without apportionment among the several states . . ." Shortly after the amendment was ratified, the modern income tax was passed by Congress with the Revenue Act of 1913.

1. **Authoritative Hierarchy**

    a. Authoritative tax law consists of legislative law, administrative law, and judicial law.

    Tax Authority Hierarchy

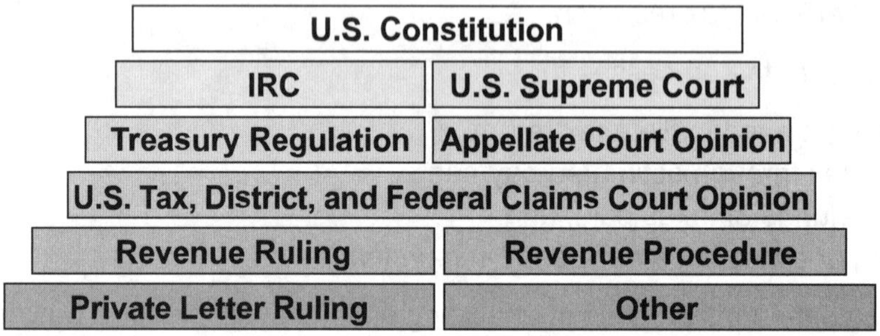

    ```
                    U.S. Constitution
              IRC           U.S. Supreme Court
       Treasury Regulation  Appellate Court Opinion
       U.S. Tax, District, and Federal Claims Court Opinion
          Revenue Ruling      Revenue Procedure
        Private Letter Ruling        Other
    ```

    Figure 3-1

    b. **Conflicting authority.** When there are conflicting sources of tax law within the same tier of the hierarchy, the most recent rule or law takes precedence.

2. **Legislative Law**

    a. Legislative law, which comes from Congress as signed by the President, is authorized by the Constitution and consists of the IRC and committee reports.

    b. *The Internal Revenue Code* of **1986** is the primary source of federal tax law. It imposes income, estate, gift, employment, miscellaneous excise taxes, and provisions controlling the administration of federal taxation. The Code is found at Title 26 of the United States Code (U.S.C.). As long as it is constitutionally valid, each IRC section is binding on the Supreme Court and, by default, all other federal courts.

    c. **Committee Reports** along with the **Congressional Record** are useful tools in determining Congressional intent behind certain tax laws and helping examiners apply the law properly.

3. **Administrative Law**

   a. Administrative tax law is a catch-all term for the rules, regulations, and procedures implemented and enforced by the Treasury Department. The IRS is a bureau of the Treasury Department. In practice, the IRS's Office of Chief Counsel writes administrative tax law, and it is approved by the Secretary of the Treasury, which is a Cabinet-level position nominated by the President and confirmed by the U.S. Senate.

      1) **Treasury Regulations** (Proposed, Temporary, or Final) are interpretations of the IRC that allow the Treasury Department to implement the IRC. They are authorized and allowed under law by the IRC, making them a primary authoritative source when conducting tax research.

         a) The IRS is bound by the regulations because it is a bureau within the Treasury Department. Courts are bound to follow them to the extent that the court does not find they conflict with the IRC.

      2) A **revenue ruling** is an official interpretation of Internal Revenue law as applied to a given set of facts and is issued by the Internal Revenue Service.

         a) Revenue rulings are published in Internal Revenue Bulletins to inform and advise taxpayers, the IRS, and others on substantive tax issues.

         b) Publication of revenue rulings is intended to promote uniform application of tax laws by IRS employees and to reduce the number of letter ruling requests.

         c) Revenue rulings may be cited as precedent and relied upon when resolving disputes, but they do not have the force and effect of regulations nor are they binding on a court.

            i) Revenue rulings are considered a primary authoritative source when conducting tax research.

      3) A **revenue procedure** is an official IRS statement that prescribes procedures that affect the rights or duties of taxpayers. They primarily address administrative and procedural matters and do not have the force of law, but they may be cited as precedent. In addition, rulings and procedures may be the basis for appealing adverse return examinations to the tax court and other federal courts.

      4) **Private Letter Rulings**

         a) In response to a request for guidance, the IRS may respond in writing to a taxpayer concerning guidance on specific facts and situations. This **Private Letter Ruling (PLR)** binds the IRS and the taxpayer requesting the ruling may rely on it, but other parties who may have similar circumstances may not rely on the PLR.

            i) Thus, third parties may not rely upon a PLR as precedent.

            ii) However, the IRS sometimes redacts personal information and responds to a request for a PLR with a Revenue Ruling, which becomes binding on all taxpayers and the IRS.

      5) **Technical Advice Memoranda (TAMs)** are requested by IRS area offices after a return has been filed, often in conjunction with an ongoing examination. Similar to a PLR, a TAM is binding on the IRS in relation to the taxpayer who is the subject of the ruling, but other parties who may have similar circumstances may not rely on the TAM.

b. The **Internal Revenue Bulletin (IRB)** is the authoritative announcement from the IRS concerning IRS rulings and procedures, Treasury Decisions, Executive Orders, Tax Conventions, legislation, court decisions, and other items of general interest. It is published on a weekly basis by the Government Printing Office.

c. IRS **Publications** explain the law in plain language for taxpayers and their advisors. They typically highlight changes in the law and provide examples illustrating Service positions. Publications are not binding on the Service and do not necessarily cover all positions for a given issue. While a good source of general information, publications should not be cited to sustain a position.

4. **Judicial Law**

    a. Judicial law is common law that originates from the federal court system and is primarily comprised of court opinions. Court cases are considered a primary authoritative source when conducting tax research.

    b. The court system is comprised as follows:

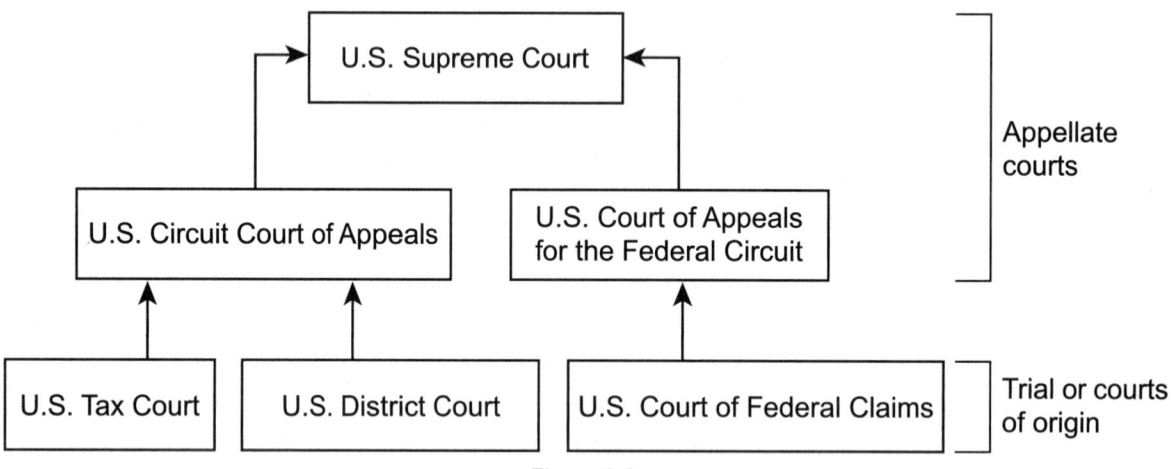

Figure 3-2

c. **Tax Court**

   1) Decisions of the Tax Court are issued as either regular decisions or memorandum decisions.

      a) **Regular decisions** establish precedent either through a new tax matter or unique facts and circumstances for a tax matter that has been previously settled.

      b) A **Tax Court memorandum** decision is a report of a Tax Court decision thought to be of little value as a precedent because the issue has been decided one or more times before.

d. Cases from the U.S. Tax Court and the U.S. District Courts are appealed to the appropriate U.S. Circuit Court of Appeals. Cases from the U.S. Court of Federal Claims are appealed to the U.S. Court of Appeals for the Federal Circuit.

e. **U.S. Supreme Court**

   1) The U.S. Supreme Court can exercise its discretionary authority to review decisions of the courts of appeals and other federal courts.

   2) A **writ of certiorari** is an order by the Supreme Court to hear a case. The court's certiorari jurisdiction (i.e., whether the court chooses to hear a case) is purely discretionary. A denial of a petition for a writ of certiorari by the Supreme Court expresses no opinion on the merits of the case, and the previous court's opinion on the case stands.

   3) If the Court determines that various lower courts are deciding a tax issue in an inconsistent manner, it may pronounce a decision and resolve the contradiction.

STOP & REVIEW

You have completed the outline for this subunit.
Study multiple-choice questions 1 through 5 beginning on page 72.

3.2 TAX PROCEDURES

1. **Tax Prepayments and Penalties for Individuals**

    a. The IRC is structured to obtain a large portion of the final tax (after nonrefundable credits) through **withholding** and **estimated tax** payments. Individuals who earn income not subject to withholding must pay estimated tax on that income in quarterly installments.

    1) For a calendar-year taxpayer, the installments are due by April 15, June 15, and September 15 of the current year and January 15 of the following year.

    2) Each of the following is treated as prepayment of tax:

        a) Overpayment of tax in a prior tax year, which has not been refunded
        b) Amounts withheld (by an employer) from wages
            i) The aggregate amount is treated as if equal parts were paid on each due date, unless the individual establishes the actual payment dates.
        c) Direct payment by the individual (or another on his or her behalf)
        d) Excess FICA withheld when an employee has two or more employers during a tax year who withheld (in the aggregate) more than the ceiling on FICA taxes
        e) Refundable tax credits

    3) Each installment must be at least 25% of the lowest of the following amounts:

        a) 100% [110% for taxpayers whose prior year's AGI exceeds $150,000 ($75,000 for married filing separately)] of the prior year's tax (if a return was filed)
        b) 90% of the current year's tax
        c) 90% of the annualized current year's tax (applies when income is uneven)

EXAMPLE 3-1   Estimated Tax Payments

John's tax liability for 2020 was $10,000 and his AGI was $100,000. John projects his tax liability for 2021 to be $12,000. In order to avoid an underpayment of estimated tax penalty, John must pay through withholdings and estimated payments throughout the year, i.e., the lesser of $10,000 (100% of prior year tax, the 110% is not applied because John's prior year AGI is less than $150,000) or $10,800 (90% of the current year tax).

---

    4) Tax refers to the sum of the regular tax, AMT, self-employment tax, and household employee tax.

From Form 1040-ES Instructions--Estimated Tax Worksheet

c	Total [Year] estimated tax. Subtract line 11b from line 11a. If zero or less, enter -0- . . . ▶	11c
12a	Multiply line 11c by 90% (66 2/3% for farmers and fishermen)	12a
b	Required annual payment based on prior year's tax (see instructions) .	12b
c	**Required annual payment to avoid a penalty.** Enter the **smaller** of line 12a or 12b . . . ▶	12c
	Caution: Generally, if you do not prepay (through income tax withholding and estimated tax payments) at least the amount on line 12c, you may owe a penalty for not paying enough estimated tax. To avoid a penalty, make sure your estimate on line 11c is as accurate as possible. Even if you pay the required annual payment, you may still owe tax when you file your return. If you prefer, you can pay the amount shown on line 11c. For details, see chapter 2 of Pub. 505.	
13	Income tax withheld and estimated to be withheld during [Year] (including income tax withholding on pensions, annuities, certain deferred income, etc.)	13
14a	Subtract line 13 from line 12c	14a
	Is the result zero or less?	
	☐ **Yes.** Stop here. You are not required to make estimated tax payments.	
	☐ **No.** Go to line 14b.	
b	Subtract line 13 from line 11c	14b
	Is the result less than $1,000?	
	☐ **Yes.** Stop here. You are not required to make estimated tax payments.	
	☐ **No.** Go to line 15 to figure your required payment.	
15	If the first payment you are required to make is due [April 15], enter ¼ of line 14a (minus any [prior year] overpayment that you are applying to this installment) here, and on your estimated tax payment voucher(s) if you are paying by check or money order	15

    b. A penalty is imposed if, by the quarterly payment date, the total of estimated tax payments and income tax withheld is less than 25% of the required minimum payment for the year.

        1) The penalty is determined each quarter.
        2) The penalty is not allowed as an interest deduction.

    c. The penalty will not be imposed if any of the following apply:

        1) Actual tax liability shown on the return for the current tax year (after reduction for withholdings and refundable credits) is less than $1,000.

EXAMPLE 3-2   Underpayment Penalty

Taxpayer has a tax liability of $11,000 for 2021. Taxpayer's employer withheld $7,000 for 2021. Taxpayer's 2020 liability was $7,000 and AGI was $160,000.

Even though only $700 [($7,000 prior year liability × 110%) – $7,000 current year withholding] is subject to the penalty, the $1,000 minimum exception does not apply due to the fact that the exception is based on the current year. The total tax liability shown on the tax return of $11,000 minus the amount paid through withholding of $7,000 is greater than $1,000. Hence, the taxpayer will be subject to an underpayment penalty.

---

        2) No tax liability was incurred in the prior tax year.
        3) The IRS waives it for reasonable cause shown.

d. Any tax liability must be paid by the original due date of the return. An automatic extension for filing the return does not extend time for payment. Interest will be charged from the original due date. Failure to file or pay on time results in a penalty based on the unpaid liability (Tax liability – Prepaid amount).

   1) A penalty of 5% per month up to 25% of unpaid liability is assessed for **failure to file** a return. Additionally, the minimum penalty for filing a return over 60 days late is the lesser of $435 (for 2021 returns filed in 2022) or 100% of tax due.

   2) A penalty of 0.5% per month up to 25% of unpaid liability is assessed for **failure to pay** tax.

      a) In general, a failure-to-pay penalty is imposed from the due date for taxes (other than the estimated taxes) shown on the return. A failure-to-pay penalty may offset a failure-to-file penalty. When an extension to file is timely requested, a failure-to-pay penalty may be avoided by paying at least 90% of the actual liability by the original due date of the return and paying the remaining balance when the return is filed. Exceptions and adjustments to these rules may apply in unique situations.

2. **Filing Requirements**

   a. An individual must file a federal income tax return if gross income is above a threshold, net earnings from self-employment is $400 or more, or (s)he is a dependent (i.e., listed on another person's tax return) with more gross income than the standard deduction or with unearned income over $1,100.

   NOTE: In contrast to individuals, corporations (including S corporations) must file an income tax return regardless of gross income.

   1) Until 2026, the gross income threshold amount generally is the standard deduction, excluding any additional amount for being blind.

   2) Net unearned income of a dependent child is taxed to the dependent at rates higher than the child's marginal tax rates. This is referred to as the **"Kiddie Tax."** This tax is designed to discourage parents from shifting unearned income to their children with lower tax rates. These higher rates are the parents' marginal tax rates. Net unearned income is unearned income minus the sum of

      a) $1,100 (first $1,100 clause) and
      b) The greater of (1) $1,100 of the standard deduction or $1,100 of itemized deductions or (2) the amount of allowable deductions that are directly connected with the production of unearned income.

EXAMPLE 3-3   **Taxable Income of a Dependent Child**

Chris, dependent child age 5, has $4,600 of unearned income and no earned income. How much of his income will be subject to the Kiddie Tax?

Unearned income	$4,600
First $1,100 clause	(1,100)
Standard deduction	(1,100)
Net unearned income	$2,400

NOTE: A dependent is allowed at least $2,200 ($1,100 + $1,100) reduction in unearned income.

SU 3: Federal Tax Authority, Procedures, and Individual Taxation 55

      c) **Unearned** income is all taxable income other than earned income. Earned income is payment received for performance of personal services and is usually reported on Form W-2.

Examples of Child Income

Earned	Unearned
Salaries	Interest
Wages	Dividends
Tips	Capital gains
Scholarships	Trusts distributions
	Gifts
	Debt cancellation
	Pension/Annuities
	Social Security
	Royalties

SUCCESS TIP: Historically, exam questions have provided the applicable standard deduction amount for dependents with unearned income, eliminating the need to memorize the specific amount. However, you should have a general idea of the amount.

3. **Due Dates and Related Extensions**

    a. **Individual** tax returns must be filed (postmarked) no later than the 15th day of the **4th** month (or 3 months and 15 days) following the close of the tax year. This is April 15 for calendar-year taxpayers.

       1) An automatic **6-month** extension is available by filing Form 4868. This extends the deadline to October 15 for calendar-year taxpayers.

       2) The extension does not grant any additional time to pay taxes due.

    b. **C corporation** tax return due dates changed significantly beginning with the 2016 tax year. Eventually, all C corporations will have original due dates on the 15th day of the 4th month following the end of the tax year, and extended due dates 6 months later on the 15th day of the 10th month following the end of the tax year.

       1) The following table shows the due dates and extension dates through 2026 when all are again unified. Changes/differences are in bold:

Tax Year Type	Through 2025	2026
June 30 Fiscal Year	Original: **3rd month** (Sept. 15) Extended: 10th month (April 15)	Original: **4th month** (Oct. 15) Extended: 10th month (April 15)
Calendar/Other Fiscal Year	Original: 4th month Extended: 10th month	

c. **S corporation** tax returns must be filed (postmarked) no later than the 15th day of the **3rd** month following the close of the tax year. This is March 15 for calendar-year taxpayers.

   1) An automatic **6-month** extension is available by filing Form 7004. This extends the deadline to September 15 for calendar-year taxpayers.
   2) The extension does not grant any additional time to pay taxes due.

d. **Partnership** tax returns must be filed (postmarked) no later than the 15th day of the **3rd** month following the close of the tax year. This is March 15 for calendar-year taxpayers.

   1) An automatic **6-month** extension is available by filing Form 7004. This extends the deadline to September 15 for calendar-year taxpayers.

e. If the 15th day falls on a Saturday, Sunday, or legal holiday, the due date is extended until the next business day.

Summary of Due Dates for Calendar-Year Taxpayers Other than C Corporations

Return Type	Original Due Date	Extension Due Date
S Corporation	March 15	September 15
Partnership	March 15	September 15
Individual	April 15	October 15

4. **Disclosure of Tax Positions**

   a. A tax position may not be adopted without **substantial authority** for the position.

      1) There is substantial authority for the tax treatment of an item only if the weight of the authorities supporting the treatment is substantial in relation to the weight of authorities supporting contrary treatment.

         a) What constitutes substantial authority is defined by statute and IRS statements.

            i) A revenue ruling, for example, constitutes legal authority that, together with other authority, may be found substantial.

      2) Statute does not generally define an exact probability percentage as substantial authority. However, the Statements on Standards for Tax Services issued by the AICPA suggests it is generally interpreted as requiring that a position has approximately a 40% likelihood of being upheld on its merits if challenged.

SU 3: Federal Tax Authority, Procedures, and Individual Taxation

b. A taxpayer's accuracy-related penalty due to disregard of rules and regulations, or substantial understatement of income tax, may be avoided if the return position is adequately disclosed and has a reasonable basis. Generally, the penalty is equal to 20% of the underpayment. The penalty is not figured on any part of an underpayment on which the fraud penalty is charged.

   1) **Reasonable basis** (generally greater than 20% probability) is a relatively high standard of tax reporting that is significantly higher than not frivolous or not patently improper.

      a) The reasonable basis standard is not satisfied by a return position that is merely arguable.

   2) Disregard of the rules and regulations includes any careless, reckless, or intentional disregard.

   3) Substantial understatement of income tax occurs when the understatement is more than the larger of 10% of the correct tax or $5,000. In addition to adequate disclosure and a reasonable basis, the amount of the understatement may be reduced to the extent the understatement is due to a tax treatment for which the taxpayer has substantial authority.

   4) Whether there is substantial authority for the tax treatment of an item depends on the facts and circumstances. Some of the items that may be considered are court opinions, Treasury regulations, revenue rulings, revenue procedures, and notices and announcements issued by the IRS and published in the IRB that involve the same or similar circumstances as the taxpayer's.

   5) To adequately disclose the relevant facts about the tax treatment of an item, use Form 8275, *Disclosure Statement*. There must also be a reasonable basis for the taxpayer's treatment of the item. Form 8275-R, *Regulation Disclosure Statement*, is used to disclose items or positions contrary to regulations.

   6) Adequate disclosure has no effect on items attributable to tax shelters.

      a) For tax shelters, tax preparers are required to have both substantial authority and a reasonable belief for their position. This belief must be "more likely than not" (generally greater than 50% probability) the proper treatment.

   7) Showing a reasonable cause also includes showing actions were taken in good faith.

5. **Recordkeeping**

   a. Books of account or records sufficient to establish the amount of gross income, deductions, credit, or other matters required to substantiate any tax or information return must be kept.

      1) Records must be maintained as long as the contents may be material in administration of any internal revenue law.

      2) Employers are required to keep records on employment taxes until at least 4 years after the due date of the return or payment of the tax, whichever is later.

6. **Claims for Refund**
    a. A claim for refund of federal income tax overpaid for the current tax year is made by filing a return (Form 1040). A refund claim for a prior year is made by filing an amended return (Form 1040X). Form 843 is used to claim a refund of any other tax.
    b. Application for a tentative carryback adjustment to get a quick refund for carryback of an unused business credit is made on Form 1045 (individuals) or Form 1139 (corporations). Corporations also use Form 1139 for carrybacks of net capital losses.
    c. A claim for refund must be made within the **statute of limitations** period for refunds. In general, most refund claims must be filed by the later of 3 years from the due date (April 15, plus the filing extension time) or 2 years after the tax was paid.
        1) An early return is treated as filed on the due date (April 15).
        2) Taxes withheld, estimated tax payments, and credits are deemed to be paid on the 15th day of the 4th month following the close of the taxpayer's tax year (April 15 for calendar-year taxpayers).

EXAMPLE 3-4	Refund Claim Expiration -- Due Date

A calendar-year taxpayer filed his Year 1 return late on June 15, Year 2. The taxpayer had taxes withheld by his employer in Year 1, which are deemed paid on April 15, Year 2. A timely claim for a refund of the taxes withheld must be made by April 15, Year 5 (3 years from the due date). Filing a return late (without an extension) does not change the deadline to file a claim for refund.

EXAMPLE 3-5	Refund Claim Expiration -- Extension

Had the taxpayer in Example 3-4 filed for an extension and timely filed his return on June 15, Year 2, the timeframe for claiming a refund of the taxes withheld would expire on June 15, Year 5 (3 years from the due date including extensions).

EXAMPLE 3-6	Refund Claim Expiration -- Payment Date

A taxpayer files his Year 1 return on April 15, Year 2. The general refund statute of limitations expires on April 15, Year 5. However, if the taxpayer pays additional tax due of $500 for tax Year 1 on June 15, Year 4, the taxpayer will have until June 15, Year 6, to request a refund of the $500 under the 2-year rule.

   3) If a taxpayer does not file a return, a refund must be claimed within 2 years from the time the tax was paid. However, a taxpayer can file a late return within 3 years of a tax return's due date (plus time on extension) and receive a refund of an overpayment of tax.

EXAMPLE 3-7	Refund Claim Expiration -- Late Return

An intern works for 3 months over the summer and has taxes withheld from their paycheck and deposited with the IRS but does not file a tax return. The intern has 3 years from the return's due date to file a late tax return requesting a refund.

   4) If the claim relates to worthless securities or bad debts, and the fact of worthlessness was not discovered until after the original return was filed, the period of limitation is increased to 7 years.

EXAMPLE 3-8	Refund Claim Expiration -- Worthless Security/Bad Debt

A taxpayer did not learn that a security had become worthless during Year 1 until Year 2, after the taxpayer had already filed the tax return. The taxpayer has 7 years (until Year 9) to amend the return.

7. **Assessment of Deficiency**

   a. A deficiency is any excess of tax imposed over the sum of amounts shown on the return plus amounts previously assessed (reduced by rebates). Assessment of tax is made by recording the liability of the taxpayer in the office of the Secretary of the Treasury. The following flowchart is provided to illustrate the process.

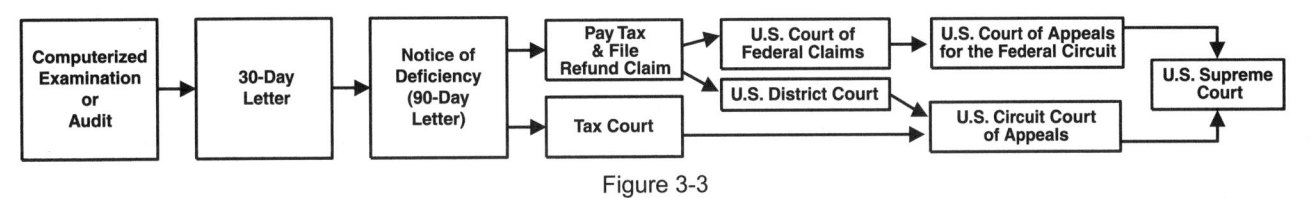

   Figure 3-3

   b. Computerized examination or audit of a return may result in an IRS examiner proposing an addition to tax. A letter stating the proposal is sent to the taxpayer. It is referred to as a **30-day letter**.

   c. If the taxpayer agrees with the proposed adjustment(s), the taxpayer accepts the changes and pays any deficiency.

   d. If consensus is not reached with the examiner in a conference with his or her supervisor or from an administrative appeal, a **notice of deficiency (ND)** is mailed to the taxpayer, but no sooner than 30 days after a 30-day letter.

      1) A notice of deficiency is referred to as a 90-day letter.
      2) A notice of deficiency is a prerequisite to assessment.
      3) However, immediate assessment, i.e., without a notice of deficiency, is allowed for the following:

         a) Tax shown on a return filed by a taxpayer
         b) Mathematical and clerical errors in a return
         c) Overstatement of credits
         d) Tax for which assessment is waived

   e. A taxpayer may institute a proceeding in the U.S. Tax Court within the 90 days following mailing of the ND (150 days if the taxpayer lives outside the U.S.). The ND is a prerequisite to a U.S. Tax Court proceeding.

      1) Payment of the deficiency is not required. Payment after the ND is mailed does not deprive the U.S. Tax Court of jurisdiction.

   f. If a petition is not filed with the U.S. Tax Court, taxes may be assessed 90 days after the ND is mailed.

      1) Filing the petition suspends the 90-day period.

   g. Partial or full payment of a deficiency prior to mailing of the ND deprives the Tax Court of jurisdiction. After full payment of any deficiency balance, the taxpayer may file a claim for refund and, if it is denied by the IRS, may institute a refund proceeding in a U.S. district court or the U.S. Court of Federal Claims.

      1) A jury is available only in a U.S. district court. One or more judges decide all issues in the U.S. Tax Court and the U.S. Court of Federal Claims.

h. Authority to assess tax liability is limited by statute to specific periods.

1) The general **statute of limitations** (S/L) for assessment of a deficiency is 3 years from the date the return was filed.

   a) A return filed before the due date is treated as filed on the due date.
   b) The IRS generally has 10 years following the assessment to begin collection of tax by levy or a court proceeding.

2) The S/L is 6 years if there is omission of items of more than 25% of gross income stated in the return. Specifically for goods or services from a trade or business, gross income includes gross receipts before deduction for cost of goods sold. Only items completely omitted are counted.

EXAMPLE 3-9   Calculation of 25% of Gross Income Threshold for 6-Year S/L

A sole proprietor had the following income transactions:

Gross receipts	$300,000
Less: COGS	(200,000)
Net business income	$100,000
Capital gains	40,000
Gross income	$140,000

For determining the 25% GI threshold, the sole proprietor's GI is as follows:

Gross receipts	$300,000
Capital gains	40,000
Gross income for 25% threshold	$340,000

Note that for the nonbusiness item, i.e., capital gains, only the gain and not the sale amount is included.

---

3) **Failure to file.** The S/L period does not commence before a return is filed.

   a) When no return has been filed, the assessment period is unlimited.

4) **Fraud.** Attempting to evade tax results in an unlimited assessment period. Fraud cannot be cured by filing a correct amended return.

5) The S/L period begins to run when a return filed late is received by the IRS.

6) Extension. The S/L period may be extended by an agreement between the taxpayer and the IRS entered into before the S/L expires.

   a) Each time an extension has been requested (or after expiration if there has been a levy), the IRS must notify the taxpayer that the taxpayer may refuse to extend the period of limitations or may limit the extension to particular issues or to a particular period of time.

SU 3: Federal Tax Authority, Procedures, and Individual Taxation

i. Mitigation of the statute of limitations. In certain circumstances, the statute of limitations may unjustly penalize the taxpayer or the government for a given return position.

EXAMPLE 3-10   **Effect of Mitigation of the Statute of Limitations**

The taxpayer reports an item of income in 2019. During an examination of the 2021 year return conducted on March 15, 2025, the IRS asserts the item should have been reported on the 2021 return. The statute of limitations to amend the 2019 return has expired. Without mitigation of the statute of limitations, the taxpayer would have to pay income tax on the item as earned in 2021. Therefore, without the mitigation provisions outlined below, the taxpayer would have to pay twice for the same item of income: once for the 2019 return, now barred by statute, and again for the 2021 return.

---

1) The mitigation provisions are limited to **income tax**, not gift, etc., when the following circumstances are met:
    a) There is a "determination" for a tax year concerning the treatment of an item of income (e.g., Tax Court decision);
    b) On the date of determination, correction of the error must be barred (i.e., statute of limitations);
    c) There must be a condition necessary for adjustment, i.e., double income (deduction); and
    d) In the proceeding of determination, the successful party must have taken a position inconsistent with the position in the closed year.

j. If unable to pay the full liability (i.e., doubt as to collectibility), the taxpayer may apply for an **offer-in-compromise**. The IRS considers the taxpayer's
   1) Ability to pay,
   2) Income,
   3) Expenses, and
   4) Asset equity.

SUCCESS TIP

The statute of limitations, both for a taxpayer claiming a refund and for the IRS assessing a deficiency, is a consistently tested topic on the exam.

---

8. **Closed Cases**
    a. Cases closed after examination will not be reopened to make adjustments unfavorable to the taxpayer except under certain circumstances. Qualifying circumstances include evidence of fraud, malfeasance, collusion, concealment, or misrepresentation of a material fact.

STOP & REVIEW

You have completed the outline for this subunit.
Study multiple-choice questions 6 through 10 beginning on page 74.

3.3 TAX PLANNING

> **BACKGROUND 3-2**   **Role of Tax Planning**
>
> Reduction of tax may always be important but should not be the deciding factor behind every financial action. The goal of maximizing "after-tax" wealth is not always the same as minimizing taxes. The role of tax planning is to assist individuals and businesses in reaching maximization of after-tax wealth in the most tax-efficient way possible.

1. Tax planning is the consideration of tax implications for individual or business decisions, usually with the intent of minimizing, or at least reducing, the tax liability. It includes, among other things, considering alternative treatments, projecting the tax consequences, and determining the role of taxes in decision making.

    a. The three most basic and common types of tax planning are

    1) Timing of income recognition,
    2) Shifting of income among taxpayers and jurisdictions, and
    3) Conversion of income among high- and low-rate activities.

2. **Timing**

    a. The timing technique accelerates or defers recognition of income and/or deductions. The advice most often heard is to defer income and accelerate deductions. This results in the lowest tax liability for the current year.

    1) However, in a year in which the taxpayer's rates are lower than the rates will be the following year, it is advisable to do just the opposite.

    b. The following items should be considered when evaluating the use of timing techniques:

    1) Time value of money (e.g., can the taxpayer make a higher return on income realized and reinvested this year than the taxpayer can save in taxes by deferring the income to a future date by not selling the capital asset until later?)
    2) Future (or likelihood of proposed) tax law (i.e., will it stay the same or change?)
    3) Individual circumstances of the taxpayer (i.e., a strategy good for one is not necessarily the best strategy for another)
    4) Doctrine of constructive receipt (covered more in Study Unit 5)

> **EXAMPLE 3-11**   **Maximizing the Depreciation Deduction**
>
> A business wants to maximize the amount of deductions in the current year related to asset depreciation. To accelerate the depreciation deduction, the business would utilize MACRS depreciation instead of electing straight-line depreciation.

    c. A taxpayer typically has more control over the recognition of some types of income (e.g., sale of capital gain property) than a taxpayer has over other types (e.g., salaries).

3. **Shifting**

    a. The basics of income shifting typically relate to moving income and therefore the accompanying tax liability from one family member to another who is subject to a lower marginal rate, or moving income between entities and their owner(s). However, tax planning also involves shifting income from one tax jurisdiction to another with different marginal tax rates.

b. Three key terms when discussing shifting income are **"assignment of income doctrine,"** **"related party transaction,"** and **"arm's-length transaction."**

   1) The assignment of income doctrine holds that a taxpayer cannot avoid tax for income the taxpayer earned by assigning it to another person.
   2) Related party transactions are transactions that occur between persons (including corporations) that are related to each other in one of the statutorily defined manners. For example, members of a family are considered related parties, as are a controlling shareholder and the controlled corporation.
   3) An arm's-length transaction occurs when the involved parties act independently, regardless of any relation. Transactions between unrelated parties are generally considered to be arm's-length. If the parties are related, a transaction is considered arm's-length if the results of the transaction are consistent with those that would have been realized if unrelated taxpayers engaged in the same transaction under the same circumstances.
   4) The purpose of the rules related to these items is to guarantee that all parties act in their own self-interest and not for the common good of all parties involved to the detriment of the IRS.

c. Other rules that may limit or otherwise make income shifting difficult include the "Kiddie Tax" rules and gift/wealth transfer rules.

d. Successful shifting of income among family members or entities depends on determining the following:

   1) Income/assets available for shifting
   2) Best strategy for realizing the shift
   3) Best recipient of income/asset within the family or entity

---

EXAMPLE 3-12   Shifting Income -- Family Members

Parents with a 32% marginal rate want to invest some of their savings and minimize the overall tax liability on the family. One way these parents can accomplish this goal is to have their adult children, who have only a 12% marginal rate, purchase a rental home and borrow the money from the parents at the lowest allowable rate (i.e., applicable federal rate). This strategy will result in the rental income being taxed at only 12% instead of the higher 32% of the parents and at the lowest cost possible (due to the low rate). The parents have also shifted income to the adult children without being subject to gift tax limits, etc.

---

e. In the case of shifting income among tax jurisdictions, the jurisdictions among which the income is moved could be city, county, or state jurisdictions within the U.S. In addition, shifting of income also could involve moving the income from U.S. jurisdiction to that of another nation.

f. In the case of multiple nations claiming the right to tax an individual or business, credit (subject to specific laws and treaties) will usually be given by each country for tax paid to the other. This helps to avoid double taxation and encourages international business.

EXAMPLE 3-13   Shifting Income -- Tax Jurisdictions

A player for the National Basketball Association is drawing near to the end of his original/rookie contract in Ohio. He has offers from franchises in Ohio, New York, Illinois, Florida, and California and wishes to minimize his overall tax liability in his next contract. All other issues being equal, the player should accept the offer from the franchise in Florida. By doing so, the player would be shifting his income from a state (Ohio) with a state income tax to the only state of those making offers with no state income tax. Though the federal income tax would go unchanged, the player's overall tax liability would be reduced.

4. **Conversion**

   a. Converting income from a less favorable category to a more favorable one can be achieved in various ways. Favorable conversions include converting ordinary income property into capital gain property. The opposite applies for losses.

   EXAMPLE 3-14   Favorable Conversion of Income

   A taxpayer wants to convert $10,000 FMV of inventory with a basis of $3,000 to capital gain property. The taxpayer will accomplish the goal by transferring the inventory to a controlled corporation for stock (the FMV would be $10,000). The taxpayer's basis in the stock is $3,000; therefore, selling the stock will result in a $7,000 capital gain for the taxpayer.

   If the taxpayer simply sells the inventory (i.e., no conversion), the $7,000 gain will be ordinary.

   ---

   b. Even better than converting property from a high tax rate to a low rate is converting it to nontaxable property. Examples of this include the following:

      1) Employee benefits, e.g., employer-paid medical reimbursement
      2) Investing in municipal bonds (i.e., nontaxable investment interest)
      3) Convert nondeductible personal expense to a business expense

   c. Some conversions involve a comparative analysis of minimization of current taxes to minimization of future taxes.

   EXAMPLE 3-15   Current vs. Future Taxes

   Contributions to an individual retirement account are deductible (subject to limitations) in the year made; however, tax applies to 100% of the withdrawals. So there is a current tax savings or deferral. On the other hand, contributions to a Roth IRA are currently taxed; however, the withdrawals are tax-exempt, including any increase in the investment over the years. This results in tax avoidance.

   ---

5. **Avoidance vs. Evasion**

   BACKGROUND 3-3   Morality of Tax Avoidance

   In a 1947 case, Judge Learned Hand stated, "Over and over again courts have said that there is nothing sinister in so arranging one's affairs as to keep taxes as low as possible. Everybody does so, rich or poor; and all do right, for nobody owes any public duty to pay more than the law demands: taxes are enforced extractions, not voluntary contributions. To demand more in the name of morals is mere cant."

   ---

   a. **Tax avoidance** is minimizing tax liability through legal arrangements and transactions. The goal of a business is to maximize profits, and tax avoidance is a key element in obtaining this goal. Avoidance maneuvers take place prior to incurring a tax liability.

   b. **Tax evasion** takes place once a tax liability has already been incurred (i.e., taxable actions have been completed). A key distinction between avoidance and evasion is taxpayer "intent." A taxpayer's intent is called into question when one of the "badges" of fraud is identified. These indicators include understatement of income, improper allocation of income, claiming of fictitious deductions, questionable conduct of the taxpayer, and accounting irregularities.

c. Concerning fraud, Sec. 7201 reads as follows: "Any person who willfully attempts in any manner to evade or defeat any tax imposed by this title or the payment thereof shall, in addition to other penalties provided by law, be guilty of a felony and, upon conviction thereof, shall be fined not more than [$250,000] ($500,000 in the case of a corporation), or imprisoned not more than five years, or both, together with the costs of prosecution."

STOP & REVIEW

You have completed the outline for this subunit.
Study multiple-choice questions 11 and 12 on page 76.

3.4 FILING STATUS

From Form 1040

Form **1040** Department of the Treasury—Internal Revenue Service (99) **U.S. Individual Income Tax Return** [Year] OMB No. 1545-0074 IRS Use Only—Do not write or staple in this space.

Filing Status ☐ Single ☐ Married filing jointly ☐ Married filing separately (MFS) ☐ Head of household (HOH) ☐ Qualifying widow(er) (QW)
Check only one box. If you checked the MFS box, enter the name of your spouse. If you checked the HOH or QW box, enter the child's name if the qualifying person is a child but not your dependent ▶

1. **Overview**
    a. The amounts of the standard deductions and applicable tax rates vary with filing status.
    b. Filing status on the last day of the year determines the filing status for the entire year.

2. **Single**
    a. An individual must file as single if (s)he neither is married nor qualifies for widow(er) or head of household status.

3. **Married Filing a Joint Return**
    a. Married individuals who file a joint return account for their items of income, deduction, and credit in the aggregate.
        1) A joint return is allowed when spouses use different accounting methods.
        2) Spouses with different tax years may not file a joint return.
    b. Two individuals are treated as legally married for the entire tax year if, on the last day of the tax year, they are
        1) Legally married and cohabiting as spouses,
        2) Legally married and living apart but not separated pursuant to a valid divorce decree or separate maintenance agreement, or
        3) Separated under a valid divorce decree that is not yet final.
    c. If a spouse dies and the surviving spouse does not remarry before the end of the tax year, a joint return may be filed.

4. **Married Filing a Separate Return**
    a. Each spouse accounts separately for items of income, deduction, and credit. A spouse who uses his or her own funds to pay expenses of jointly owned property is entitled to any deduction attributable to the payments.
    b. If one spouse files separately, so must the other.
    c. Filing separately is required when the spouses have different tax year ends.

5. **Head of Household**

   a. An individual qualifies for head of household status if (s)he satisfies conditions with respect to filing status, marital status, and household maintenance.

   b. **Filing status.** The individual may not file as a qualifying widow(er).

   c. **Marital status.** A married person does not qualify for head of household status unless the conditions below are satisfied. A married individual who lives with a dependent apart from the spouse qualifies for head of household status if, for the tax year,

   1) (S)he files separately;
   2) (S)he pays more than 50% toward maintaining the household; and
   3) For the last 6 months,

      a) The spouse is not a member of the household,
      b) The household is the principal home of a child of the individual, and
      c) The individual can claim the child as a dependent.

   d. **Household maintenance.** To qualify for head of household status, an individual must maintain a household that is the principal place of abode for a qualifying individual for at least half of the tax year.

   1) To maintain a household for federal filing status purposes, an individual must furnish more than 50% of the qualifying costs, of mutual benefit, of maintaining the household during the tax year.

Qualifying Costs	Nonqualifying Costs
Property tax	Clothing
Mortgage interest	Education
Rent	Medical treatment
Utilities	Life insurance
Upkeep	Transportation
Repair	Vacations
Property insurance	Services by the taxpayer
Food consumed in-home	Services by the dependent

   NOTE: Nonresident aliens cannot qualify for the head of household status.

   2) **Qualifying person and time.** The taxpayer must maintain a household that constitutes the principal place of abode for more than half of the taxable year for at least one qualified individual who is

      a) A qualifying child or
      b) A qualifying relative. (Both of these are defined in Subunit 3.5.)

   3) There are two special rules concerning a qualifying person.

      a) First, the taxpayer with a dependent parent qualifies even if the parent does not live with the taxpayer. Otherwise, the IRS maintains that the qualifying individual must occupy the same household (except for temporary absences).
      b) Second, in the case of divorce, the custodial parent of a qualifying child qualifies for head of household status even if the noncustodial parent claims the child as his or her dependent.

   4) On the following page is a summary of the qualifications for a person qualifying the taxpayer as head of household.

Who Is a Qualifying Person Qualifying the Taxpayer to File as Head of Household?

IF the person is the taxpayer's . . .	AND . . .	THEN that person is . . .
qualifying child (such as a son, daughter, or grandchild who lived with the taxpayer more than half the year and meets certain other tests)	he or she is single	a qualifying person, whether or not the child meets the citizen or resident test (i.e., U.S. citizen, resident alien or national, or resident of Canada or Mexico).
	he or she is married **and** the taxpayer can claim him or her as a dependent	a qualifying person.
	he or she is married **and** the taxpayer cannot claim him or her as a dependent other than just because they are married	not a qualifying person.
qualifying relative who is the taxpayer's father or mother	the taxpayer can claim him or her as a dependent	a qualifying person.[1]
	the taxpayer cannot claim him or her as a dependent	not a qualifying person.
qualifying relative other than the taxpayer's father or mother.	he or she lived with the taxpayer more than half the year, **and** the taxpayer can claim him or her as a dependent, **and** is one of the following: son, daughter, stepchild, foster child, or a descendant of any of them; the taxpayer's brother, sister, half-brother, half-sister, or a son or daughter of any of them; an ancestor or sibling of the taxpayer's father or mother; or stepbrother, stepsister, stepfather, stepmother, son-in-law, daughter-in-law, father-in-law, mother-in-law, brother-in-law, or sister-in-law	a qualifying person.
	he or she did not live with the taxpayer more than half the year	not a qualifying person.
	he or she is not related to the taxpayer in one of the ways listed above **and** is the taxpayer's qualifying relative only because he or she lived with the taxpayer all year as a member of the taxpayer's household (for example, a companion or a friend)	not a qualifying person.
	the taxpayer cannot claim him or her as a dependent	not a qualifying person.

[1] The taxpayer is eligible to file as head of household even if the taxpayer's parent, whom the taxpayer can claim as a dependent, does not live with the taxpayer. The taxpayer must pay more than half the cost of keeping up a home that was the main home for the entire year for the taxpayer's parent. This requirement is met if the taxpayer pays more than half the cost of keeping the taxpayer's parent in an assisted living or nursing facility.

6. **Qualifying Widow(er) or Surviving Spouse**

    a. The qualifying widow(er) status is available for 2 years following the year of death of the spouse if the following conditions are satisfied:

        1) The taxpayer did not remarry during the tax year.
        2) The widow(er) qualified (with the deceased spouse) for married filing joint return status for the tax year of the death of the spouse.
        3) A qualifying widow(er) maintains a household for the entire taxable year. Maintenance means the widow(er) furnishes more than 50% of the costs to maintain the household for the tax year.

            a) The household must be the principal place of abode of a qualifying dependent of the widow(er).
            b) The dependent must be a son or daughter, a stepson or daughter, or an adopted child. This does not include a foster child. (This is an exception to the general dependent rules covered in detail in the next subunit.)

        4) A widow(er) can file a joint return in the tax year of the death of the spouse.

STOP & REVIEW

You have completed the outline for this subunit.
Study multiple-choice questions 13 through 17 beginning on page 77.

3.5 DEPENDENTS

SUCCESS TIP

The AICPA has consistently tested the rules and regulations pertaining to qualification as a dependent. Take the time necessary to understand this information, as the requirements for each can easily be confused. The excerpt from Form 1040 below emphasizes the portions related to dependents. Work through the questions in the Gleim materials to reinforce your knowledge of these topics.

From Form 1040

Dependents (see instructions): If more than four dependents, see instructions and check here ▶ ☐	(2) Social security number	(3) Relationship to you	(4) ✔ if qualifies for (see instructions):
(1) First name Last name			Child tax credit / Credit for other dependents
			☐ / ☐
			☐ / ☐
			☐ / ☐
			☐ / ☐

1. **Overview**

    a. Until 2018, taxpayers were allowed personal exemptions to reduce their adjusted gross income for themselves and any of their qualified dependents. From 2018 through 2025, the exemption amount is $0, essentially eliminating the personal exemption for these years. For that reason, this review course has removed coverage of personal exemptions.

        1) However, the rules pertaining to qualified dependents still apply because dependency status affects more than just the exemption. For example, in the prior subunit discussing filing status, having dependents is required for qualifying for head of household. Similarly, dependents may qualify the taxpayer for the child tax credit or credit for other dependents. Therefore, it is important to learn the rules qualifying someone as a dependent of the taxpayer.

2. Qualified Dependent

a. To qualify as a dependent, the individual must be a qualifying child or a qualifying relative.

Overview of the Rules for Claiming a Dependent

Caution: This table is only an overview of the rules.
• The taxpayer cannot claim any dependents if the taxpayer, or the taxpayer's spouse if filing jointly, could be claimed as a dependent by another taxpayer.
• The taxpayer cannot claim a married person who files a joint return as a dependent unless that joint return is only to claim a refund of income tax withheld or estimated tax paid.
• Example: Robert, a full-time graduate student under the age of 24 at the end of the year, and his wife Claire lived with Robert's father, Mark. Robert had no income but filed a joint return for 2021, owing an additional $500 in taxes on Claire's income. Because Robert and Claire filed a joint return, for reasons other than to claim a refund, Mark cannot claim Robert as a dependent.
• The taxpayer cannot claim a person as a dependent unless (s)he is the taxpayer's **qualifying child** or **qualifying relative**.

Tests To Be a Qualifying Child	**Tests To Be a Qualifying Relative**
1. **Relationship.** The child must be the taxpayer's son, daughter, stepchild, foster child, brother, sister, half brother, half sister, stepbrother, stepsister, or a descendant of any of them. Adopted individuals qualify.	1. **Relationship.** The relationship requirement is satisfied if the person is related as indicated in **item 3., Qualifying Relative Relationship Criteria**, on the next page, or meets the member of the household test.
2. **Member of the Household Test.** The child must have lived with the taxpayer for more than half of the year.	a) **Member of the Household Test.** The requirement is satisfied if an unrelated person lives with the taxpayer all year as a member of the taxpayer's household.
3. **Age.** The child must be: (a) under age 19 at the end of the year, (b) under age 24 at the end of the year and a full-time student,[1] or (c) any age if permanently and totally disabled.	2. **Gross Taxable Income.** The person's gross income for the year must be less than $4,300. Gross income means all income the person received in the form of money, goods, property, and services that is not exempt from tax (e.g., taxable interest income and taxable scholarships). Does not include Social Security benefits for low-income taxpayers.
4. **Not Self-Supporting.** The child must not have provided more than half of his or her own support for the year.	3. **Support.** The taxpayer must provide more than half of the person's total (economic) support for the year. **Item 4., Qualifying Relative Support Criteria**, beginning on the next page, has a detailed explanation.
5. If the child meets the rules to be a qualifying child of more than one person, tie-breaking rules apply.	4. The person cannot be the taxpayer's qualifying child or the qualifying child of any other taxpayer. A child is not the qualifying child of any other taxpayer if the child's parent (or any other person for whom the child is defined as a qualifying child) is not required to file an income tax return or files an income tax return only to get a refund of income tax withheld.

[1] To qualify as a full-time student, the dependent must be enrolled at an educational organization for at least 5 months during the tax year.

3. **Qualifying Relative Relationship Criteria**

   a. The relationship requirement is satisfied by existence of an extended (by blood) or immediate (by blood, adoption, or marriage) relationship. The relationship need be present to only one of the two married persons who file a joint return. Any relationship established by marriage is not treated as ended by divorce or by death.

      1) Extended relationships: Grandparents and ancestors, grandchildren and descendants, uncles or aunts, nephews or nieces
      2) Immediate relationships

         a) Parent: Natural, adoptive, stepparent, father- or mother-in-law
         b) Child: Natural, adoptive, stepchild, son- or daughter-in-law, foster child (who lives with the claimant for the entire tax year)
         c) Sibling: Full or half brother or sister, adoptive brother or sister, stepbrother or sister, brother- or sister-in-law

      NOTE: Cousins do not meet the relationship test. However, if they lived with the taxpayer all year, they meet the relationship requirement through the member of the household test.

4. **Qualifying Relative Support Criteria**

   a. Support includes welfare benefits, Social Security benefits, and any support provided by the exemption claimant, the dependent, and any other person.

   > **EXAMPLE 3-16   Total Support**
   >
   > A dependent earns $2,000 and the exemption claimants provide $3,000 of support to the dependent. The total support equals $5,000 ($2,000 provided by dependent + $3,000 provided by exemption claimants).

   b. Only amounts provided during the calendar year qualify as support.

      1) Amounts paid in arrears (i.e., payment for child support for a previous year) are not considered support for the current year.

   c. Support includes money and items, or amounts spent on items, such as

      1) Food, clothing, shelter, utilities
      2) Medical and dental care and insurance
      3) Education
      4) Child care, vacations, etc.

   d. **Excluded.** Certain items (or amounts spent on them) have not been treated as support, e.g., scholarship received by a dependent child, taxes, or life insurance premiums.

   e. A **divorced or separated** individual need not meet the support test if (s)he and the (ex-)spouse meet (or have met) the following conditions:

      1) Provided more than 50% of the support
      2) Had (between them) custody for more than 50% of the year
      3) Lived apart for the last half of the year
      4) Did not have a multiple support agreement in effect

      NOTE: The parent having custody for more than 50% of the year is entitled to claim the child, but the ability to claim the child may be allocated to the noncustodial parent if there is an agreement signed by both parents and attached to the noncustodial parent's return.

f. **Multiple support agreement.** One person of a group that together provides more than 50% of the support of an individual may, pursuant to an agreement, be allowed the dependency exemption amount.

1) The person must be otherwise eligible to claim the exemption and must provide more than 10% of the support.
2) No other person may provide more than 50% of the support.
3) Each other person in the group who provides more than 10% of the support must sign a written consent filed with the return of the taxpayer who claims the exemption.

5. **Dependent Rules**

    a. There are special rules that apply to an individual qualifying as a dependent.

    1) **Filing status** (occasionally referred to as the joint return test). An individual does not qualify as a dependent on another's return if the individual is married and files a joint return.

        a) However, such an individual can qualify as a dependent if (s)he files a joint return solely to claim a refund of withheld tax without regard to the citizenship test.

    > **EXAMPLE 3-17**   **Filing by Dependents to Obtain a Refund**
    >
    > Mr. and Mrs. Kind provided more than half the support for their married daughter and son-in-law who lived with the Kinds all year. Neither the daughter nor the son-in-law is required to file a 2021 tax return. They do so only to get a refund of withheld taxes. The Kinds may claim the daughter and the son-in-law as dependents on their 2021 joint return.

    2) The individual must **not be a qualifying child** of any other taxpayer.

        a) A child being adopted is eligible to be claimed as a dependent by the adopting parents if the adoption taxpayer identification number (ATIN) is assigned.
        b) Both a dependent who dies before the end of the year and a child born during the year may be claimed as dependents.

    3) **Citizenship.** To qualify as a dependent, an individual must generally be, for any part of the year, a U.S. citizen, resident, or national.

    4) **Taxpayer identification number (TIN).** The taxpayer must provide the correct TIN of a dependent on the income tax return.

STOP & REVIEW

You have completed the outline for this subunit.
Study multiple-choice question 18 on page 78.

QUESTIONS

3.1 Tax Authority

1. Which of the following is the primary source of Federal Tax Law?

A. The Internal Revenue Code of 1939.
B. Treasury Regulations.
C. The Internal Revenue Code of 1986.
D. The Internal Revenue Bulletin.

Answer (C) is correct.
REQUIRED: The primary source of Federal Tax Law.
DISCUSSION: The Internal Revenue Code of 1986 is the primary source of Federal Tax Law. It imposes income, estate, gift, employment, and miscellaneous excise taxes and provisions controlling the administration of federal taxation. The Code is found at Title 26 of the United States Code.
Answer (A) is incorrect. The Internal Revenue Code (IRC) of 1939 was the first codification of federal tax laws and is superseded by the 1986 Code. **Answer (B) is incorrect.** Treasury Regulations are administrative pronouncements that interpret and illustrate the rules contained in the Internal Revenue Code. Though authoritative, they are not as authoritative as the IRC. **Answer (D) is incorrect.** The Internal Revenue Bulletin is an instrument used to publish treasury decisions, executive orders, tax conventions, legislation, court decisions, and other items of general interest.

2. When a revenue ruling conflicts with a revenue procedure, which of the two tax authorities has precedence?

A. Revenue ruling.
B. The one established first.
C. Revenue procedure.
D. The most recently established.

Answer (D) is correct.
REQUIRED: The tax authority with precedence when there is a conflict.
DISCUSSION: When there are conflicting sources of tax law within the same tier of the hierarchy (as is the case with revenue rulings and procedures), the most recent rule/law takes precedence.
Answer (A) is incorrect. Revenue rulings are in the same hierarchical tier as revenue procedures. **Answer (B) is incorrect.** More recent tax law within the same hierarchical tier has precedence. **Answer (C) is incorrect.** Revenue procedures are in the same hierarchical tier as revenue rulings.

3. In order to show that a tax preparer's application of tax law was in line with the intent of the tax law, the preparer should cite which of the following types of authoritative sources to make the most convincing case?

A. IRS publication.
B. Technical advice memorandum of another, similar case.
C. Committee report.
D. Delegation order.

Answer (C) is correct.
REQUIRED: The authoritative source for determining the intent behind certain tax law.
DISCUSSION: Committee reports are useful tools in determining Congressional intent behind certain tax laws and helping examiners apply the law properly. The committee reports are very high authority.
Answer (A) is incorrect. Publications do an excellent job of plainly explaining the law; however, they are not binding on the IRS or courts. **Answer (B) is incorrect.** TAMs are binding on the IRS only in relation to the taxpayer who is the subject of the ruling. **Answer (D) is incorrect.** Delegation orders are not authoritative sources for tax research. They simply delegate authority to perform tasks/make decisions to specified IRS employees.

SU 3: Federal Tax Authority, Procedures, and Individual Taxation

4. Which of the following statements with respect to revenue rulings and revenue procedures is **false**?

A. Revenue procedures are official statements of procedures that either affect the rights or duties of taxpayers or other members of the public or should be a matter of public knowledge.

B. The purpose of revenue rulings is to promote uniform application of the tax laws.

C. Taxpayers cannot appeal adverse return examination decisions based on revenue rulings and revenue procedures to the courts.

D. IRS employees must follow revenue rulings and revenue procedures.

Answer (C) is correct.
REQUIRED: The false statement regarding revenue rulings and revenue procedures.
DISCUSSION: Revenue rulings and revenue procedures do not have the force and effect of regulations but are published to provide precedents to be used in the disposition of other cases. While taxpayers may rely on the rulings and procedures, they can also appeal adverse return examination decisions based on those rulings to the Tax Court or other federal courts.

5. To research whether the Internal Revenue Service has announced an opinion on a Tax Court decision, refer to which of the following references for the original announcement?

A. Circular 230.
B. Federal Register.
C. Internal Revenue Bulletin.
D. Tax Court Reports.

Answer (C) is correct.
REQUIRED: The reference that contains the original announcement of an IRS opinion on a Tax Court decision.
DISCUSSION: The Internal Revenue Bulletin is published weekly and includes Treasury decisions, statutes, committee reports, U.S. Supreme Court decisions affecting the IRS, lists of the acquiescences and nonacquiescences of the IRS to decisions of the courts, and administrative rulings.
Answer (A) is incorrect. Circular 230 does not contain the original announcement of an IRS opinion on a Tax Court decision. **Answer (B) is incorrect.** The Federal Register does not contain the original announcement of an IRS opinion on a Tax Court decision. **Answer (D) is incorrect.** Tax Court Reports do not contain the original announcement of an IRS opinion on a Tax Court decision.

3.2 Tax Procedures

6. A taxpayer understated the tax liability by $10,000. The total tax liability was $50,000. No disclosure of the return position was made by the taxpayer; however, the basis for the position is reasonable. How much of an accuracy-related penalty will the taxpayer be assessed?

A. $0
B. $1,000
C. $2,000
D. $10,000

Answer (C) is correct.
REQUIRED: The amount of an accuracy-related penalty.
DISCUSSION: A taxpayer's accuracy-related penalty due to disregard of rules and regulations, or substantial understatement of income tax, may be avoided if the return position is adequately disclosed and has a reasonable basis. Generally, the penalty is equal to 20% of the underpayment. Substantial understatement of income tax occurs when the understatement is more than the larger of 10% of the correct tax ($5,000 is 10% of the correct tax) or $5,000. This taxpayer failed to adequately disclose or achieve substantial authority for the return position. The penalty is $2,000 ($10,000 understatement × 20%).
Answer (A) is incorrect. Because the taxpayer substantially understated the liability and failed to adequately disclose the return position, an accuracy-related penalty is due. Answer (B) is incorrect. The penalty is greater than 10%. Answer (D) is incorrect. The penalty is less than 100% of the understatement.

7. Keen, a calendar-year taxpayer, reported gross income of $100,000 on his 2021 income tax return. Inadvertently omitted from gross income was a $20,000 commission that should have been included in 2021. Keen filed his 2021 return on March 17, 2022. To collect the tax on the $20,000 omission, the Internal Revenue Service must assert a notice of deficiency no later than

A. March 17, 2025.
B. April 15, 2025.
C. March 17, 2028.
D. April 15, 2028.

Answer (B) is correct.
REQUIRED: The statute of limitations on assessment of a deficiency.
DISCUSSION: The general statute of limitations for assessment of a deficiency is 3 years from the date the return was filed. An income tax return filed before the due date for the return is treated as if filed on the due date for statute of limitations purposes. Since Keen's return was due April 15, 2022, the statute of limitations will expire 3 years from that date.
Answer (A) is incorrect. An income tax return filed before the due date for the return is treated as if filed on the due date. Answer (C) is incorrect. A 6-year statute applies only when income items that would increase stated gross income by more than 25% are omitted. Answer (D) is incorrect. A 6-year statute applies only when income items that would increase stated gross income by more than 25% are omitted.

8. A taxpayer filed his income tax return after the due date but neglected to file an extension form. The return indicated a tax liability of $50,000 and taxes withheld of $45,000. On what amount is the penalties for late filing and late payment computed?

A. $0
B. $5,000
C. $45,000
D. $50,000

Answer (B) is correct.
REQUIRED: The amount used to assess late filing and late payment penalties.
DISCUSSION: When an income tax return is filed later than its due date and no extension has been filed, the IRS may assess a penalty on the taxpayer. The penalty is assessed only on the outstanding taxes due. The taxpayer therefore receives credit for the $45,000 in withholding taxes and the penalty is only assessed on the difference, $5,000 [Sec. 6651(b)].
Answer (A) is incorrect. The net tax due is used to assess the penalty. Answer (C) is incorrect. Only the net tax still due, not the tax already remitted, is used to assess the penalty. Answer (D) is incorrect. The taxpayer receives a credit for the taxes withheld.

9. A claim for refund of erroneously paid income taxes, filed by an individual before the statute of limitations expires, must be submitted on Form

A. 1139.
B. 1045.
C. 1040X.
D. 843.

Answer (C) is correct.
REQUIRED: The required form for submitting a claim for refund of individual income taxes.
DISCUSSION: A claim for refund of previously paid income taxes is made by filing an amended return on Form 1040X within the appropriate statute of limitations period.
Answer (A) is incorrect. Application for a tentative carryback adjustment to get a quick refund for carryback of a corporate net capital loss and general business credit may be made on Form 1139 for corporations. **Answer (B) is incorrect.** Form 1045 is used to apply for a quick refund on a carryback for individuals. **Answer (D) is incorrect.** Form 843 is used to file a claim for refund of taxes paid other than income taxes.

10. Krete is an unmarried taxpayer with income exclusively from wages. By December 31, Year 1, Krete's employer had withheld $16,000 in federal income taxes, and Krete had made no estimated tax payments. On April 15, Year 2, Krete timely filed an extension request to file her individual tax return and paid $300 of additional taxes. Krete's Year 1 income tax liability was $16,500 when she timely filed her return on April 30, Year 2, and paid the remaining income tax liability balance. What amount is subject to the penalty for the underpayment of estimated taxes?

A. $0
B. $500
C. $1,650
D. $16,500

Answer (A) is correct.
REQUIRED: The amount subject to penalty for underpayment of estimated taxes.
DISCUSSION: No amount is subject to the penalty for the underpayment of estimated taxes. The amount withheld from wages by Krete's employer, $16,000, is treated as if an equal part was paid on each due date. Each of these installments meets the 25% of 90% of the current year's tax threshold.
Answer (B) is incorrect. This amount is the additional $500 income tax liability computed on the filed return. **Answer (C) is incorrect.** This amount results from multiplying the entire amount of income tax liability, $16,500, by 10% ($16,500 × .10 = $1,650). **Answer (D) is incorrect.** This figure is the entire amount of income tax liability computed on the filed return.

3.3 Tax Planning

11. Company A, a U.S. company, deducted costs from research and development of a product in the U.S., then licensed rights to the product to a foreign subsidiary in a lower tax jurisdiction. The subsidiary then manufactured the product and sold each unit back to Company A (the parent company). This is an example of which tax planning technique?

A. Timing of income/deductions.
B. Shifting of income.
C. Conversion of income property.
D. Deferral of income.

Answer (B) is correct.
REQUIRED: The tax planning technique exemplified in the question.
DISCUSSION: In addition to moving income among related parties, shifting of income also involves moving income from one tax jurisdiction to another with a lower tax rate. By deducting all of the R&D expenses in the U.S. and licensing the rights to a foreign subsidiary, Company A minimized their U.S. taxable income and shifted profits to a foreign tax jurisdiction with a lower tax rate.
Answer (A) is incorrect. Timing of income deals with the recognition period of income, not the jurisdiction. **Answer (C) is incorrect.** Conversion of income property relates to the change in the type of income property, resulting in a different tax liability, not the jurisdiction. **Answer (D) is incorrect.** Deferral of income is an element of timing of income/deductions and is not exemplified in the question.

12. Utilizing MACRS depreciation (accelerating the depreciation deduction) instead of electing straight-line depreciation is an example of which tax planning technique?

A. Conversion.
B. Shifting.
C. Timing.
D. Assignment.

Answer (C) is correct.
REQUIRED: The tax planning technique exemplified by choice of a depreciation method.
DISCUSSION: The three most basic and common types of tax planning are

1. Timing of income recognition,
2. Shifting of income among taxpayers and jurisdictions, and
3. Conversion of income among high and low rate activities.

The timing technique accelerates or defers recognition of income and/or deductions. Because choice of depreciation methods accelerate or defer the depreciation deduction, it is a timing strategy.
Answer (A) is incorrect. Conversion of income involves changing the type/class of income producing property. Choosing a depreciation method does not change the income property but does change the period of income recognition. **Answer (B) is incorrect.** Shifting of income involves a change in ownership of the income or change in the tax jurisdiction of the income. Choosing a depreciation method does not change the ownership or jurisdiction of income but does change the period of income recognition. **Answer (D) is incorrect.** Assignment of income is an element of income shifting and is not related to the effects of choosing a depreciation method.

3.4 Filing Status

13. A married couple can file a joint return even if

- A. The spouses have different tax years, provided that both spouses are alive at the end of the year.
- B. The spouses have different accounting methods.
- C. Either spouse was a nonresident alien at any time during the tax year, provided that at least one spouse makes the proper election.
- D. They were divorced before the end of the tax year.

Answer (B) is correct.
REQUIRED: The condition under which a married couple may file a joint return.
DISCUSSION: There is no provision disallowing spouses from filing a joint return because they have different accounting methods.
Answer (A) is incorrect. The IRC disallows spouses with different tax years from filing a joint return. **Answer (C) is incorrect.** The IRC provides that neither spouse can be a nonresident alien during the tax year and still file a joint return, unless the nonresident alien spouse is married to a U.S. citizen or resident alien at year end and both spouses elect to have the nonresident alien treated as a resident alien. **Answer (D) is incorrect.** Spouses must be married on the last day of the tax year to be allowed to file a joint return.

14. Which of the following, if any, are among the requirements to enable a taxpayer to be classified as a "qualifying widow(er)"?

I. A dependent has lived with the taxpayer for 6 months.

II. The taxpayer has maintained the cost of the principal residence for 6 months.

- A. I only.
- B. II only.
- C. Both I and II.
- D. Neither I nor II.

Answer (D) is correct.
REQUIRED: The requirements, if any, to file as a qualifying widow(er).
DISCUSSION: Filing as a surviving spouse or qualifying widow(er) requires the individual's spouse to have died during one of the previous 2 tax years. In addition, the survivor must maintain a household that is the principal place of residence for a dependent child. "Maintain" means the spouse furnishes over 50% of the costs of the household for the entire year.

15. A taxpayer's spouse dies in August of the current year. Which of the following is the taxpayer's filing status for the current year?

- A. Single.
- B. Qualifying widow(er).
- C. Head of household.
- D. Married filing jointly.

Answer (D) is correct.
REQUIRED: The taxpayer's filing status for the current year.
DISCUSSION: The qualifying widow(er) status is available for 2 years following the year of death of the husband or wife; however, the surviving spouse can file a joint return or a married filing separate return in the tax year of the death of the deceased spouse.
Answer (A) is incorrect. A taxpayer cannot file as single in the year his or her spouse dies. **Answer (B) is incorrect.** A taxpayer cannot file as a qualifying widow(er) in the year his or her spouse dies. However, the qualifying widow(er) status is available for the 2 years following the year of death of the spouse under certain conditions. **Answer (C) is incorrect.** A taxpayer cannot file as head of household in the year his or her spouse dies because the taxpayer will not be considered unmarried.

16. A couple filed a joint return in prior tax years. During the current tax year, one spouse died. The couple has no dependent children. What is the filing status available to the surviving spouse for the first subsequent tax year?

A. Qualified widow(er).
B. Married filing separately.
C. Single.
D. Head of household.

Answer (C) is correct.
REQUIRED: The filing status of the surviving spouse for years subsequent to death.
DISCUSSION: For the year of death, the living spouse may choose MFJ status. Because the surviving spouse has no dependents (qualifying individuals), the only filing status available for subsequent years is single.
Answer (A) is incorrect. In order to elect to file as widow(er), the household must be the principal place of abode of a qualifying dependent of the surviving spouse.
Answer (B) is incorrect. Both filing statuses for married individuals require the taxpayer to be married. Married status is terminated for years subsequent to death.
Answer (D) is incorrect. The surviving spouse does not have any qualifying (dependent) individuals as required for head of household status.

17. For head of household filing status, which of the following costs are considered in determining whether the taxpayer has contributed more than one-half the cost of maintaining the household?

	Food Consumed in the Home	Value of Services Rendered in the Home by the Taxpayer
A.	Yes	Yes
B.	No	No
C.	Yes	No
D.	No	Yes

Answer (C) is correct.
REQUIRED: The item(s) considered keeping up a home for head of household filing status.
DISCUSSION: The cost of maintaining a household for head of household status includes expenditures for the mutual benefit of the occupants, e.g., food consumed in the home, rent, or real estate taxes. Not included is the value of services rendered in the home by the taxpayer or the rental value of a home owned by the taxpayer.

3.5 Dependents

18. Jim and Kay Ross contributed to the support of their two children, Dale and Kim, and Jim's widowed parent, Grant. For 2021, Dale, a 19-year-old, full-time college student, earned $6,450 as a bookkeeper. Kim, a 23-year-old bank teller, earned $13,950. Grant received $8,125 in dividend income and $7,125 in nontaxable Social Security benefits. Grant, Dale, and Kim are U.S. citizens and were over one-half supported by Jim and Kay. How many dependents can Jim and Kay claim on their 2021 joint income tax return?

A. 2
B. 1
C. 3
D. 5

Answer (B) is correct.
REQUIRED: The number of dependents that a married couple filing a joint return can claim.
DISCUSSION: Kim does not qualify as a dependent because she had gross income in excess of $4,300 in 2021. Although a parent can also qualify as a dependent, Grant has gross income in excess of $4,300 and therefore cannot be claimed. The gross income test does not apply to a person such as Dale, who is a child of the claimant, under age 24, and a full-time student. Jim and Kay cannot claim themselves. Thus, only Dale qualifies.

STUDY UNIT FOUR
GROSS INCOME AND EXCLUSIONS

(21 pages of outline)

4.1 Gross Income	80
4.2 Exclusions	94

This study unit presents taxable and nontaxable income items, income items for which there are no exclusions, and income items for which the Internal Revenue Code provides partial or complete exclusion from gross income.

The following table provides an overview of the steps to compute federal income tax liability for individual taxpayers and each corresponding study unit. It will be a useful reference throughout this course's tax-related knowledge transfer outline.

Individual Income Tax FORMULA	Information covered in
GROSS INCOME	SU 4
− Adjustments (above the line)	
= **ADJUSTED GROSS INCOME**	
− Itemized Deductions or Standard Deduction	
− Qualified Business Income Deduction	SU 7
= **TAXABLE INCOME**	
× Tax Rate	
= **GROSS TAX** Liability	
− Credits	SU 8
= **NET TAX** Liability or Refund Receivable	

Some candidates find it helpful to have the entire tax form side-by-side with our Knowledge Transfer Outline when studying, and others may prefer to see the final draft of a form when it is released. The full versions of the most up-to-date forms are easily accessible at www.gleim.com/taxforms. These forms and the form excerpts used in our outline are periodically updated as the latest versions are released by the IRS.

4.1 GROSS INCOME

1. **Overview**

    a. The Internal Revenue Code (IRC) defines gross income as all income from whatever source derived except as otherwise provided.

    b. The IRC enumerates a non-exhaustive list of the types of income that constitute gross income as follows:

    1) Compensation for services, including fees, commissions, and fringe benefits
    2) Gross income derived from business
    3) Gains derived from dealings in property
    4) Interest
    5) Rents
    6) Royalties
    7) Dividends
    8) Alimony and separate maintenance payments (divorces executed before 2019)
    9) Annuities
    10) Income from life insurance and endowment contracts
    11) Pensions
    12) Income from discharge of indebtedness
    13) Distributive share of partnership gross income
    14) Income in respect of a decedent (income earned but not received before death)
    15) Income from an interest in an estate or trust

    c. Some types of gross income not enumerated in Sec. 61 are specifically included by other IRC sections or case law.

    1) Other types of income also constitute gross income unless a statute specifically excludes them.

EXAMPLE 4-1   Gross Income -- Lump Sum for Noncompete Agreement

John receives a lump sum for signing a noncompete agreement. John should recognize the entire lump sum as ordinary income in the year received.

NOTE: To enable better understanding of the numerous gross income categories, we have provided a "snap-shot" of the applicable Form 1040 line number(s), forms, and schedules with which the gross income items are associated. The forms referenced on the following pages may be accessed at www.gleim.com/taxforms.

2. Compensation for Services

From Form 1040

| 1 | Wages, salaries, tips, etc. Attach Form(s) W-2 . . . . | 1 | |

a. **All compensation for personal services (including fees, commissions, and similar items) is gross income** regardless of form of payment.

   1) If property or credit is given in lieu of cash or check, the FMV of the property or credit is included in gross income.

   2) Gross income of an employee includes any amount paid by an employer for a liability (including taxes) or an expense of the employee.

> **EXAMPLE 4-2   Employer Payment of a Liability**
>
> Rick's employer pays his car payment in lieu of direct deposit into Rick's personal account, and the payment is reported as gross income.

b. All wages (including tips) received by the taxpayer are listed on Form W-2, *Wage and Tax Statement*. A sample of Form W-2 appears below.

c. The following types of income must also be included on Form W-2 and in the total on line 1 of Form 1040.
   1) All wages received as a household employee. An employer is not required to provide a Form W-2 to the taxpayer if the employer paid the taxpayer wages of less than $2,300 in 2021.
   2) Tip income the taxpayer did not report to the employer. This should include any allocated tips reported in box 8 on Form W-2. Also include the value of any noncash tips the taxpayer received, such as tickets, passes, or other items of value.
   3) Dependent care benefits that are reported in box 10 of Form W-2.
   4) Employer-provided adoption benefits, which should be shown in box 12 of Form(s) W-2 with code T.
   5) Excess salary deferrals. The amount deferred is reported in box 12 of Form W-2.
d. If an employer transfers property to an employee at less than its FMV **(bargain purchase)**, the difference may be income to the employee and treated as compensation for personal services.
e. **Scholarships or fellowships** received for room, board, or incidental expenses are gross income.
f. **Reimbursed employee expenses** plans include those that are
   1) Nonaccountable. Under nonaccountable plans, employee reimbursements (advances) are included in gross income.
   2) Accountable. Under accountable plans, employees must submit requests for reimbursement. Only reimbursements in excess of expenses must be included in gross income.

EXAMPLE 4-3	Refund of Amount Reimbursed by Employer

John submitted reimbursement requests to his employer for $10,500 in airfare. John was later refunded for $500 of the airfare. If John does not remit the funds to his employer, John must include the $500 in gross income.

g. **Qualified reimbursements for moving expenses** incurred by members of the military are excluded from gross income. If the reimbursement is not for qualified moving expenses or the taxpayer is not a member of the military, the reimbursement is included in gross income.
h. Employer contributions to qualified retirement plans and elective deferrals are not included in income upon contribution. Instead, the contributions and earnings are included in income and taxed at distribution.

SU 4: Gross Income and Exclusions

3. **Interest and Dividends**

    From Form 1040

Attach Sch. B if required.	2a Tax-exempt interest ... 2a [ ]	b Taxable interest ... 2b [ ]
	3a Qualified dividends ... 3a [ ]	b Ordinary dividends ... 3b [ ]

    a. **Interest income** is gross income for tax purposes unless an exclusion applies. Examples of interest income include

        1) Merchandise premium (e.g., a toaster given to a depositor for opening an interest-bearing account).
        2) Imputed interest on below-market term loans.
        3) Interest on state, local, and federal tax refunds.
        4) Interest from U.S. treasury bonds.

    b. Generally, payers of interest income send the taxpayer Form 1099-INT listing the interest income amount.

        1) **Taxable interest** is reported on Form 1040 with Schedule B (sample provided on the next page) attached if the total is over $1,500.

    c. Generally, payers of dividends send the taxpayer Form 1099-DIV listing ordinary and qualified dividends amounts.

        1) **Ordinary dividends** are reported on Form 1040 with Schedule B attached if the total is over $1,500 or the taxpayer received, as a nominee, ordinary dividends that actually belong to someone else.
        2) **Qualified dividends** are reported on Form 1040 and are also included in the ordinary dividend total.

4. **Taxable State and Local Refunds or Credits**

    From Form 1040 Schedule 1

    1 Taxable refunds, credits, or offsets of state and local income taxes .... 1 [ ]

    a. Payers of state or local income tax refunds, credits, or offsets send the taxpayer Form 1099-G listing the amount to be reported.
    b. None of the refund is taxable if, in the year the taxpayer paid the tax, the taxpayer either

        1) Did not itemize deductions or
        2) Did not deduct state and local income taxes.

    > **EXAMPLE 4-4   Inclusion of Refunded Tax in Gross Income**
    >
    > In 2021, a taxpayer who files single elected to itemize deductions, claiming $10,000 of state income tax paid and $4,000 of investment interest paid for a total itemized deduction of $14,000. In 2022, the state refunded $2,000. The taxpayer must include the refund in gross income for 2022 to the extent the total 2021 itemized deduction exceeded the 2021 standard deduction, which is $1,450 ($14,000 itemized deduction − $12,550 standard deduction for 2021).

    c. This is referred to as the recovery of tax benefit rule and is covered in general in item 11.d. of this subunit.

SCHEDULE B (Form 1040) Department of the Treasury Internal Revenue Service (99)	Interest and Ordinary Dividends ▶ Go to *www.irs.gov/ScheduleB* for instructions and the latest information. ▶ Attach to Form 1040 or 1040-SR.	OMB No. 1545-0074 **[Year]** Attachment Sequence No. 08
Name(s) shown on return		Your social security number

Part I **Interest** (See instructions and the instructions for Forms 1040 and 1040-SR, line 2b.) **Note:** If you received a Form 1099-INT, Form 1099-OID, or substitute statement from a brokerage firm, list the firm's name as the payer and enter the total interest shown on that form.	1	List name of payer. If any interest is from a seller-financed mortgage and the buyer used the property as a personal residence, see the instructions and list this interest first. Also, show that buyer's social security number and address ▶		**Amount**
			1	
	2	Add the amounts on line 1	2	
	3	Excludable interest on series EE and I U.S. savings bonds issued after 1989. Attach Form 8815	3	
	4	Subtract line 3 from line 2. Enter the result here and on Form 1040 or 1040-SR, line 2b . . . . ▶	4	
	Note: If line 4 is over $1,500, you must complete Part III.			**Amount**
Part II **Ordinary Dividends** (See instructions and the instructions for Forms 1040 and 1040-SR, line 3b.) **Note:** If you received a Form 1099-DIV or substitute statement from a brokerage firm, list the firm's name as the payer and enter the ordinary dividends shown on that form.	5	List name of payer ▶		
			5	
	6	Add the amounts on line 5. Enter the total here and on Form 1040 or 1040-SR, line 3b . . . . ▶	6	
	Note: If line 6 is over $1,500, you must complete Part III.			

Part III **Foreign Accounts and Trusts** **Caution:** If required, failure to file FinCEN Form 114 may result in substantial penalties. See instructions.	You must complete this part if you **(a)** had over $1,500 of taxable interest or ordinary dividends; **(b)** had a foreign account; or **(c)** received a distribution from, or were a grantor of, or a transferor to, a foreign trust.	Yes	No
	7a At any time during [Year], did you have a financial interest in or signature authority over a financial account (such as a bank account, securities account, or brokerage account) located in a foreign country? See instructions		
	If "Yes," are you required to file FinCEN Form 114, Report of Foreign Bank and Financial Accounts (FBAR), to report that financial interest or signature authority? See FinCEN Form 114 and its instructions for filing requirements and exceptions to those requirements		
	b If you are required to file FinCEN Form 114, enter the name of the foreign country where the financial account is located ▶		
	8 During [Year], did you receive a distribution from, or were you the grantor of, or transferor to, a foreign trust? If "Yes," you may have to file Form 3520. See instructions		

For Paperwork Reduction Act Notice, see your tax return instructions.   Cat. No. 17146N   Schedule B (Form 1040) [Year]

SU 4: Gross Income and Exclusions 85

5. **Alimony and separate maintenance payments** are included in the gross income of the recipient (payee) and are deducted from the gross income of the payor for divorce decrees executed (i.e., established) prior to 2019.

   From Form 1040 Schedule 1

   | 2a | Alimony received . . . . | 2a | |

   a. A payment is considered to be alimony (even if paid to a third party) when it is
      1) Paid in cash
      2) Paid pursuant to a written divorce or separation instrument
      3) Terminated at death of recipient
      4) Not designated as other than alimony (e.g., child support)
      5) Not paid to a member of the same household
      6) Not paid to a spouse with whom the taxpayer is filing a joint return

   b. **Payments to a third party** for the benefit of the payor's ex-spouse are considered qualified alimony payments if all other requirements are met.

   c. **Property settlements** are not treated as alimony.
      1) Property transferred to a spouse or former spouse incident to a divorce is treated as a transfer by gift, which is specifically excluded from gross income.
         a) **"Incident to a divorce"** means a transfer of property within 1 year after the date the marriage ceases or a transfer of property related to the cessation of the marriage.
         b) This exclusion does not apply if the spouse or former spouse is a nonresident alien.

   d. **Child support** payments are an exclusion from the gross income of the recipient and are not deductible by the payor. These payments are not alimony.
      1) If the divorce or separation instrument specifies payments of both alimony and child support and only **partial payments** are made, the payments are considered to be child support until this obligation is fully paid, and any excess is then treated as alimony.
      2) If the payment amount is to be reduced based on a contingency relating to a child (e.g., attaining a certain age, marrying), the amount of the **payment reduction** will be treated as child support.

   e. For a divorce finalized (i.e., established) after 2018, alimony is not deductible by the payor and is not included in the gross income of the recipient.

6. **Business and Supplemental Income**

   From Form 1040 Schedule 1

   | 3 | Business income or (loss). Attach Schedule C . . . . | 3 | |
   | 5 | Rental real estate, royalties, partnerships, S corporations, trusts, etc. Attach Schedule E . . . . . | 5 | |

   a. **Business income** includes service and non-service income.
      1) Gross income is calculated in a manner similar to individuals.
      2) Supplemental income is reported on Schedule E and includes rental real estate, royalties, partnerships and LLCs (from Schedule K-1), S corporations (K-1), estates (K-1), and trusts (K-1).

b. Net earnings reported on Schedule C (Form 1040) or other schedules used for reporting self-employment income are included in gross income.

   1) The director of a corporation who is not employed by the corporation is considered self-employed, and all director and consulting fees received are included in gross income.
   2) Generally, amounts that are received in advance for future goods and services are required to be included in the year of receipt. However, accrual-basis taxpayers can elect to defer recognition until the time of performance, up to the year after the payment date.

> **EXAMPLE 4-5　　Prepaid Income Allocation**
>
> Beth is a piano instructor. She is a calendar-year taxpayer using the accrual method of accounting and has elected to defer advance payments for services. On November 2 of Year 1, she received $4,800 for a contract for 96 1-hour lessons beginning on that date. The contract provided Beth give 8 lessons in Year 1 and 48 lessons in Year 2, with the remaining lessons to be given in Year 3. Beth should report $400 on her Year 1 return and the remaining prepayment of $4,400 on her Year 2 return.

c. **Rent** is income from an investment, not from the operation of a business. Lessor gross income includes

   1) A bonus received for granting a lease. However, a lessee's refundable deposit is not income to the lessor.
   2) Value received to cancel or modify a lease. Amounts received by a lessee to cancel a lease, however, are treated as amounts realized on disposition of an asset/property (a capital gain).
   3) An amount paid by a lessee to maintain the property in lieu of rent, e.g., property tax payments. The lessor includes the payment in gross income and may be entitled to a corresponding deduction, e.g., a property tax deduction.
   4) The FMV of lessee improvements made to the property in lieu of rent. The **cost of maintenance** may be deducted by the lessor as a rental expense. The **cost of capital expenditures** may be capitalized and depreciated by the lessor. The FMV of lessee improvements not made in lieu of rent are excluded.

   NOTE: Study Unit 9, Subunit 1, has more detailed coverage of when to expense and when to capitalize costs.

   5) Prepaid rent, with no restriction as to its use, which is income when received regardless of the method of accounting.
   6) Rental income from a residence unless the residence is rented out for less than 15 days a year.
      a) If rental income is excluded, the corresponding rental deductions are also disallowed.

> **EXAMPLE 4-6　　Less than 15-Day Rental**
>
> Betty, who lives in a college town, rents out her home for homecoming weekend for $10,000. She does not rent out her home for any other portion of the year. Because Betty rented her home for less than 15 days, the rental income is excluded from gross income. Any corresponding expenses are nondeductible.

d. **Bartered services or goods** are included in gross income at the fair market value of the item(s) received in exchange for the services.

   1) Bartered exchanges are required to file Form 1099-B, and the transaction is recorded on Form 1040 Schedule C.

e. **Royalties** are payments to an owner by people who use some right belonging to that owner; thus, royalties constitute gross income.

f. A partner's share of **partnership income** is included in the partner's gross income, whether distributed or not. An owner's pro rata share of **S corporation income** is also included, whether distributed or not.

g. **Income in respect of a decedent** (income earned but not received before death) and distributed **income from an interest in an estate or trust** is included in gross income.

NOTE: Gross Income from Self-Employment (Schedule C) is discussed in detail in Study Unit 6.

7. **Investment income (including gains derived from dealings in property).** An investor in property seeks a return of the investment (capital) and gross income from the investment, which may be in the form of gains, interest, rents, royalties, or dividends.

From Form 1040

| 7 | Capital gain or (loss). Attach Schedule D if required. If not required, check here ▶ ☐ | 7 | |

From Form 1040 Schedule 1

| 4 | Other gains or (losses). Attach Form 4797 | 4 | |

a. A gain on disposition of investment property is generally the net increase (appreciation) in the value of the property.

1) **Realization** of investment income occurs upon a taxable event such as a disposition of the property by a sale or an exchange. **Realized gain** is calculated as follows:

$$
\begin{aligned}
&\text{Total money received and to be received} \\
&+ \text{FMV}^1 \text{ of property received and to be received} \\
&+ \text{Amount of liabilities transferred with the property} \\
&- \text{Any selling expenses} \\
&\underline{- \text{Liabilities assumed}} \\
&= \textbf{Amount realized} \\
&\underline{- \text{Adjusted basis}} \\
&= \textbf{Gain (or loss) realized}
\end{aligned}
$$

^{1}FMV = Fair market value at time of disposition

b. All gain realized is **recognized gain** unless a statutory provision provides for its nonrecognition by way of exclusion or deferral. Recognition means the income is to be included in gross income.

c. **Adjusted basis (AB)** indicates the amount of capital invested in the property and not yet recovered by tax benefit (i.e., depreciation). Adjusted basis generally is computed as follows:

$$
\begin{aligned}
&\text{Basis on acquisition (e.g., acquisition cost, acquisition debt, assumed liabilities)} \\
&\underline{\pm \text{ Adjustments to basis (e.g., } - \text{ depreciation, } + \text{ improvements)}} \\
&= \text{AB}
\end{aligned}
$$

d. If the taxpayer **sold a capital asset** (e.g., stock), the taxpayer must attach Form 8949, *Sales and Other Dispositions of Capital Assets,* Schedule D, *Capital Gains and Losses*, and Form 4797, *Sales of Business Property.*

e. If the taxpayer **sold or exchanged assets used in a trade or business** (e.g., delivery trucks), the taxpayer must complete and attach Form 4797, *Sales of Business Property.*

8. **Retirement Income**

    From Form 1040

4a	IRA distributions	4a		b Taxable amount	4b	
5a	Pensions and annuities	5a		b Taxable amount	5b	

    a. An **individual retirement account (IRA)** is a personal savings plan that gives the taxpayer tax advantages for setting aside money for retirement. Advantages of an IRA include
        1) Contributions the taxpayer makes to an IRA may be fully or partially deductible, depending on which type of IRA the taxpayer has and the taxpayer's circumstances.
        2) Generally, amounts in the taxpayer's IRA (including earnings and gains) are not taxed until distributed. In some cases, amounts are not taxed at all (or partially taxed) if distributed according to the rules.
    b. Payers of IRA distributions send the taxpayer Form 1099-R listing the gross distribution and the taxable amount (if known) before income tax or other deductions were withheld.
    c. A **pension** is generally a series of definitely determinable payments (most often paid in the form of an annuity) made to a taxpayer after the taxpayer retires from work.
        1) Pension payments are made regularly and are based on such factors as years of service and prior compensation. Therefore, the rules for pensions are similar to the rules for annuities.
            a) The investment in the pension is the amount contributed by the employee in after-tax dollars.
            b) Amounts withdrawn early are treated as a recovery of the employee's contributions (excluded from gross income) and of the employer's contributions (included in gross income). After all of the employee's contributions are recovered, additional withdrawals are fully included in gross income.
                i) However, a noncontributory plan results in all withdrawals being included in gross income (i.e., the employee made no contribution).
    d. **Annuity** payments are included in gross income unless a statute provides for their exclusion.
        1) Retirees are able to recover their contributions to their pensions (cost of annuity) tax-free.
        2) Any proceeds in excess of the cost of the annuity or contributions are included in gross income.
    e. Generally, the taxpayer will receive Form 1099-R listing the total amount of the taxpayer's pension and annuity payments before income tax or other deductions were withheld.

    From Form 1040 Schedule 1

7	Unemployment compensation	7	

9. **Unemployment benefits** received under a federal or state program are gross income.
    a. The payer of unemployment compensation sends the taxpayer Form 1099-G listing the amount to be reported.
    b. **Supplemental unemployment benefits** from a noncontributory fund that is company financed are taxable as wages (not unemployment).
        1) Supplemental unemployment benefits to be reported are listed on Form W-2.

    From Form 1040

6a	Social security benefits	6a		b Taxable amount	6b	

10. **Social Security Benefits (SSB)** are generally not taxable unless additional income is received. The gross income inclusion is dependent upon the relation of provisional income (PI) to the base amount (BA) and the adjusted base amount (ABA).

    a. Only the portion of SSB that exceeds a base amount related to other sources of income is subject to tax. SSB are calculated as follows:

    1) PI = Adjusted gross income (AGI) + Tax-exempt interest + Excluded foreign income + 50% of SSB
    2) Base amount (BA) is $32,000 if married filing jointly (MFJ), $0 if married filing separately and having lived with spouse at any time during the tax year (MFSLT), or $25,000 for all others.
    3) Adjusted base amount (ABA) is $44,000 if MFJ, $0 if MFSLT, or $34,000 for all others.
    4) If PI < BA, there is no inclusion (i.e., the SSB is excluded from gross income). If PI > BA but ≤ ABA, up to 50% of SSB will be included in gross income. If PI > ABA, up to 85% of SSB will be included in gross income.

EXAMPLE 4-7   Taxable Social Security Benefits

Mr. and Mrs. Slom, both over 65 and filing jointly, received $20,000 in Social Security benefits. Additionally, they reported $30,000 of taxable interest, $15,000 of tax-exempt interest, $18,000 in dividends, and a taxable pension of $16,000. Therefore, their AGI, excluding Social Security benefits, is $64,000 ($30,000 taxable interest + $18,000 dividends + $16,000 taxable pension payments).

- Provisional income is $89,000 [$64,000 AGI + $15,000 tax-exempt interest + 50% of SS benefits ($10,000)].
- The adjusted base amount is $44,000.
- The amount of $17,000 (85% of SS benefits) will be included in gross income since it is less than 85% of the excess of PI over the ABA plus the lesser of 50% of the incremental BA ($6,000) or 50% of SS benefits.
- Calculation of included Social Security benefits is as follows:

1) AGI, excluding SS benefits		$64,000
2) + Tax-exempt interest (excluded foreign income)	+	15,000
3) = Modified AGI	=	$79,000
4) + 50% of SS benefits	+	10,000
5) = Provisional income (PI)	=	$89,000
6) − BA ($32,000, $25,000, or $0)	−	32,000
7) = Excess PI (If < $0, then $0 inclusion)	=	$57,000
8) − Incremental base amount ($12,000, $9,000, or $0)	−	12,000
9) = Excess PI	=	$45,000
10) Smaller of amount in line 7 or 8		$12,000
11) 50% of line 10		6,000
12) Smaller of amount in line 4 or 11		6,000
13) Multiply line 9 by 85%		38,250
14) Add lines 12 and 13		44,250
15) SS benefits × 85%		17,000
16) Taxable benefits = Smaller of amount in line 14 or 15		17,000

SUCCESS TIP: While it is unlikely you would need to complete a detailed calculation like above on the CPA Exam, you should remember the PI calculation and the BA and ABA amounts so you can approximate whether a taxpayer's SSB are 0%, 50%, or 85% includible.

NOTE: SSB are listed on Form SSA-1099 and reported on Form 1040.

FORM SSA-1099 – SOCIAL SECURITY BENEFIT STATEMENT

[Year]
- PART OF YOUR SOCIAL SECURITY BENEFITS SHOWN IN BOX 5 MAY BE TAXABLE INCOME.
- SEE THE REVERSE FOR MORE INFORMATION.

Box 1. Name	Box 2. Beneficiary's Social Security Number

Box 3. Benefits Paid in [Year]	Box 4. Benefits Repaid to SSA in [Year]	Box 5. Net Benefits for [Year] *(Box 3 minus Box 4)*

DESCRIPTION OF AMOUNT IN BOX 3	DESCRIPTION OF AMOUNT IN BOX 4

Box 6. Voluntary Federal Income Tax Withheld

Box 7. Address

Box 8. Claim Number *(Use this number if you need to contact SSA.)*

Form **SSA-1099-SM**   **DO NOT RETURN THIS FORM TO SSA OR IRS**

11. Other Income

From Form 1040 Schedule 1

8 Other income. List type and amount ▶ _____ | 8 |

a. **Gambling winnings** are reported in gross income and later in the return can be offset by gambling losses (e.g., non-winning lottery tickets) only to the extent of winnings and only as other itemized deductions. However, gambling losses over winnings for the taxable year cannot be used as a carryover or carryback to reduce gambling income from other years.

b. **Prizes or awards** in a form other than money are included in gross income at the FMV of the property.

   1) The honoree may avoid inclusion by rejecting the prize or award.
   2) Some prizes and awards are excludable (e.g., transfers to charities, employee achievement).

c. **Business inducements** transfer value (even as "gifts") in exchange for past or anticipated economic benefits.

   1) The FMV of the inducement is income to the recipient.

d. Gross income includes the **recovery of tax benefit** items in a prior year.

EXAMPLE 4-8   Recovery of Tax Benefit -- Bad Debt

Taxpayer writes off bad debt in Year 1. In Year 7, the debtor pays Taxpayer the principal of the debt written off, which must be included in gross income because the deduction in Year 1 reduced the tax liability.

---

e. **Treasure troves** that are undisputedly in the taxpayer's possession are gross income for the tax year.

EXAMPLE 4-9   Reporting of a Treasure Trove

Rich purchased an old piano for $500 last year. In the current year, Rich finds $10,000 hidden in the piano. Rich must report the $10,000 as gross income in the current year.

---

f. Income from **illegal activities**, such as money from dealing illegal drugs, must be included in the taxpayer's income on Form 1040 or on Schedule C (Form 1040) if from the taxpayer's self-employment activity.

g. Gross income includes **discharge (cancellation) of indebtedness** when a debt is canceled in whole or part for consideration.
   1) If a debtor performs services to satisfy a debt, the debtor must recognize the amount of the debt as income.
   2) If a creditor gratuitously cancels a debt, the amount forgiven is treated as a gift.
   3) Gross income **does not include** discharges that
      a) Occur in bankruptcy (except a stock for debt transfer).
      b) Occur when the debtor is insolvent but not in bankruptcy.
         i) The maximum amount that can be excluded is the amount by which liabilities exceed the FMV of assets.
      c) Are related to qualified farm indebtedness.
      d) Are related to a purchase-money debt reduction in which a seller reduces the debt and the debtor is not in bankruptcy and is not insolvent. The discharge is treated as a purchase price adjustment.
      e) Are secured by a principal residence and were incurred in the acquisition, construction, or substantial improvement of the principal residence pursuant to the Mortgage Forgiveness Debt Relief Act (extended through 2025). The exclusion applies for discharges of up to $2 million ($1 million if married filing separately).
      f) Are related to certain qualified student loans.
      g) Are for Paycheck Protection Program loans.
   4) When a taxpayer excludes discharge of indebtedness under g.1), g.2), or g.3) above, the taxpayer must reduce his or her tax attributes in the following order:
      a) NOLs
      b) General business credit
      c) Capital loss carryovers
      d) Basis reductions

      NOTE: However, the taxpayer may first elect to decrease the basis in depreciable property.
   5) Generally, the creditor will send the taxpayer Form 1099-C listing the amount of cancellation of debt to be reported.

h. **Subpart F income** provisions were enacted to prevent U.S. persons from deferring income recognition by shifting income to low- or no-tax jurisdictions.

1) In general, qualified income from controlled foreign corporations (CFC) is included in income for the U.S. shareholder. The following defines the key terms for understanding what is qualified income:

    a) CFC: A foreign corporation owned more than 50% by U.S. shareholders.
    b) U.S. Shareholder: A U.S. person with 10% or more voting-ownership in the CFC.
    c) U.S. Person: A U.S. citizen, resident alien, domestic corporation, partnership, estate, or trust.

2) Qualified income includes a variety of sources; however, the most significant and only source covered in this review is foreign-base-company income (FBCI). FBCI consists of

    a) Foreign-personal-holding-company income,
    b) Foreign-base-company sales income, and
    c) Foreign-base-company services income.

3) The sales income does not qualify if the item sold was manufactured or sold within the country of the CFC.

    a) The service income only qualifies if the service is performed outside the country of the CFC.

EXAMPLE 4-10   **Subpart F Income for a CFC**

U.S. shareholders own more than 50% of an Ireland-based corporation, making the Irish corporation a CFC. Any service income performed in another country, e.g., Denmark, creates Subpart F income for the CFC (i.e., Irish corporation).

---

4) The provisions of Subpart F are exceedingly intricate and contain numerous general rules, special rules, definitions, exceptions, exclusions, and limitations, which require careful consideration. Only the basics required for the CPA Exam are covered in this course.

SUCCESS TIP

The AICPA has regularly tested candidates' knowledge of what types of income constitute gross income. Both theoretical and calculation questions have covered this topic.

STOP & REVIEW

You have completed the outline for this subunit.
Study multiple-choice questions 1 through 11 beginning on page 100.

4.2 EXCLUSIONS

1. **Specifically Stated**

   a. An item of income generally constitutes gross income unless a provision of the IRC **specifically states** that all or part of it is not treated as income, i.e., is excluded.

2. **Not Specifically Stated**

   a. Certain items are not treated as income for federal income tax purposes even though no IRC section specifically excludes them. The following are examples:

      1) **Unrealized income.** Income must be realized before it constitutes gross income. Generally, a gain is not realized until the property is sold or disposed. Mere fluctuations in market value are not treated as income for tax purposes.

      2) **Return of capital.** An amount invested in an asset is generally not treated as income for tax purposes upon an otherwise taxable disposition of the asset. Receipt of payment of debt principal is return of capital and not income. The value of one's own services, however, is not treated as capital invested.

      3) **Loans.** Receipt of loan funds does not give rise to income.

      4) **Intra-family services.** The value of services rendered by a person for himself or herself is not treated as income for tax purposes. The same applies for gratuitous services performed by one member of a family for another.

      5) **Use of one's own property.** Income is not imputed for the economic benefit of the use of property owned by oneself.

3. **Survivor benefits for public safety officers killed in the line of duty.** The annuity must be a result of a governmental plan meeting certain requirements and is attributable to the officer's service as a public safety officer.

4. **Life Insurance Proceeds**

   a. In general, proceeds of a life insurance policy paid by reason of the death of the insured (i.e., death benefit) are excluded from gross income.

   NOTE: Benefits from "employer-owned" life insurance contracts are to be included in gross income to the extent they exceed premiums paid.

   b. The exclusion is allowed regardless of form of payment or recipient. Interest earned on proceeds (after death of the insured) is gross income to the beneficiary.

   c. The amount of each payment in excess of the death benefit principal amount is interest income.

EXAMPLE 4-11   Life Insurance Proceeds Paid in Installments

A $75,000 policy pays off in $6,000 installments over 15 years. The principal amount per installment, $5,000 ($75,000 ÷ 15 years), is excluded. The remaining $1,000 ($6,000 − $5,000) is taxable interest income.

---

   d. If the owner of a policy transfers the policy to another person for consideration, the proceeds are taxable. However, amounts paid to acquire the policy and subsequent premium payments are treated as return of investment capital.

SU 4: Gross Income and Exclusions

e. Amounts received as accelerated death benefits under a life insurance contract for individuals who are either terminally ill (certified by a physician that death can be reasonably expected to result within 24 months) or chronically ill (unable to perform basic tasks) are excluded from gross income.

   1) A chronically ill person must use the funds for medical care to qualify for the exclusion.

f. Dividends paid on insurance policies are excluded from gross income to the extent cumulative dividends do not exceed cumulative premiums and provided the cash value does not exceed the net investment, which it normally does not.

   1) Interest on Veterans Administration (VA) insurance dividends left on deposit with the VA is excluded from gross income.

5. **Annuity Contracts**

   a. Taxpayers are permitted to recover the cost of the annuity (the price paid) tax-free (e.g., dividends from life insurance policy up to the amount of premiums paid). The nontaxable portion of an annuity is determined as follows:

      1) Calculate the expected return, which is equal to the annual payment multiplied by the expected return multiple (life expectancy determined from an actuarial table).

      2) The exclusion ratio is equal to the investment in the contract (or its cost) divided by the expected return.

      3) The current exclusion is calculated by multiplying the exclusion ratio by the amount received during the year.

EXAMPLE 4-12   Annual Exclusion for an Annuity Contract

Xavier, age 56, purchased an annuity contract to provide monthly payments of $150 until his death. The annuity cost is $35,000. The annual exclusion is calculated as follows:

		Age	Exclusion Multiple
Annual payment	$ 1,800	55	28.6
Exclusion multiple	× 27.7	56	27.7
Expected return	$49,860	57	26.8
Exclusion ratio	$35,000 / $49,860 = 70%		

Annual exclusion = $150 per month × 12 months × 70% exclusion ratio = $1,260

---

      4) A simplified method is required for retirement plan (employee) annuities with starting dates after November 18, 1996. The nontaxable portion is calculated by dividing the investment in the contract, as of the annuity starting date, by the number of anticipated monthly payments.

Age of Primary Annuitant on the Annuity Starting Date	Number of Anticipated Monthly Payments
55 and under	360
56-60	310
61-65	260
66-70	210
71 and over	160

         a) If the annuity has a fixed number of payments, use that number instead.

6. **Gifts**
    a. A gift is a transfer for less than full or adequate consideration. The IRC excludes from the gross income of the recipient the value of property acquired by gift.
        1) Voluntary transfers from employer to employee are presumed to be compensation, not gifts.

7. **Prizes and Awards**
    a. A prize or award may qualify for exclusion as a scholarship. Additionally, a recipient may exclude the FMV of the prize or award if
        1) The amount received is in recognition of religious, scientific, charitable, or similar meritorious achievement;
        2) The recipient is selected without action on his or her part;
        3) The receipt of the award is not conditioned on substantial future services; and
        4) The amount is paid by the organization making the award to a tax-exempt organization (including a governmental unit) designated by the recipient.
    b. A qualified employee achievement plan award is provided under an established written program that does not discriminate in favor of highly compensated employees.
        1) Employee achievement awards may qualify for exclusion from the recipient employee's gross income if they are awarded as part of a meaningful presentation for safety achievement or length of service and
            a) The awards do not exceed $400 for all nonqualified plan awards or
            b) The awards do not exceed $1,600 for all qualified plan awards.
            c) The award is tangible personal property (e.g., plaque, watch, etc.). Cash, cash equivalents, and gift cards are not tangible personal property.

8. **Scholarships and Tuition Reduction**
    a. Amounts received by an individual as scholarships or fellowships are excluded from gross income to the extent that the individual is a candidate for a degree from a qualified educational institution and the amounts are used for required tuition or fees, books, supplies, or equipment (not personal expenses).
    b. Gross income includes any amount received, e.g., as tuition reduction, in exchange for the performance of such services as teaching or research.
    c. Generally, a reduction in undergraduate tuition for an employee of a qualified educational organization does not constitute gross income.
        1) The exclusion is not allowed for amounts representing payments for services (e.g., research, teaching) performed by the student as a condition for receiving the qualified scholarship.

9. **Student Loan Forgiveness and Employer Payments**
    a. Federal, state, and/or local government student loan indebtedness may be discharged and excluded from income if the former student engages in certain employment (e.g., in a specified location, for a specified period, or for a specified employer) or the discharge is due to death or total and permanent disability.
    b. Payments made by an employer to an employee or lender (up to $5,250 per employee) during the current year on any qualified educational loan incurred by the employee for the employee's education may be excluded by the employer from the employee's taxable wages.

10. **Redemption of U.S. Savings Bonds to Pay Educational Expenses**
    a. If a taxpayer pays qualified higher education expenses during the year, a portion of the interest on redemption of a Series EE U.S. Savings Bond is excluded.
    b. The exclusion rate equals qualified expenses divided by the total of principal and interest (not to exceed 100% or 1.0).
    c. The amount of qualified expenses is reduced by the total of qualified scholarships (excluded from income), employer-provided educational assistance, expenses for American Opportunity and Lifetime Learning credits, and other higher education related benefits. In order to qualify,
        1) The taxpayer, the taxpayer's spouse, or a dependent incurs tuition and fees to attend an eligible educational institution.
        2) The taxpayer's modified AGI (MAGI) must not exceed a certain limit. For 2021, the exclusion is reduced when MAGI exceeds a threshold of $83,200 ($124,800 if a joint return). The amount at which the benefit is completely phased out is $98,200 ($154,800 if a joint return).
        3) The purchaser of the bonds must be the sole owner of the bonds (or joint owner with his or her spouse).
        4) The issue date of the bonds must follow the 24th birthday(s) of the owner(s).

11. **Interest on State and Local Government Obligations**

    From Form 1040

2a	Tax-exempt interest . . .	2a	

    a. Interest to a holder of a debt obligation incurred by a state or local governmental entity is generally exempt from federal income tax.

    > **BACKGROUND 4-1   State and Local Government Interest Exemption**
    >
    > Historically, this exemption has been extremely important to state and local governments. It allows them to offer their debt at lower interest rates, thereby lowering their cost of capital.

    b. The interest on certain private activity bonds and arbitrage bonds is not excluded.
        1) Private activity bonds are bonds of which more than 10% of the proceeds are to be used in a private business and more than 10% of the principal or interest is secured or will be paid by private business property or more than 5% or $5 million of the proceeds are to be used for private loans, whichever is lesser.
        2) Interest on private activity bonds can still be excluded if the bond is for residential rental housing developments, public facilities (such as airports or waste removal), or other qualified causes.

12. **Compensation for Injury or Sickness**
    a. Gross income does not include benefits specified that might be received in the form of disability pay, health or accident insurance proceeds, workers' compensation awards, or other "damages" for personal physical injury or physical sickness.
    b. Specifically **included** in gross income are
        1) Compensation for slander of reputation.
        2) Damages for lost profits in a business.
        3) Punitive damages received.
            a) If a judgment results in both actual and punitive damages, the judgment must be allocated.
        4) Damages received **solely** for emotional distress.
    c. Interest earned on an award for personal injuries is not excluded from gross income.
    d. Recovery of deductions
        1) If the taxpayer incurred medical expenses in Year 1, deducted these expenses on his or her Year 1 tax return, and received reimbursement for the same medical expenses in Year 2, the reimbursement is included in gross income on the Year 2 return in an amount equal to the previous deduction.

13. **Recovery of Tax Benefit Item**
    a. Amounts recovered during the tax year that did not provide a tax benefit in the prior year are excluded.

EXAMPLE 4-13   Recovery Not Providing a Tax Benefit

Taxpayer pays state income tax in excess of the standard deduction and itemizes deductions. Subsequent refunds in excess of the applicable standard deduction must be included in gross income. However, if Taxpayer elected the standard deduction, the refund would not be included because no tax benefit from payment of state income tax was realized.

---

    b. A similar rule applies to credits.

14. **Gain on Sale of Principal Residence**
    a. In general, a taxpayer may exclude up to $250,000 ($500,000 for married taxpayers filing jointly) of realized gain on the sale of a principal residence.

15. **Stock Dividends**
    a. Generally, a shareholder does not include in gross income the value of a stock dividend (or right to acquire stock) declared on its own shares unless one of the following exceptions applies:
        1) Any shareholder can elect to receive cash or other property.
        2) Some common stock shareholders receive preferred stock, while other common stock shareholders receive common stock.
        3) The distribution is on preferred stock (but a distribution on preferred stock merely to adjust conversion ratios as a result of a stock split or dividend is excluded).
        4) If a shareholder receives common stock and cash for a fractional portion of stock, then only the cash received for the fractional portion is included in gross income.

SU 4: Gross Income and Exclusions

16. **Foreign-Earned Income Exclusion**
    a. U.S. citizens may exclude up to $108,700 (in calendar year 2021) of foreign-earned income and a statutory housing cost allowance from gross income.
    b. **To qualify for exclusion**, the taxpayer must either be a resident of one or more foreign countries for the entire taxable year or be present in one or more foreign countries for 330 days during a consecutive 12-month period.
    c. The $108,700 limitation must be prorated if the taxpayer is not present in (or a resident of) the foreign country for the entire year.
    d. This exclusion is in lieu of the Foreign Tax Credit.
    e. Deductions attributed to the foreign-earned income (which is excluded) are disallowed.

17. **Lease Improvements**
    a. The value of improvements made by the real property lessee, including buildings erected, is excludable by the lessor unless the lessee provided the improvements in lieu of rent. Income realized by the lessor from the improvements subsequent to termination of the lease is included.
    b. Amounts received by a retail lessee as cash or rent reductions are not included in gross income of the lessee if used for qualified construction or improvements to the retail space.

18. **Insurance Payments for Living Expenses**
    a. If an individual's principal residence is damaged by casualty or the individual is denied access by governmental authorities to the casualty, then amounts paid to reimburse for living expenses are excluded from gross income. The exclusion is limited to actual living expenses incurred less the normal living expenses the taxpayer would have incurred during the period.

19. **Rental Value of Parsonage**
    a. Ministers may exclude from gross income the rental value of a home or a rental allowance to the extent the allowance is used to provide a home. However, the rental value or allowance is included in self-employment income when calculating self-employment tax.

20. **Foster Care**
    a. Amounts received in return for foster care are excluded.

SUCCESS TIP

Candidates should expect to see questions testing exclusions from gross income on the exam and may see questions that give a list of items and ask for the amount of those items excluded from gross income.

STOP & REVIEW

You have completed the outline for this subunit.
Study multiple-choice questions 12 through 20 beginning on page 105.

QUESTIONS

4.1 Gross Income

1. Which of the following conditions must be present in a post-1984 but pre-2019 divorce agreement for a payment to qualify as deductible alimony?

I. Payments must be in cash.
II. The payments must end at the recipient's death.

A. I only.
B. II only.
C. Both I and II.
D. Neither I nor II.

Answer (C) is correct.
REQUIRED: The conditions required in a post-1984 but pre-2019 divorce agreement for payments to qualify as deductible alimony.
DISCUSSION: In order for payments to qualify as deductible alimony, they must meet all of the following requirements:

1) Paid in cash
2) Paid pursuant to a written divorce or separation instrument
3) Not designated as other than alimony
4) Terminated at death of recipient
5) Not paid to a member of the same household
6) Not paid to a spouse with whom the taxpayer is filing a joint return

2. Pierce Corp., an accrual-basis, calendar-year C corporation, had the following 2021 receipts:

2022 advance rental payments for a lease ending in 2023	$250,000
Lease cancellation payment from a 5-year lease tenant	100,000

Pierce had no restrictions on the use of the advance rental payments and renders no services in connection with the rental income. What amount of gross income should Pierce report on its 2021 tax return?

A. $350,000
B. $250,000
C. $100,000
D. $0

Answer (A) is correct.
REQUIRED: The amount of gross income for the current year.
DISCUSSION: Both cash- and accrual-basis taxpayers must include rental payments in gross income upon actual or constructive receipt if the taxpayer has an unrestricted claim to the amount. A lease cancellation payment is in lieu of rent and is included in income like rent. Because Pierce had no restrictions on the use of the payments, the entire amount of the payments is included in income.
Answer (B) is incorrect. A lease cancellation payment is a payment made in lieu of rent and is included in income like rent. **Answer (C) is incorrect.** Without restrictions on the use, prepaid rent is income when received even if the lessor uses the accrual method of accounting. **Answer (D) is incorrect.** Without restrictions on the use, prepaid rent is income when received, and lease cancellation payments are made in lieu of rent and are included in income like rent.

SU 4: Gross Income and Exclusions

3. Fred and Rosanne Mott's divorce agreement was executed in February 2021. In accordance with the agreement, Rosanne transferred the title in their home to Fred in 2021. The home, which had a fair market value of $150,000, was subject to a $50,000 mortgage that had 20 more years to run. Monthly mortgage payments amount to $1,000. Under the terms of settlement, Rosanne is obligated to make the mortgage payments on the home for the full remaining 20-year term of the indebtedness, or until Fred's death, whichever is sooner. Rosanne made 11 mortgage payments in 2021. What amount is taxable as alimony in Fred's 2021 return?

A. $0
B. $11,000
C. $100,000
D. $111,000

Answer (A) is correct.
   REQUIRED: The taxable alimony.
   DISCUSSION: Regardless of the requirements to qualify as alimony, for divorces executed after 2018, maintenance and separation payments to a former spouse are not deductible by the payor or income to the payee. Therefore, Fred has no taxable alimony from Rosanne for 2021.
   Answer (B) is incorrect. If the divorce was executed prior to 2019, Fred would have $11,000 in taxable income, but it was not effective until 2021, resulting in no taxable income for Fred. **Answer (C) is incorrect.** The transfer of title to the property is not a payment in cash. In addition, the divorce agreement was not executed until 2021. **Answer (D) is incorrect.** To be included in the payee spouse's taxable income, the payment must be in cash and the divorce must be effective prior to 2019.

4. Darr, an employee of Source C corporation, is not a shareholder. Which of the following should be included in Darr's gross income?

A. Employer-provided medical insurance coverage under a health plan.
B. A $16,000 gift from the taxpayer's grandparents.
C. The fair market value of land that the taxpayer inherited from an uncle.
D. The dividend income on shares of stock that the taxpayer received for services rendered.

Answer (D) is correct.
   REQUIRED: The item included in the gross income of an employee.
   DISCUSSION: The dividend income as well as the FMV of the stock would be included in Darr's gross income. The FMV of the stock is classified as compensation.
   Answer (A) is incorrect. Employer-provided medical coverage is excluded from an employee's gross income. However, any benefits (reimbursement) from the employer-provided plan in excess of expenses should be included. **Answer (B) is incorrect.** Gifts are excluded from gross income. **Answer (C) is incorrect.** Land acquired by inheritance is excluded.

5. An individual received $50,000 during the current (2021) year pursuant to a pre-2019 divorce decree. A check for $25,000 was identified as annual alimony, checks totaling $10,000 were identified as annual child support, and a check for $15,000 was identified as a property settlement. What amount should be included in the individual's gross income?

A. $50,000
B. $40,000
C. $25,000
D. $0

Answer (C) is correct.
REQUIRED: The amount included in an individual's gross income.
DISCUSSION: For divorces executed before 2019, alimony is gross income to the recipient and deductible by the payor. Alimony is payment in cash, paid pursuant to a written divorce decree, not designated as other than alimony (e.g., child support), terminated at death of recipient, not paid to a member of the same household, and not paid to a spouse with whom the taxpayer is filing a joint return. Child support and property settlement payments are not alimony. Thus, the $25,000 of alimony is included in gross income.
Answer (A) is incorrect. Child support payments are an exclusion from gross income of the recipient and are not deductible by the payor. These payments are not alimony. Property settlement payments are not treated as alimony. They are treated as a transfer by gift, which is specifically excluded from gross income. **Answer (B) is incorrect.** Property settlement payments are not treated as alimony. They are treated as a transfer by gift, which is specifically excluded from gross income. **Answer (D) is incorrect.** Alimony is gross income to the recipient and deductible by the payor. Thus, $25,000 of alimony is included in gross income.

6. With regard to the alimony deduction in connection with a 2018 divorce, which one of the following statements is true?

A. Alimony is deductible by the payor spouse, and includible by the payee spouse, to the extent that payment is contingent on the status of the divorced couple's children.

B. The divorced couple may be members of the same household at the time alimony is paid, provided that the persons do not live as husband and wife.

C. Alimony payments must terminate on the death of the payee spouse.

D. Alimony may be paid either in cash or in property.

Answer (C) is correct.
REQUIRED: The payments deductible as alimony.
DISCUSSION: Payments to a former spouse under a pre-2019 divorce decree are treated as alimony if made in cash and if the divorce decree does not designate the payments as other than alimony and the payments are deductible by the payor. If payments are required to continue after the death of the recipient spouse, however, they are not alimony.
Answer (A) is incorrect. Any portion that is for support of a minor child is excluded from gross income of the recipient and is not deductible by the payor. **Answer (B) is incorrect.** Alimony can only include payments when the payor and the payee are not members of the same household. **Answer (D) is incorrect.** Only payments made in cash can constitute deductible alimony.

SU 4: Gross Income and Exclusions

7. In which of the following situations will a controlled foreign corporation located in Ireland be deemed to have Subpart F income?

A. Services are provided by an Irish company in England under a contract entered into by its U.S. parent.

B. Property is produced in Ireland by the Irish company and sold outside its country of incorporation.

C. Services are performed in Ireland by the Irish company under a contract entered into by its U.S. parent.

D. Property is bought from the controlled foreign corporation's U.S. parent and is sold by an Irish company for use in an Irish manufacturing plant.

Answer (A) is correct.
REQUIRED: The proper identification of Subpart F income.
DISCUSSION: Section 954 of Subpart F defines foreign base company income (which is a component of Subpart F income) as including foreign base company services income. Foreign base company services income is income derived from the performance of a service of a skill on behalf of a related party and performed outside of the country of incorporation of the foreign subsidiary. Taxing Subpart F income ensures that companies cannot defer income tax by setting up corporations in low tax jurisdictions. Flowing the money into Ireland's low tax jurisdiction for service performed in England's higher tax jurisdiction creates Subpart F income.
Answer (B) is incorrect. Subpart F income does not include income from manufacturing and exporting goods. **Answer (C) is incorrect.** Foreign base company services income does not include income from providing services within the country of incorporation, only those services performed outside the country of incorporation. **Answer (D) is incorrect.** Subpart F income does not include income derived from the sale of personal property within the country of incorporation.

8. Easel Co. has elected to reimburse employees for business expenses under a nonaccountable plan. Easel does not require employees to provide proof of expenses and allows employees to keep any amount not spent. Under the plan, Mel, an Easel employee for a full year, gets $400 per month for business automobile expenses. At the end of the year, Mel informs Easel that the only business expense incurred was for business mileage of 8,036 at a rate of 56 cents per mile, the IRS standard mileage rate at the time of travel. Mel encloses a check for $300 to refund the overpayment to Easel. What amount should be reported in Mel's gross income for the year?

A. $0
B. $300
C. $4,500
D. $4,800

Answer (D) is correct.
REQUIRED: The gross income reported for reimbursements from a nonaccountable plan.
DISCUSSION: In a nonaccountable plan, the reimbursements are included in the employee's gross income. These expenses are not deductible from 2018 to 2025. Since the employee accounted to the employer and returned the excess reimbursement, this could have qualified as an "accountable plan." Under an accountable plan, the employee would include nothing in income. However, the company uses a nonaccountable plan, and Mel must include $4,800 ($400 × 12 months) in his gross income.
Answer (A) is incorrect. Under a nonaccountable plan, Mel must include all reimbursements in gross income ($4,800). **Answer (B) is incorrect.** With a nonaccountable plan, the amount included in gross income is the total reimbursement (not limited to overpayment of the reimbursement). **Answer (C) is incorrect.** Under a nonaccountable plan, Mel must include all reimbursements in gross income ($4,800).

9. In 2021, Emil Gow won $16,000 in a state lottery and spent $800 for the purchase of lottery tickets. Emil elected the standard deduction on his 2021 income tax return. The amount of lottery winnings that should be included in Emil's 2021 gross income is

A. $0
B. $2,650
C. $3,450
D. $16,000

Answer (D) is correct.
REQUIRED: The amount of state lottery winnings included in gross income.
DISCUSSION: Gambling winnings (whether legal or illegal) are included in gross income. Therefore, Emil must include the full $16,000 in gross income. Gambling losses, i.e., amounts spent on nonwinning tickets, may be deductible but only as an itemized deduction to the extent of gambling winnings.
Answer (A) is incorrect. All gambling winnings constitute gross income. Answer (B) is incorrect. If the standard deduction is claimed, itemized deductions are not allowed. In addition, the standard deduction reduces AGI, not the amount included in gross income. Answer (C) is incorrect. Although gambling losses are an itemized deduction, they do not reduce the amount of gambling winnings included in gross income.

10. Porter was unemployed for part of 2021. Porter received $35,000 of wages, $4,000 from a state unemployment compensation plan, and $2,000 from his former employer's company-paid supplemental unemployment benefit plan. What is the amount of Porter's gross income?

A. $35,000
B. $37,000
C. $39,000
D. $41,000

Answer (D) is correct.
REQUIRED: The total amount of gross income.
DISCUSSION: Gross income is all income from whatever source derived except as otherwise provided. All compensation (wages) for personal services is gross income. Unemployment benefits received under a federal or state program are gross income. Supplemental unemployment is included in gross income as wages (not under unemployment). Porter's total gross income is $41,000 ($35,000 wages + $4,000 state unemployment + $2,000 supplemental unemployment).
Answer (A) is incorrect. Although the $35,000 he received as wages is included in gross income, so are the $4,000 of state unemployment and the $2,000 of supplemental unemployment, for a total of $41,000. Answer (B) is incorrect. Although both the $35,000 of wages and $2,000 of supplemental unemployment are included in gross income, so is the $4,000 of state unemployment. Answer (C) is incorrect. Although both the $35,000 of wages and $4,000 of state unemployment are included in gross income, so is the $2,000 of supplemental unemployment.

11. Paul Crane, age 25, is single with no dependents and had an adjusted gross income of $30,000 in 2021, exclusive of $2,000 in unemployment compensation benefits received in 2021. The amount of Crane's unemployment compensation benefits taxable for 2021 is

A. $2,000
B. $1,000
C. $500
D. $0

Answer (A) is correct.
REQUIRED: The amount of taxable unemployment compensation.
DISCUSSION: All unemployment compensation constitutes gross income. The IRC does not allow exclusion or deduction of any of it.

4.2 Exclusions

12. Klein, a master's degree candidate at Briar University, was awarded a $12,000 scholarship from Briar in Year 1. The scholarship was used to pay Klein's Year 1 university tuition and fees. Also in Year 1, Klein received $5,000 for teaching two courses at a nearby college. What amount must be included in Klein's Year 1 gross income?

A. $0
B. $5,000
C. $12,000
D. $17,000

Answer (B) is correct.
REQUIRED: The amount of scholarship received that is includible in gross income.
DISCUSSION: Scholarships may be excluded from gross income provided a student is enrolled in a degree-seeking program and that the scholarship is used for qualified expenses such as tuition and fees. However, amounts received for services such as teaching must be included in gross income.
Answer (A) is incorrect. Klein must include the $5,000 received for teaching the two courses. Answer (C) is incorrect. Klein may exclude the $12,000 scholarship but must include the $5,000 for teaching. Answer (D) is incorrect. Klein may exclude the $12,000 scholarship.

13. Sam and Ann Hoyt filed a joint federal income tax return for the calendar year 2021. Among the Hoyts' cash receipts during 2021 was the following: $6,000 first installment on a $75,000 life insurance policy payable to Ann in annual installments of $6,000 each over a 15-year period, as beneficiary of the policy on her uncle, who died in 2020. What portion of the $6,000 installment on the life insurance policy is excludable from 2021 gross income in arriving at the Hoyts' adjusted gross income?

A. $0
B. $1,000
C. $5,000
D. $6,000

Answer (C) is correct.
REQUIRED: The life insurance proceeds excluded from gross income.
DISCUSSION: Proceeds under a life insurance contract paid by reason of death of the insured are excluded from gross income. But the amount of each payment in excess of the death benefit prorated over the period of payment ($75,000 ÷ 15 years = $5,000 per year) is interest income ($6,000 – $5,000), which is included in gross income.
Answer (A) is incorrect. The portion paid by reason of death, i.e., the amount of coverage, is excluded. Answer (B) is incorrect. The amount of interest included in gross income is $1,000. Answer (D) is incorrect. Only the portion paid by reason of death, i.e., the amount of coverage, is excluded.

14. DAC Foundation awarded Kent $75,000 in recognition of lifelong literary achievement. Kent was not required to render future services as a condition to receive the $75,000. What condition(s) must have been met for the award to be excluded from Kent's gross income?

I. Kent was selected for the award by DAC without any action on Kent's part.

II. Pursuant to Kent's designation, DAC paid the amount of the award either to a governmental unit or to a charitable organization.

A. I only.
B. II only.
C. Both I and II.
D. Neither I nor II.

Answer (C) is correct.
REQUIRED: The conditions under which an award may be excluded from a taxpayer's gross income.
DISCUSSION: Prizes and awards made primarily in recognition of charitable, scientific, educational, etc., achievement are excluded from gross income only if the recipient was selected without any action on his or her part, is not required to render substantial future services as condition of receiving the prize or award, and assigns it to charity.
Answer (A) is incorrect. Kent must also assign the award to charity. Answer (B) is incorrect. Kent must have been selected without any action on his or her part. Answer (D) is incorrect. Prizes and awards made primarily in recognition of charitable, scientific, educational, etc., achievement are excluded from gross income only if the recipient was selected without any action on his or her part, is not required to render substantial future services as condition of receiving the prize or award, and assigns it to charity.

15. Clark filed Form 1040 for the 2020 taxable year and claimed the standard deduction. In July 2021, Clark received a state income tax refund of $900, plus interest of $10, for overpayment of 2020 state income tax. What amount of the state tax refund and interest is taxable in Clark's 2021 federal income tax return?

A. $0
B. $10
C. $900
D. $910

Answer (B) is correct.
REQUIRED: The amount of a recovered item that produced no tax benefit, and interest, includible in gross income.
DISCUSSION: If a taxpayer obtains a deduction for an item that reduces taxes in one year and later recovers all or a portion of the prior deduction, the recovery is included in gross income in the year it is received. To the extent the expense did not reduce federal income taxes in the earlier year, the recovery is excluded from income. Clark opted for the standard deduction in lieu of itemizing and claiming the state income tax deduction. Thus, the state tax paid produced no tax benefit and is excluded from gross income. Interest on state income tax refunds is not excludable. It is expressly included in gross income.
Answer (A) is incorrect. The interest on the tax refund is not excludable. **Answer (C) is incorrect.** The state income tax paid was not deducted on the Form 1040 and is thus excluded from gross income. Furthermore, the interest on the tax refund is not excludable. **Answer (D) is incorrect.** The state income tax paid was not deducted on the Form 1040 and is thus excluded from gross income.

16. Clark bought Series EE U.S. Savings Bonds. Redemption proceeds will be used for payment of college tuition for Clark's dependent child. One of the conditions that must be met for tax exemption of accumulated interest on these bonds is that the

A. Purchaser of the bonds must be the sole owner of the bonds (or joint owner with his or her spouse).
B. Bonds must be bought by a parent (or both parents) and put in the name of the dependent child.
C. Bonds must be bought by the owner of the bonds before the owner reaches the age of 24.
D. Bonds must be transferred to the college for redemption by the college rather than by the owner of the bonds.

Answer (A) is correct.
REQUIRED: The stated requirement for exclusion of interest on Series EE U.S. Savings Bonds.
DISCUSSION: Exclusion of accumulated interest on U.S. savings bonds issued at a discount is permitted. The bonds must be issued after 1989. Exclusion of interest is conditioned on each of the following: (1) The purchaser of the bonds must be the sole owner (or joint owner with his or her spouse) of the bonds; (2) the issue date of the bonds must follow the 24th birthday(s) of the owner(s); and (3) the redemption proceeds must be used to pay tuition and fees of the taxpayer, spouse, or dependent to attend a college, a university, or certain vocational schools.
Answer (B) is incorrect. The purchaser must be the sole owner (or joint owner with his or her spouse) of the bonds. **Answer (C) is incorrect.** The requirement is that the bond's issue date must follow the owner's 24th birthday. **Answer (D) is incorrect.** The requirement is that the proceeds be used to pay qualified higher education expenses.

17. Charles and Marcia are married cash-basis taxpayers. In 2021, they had interest income as follows:

- $500 interest on federal income tax refund
- $600 interest on state income tax refund
- $800 interest on federal government obligations
- $1,000 interest on state government obligations

What amount of interest income is taxable on Charles and Marcia's 2021 joint income tax return?

A. $500
B. $1,100
C. $1,900
D. $2,900

Answer (C) is correct.
REQUIRED: The amount of interest income included in gross income.
DISCUSSION: Unless otherwise excluded in another section, the IRC includes interest in gross income. The IRC excludes from gross income interest on most obligations of states or political subdivisions of a state (e.g., municipal bonds). This exclusion does not apply to the obligations of the United States (with the exception of EE bonds used for qualifying education expenses) or interest on state income tax overpayments. Interest income is taxable unless specifically excluded from gross income.

18. During 2021, Adler had the following cash receipts:

Wages	$18,000
Interest income from investments in municipal bonds	400
Unemployment compensation	1,500

What is the total amount that must be included in gross income on Adler's 2021 income tax return?

A. $18,000
B. $18,400
C. $19,500
D. $19,900

Answer (C) is correct.
REQUIRED: The amount included in gross income on a taxpayer's income tax return.
DISCUSSION: The IRC specifically includes wages and unemployment compensation as gross income. Furthermore, the IRC excludes from gross income interest on most obligations of states or political subdivisions of a state (e.g., municipal bonds).
Answer (A) is incorrect. Unemployment compensation is also included in gross income.
Answer (B) is incorrect. Interest on state and local government obligations is specifically excluded from gross income, and unemployment compensation is included in gross income. **Answer (D) is incorrect.** Interest on state and local government obligations is specifically excluded from gross income.

19. Cassidy, an individual, reported the following items of income and expense during the current year (2021):

Salary	$50,000
Alimony paid to a former spouse (pre-2019 divorce agreement)	10,000
Inheritance from a grandparent	25,000
Proceeds of a lawsuit for physical injuries	50,000

What is the amount of Cassidy's adjusted gross income?

A. $40,000
B. $50,000
C. $115,000
D. $125,000

Answer (A) is correct.
REQUIRED: The taxpayer's adjusted gross income, including determining which items are gross income and which items are deducted from gross income.
DISCUSSION: A taxpayer's adjusted gross income equals all gross income items, as defined by Sec. 61 of the Internal Revenue Code, less any available deductions from gross income, as defined by the Internal Revenue Code.

Salary	$ 50,000
Alimony Paid	(10,000)
AGI	$ 40,000

The inheritance and proceeds for physical injury are excluded from gross income.
Answer (B) is incorrect. A deduction is allowed for alimony paid to a former spouse. **Answer (C) is incorrect.** Inheritances are excluded from the gross income of the recipient as gifts, and proceeds of a lawsuit for physical injuries, provided they are for actual damages, are specifically excluded from gross income as compensation for injury or sickness. **Answer (D) is incorrect.** Only one item is includible in gross income, and a deduction is allowed for alimony paid to a former spouse.

20. During 2021, Clark received the following interest income:

On Veterans Administration insurance dividends left on deposit with the V.A.	$20
On state income tax refund	30

What amount should Clark include for interest income in his 2021 return?

A. $50
B. $30
C. $20
D. $0

Answer (B) is correct.
REQUIRED: The amount of interest income included in gross income.
DISCUSSION: Interest income is included in gross income unless specifically excluded by an IRC section. Although an exclusion for interest on certain obligations of states and municipalities is provided, it does not apply to interest on state income tax refunds. The interest on V.A. insurance dividends left on deposit with the V.A. is excluded from gross income.
Answer (A) is incorrect. The interest on V.A. insurance dividends is excluded from gross income. **Answer (C) is incorrect.** Interest on state income tax refunds is included in gross income, but interest on V.A. insurance dividends is excluded from gross income. **Answer (D) is incorrect.** Interest on state income tax refunds is included in gross income.

Access the **Gleim CPA Premium Review System** featuring our SmartAdapt technology from your Gleim Personal Classroom to continue your studies. You will experience a personalized study environment with exam-emulating multiple-choice questions.

STUDY UNIT FIVE
ACCOUNTING METHODS AND SPECIAL ENTITIES

(15 pages of outline)

5.1	Accounting Methods	109
5.2	Exempt Organizations	119
5.3	Trusts	122

Explanation of the timing of inclusions, exclusions, and deductions is integrated into the discussion of accounting methods in the first subunit of this study unit.

The final two subunits cover the very basics (i.e., definitions and qualifications) of organizations exempt from federal income tax and taxation of trusts. Certain organizations may qualify for exemption from federal income tax under Sec. 501(a). They are referred to as nonprofit organizations. Most organizations seeking recognition of exemption from federal income tax must use application forms specifically prescribed by the IRS. Trusts are legal entities defined by the assets they hold. These assets produce income, and the entities are subject to tax on that income. This is referred to as fiduciary income taxation. The formula for computing this fiduciary tax is the individual income tax formula presented in Study Unit 4, with some modification beyond the scope of the exam. Furthermore, the beneficiaries of these fiduciary entities, rather than the fiduciary, are personally subject to income tax on certain fiduciary income.

The exam scope of Subunits 5.2-5.3 has been significantly reduced, and this outline reflects those changes.

5.1 ACCOUNTING METHODS

1. **Background**
    a. A person must use the method of accounting regularly used to compute income in keeping books and records. The method must clearly reflect income. The **cash method** and the **accrual method** are the most common. Specific provisions of the Internal Revenue Code (IRC) may override and require specific treatment of certain items.
    b. Generally, IRS consent is required for **changes in accounting method**, which include, but are not limited to, change in either the overall system of accounting for gross income or deductions or treatment of any material item used in the system.
    c. Income is reported when it can be estimated with reasonable accuracy. Adjustments are made in a later year for any differences between the actual amount and the previously reported amounts.

2. **Tax Year**
   a. The accounting method determines the tax year, which is the annual accounting period used to keep the person's books and records, in which an item is includible or deductible in computing taxable income. Federal income tax is imposed on taxable income.
   b. The taxable period is adopted in a person's first tax year and includes the following:
      1) A **calendar year** is the 12-month period ending on December 31.
      2) A **fiscal year** is any 12-month period ending on the last day of a month.
      3) A **52- or 53-week tax year** is also allowed.
      4) A **short tax year** is allowed for a business not in existence for an entire year (365 or 366 days), e.g., the start-up year or the year at dissolution.
      5) A change of tax year generally requires IRS consent, and a short tax year return is then required.

3. **Cash Method**
   a. A cash-method taxpayer accounts for income when one of the following occurs:
      1) Cash or its equivalent is actually received
      2) Cash or its equivalent is constructively received
   b. At the time a person receives noncash forms of income, such as property or services, the fair market value is included in gross income. This applies even if the property or service can be currently converted into cash at an amount lower than face value.
      1) A **cash equivalent** is property that is readily convertible into cash and typically has a maturity of 3 months or less. Cash equivalents are so near to maturity that the risk of loss due to a change in value is immaterial. Cash equivalents include
         a) Checks (valued at face)
         b) Promissory notes (valued at FMV)
         c) Property (e.g., land, transferable at current FMV)
      2) If the value of property received cannot be determined, the value of what was given in exchange for it is treated as the amount of income received.

> **EXAMPLE 5-1   Indeterminate Value of Property**
>
> A CPA performs various services for a start-up company in exchange for stock options. If the value of the stock options cannot be determined, the value of the services performed is included in income.

      3) If both the property received and the property given are impossible to value (e.g., an unsecured promise to pay from a person with unknown creditworthiness), the transaction is treated as open, and the consideration is not viewed as income until its value can be ascertained.
   c. Under the doctrine of **constructive receipt**, an item is included in gross income when a person has an unqualified right to immediate possession.
      1) A person constructively receives income in the tax year during which it is credited to his or her account, set apart for him or her, or otherwise made available so that (s)he may draw upon it at any time.
         a) It is more than a billing, offer, or promise to pay.
         b) It includes ability to use on demand, as with escrowed funds subject to a person's order.
         c) Deferring deposit of a check does not defer income. However, dishonor (i.e., bounced or returned checks) retroactively negates the income.

2) Constructive receipt **by an agent** is imputed to the principal.
3) Income is not constructively received if the taxpayer's control of its receipt is subject to substantial restrictions or limitations (e.g., a valid deferred compensation agreement).

EXAMPLE 5-2 Income Not Constructively Received

John is awarded a $10,000 bonus in 2021. If only half of the bonus is payable in 2021 with the other half paid at the end of 2022, contingent upon John completing another year of service for his employer, only $5,000 is taxable in 2021.

---

d. The **claim-of-right** doctrine indicates that a taxpayer receiving payments under a claim of right and without restrictions on its use includes the payment in income in the year received even though the right to retain the payment is not yet fixed or the taxpayer may later be required to return it.
   1) If payment is not received, the payment is not included in income.
e. The **economic or financial benefit** conferred on an employee as compensation has been determined by the courts to be included in the definition of gross income. This economic benefit theory is applied by the IRS in situations in which an employee or independent contractor receives a transfer of property that confers an economic benefit that is equivalent to cash.
   1) The economic benefit theory applies even when the taxpayer cannot choose to take the equivalent value of the income in cash.

EXAMPLE 5-3 Economic Benefit of Property Received Included in Gross Income

The fair rental value of a car that a dealership provides for the personal use of its president is gross income.

---

f. **Dividends** are constructively received when made subject to the unqualified demand of a shareholder.
   1) If a corporation declares a dividend in December and pays such that the shareholders receive it in January, the dividend is not treated as received in December.
g. When a **bond** is sold between interest payment dates, the interest accrued up to the sale date is added to the selling price of the bond. The seller includes the accrued interest in gross income as interest income. The buyer reduces interest income, as a return of capital, by the same amount.
h. **Prepaid rent** is included in gross income when received (the same as for cash-method and accrual-method taxpayers).
   1) Lease cancellations are included.
   2) Tenant improvements, in lieu of rent, are included.
   3) Security deposits are not considered income when the property owner is obligated to return it to the tenant.
   4) Advance rental payments must be deducted by the payee during the tax periods to which the payments apply.
i. Tips are gross income when reported. An employee who receives $20 or more in tips per month working for any employer must report the tips to the employer by the 10th day of the following month.

j. A cash-method taxpayer's **deductions** include expenditures when actually paid, except generally for prepaid expenses (e.g., rent or insurance). Item k. below explains this in more detail. Rules regarding actual payment include the following:

1) A promise to pay (e.g., promissory note), without more, is not payment.
2) A check represents payment when delivered or sent.
3) A third-party (e.g., bank) credit card charge transaction represents current payment with loan proceeds. A second-party (e.g., store) credit card charge transaction is not paid until the charge is paid off.
4) Adjusted basis in accounts receivable is deductible when the debt becomes worthless. Since a cash-method taxpayer usually has no basis in accounts receivable, (s)he may not deduct bad debts.
5) Interest on a loan issued at discount, or unstated (imputed) interest, is deductible pro rata over the life of the loan.
6) A person who uses the cash method to report gross income must use the cash method to report expenses.

k. For cash-method taxpayers, prepaid expenses are generally not deductible when paid. Instead, prepaid expenses are prorated over the period of the expense.

EXAMPLE 5-4   Prepaid Expenses

A cash-basis, calendar-year taxpayer pays $24,000 for 2 years of rent on January 1, 2021. The rental period covered by the payment is from January 1, 2021, through December 31, 2022. The taxpayer cannot deduct the full $24,000 payment in 2021. Instead, the expense will be prorated based on the actual contract period, making $12,000 deductible in Year 1 (12 months/24 months) and $12,000 deductible in 2022.

---

1) An important exception to the rule above is the **12-month rule**. The 12-month rule allows a cash-basis taxpayer to deduct a prepaid expense in the year of payment if two conditions are met.

    a) First, the contract period of the expense cannot exceed 12 months (i.e., a taxpayer cannot prepay for 13 months of a service).
    b) Second, the contract period cannot extend beyond the end of the next taxable year (i.e., a payment in Year 1 cannot be for a benefit in Year 3).

2) Though common expenses like prepaid rent or prepaid insurance expense are allowed deductions under the 12-month rule, prepaid interest is not allowed a deduction until the year to which the interest relates.

EXAMPLE 5-5   12-Month Rule

A cash-basis, calendar-year taxpayer pays $12,000 for 1 year of rent on July 1, 2021. The rental period covered by the payment is from July 1, 2021, through June 20, 2022. Because the contract period is 12 months or less and does not extend beyond the end of the next taxable year, the entire $12,000 payment is deductible in 2021.

SU 5: Accounting Methods and Special Entities

4. **Accrual Method**
    a. Generally, an accrual-method taxpayer accounts for income in the period it is actually earned. For taxpayers with **applicable financial statements (AFSs)**, the inclusion is generally no later than the inclusion for financial accounting purposes. This AFS rule does not apply to special methods of accounting (e.g., long-term contracts, installment agreements) or mortgage servicing contracts. For taxpayers without AFSs, **income** is included when all the events have occurred that fix the right to receive it and the amount can be determined with reasonable accuracy.
        1) A right is not fixed if it is contingent on a future event.
        2) The all-events test is satisfied when goods shipped on consignment are sold.
        3) Only in rare and unusual circumstances, in which neither the FMV received nor the FMV given can be ascertained, will the IRS respect holding a transaction open once the right to receive income is fixed. In those circumstances, income is accrued upon receipt.
            a) Proceeds from settlement of a lawsuit are determinable in amount with reasonable accuracy when received.
    b. **Prepaid income** must generally be included in income when received.
        1) Prepaid income for **services** may be accrued over the period for which the services are to be performed, but only if it does not extend beyond the end of the next tax year.
            a) The taxpayer recognizes income as it is earned in Year 1, and the balance of the prepaid income is recognized in Year 2, even if it might be earned in Year 3 or later.
        2) Prepaid **rent** is includible in gross income in the year received (the same as for cash-method and accrual-method taxpayers).
        3) Prepayments for **merchandise sales** must be included when reported for accounting purposes if reported earlier than when earned.
            a) The right to income is fixed when it is earned (e.g., when goods are shipped).
    c. **Expenses** are generally deductible in the period in which they accrue. A taxpayer who uses the accrual method to report gross income must use the accrual method to report expenses.
        1) The accrual-method taxpayer may claim an allowable deduction when both of the following requirements are met:
            a) All events have occurred that establish the fact of the liability, including that economic performance has occurred.
            b) The amount can be determined with reasonable accuracy.
        2) To the extent the amount of a liability is disputed, the test is not met. But any portion of a (still) contested amount that is paid is deductible.
        3) **Economic performance** occurs as services are performed or as property is provided or used.
            a) For expense items that are recurring in nature, a deduction can be taken in the year before economic performance occurs with the recurring item exception.
                i) In other words, under the recurring item exception a deduction can be taken in Year 1 even though economic performance occurs in Year 2.
                ii) Economic performance in Year 2 must occur before the earlier of the return filing or 8.5 months.

EXAMPLE 5-6 — Recurring Item

ABC, Inc., a calendar-year, accrual-method taxpayer has a year-end accrual for $10,000 of real property taxes assessed for 2021, but payment is not due until March 1, 2022. Economic performance for property taxes due is considered to occur when the tax is paid. Under the general rules for accrual-method taxpayers, ABC could deduct the property taxes in the year paid (i.e., the all-events test is met and economic performance has occurred). However, with the recurring item exception, ABC will be able to deduct in 2021 the property tax payment made in 2022 (the all-events test is met and economic performance occurs in Year 2 prior to the earlier of return filing or 8.5 months).

4) Under current case law, reserves for contingent liabilities (such as product warranties) are not determinable in amount with reasonable accuracy.

Warranty Reserve Account
Beginning balance
+ Accrued warranty expense
− Ending balance
= Tax deductible warranty expense

a) Therefore, only amounts paid are deductible. Both cash-basis and accrual-method taxpayers must use the direct write-off method. For example, the formula to the left is used to calculate deductible warranty expense.

5) Accrued vacation pay is generally deductible by the employer when paid or in the year accrued if paid within 2.5 months of year end.

6) Deduction of an amount payable to a related party is allowed only when includible in gross income of the related party.

EXAMPLE 5-7 — Deduction of a Payable to a Related Party

An individual cash-method taxpayer owns 55% of an accrual-method corporation. The corporation owes the individual $5,000 for rent incurred in Year 1. In Year 2, $5,000 was paid and reported as income by the individual. Because the corporation and individual are related parties, the corporation must wait to take the deduction of $5,000 until Year 2, the year it was reported as income by the related party.

d. The accrual method is required of certain persons and for certain transactions.

1) If the accrual method is used to report expenses, it must be used to report income items.

2) Generally, C corporations, partnerships with a C corporation as a partner, charitable trusts with unrelated income, and tax shelters must use the accrual method. **Tax shelters** include any arrangement for which the principal purpose is avoidance of tax, any syndicates, and any enterprise in which the interests must be registered as a security. Exceptions to the general rule allow the following taxpayers to use the cash method if the entity is not a tax shelter:

a) Qualified personal service corporations
b) Entities that meet the gross receipts test by having $26 million or less average gross receipts in the 3 preceding years
c) Farming or tree-raising businesses

SUCCESS TIP

The accounting rules for income and deduction items under both the cash and accrual methods have often been tested. The AICPA has used questions that have focused on the timing of the inclusions of various income and expense items under each method.

5. **Inventory Method**
   a. A taxpayer who maintains inventory must use the accrual method with regard to purchases and sales. Exceptions to this inventory rule include **qualifying taxpayers** who satisfy the gross receipts test for each test year. The average annual gross receipts (consisting of the test year and the preceding 2 years) for each test year must be $26 million or less.
      1) S corporations are not subject to the $26 million limitation; however, if inventory sales are a material part of the S corporation's operations, the accrual method must be used to calculate gross profit.
   b. The inventory method used must clearly reflect income and conform to generally accepted accounting principles of the trade or business.
      1) Gross income includes receipts reduced by cost of goods sold (COGS), whether purchased or manufactured.
      2) Regulations require the particular treatment of certain items or an acceptable alternative treatment.
   c. Inventory may be valued at cost or at the lower of cost or market.
   d. **Purchased merchandise** is valued at invoice price reduced by trade discounts and increased by handling charges, such as freight. Cash discounts may instead be treated as income.

   Cost = Purchase price − Trade discounts + Handling charges

   1) The uniform capitalization rules require the costs for acquiring property for sale to customers (retail) to be capitalized.
      a) The uniform capitalization rules do not apply if property is acquired for resale and the company's annual gross receipts (for the past 3 years) do not exceed $26 million.
      b) Both direct and most allocable indirect costs necessary to prepare the inventory for its intended use must be capitalized.
   e. **Produced merchandise** cost must be calculated using the full absorption costing method.
      1) **Direct costs** of material and labor are included in inventory.
      2) **Overhead costs** for manufacturing are also included (e.g., costs for plant administration, plant maintenance such as rent, utilities, insurance, and support costs such as payroll and warehousing).
      3) **Nonmanufacturing costs** (e.g., marketing) need not be included in inventory, but interest must be included in inventory on property that is real or requires more than 2 years of production (1 year if it costs more than $1 million).

f. Any of the following **standard methods** may be used to determine inventory costs: specific identification, average cost, FIFO, and LIFO.

   1) **FIFO** assumes that the first items acquired are the first items sold. Ending inventory contains the most recently acquired items.
   2) **LIFO** assumes that the latest items acquired are the first items sold. If LIFO is used, inventory must be valued at cost. In a period of rising prices, LIFO results in a higher cost of goods sold than FIFO. Because COGS is higher, net income (NI) is lower, resulting in lower current tax liability.

Inventory Prices ↑			
LIFO:	COGS ↑	Taxable income ↓	Tax liability ↓
FIFO:	COGS ↓	Taxable income ↑	Tax liability ↑

   a) LIFO may only be used for tax purposes if it is used for financial reporting.

   NOTE: Taxpayers using a rolling-average method for financial accounting purposes are allowed to use the same method for tax purposes if the related safe harbor rules are satisfied.

6. **Long-Term Contracts**

   a. A long-term contract is a contract completed in a tax year subsequent to the one in which it was entered into for building, construction, installation, or manufacturing. Long-term manufacturing contracts are for items that normally require more than 12 months to complete or that are unique and not usually inventory items.

      1) A trade or business of a taxpayer must use the same method for each of its long-term contracts.
      2) Long-term contract rules apply to direct costs and allocable portions of labor, material, and overhead costs.
      3) Costs of the following do not need to be allocated to a specific contract:
         a) Unaccepted bids
         b) Marketing
         c) Research and development (if not restricted to the specific contract)

   b. The **completed-contract method** accounts for (reports) receipts and expenditures in the tax year in which the contract is completed. The method is allowed only for

      1) Home construction projects or
      2) Small businesses (average annual gross receipts not greater than $26 million for the 3 preceding tax years) whose construction contracts are expected to take not greater than 2 years to complete.

c. The **percentage-of-completion method** reports as income that portion of the total contract price that represents the percentage of total work completed in the year. It may be measured by the ratio of costs for the tax year to total expected costs.

Formula:

Contract price	$ XXX
Minus: Total estimated cost **of contract**[1]	(XXX)
Estimated total gross profit	$ XXX
Times: Percent completed[2]	XXX
Gross profit recognized to date	$ XXX
Minus: Gross profit recognized in prior periods	(XXX)
Gross profit recognized in current period	$ XXX

[1] Cost incurred to date plus remaining estimated cost **to complete**

[2] Total cost to date ÷ Total estimated cost **of contract**

1) When the contract is complete, the taxpayer must pay interest on any additional tax that would have been incurred if actual total costs had been used instead of expected costs.
2) The taxpayer may elect not to apply the above rule if the cumulative taxable income or loss using estimated costs is within 10% of the cumulative taxable income or loss using actual costs.

7. **Installment Method**

a. The installment method is required for installment sales by both cash-method and accrual-method taxpayers, unless an election is made not to apply the method.

1) An installment sale is a disposition of property in which at least one payment is received after the year of sale.
2) The method applies only to gains.
3) A loss on an installment sale is fully recognized in the year realized (unless recognition would be deferred even if the sale was not an installment sale).

b. The installment sales method is generally not applied to the following sales:

1) Inventory personal property sales
2) Revolving credit personal property sales
3) Dealer dispositions
4) Securities, generally, if publicly traded
5) Sales by manufacturers of tangible personal property

c. Installment sale income is determined as follows:
1) Calculate cost of goods sold:

$$\text{Adjusted basis + Selling expense}$$

2) Calculate gross profit:

$$\text{Contract (sale) price} - \text{Cost of goods sold}$$

3) Calculate gross profit percentage:

$$\frac{\text{Gross profit}}{\text{Contract (sale) price}}$$

4) Calculate current-year installment sale income:

$$\text{Current-year receipts} \times \text{Gross profit percentage}$$

EXAMPLE 5-8   **Current-Year Installment Sale Income**

A company sold a building for $500,000 with an adjusted basis of $400,000. The company received a down payment of $80,000, as well as principal payments of $105,000 for each of the subsequent 4 years. The gain recognized is $16,000 (20% gross profit percentage × $80,000 proceeds).

---

d. The full amount of any depreciation recapture recharacterized as ordinary income must be recognized in the year of sale, regardless of the payments received. This does not apply to unrecaptured Sec. 1250 gains because it is not recharacterized as ordinary income.

8. **Hybrid Methods**

   a. Any combination of permissible accounting methods may be employed if the combination clearly reflects income and is consistently used.

   b. A person may use different methods for separate businesses.

STOP & REVIEW

You have completed the outline for this subunit.
Study multiple-choice questions 1 through 9 beginning on page 124.

5.2 EXEMPT ORGANIZATIONS

1. **Exempt Status**

    a. Exempt status generally depends on the nature and purpose of an organization.

        1) An organization is tax-exempt only if it is of a class specifically described by the IRC as one on which exemption is conferred.
        2) It may be organized as a corporation, trust, foundation, fund, community chest, society, etc.
        3) An organization operated for the primary purpose of carrying on a trade or business for profit is generally not tax-exempt.

    b. Examples of organization types that may be exempt are religious or apostolic organizations, political organizations, social clubs, athletic clubs, fraternal beneficiary associations, chambers of commerce, real estate boards, labor organizations, civic welfare associations, and certain domestic and foreign corporations.

    c. Organizations that foster national or international amateur sports competition may be exempt if they do not provide athletic facilities or equipment.

    d. Fraternal beneficiary associations that operate under the lodge system and provide payment of life, sick, accident, or other benefits to members and their dependents are an exempt class.

    e. Social clubs organized for pleasure, recreation, and other nonprofitable purposes, substantially all of the activities of which are for such purposes, are an exempt class.

        1) No part of net earnings may inure to the benefit of any private shareholder.
        2) Exempt status is lost if 35% or more of its receipts are from sources other than membership fees, dues, and assessments.

    f. **Prohibited Transactions**

        1) Certain employee trusts lose exempt status if they engage in prohibited transactions, e.g., lending without adequate security or reasonable interest, or paying unreasonable compensation for personal services.

    g. **Religious, Charitable, Scientific, Educational, Literary**

        1) Organizations formed and operated exclusively for religious, charitable, scientific, educational, literary, or similar purposes are a broad class of exempt organizations.
        2) No part of net earnings may inure to the benefit of any private shareholder or individual.
        3) No substantial part of its activities may attempt to influence legislation or a political candidacy (e.g., Political Action Committees).
        4) In general, if a substantial part of the activities of an organization consists of attempting to influence legislation, the organization will lose its exempt status. However, most organizations can elect to replace the substantial part of activities test with a lobbying expenditure limit.
        5) If an election for a tax year is in effect for an organization and that organization exceeds the lobbying expenditure limits, an excise tax of 25% will be imposed on the excess amount.
        6) Exempt status will be lost if the organization directly participates in a political campaign.

h. Private Foundations

1) Each domestic or foreign exempt organization is a private foundation unless, generally, it receives more than a third of its support (annually) from its members and the general public. In this case, the private foundation status terminates, and the organization becomes a public charity.
2) Exempt status of a private foundation is subject to statutory restrictions, notification requirements, and excise taxes.
3) A charitable, religious, or scientific organization is presumed to be a private foundation unless it either
   a) Is a church or has annual gross receipts under $5,000 or
   b) Notifies the IRS that it is not a private foundation (on Form 1023) within 27 months from the end of the month in which it was organized.

i. Feeder Organization

1) An organization must independently qualify for exempt status. It is not enough that all of its profits are paid to exempt organizations.

j. Homeowners' Association

1) It is treated as a tax-exempt organization.
2) A homeowners' association is one organized for acquisition, construction, management, maintenance, etc., of residential real estate or condominiums. A cooperative housing corporation is excluded.
3) A condominium management association, to be treated as a tax-exempt housing association, must file a separate election for each tax year by the return due date of the applicable year.

Tax-Exempt Organization Internal Revenue Code Chart

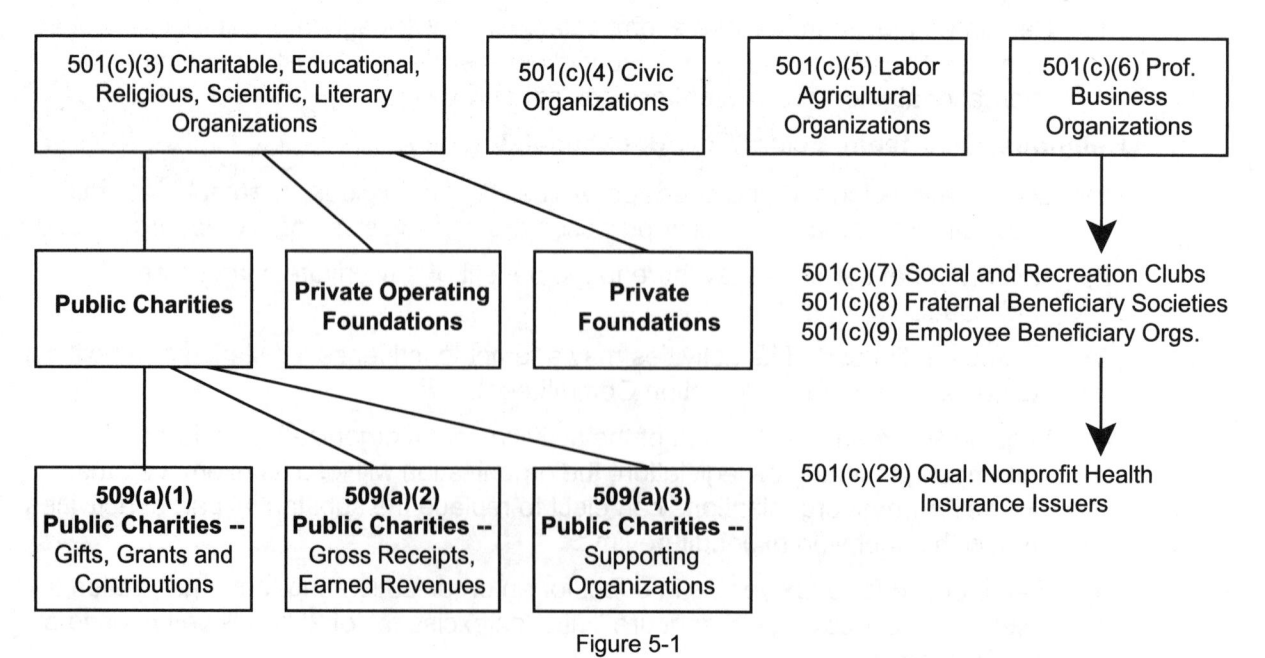

```
┌─────────────────────────┐  ┌──────────────┐  ┌──────────────┐  ┌──────────────┐
│ 501(c)(3) Charitable,   │  │ 501(c)(4)    │  │ 501(c)(5)    │  │ 501(c)(6)    │
│ Educational, Religious, │  │ Civic        │  │ Labor        │  │ Prof.        │
│ Scientific, Literary    │  │ Organizations│  │ Agricultural │  │ Business     │
│ Organizations           │  │              │  │ Organizations│  │ Organizations│
└─────────────────────────┘  └──────────────┘  └──────────────┘  └──────────────┘
```

- 501(c)(7) Social and Recreation Clubs
- 501(c)(8) Fraternal Beneficiary Societies
- 501(c)(9) Employee Beneficiary Orgs.

- 501(c)(29) Qual. Nonprofit Health Insurance Issuers

Boxes below: **Public Charities**, **Private Operating Foundations**, **Private Foundations**

- **509(a)(1) Public Charities --** Gifts, Grants and Contributions
- **509(a)(2) Public Charities --** Gross Receipts, Earned Revenues
- **509(a)(3) Public Charities --** Supporting Organizations

Figure 5-1

2. **Unrelated Business Income Tax**
    a. Tax-exempt organizations are generally subject to tax on income from unrelated business income (UBI).
    b. An unrelated business is a trade or business activity regularly carried on for the production of income (even if a loss results) that is not substantially related to performance of the exempt purpose or function, i.e., that does not contribute more than insubstantial benefits to the exempt purposes.
    c. Certain qualified sponsorship payments received by an exempt organization have not been subject to unrelated business income tax.
        1) A qualified sponsorship payment is one from which the payor does not expect any substantial return or benefit other than the use or acknowledgment of the payor's name or logo.
        2) The payor may not receive a substantial return.
    d. Exempt organizations subject to tax on UBI are required to comply with the Code provisions regarding installment payments of estimated income tax by corporations [Sec. 6655(g)(3)].
    e. Generally, losses from an unrelated trade or business are not permitted to be offset against income from another unrelated trade or business (except for NOL from tax periods before January 1, 2018).
    f. An unrelated business income tax return (Form 990-T) is required of an exempt organization with at least $1,000 of gross income used in computing the UBI tax for the tax year [Reg. 1.6012-2(e)].

3. **Charitable Deduction**
    a. Solicitations for contributions or other payments by tax-exempt organizations must include a statement if payments to that organization are not deductible as charitable contributions for federal income tax purposes. Donations to the following organizations are tax deductible:
        1) Corporations organized under an Act of Congress
        2) All 501(c)(3) organizations except those testing for public safety
        3) Cemetery companies
        4) Cooperative hospital service organizations
        5) Cooperative service organizations of operating educational organizations
        6) Child-care organizations

4. **Executive Compensation**
    a. Exempt organizations generally will incur an excise tax of 21% on the sum of
        1) Compensation in excess of $1 million paid to a covered employee and
        2) Any excess parachute payment paid to a covered employee.
            a) A covered employee includes an employee who is one of the five highest-compensated employees for the current year or who is designated as a covered employee for tax years beginning January 1, 2017.

You have completed the outline for this subunit.
Study multiple-choice questions 10 through 16 beginning on page 128.

5.3 TRUSTS

1. **Simple Trust**

    a. A simple trust is formed under an instrument having the following characteristics:

    1) Requires current distribution of all its income
    2) Requires no distribution of the res (i.e., principal, corpus)
    3) Provides for no charitable contributions by the trust

2. **Complex Trust**

    a. A complex trust is any trust other than a simple trust. A complex trust can

    1) Accumulate income,
    2) Provide for charitable contributions, and
    3) Distribute amounts other than income.

3. **Grantor Trust**

    a. A grantor trust is any trust to the extent the grantor is the effective beneficiary.

    1) The income attributable to a trust principal that is treated as owned by the grantor is taxed to the grantor.
    2) The trust is disregarded.

        a) A trust is considered a grantor trust when the grantor has greater than 5% reversionary interest.
        b) A grantor is treated as the owner of a trust in which the income may be distributed or accumulated for the grantor's spouse.
        c) The grantor is also taxed on income from a trust in which the income may be applied for the benefit of the grantor. Use of income for the support of a dependent is considered the application of income for the benefit of the grantor. The income that may be applied for the support of a dependent is not taxable to the grantor if it is not actually used.

    3) All revocable trusts are grantor trusts.

4. **Application of Rules**

    a. The rules for classifying trusts are applied on a year-to-year basis.

5. **Principal vs. Income**

    a. Tax is imposed on taxable income (TI) of trusts, not on items treated as fiduciary principal.
    b. State law defines **principal** and **income** of a trust for federal income tax purposes.

    1) Many states have adopted the Revised Uniform Principal and Income Act, some with modifications.

        a) The act and state laws provide that trust instrument designations of fiduciary principal and interest components control.
        b) The act and state law also provide default designations.

    c. Generally, principal is property held eventually to be delivered to the remainderman (the person who inherits or is entitled to inherit the property).

    1) Change in form of principal is not taxable income.
    2) Income is return on, or for use of, the principal.
    3) It is held for or distributed to the income beneficiary.

    d. Principal is also referred to as the corpus or res.

Allocation of Fiduciary Receipts and Disbursements

Principal	Income
Receipts	
Consideration for property, e.g., gain on sale	Business income
Replacement property	Insurance proceeds for lost profits
Nontaxable stock dividends	Interest
Stock splits	Rents
Stock rights	Dividends (taxable)
Liquidating dividends	Extraordinary dividends
Depletion allowance (natural resource property) – royalties (90%)	Taxable stock dividends
	Depletion allowance (natural resource property) – royalties (10%)
Disbursements	
Principal payments on debt	Business (ord. & nec.) expenses, e.g., interest expense
Capital expenditures	Production of income expenses, e.g., maintenance/repair
• Major repairs	• Insurance
• Modifications	• Rent collection fee
Fiduciary fees (e.g., management of principal)	• Tax on fiduciary income
Tax on principal items, e.g., capital gains	Depreciation
	Fiduciary fees (e.g., probate court fees and costs)

6. **Tax Rates**

   a. Tax is imposed on taxable income of a trust at the following rates for 2021:

Fiduciary Taxable Income Brackets	Applicable Rate
$ 0 - $ 2,650	10%
2,651 - 9,550	24% (+ $265)
9,551 - 13,050	35% (+ $1,921)
> 13,050	37% (+ $3,146)

STOP & REVIEW

You have completed the outline for this subunit.
Study multiple-choice questions 17 through 19 beginning on page 130.

QUESTIONS

5.1 Accounting Methods

1. Aviary Corp. sold a building for $600,000. Aviary received a down payment of $120,000, as well as annual principal payments of $120,000 for each of the subsequent 4 years. Aviary purchased the building for $500,000 and claimed depreciation of $80,000. What amount of gain should Aviary report in the year of sale using the installment method?

A. $180,000
B. $120,000
C. $54,000
D. $36,000

Answer (D) is correct.
REQUIRED: The amount of gain reported under the installment method.
DISCUSSION: Under the installment method, the gain recognized is equal to the proceeds received in the current year multiplied by the gross profit percentage. The gross profit percentage is the gross profit divided by the sales price. The gross profit of $180,000 is the sales price less the AB. The AB of the asset is the $500,000 initial cost reduced by the $80,000 depreciation, or $420,000. Thus, the gross profit percentage is equal to 30% ($180,000 gross profit ÷ $600,000 sales price). The only installment received this period is the down payment of $120,000, which is multiplied by the gross profit percentage (30%) for a reported gain of $36,000 currently. The building is 1250 property and would have been depreciated over S/L, therefore there is no depreciation recaptured as ordinary income (i.e., all $80,000 depreciation is unrecaptured) and the reported gain is not increased to $80,000.
Answer (A) is incorrect. The entire gross profit is not reported in the current period under the installment method. **Answer (B) is incorrect.** The entire $120,000 down payment should not be reported as a gain in the current period. The reported gain must consider the gross profit percentage, which is multiplied by the current proceeds. **Answer (C) is incorrect.** Multiplying the gross profit percentage by the gross profit equals $54,000; however, the gain reported in the current period is the gross profit percentages multiplied by the installments received currently.

2. Soma Corp. had $600,000 in compensation expense for book purposes in Year 1. Included in this amount was a $50,000 accrual for Year 1 nonshareholder bonuses. Soma paid the actual Year 1 bonus of $60,000 on March 1, Year 2. In its Year 1 tax return, what amount should Soma deduct as compensation expense?

A. $600,000
B. $610,000
C. $550,000
D. $540,000

Answer (B) is correct.
REQUIRED: The amount of compensation expense deductible when paid.
DISCUSSION: A deduction is allowed for all ordinary and necessary business expenses paid or incurred during the taxable year, including a reasonable allowance for salaries or other compensation for personal services actually rendered. Because the bonuses were compensation to unrelated parties, Soma accrues and deducts $50,000 of them in Year 1 and an additional $10,000 in Year 1 because the payment in Year 2 was attributable to the Year 1 tax year of an accrual-method taxpayer.
Answer (A) is incorrect. The additional $10,000, although paid in Year 2, was attributable to services rendered in a prior tax year to an accrual-method taxpayer. **Answer (C) is incorrect.** The amount of $550,000 results from subtracting the accrued nonshareholder bonuses from compensation expense. **Answer (D) is incorrect.** The amount of $540,000 results from subtracting the actual Year 1 bonuses paid in Year 2 from compensation expense.

3. A cash-basis taxpayer should report gross income

A. Only for the year in which income is actually received in cash.
B. Only for the year in which income is actually received whether in cash or in property.
C. For the year in which income is either actually or constructively received in cash only.
D. For the year in which income is either actually or constructively received, whether in cash or in property.

Answer (D) is correct.
REQUIRED: The time for a cash-basis taxpayer to report gross income.
DISCUSSION: A cash-basis taxpayer should report gross income for the year in which income is either actually or constructively received in cash or property. Constructive receipt is when the payment is made available to the taxpayer or when the taxpayer has economic benefit of the funds.
Answer (A) is incorrect. Gross income is reported by a cash-basis taxpayer when actually or constructively received in cash. **Answer (B) is incorrect.** Gross income is reported by a cash-basis taxpayer when actually or constructively received in cash or property. **Answer (C) is incorrect.** Gross income is not limited to cash.

4. Nare, an accrual-basis taxpayer, owns a building which was rented to Mott under a 10-year lease expiring August 31, Year 4. On January 2, Year 1, Mott paid $30,000 as consideration for canceling the lease. On November 1, Year 1, Nare leased the building to Pine under a 5-year lease. Pine paid Nare $10,000 rent for the 2 months of November and December, and an additional $5,000 for the last month's rent. What amount of rental income should Nare report in its Year 1 income tax return?

A. $10,000
B. $15,000
C. $40,000
D. $45,000

Answer (D) is correct.
REQUIRED: The landlord's rental income from various types of payments.
DISCUSSION: Both cash- and accrual-basis taxpayers must include amounts in gross income upon actual or constructive receipt if the taxpayer has an unrestricted claim to such amounts. Since Nare has an unrestricted claim to the $5,000 of rent paid in advance, it is included in his rental income. The amounts received by a lessee to cancel a lease are treated as an amount realized on a disposition of property. However, value received by a lessor to cancel a lease is gross income from rent as if received in lieu of rent.
Answer (A) is incorrect. Money paid as consideration for canceling a lease is also included in rental income. The $5,000 payment by Pine for the last month's rent is also included in rental income for Year 1. **Answer (B) is incorrect.** The amount of $15,000 does not include the money paid as consideration for canceling the lease. **Answer (C) is incorrect.** Prepaid rent is income when received even if the lessor uses the accrual method of accounting.

5. Unless the Internal Revenue Service consents to a change of method, the accrual method of tax reporting is mandatory for a non-small business sole proprietor when there are

	Accounts Receivable for Services Rendered	Year-End Merchandise Inventories
A.	Yes	Yes
B.	Yes	No
C.	No	No
D.	No	Yes

Answer (D) is correct.
REQUIRED: The circumstances in which the accrual method is mandatory.
DISCUSSION: A person must generally use the method of accounting regularly used to compute income in keeping books and records. But a taxpayer that maintains inventory must use the accrual method with regard to purchases and sales. The accrual method is not mandatory when there are accounts receivable.

6. Dart, a C corporation, distributes software over the Internet and has had average revenues in excess of $40 million per year for the past 3 years. To purchase software, customers enter their credit card number to a secure website and receive a password that allows the customer to immediately download the software. As a result, Dart does not record accounts receivable or inventory on its books. Which of the following statements is correct?

A. Dart may use either the cash or accrual method of accounting as long as Dart elects a calendar year end.

B. Dart may use any method of accounting Dart chooses as long as Dart consistently applies the method it chooses.

C. Dart must use the accrual method of accounting.

D. Dart may use the cash basis method of accounting until it incurs an additional $30 million to develop additional software.

Answer (C) is correct.
REQUIRED: The method of accounting required to be used by Dart Corporation.
DISCUSSION: The accrual method of accounting must be used for C corporations unless they have less than $26 million average annual gross receipts in the preceding 3 years. If average revenues exceeded $40 million, the gross receipts must have been at least this amount.
Answer (A) is incorrect. The calendar year end does not affect the method of accounting, which relies on other factors. The accrual method must be used for Dart because its average gross receipts exceed the applicable limit. **Answer (B) is incorrect.** Dart must use the accrual method because the average gross receipts test is not met for C corporations. **Answer (D) is incorrect.** The average gross receipts test for a C corporation is equal to $26 million over the preceding 3 years.

7. In Year 1, Stewart Corp. properly accrued $5,000 for an income item on the basis of a reasonable estimate. In Year 2, after filing its Year 1 federal income tax return, Stewart determined that the exact amount was $6,000. Which of the following statements is true?

A. No further inclusion of income is required, as the difference is less than 25% of the original amount reported and the estimate had been made in good faith.

B. The $1,000 difference is includible in Stewart's Year 2 income tax return.

C. Stewart is required to notify the IRS within 30 days of the determination of the exact amount of the item.

D. Stewart is required to file an amended return to report the additional $1,000 of income.

Answer (B) is correct.
REQUIRED: The true statement about accrual of a reasonable estimate when the exact amount is greater than the estimate.
DISCUSSION: Under the accrual method of accounting, income is includible in gross income when all the events have occurred that fix the right to receive the income and the amount can be determined with reasonable accuracy. If an amount of income is properly accrued on the basis of a reasonable estimate and the exact amount is subsequently determined, the difference, if any, shall be taken into account for the taxable year in which such determination is made.

8. During Year 3, Scott charged $4,000 on his credit card for his dependent son's medical expenses. Payment to the credit card company had not been made by the time Scott filed his income tax return in Year 4. However, in Year 3, Scott paid a physician $2,800 for the medical expenses of his wife, who died in Year 1. Disregarding the adjusted gross income percentage threshold, what amount could Scott claim in his Year 3 income tax return for medical expenses?

A. $0
B. $2,800
C. $4,000
D. $6,800

Answer (D) is correct.
REQUIRED: The tax year in which medical expense is deductible.
DISCUSSION: Generally, only qualified medical expenses paid during the year on behalf of the taxpayer, his or her spouse, or a dependent are deductible. Charging to a third-party credit card is treated as a current payment. Thus, Scott is treated as having paid $6,800 of deductible medical expense in Year 3.
Answer (A) is incorrect. Qualified medical expenses paid during the year are deductible. **Answer (B) is incorrect.** Charging to a third-party credit card is treated as current payment. **Answer (C) is incorrect.** A taxpayer may deduct medical expense for his or her spouse paid during the year.

9. Pierre, a pizza delivery person, received tips totaling $1,000 in December Year 1. On January 5, Year 2, Pierre reported this tip income to his employer in the required written statement. At what amount, and in which year, should this tip income be included in Pierre's gross income?

A. $1,000 in Year 1.
B. $1,000 in Year 2.
C. $500 in Year 1 and $500 in Year 2.
D. $83 in Year 1 and $917 in Year 2.

Answer (B) is correct.
REQUIRED: The tax year in which tips are included in income.
DISCUSSION: Normally, a cash-basis taxpayer includes income when received. However, tips receive special treatment. An employee who receives $20 or more in tips in a month (as a result of working for one employer, and not combined from several jobs) must report the total tips to the employer by the 10th day of the next month. These tips are treated as paid when the report is made to the employer. Since Pierre properly reported his December Year 1 tips to his employer in January Year 2, the tips are not included in gross income until Year 2.
Answer (A) is incorrect. The $1,000 tip income is not included in gross income until Year 2. **Answer (C) is incorrect.** The entire $1,000 tip income is not included in gross income until Year 2. **Answer (D) is incorrect.** The entire amount of tip income reported to an employer in the required written statement must be included in gross income in the year the statement is submitted.

5.2 Exempt Organizations

10. Which of the following is **not** an exempt organization?

A. American Society for Prevention of Cruelty to Animals.
B. Red Cross.
C. State-chartered credit unions.
D. Privately owned nursing home.

Answer (D) is correct.
REQUIRED: The organization that does not qualify as exempt.
DISCUSSION: Exempt status generally depends on the nature and purpose of an organization. Among the types of organizations that may qualify as exempt are corporations, trusts, foundations, funds, community funds, etc. A more complete list can be found in Sec. 501(c) along with the permitted stated purposes and requirements.
Answer (A) is incorrect. The American Society for Prevention of Cruelty to Animals is an exempt organization according to Sec. 501(c). **Answer (B) is incorrect.** The Red Cross is an exempt organization according to Sec. 501(c). **Answer (C) is incorrect.** State-chartered credit unions are exempt organizations.

11. Which of the following organizations may request exempt status under the Internal Revenue Code as charitable organizations?

A. Religious organization.
B. School.
C. Animal welfare organization.
D. All of the answers are correct.

Answer (D) is correct.
REQUIRED: The organization that could request tax-exempt status under Sec. 501(c)(3) as a charitable organization.
DISCUSSION: Exempt status generally depends on the nature and purpose of an organization. An organization is tax-exempt only if it is a class specifically described by the IRC as one on which exemption is conferred. An organization operated for the primary purpose of carrying on a trade or business for profit is generally not tax-exempt. Religious organizations, schools, and animal welfare organizations are all considered exempt because their activities do not involve making a profit.

12. Of the organizations listed below, which organization could **not** receive approval for tax-exempt status under Internal Revenue Code Sec. 501(c)(3)?

A. A local chapter of the Salvation Army.
B. A partnership for scientific research.
C. A college alumni association.
D. A local boys club.

Answer (B) is correct.
REQUIRED: The organization that is not tax-exempt under Sec. 501(c)(3).
DISCUSSION: Organizations formed and operated exclusively for religious, charitable, scientific, educational, literary, or similar purposes are a broad class of exempt organizations. A partnership cannot qualify as an exempt organization, and no part of the net earnings may accrue to the benefit of any private shareholder or individual.
Answer (A) is incorrect. The Salvation Army operates exclusively for charitable purposes with no part of net earnings accrued for the benefit of a private shareholder or individual. **Answer (C) is incorrect.** A college alumni association does not accrue any part of its net earnings for the benefit of an individual. **Answer (D) is incorrect.** A boys club operates exclusively for charitable purposes with no part of net earnings accrued for the benefit of a private shareholder or individual.

SU 5: Accounting Methods and Special Entities

13. With respect to tax-exempt organizations, which of the following statements is **false**?

A. A foundation may qualify for exemption from federal income tax if it is organized for the prevention of cruelty to children.

B. An individual may qualify as an organization exempt from federal income tax.

C. A corporation organized for the prevention of cruelty to animals may qualify for exemption from federal income tax.

D. A trust organized and operated for the purpose of testing for public safety may qualify for exemption from federal income tax.

Answer (B) is correct.
REQUIRED: The false statement regarding tax-exempt organizations.
DISCUSSION: To qualify for tax-exempt status, an organization must be a corporation, community chest fund, or foundation. An individual or a partnership cannot qualify.

14. Which of the following statements is true with respect to tax-exempt organizations?

A. A foundation may qualify for exemption from federal income tax if it is organized for the prevention of cruelty to animals.

B. A partnership may qualify as an organization exempt from federal income tax if it is organized and operated exclusively for one or more of the purposes found in Sec. 501(c)(3).

C. An individual can qualify as an organization exempt from federal income tax.

D. In order to qualify as an exempt organization, the organization must be a corporation.

Answer (A) is correct.
REQUIRED: The true statement with respect to tax-exempt organizations.
DISCUSSION: Exempt status generally depends on the nature and purpose of an organization. Among the types of organizations that may qualify as exempt are corporations, trusts, foundations, funds, community funds, etc. A more complete list can be found in Sec. 501(c) along with the permitted stated purposes and requirements.
Answer (B) is incorrect. A partnership is, by definition, a for-profit association. Also, a partnership is not listed as a type of organization that may qualify for exempt status in Sec. 501(c) or (d). **Answer (C) is incorrect.** An individual is not an organization described in Sec. 501(c) or (d) that may qualify for exempt status. **Answer (D) is incorrect.** Other types of organizations listed in Sec. 501(c) or (d) may also qualify.

15. An incorporated exempt organization subject to tax on its current-year unrelated business income (UBI)

A. Must make estimated tax payments if its tax can reasonably be expected to be $100 or more.

B. Must comply with the Code provisions regarding installment payments of estimated income tax by corporations.

C. Must pay at least 70% of the tax due as shown on the return when filed, with the balance of tax payable in the following quarter.

D. May defer payment of tax for up to 9 months following the due date of the return.

Answer (B) is correct.
REQUIRED: The timing of payment obligations with respect to UBI tax.
DISCUSSION: Exempt organizations subject to tax on UBI are required to comply with the Code provisions regarding installment payments of estimated income tax by corporations [Sec. 6655(g)(3)].
Answer (A) is incorrect. Like a corporation, quarterly payments of estimated tax are required of an exempt organization that expects estimated tax on UBI to equal or exceed $500 for the tax year. **Answer (C) is incorrect.** Tax on UBI is due in full when the UBI return and annual information return are due. **Answer (D) is incorrect.** Tax on UBI is due in full when the UBI return and annual information return are due.

16. Which transaction will **not** always cause an employee trust to lose exempt status?

A. Compensating an employee for personal services.
B. Lending at below market rates.
C. Lending without security.
D. Lending with some, but not adequate, security.

Answer (A) is correct.
REQUIRED: The permissible transaction for an exempt employee trust.
DISCUSSION: Certain employee trusts lose exempt status if they engage in prohibited transactions, e.g., lending without adequate security or reasonable interest, or paying unreasonable compensation for personal services. Reasonable compensation is permissible.
Answer (B) is incorrect. Lending without reasonable interest is a prohibited transaction and will cause the trust to lose exempt status. **Answer (C) is incorrect.** Lending without adequate security is a prohibited transaction. **Answer (D) is incorrect.** Lending without adequate security will cause a trust to lose exempt status.

5.3 Trusts

17. A complex trust is a trust that

A. Must distribute income currently but is prohibited from distributing principal during the taxable year.
B. Invests only in corporate securities and is prohibited from engaging in short-term transactions.
C. Permits accumulation of current income, provides for charitable contributions, or distributes principal during the taxable year.
D. Is exempt from payment of income tax since the tax is paid by the beneficiaries.

Answer (C) is correct.
REQUIRED: The characteristics of a complex trust.
DISCUSSION: Complex trusts can accumulate income, provide for charitable contributions, or distribute amounts other than income. These characteristics distinguish a complex trust from a simple trust.
Answer (A) is incorrect. A complex trust may distribute principal. **Answer (B) is incorrect.** A complex trust is not required to invest only in corporate securities and is not prohibited from engaging in short-term transactions. **Answer (D) is incorrect.** A complex trust, like a simple trust, is taxed on income not distributed to beneficiaries.

18. The Revised Uniform Principal and Income Act, with some modifications, has been adopted by many states to establish the definitions of the principal and income of a trust or estate for federal income tax purposes. In general, the act treats which of the following as income to a trust or estate?

I. Rents
II. Gain on the sale of property
III. Stock rights
IV. Interest

A. I and II.
B. I and IV.
C. II and III.
D. III and IV.

Answer (B) is correct.
REQUIRED: The items generally treated as trust or estate income.
DISCUSSION: The distinction between trust or estate income and principal is an important one. Tax is imposed on the taxable income (TI) of trusts or estates, but not on items treated as fiduciary principal. The Revised Uniform Principal and Income Act specifies that certain items, including business income, interest, rents, and taxable dividends, are to be treated as income to the trust or estate. The act also lists certain items to be treated as principal, including consideration for property (e.g., gain on sale), stock splits, stock rights, and liquidating dividends.
Answer (A) is incorrect. The gain on the sale of property is an item allocated to principal. **Answer (C) is incorrect.** Both the gain on the sale of property and the stock rights are items allocated to principal. **Answer (D) is incorrect.** The stock rights are an item allocated to principal.

19. Gardner, a U.S. citizen and the sole income beneficiary of a simple trust, is entitled to receive current distributions of the trust income. During the year, the trust reported:

Interest income from corporate bonds	$5,000
Fiduciary fees allocable to income	750
Net long-term capital gain allocable to corpus	2,000

What amount of the trust income is includible in Gardner's gross income?

A. $7,000
B. $5,000
C. $4,250
D. $0

Answer (C) is correct.
REQUIRED: The amount of trust income included in Gardner's gross income.
DISCUSSION: A simple trust is formed under an instrument having the following characteristics:

1. Requires current distribution of all its income
2. Requires no distribution of the principal
3. Provides for no charitable contribution by the trust

Trust income is taxed to the beneficiary of the trust whether distributed or not. Income related to the disposition of corpus is not taxable to the beneficiary because it is not earned income. The fees paid to the fiduciary are deductible from the trust income. Therefore, the trust income equals $5,000 of interest income less $750 of fiduciary fees for a total of $4,250.

Answer (A) is incorrect. The long-term capital gain allocable to the corpus is not taxable to Gardner and the fiduciary fees are deductible. **Answer (B) is incorrect.** The $750 of fiduciary fees are deductible in arriving at gross income for Gardner. **Answer (D) is incorrect.** The income of a simple trust is taxable whether or not it is distributed to Gardner.

Access the **Gleim CPA Premium Review System** featuring our SmartAdapt technology from your Gleim Personal Classroom to continue your studies. You will experience a personalized study environment with exam-emulating multiple-choice questions.

Notes

STUDY UNIT SIX
SELF-EMPLOYMENT

(18 pages of outline)

6.1	Business Income and Expenses	135
6.2	FICA and FUTA Taxes	144
6.3	Employee Benefits	147

Gross income is reduced by deductions to compute taxable income. No amount can be deducted from gross income unless allowed by the Internal Revenue Code (IRC). Deductible business expenses apply to sole proprietorships (Form 1040 Schedule C) as well as other business entities. Employers who pay wages are required to pay employment taxes based on employees' pay. These taxes include Social Security tax, Medicare tax, and unemployment tax. Not all payments made to employees are includible in their gross income.

SUCCESS TIP: Deductions to compute taxable income are heavily tested on the CPA Exam. The business expense deductions explained in this study unit are also tested in the corporate context. The CPA Exam has decreased its testing of exact amounts of limits. Nevertheless, you should be familiar with limit and threshold amounts.

Some candidates find it helpful to have the entire tax form side-by-side with our Knowledge Transfer Outline when studying, and others may prefer to see the final draft of a form when it is released. The full versions of the most up-to-date forms are easily accessible at www.gleim.com/taxforms. These forms and the form excerpts used in our outline are periodically updated as the latest versions are released by the IRS.

SCHEDULE C
(Form 1040)

Department of the Treasury
Internal Revenue Service (99)

Profit or Loss From Business
(Sole Proprietorship)

▶ Go to *www.irs.gov/ScheduleC* for instructions and the latest information.
▶ **Attach to Form 1040, 1040-SR, 1040-NR, or 1041; partnerships generally must file Form 1065.**

OMB No. 1545-0074

[Year]

Attachment
Sequence No. **09**

Name of proprietor | Social security number (SSN)

A Principal business or profession, including product or service (see instructions) | **B** Enter code from instructions ▶
C Business name. If no separate business name, leave blank. | **D** Employer ID number (EIN) (see instr.)
E Business address (including suite or room no.) ▶
City, town or post office, state, and ZIP code
F Accounting method: (1) ☐ Cash (2) ☐ Accrual (3) ☐ Other (specify) ▶
G Did you "materially participate" in the operation of this business during [Year]? If "No," see instructions for limit on losses . ☐ Yes ☐ No
H If you started or acquired this business during [Year], check here . . . . ▶ ☐
I Did you make any payments in [Year] that would require you to file Form(s) 1099? See instructions . . . . ☐ Yes ☐ No
J If "Yes," did you or will you file required Form(s) 1099? . . . . ☐ Yes ☐ No

Part I Income

1	Gross receipts or sales. See instructions for line 1 and check the box if this income was reported to you on Form W-2 and the "Statutory employee" box on that form was checked . . . . ▶ ☐	1
2	Returns and allowances	2
3	Subtract line 2 from line 1	3
4	Cost of goods sold (from line 42)	4
5	**Gross profit.** Subtract line 4 from line 3	5
6	Other income, including federal and state gasoline or fuel tax credit or refund (see instructions)	6
7	**Gross income.** Add lines 5 and 6 . . . . ▶	7

Part II Expenses. Enter expenses for business use of your home **only** on line 30.

8	Advertising	8		18	Office expense (see instructions)	18
9	Car and truck expenses (see instructions)	9		19	Pension and profit-sharing plans	19
				20	Rent or lease (see instructions):	
10	Commissions and fees .	10		a	Vehicles, machinery, and equipment	20a
11	Contract labor (see instructions)	11		b	Other business property . . .	20b
12	Depletion	12		21	Repairs and maintenance . . .	21
13	Depreciation and section 179 expense deduction (not included in Part III) (see instructions)	13		22	Supplies (not included in Part III) .	22
				23	Taxes and licenses	23
				24	Travel and meals:	
14	Employee benefit programs (other than on line 19) . .	14		a	Travel	24a
15	Insurance (other than health)	15		b	Deductible meals (see instructions)	24b
16	Interest (see instructions):			25	Utilities	25
a	Mortgage (paid to banks, etc.)	16a		26	Wages (less employment credits) .	26
b	Other	16b		27a	Other expenses (from line 48) .	27a
17	Legal and professional services	17		b	Reserved for future use . . .	27b

28	**Total expenses** before expenses for business use of home. Add lines 8 through 27a . . . ▶	28
29	Tentative profit or (loss). Subtract line 28 from line 7	29
30	Expenses for business use of your home. Do not report these expenses elsewhere. Attach Form 8829 unless using the simplified method. See instructions. **Simplified method filers only:** Enter the total square footage of (a) your home: _____ and (b) the part of your home used for business: _____ . Use the Simplified Method Worksheet in the instructions to figure the amount to enter on line 30	30
31	**Net profit or (loss).** Subtract line 30 from line 29. • If a profit, enter on both **Schedule 1 (Form 1040), line 3,** and on **Schedule SE, line 2.** (If you checked the box on line 1, see instructions). Estates and trusts, enter on **Form 1041, line 3.** • If a loss, you **must** go to line 32.	31
32	If you have a loss, check the box that describes your investment in this activity. See instructions. • If you checked 32a, enter the loss on both **Schedule 1 (Form 1040), line 3,** and on **Schedule SE, line 2.** (If you checked the box on line 1, see the line 31 instructions). Estates and trusts, enter on **Form 1041, line 3.** • If you checked 32b, you **must** attach **Form 6198.** Your loss may be limited.	32a ☐ All investment is at risk. 32b ☐ Some investment is not at risk.

For Paperwork Reduction Act Notice, see the separate instructions. Cat. No. 11334P Schedule C (Form 1040) [Year]

6.1 BUSINESS INCOME AND EXPENSES

1. **Self-Employment Income**
   a. Self-employment income is generally earned by a sole proprietor or independent contractor from a trade or business.
   b. A sole proprietor generally reports all self-employment income and expense on Schedule C.
   c. Gross income (GI) includes all income from a trade or business.
      1) Gross income from a business that sells products or commodities is

      Gross sales (receipts)
      − Cost of goods sold
      + Other GI (e.g., rentals)
      = **GI from the business**

      2) Cost of goods sold (COGS) is treated as a return of capital, which is not income for tax purposes. COGS for a tax year, typically, is

      Beginning inventory
      + Inventory-related purchases during year
      + Costs to produce inventory (i.e., labor, depreciation, material, and supplies)
      − Year-end inventory
      = **COGS**

      3) COGS should be determined in accordance with the accounting method consistently used by the business.

2. **Ordinary and Necessary Expenses**
   a. A deduction from gross income is allowed for all ordinary and necessary expenses paid or incurred during a tax year in carrying on a trade or business.
   b. These deductions apply to sole proprietors as well as other business entities.

3. **Trade/Business and Expenses Defined**
   a. A trade or business is a regular and continuous activity that is entered into with the expectation of making a profit.
      1) "Regular" means the taxpayer devotes a substantial amount of business time to the activity.
   b. An activity that is not engaged in for a profit is a hobby (personal).
      1) An activity that results in a profit in any 3 of 5 consecutive tax years (2 of 7 for the breeding and racing of horses) is presumed not to be a hobby.
      2) Expenses related to a hobby are not deductible, but any income is included in gross income.
   c. An expense must be **both** ordinary and necessary to be deductible.
      1) "Ordinary" implies that the expense normally occurs or is likely to occur in connection with businesses similar to the one operated by the taxpayer claiming the deduction.
         a) The expenditures need not occur frequently.
      2) "Necessary" implies that an expenditure must be appropriate and helpful in developing or maintaining the trade or business.
      3) Implicit in the "ordinary and necessary" requirement is the requirement that the expenditures be reasonable.

4. **Compensation**
    a. Cash and the FMV of property paid to an employee as reasonable compensation are deductible by the employer.

5. **Rent**
    a. Advance rental payments may be deducted by the lessee only during the tax periods to which the payments apply.
    b. Generally, even a cash-method taxpayer must amortize prepaid rent expense over the period to which it applies. The exception to this rule is if the rental contract is for 12 months or less and the payments do not extend beyond the end of the next taxable year (i.e., the 12-month rule).

EXAMPLE 6-1   Cash-Method Prepaid Rent

A cash-method calendar-year taxpayer leases a building at a monthly rental rate of $1,000 beginning July 1, 2021. On June 30, 2021, the taxpayer pays advance rent of $12,000 for the last 6 months of 2021 and the first 6 months of 2022. The taxpayer may deduct the entire $12,000 payment for 2021. The payment applies to the right to use the property that does not extend beyond 12 months after the date the taxpayer received this right. If the taxpayer deducts the $12,000 in 2021, then there is no deduction left for 2022.

---

6. **Business Meals**
    a. Business meals include food and beverages provided to a business associate.
        1) "Business associate" is defined as a person with whom the taxpayer could reasonably expect to engage or deal in the active conduct of the taxpayer's trade or business, such as the taxpayer's customer, client, supplier, employee, agent, partner, or professional advisor, whether established or prospective.
        2) The cost of meals includes any sales tax, delivery fees, or tips.
    b. Meal expenses are not deductible if neither the taxpayer nor an employee of the taxpayer is present at the meal.
    c. There is a 50% limit to deductible amounts for allowable meal expenses and related expenses, such as taxes, tips, and parking fees.
        1) No deduction is allowed for meals (or any portion thereof) that are lavish or extravagant under the circumstances.
        2) Transportation to and from a business meal is not limited.
        3) The IRS denies deductions for any meal expense over $75 for which the claimant did not provide substantiating evidence.
    d. Meals while traveling for business are also 50% deductible.

> **EXAMPLE 6-2**   Deductible Business Travel Expenses
>
> A taxpayer's business travel expenses include hotel costs ($1,300), plane fares ($2,500), employee meals ($1,000), and business meals with clients ($400). Of the $5,200 of expenses incurred, how much can the taxpayer claim as tax deductible?
>
> | Expense | Amount | % Allowed | Deduction |
> |---|---|---|---|
> | Hotel costs | $1,300 | 100% | $1,300 |
> | Plane fares | 2,500 | 100% | 2,500 |
> | Employee meals | 1,000 | 50% | 500 |
> | Business meals with clients | 400 | 50% | 200 |
> | Total | $5,200 | | $4,500 |

7. **Travel**
   a. While away from home overnight on business, travel expenses are deductible. Travel expenses include transportation, lodging, and meal expenses in an employment-related context.
   b. No deduction is allowed for
      1) Travel that is primarily personal in nature except for
         a) Directly related business expenses while at the destination.
      2) The travel expenses of the taxpayer's spouse unless
         a) There is a bona fide business purpose for the spouse's presence,
         b) The spouse is an employee, and
         c) The expenses would be otherwise deductible.
      3) Commuting between home and work
      4) Attending investment meetings
      5) Travel as a form of education (e.g., a Spanish teacher cannot deduct a trip to Spain to improve his or her Spanish language skills)
   c. A rule allows for lodging deductions when not traveling away from home (e.g., a conference or trade show held at a local hotel with evening events), if qualified under one of two tests or rules.
      1) The deduction is allowed if all the facts and circumstances indicate the lodging is for carrying on a taxpayer's trade or business. One factor under this test is whether the taxpayer incurs an expense because of a bona fide condition or requirement of employment imposed by the taxpayer's employer.
      2) A safe harbor rule applies if
         a) The lodging is necessary for the individual to participate fully in, or be available for, a bona fide business meeting, conference, training activity, or other business function;
         b) The lodging is for a period that does not exceed 5 calendar days and does not recur more frequently than once per calendar quarter;
         c) The employee's employer requires the employee to remain at the activity or function overnight (if the individual is an employee); and
         d) The lodging is not lavish or extravagant under the circumstances and does not provide any significant element of personal pleasure, recreation, or benefit.

8. **Foreign Travel**

    a. Traveling expenses of a taxpayer who ventures outside of the United States away from home must be allocated between time spent on the trip for business and time spent for pleasure.

    > **EXAMPLE 6-3　　Deductible Foreign Travel Expenses**
    >
    > Scott's foreign trip lasts longer than a week, and he spends 35% of his time on a personal vacation. However, he spends the other 65% providing business-related services.
    >
    > Only 65% of the expenses related to the time providing business services, including transportation, lodging, local travel, etc., may be deducted.

    b. No allocation is required for costs of getting to and from the destination when

     1) The trip is for no more than 1 week,
     2) The taxpayer can establish that a personal vacation was not the major consideration, or
     3) The personal time spent on the trip is less than 25% of the total time away from home.

9. **Entertainment**

    a. Generally, expenses for entertainment that are ordinary and necessary to the business are no longer deductible. An exception to this disallowance is social events primarily for the benefit of employees (e.g., a company picnic or holiday party).

    b. Any item that might be considered either a gift (discussed on page 140) or entertainment generally will be considered entertainment and, therefore, not deductible.

10. **Automobile Expenses**

    a. Actual expenses for automobile use are deductible (e.g., services, repairs, gas).

    b. Alternatively, the taxpayer may deduct the standard mileage rate ($0.56 per mile for 2021), plus parking fees, tolls, etc.

11. **Taxes**

    a. Taxes paid or accrued in a trade or business are deductible.

    b. Taxes paid or accrued to purchase property are treated as part of the cost of the property.

    c. Sales tax is treated as part of the property's cost.

     1) If capitalized, the sales tax may be recoverable as depreciation.
     2) If the cost of the property is currently expensed and deductible, so is the tax.

    d. Occupational license taxes are deductible.

    e. Property tax.

     1) Tax on real and personal property is an itemized deduction for individuals.
     2) Tax on business property is a business expense (i.e., deducted on a business return, for example, Schedule C or E).
     3) Local improvements.

         a) Taxes assessed for local benefit that tend to increase the value of real property are added to the property's adjusted basis and are not currently deductible as tax expense.

f. Income taxes.
   1) State and local taxes imposed on net income of an individual are NOT deductible on Schedule C.
      a) They are deductible as a personal, itemized deduction.
      b) They are not a business expense of a sole proprietorship.
   2) Federal income taxes generally are not deductible.
   3) Individual taxpayers may claim an itemized deduction for either general state and local sales taxes or state income taxes, but not both.

   NOTE: The itemized deduction for the sum total of all taxes paid (e.g., property, income) is limited to $10,000 ($5,000 if MFS).

g. Employment taxes.
   1) Deductible FICA and FUTA taxes are covered in detail in Subunit 6.2.

12. **Insurance Expense**
    a. Trade or business insurance expense paid or incurred during the tax year is deductible.
    b. A cash-method taxpayer may not deduct a premium before it is paid.
    c. Prepaid insurance must be apportioned over the period of coverage. However, a cash-method taxpayer can deduct prepaid premiums if the 12-month rule applies (contract is 12 months or less and does not extend beyond the next taxable year).

13. **Bad Debts**
    a. A bad debt is the loss that occurs when a customer does not pay amounts owed or an investment becomes worthless. Generally, a bad debt is related to a company's accounts or trades receivables that cannot be collected.
    b. A bad debt deduction is allowed only for a bona fide debt arising from a debtor-creditor relationship based upon a valid and enforceable obligation to pay a fixed or determinable sum of money.
    c. Worthless debt is deductible only to the extent of adjusted basis in the debt.
       1) A cash-basis taxpayer has no basis in accounts receivable and generally has no deduction for bad debts.
    d. A **business bad debt** is one incurred or acquired in connection with the taxpayer's trade or business.
       1) Partially worthless business debts may be deducted to the extent they are worthless and specifically written off.
       2) A business bad debt is treated as an ordinary loss.
    e. A **nonbusiness bad debt** is a debt other than one incurred or acquired in connection with the taxpayer's trade or business.
       1) Investments are not treated as a trade or business.
       2) A partially worthless nonbusiness bad debt is not deductible.
       3) A wholly worthless nonbusiness debt is treated as a short-term capital loss.
    f. Worthless corporate securities are not considered bad debts. They are generally treated as a capital loss.
    g. The **specific write-off method** must generally be used for tax purposes. The allowance method is generally used only for financial accounting purposes.

14. **Loan Costs**

    a. Costs of business borrowing are generally deductible.
    b. Costs of obtaining a loan, other than interest, are deductible over the period of the loan. Examples of such costs are recording fees and mortgage commissions.
    c. Interest is deductible when paid, as are payments in lieu of interest, for cash-basis taxpayers.
        1) Prepayment penalties are treated as interest and are deductible when paid.
        2) Points are treated as interest. They must be amortized over the period of the loan.
            a) However, ordinary points on acquisition indebtedness of a principal residence may be treated as currently deductible loan costs.
            b) Points paid on refinancing must be amortized.
        3) Prepaid interest in any form must be amortized over the period of the loan.
            a) Any undeducted balance is deductible in full when the loan is paid off.

EXAMPLE 6-4   Deductible Business Interest

On December 1, Year 1, a self-employed cash-basis taxpayer borrowed $500,000 for a business purpose use. The loan was to be repaid on November 30, Year 2. The taxpayer paid the entire interest amount of $60,000 on December 1, Year 1. The amortization of prepaid interest is calculated as follows:

Prepaid interest	$60,000
Period of amortization	12 months
1 month amortization expense	$60,000 ÷ 12 = $5,000 deduction limit for Year 1

The remaining $55,000 of interest is deductible for Year 2 when the loan is paid in full.

---

15. **Business Gifts**

    a. Expenditures for business gifts are deductible. They must be ordinary and necessary.
    b. The deduction is limited to $25 per recipient per year for excludable items.
        1) The $25 limit does not apply to incidental (e.g., advertising) items costing (the giver) $4 each or less, and other promotional materials, including signs and displays.
        2) A husband and wife are treated as one taxpayer, even if they file separate returns and have independent business relationships with the recipient.
    c. Any item that might be considered either a gift or entertainment generally will be considered entertainment and, therefore, not deductible.

16. **Employee Achievement Awards**

    a. Up to $400 of the cost of employee achievement awards is deductible by an employer for all nonqualified plan awards.
        1) An employee achievement award is tangible personal property awarded as part of a meaningful presentation for safety achievement or length of service.
            a) Tangible personal property does not include cash, cash equivalents, gift cards/coupons/certificates, vacations, meals, lodging, event tickets (e.g., theater, sporting), stocks, bonds, and other securities.

b. Deduction of qualified plan awards is limited to $1,600 per year.

1) A qualified plan award is an employee achievement award provided under an established written program that does not discriminate in favor of highly compensated employees.
2) If the average cost of all employee achievement awards is greater than $400, then it is not a qualified plan award.

17. **Start-Up and Organizational Costs**

    a. Taxpayers can deduct up to $5,000 of start-up costs and $5,000 of organizational costs in the taxable year in which the business begins. All deductible expenses occur prior to the start or purchase of the business.

        1) Examples of start-up costs are costs incurred to prepare to enter into the trade or business, to secure suppliers and customers, and to obtain certain supplies and equipment (noncapital).
        2) Examples of organizational costs are legal and accounting fees to draft a corporate charter; costs of state filings; and expenses of meetings with directors, shareholders, or partners.
        3) Any start-up or organizational costs in excess of $5,000 are capitalized and amortized proportionally over a 180-month period beginning with the month in which the active trade or business begins. The total start-up or organizational costs deducted for the first year equal the sum total of the $5,000 limit and the amortized amount allocated to the first year.

            a) These amounts are reduced, but not below zero, by the cumulative cost of the start-up costs or organizational costs that exceed $50,000.

        4) Taxpayers are not required to file a separate election statement. The taxpayer needs only to expense or capitalize the cost; from there, the election is irrevocable.

EXAMPLE 6-5   Deduction for Start-Up Costs and Organizational Costs

A cash-basis sole proprietor began her calendar-year business on April 1, Year 1. In February of Year 1, she incurred and paid $8,000 to secure suppliers and customers. At the end of Year 1, $12,000 was paid to her accountant to prepare financial statements.

The maximum deduction that can be taken on the Year 1 return is calculated as follows:

		Deduction in Year 1
Start-up costs	$8,000	$5,000
Organizational costs	0	0
First $5,000 expense		$5,000
Less: First $5,000	(5,000)	
Remaining start-up balance	$3,000	
Amortization period	÷ 180 months	
	$16.67/month	
Applicable months in Year 1	× 9 months	
Year 1 amortization		150
Total Schedule C deduction for Year 1		$5,150

The $12,000 paid to the accountant to prepare financial statements occurs after the start of business and therefore is neither a start-up cost nor an organizational expense.

18. **Vacant Land**

    a. Interest and taxes on vacant land are deductible.

19. **Medical Reimbursement Plans**

    a. The cost of such a plan for employees is deductible by the employer.

20. **Political Contributions and Lobbying Expenses**

    a. Contributions to a political party or candidate and lobbying expenses are not deductible.

21. **Intangibles**

    a. The cost of intangibles must generally be capitalized.

    b. Amortization is allowed if the intangible has a determinable useful life or was acquired as part of an acquisition of another business.

22. **Tax-Exempt Income**

    a. An expenditure related to producing tax-exempt income is not deductible, e.g., interest on a loan used to purchase tax-exempt bonds.

23. **Public Policy**

    a. A trade or business expenditure that is ordinary, necessary, and reasonable may be nondeductible if allowing the deduction would frustrate public policy.

    b. Examples are

    1) Fines and penalties paid to the government for violation of the law
    2) Illegal bribes and kickbacks
    3) Two-thirds of damages for violation of federal antitrust law
    4) Expenses of dealers in illegal drugs (as determined at the federal level)

        a) However, adjustment to gross receipts is permitted for the cost of merchandise.

24. **Miscellaneous Ordinary and Necessary Business Expenses**

    a. Miscellaneous ordinary and necessary business expenses are deductible.

    b. Examples include costs of advertising, bank fees, depreciation, amortization, office supplies, etc.

25. **Capital Expenditures**

    a. Capital expenditures are made in acquiring or improving property that will have a useful life of longer than 1 year.

    1) For example, replacing machinery is generally a capital expenditure. Also, wages paid to employees for constructing a new building to be used in the business are capitalized.

    b. If the property is a depreciable asset, the cost is recovered through depreciation.

    c. If the property is not a depreciable asset, the amount of the capital expenditure might be recovered at the time of disposition.

SU 6: Self-Employment

26. **Rental Property Income and Expense**
    a. Generally, rental property activity is **reported on Schedule E** for individuals.
    b. Expenses related to the production of rental income are generally deductible to arrive at adjusted gross income.
    c. Rental property expenditures may be deducted by depreciation. Generally, a Sec. 179 deduction (i.e., "bonus depreciation") is not allowed for rental property. (Study Unit 9, Subunit 2, "Depreciation and Amortization," has more detail on the Sec. 179 deduction.) The exceptions to this include a deduction for qualified improvement property.
    d. Special rules limit deductions on the rental of a residence or a vacation home.
        1) **Minimum rental use.** The property must be rented for more than 14 days during the year for deductions to be allowable.
        2) **Minimum personal use.** The vacation-home rules apply when the taxpayer uses the residence for personal purposes for the greater of (a) more than 14 days or (b) more than 10% of the number of days for which the residence is rented.
            a) When the residence is rented for less than 15 days, the rental income does not need to be reported. Any corresponding rental expenses cannot be deducted.
    e. If the property passes the minimum rental-use test but fails the minimum personal-use test, the property is considered a vacation home, and rental deductions may not exceed the gross income derived from rental activities.
        1) When deductions are limited to gross income, the order of deductions is
            a) The allocable portion of expenses deductible regardless of rental income (e.g., mortgage interest and property taxes)
            b) Deductions that do not affect basis (e.g., ordinary repairs and maintenance)
            c) Deductions that affect basis (e.g., depreciation)
        2) Expenses must be allocated between the personal use and the rental use based on the number of days of use of each.
    f. If the property passes both the minimum rental-use test and the minimum personal-use test, then all deductions may be taken and a loss may occur, subject to the passive loss limits.

Minimum Use Tests

	Rental Use	Personal Use
Pass	> 14 days	≤ 14 days or < 10%
Fail	≤ 14 days	greater of > 14 days or > 10%

STOP & REVIEW

You have completed the outline for this subunit.
Study multiple-choice questions 1 through 10 beginning on page 151.

6.2 FICA AND FUTA TAXES

1. **Federal Insurance Contributions Act (FICA) -- Social Security & Medicare Tax**
   a. While assessed on both employees and employers, employers are the ones required to deposit to the IRS this payroll tax based on the employee's pay.
   b. The **employer** must pay
      1) 6.2% of the first $142,800 (2021) of wages paid for Social Security (i.e., OASDI) tax, plus
      2) 1.45% of all wages for Medicare tax. There is no cap on this tax.
   c. The employer must withhold the following amounts from the **employee's** wages:
      1) Tier 1 – From $0 to $142,800; Employee's wages × 7.65% (6.2% Social Security + 1.45% Medicare)
      2) Tier 2 – Above $142,800 to $200,000; Employee's wages × 1.45% (Medicare)
      3) Tier 3 – Above $200,000 of earned income; Employee's wages × 2.35% (1.45% Medicare + 0.9% Additional Medicare)
         a) The Additional Medicare Tax on earned income is a 0.9% tax on wages and net self-employment income in excess of a threshold.
            i) This additional tax applies to earned income exceeding $200,000 for single, head-of-household, or surviving spouse; $250,000 for married filing jointly; and $125,000 for married filing separately. Employers withhold an additional 0.9% for income beyond $200,000 regardless of filing status.
   d. When overwithholding occurs, e.g., as a result of an employee having multiple employers, the overwithholding is alleviated as a credit against the employee's income tax.
   e. Contributions made by the employee are not tax deductible by the employee, while those made by the employer are deductible by the employer.
   f. An employer must pay FICA taxes for all household employees who are paid more than $2,300 during tax year 2021.
   g. The CARES Act allows a refundable credit against employment taxes for eligible employers carrying on a trade or business during calendar year 2021 if
      1) The operation of the trade or business is fully or partially suspended by an appropriate governmental authority due to COVID-19 during any calendar quarter or
      2) The employer suffers a significant decline in gross receipts such that the gross receipts for the calendar quarter are less than 80% of gross receipts for the same calendar quarter in 2019.
         a) Employers that did not exist in 2019 can use the corresponding quarter in 2020 to measure the decline in their gross receipts.

   NOTE: The provision only applies to wages paid after March 12, 2020, and before July 1, 2021.

2. **Net Investment Income Tax (NIIT)**
    a. All investment income in excess of deductions allowable for such income and income from passive activities are subject to a 3.8% **net investment income tax**. This tax essentially applies FICA taxes to income that previously was not subject to the taxes.
    b. The tax is imposed on the lesser of an individual's net investment income or any excess of modified adjusted gross income (MAGI) for the tax year over a specified threshold.

Filing Status	Threshold Amount
Married filing jointly, surviving spouse	$250,000
Single, head of household	$200,000
Married filing separately	$125,000

    c. MAGI is the sum of AGI and excludable foreign-earned income/housing costs after any deductions, exclusions, or credits applicable to the foreign-earned income.
    d. Net investment income tax does not apply to nonresident aliens.

3. **Self-Employment Tax**
    a. Self-employment taxes are paid through estimated payments, not withholding.
    b. The FICA tax liability is imposed on net earnings from self-employment at the employer rate plus the employee rate as follows:
        1) Tier 1 – From $0 to $142,800; Net earnings from self-employment × 15.3%
        2) Tier 2 – Above $142,800 to $200,000; Net earnings from self-employment × 2.9%
        3) Tier 3 – Above $200,000 ($250,000 MFJ, $150,000 MFS); Net earnings from self-employment × 3.8% (2.9% Medicare + 0.9% Additional Medicare)
    c. Net income from self-employment − (Net income from self-employment × .0765) = Net earnings from self-employment.
    d. Net income from self-employment does not include the following:
        1) Rents
        2) Gain or loss from disposition of business property
        3) Capital gain or loss
        4) Nonbusiness interest
        5) Dividends
        6) Income or expenses related to personal activities
        7) Wages, salaries, or tips received as an employee
        8) Self-employment tax
        9) Self-employment health insurance
    e. A self-employed person is allowed a deduction for the employer's portion of the FICA taxes paid to arrive at his or her AGI. For 2021, this equals
        1) 6.2% of the first $142,800 of net earnings from self-employment plus
        2) 1.45% of net earnings from self-employment (no cap).

f. The additional 0.9% Medicare tax is only imposed on the employee portion of self-employment tax. Therefore, it is not deductible.

1) Individuals with wages and self-employment net earnings calculate their liabilities in three steps:

   a) Calculate the tax on any wages in excess of the applicable threshold without regard to any withholding;
   b) Reduce the applicable threshold by the total amount of Medicare wages received, but not below zero; and
   c) Calculate the tax on any self-employment net earnings in excess of the reduced threshold.

> **EXAMPLE 6-6**   **Tax on Self-Employment Net Earnings**
>
> C, a single filer, has $130,000 in wages and $145,000 in self-employment net earnings. C's wages are not in excess of the $200,000 threshold for single filers, so C is not liable for the surtax on these wages. Before calculating the tax on self-employment net earnings, the $200,000 threshold for single filers is reduced by C's $130,000 in wages, resulting in a reduced self-employment threshold of $70,000. C is liable to pay the additional 0.9% tax on $75,000 of self-employment net earnings ($145,000 − $70,000).

g. The employee's portion of the FICA taxes is not deductible.

4. **Federal Unemployment Taxes (FUTA)**

   a. This tax is imposed on employers. The tax is 6.0% of the first $7,000 of wages paid to each employee. The employee does not pay any portion of FUTA.

5. Taxpayers have different reporting responsibilities for payments to employees than to independent contractors. The basic differences are covered in the following chart.

FICA and FUTA Reporting Requirement Chart

Employee	Independent Contractor
The employer must withhold federal income tax and the employee's half of FICA.	Generally, the contractor is responsible for federal income taxes and FICA.
The employer must pay the employer's half of FICA, as well as FUTA.	Generally, the contractor is responsible for federal income taxes and FICA. No FUTA responsibility.
The employer must issue Form W-2, *Wage and Tax Statement*, to the employee and send copies to the IRS.	The taxpayer must issue the contractor Form 1099-NEC and file copies with the IRS if the taxpayer pays the contractor $600 or more during the year.

STOP & REVIEW

You have completed the outline for this subunit.
Study multiple-choice questions 11 through 14 beginning on page 155.

6.3 EMPLOYEE BENEFITS

1. **Fringe Benefits**
   a. An employee's gross income does not include the cost of any qualified fringe benefit supplied or paid for by the employer.

2. **Employee Discounts**
   a. Certain employee discounts on the selling price of qualified property or services of their employer are excluded from gross income.
   b. The employee discount may not exceed
      1) The gross profit percentage normally earned on merchandise or
      2) 20% of the price offered to customers in the case of qualified services.

3. **De Minimis**
   a. The value of property or services (not cash) provided to an employee is excludable as a de minimis fringe benefit if the value is so minimal that accounting for it would be unreasonable or impracticable.
   b. The following are examples of de minimis fringe benefits. The list is not exhaustive.
      1) Occasional use of company copy machines
      2) Occasional company parties or picnics
      3) Occasional tickets to entertainment/sporting events (not season tickets)
      4) Occasional taxi fare or meal money due to overtime work
      5) Traditional noncash holiday gifts with a small FMV

      NOTE: Use of an employer-provided car more than once a month for commuting and membership to a private country club or athletic facility are never excludable as de minimis fringe benefits.
   c. The value of an on-premises athletic facility provided by an employer is generally excluded from gross income of employees.

4. **Qualified Transportation Fringe Benefits**
   a. Up to $270 a month may be excluded for the value of employer-provided transit passes and transportation in an employer-provided "commuter highway vehicle."
   b. Additionally, an exclusion of up to $270 per month is available for employer-provided parking.
   c. Employees may use both of these exclusions.

5. **Employer-Provided Educational Assistance**
   a. Up to $5,250 may be excluded by the employee for employer-provided educational assistance.
   b. Under the CARES Act, payments made by an employer to an employee or lender between March 27, 2020, and January 1, 2026, on any qualified educational loan incurred by the employee for his or her education may be excluded by the employer from the employee's taxable wages.
   c. Excludable assistance payments may not include the cost of meals, lodging, transportation, tools, or supplies that the employee retains after the course.

6. **Employer-Provided Life Insurance**

    a. Proceeds of a life insurance policy for which the employer paid the premiums may be excluded from the employee's gross income.

    b. The cost (e.g., premiums paid by the employer) of group term life insurance up to a coverage amount of $50,000 is excluded from the employee's gross income. In addition, the plan cannot discriminate in favor of highly compensated employees.

    c. Premiums paid by the employer for excess coverage (coverage over $50,000) are included in gross income.

    > **EXAMPLE 6-7   Employer-Provided Life Insurance**
    >
    > Janet, who is 40 years old, is provided with $150,000 of nondiscriminatory group term life insurance by her employer. Based on the IRS uniform premium cost table, the total annual cost of a policy of this type is $1.20 per $1,000 of coverage. Janet contributed $50 toward the policy. Janet should include $70 in gross income.
    >
    > | | |
    > |---|---:|
    > | Amount in excess of $50,000 | $100,000 |
    > | Cost of $100,000 policy | 120 |
    > | – Janet's contribution | 50 |
    > | Gross income to Janet | $ 70 |

    d. The employer must report the amount taxable to the employee on Form W-2.

    e. The exclusion applies only to coverage of the employee. Payments for coverage of an employee's spouse or dependent are included as gross income.

7. **Accident and Health Plans**

    a. Benefits received by an employee under an accident and health plan under which the employer paid the premiums or contributed to an independent fund are excluded from gross income of the employee.

    b. The benefits must be either

        1) Payments made due to permanent injury or loss of bodily functions or

        2) Reimbursement paid to the employee for medical expenses of the employee, spouse, or dependents. Any reimbursement in excess of medical expenses is included in income.

8. **Death Benefits**

    a. All death benefits received by the beneficiaries or the estate of an employee from or on behalf of an employer are included in gross income.

        1) This is for employer paid death benefits, not to be confused with death benefits of a life insurance plan provided by an employer.

SU 6: Self-Employment

9. **Meals and Lodging**

    a. The value of meals furnished to an employee by or on behalf of the employer is excluded from the employee's gross income if the meals are furnished on the employer's business premises and for the employer's convenience. The exclusion does not cover meal allowances.

    > **EXAMPLE 6-8   Employer-Provided Meals**
    >
    > An accounting firm provides catering some nights during busy season so employees can work longer hours. These meals would be excluded from the employee's gross income.

    b. The value of lodging is excluded from gross income if the lodging is on the employer's premises, is for the convenience of the employer, and must be accepted as a condition of employment.

    > **EXAMPLE 6-9   Employer-Provided Lodging**
    >
    > A hotel requires its manager to reside in a room at the hotel so she is readily available. The FMV of the lodging is excluded from the manager's gross income.

10. **Incentive Stock Options**

    a. An employee may not recognize income when an incentive stock option is granted or exercised depending upon certain restrictions.

    b. The employee recognizes long-term capital gain if the stock is sold 2 years or more after the option was granted and 1 year or more after the option was exercised.

        1) The employer is not allowed a deduction.

    c. Otherwise, the excess of the stock's FMV on the date of exercise over the option price is ordinary income to the employee when the stock is sold.

        1) The employer may deduct this amount.
        2) The gain realized is short-term or long-term capital gain.

    d. Nonqualified stock option.

        1) An employee stock option is not qualified if it does not meet numerous technical requirements to be an incentive stock option.
        2) If the option's FMV is ascertainable on the grant date,
            a) The employee has gross income equal to the FMV of the option.
            b) The employer is allowed a deduction.
            c) There are no tax consequences when the option is exercised.
            d) Capital gain or loss is reported when the stock is sold.
        3) If the option's FMV is not ascertainable on the grant date,
            a) The excess of FMV over the option price is gross income to the employee when the option is exercised.
            b) The employer is allowed a corresponding compensation deduction.
            c) The employee's basis in the stock is the exercise price plus the amount taken into ordinary income.

11. **Cafeteria Plans**
    a. A cafeteria plan is a benefit plan under which all participants are employees, and each participant has the opportunity to select between cash and nontaxable benefits.
        1) If the participant chooses cash, such cash is gross income.
        2) If qualified benefits are chosen, they are excludable to the extent permitted by the IRC.
    b. The employee must choose the benefit before the tax year begins. Under the CARES Act, mid-year elections are permitted during calendar year 2021.
    c. Any unused benefit is forfeited. However, an employer, in its discretion, may permit extended claim periods for unused amounts during calendar years 2020 and 2021.
    d. Self-employed individuals are not included.
    e. Employers **may** offer participation in a cafeteria plan to an employee on the employee's first day of employment, but employers **must** offer participation after the employee completes 3 years of employment.
    f. The plan cannot discriminate in favor of highly compensated employees.
    g. Every employer maintaining a cafeteria plan must file an information return, reporting the number of eligible and participating employees, the total cost of the plan for the tax year, and the number of highly compensated employees.
    h. Nontaxable benefits include
        1) Dependent care assistance
        2) Group term life insurance coverage up to $50,000
        3) Disability benefits
        4) Accident and health benefits
        5) Group legal services
    i. Plans may not offer scholarships, educational assistance, or meals and lodging (for the convenience of the employer).
    j. Deferred compensation plans other than 401(k) plans do not qualify for exclusion under a cafeteria plan.
    k. Nonemployee beneficiaries (e.g., spouses) may not participate in a cafeteria plan. They might benefit, however, depending on the plan selection.

12. **No Additional Cost Services**
    a. Employees can exclude from gross income the value of no additional cost services provided by their employer.
    b. The service provided to the employee must be in the employer's line of business and offered to customers in the ordinary course of business.

EXAMPLE 6-10   **No Additional Cost Service**

An airline allows its employees to fly for free on flights that are not full (i.e., no revenue is forgone). The value of the flight is excluded from the employee's gross income.

You have completed the outline for this subunit.
Study multiple-choice questions 15 through 20 beginning on page 157.

STOP & REVIEW

SU 6: Self-Employment

QUESTIONS

6.1 Business Income and Expenses

1. On December 1, 2021, Krest, a self-employed cash-basis taxpayer, borrowed $200,000 to use in her business. The loan was to be repaid on November 30, 2022. Krest paid the entire interest amount of $24,000 on December 1, 2021. What amount of interest was deductible on Krest's 2021 income tax return?

A. $0
B. $2,000
C. $22,000
D. $24,000

Answer (B) is correct.
REQUIRED: The amount of prepaid interest deductible on Krest's tax return for the current year.
DISCUSSION: Costs of business borrowing are generally deductible, but prepaid interest in any form must be amortized over the period of the loan. Only 1 month of the loan has expired, so $2,000 [$24,000 × (1 ÷ 12)] is deductible.
Answer (A) is incorrect. The interest related to the expired portion of the loan is deductible. **Answer (C) is incorrect.** The amount of $22,000 is the prepaid interest that should be amortized in 2021. **Answer (D) is incorrect.** Only one month of interest is deductible, not the entire interest amount of $24,000.

2. Mock operates a retail business selling illegal narcotic substances. When Mock calculates business income, he may adjust for

I. Cost of merchandise
II. Business expenses other than the cost of merchandise

A. I only.
B. II only.
C. Both I and II.
D. Neither I nor II.

Answer (A) is correct.
REQUIRED: The deductible items allowed to arrive at business income.
DISCUSSION: An adjustment to gross receipts is permitted for the cost of merchandise related to the selling of illegal narcotic substances (Sec. 280E), even if the narcotics are listed in the Controlled Substances Act. However, all other business expenses related to the sales are not deductible.
Answer (B) is incorrect. Business expenses for the sale of narcotics are not deductible. **Answer (C) is incorrect.** An adjustment for cost of merchandise is allowed, but business expenses associated with the sale of narcotics are not deductible. **Answer (D) is incorrect.** An adjustment to gross receipts is permitted for the cost of merchandise related to the selling of illegal narcotic substances.

3. Phil Armonic is actively engaged in the oil business and owns numerous oil leases in the Southwest. During 2021, he made several trips to inspect oil wells on the leases. As a result of these overnight trips, he paid the following:

Plane fares	$4,000
Hotels	1,000
Meals	800
Entertaining lessees	500

Of the $6,300 in expenses incurred, he can claim as deductible expenses

A. $6,300
B. $5,400
C. $5,000
D. $4,400

Answer (B) is correct.
REQUIRED: The deductible amount of expenses incurred on overnight trips.
DISCUSSION: A deduction is allowed for travel expenses while away from home in the pursuit of a trade or business. Meals expenses are limited to 50% of their cost. Generally, entertainment expenses are not deductible. Assuming that Armonic's expenses meet the business relation requirements, his total deduction is

Plane fares	$4,000
Hotels	1,000
Meals ($800 × 50%)	400
Total deduction	$5,400

Answer (A) is incorrect. Only part of the expenses may be deducted. **Answer (C) is incorrect.** Meals expenses are deductible but limited to 50% of their cost. **Answer (D) is incorrect.** The cost of lodging is deductible as travel expense.

4. The following 2021 information pertains to Sam and Ann Hoyt, who filed a joint federal income tax return for the calendar year 2021:

Adjusted gross income -- $34,000
$100 contribution to a recognized political party

The Hoyts itemized their deductions. What amount of the $100 political contribution were the Hoyts entitled to claim as a deduction against their 2021 tax?

A. $0
B. $25
C. $50
D. $100

Answer (A) is correct.
REQUIRED: The amount taxpayers are entitled to claim as a deduction for political contributions.
DISCUSSION: Contributions to a political party or candidate are not deductible.

5. Recasto owns a second residence that is used for both personal and rental purposes. During 2021, Recasto used the second residence for 50 days and rented the residence to Louis for 200 days. Which of the following statements is true?

A. Depreciation may not be deducted on the property under any circumstances.
B. A rental loss may be deducted if rental-related expenses exceed rental income.
C. Utilities and maintenance on the property must be divided between personal and rental use.
D. All mortgage interest and taxes on the property will be deducted to determine the property's net income or loss.

Answer (C) is correct.
REQUIRED: The true statement regarding Recasto's second residence.
DISCUSSION: The expenses for rental property must be allocated between personal and rental use. Deductions are only allowed for those expenses related to the rental expense. In order to qualify to deduct these amounts, the taxpayer must pass the "Minimum Rental Use" test, which states that the property must be rented for at least 15 days to qualify as business use. In addition, if the taxpayer uses the residence for personal use more than either 14 days or 10% of the days it is rented, the deductions are further limited.
Answer (A) is incorrect. Expenses allocable to the rental use are deductible. **Answer (B) is incorrect.** Although the minimum rental use test was passed, the residence failed the minimum personal use test. Therefore, it cannot qualify for any passive activity loss deduction. **Answer (D) is incorrect.** The expenses must be allocated between personal and rental use.

6. On December 1, 2020, Michael, a self-employed cash-basis taxpayer, borrowed $100,000 to use in his business. The loan was to be repaid on November 30, 2021. Michael paid the entire interest of $12,000 on December 1, 2020. What amount of interest was deductible on Michael's 2021 income tax return?

A. $12,000
B. $11,000
C. $1,000
D. $0

Answer (B) is correct.
REQUIRED: The amount of interest deductible by a cash-method taxpayer.
DISCUSSION: Deductions are allowed under the cash method of accounting in the taxable year when paid. However, prepaid interest must be capitalized. Thus, $11,000 of interest attributable to the 2021 tax year may be deducted on Michael's 2021 income tax return and not earlier.
Answer (A) is incorrect. The cash-basis taxpayer deducts the $11,000 of interest attributable to the 2021 tax year in 2021. **Answer (C) is incorrect.** The amount of interest attributable to 2020 is $1,000. **Answer (D) is incorrect.** A cash-basis taxpayer may not deduct prepaid interest when paid.

7.
Gary Judd is an individual proprietor trading as Lake Stores, an accrual basis enterprise that had been using the allowance method for determining bad debt expense for book purposes. At December 31, 2020, Lake's allowance for doubtful accounts ("bad debt reserve") was $20,000. In Lake's 2021 budget, it was estimated that $3,000 of trade accounts receivable would become worthless in 2021. However, actual bad debts amounted to $4,000 in 2021. In Lake's 2021 Schedule C of Form 1040, Lake is allowed

A. A $4,000 deduction for bad debts but must also include $5,000 of the "reserve" in taxable income.

B. A $4,000 deduction for bad debts and does not have to include any portion of the "reserve" in taxable income.

C. No deduction for bad debts since these bad debts should be charged against the "reserve."

D. A $1,000 deduction for bad debts, which is the excess of actual bad debts over the amount estimated.

Answer (B) is correct.
REQUIRED: The amount allowable as a deduction for business bad debts.
DISCUSSION: An accrual-basis taxpayer includes trade receivables in gross income, and a trade receivable is deductible as a business bad debt to the extent it is worthless. The allowance method of deducting bad debts is not allowed, so Gary must use the specific write-off method.
Answer (A) is incorrect. Although "reserve" was not deductible, no portion need be included in gross income when an actual bad debt is specifically written off. Answer (C) is incorrect. The actual bad debts are deductible. Adjustment should be made to the reserve for financial accounting, not tax purposes. Answer (D) is incorrect. The debts actually written off, not the estimated amount, are deductible.

8.
Basic Partnership, a cash-basis, calendar-year entity, began business on February 1, 2021. Basic incurred and paid the following in 2021:

Filing fees incident to the creation of the partnership	$ 3,600
Accounting fees to prepare the representations in offering materials	12,000

Basic elected to amortize costs. What is the maximum amount that Basic may deduct on the 2021 partnership return?

A. $5,000
B. $3,300
C. $0
D. $3,600

Answer (D) is correct.
REQUIRED: The amount of organizational costs that is deductible in the current tax year.
DISCUSSION: A partnership may elect to deduct up to $5,000 of any qualified organizational expenses (in addition to $5,000 of any startup costs) it incurs in the tax year in which it begins business. The $5,000 deducted for organizational expenses must be reduced by the amount by which the expenses exceed $50,000. Any remaining balance of organizational expenditures that are not immediately deductible must be amortized over a 15-year period. Organizational costs include costs associated with the formation of the partnership. They do not include syndication fees. Thus, the filing fees are the only fees that may be deducted. The maximum amount that Basic may deduct is $3,600.
Answer (A) is incorrect. A $5,000 deduction includes the syndication fees. Answer (B) is incorrect. The amount of $3,300 is the result of amortizing the organizational costs over 11 months. Answer (C) is incorrect. The amount of $0 does not include the filing fees.

9. Nan, a cash basis taxpayer, borrowed money from a bank and signed a 10-year interest-bearing note on business property on January 1 of the current year. The cash flow from Nan's business enabled Nan to prepay the first 3 years of interest attributable to the note on December 31 of the current year. How should Nan treat the prepayment of interest for tax purposes?

A. Deduct the entire amount as a current expense.

B. Deduct the current year's interest and amortize the balance over the next 2 years.

C. Capitalize the interest and amortize the balance over the 10-year loan period.

D. Capitalize the interest as part of the basis of the business property.

Answer (B) is correct.
REQUIRED: The appropriate treatment for the prepayment of interest on business property.
DISCUSSION: Despite being a cash-basis taxpayer, the interest expense must be apportioned to the periods to which it is attributable. As the first 3 years' portion is paid in Year 1, the Year 1 portion is currently deductible. The remainder must be deducted in the year to which it is attributable (Year 2 in Year 2 and Year 3 in Year 3), regardless of when paid.
Answer (A) is incorrect. The interest expense must be allocated to the period which it benefited and may not be entirely deducted presently. **Answer (C) is incorrect.** As the prepayment of interest does not benefit the periods after the end of Year 3, it is not reasonable to allocate the interest to periods beyond Year 3. **Answer (D) is incorrect.** The appropriate treatment for the prepayment of interest on business property is to capitalize and amortize the interest in the period to which it applies.

10. Dr. Merry, a self-employed dentist, incurred the following expenses:

Investment expenses	$ 700
Custodial fees related to Dr. Merry's Keogh plan	40
Work uniforms for Dr. Merry and Dr. Merry's employees	320
Subscriptions for medical periodicals used in the waiting room	110
Dental education seminar	1,300

What is the amount of expenses the doctor can deduct as business expenses on Schedule C, *Profit or Loss from Business*?

A. $1,620

B. $1,730

C. $1,770

D. $2,430

Answer (B) is correct.
REQUIRED: The expenses deductible on Schedule C.
DISCUSSION: A deduction from gross income is allowed for all ordinary and necessary expenses paid or incurred during a tax year in carrying on a trade or business. Dr. Merry's deductible business expenses include work uniforms, subscriptions for medical periodicals related to the trade or business, and the dental education seminar. Thus, total deductible expenses on Schedule C equal $1,730 ($320 + $110 + $1,300).
Answer (A) is incorrect. The subscriptions for periodicals related to the dentist's trade or business used in the waiting room are deductible on Schedule C. **Answer (C) is incorrect.** The custodial fees related to Dr. Merry's Keogh plan are not deductible on Schedule C. **Answer (D) is incorrect.** The investment expenses are not deductible.

6.2 FICA and FUTA Taxes

11. Michael operates his health food store as a sole proprietorship out of a building he owns. Based on the following information regarding Year 6, compute his net self-employment income (for SE tax purposes) for Year 6.

Gross receipts	$100,000
Cost of goods sold	49,000
Utilities	6,000
Real estate taxes	1,000
Gain on sale of business truck	2,000
Depreciation expense	5,000
Section 179 expense	1,000
Mortgage interest on building	7,000
Contributions to Keogh retirement plan	2,000
Net operating loss (NOL) from Year 5	10,000

A. $14,000
B. $16,000
C. $24,000
D. $31,000

Answer (D) is correct.
REQUIRED: The sole proprietor's net self-employment income.
DISCUSSION: Net earnings from self employment are gross income derived from a trade or business, less allowable deductions attributable to the trade or business. Capital gains and losses and contributions to retirement plans are not considered income or expenses for self-employment purposes. Also, net operating losses are not considered for self-employment purposes. Michael's net self-employment income is computed as follows:

Gross receipts	$100,000
Cost of goods sold	(49,000)
Utilities	(6,000)
Real estate taxes	(1,000)
Depreciation expense	(5,000)
Section 179 expense	(1,000)
Mortgage interest	(7,000)
Net self-employment income	$ 31,000

Answer (A) is incorrect. The NOL is not considered when computing self-employment income. **Answer (B) is incorrect.** The NOL is not considered when computing self-employment income. **Answer (C) is incorrect.** The gain on the sale of the business truck, contributions to the Keogh retirement plan, and the NOL are not considered when computing self-employment income.

12. The self-employment tax is

A. Fully deductible as an itemized deduction.
B. Fully deductible in determining net income from self-employment.
C. Partially deductible from gross income in arriving at adjusted gross income.
D. Not deductible.

Answer (C) is correct.
REQUIRED: The true statement concerning deductibility of the self-employment tax.
DISCUSSION: To arrive at AGI, a self-employed person may deduct the employer's portion of the self-employment tax paid. This is an above-the-line deduction.
Answer (A) is incorrect. Only a portion of the self-employment tax may be deducted, and the deduction is above-the-line. **Answer (B) is incorrect.** Only a portion of the self-employment tax may be deducted to arrive at AGI. **Answer (D) is incorrect.** A deduction for self-employment tax is available.

13. Juan recently started operating a flower shop as a proprietorship. In its first year of operations, the shop had a taxable income of $60,000. Assuming that Juan had **no** other employment-related earnings,

A. The flower shop must withhold FICA taxes from Juan's earnings.
B. Juan must pay self-employment tax on the earnings of the business.
C. Juan will be exempt from self-employment taxes for the first 3 years of operations.
D. Juan will be exempt from the Medicare tax because the business earnings are below the threshold amount.

Answer (B) is correct.
REQUIRED: The correct action for self-employment tax.
DISCUSSION: Self-employed taxpayers must pay a self-employment tax on the earnings of their business. The FICA tax liability is imposed on net earnings from self-employment at the employer rate plus the employee rate.
Answer (A) is incorrect. Self-employment taxes are paid through estimated payments, not withholding. **Answer (C) is incorrect.** There is no exemption from self-employment taxes for the first 3 years of operation. **Answer (D) is incorrect.** While Juan's earnings are below the additional Medicare tax threshold, there is no threshold for the Medicare portion of FICA taxes.

14. Rich is a cash-basis, self-employed air-conditioning repair technician with current-year gross business receipts of $20,000. Rich's cash disbursements were as follows:

Air-conditioning parts	$2,500
Social media advertising	2,000
Estimated federal income taxes on self-employment income	1,000
Business telecommunication fees	400
Charitable contributions	200

What amount should Rich report as net earnings from self-employment?

A. $15,100
B. $14,900
C. $14,100
D. $13,945

Answer (D) is correct.
REQUIRED: The amount of net earnings from self-employment.
DISCUSSION: The $20,000 gross receipts would be reduced by the $2,500 for parts, the $2,000 in advertising expense, and the $400 in telecommunication expense. This $15,100 is net income from self-employment. Net earnings from self-employment is net income from self-employment reduced by the employer's portion of FICA taxes (0.0765) times the taxpayer's net income from self-employment. Thus, the $15,100 should be reduced by an additional $1,155 ($15,100 × 0.0765), resulting in net earnings from self-employment of $13,945.
Answer (A) is incorrect. Net income from self-employment is $15,100. **Answer (B) is incorrect.** Net income is gross business income less business deductions. Charitable contributions do not reduce self-employment income. **Answer (C) is incorrect.** Federal income taxes are not a reduction in computing net self-employment income.

6.3 Employee Benefits

15. Under a "cafeteria plan" maintained by an employer,

A. Participation must be restricted to employees and their spouses and minor children.
B. At least 3 years of service are required before an employee can participate in the plan.
C. Participants may select their own menu of benefits.
D. Provision may be made for deferred compensation other than 401(k) plans.

Answer (C) is correct.
REQUIRED: The true statement about a cafeteria plan maintained by an employer.
DISCUSSION: Section 125 defines a cafeteria plan as a written plan under which all participants are employees and the participants may choose among benefits consisting of cash and qualified benefits. Participation is restricted to the employee. There is no minimum period of employment required. Benefits that do not qualify include (1) deferred compensation plans other than Sec. 401(k) plans, (2) scholarships and fellowship grants or tuition reductions, (3) educational assistance, and (4) other fringe benefits.
Answer (A) is incorrect. Spouses and other nonemployee beneficiaries may not participate in a cafeteria plan. **Answer (B) is incorrect.** No minimum period of employment is required. The maximum period of employment an employer may require is 3 years. **Answer (D) is incorrect.** Deferred compensation plans other than Sec. 401(k) plans do not qualify for exclusion under a cafeteria plan.

16. John Budd files a joint return with his wife. Budd's employer pays 100% of the cost of all employees' group term life insurance under a qualified plan. Under this plan, the maximum amount of tax-free coverage that may be provided for Budd by his employer is

A. $100,000
B. $50,000
C. $10,000
D. $5,000

Answer (B) is correct.
REQUIRED: The maximum amount of employer-paid group term life insurance cost excludable by the employee.
DISCUSSION: Benefits received from an employer are compensation for services and are included in gross income unless provided otherwise. Included in gross income is the cost of group term life insurance paid by the employer, but only to the extent that such cost exceeds the cost of $50,000 of such insurance. The plan cannot discriminate in favor of highly-compensated employees.

17. In 2017, Ross was granted an incentive stock option (ISO) by his employer as part of an executive compensation package. Ross exercised the ISO in 2019 and sold the stock in 2021 at a gain. Ross's profit was subject to the income tax for the year in which the

A. ISO was granted.
B. ISO was exercised.
C. Stock was sold.
D. Employer claimed a compensation deduction for the ISO.

Answer (C) is correct.
REQUIRED: The year in which the taxpayer's profit on an ISO is subject to the income tax.
DISCUSSION: According to the Internal Revenue Code, an employee will have no income tax consequences on the grant date or the exercise date of an incentive stock option if that employee meets two requirements. First, the employee cannot dispose of the stock within 2 years after the grant date or within 1 year after the exercise date. Second, the employee must be employed by the company on the grant date until 3 months prior to the exercise date. Since Ross meets these requirements, he is not subject to any tax on the grant or exercise dates. Ross did, however, recognize a capital gain when he sold the stock in 2021.
Answer (A) is incorrect. There are no income tax consequences on the grant date. **Answer (B) is incorrect.** There are no income tax consequences on the exercise date. **Answer (D) is incorrect.** An employer may not take a deduction for the amount of the profit on an incentive stock option.

SU 6: Self-Employment

18. Howard, an employee of Ogden Corporation, died on June 30, 2021. During July, Ogden made employee death payments of $10,000 to his widow and $10,000 to his 15-year-old son. What amounts should be included in gross income by the widow and son in their respective tax returns for 2021?

	Widow	Son
A.	$0	$0
B.	$10,000	$10,000
C.	$5,000	$5,000
D.	$7,500	$7,500

Answer (B) is correct.
REQUIRED: The employee death benefits a widow and son should each include in gross income.
DISCUSSION: All death benefits received by the beneficiaries or the estate of an employee from or on behalf of an employer are included in gross income. Therefore, the widow and the son should each include the full $10,000 received as employee death benefits.

19. Frank Clarke, an employee, was covered under a noncontributory pension plan. Frank died on April 15, 2021, at age 64 and, pursuant to the plan, his widow received monthly pension payments of $500 beginning May 1, 2021. Mrs. Clarke also received an employee death payment of $10,000 in May 2021. How much should she include in her gross income for 2021?

A. $5,000
B. $9,000
C. $10,000
D. $14,000

Answer (D) is correct.
REQUIRED: The amount of monthly pension payments and/or the amount of a lump-sum death benefit that is included in gross income.
DISCUSSION: All death benefits received by the beneficiaries or the estate of an employee from, or on behalf of, an employer are included in gross income. The pension payments must be included unless Frank made contributions to the pension plan.

20. Which of the following fringe benefits is **not** excludable from an employee's wages?

A. Qualified employee discount.
B. Educational assistance expenses of $5,250 provided through an educational assistance program.
C. $2,500 of group term life insurance covering the death of an employee's spouse or dependent.
D. Qualified transportation benefits.

Answer (C) is correct.
REQUIRED: The fringe benefit not excludable from an employee's wages.
DISCUSSION: Under the IRC, the cost of qualified group term life insurance paid by an employer is included in the employee's gross income to the extent that such cost exceeds the cost of $50,000 of such insurance. The exclusion only applies to coverage of the employee. Payments for coverage of an employee's spouse or dependent are included in an employee's wages.
Answer (A) is incorrect. Qualified employee discounts are excludable. **Answer (B) is incorrect.** Under an employer's educational assistance program, the employee may exclude up to $5,250 from his or her gross income. **Answer (D) is incorrect.** Qualified transportation benefits are excludable up to $270.

Access the **Gleim CPA Premium Review System** featuring our SmartAdapt technology from your Gleim Personal Classroom to continue your studies. You will experience a personalized study environment with exam-emulating multiple-choice questions.

STUDY UNIT SEVEN
ADJUSTMENTS AND DEDUCTIONS FROM AGI

(27 pages of outline)

7.1	Above-the-Line Deductions	160
7.2	Standard and Itemized Deductions	166
7.3	Qualified Business Income Deduction (QBID)	179

Above-the-line deductions are adjustments deducted from gross income to arrive at adjusted gross income (AGI) for individual taxpayers.

Individual taxpayers are also allowed to take certain deductions from AGI, including the greater of the standard or itemized deductions, and the new qualified business income deduction. The following are common deductions tested on the CPA Exam:

Adjustments to Gross Income	Itemized Deductions
• Educator expenses • Health savings account deduction • Moving expenses for military • Deductible part of self-employment tax • Self-employed SEP and qualified plans • Self-employed health insurance deduction • Penalty on early withdrawal of savings • Alimony paid pursuant to a divorce finalized prior to 2019 • IRA deduction • Student loan interest deduction • Jury duty repayments	• Medical and dental expenses • Taxes paid • Interest paid • Gifts to charity • Casualty losses in federally declared disaster areas • Other

The CPA Exam tests the method of computing income tax liability. In the past, however, candidates have generally not been required to memorize the tax rates for each bracket for each filing status. The computation questions have generally provided brackets and rates to be applied for specific questions. Nevertheless, candidates should be prepared to answer questions on the current rate-bracket structure (e.g., what is the highest marginal rate?).

2021 Individual Income Tax Rates and Brackets

Rate Taxable Income Filing Status	10% The First	12% From 10% Max. up to	22% From 12% Max. up to	24% From 22% Max. up to	32% From 24% Max. up to	35% From 32% Max. up to	37% From 35% Max. up to
Married Filing Jointly and Qualifying Widow(er)	$19,900	$81,050	$172,750	$329,850	$418,850	$628,300	$Balance
Head of Household	$14,200	$54,200	$86,350	$164,900	$209,400	$523,600	$Balance
Single	$9,950	$40,525	$86,375	$164,925	$209,425	$523,600	$Balance
Married Filing Separately	$9,950	$40,525	$86,375	$164,925	$209,425	$314,150	$Balance

Some candidates find it helpful to have the entire tax form side-by-side with our Knowledge Transfer Outline when studying, and others may prefer to see the final draft of a form when it is released. The full versions of the most up-to-date forms are easily accessible at www.gleim.com/taxforms. These forms and the form excerpts used in our outline are periodically updated as the latest versions are released by the IRS.

7.1 ABOVE-THE-LINE DEDUCTIONS

1. **Overview**

    a. Above-the-line deductions are deducted from gross income to arrive at adjusted gross income (AGI).

    Gross income − Above-the-line deductions = Adjusted gross income (AGI)

    1) "Above-the-line deductions" is a term used in our materials, but they can also be referred to as "adjustments," "deductions to arrive at AGI," and "deductions for AGI."

2. **Educator Expenses**

    From Form 1040 Schedule 1

10	Educator expenses	10	

    a. Elementary (primary) and middle/high (secondary) school educators may claim an above-the-line deduction for unreimbursed expenses paid or incurred for books and supplies used in the classroom up to $250 annually. Each taxpayer (educator) on a joint return may deduct up to the maximum amount.

    1) Books, supplies (including personal protective equipment such as face masks and disinfectants), computer equipment (including related software and services) and other equipment, and supplementary materials used in the classroom qualify for the deduction.

    2) An eligible educator is an individual who, for at least 900 hours during a school year, is a kindergarten through grade 12 teacher, instructor, counselor, principal, or aide.

3. **Health Savings Account Deduction**

    From Form 1040 Schedule 1

12	Health savings account deduction. Attach Form 8889	12	

    a. **Health Savings Account**

    1) A Health Savings Account is a tax-exempt account the taxpayer sets up with a U.S. financial institution to save money used exclusively for future medical expenses.

        a) This account must be used in conjunction with a High Deductible Health Plan.

    2) The amount that may be contributed to a taxpayer's Health Savings Account depends on the nature of his or her coverage and his or her age.

        a) For self-only coverage, the taxpayer or his or her employer can contribute up to $3,600 ($4,600 for taxpayers who have reached age 55).

        b) For family coverage, the taxpayer or his or her employer can contribute up to $7,200 ($9,200 for taxpayers who have both reached age 55).

    3) Contributions to a Health Savings Account for 2021 may include contributions made until April 15, 2022.

SU 7: Adjustments and Deductions from AGI

4. **Moving Expenses**

    From Form 1040 Schedule 1

13	Moving expenses for members of the Armed Forces. Attach Form 3903	13	

    a. Military members on active duty who move pursuant to a military order and due to a permanent change of station are allowed a deduction for relocation expenses.

5. **Self-Employment**

    From Form 1040 Schedule 1

14	Deductible part of self-employment tax. Attach Schedule SE	14	
15	Self-employed SEP, SIMPLE, and qualified plans	15	
16	Self-employed health insurance deduction	16	

    a. **Self-Employment Tax**

       1) A self-employed person is allowed a deduction for the employer's portion of the FICA taxes paid to arrive at his or her AGI. The deduction for the employer's share is equal to 50% of the self-employment tax. For 2021, the deduction equals

          a) 6.2% of the first $142,800 of net earnings from self-employment plus
          b) 1.45% of net earnings from self-employment (no cap).

       NOTE: The calculation of net earnings from self-employment is explained in item 3.c. in Study Unit 6, Subunit 2.

       2) The 0.9% additional Medicare tax is on the employee's portion of FICA taxes. Therefore, the 0.9% tax is not deductible.

    b. **Self-Employed SEP and Qualified Plans**

       1) A self-employed individual can deduct specified amounts paid on his or her behalf to a qualified retirement or profit-sharing plan, such as a SEP plan.

       2) The most common self-employed retirement plan used is a SEP (Keogh) plan.

          a) The maximum annual contribution is limited to the lesser of 25% of the self-employed earnings or $58,000 in 2021.
          b) Self-employed earnings are reduced by the deductible part of self-employment taxes.
          c) Contributions to the plan are subtracted from net earnings to calculate self-employed earnings, creating a circular computation. For convenience, a standard rate of 20% is used to calculate the allowed deduction.

    EXAMPLE 7-1   Self-Employed SEP and Qualified Plans Deductions

    Alice has business income of net self-employed earnings of $125,000 before the deductible part of self-employment taxes of $9,563. The maximum annual deduction is calculated as follows:

    ($125,000 − $9,563) × 20% = $23,087 (rounded)

    ---

    c. **Self-Employed Health Insurance Deduction**

       1) Self-employed individuals can deduct 100% of payments made for health insurance coverage for the individual, his or her spouse, and dependents.

       2) The deduction is limited to the taxpayer's earned income derived from the business for which the insurance plan was established.

162　SU 7: Adjustments and Deductions from AGI

6. **Penalty on Early Withdrawal of Savings**

    From Form 1040 Schedule 1

    17　Penalty on early withdrawal of savings . . . . 　17

    a. Deduction is allowable for penalties from an early withdrawal of funds from certificates of deposit or other time savings accounts.
    b. The deduction is taken in the year the penalty is incurred.

7. **Alimony**

    From Form 1040 Schedule 1

    18a　Alimony paid . . . . 　18a
    　b　Recipient's SSN . . . . ▶
    　c　Date of original divorce or separation agreement (see instructions) ▶ _____

    a. Divorces Executed before 2019
        1) Alimony is gross income to the recipient and deductible by the payor.
        2) Alimony payments may not extend past the death of the payee spouse.
    b. Divorces Executed or Modified after 2018
        1) Alimony is nondeductible to the payor and not included in the gross income of the recipient. Thus, whether alimony is deductible or not depends on when the divorce was executed.
    c. Child support is neither gross income to the recipient nor deductible by the payor.

8. **IRA Deduction**

    From Form 1040 Schedule 1

    19　IRA deduction . . . . 　19

    a. **Individual Retirement Arrangement (IRA) Contributions (Traditional IRAs)**
        1) For 2021, contributions are fully deductible (subject to certain qualifying rules and limitations) up to the lesser of $6,000 ($7,000 for taxpayers age 50 and over) or 100% of includible compensation. Because contributions are deducted from gross income, all distributions are included as ordinary gross income.
        2) To qualify for the return year, contributions must be made by the due date of the return without regard to extensions.
        3) Compensation includes alimony and earned income but not pensions, annuities, or other deferred compensation distributions.
        4) An additional $6,000 ($7,000 for taxpayers age 50 and over) may be contributed to the IRA for the taxpayer's nonworking spouse, or a spouse earning less income, if a joint return is filed.
            a) The combined IRA contributions by both spouses cannot exceed their combined compensation for the year.

SU 7: Adjustments and Deductions from AGI

5) If the taxpayer is an active participant in an employer-sponsored retirement plan and has earned income of over $105,000 [married filing jointly or qualifying widow(er)] in 2021 ($66,000 in 2021 for head of household or single taxpayers, and $0 for married filing separate), the IRA deduction is proportionately reduced over a phaseout range (fully phased out at $125,000).

   a) An individual is not labeled an active plan participant due to the status of that individual's spouse.
   b) If an individual's spouse is an active plan participant, that individual's deductible contribution will be phased out when AGI is between $198,000 and $208,000.

6) Excessive contributions may be subject to a 6% excise tax.

7) The owner of an IRA must begin receiving distributions by April 1 of the calendar year following the later of the calendar year in which the employee attains age 72 or the calendar year in which the employee retires.

8) Contributions can still be made to an IRA (up to the $6,000/$7,000 limits) even if nondeductible. This is often called a nondeductible IRA. Because there is no deduction upon contribution, and because earnings are taxed upon withdrawal, the nondeductible IRA is less advantageous than a deductible IRA or a Roth IRA. But, like a traditional IRA, a nondeductible IRA does allow earnings to grow tax-free until withdrawal.

9) IRA distributions made before age 59 1/2 are subject to taxation plus a 10% penalty tax. Some exceptions to the penalty include distributions for

   a) Death or disability
   b) Medical expenses in excess of 7.5% of AGI
   c) Qualified higher education expenses
   d) The purchase of a first home (up to $10,000)
   e) Birth or adoption of a child (up to $5,000)

b. **Roth IRAs and Roth 401(k)s**

   1) Contributions to a Roth IRA are **nondeductible**.
   2) Earnings on contributions are not taxed, provided they meet certain requirements to be considered a qualified distribution. To be a qualified distribution, the distribution must

      a) Satisfy the 5-year holding period.
         i) The distribution may not be made before the end of the 5-tax-year period.
         ii) The holding period begins with the tax year to which the contribution relates, not the year of contribution.

EXAMPLE 7-2   Roth IRA Withdrawals

A contribution made on April 6, 2017, designated as a 2016 contribution, may be withdrawn tax-free in 2021 if it is otherwise a qualified distribution.

---

      b) Meet one of four other requirements. It must be
         i) Made on or after the date on which the individual attains age 59 1/2,
         ii) Made to a beneficiary or the individual's estate on or after the individual's death,
         iii) Attributed to the individual's disability, or
         iv) To pay for qualified first-time homebuyer expenses.

3) Distributions are treated as made from contributions first; thus, no portion of a distribution is treated as attributable to earnings or, if nonqualified, includible in gross income until the total of all distributions from the Roth IRA exceeds the amount of contributions.

   a) Nonqualified distributions are included in income after recovery of contribution, and they are subject to the 10% early withdrawal penalty.

EXAMPLE 7-3   Roth IRA -- 10% Penalty

John made $6,000 in contributions to his Roth IRA over the last decade. The value of John's Roth IRA is now $9,000. If the $9,000 is distributed and the distribution is qualified, John will not owe any tax or 10% penalty. If the distribution is unqualified, John will owe taxes at his marginal tax rate on the $3,000 in earnings and will owe a penalty ($300) of 10% of the earnings.

---

4) The overall limit for contributions to IRAs, both traditional and Roth, is $6,000 ($7,000 for taxpayers age 50 and over).

5) Contributions to Roth IRAs are phased out based on AGI (i.e., you cannot contribute to a Roth above these phaseouts):

	AGI Phaseout Range
MFJ	$198,000 to $208,000
Single, Head of Household	$125,000 to $140,000
MFS	$0 to $10,000

9. **Education**

   a. **Student Loan Interest Deduction**

   From Form 1040 Schedule 1

   20 Student loan interest deduction 20

   1) Taxpayers may deduct $2,500 of interest paid on qualified educational loans in 2021. This deduction is available for each year interest is paid.

   2) The deduction is subject to income limits.

	AGI Phaseout Range
MFJ	$140,000 to $170,000
Single, HH, MFS	$70,000 to $85,000

   3) The amount of reduction in the deduction can be calculated as follows:

   $$\$2,500 \times \frac{(\text{AGI} - \$70,000)}{\$15,000 \text{ phaseout range}}$$

SU 7: Adjustments and Deductions from AGI

b. **Coverdell Education Savings Accounts (CESA)**

1) Taxpayers may make **nondeductible contributions** of $2,000 per child (beneficiary) to a CESA.
2) Contributions to CESAs are phased out based on AGI:

	AGI Phaseout Range
MFJ	$190,000 to $220,000
Single, HH, MFS	$95,000 to $110,000

3) The earnings may be distributed tax free, provided they are used for qualified education expenses.
4) This income exclusion is not available for any year in which the American Opportunity Credit or Lifetime Learning Credit is claimed.

10. **Jury Duty Pay**

From Form 1040 Schedule 1

| 22 | Add lines 10 through 21. These are your **adjustments to income.** Enter here and on Form 1040, 1040-SR, or 1040-NR, line 10a . . . . | 22 | |

a. Jury duty pay is included in gross income.
b. However, jury duty pay remitted to an employer in exchange for regular pay is an above-the-line deduction.
c. Jury duty pay is considered a "write-in" adjustment, with the description and amount required to be entered on the dotted portion of line 22.

11. **Charitable Contributions**

a. An above-the-line charitable contribution deduction of up to $300 is allowed for the 2021 tax year for individual taxpayers who do not itemize. A qualified contribution is any charitable cash contribution for which a deduction is allowable that is made to a

1) Church or association of churches;
2) Nonprofit educational organization; or
3) Nonprofit medical or hospital care organization, including one for medical education or medical research.

STOP & REVIEW

You have completed the outline for this subunit.
Study multiple-choice questions 1 through 5 beginning on page 186.

7.2 STANDARD AND ITEMIZED DEDUCTIONS

1. **Taxable Income**
   a. Taxable income is adjusted gross income (AGI) minus
      1) Itemized deductions or the standard deduction and
      2) The qualified business income deduction (QBID).
   b. Below-the-line deductions are all the deductions that may be subtracted from AGI to arrive at taxable income.

   $$\text{Taxable income} = \text{AGI} - \begin{array}{c}\text{Itemized deductions on Schedule A}\\\text{or the standard deduction}\end{array} - \text{QBID}$$

2. **Itemized vs. Standard**
   a. Generally, the taxpayer itemizes deductions if the total amount of allowable itemized deductions is greater than the amount of the standard deduction. Otherwise, the taxpayer claims the standard deduction. A taxpayer must elect to itemize, or no itemized deductions will be allowed.
      1) Election is made by filing Schedule A of Form 1040 or Form 1040-SR.
      2) Election made in any other taxable year is not relevant.
      3) Election may be changed by filing an amended return (Form 1040X).

3. **Standard Deduction Unavailable**
   a. The following taxpayers are **not allowed** the standard deduction:
      1) Persons who itemize deductions
      2) Nonresident alien individuals
      3) Individuals who file a "short period" return
      4) A married individual who files a separate return and whose spouse itemizes
      5) Partnerships, estates, and trusts
      6) Corporations

4. **Standard Deduction**

   STANDARD DEDUCTION AMOUNTS -- 2021

Filing Status	Basic	Additional Age 65/Blind
Married Filing Jointly (MFJ)	$25,100	$1,350
Qualifying Widow(er)	25,100	1,350
Head of Household (HH)	18,800	1,700
Single (other than above)	12,550	1,700
Married Filing Separately (MFS)	12,550	1,350

   a. The standard deduction is the sum of the basic standard deduction and the additional standard deductions.

SU 7: Adjustments and Deductions from AGI

b. The **basic standard deduction** amount (shown in the table on the previous page) depends on filing status and dependency status on another's return.
   1) The basic standard deduction amount of a child under age 19 or a student under age 24 who can be claimed as a dependent on another individual's income tax return is limited to the greater of either
      a) $1,100 or
      b) Earned income for the year plus $350 up to $12,550 (i.e., applicable single standard deduction).
         i) Earned income does not include either dividends or capital gains from the sale of stock.
c. **Additional standard deduction** amounts, indexed for inflation, appear in the table on the previous page.
   1) An individual who has reached age 65 or is blind is entitled to the amount.
   2) An individual who both has reached age 65 and is blind is entitled to twice the amount.
   3) The individual is entitled to the amount if (s)he reaches age 65 before the end of the tax year
      a) Even if (s)he dies before the end of the year, but
      b) Not if (s)he dies before reaching age 65 even if (s)he would have otherwise reached age 65 before year's end.
   4) A person who becomes blind on or before the last day of the taxable year is entitled to the amount.
   5) Once qualified, the standard deduction is allowed in full.
      a) It is not prorated if a person dies during a tax year.
d. As mentioned in Study Unit 3, Subunit 2, under Filing Requirements, the threshold requiring a tax return to be filed is generally the standard deduction (excluding any amount for being blind).

> **SUCCESS TIP**: Traditionally, the AICPA has heavily tested itemized deductions, mostly with questions requiring calculations. Always read the questions very carefully. A question may contain one small, easily missed detail that changes the amount of the deduction.

5. **Itemized Deductions**
   a. Schedule A is the form where itemized deductions are reported.
   b. Itemized deductions include
      1) Medical and dental expenses
      2) Taxes paid
      3) Interest paid
      4) Charitable contributions
      5) Casualty and theft losses
      6) Other itemized deductions

6. **Medical and Dental Expenses**

From Form 1040 Schedule A

Medical and Dental Expenses	**Caution:** Do not include expenses reimbursed or paid by others.		
	1 Medical and dental expenses (see instructions)	1	
	2 Enter amount from Form 1040 or 1040-SR, line 11 2		
	3 Multiply line 2 by 7.5% (0.075)	3	
	4 Subtract line 3 from line 1. If line 3 is more than line 1, enter -0-		4

    a. Amounts paid for qualified medical expenses that exceed 7.5% of AGI may be deducted.

    b. To qualify for a deduction, an expense must be paid during the taxable year for the taxpayer, the taxpayer's spouse, or a dependent and must not be compensated for by insurance or otherwise during the taxable year. The service (expense) could have been rendered (incurred) in a prior year.

    c. The expenses must be primarily to alleviate or prevent a physical or mental disability or illness.

    d. Deductible medical expenses are amounts paid for

        1) Diagnosis, cure, mitigation, treatment or prevention of disease, or for the purpose of affecting any structure or function of the body

        2) Transportation primarily for and essential to medical care

        3) Medical insurance

        4) Qualified long-term care premiums and services

    e. A medical expense deduction is not allowed for amounts paid for any activity or treatment designed merely to improve an individual's general health or sense of wellness, even if recommended by a physician.

        1) Examples include participation in a health club, a stop-smoking clinic, or a weight-loss institute.

            a) Such expenses may be deductible if the services are prescribed by a physician who provides a written statement that they are necessary to alleviate a physical or mental defect or illness.

    f. The cost of in-patient hospital care (including meals and lodging) is deductible as a medical expense.

        1) If the principal reason an individual is in an institution (e.g., nursing home, rehabilitation facility, or disability-specific school) other than a hospital is the need for and availability of the medical care furnished by the institution, the full costs of meals, lodging, and other services necessary (including special schooling) for furnishing the medical care are all deductible.

    g. Only drugs that require a prescription are qualified medical expenses.

    h. The following are also considered deductible medical expenses:

        1) Eyeglasses and contact lenses

        2) A guide dog

        3) Wheelchair, crutches, or artificial limbs

        4) Special beds

        5) Air conditioning

        6) Dehumidifying equipment

SU 7: Adjustments and Deductions from AGI

i. Expenditures for new building construction or for permanent improvements to existing structures may be deductible in part.
   1) The excess of the cost of a permanent improvement over the increase in value of the property is a deductible medical expense.
      a) Even when the cost of the capital asset is not deductible, the cost of operating and maintaining the asset may be deductible when the asset is operated primarily for medical care.
   2) Construction of ramps for the disabled, installation of elevators, widening of doorways, or lowering of kitchen cabinets or equipment may each qualify.
j. Insurance
   1) Premiums paid for medical insurance that provides for reimbursement of medical care expenses are deductible.
   2) Self-employed health insurance payments may be deducted as an above-the-line deduction.

7. **Taxes Paid**

From Form 1040 Schedule A

Taxes You Paid	5 State and local taxes.	
	a State and local income taxes or general sales taxes. You may include either income taxes or general sales taxes on line 5a, but not both. If you elect to include general sales taxes instead of income taxes, check this box . . . . ▶ ☐	5a
	b State and local real estate taxes (see instructions)	5b
	c State and local personal property taxes	5c
	d Add lines 5a through 5c	5d
	e Enter the smaller of line 5d or $10,000 ($5,000 if married filing separately)	5e
	6 Other taxes. List type and amount ▶ _____	6
	7 Add lines 5e and 6	7

a. A taxpayer who itemizes deductions is permitted to deduct the full amount of certain taxes that are paid and incurred during the taxable year, subject to the $10,000 limit on total state and local taxes.
b. Real Property
   1) The owner may deduct state and local real property taxes.
   2) If real property is bought or sold during the year, the real property tax is apportioned between the buyer and the seller on the basis of the number of days each one held the property during the real property tax year (regardless of nonproration agreements between buyers and sellers).
      a) The purchaser is presumed to own the property on the date of sale.
   3) Special assessments for local improvements increase the basis of the property and are not deductible.
c. Ad Valorem, Personal Property Taxes
   1) These state and local taxes are deductible, but only if the tax is
      a) Substantially in proportion to the value of the property,
      b) Imposed on an annual basis, and
      c) Actually imposed.

d. Income Taxes

1) State and local income taxes are deductible.
2) Foreign income taxes paid are deductible, unless the foreign tax credit is claimed.
3) Individual taxpayers may claim an itemized deduction for general state and local sales tax in lieu of state income tax. That is, either the state sales tax or the state income tax, but not both, can be claimed.

e. The sum total of deductible state and local taxes is limited to $10,000 ($5,000 for MFS).

f. The following taxes are not deductible:

1) Federal taxes on income, estates, gifts, inheritances, legacies, and successions
2) State taxes on cigarettes and tobacco, alcoholic beverages, gasoline, registration, estates, gifts, inheritances, legacies, and successions
3) Licensing fees of highway motor vehicles (if based on the weight of the vehicle)

8. **Interest Paid**

From Form 1040 Schedule A

Interest You Paid

Caution: Your mortgage interest deduction may be limited (see instructions).

8 Home mortgage interest and points. If you didn't use all of your home mortgage loan(s) to buy, build, or improve your home, see instructions and check this box . . . . ▶ ☐

a Home mortgage interest and points reported to you on Form 1098. See instructions if limited . . . . | 8a |

b Home mortgage interest not reported to you on Form 1098. See instructions if limited. If paid to the person from whom you bought the home, see instructions and show that person's name, identifying no., and address . . . .

▶ _____
_____ | 8b |

c Points not reported to you on Form 1098. See instructions for special rules . . . . | 8c |

d Mortgage insurance premiums (see instructions) . . . . | 8d |

e Add lines 8a through 8d . . . . | 8e |

9 Investment interest. Attach Form 4952 if required. See instructions . | 9 |

10 Add lines 8e and 9 . . . . | 10 |

a. **Qualified Residence Interest**

1) Qualified residence interest is deductible on no more than $750,000 of the sum of acquisition and home equity indebtedness ($375,000 if married filing separately).
2) It is interest paid or accrued during the tax year on acquisition or home equity indebtedness that is secured by a qualified residence.
3) A qualified residence includes the principal residence of the taxpayer and one other residence owned by the taxpayer.
4) A taxpayer who has more than two residences may select, each year, the residences used to determine the amount of qualified residence interest.
5) Acquisition indebtedness is debt incurred in acquiring, constructing, or substantially improving a qualified residence. The debt must be secured by the residence.
6) Home equity indebtedness is all debt other than acquisition debt that is secured by a qualified residence to the extent it does not exceed the fair market value of the residence reduced by any acquisition indebtedness. For tax years 2018-2025, the home equity debt must be used to buy, build, or substantially improve the qualified residence. This means the prior allowance to use the funds for other personal expenses, such as college tuition, is suspended until 2026.

7) Points paid by the borrower are prepaid interest, which is typically deductible over the term of the loan.
   a) Amounts paid as points may be deducted in the year paid if
      i) The loan is used to buy or improve a taxpayer's principal home and is secured by that home;
      ii) Payment of points is an established business practice in the area where the loan is made; and
      iii) The points paid do not exceed points generally charged in the area.
8) Points paid by the seller are a selling expense that reduces the amount realized on the sale.
   a) The purchaser can elect to deduct points on the acquisition indebtedness of a principal residence by reducing the basis.

b. **Investment Interest Expense**
   1) The IRC allows the deduction of a limited amount of investment interest as an itemized deduction.
   2) Investment interest is interest paid or incurred (on debt) to purchase or carry property held for investment.
   3) Investment interest does **not** include qualified residence interest or passive activity interest.
      a) Passive activity interest is includible with passive activities and deductible within the passive loss rules.
   4) Limit
      a) Investment interest may be deducted only to the extent of net investment income, which is any excess of investment income over investment expense.
      b) Investment income is
         i) Non-trade or nonbusiness income from (a) interest; (b) dividends not subject to the capital gains tax; and (c) annuities, royalties, and other gross income from property held for investment.
         ii) Net gain on the disposition of property held for investment. A taxpayer may elect to treat all or a portion of long-term capital gains and qualified dividends as investment income.
         iii) Income treated as gross portfolio income under the PAL rules.
         iv) Income from interests in activities that involve a trade or business in which the taxpayer does not materially participate, if the activity is not treated as passive activity under the PAL rules.
      c) Investment income is **not** from rental real estate activity in which the taxpayer actively participates.
   5) Disallowed investment interest is carried forward indefinitely. It is deductible to the extent of investment income in a subsequent tax year.
   6) Interest related to producing tax-exempt income is not deductible.

c. **Personal Interest Expense**
   1) The general rule is that personal interest expense may **not** be deducted.
   2) This includes interest on credit card debt, revolving charge accounts and lines of credit, car loans, medical fees, premiums, home acquisition debt greater than the allowed deduction limit, etc.
   3) Personal interest expense does not include
      a) Interest on trade or business debt
      b) Investment interest
      c) Passive activity interest
      d) Qualified residence interest
      e) Interest on the unpaid portion of certain estate taxes
      f) Student loan interest

EXAMPLE 7-4   Itemized Deductions -- Interest

A taxpayer with AGI of $100,000 made the following transactions in Year 1:
- Paid $3,000 interest on a bank loan
- Using the loan, purchased interest-bearing bonds with interest income of $10,000 in Year 1
  - No other investment income was earned in Year 1.
- Paid personal credit card interest of $650
- Paid interest in the amount of $12,000 on home mortgage for Year 1

The $15,000 total interest expense in calculating itemized deductions for Year 1 is calculated as follows:

Net investment income	$10,000	
Investment interest expense	3,000	
Deductible investment interest expense (Lesser of NII and investment interest expense)		$ 3,000
Home mortgage interest		12,000
Total interest		$15,000

NOTE: Deductible investment interest is limited to net investment income. In this example, net investment income is greater than investment interest expense, therefore the total expense of $3,000 is deductible. Credit card interest is a personal interest expense in this example and not deductible.

9. Charitable Contributions

From Form 1040 Schedule A

Gifts to Charity

Caution: If you made a gift and got a benefit for it, see instructions.

11	Gifts by cash or check. If you made any gift of $250 or more, see instructions	11
12	Other than by cash or check. If you made any gift of $250 or more, see instructions. You **must** attach Form 8283 if over $500. . . .	12
13	Carryover from prior year	13
14	Add lines 11 through 13	14

a. A nonitemizer can claim up to $300 of charitable contributions as an above-the-line deduction. If the taxpayer itemizes, all charitable contributions are deducted on Schedule A (Itemized Deductions).

b. Charitable contributions are deductible only if they are made to qualified organizations.

c. Qualified organizations can be either public charities or private foundations.

   1) Generally, a public charity is one that derives more than one-third of its support from its members and the general public.

d. Donations can be made in the form of cash or noncash property.

e. Individuals may carry forward excess contributions for 5 years.

f. All rights and interest to the donation must be transferred to the qualified organization.

g. Additional donation requirements:

   1) Clothing and household items donated must be in good or better condition.

      a) The exception to this rule is that a single item donation in less than good condition but still a $500 value or more is deductible with a qualified appraisal.

   2) Cash or cash equivalent donations require a bank record alone or a receipt, letter, etc., from the donee regardless of the amount. These must

      a) Be provided at the time of donation,
      b) State the name of the organization, and
      c) Include the date and amount of the donation.

   3) Donations of $250 or more continue to require substantiation by a written receipt from the organization (the bank record alone is insufficient).

   4) A qualified appraisal for real property donations is required to be attached to the tax return for property valued over $5,000.

h. If a donation is in the form of property, the amount of the donation depends on the type of property and the type of organization that receives the property.

   1) Capital gain property is property on which a long-term capital gain would be recognized if it were sold on the date of the contribution.

   2) Ordinary income property is property on which ordinary income or short-term capital gain would be recognized if it were sold on the date of the contribution.

Examples of Charitable Contributions

Deductible as Charitable Contributions	Not Deductible as Charitable Contributions

Donations to
 	
    Churches, synagogues, temples, mosques, and other religious organizations
 	
    Federal, state, and local governments, if the taxpayer's contribution is solely for public purposes (for example, a gift to reduce the public debt or maintain a public park)
 	
    Nonprofit schools and hospitals
 	
    The Salvation Army, American Red Cross, CARE, Goodwill Industries, United Way, Boy Scouts of America, Girl Scouts of America, Boys and Girls Clubs of America, etc.
 	
    War veterans' groups
 	
Expenses paid for a student living with the taxpayer, sponsored by a qualified organization
 	
Out-of-pocket expenses when the taxpayer serves a qualified organization as a volunteer
	Donations to
	
	    Civic leagues, social and sports clubs, labor unions, and chambers of commerce
	
	    Foreign organizations (exceptions exist)
	
	    Groups that are run for personal profit
	
	    Groups whose purpose is to lobby for law changes
	
	    Homeowners' associations
	
	    Individuals
	
	    Political groups or candidates for public office
	
	Cost of raffle, bingo, or lottery tickets
	
	Dues, fees, or bills paid to country clubs, lodges, fraternal orders, or similar groups
	
	Tuition
	
	Cost for rights to buy tickets at an athletic event (including at a college or university)
	
	Value of the taxpayer's time or services
	
	Value of blood given to a blood bank

SU 7: Adjustments and Deductions from AGI

i. There are basically two types of charitable organizations: those classified as **50% limit organizations** and those classified as **non-50% limit organizations**.
   1) 50% limit organizations, which encompass the majority of qualified charitable organizations, are generally public organizations. The following list represents some 50% organizations (IRS Publication 526 contains a complete, detailed list):
      a) Churches
      b) Educational organizations
      c) Hospitals and certain medical research organizations
      d) Organizations that are operated only to receive, hold, invest, and administer property and to make expenditures to or for the benefit of state and municipal colleges and universities
      e) The United States or any state, the District of Columbia, a U.S. possession (including Puerto Rico), a political subdivision of a state or U.S. possession, or an Indian tribal government
      f) Private operating foundations
      g) Private nonoperating foundations that make qualifying distributions of 100% of contributions within 2 1/2 months following the year they receive the contribution
   2) Non-50% limit organizations are all qualified charities that are not designated as 50% limit organizations.
      a) They are generally other private organizations.
j. Charitable contribution deductions are subject to limitations.
   1) The overall limitation on charitable deductions is 50% (60% for cash contributions) of AGI (applicable to the total of all charitable contributions during the year), but certain contributions may be further limited to 30% or 20% of AGI, depending on the type of contribution given and the type of organization to which it is given.
      a) The table on the next page summarizes the limitations.
      b) The limitation for certain cash contributions paid in 2021 has been suspended for taxpayers who itemize deductions. Taxpayers may deduct up to the amount by which their contribution base (AGI without regard to NOL carrybacks) exceeds the deduction for other charitable contributions. This covers the vast majority of contributions, i.e., those made to churches, nonprofit educational and medical institutions, and public charities.
   2) Any donations that exceed this limitation can be carried forward and potentially deducted in the next 5 tax years.
   3) Further limitations:
      a) 30% limitation. A 30% limit applies to gifts to all qualified charitable organizations other than 50% limit organizations.
      b) Special 30% limitation for capital gain property. A special 30% limitation applies to gifts of capital gain property given to 50% limit organizations. (Study Unit 9, Subunit 3, defines capital assets.)
         i) It is only applicable if the donor elects **not** to reduce the fair market value of the donated property by the amount that would have been long-term capital gain if (s)he had sold the property.
         ii) If the reduction is elected, only the 50% [60% (100% in 2021) for cash contributions] limitation applies.

c) 20% limitation. This limitation applies to capital gain property donated to non-50% limit charities. The limit is actually the lesser of 20% of AGI or 30% of AGI minus capital gain contributions to public charities.
d) In accounting for the different limitations, all donations subject to the 50% [60% (100% in 2021) for cash contributions] limit are considered before the donations subject to the 30% limit.
e) In carrying over excess contributions to subsequent tax years, the excess must be carried over to the appropriate limitation categories. If a contribution in the 30% category is in excess of the limit, the excess is carried over and subject to the 30% limitation in the next year.

k. The value of services provided to a charitable organization is not deductible.
   1) However, out-of-pocket, unreimbursed expenses incurred in rendering the services are deductible.
l. The value of a ticket to a charitable event is a deductible contribution to the extent the purchase price exceeds the FMV of the event's admission.
m. Generally, a deduction is allowed in the year the contribution is paid, including amounts charged to a bank credit card.
n. Up to $50 per month of actual expenses incurred for maintaining a qualified student may be deducted if there is a written agreement with the sponsoring charitable organization.

Form of Property	Amount of Donation	Limitation
50% Limit Organizations (Mainly Public)		
Cash	Cash amount	60% AGI (100% in 2021)
Capital Gain Property	FMV (elect not to reduce FMV by potential long-term capital gain)	30% AGI (special limit)
• Tangible personal property unrelated to donee's purpose	Lower of FMV or AB	50% AGI
• Election to reduce property to adjusted basis	Lower of FMV or AB	50% AGI
Ordinary Income Property	Lower of FMV or AB	50% AGI
Services	Unreimbursed expenses	50% AGI
Non-50% Limit Organizations (Mainly Private)		
Cash	Cash amount	30% AGI (regular limit)
Capital Gain Property	Lower of FMV or AB	Lesser of: 20% AGI or excess of 30% AGI over contributions to public charities
Ordinary Income Property	Lower of FMV or AB	30% AGI (regular limit)
Services	Unreimbursed expenses	30% AGI (regular limit)

> **EXAMPLE 7-5   Charitable Contribution Deduction**
>
> A single taxpayer had AGI of $80,000 in Year 6. On June 5, Year 6, the taxpayer donated land and stock to a church. The taxpayer purchased the land as an investment in Year 1 for $5,000 and purchased the stock on January 14, Year 6, for $1,500. On the day of donation, the land's fair market value was $9,000 and the stock's fair market value was $1,860. Calculate the taxpayer's charitable contribution deduction for Year 6.
>
> The charitable contribution deduction in the amount of $10,500 is calculated as follows:
>
> | Property | Form of Property | Nature of Deduction | Deductible Amount |
> |---|---|---|---|
> | Land held for investment greater than 1 year | Capital gain property | FMV | $ 9,000 |
> | Stock held for investment less than 1 year | Ordinary income property | Lower of FMV or adjusted basis | 1,500 |
> | **Total deductible contribution** | | | **$10,500** |

10. Casualty and Theft Losses

From Form 1040 Schedule A

Casualty and Theft Losses   15   Casualty and theft loss(es) from a federally declared disaster (other than net qualified disaster losses). Attach Form 4684 and enter the amount from line 18 of that form. See instructions . . . . |15|

    a. Generally, the itemized deduction for personal casualty and theft losses for tax years 2018 through 2025 has been suspended. Exceptions to the suspension include

        1) Losses attributed to a federally declared disaster and
        2) Non-federally declared disaster losses limited to casualty gains.

    b. Limitations

        1) Only the amount of loss over $100 is deductible.
        2) Only the aggregate amount of all losses in excess of 10% of AGI is deductible.

11. Other Itemized Deductions

From Form 1040 Schedule A

Other Itemized Deductions	16 Other—from list in instructions. List type and amount ▶ _____	16

a. The following expenses are deductible as other itemized deductions:

1) Amortizable premium on taxable bonds
2) Casualty and theft losses from income-producing property
3) Federal estate tax on income in respect of a decedent
4) Gambling losses up to the amount of gambling winnings
5) Impairment-related work expenses of persons with disabilities
6) Repayments of more than $3,000 under a claim of right
7) Unrecovered investment in a pension

12. Recovery of Tax Benefits

a. Recovery of a tax benefit item is generally included in gross income.

b. The recovered amount is included in income to the extent total allowable itemized deductions (for the applicable year) exceed the standard deduction (for the same year).

EXAMPLE 7-6   Recovery of Tax Benefit

Anne deducted $6,000 in state and local taxes on her 2020 Schedule A. Anne's total itemized deductions were $13,400 ($1,000 more than the $12,400 standard deduction in effect during 2020). If Anne receives a $1,500 state and local tax refund in 2021 (i.e., on the 2020 return filed in 2021), $1,000 of the refund will be taxable on her 2021 federal return under the tax benefit rule. Only $1,000 is taxable because this is the amount that actually produced a tax benefit. The remaining $500 is not included in gross income because it did not produce a tax benefit (Anne could have taken the standard deduction instead of deducting the recovered $500).

STOP & REVIEW

You have completed the outline for this subunit.
Study multiple-choice questions 6 through 15 beginning on page 188.

7.3 QUALIFIED BUSINESS INCOME DEDUCTION (QBID)

From Form 1040

| 13 | Qualified business income deduction. Attach Form 8995 or Form 8995-A . . . . | 13 | |

1. **Qualified Business Income Deduction (Section 199A)**

    a. Because of the low, flat tax rate of 21% for C corporations, the qualified business income deduction (QBID) was created to provide similar tax reductions to pass-through business entities (sole proprietorships, S corporations, and partnerships).

    b. The QBID is available to noncorporate taxpayers (e.g., individuals, trusts, estates) and is generally equal to 20% of qualified business income (QBI). This subunit focuses on the QBID in the context of individual taxpayers—the setting the CPA Exam is most likely to test.

    1) The impact of this deduction, when fully available, is to make 20% of qualifying income nontaxable.

    c. The QBID is a below-the-line deduction (deduction from AGI), but it is not an itemized deduction. Thus, the QBID can be paired with either the standard deduction or itemized deductions.

2. **Qualifying Business Income (QBI)**

    a. Conceptually, Congress's intent was to use the QBID to incentivize small business owners to grow their core business rather than speculate on side ventures unrelated to their main business objectives. Therefore, income from non-core activities is not considered QBI.

    b. To calculate the QBI and, ultimately, the QBID, the following steps must be performed:

    1) Ensure the income is effectively connected with the conduct of a trade or business within the United States or Puerto Rico **and** is included in the determination of taxable income for the tax year.

        a) Income disallowed or limited by tax basis, at-risk, passive losses, and excess business loss rules (TAPE) is not included in taxable income for determining QBI.

    2) Ensure the income comes from a flow-through entity. These include

        a) Sole proprietorships (reported on Schedule C of Form 1040)
        b) Partnerships (reported on Form 1065)
        c) S corporations (reported on Form 1120-S)

3) Further reduce the net income by items
    a) From non-core activities, such as
        i) Capital gains and losses
        ii) Dividend income
        iii) Nonoperating interest income
        iv) Interest income attributable to working capital
        v) Foreign currency gains (in excess of gains of core businesses)
    b) From businesses as reasonable compensation, such as
        i) Salaries and wages from S corporations
        ii) Guaranteed payments from partnerships

EXAMPLE 7-7   Compensation

Aly is a 50% owner of ABC, Inc. (an S corporation). Aly is also the president of ABC. For her services as president, Aly receives a salary of $200,000. Aly's salary will not constitute QBI. However, her 50% share of the corporation's ordinary income will constitute QBI.

---

3. **Computation of QBID**
    a. The **overall QBID limitation** is the **lesser of**
        1) 20% × Qualified business income, or
        2) 20% × (Taxable income – Net capital gains).
            a) Net capital gains is defined as net long-term capital gains in excess of any net short-term capital loss. This income is excluded because this income is already taxed at preferential rates.
    b. For taxpayers above certain taxable income thresholds, the overall QBID limitation applies after the specific limitations discussed on the following pages have been applied.

4. **Additional Considerations**
    a. Specified Service Trades or Businesses (SSTBs)
        1) For taxpayers above the taxable income threshold discussed in item b. on page 182, certain types of business income are disqualified from being QBI and are referred to as income from SSTBs.

2) Generally, SSTB refers to trades or businesses where the principal asset is the reputation of one or more of its employees or owners.

   a) Examples of SSTBs include
      i) Health (e.g., physicians, nurses, dentists)
      ii) Law
      iii) Accounting
      iv) Actuarial science
      v) Performing arts
      vi) Consulting
      vii) Athletics
      viii) Financial services (e.g., financial advisors, wealth planners, retirement advisors, investment bankers)
      ix) Brokerage services
      x) Any trade or business where the principal asset of such trade or business is the reputation or skill of one or more of its employees or owners.

      NOTE: While the provision of reputation as a principal asset sounds like it could encompass many businesses, regulations indicate that the Treasury will only interpret this provision to include businesses that generate income from (1) endorsements, (2) compensation for use of one's likeness, and (3) appearance fees.

EXAMPLE 7-8   Reputation and Skill

Bill owns Bill's Plumbing, a sole proprietorship. Bill's Plumbing's motto is "Bill is a very skilled plumber with a great reputation." According to the regulations, because Bill's Plumbing does not involve endorsements, compensation for use of one's likeness, or appearance fees, Bill's Plumbing's principal asset is not the reputation or skill of one or more of its employees or owners. Thus, Bill's Plumbing is not considered a specified service business.

---

   b) While many categories of professional services are classified as SSTBs, Congress specifically excluded (1) architecture and (2) engineering from SSTBs.

EXAMPLE 7-9   SSTB

Danny is a partner at XYZ, LLP, a public accounting firm. Danny is single with taxable income of $500,000. Because Danny's taxable income is above the taxable income threshold, the specified service business limitation applies. Thus, because XYZ is a specified service business (and Danny's taxable income is above the phase-in range), XYZ's business income is not QBI and thus is not eligible for the QBID. However, if Danny's taxable income had instead been $100,000, XYZ's business income would have been eligible for the QBID because the specified service business limitation would not have applied.

3) A flow-through entity not considered an SSTB is a qualified trade or business (QTB).
4) Regulations have been issued that define how much of a specified service activity will render an entire business as an SSTB. Under this de minimis rule, if gross receipts of a business are $25 million or less for the current tax year, then up to 10% of gross receipts can be attributable to a specified service without the overall business being considered a specified service business. For businesses with gross receipts greater than $25 million, the de minimis threshold is 5%.

EXAMPLE 7-10   SSTB De Minimus Rule

Acme, Inc. (an S corporation), is primarily a retailer with $24 million in gross receipts during the current year. Of Acme's $24 million in gross receipts, $22 million comes from retail activities and $2 million comes from consulting. Consulting is a specified service. However, because Acme's gross receipts are below $25 million, Acme will only be considered a specified service business if greater than 10% of its total gross receipts come from specified services. In this case, because less than 10% of Acme's gross receipts come from consulting, Acme is not considered a specified service business under the de minimis rule.

---

b. Taxable Income Thresholds
1) QBID limitations apply when the taxable income reaches the threshold. For 2021, the lower threshold is $329,800 for married filing jointly taxpayers and $164,900 for single filers. The upper threshold is $429,800 for married filing jointly taxpayers and $214,900 for single filers.
   a) If the taxable income is below the lower threshold, no limitation to QBID except the overall exception applies.
   b) If the taxable income is above the upper threshold,
      i) There is no QBID for SSTBs.
      ii) The QBID is limited based on wages paid and/or property owned.
   c) If the taxable income falls between the lower and upper thresholds, application of the above limitations is phased in.

c. Wages and Property Limitations
1) If the taxable income of a taxpayer exceeds the lower taxable income threshold, the QBID is further limited by the wages and property limitations (W-2 limits).
2) The W-2 limit is the greater of
   a) 50% of W-2 wages paid or
   b) 25% of W-2 wages paid plus 2.5% of the unadjusted basis of qualifying property immediately after acquisition.
      i) Qualifying property is generally depreciable property. Land is not depreciable and is thus excluded.

SU 7: Adjustments and Deductions from AGI

5. The following flowchart outlines the computation of QBID per entity.

QUALIFIED BUSINESS INCOME DEDUCTION

Taxable Income*

Lower Threshold
- ≤ $164,900 Single
- ≤ $329,800 Married Filing Jointly

Any income from either
1) Qualified trade or business or
2) Specified service trade or business

- No → **No QBI Deduction Allowed**
- Yes → **QBI Deduction Allowed** → Multiply qualified business income (QBI) by 0.2 to arrive at the taxpayer's allowed QBI.

Phase-in Range of W-2 Wage Limit
Income between lower and upper threshold

- Income from qualified trade or business → Conduct the following W-2 Wage Limit Test
- Income from specified service trade or business → Conduct the following W-2 Wage Limit Test

Step 1: Calculate Reduction Ratio

Single
$$= \frac{\text{Taxable income} - \$164,900}{\$50,000}$$

Married Filing Jointly
$$= \frac{\text{Taxable income} - \$329,800}{\$100,000}$$

Step 2: Calculate Applicable Percentage
= 100% − Reduction ratio

Step 3: Apply Applicable Percentage
Includible QBI = QBI × Applicable %
Includible wages = Wages × Applicable %
Includible unadjusted = Unadjusted basis immediately after acquisition

Step 4: Calculate W-2 Limit
Greater of
- 50% includible wages or
- 25% includible wages + 2.5% includible unadjusted basis immediately after acquisition

If W-2 limit > 20% × QBI, then QBI allowed = 20% × QBI. Otherwise, continue below.

Step 5: Calculate Excess Amount
= (0.2 × Includible QBI) − W-2 limit

Step 6: Calculate Allowed QBI Amount
= (0.2 × Includible QBI) − (Reduction ratio × Excess amount)

For qualified trade or business path (phase-in):

Step 2: Calculate W-2 Limit
Greater of
- 50% all employee wages or
- 25% wages + 2.5% unadjusted basis immediately after acquisition

Step 3: Calculate Excess Amount
= (0.2 × QBI) − W-2 limit

Step 4: Calculate Allowed QBI Amount
= (0.2 × QBI) − (Reduction ratio × Excess amount)

Upper Threshold
- ≥ $214,900 Single
- ≥ $429,800 Married Filing Jointly

- Income from specified service trade or business → **No QBI Deduction Allowed**
- Income from qualified trade or business → **QBI Deduction Allowed** → Conduct the following W-2 Wage Limit Test

Step 1: Calculate W-2 Limit
Greater of
- 50% all employee wages or
- 25% wages + 2.5% unadjusted basis immediately after acquisition

Step 2: QBI Allowed Equals
Lesser of
- 20% of QBI or
- W-2 limit

*Taxable income equals adjusted gross income (line 8b of Form 1040) minus standard or itemized deductions (line 9 of Form 1040).

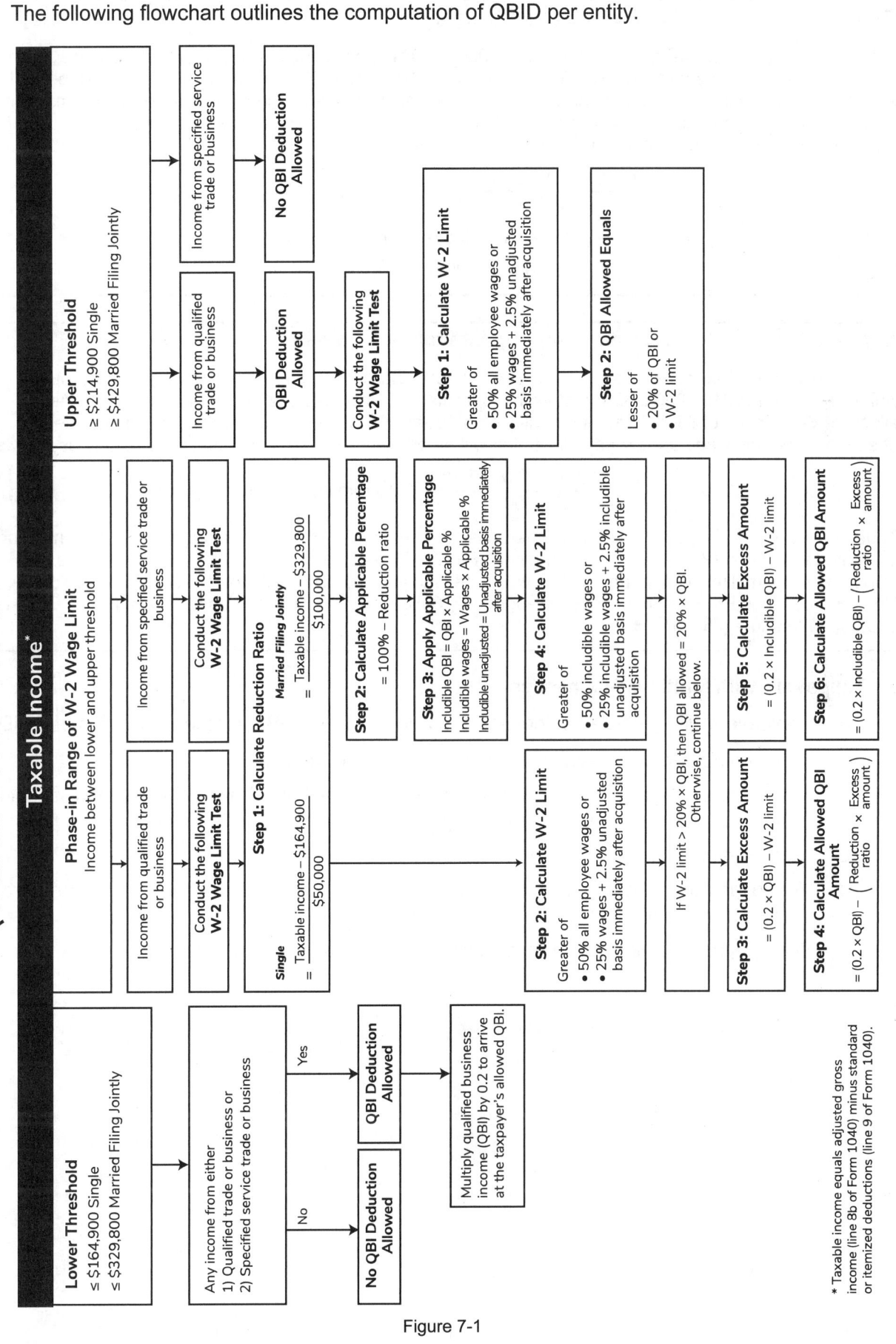

Figure 7-1

> **EXAMPLE 7-11   SSTB Limitation Phase-In**
>
> Earl, a single taxpayer, has taxable income of $199,900. Thus, he is subject to the specified service business limitation and the wages and property limitation. Earl has $100,000 of business income that would be QBI but for the fact it was generated by a specified service business. However, because Earl's taxable income is in the phase-in range, he will be eligible for a partial QBID. Assuming Earl is not also limited by the wages and property limitation, his partial deduction would be computed as follows:
>
> $$\frac{\$199{,}900 - \$164{,}900}{\$50{,}000} = 70\% \text{ reduction ratio}$$
>
> $$(1 - 70\%) \times \$100{,}000 = \$30{,}000 \text{ of QBI}$$
>
> $$\$30{,}000 \times 20\% = \$6{,}000 \text{ QBID}$$

> **EXAMPLE 7-12   Wage and Property Limitation Phase-In**
>
> Fran, a single taxpayer, has taxable income of $179,900. Thus, she is subject to the wages and property limitation. Fran has $100,000 of QBI (not from a specified service business). However, Fran only has allocable W-2 wages of $30,000 and no qualifying property. Because Fran's taxable income is in the phase-in range, the wage and property limitation will be phased in. Fran's deduction is computed as follows:
>
> $$\frac{\$179{,}900 - \$164{,}900}{\$50{,}000} = 30\% \text{ reduction ratio}$$
>
> Thus, any wage and property limitation will be phased in by 30%. In other words, only 30% of any limitation computed will apply. Therefore, Fran's tentative QBID is $20,000 ($100,000 × 20%). However, under the wage and property limitation, her deduction would be limited to $15,000, a limitation (decrease) of $5,000. However, because Fran is in the phase-in range, only 30% of this limitation will apply. Thus, Fran's QBID is $18,500 [$20,000 – ($5,000 × 30%)].

6. **Taxpayers with Multiple Businesses**

    a. Taxpayers with multiple businesses can aggregate the QBIs for the calculation of QBID if

    1) All aggregated businesses have the same tax year and
    2) The same taxpayer or group of persons (e.g., a family) owns 50% of more of each trade or business after satisfying certain criteria.

    b. Aggregation is only allowed for QTBs.

    c. An advantage of aggregation is that it allows QTBs with insufficient wages and property to use those of other QTBs to generate a larger QBID.

    d. If aggregation is elected, QBIs for subsequent years must be aggregated.

7. **QBI Loss Carryover**

   a. If the net QBI for the year from all entities is negative, the QBI is treated as a qualified business loss (QBL).

   b. QBLs are carried forward to later years (losses cannot be carried back). QBL carryforwards reduce the amount of QBI in the later years.

   c. A QBL carryforward is used only to compute future QBIDs. It does not affect the determination of whether a business loss is deductible in the computation of taxable income (e.g., a net operating loss).

> **EXAMPLE 7-13**   **Carryover**
>
> Charlie has QBI in 2020 of negative $100. This $(100) is a QBL that will carry forward to 2021. If Charlie has a positive QBI of $500 in 2021, the amount eligible for the QBID will be reduced by the $100 QBL carryforward. Thus, Charlie's maximum QBID would be $80 [20% × ($500 – $100)].

8. **Other Sec. 199A Rules**

   a. The Sec. 199A deduction does not affect the taxpayer's basis in the pass-through entity.

STOP & REVIEW

You have completed the outline for this subunit.
Study multiple-choice questions 16 through 19 beginning on page 192.

QUESTIONS

7.1 Above-the-Line Deductions

1. In 2021, a self-employed taxpayer had gross income of $57,000. The taxpayer paid self-employment tax of $8,000, health insurance of $6,000, and $5,000 of alimony per a 2018 divorce agreement. The taxpayer also contributed $2,000 to a traditional IRA. What is the taxpayer's adjusted gross income?

A. $55,000
B. $50,000
C. $46,000
D. $40,000

Answer (D) is correct.
REQUIRED: The taxpayer's AGI.
DISCUSSION: In 2021, self-employed individuals can deduct 50% of FICA taxes paid and 100% of payments made for health insurance coverage for the individual and his or her family. Alimony is gross income to the recipient and deductible by the payor. Contributions of up to $6,000 to an individual retirement account are deductible. The taxpayer's AGI is $40,000 [$57,000 GI – $4,000 SE tax paid – $6,000 health insurance – $5,000 alimony (paid pursuant to a pre-2019 divorce) – $2,000 contribution to IRA].
Answer (A) is incorrect. Self-employment taxes and health insurance, along with alimony paid, also reduce gross income to arrive at AGI. **Answer (B) is incorrect.** Self-employment taxes and health insurance paid also reduce gross income to arrive at AGI. **Answer (C) is incorrect.** Self-employment health insurance paid also reduces gross income to arrive at AGI.

2. A 33-year-old taxpayer withdrew $30,000 (pretax) from a traditional IRA. The taxpayer has a 28% effective tax rate and a 35% marginal tax rate. What is the total tax liability associated with the withdrawal?

A. $10,000
B. $10,500
C. $13,000
D. $13,500

Answer (D) is correct.
REQUIRED: The tax liability associated with an early distribution from a traditional IRA.
DISCUSSION: IRA distributions made before age 59 1/2 are subject to taxation as well as a 10% penalty. Each amount is calculated based on the distribution. No penalty is applied if the distribution is used for death or disability, medical expenses in excess of the percent limitation, the purchase of a first home (up to $10,000), higher education expenses, or the birth or adoption of a child (up to $5,000). None of these circumstances are applicable; therefore, the tax and penalty apply to the entire $30,000. The applicable tax rate is 35% for a tax liability of $10,500 ($30,000 × 35%), which is added to the penalty of $3,000 ($30,000 × 10%), for a total of $13,500.
Answer (A) is incorrect. Early distributions from a traditional IRA must be taxed as well as penalized. **Answer (B) is incorrect.** In addition to the tax at a rate of 35%, a 10% penalty is also applicable. **Answer (C) is incorrect.** The tax rate used should be the marginal rate, not the effective rate.

SU 7: Adjustments and Deductions from AGI

3. With regard to tax recognition of alimony paid in 2021 per a 2018 divorce, which one of the following statements is true?

A. The divorced couple may be members of the same household when payments are made.
B. Payments may be made in cash or property.
C. If the payor spouse pays premiums for insurance on his life as a requirement under the divorce agreement, the premiums are alimony if the payor spouse owns the policy.
D. Payments must terminate at the death of the payee spouse.

Answer (D) is correct.
REQUIRED: The amounts deductible as alimony.
DISCUSSION: Only amounts that are required to be included as gross income of the recipient as alimony are deductible by the payor in calculating AGI. A component of the alimony definition is that the payor has no liability to make the payment for any period after the death of the payee spouse.
Answer (A) is incorrect. Alimony consists of payments when the payor and payee are not members of the same household. **Answer (B) is incorrect.** Alimony payments must be made in cash. **Answer (C) is incorrect.** The payments are not made to the payee spouse (the payor spouse owns the policy).

4. In the current year, an unmarried individual with modified adjusted gross income of $25,000 paid $1,000 interest on a qualified education loan entered into on July 1. How may the individual treat the interest for income tax purposes?

A. As a $500 deduction to arrive at AGI for the year.
B. As a $1,000 deduction to arrive at AGI for the year.
C. As a $1,000 itemized deduction.
D. As a nondeductible item of personal interest.

Answer (B) is correct.
REQUIRED: The treatment of interest paid for qualified higher education loans.
DISCUSSION: Taxpayers may deduct up to $2,500 of interest paid on qualified educational loans. The deduction is subject to income limits. The phaseout range begins when AGI exceeds $70,000 for unmarried individuals and ends at $85,000. The deduction is taken above-the-line to arrive at AGI for the year.
Answer (A) is incorrect. The reduction in the deduction does not begin until AGI exceeds $70,000. **Answer (C) is incorrect.** The deduction is taken above-the-line to arrive at AGI for the year. **Answer (D) is incorrect.** Taxpayers may take an above-the-line deduction up to $2,500 of interest paid on qualified educational loans.

5. Dale received $1,000 in 2021 for jury duty. In exchange for regular compensation from her employer during the period of jury service, Dale was required to remit the entire $1,000 to her employer in 2021. In Dale's 2021 income tax return, the $1,000 jury duty fee should be

A. Claimed in full as an itemized deduction.
B. Claimed as an other itemized deduction.
C. Deducted from gross income in arriving at adjusted gross income.
D. Included in taxable income without a corresponding offset against other income.

Answer (C) is correct.
REQUIRED: The deductibility of jury duty pay.
DISCUSSION: Pay for jury duty is compensation gross income. Jury duty pay remitted to an employer (in return for being paid during the duty) is deductible for AGI.

7.2 Standard and Itemized Deductions

6. Which of the following requirements must be met in order for a single individual to qualify for an additional standard deduction?

	Must Be Age 65 or Older or Blind	Must Support Dependent Child or Aged Parent
A.	Yes	Yes
B.	No	No
C.	Yes	No
D.	No	Yes

Answer (C) is correct.
REQUIRED: The requirement for a single individual to qualify for the additional standard deduction.
DISCUSSION: An additional standard deduction is allowed for a taxpayer if, during the year, the taxpayer is age 65 or over or blind. The respective amounts are doubled if the taxpayer is both elderly and blind. Support of a dependent is not a condition for an increase to the standard deduction.
Answer (A) is incorrect. The additional standard deduction amount is not available to single individuals merely supporting a dependent child or aged parent. Answer (B) is incorrect. The additional standard deduction amount is available to individuals 65 (or over) or blind. Answer (D) is incorrect. The additional standard deduction amount is available for taxpayers who are age 65 or over or blind.

7. In 2021, Moore, a single taxpayer, had $50,000 in adjusted gross income. During 2021, she contributed $23,000 in cash to her church. She had a $10,000 charitable contribution carryover from her 2020 church contribution. What was the maximum amount of properly substantiated charitable contributions that Moore could claim as an itemized deduction for 2021?

A. $10,000
B. $23,000
C. $30,000
D. $33,000

Answer (D) is correct.
REQUIRED: The amount of deductible charitable contributions.
DISCUSSION: The limitation for certain cash contributions paid in 2021 has been suspended for taxpayers who itemize deductions. Taxpayers may deduct up to the amount by which their contribution base (AGI without regard to NOL carrybacks) exceeds the deduction for other charitable contributions. Moore's charitable cash contribution deduction in 2021 is limited to 100% of AGI ($50,000), less deductions for other noncash contributions made. As there are no other contributions in 2021, the $23,000 cash contribution to the church may be deducted. The 2020 cash contribution is also limited to 100% of AGI. Thus, the entire $10,000 of carryover is deductible.

8. In 2021, the Browns borrowed $20,000, secured by their home, to pay their son's college tuition. At the time of the loan, the fair market value of their home was $400,000, and it was unencumbered by other debt. The interest on the loan qualifies as

A. Deductible personal interest.
B. Deductible qualified residence interest.
C. Nondeductible interest.
D. Investment interest expense.

Answer (C) is correct.
REQUIRED: The nature and deductibility of interest.
DISCUSSION: Qualified residence interest is deductible. It is interest paid or accrued during the tax year on home acquisition or home equity indebtedness. Home equity indebtedness is all debt other than acquisition debt that is secured by a qualified residence to the extent it does not exceed the fair market value of the residence, reduced by any acquisition indebtedness. However, for tax years 2018-2025, the home equity debt must be used to buy, build, or substantially improve a qualified residence. Therefore, the Browns may not deduct the interest.
Answer (A) is incorrect. Personal interest is generally not deductible. Answer (B) is incorrect. The interest is not deductible as it is not used to buy, build, or improve a qualified residence. Answer (D) is incorrect. It is not investment interest.

SU 7: Adjustments and Deductions from AGI

9. In 2021, Smith paid $6,000 to the tax collector of Big City for realty taxes on a two-family house owned by Smith's mother. Of this amount, $2,800 covered back taxes for 2020, and $3,200 covered 2021 taxes. Smith resides on the second floor of the house, and his mother resides on the first floor. In Smith's itemized deductions on his 2021 return, what amount was Smith entitled to claim for realty taxes?

A. $6,000
B. $3,200
C. $3,000
D. $0

10. In 2021, Welch paid the following expenses:

Premiums on an insurance policy against loss of earnings due to sickness or accident	$3,000
Physical therapy after spinal surgery	2,000
Premium on an insurance policy that covers reimbursement for the cost of prescription drugs	500

In 2021, Welch recovered $1,500 of the $2,000 that she paid for physical therapy through insurance reimbursement from a group medical policy paid for by her employer. Disregarding the adjusted gross income percentage threshold, what amount could be claimed on Welch's 2021 income tax return for medical expenses?

A. $4,000
B. $3,500
C. $1,000
D. $500

Answer (D) is correct.
REQUIRED: The amount of deductible property taxes.
DISCUSSION: Taxes may be deducted only by the person on whom they are legally levied or by someone with a legally recognized interest in the property. Smith does not own the house, therefore none of the taxes paid can be deducted on his tax return and the payment is treated as a gift to Smith's mother. Smith's mother is entitled to the deduction only if she pays the taxes.
Answer (A) is incorrect. The total amount of taxes are not levied on Smith. **Answer (B) is incorrect.** Had Smith owned the property, the deduction would not have been limited to current taxes. Assuming he is a cash-basis taxpayer, the deductions are taken when amounts are paid. **Answer (C) is incorrect.** The IRC generally does not allow a deduction for paying the liability of another. It is treated as a gift.

Answer (C) is correct.
REQUIRED: The amount of deductible medical expenses.
DISCUSSION: Medical expenses are deductible to the extent they exceed 7.5% of AGI. Medical care expenses include amounts paid for the diagnosis, cure, medication, treatment, or prevention of a disease or physical handicap or for the purpose of affecting any structure or function of the body. The term medical care also includes amounts paid for insurance covering medical care. However, the amount deductible for expenses incurred for medical care is reduced by the amount of reimbursements. The cost of insurance against loss of earnings is not deductible. Therefore, deductible medical expenses are $1,000 [($2,000 – $1,500 reimbursement) + $500].
Answer (A) is incorrect. The cost of insurance against loss of earnings is not deductible. **Answer (B) is incorrect.** The cost of insurance against loss of earnings is not deductible. The cost of insurance for medical care, which includes the cost of prescription drugs, is deductible. **Answer (D) is incorrect.** The cost of insurance covering medical expenses is deductible.

11.
The 2021 deduction by an individual taxpayer for interest on investment indebtedness is

A. Limited to investment interest paid in 2021.
B. Limited to the taxpayer's 2021 interest income.
C. Limited to the taxpayer's 2021 net investment income.
D. Not limited.

Answer (C) is correct.
REQUIRED: The true statement concerning limits on deductibility of interest on investment indebtedness.
DISCUSSION: The deduction for interest on investment indebtedness is limited to the amount of net investment income for the taxable year. Any disallowed investment interest may be carried over and treated as investment interest paid or accrued in the succeeding taxable year.
Answer (A) is incorrect. Interest on investment indebtedness is deductible only to the extent of net investment income for the taxable year, not investment interest paid. **Answer (B) is incorrect.** The deduction for interest on investment indebtedness is not tied to general interest income. **Answer (D) is incorrect.** The deduction for interest on investment indebtedness is limited.

12.
Which of the following is **not** an itemized deduction?

A. Gambling losses up to the amount of gambling winnings.
B. Medical expenses.
C. Real estate tax.
D. Employee business expenses.

Answer (D) is correct.
REQUIRED: The nonitemized deduction.
DISCUSSION: The miscellaneous itemized deductions subject to a 2%-of-AGI exclusion were suspended after 2017. The three categories of these miscellaneous itemized deductions were employee expenses, tax determination expenses, and other expenses.
Answer (A) is incorrect. Gambling losses up to the amount of gambling winnings are reported on Schedule A as an other itemized deduction. **Answer (B) is incorrect.** Medical expenses are itemized deductions subject to a 7.5% of AGI floor. **Answer (C) is incorrect.** Real estate taxes are itemized deductions.

13.
Jimet, an unmarried taxpayer, qualified to itemize 2021 deductions. Jimet's 2021 adjusted gross income was $30,000, and he made a $2,000 cash donation directly to a needy family. In 2021, Jimet also donated stock, valued at $3,000, to his church. Jimet had purchased the stock 4 months earlier for $1,500. What was the maximum amount of the charitable contribution allowable as an itemized deduction on Jimet's 2021 income tax return?

A. $0
B. $1,500
C. $2,000
D. $5,000

Answer (B) is correct.
REQUIRED: The maximum allowed charitable contribution deduction.
DISCUSSION: A deduction is allowed for contributions to a qualified organization. Therefore, no deduction is allowed for the contribution to the family. However, a deduction is available for the donation of stock in the amount of $1,500. Since the stock has not been held long term, it is ordinary income property, and the deduction is equal to the lesser of FMV or AB.
Answer (A) is incorrect. A deduction is allowed. **Answer (C) is incorrect.** The cash may not be deducted. **Answer (D) is incorrect.** Only the stock is allowed as a deduction, and the deduction amount is $1,500.

SU 7: Adjustments and Deductions from AGI

14. Smith paid the following unreimbursed medical expenses:

Dentist and eye doctor fees	$ 5,000
Contact lenses	500
Facial cosmetic surgery to improve Smith's personal appearance (surgery is unrelated to personal injury or congenital deformity)	10,000
Premium on disability insurance policy to pay him if he is injured and unable to work	2,000

What is the total amount of Smith's tax-deductible medical expenses before the adjusted gross income limitation?

A. $17,500
B. $15,500
C. $7,500
D. $5,500

Answer (D) is correct.
   REQUIRED: The amount of deductible medical expenses.
   DISCUSSION: Medical expenses are deductible to the extent they exceed 7.5% of AGI. Medical care expenses include amounts paid for the diagnosis, cure, medication, treatment, or prevention of a disease or physical handicap or for the purpose of affecting any structure or function of the body. Therefore, $5,500 ($5,000 dentist and eye doctor fees + $500 contact lenses) qualifies for the deduction before the AGI limitation.
   Answer (A) is incorrect. The expenses must be primarily to alleviate or prevent a physical disability or illness. Cosmetic surgery is not deductible unless it corrects a congenital deformity, a personal injury from an accident or trauma, or a deformity from a disease. Furthermore, only premiums paid for medical insurance that provides for reimbursement of medical care expenses are deductible. **Answer (B) is incorrect.** The expenses must be primarily to alleviate or prevent a physical disability or illness. Cosmetic surgery is not deductible unless it corrects a congenital deformity, a personal injury from an accident or trauma, or a deformity from a disease. **Answer (C) is incorrect.** Only premiums paid for medical insurance that provides for reimbursement of medical care expenses are deductible.

15. How may taxes paid by an individual to a foreign country be treated?

A. As an other itemized deduction.
B. As a credit against federal income taxes due.
C. As an adjustment to gross income.
D. As a nondeductible expense.

Answer (B) is correct.
   REQUIRED: The treatment of taxes paid to a foreign country.
   DISCUSSION: A taxpayer may elect either a credit or an itemized deduction for "taxes you paid" to other countries or U.S. possessions.
   Answer (A) is incorrect. If treated as an itemized deduction, it is taken under "taxes you paid," not under "other itemized deductions." **Answer (C) is incorrect.** The foreign tax can be treated as a credit or deduction, not an adjustment. **Answer (D) is incorrect.** Foreign taxes paid can be deductible.

7.3 Qualified Business Income Deduction (QBID)

16. Which of the following comments is **not** correct regarding the QBI deduction?

A. Taxpayers with taxable income above the lower threshold are subject to limitations based on W-2 wages and/or the unadjusted basis in acquired qualified property.

B. For the most part, the deduction is 21% of a taxpayer's QBI from a partnership, S corporation, or sole proprietorship.

C. The QBI deduction is available to taxpayers who elect the standard deduction.

D. The W-2 wage limit begins to phase in if the taxpayer's taxable income exceeds the threshold amount of $164,900 ($329,800 for a joint return).

Answer (B) is correct.
   REQUIRED: The incorrect statement about QBID.
   DISCUSSION: Generally, the deduction is 20%, not 21%, of a taxpayer's QBI from a partnership, S corporation, or sole proprietorship. The deduction is intended to reduce the tax rate on QBI to a rate that is closer to the corporate tax rate of 21%.
   Answer (A) is incorrect. Based on taxable income, taxpayers may be subject to limitations based on the W-2 wages and the unadjusted basis in acquired qualified property. **Answer (C) is incorrect.** The QBI deduction is available to taxpayers who elect the standard deduction. **Answer (D) is incorrect.** The W-2 wage limit begins to phase in if the taxpayer's taxable income exceeds the threshold amount of $164,900 ($329,800 for a joint return).

17. Which of the following statements about qualified business income (loss) is correct under Sec. 199A?

A. If the net amount of qualified income, gain, deduction, and loss is greater than zero, the deduction must be carried over to the next year.

B. If the net amount of qualified income, gain, deduction, and loss is less than zero, the loss must be carried back to the prior year.

C. If the net amount of qualified income, gain, deduction, and loss is less than zero, the loss must be carried over to the next year.

D. The net amount of qualified income, gain, deduction, and loss is always greater than zero.

Answer (C) is correct.
   REQUIRED: The correct QBI statement.
   DISCUSSION: If the net amount of qualified income, gain, deduction, and loss is less than zero, the loss must be carried over to the next year, allocated proportionately among that year's QBI per entity.
   Answer (A) is incorrect. If the net amount of qualified income, gain, deduction, and loss is greater than zero, the deduction cannot be carried over to the next year. **Answer (B) is incorrect.** If the net amount of qualified income, gain, deduction, and loss is less than zero, the loss cannot be carried back. **Answer (D) is incorrect.** The net amount of qualified income, gain, deduction, and loss can be less than zero.

18. Forrest, a single taxpayer, has taxable income of $319,800. He considers investing in some entities to earn extra income. In which of the following entities should Forrest invest so that he may be able to claim the Sec. 199A deduction?

A. A tax services partnership.
B. A limited liability partnership that performs brokerage services.
C. An S corporation that performs architecture services.
D. A C corporation that performs engineering services.

Answer (C) is correct.
REQUIRED: The qualified business for QBID.
DISCUSSION: Because Forrest has taxable income greater than $214,900, only investing in qualified businesses enables him to claim a Sec. 199A deduction (i.e., non-SSTB). A qualified trade or business is any trade or business other than a specified service trade or business and other than the trade or business of performing services as an employee. A "specified service trade or business" under Sec. 199A includes any trade or business that involves the performance of services in the fields of health, law, accounting, actuarial science, performing arts, consulting, athletics, financial services, and brokerage services. "Specified service activity" is modified to exclude engineering and architecture services under Sec. 199A. In addition, an S corporation is a qualified pass-through entity. Thus, Forrest should invest in an S corporation that performs architecture services so that he may be able to claim the Sec. 199A deduction.

Answer (A) is incorrect. A tax services partnership is a specified service trade or business that disqualifies Forrest from taking the Sec. 199A deduction because his taxable income is greater than $214,900. **Answer (B) is incorrect.** A limited liability partnership that performs brokerage services is a specified service trade or business that disqualifies Forrest from taking the Sec. 199A deduction because his taxable income is greater than $214,900. **Answer (D) is incorrect.** The Sec. 199A deduction is available to noncorporate taxpayers who have qualified business income from qualified pass-through entities. Qualified pass-through entities include sole proprietorships, S corporations, partnerships, trusts, and estates. A C corporation is not a qualified pass-through entity. Thus, Forrest cannot claim the Sec. 199A deduction if he chooses to invest in a C corporation.

19. Zachary owns 40% of an S corporation that pays him $70,000 of wages, $10,000 of dividends, and allocates to him $89,000 of income. What is Zachary's qualified business income (QBI)?

A. $70,000
B. $89,000
C. $159,000
D. $99,000

Answer (B) is correct.
REQUIRED: The QBI amount.
DISCUSSION: QBI is the net amount of income, gain, deduction, and loss with respect to any qualified trade or business of the taxpayer conducted within the United States and included or allowed in determining taxable income for the taxable year. Wages and dividends are not included.

Answer (A) is incorrect. The amount of $70,000 represents employee compensation, which is not QBI. **Answer (C) is incorrect.** QBI does not include employee compensation. **Answer (D) is incorrect.** QBI does not include any dividend or income equivalent to a dividend.

GLEIM® CPA REVIEW

#1 CPA EXAM PREP

KNOW WHAT TO STUDY. KNOW WHEN YOU'RE READY.

FEATURES OUR INNOVATIVE SMARTADAPT™ TECHNOLOGY

SmartAdapt identifies where you need to focus (and where you don't) throughout your studies.

Also featuring:

- Personalized support from our team of Exam Experts
- Comprehensive test bank of exam-emulating simulation and multiple-choice questions
- One-of-a-kind, no-hassle Access Until You Pass® guarantee
- Two Exam Rehearsals (full-length mock exams) to help you get exam-day ready

GleimCPA.com | 800.874.5346

STUDY UNIT EIGHT
CREDITS AND LOSSES

(20 pages of outline)

8.1	Tax Credits	195
8.2	Losses and Limits	206

Tax credits, dollar for dollar, are a greater benefit to taxpayers than deductions, which depend on individual income tax rates and brackets.

The various loss deductions available are always subject to some limiting amount or qualification. This study unit analyzes available losses and the applicable limitations of each.

Some candidates find it helpful to have the entire tax form side-by-side with our Knowledge Transfer Outline when studying, and others may prefer to see the final draft of a form when it is released. The full versions of the most up-to-date forms are easily accessible at www.gleim.com/taxforms. These forms and the form excerpts used in our outline are periodically updated as the latest versions are released by the IRS.

8.1 TAX CREDITS

1. **Overview**

    a. Tax credits are used to achieve policy objectives, such as encouraging energy conservation or providing tax relief to low-income taxpayers. A $1 credit reduces gross tax liability by $1.

       1) Most credits are nonrefundable, meaning that once tax liability reaches zero, no more credits can be taken to produce refunds.

       2) However, there are a few refundable credits, including a credit for taxes withheld, a portion of the Child Tax Credit (called the Additional Child Tax Credit), and the Earned Income Credit.

2. **Nonrefundable Personal Credits**

    a. These credits include the

       1) Foreign Tax Credit
       2) Child and Dependent Care Credit
       3) Lifetime Learning Credit
       4) Retirement Savings Contribution Credit
       5) Child and Other Dependents Tax Credit
       6) Credit for the Elderly or the Disabled
       7) General Business Credit
       8) Adoption Credit

b. **Foreign Tax Credit.** This is an alternative to deduction of the tax. The credit is equal to the lesser of

1) Foreign taxes paid/accrued during the tax year or
2) The portion of U.S. tax liability (before credits) attributed to all foreign-earned income.

$$\text{FTC} = \text{U.S. income tax before FTC} \times \frac{\text{Foreign-earned taxable income}}{\text{Worldwide taxable income}}$$

   a) If the credit is limited to the amount in 2) above, unused foreign tax credits will equal the difference between 1) and 2).
   b) The unused credits can be carried back for 1 year and then carried forward for 10 years.
   c) The FTC in the GILTI basket (discussed in Study Unit 13) is limited to 80% of the otherwise allowable credit, and any excess cannot be carried to other years.

c. **Child and Dependent Care Credit.** This credit is for offsetting child and dependent care expenses. A taxpayer is eligible for this credit only if 1) and 2) below are satisfied.

   1) Child and dependent care expenses are incurred to enable a taxpayer to maintain gainful employment.
      a) The expenses may be incurred when the taxpayer is employed or actively seeking employment.
   2) The taxpayer provides more than half the cost of maintaining a household for a dependent under age 13 or an incapacitated spouse or dependent.
      a) Qualifying expenses include household services such as babysitting, housekeeping, and nursing. Outside services, such as day care facilities, must be in qualified facilities. Outside expenses for the care of an incapacitated spouse or dependent qualify only if the individual spends more than 8 hours a day in the taxpayer's home.
      b) Total child and dependent care expenses cannot exceed the taxpayer's earned income. For married taxpayers, the income for this limitation is the smaller income of the two.

EXAMPLE 8-1   Child and Dependent Care Credit

The taxpayer remarried on December 3 and the taxpayer's earned income for the year was $18,000. The taxpayer's new spouse's earned income for the year was $2,000. The taxpayer paid work-related expenses of $3,000 for the care of the taxpayer's 5-year-old child and qualified to claim the credit. The amount of expenses the taxpayer uses to figure the taxpayer's credit cannot be more than $2,000 (i.e., the smaller of the taxpayer's earned income or that of the taxpayer's spouse).

---

      i) If one of the spouses is a full-time student at an educational institution or is unable to care for himself or herself, (s)he is considered to have earned $250 per month if there is one qualifying individual and $500 per month if there are two or more qualifying individuals.
   c) Child and dependent care expenses are limited to $3,000 for one qualifying individual and $6,000 for two or more individuals.
   d) The credit is equal to 35% of the child and dependent care expenses. This rate is reduced by 1% (but not below 20%) for each $2,000 (or part thereof) by which AGI exceeds $15,000. Therefore, taxpayers with AGI over $43,000 will have a credit of 20%.

SU 8: Credits and Losses

d. **Lifetime Learning Credit.** This credit is 20% of qualified tuition expenses paid by the taxpayer. The maximum credit allowed per year is $2,000 and is limited to 20% of the first $10,000 of expenses. The Lifetime Learning Credit

   1) Phases out for AGI between $59,000 and $69,000 for singles and between $119,000 and $139,000 on a joint return.

   2) Is available in years that the American Opportunity Credit is not claimed with respect to the same student.

   3) Is available for an unlimited number of years and can be used for both graduate- and undergraduate-level courses.

   NOTE: The tuition statement (Form 1098-T) provided to the taxpayer must include the name, address, and TIN (Taxpayer Identification Number) of the student.

EXAMPLE 8-2   Lifetime Learning Credit

Weasley and Brandy Kat, who file a joint tax return, have an adjusted gross income (AGI) of $117,000 for 2021. Their daughter Honey began her first year of graduate school on July 21, 2020. Weasley and Brandy incurred expenses in 2021 of $12,000 for tuition.

A Lifetime Learning Credit is limited to the amount of 20% of the first $10,000 of tuition paid. The Lifetime Learning Credit is available in years the American Opportunity Credit is not claimed. The Kats' credit for 2021 will be $2,000 ($10,000 × 20%). There is no phaseout of the Lifetime Learning Credit for the Kats because the credit phaseout for married taxpayers filing jointly commences when modified AGI is $119,000 and ends at $139,000.

---

e. **Retirement Savings Contribution Credit.** Unlike most other tax topics allowing a credit or deduction, this credit is in addition to the exclusion or deduction from gross income for qualified contributions. In general, a taxpayer may claim a credit for an eligible contribution to an eligible retirement plan.

   1) The credit is a percentage based on AGI on a retirement contribution of up to $2,000 ($4,000 if married filing jointly). The following table provides the 2021 AGI thresholds and corresponding percentages:

Applicable % and Threshold Amounts

Credit Rate (% of taxpayer contributions)	Married Filing Jointly (AGI)	Head of Household (AGI)	All Other Filers (AGI)
50%	≤ $39,500	≤ $29,625	≤ $19,750
20%	$39,501-$43,000	$29,626-$32,250	$19,751-$21,500
10%	$43,001-$66,000	$32,251-$49,500	$21,501-$33,000
0%	> $66,000	> $49,500	> $33,000

EXAMPLE 8-3   Retirement Savings Contribution Credit

Stephanie, who works at a retail store, is married and earned $39,000 in 2021. Stephanie's husband was unemployed in 2021 and did not have any earnings. Stephanie contributed $1,000 to her IRA in 2021. After deducting her IRA contribution, the adjusted gross income shown on her joint return is $38,000. Stephanie may claim a 50% credit ($500) for her $1,000 IRA contribution.

f. **Child Tax Credit and Credit for Other Dependents**
   1) Taxpayers who have qualifying children or qualifying relatives are entitled to the Child Tax Credit of $2,000 per qualifying child and a Credit for Other Dependents of $500 per qualifying relative.
      a) **Qualifying child**, for this credit, is defined the same as it is for dependents in Study Unit 3, Subunit 5, but the child must be under the age of 17.
         i) A dependent that meets the qualifying child test from Study Unit 3, Subunit 5, but is age 17 or older is not eligible for the $2,000 Child Tax Credit but is eligible for the $500 Credit for Other Dependents.
      b) **Qualifying relative**, for this credit, is defined the same as it is for dependents in Study Unit 3, Subunit 5.
   2) The credit begins to phase out when modified AGI reaches $400,000 for joint filers and $200,000 for all other filing statuses. The credit is reduced by $50 for each $1,000 of modified AGI above the thresholds.

g. **Elderly or Disabled Credit.** An individual may be eligible for this credit if (s)he was age 65 before the close of the tax year or retired before the close of the tax year due to a total and permanent disability.
   1) The credit is equal to 15% multiplied by the initial base amount, which is
      a) $5,000 for single filers and married filing jointly with only one qualified spouse
      b) $7,500 for married filing jointly (both aged 65 or older)
      c) $3,750 for married filing separately
   2) The initial base amount is reduced by the following:
      a) Tax-exempt Social Security benefits
      b) Pension or annuity benefits excluded from gross income
      c) Disability income if under 65
      d) One-half the excess of AGI over
         i) $7,500 for single
         ii) $10,000 for married filing jointly
         iii) $5,000 for married filing separately
   3) A married person filing separately who lives with the spouse at any time during the year may not claim the credit.

Elderly or Disabled Credit Eligibility Decision Chart

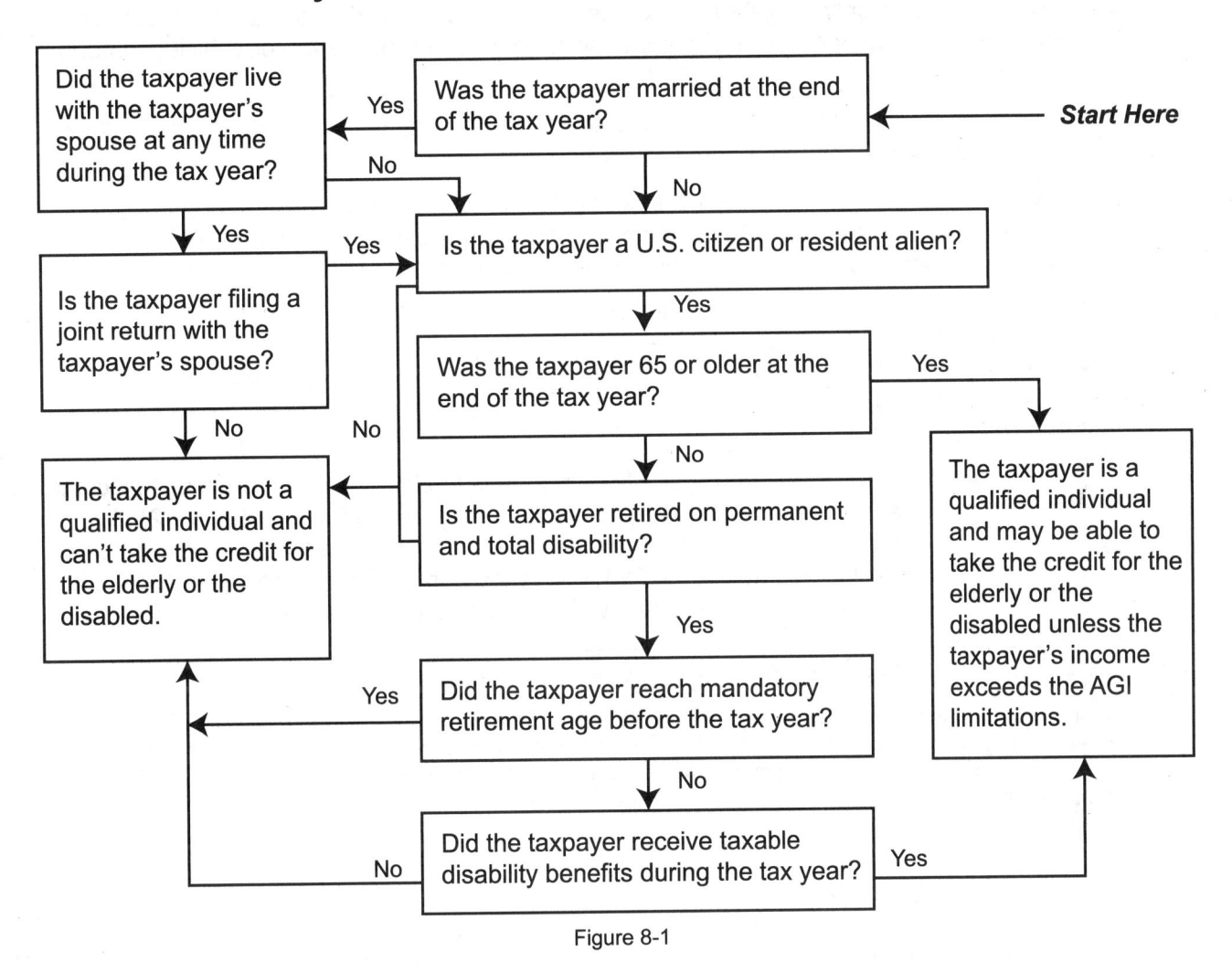

Start Here → Was the taxpayer married at the end of the tax year?

- **Yes** → Did the taxpayer live with the taxpayer's spouse at any time during the tax year?
  - **Yes** → Is the taxpayer filing a joint return with the taxpayer's spouse?
    - **Yes** → Is the taxpayer a U.S. citizen or resident alien?
    - **No** → The taxpayer is not a qualified individual and can't take the credit for the elderly or the disabled.
  - **No** → Is the taxpayer a U.S. citizen or resident alien?
- **No** → Is the taxpayer a U.S. citizen or resident alien?

Is the taxpayer a U.S. citizen or resident alien?
- **No** → The taxpayer is not a qualified individual and can't take the credit for the elderly or the disabled.
- **Yes** → Was the taxpayer 65 or older at the end of the tax year?
  - **Yes** → The taxpayer is a qualified individual and may be able to take the credit for the elderly or the disabled unless the taxpayer's income exceeds the AGI limitations.
  - **No** → Is the taxpayer retired on permanent and total disability?
    - **No** → The taxpayer is not a qualified individual and can't take the credit for the elderly or the disabled.
    - **Yes** → Did the taxpayer reach mandatory retirement age before the tax year?
      - **Yes** → The taxpayer is not a qualified individual and can't take the credit for the elderly or the disabled.
      - **No** → Did the taxpayer receive taxable disability benefits during the tax year?
        - **No** → The taxpayer is not a qualified individual and can't take the credit for the elderly or the disabled.
        - **Yes** → The taxpayer is a qualified individual and may be able to take the credit for the elderly or the disabled unless the taxpayer's income exceeds the AGI limitations.

Figure 8-1

h. **General Business Credit.** The General Business Credit (GBC) is a set of more than 30 credits commonly available to businesses. The GBC includes credits for investment, research, work opportunity, low-income housing, and alternative motor vehicles, among others.

1) Overall limit. The GBC is limited to net income tax minus the greater of the tentative minimum tax or 25% of net regular tax over $25,000.

NOTE: As of 2018, corporations are not subject to alternative minimum tax (AMT), and therefore, do not have tentative minimum tax for this limitation. The corporate limit is simply the net income tax minus 25% of net regular tax over $25,000.

From Form 1040

16	Tax (see instructions). Check if any from Form(s): 1 ☐ 8814 2 ☐ 4972 3 ☐ _____	16	
17	Amount from Schedule 2, line 3	17	
18	Add lines 16 and 17	18	

a) On Form 1040, the regular tax (line 16) is the tax computed on taxable income. The income tax is the regular tax (line 16) plus the AMT (Schedule 2) plus excess advance premium tax credit repayment (Schedule 2). The net income tax is the income tax (line 18) minus the nonrefundable credits other than the GBC. The GBC will not be available when the AMT exceeds the regular tax.

EXAMPLE 8-4   General Business Credit

The noncorporate taxpayer has a regular tax of $60,000 and a tentative minimum tax of $57,000. The taxpayer also has $10,000 of potential general business credits. Since the regular tax exceeds the tentative minimum tax, there is no alternative minimum tax. The taxpayer is allowed a General Business Credit computed as follows:

$60,000	Regular tax
(0)	Alternative minimum tax
$60,000	Income tax
(0)	Nonrefundable credits other than General Business Credit
$60,000	Net income tax
(57,000)	Greater of tentative minimum tax or 25% of net regular tax over $25,000
$ 3,000	General Business Credit

---

b) Tentative minimum tax is an amount used in computing the alternative minimum tax.

c) Net regular tax is the taxpayer's regular income tax liability (i.e., without alternative minimum tax) reduced by nonrefundable credits.

d) Excess over the limit may be allowable as a current deduction to the extent it is attributable to the Work Opportunity Tax Credit, among others.

e) Any excess of the combined GBC over the limit (and not allowed as a current deduction) may be carried back 1 year and forward 20 as a credit. It is carried to the earliest year to which it could be used, then to the next, and so on.

2) **Work Opportunity Tax Credit (WOTC).** Employers may take a credit equal to 40% (reduced to 25% for employment of more than 120 hours but less than 400) of the first $6,000 paid to employees from certain targeted groups who work at least 400 hours ($10,000 for LT Family Assistance Recipients and $3,000 for Qualified Summer Youth Employees).

   a) Generally, the maximum credit is $2,400 ($6,000 × 0.40) [$4,000 for LT Family Assistance Recipients ($10,000 × 0.40) and $1,200 for Qualified Summer Youth Employees ($3,000 × 0.40)] for non-veteran groups ($4,800, $5,600, or $9,600 for various veteran groups).

   b) The credit is not available for an individual with less than 120 hours of service performed for the employer.

   c) The second-year credit allowed only for LT Family Assistance Recipients is 50% of the first $10,000. The maximum credit for both years is $9,000 ($4,000 + $5,000).

      i) Qualified wages include
         - Remuneration for employment
         - Amount received under accident and health plans
         - Contributions by employers to accident and health plans
         - Educational assistance
         - Dependent care expenses

   d) Wages paid or incurred to an employee who begins work after December 31, 2025, are not eligible for this credit.

3) **Research Credit.** A credit is allowed for 20% of the amount by which the taxpayer's qualified research expenditures for a tax year exceed its base-period amount. Taxpayers may elect an alternative simplified credit equal to 14% of expenses in excess of 50% of the average expense for the preceding 3 years.

4) A $500 credit is allowed for employers who include an automatic contribution arrangement in a qualified employer plan. The credit is for the first 3 years of the automatic arrangement.

i. **Adoption Credit.** A credit is allowed for qualified adoption expenses incurred by the taxpayer.

   1) Qualified adoption expenses are reasonable and necessary adoption expenses, including adoption fees, court costs, attorney fees, and other directly related expenses.

   2) The maximum credit is $14,440 per qualified child, including a special-needs adoption.

      a) The maximum credit amount is allowed for the adoption of a child with special needs regardless of the actual expenses paid or incurred in the year the adoption becomes final.

      b) The amount of the credit allowable for any tax year is phased out for taxpayers with modified adjusted gross income (MAGI) in excess of $216,660 and is fully eliminated when MAGI reaches $256,660.

   3) Any unused credit may be carried forward for up to 5 years and is not subject to the MAGI phaseout.

3. **Refundable Credits**
   a. A refundable credit is payable as a refund to the extent the credit amount exceeds tax otherwise due. Refundable credits include the following:
      1) Credit for taxes withheld
      2) Earned Income Credit
      3) Additional Child Tax Credit
      4) American Opportunity Credit
      5) Premium Tax Credit
   b. Withholdings from employee wages for income tax are treated as a refundable credit. Withholdings from wages for Social Security (FICA) tax are also refundable but only if an aggregate is withheld in excess of the maximum by two or more employers.
   c. **Earned Income Credit (EIC)**
      1) To qualify for EIC, the taxpayer and spouse (if married and filing a joint return), must meet all of the following criteria:
         a) Have a valid Social Security number
         b) Have earned income from employment, self-employment, or another source
         c) Cannot use the married filing separately filing status (Spouses must file jointly, which also means one spouse cannot be a dependent of the other.)
         d) Must be a U.S. citizen or resident alien all year or a nonresident alien married to a U.S. citizen or resident alien and choose to file a joint return and be treated as a resident alien
         e) Cannot be the qualifying child (QC) of another person
         f) Have adjusted gross income and earned income less than the thresholds in item 6) on the next page
         g) Have investment income less than $3,650 for 2021
      2) Earned income includes wages, salaries, tips, and net earnings from self-employment. Disqualified income includes interest, dividends, capital gain net income, net passive income, unemployment compensation, and any compensation that is not taxable (other than excluded combat-zone pay).
      3) An individual without a QC must have his or her principal residence in the U.S. for more than half of the tax year, be at least 25 but not over 64 years old, and not be a dependent of another.
      4) Taxpayers with one or more QCs are eligible for a higher applicable percentage and a more lenient phaseout amount. For a child to be a QC, three tests must be met:
         a) Relationship. The child must be related by birth or adoption or be an eligible foster child or stepchild.
         b) Residency. The taxpayer must provide the child's principal place of abode for more than half of the year.
         c) Age. The child must be under age 19 at the close of the tax year, be permanently disabled, or be a student under the age of 24.
      5) To calculate EIC, multiply the individual's earned income by the applicable percentage.

EIC: Maximum Amounts, 2021

Type of Taxpayer	Applicable Percentage	Earned Income Amount	Maximum EIC
0 QC	7.65%	$ 7,100	$ 543
1 QC	34%	$10,640	$3,618
2 QC	40%	$14,950	$5,980
3 or more QC	45%	$14,950	$6,728

6) Phaseout of EIC. Decrease the maximum EIC by any phaseout, which is determined by multiplying the applicable phaseout percentage by the excess of the individual's AGI amount (or earned income, if greater) over the beginning amount. No EIC is available when AGI or earned income exceeds the completed phaseout amount.

EIC: Phaseout Amounts, 2021

Type of Taxpayer	Applicable Phaseout Percentage	Beginning Phaseout Amount	Beginning Phaseout Amt. for Joint Filers	Completed Phaseout Amount	Completed Phaseout Amt. for Joint Filers
0 QC	7.65%	$ 8,880	$14,820	$15,980	$21,920
1 QC	15.98%	$19,520	$25,470	$42,158	$48,108
2 QC	21.06%	$19,520	$25,470	$47,915	$53,865
3 or more QC	21.06%	$19,520	$25,470	$51,464	$57,414

Tests for Qualifying Child

Relationship

A qualifying child who is the taxpayer's . . .

Son, daughter, stepchild, foster child, or a descendant of any of them (for example, the taxpayer's grandchild)

OR

Brother, sister, half brother, half sister, stepbrother, stepsister, or a descendant of any of them (for example, the taxpayer's niece or nephew)

AND

Age

was . . .

Under age 19 at the end of the tax year and younger than the taxpayer (or taxpayer's spouse, if filing jointly)

OR

Under age 24 at the end of the tax year, a student, and younger than the taxpayer (or the taxpayer's spouse, if filing jointly)

OR

Permanently and totally disabled at any time during the year, regardless of age

AND

Residency

Who lived with the taxpayer in the United States for more than half of the tax year

Figure 8-2

d. **Additional Child Tax Credit**
   1) This credit is available for certain taxpayers who get less than the full amount of the Child Tax Credit.
   2) The credit is refundable up to the lesser of 15% of earned income in excess of $2,500 or the unclaimed portion of the nonrefundable credit. The refund is capped at $1,400 per child, though the $500 credit for qualifying relatives is not refundable.

e. **American Opportunity Credit.** This credit provides a maximum allowed credit of $2,500 per student per year for the first 4 years of post-secondary education. The credit may be used for qualified tuition and expenses.
   1) The credit is computed as 100% of the first $2,000 of expenses and 25% of the second $2,000 of expenses.
   2) Qualified expenses include required tuition, fees, and course materials. The credit is not allowed for room and board, activity fees, and any other fees or expenses not related to the student's academic course of instruction.
   3) The credit phases out for AGI between $80,000 ($160,000 for joint filers) and $90,000 ($180,000 for joint filers). The amount of reduction in credit can be calculated as follows:

   $$\text{Amount of credit allowed} \times \frac{\text{AGI} - \$80,000 \text{ (or } \$160,000 \text{ for joint filers)}}{\$10,000 \text{ (or } \$20,000 \text{ for joint filers)}}$$

   4) Up to 40% of the credit is refundable.
   5) The American Opportunity Credit is allowed per student, whereas the Lifetime Learning Credit is calculated per taxpayer without reference to the number of students.

   NOTE: The tuition statement (Form 1098-T) provided to the taxpayer must include the name, address, and TIN (Taxpayer Identification Number) of the student.

f. **Premium Tax Credit (PTC).** Taxpayers who obtain health insurance coverage through the Health Insurance Marketplace may be eligible for the Health Insurance Premium Tax Credit. The PTC is a refundable credit.

   1) The credit is available to households with income no greater than 400% of the federal poverty line for their family size.
   2) The amount of the credit is generally equal to the premium for the second lowest cost silver plan available through the Marketplace minus a certain percentage of household income (the taxpayer's required share of the premiums).
      a) A taxpayer's required share of premiums increases as the taxpayer's income increases, up to a maximum required contribution of 9.83% of household income.
   3) To be eligible for the credit, a taxpayer must
      a) Buy health insurance through the Marketplace,
      b) Be ineligible for coverage through an employer or government plan (e.g., Medicare or Medicaid),
      c) Not file a return as married filing separately (unless the taxpayer is a victim of domestic violence), and
      d) Not be claimed as a dependent by another person.
   4) Eligible taxpayers may either receive advance payments toward their health insurance premiums or receive a regular credit at the end of the year.
      a) Taxpayers who receive advance payments must file a tax return regardless of whether their income is below the filing threshold.

STOP & REVIEW

You have completed the outline for this subunit.
Study multiple-choice questions 1 through 8 beginning on page 215.

8.2 LOSSES AND LIMITS

1. **Casualty and Theft Losses**

    a. The IRC allows deduction for losses caused by theft or casualties, whether business or personal. However, as of 2018, personal casualty and theft losses only apply to **federally declared disasters** and **losses to the extent of casualty gains**.

    NOTE: Though the changes to personal losses significantly reduce the likelihood of any related questions on the exam, the details for casualty and theft losses are covered in this subunit for application to business losses.

    b. A casualty loss arises from a sudden, unexpected, or unusual event caused by an external force, such as fire, storm, shipwreck, earthquake, sonic boom, etc.

    1) Losses resulting from ordinary accidents are not deductible. Examples of these include dropping a vase or progressive deterioration, such as rust or insect damage.

    c. Theft includes robbery, larceny, etc. It may also include loss from extortion, blackmail, etc.

    1) Misplacing or losing items or having them confiscated by a foreign government is not considered theft.

    d. In general, the loss amount is the lesser of the decline in FMV or the AB minus insurance reimbursements.

    1) However, if business or investment property is completely lost or stolen, FMV is disregarded and AB is used to compute the loss.

EXAMPLE 8-5   Casualty Losses

Kaitlyn is a veterinarian. She had business equipment with a FMV of $15,000 and adjusted basis of $20,000 and had a business computer with a FMV of $1,000 and adjusted basis of $500. Both the equipment and computer were completely destroyed by a storm. She did not have insurance on these assets. Kaitlyn is able to deduct a loss of the combined adjusted bases since the assets are business assets equal to $20,500 ($20,000 + $500). If the same assets were personal-use assets and not business assets, and the storm was a federally declared disaster, the loss would be the lower of the decline in adjusted basis and fair market value (subject to a per-event and AGI floor). Since there was one event, look at the items' combined value. If it was not a federally declared disaster, there would be no loss deduction for personal-use assets.

---

   e. Reimbursement

   1) Only the amount of loss not compensated by insurance is deductible.
   2) Any excess recovered over the amount of property basis is gain.

   f. Timing

   1) A casualty loss is deductible in the tax year in which it occurs.
   2) A theft loss is deductible when it is discovered.

g. There are two ways a casualty loss of inventory, including items held for sale to customers, may be deducted: through cost of goods sold or deducting the loss separately.

1) Under the first of those methods, a taxpayer may deduct the loss through the increase in the cost of goods sold by properly reporting the opening and closing inventories. The loss is not claimed again as a casualty loss. Any insurance or other reimbursement received for the loss is included in gross income.

2) Under the second of those methods, a taxpayer may eliminate the affected inventory items from the cost of goods sold by making a downward adjustment to opening inventory or purchases. Any reimbursement received reduces the loss and is not included in gross income.

h. Business casualty losses are taken above the line. Personal casualty losses are taken below the line as an itemized deduction.

2. **Disaster Areas**

a. A taxpayer is subject to a special rule if (s)he sustains a loss from a federally declared disaster area.

b. The taxpayer has the option of deducting the loss on

1) The return for the year in which the loss actually occurred or
2) The preceding year's return (by filing an amended return).

c. Revocation of the election may be made before the expiration of time for filing the return for the year of loss.

d. A disaster loss deduction is computed the same way as a casualty loss, but personal losses are claimed on Schedule A as an itemized deduction.

1) The deduction is limited by a $100 per-event floor and a 10%-of-AGI floor. In other words, only disaster losses exceeding $100 plus 10% of AGI are deductible.

2) If the disaster loss is claimed on the preceding year's return, the AGI limitation is based on the prior year's AGI.

e. The loss is calculated on Form 4684, *Casualties and Thefts*, and carried over to Schedule A, *Itemized Deductions*.

3. **Capital Losses**
    a. Capital gain or loss realized on the sale or exchange of a capital asset is discussed in Study Unit 9, Subunit 3.
        1) An individual taxpayer may deduct net capital losses to the extent that they do not exceed the lesser of ordinary income or $3,000 ($1,500 if married filing separately).
        2) The individual may carry forward any excess capital losses indefinitely.
    b. Corporate and noncorporate capital losses in relation to net operating loss
        1) The amount of capital loss (CL) included in the NOL of a noncorporate taxpayer is limited.
        2) Before the limit is applied, the CL must be separated into business CL and nonbusiness CL.
        3) Capital losses are included in the NOL only as follows:
            a) Nonbusiness CL is deducted to the extent of nonbusiness capital gain (CG).
                i) Any excess nonbusiness CL is not deductible.
            b) If nonbusiness CG exceeds nonbusiness CL [in a) above], then such excess is applied against any excess of nonbusiness deductions over nonbusiness income.
            c) If nonbusiness CG exceeds excess nonbusiness deductions [in b) above], then the excess nonbusiness CG may offset business CL.
                i) Business CL may also be deducted to the extent of business CG.
            d) A corporation may use capital losses only to offset capital gains each year. A corporation must carry the excess capital loss back 3 years and forward 5 years and characterize all carryovers as short-term capital losses (regardless of character).

4. **Net Operating Loss (NOL)**
    a. A net operating loss occurs when business expenses exceed business income.
    b. The treatment of an NOL in the current year depends on the year in which the NOL originally arose (i.e., the year the loss was incurred). The NOL is deductible when carried to a year in which there is taxable income. Apply NOLs as a deduction in the following manner.
        1) NOLs that arose prior to 2018 can be carried back 2 years and carried forward for 20 years. The usage of the NOL is not limited by taxable income. Any excess carries over to future years until the NOL is exhausted or expires after 20 years.
        2) Under the CARES Act, NOLs for tax years 2018, 2019, and 2020 may be carried back 5 years and carried forward indefinitely. The carryback or carryforward period may offset the taxpayer's entire taxable income until 2021.
        3) NOLs that arise in 2021 and later may be carried forward indefinitely, but no carryback is allowed. The carryover is limited to 80% of the taxable income for the year it is carried to. Any excess continues to carry over to future years until exhausted.

        NOTE: If the CARES Act had not been passed, the elimination of the carryback and the 80% offset limit would have applied to tax years 2018, 2019, and 2020.

        4) When utilizing NOLs, the earliest year is used first.

        NOTE: There are exceptions to these general rules, but they are beyond the scope of the exam.

c. Although NOLs are typically business deductions, an individual may have an NOL.
d. To calculate NOL, start with taxable income (a negative amount) and make the following adjustments:
   1) Add back NOLs carried forward into the current tax year.
   2) Add back the Qualified Business Income Deduction.
   3) Add back excess of nonbusiness deductions over nonbusiness income.
      a) For this purpose, nonbusiness deductions are
         i) Alimony (for divorce agreements executed before 2019),
         ii) Contributions to self-employed retirement plans,
         iii) Loss from the sale of investment property, and
         iv) Either the standard deduction or all itemized deductions.

         NOTE: Business deductions include all (even personal) casualty losses.
      b) Nonbusiness income includes
         i) Interest,
         ii) Dividends,
         iii) Gain on the sale of investment property, and
         iv) Treasure trove.
      c) Rents and wages are business income.

EXAMPLE 8-6   NOL

For 2021, Sally realized a $30,000 net loss (sales of $200,000 less expenses of $230,000) from operating a sole proprietorship without regard to dispositions of property other than inventory. Other than this, the income tax return showed gross income of $10,000 ($4,500 of wages, $1,000 interest on personal savings, and a $4,500 long-term capital gain on business property). The excess of deductions over income was $32,550 ($10,000 gross income – $30,000 loss from business operations – $12,550 standard deduction).

To compute Sally's NOL, add back the $11,550 excess of nonbusiness deductions over nonbusiness income ($12,550 standard deduction – $1,000 interest).

Thus, Sally's NOL for the current tax year is $21,000 [$(32,550) "negative taxable income" + $11,550].

---

e. An NOL carried forward is a deduction to arrive at AGI.

5. **At-Risk Rules**

    a. The amount of a loss allowable as a deduction is limited to the amount a person has at risk in the activity.
    b. A loss is the excess of deductions over gross income attributable to the activity.
    c. The amount at risk and any deductible loss are calculated on Form 6198.
    d. The rules apply to individuals, partners in partnerships, members in limited liability companies, shareholders of S corporations, trusts, estates, and certain closely held C corporations.
    e. The rules are applied separately to each trade, business, or income-producing activity.
    f. A person's amount at risk in an activity is determined at the close of the tax year.

        1) A person's initial at-risk amount includes money contributed, the adjusted basis of property contributed, and borrowed amounts.
        2) Recourse Debt

            a) A person's at-risk amount includes amounts borrowed only to the extent that, for the debt, the person has either personal liability or pledged property as security.
            b) The at-risk amount does not include debt if one of the following applies:

                i) Property pledged as security is used in the activity.
                ii) Personal liability is protected against by insurance, guarantees, stop-loss agreements, or similar arrangements.
                iii) The creditor is a person with an interest in the activity or one related to the taxpayer.

        3) Nonrecourse debt is generally excluded from the amount at risk.

            a) The amount at risk in the activity of holding real property includes qualified nonrecourse financing (QNRF).
            b) In qualified nonrecourse financing, the taxpayer is not personally liable, but the financing is

                i) Incurred in a real estate activity;
                ii) Secured by the real property;
                iii) Not convertible to an ownership interest; and
                iv) From an unrelated third party (but not the seller or the seller's relative), from a related party but on commercially reasonable terms, or guaranteed by a governmental entity.

EXAMPLE 8-7   At-Risk Rules

Mooch Financial purchased rental real estate with some money borrowed from a related bank at commercially reasonable terms and the rest of the money borrowed from the seller. Both loans were nonrecourse and only secured by the property. Mooch Financial is at risk for the loan from the related bank because of the commercially reasonable terms and the nonrecourse loan is for real property. Regardless of the terms, Mooch Financial is not at risk for the seller's loan.

g. Adjustments to an at-risk amount are made for events that vary the investors' economic risk of loss.
   1) Add contributions of money and property (its AB), recourse debt increases, QNRF increase, and income from the activity.
   2) Subtract distributions, liability reductions, and tax deductions allowable (at year end), but only to the extent they reduce the at-risk amount to zero.
      a) If the amount at risk decreases below zero, previously allowed losses must be recaptured as income.
h. Disallowed losses are carried forward.
i. If a deduction would reduce basis in property and part or all of the deduction is disallowed by the at-risk rules, the basis is reduced anyway.

6. **Passive Activity Loss (PAL) Limitation Rules**
   a. The amount of a loss attributable to a person's passive activities is allowable as a deduction or credit only against, and to the extent of, gross income or tax attributable to those passive activities (in the aggregate).
      1) The excess is deductible or creditable in a future year, subject to the same limits.

EXAMPLE 8-8   PAL Limitation

A wealthy taxpayer invested in an architecture partnership as a passive investor. Because the taxpayer does not engage in the business outside of occasional business consulting, any income or loss derived from the business is passive in nature. Therefore, any losses derived from the partnership may only offset passive activity gains.

---

   b. The passive activity rules apply to individuals, estates, trusts (other than grantor trusts), personal service corporations, and closely held corporations.
      1) Although passive activity rules do not apply to grantor trusts, partnerships, and S corporations directly, they do apply to the owners of these entities.
   c. A passive activity is either a trade or business in which the person does not materially participate or a rental activity.
      1) A taxpayer materially participates in an activity during a tax year if (s)he satisfies one of the following tests:
         a) Participates more than 500 hours.
         b) The taxpayer's participation constitutes substantially all of the participation in the activity.
         c) Participates more than 100 hours and exceeds the participation of any other individual.
         d) Materially participated in the activity for any 5 years of the preceding 10 years before the year in question.
         e) Materially participated in a personal service activity for any 3 years preceding the year in question.
         f) Participates in the activity on a regular, continuous, and substantial basis.

d. Passive activity rules do not apply to
　1) Active income/loss/credit
　2) Portfolio income/loss/credit
　3) Casualty and theft losses, vacation home rental, qualified home mortgage interest, business use of home, or a working interest in an oil or gas well held through an entity that does not limit the person's liability

> **SUCCESS TIP**
> Whether the participation is active or passive is usually given on the REG exam, except for limited partnerships, which you should assume to be passive.

e. Rental Real Estate
　1) All rental activity is passive.
　2) However, a person who actively participates in rental real estate activity is entitled to deduct up to $25,000 of losses from the passive activity from other than passive income. This is often referred to as the "small landlord" exception or "mom and pop" exception.
　3) This exception to the general PAL limitation rule applies to a person who
　　a) Actively participates in the activity
　　b) Owns 10% or more of the activity (by value) for the entire year
　　c) Has MAGI of less than $150,000 [phaseout begins at $100,000; shown in 4)a) below]
　4) $25,000 of a tax year loss from rental real estate activities in excess of passive activity gross income is deductible against portfolio or active income.
　　a) The $25,000 limit is reduced by 50% of the person's MAGI [i.e., AGI without regard to PALs, Social Security benefits, and qualified retirement contributions (e.g., IRAs)] over $100,000.
　　b) Excess rental real estate PALs are suspended. They are treated as other PALs carried over.

EXAMPLE 8-9　　Allowed Rental Loss

A MFJ taxpayer actively participated in rental activity and incurred a rental loss of $30,000 in the current year. If the taxpayer's MAGI is $120,000, what is the amount of rental loss that is deductible?

MAGI	$120,000	Loss limit	$25,000
Threshold	(100,000)	Reduction	(10,000)
Excess	$ 20,000	Allowed loss	$15,000
Reduction %	× 50%		
Reduction	$ 10,000		

5) Active participation is a less stringent requirement than material participation.

   a) It is met with participation in management decisions or arranging for others to provide services (such as repairs).
   b) There will not be active participation if at any time during the period there is ownership of less than 10% of the interest in the property (including the spouse's interest).

6) Real Property Trades or Businesses

   a) The passive activity loss rules do not apply to certain taxpayers who are involved in real property trades or businesses.
   b) An individual may avoid passive activity loss limitation treatment on a rental real estate activity if two requirements are met:
      i) More than 50% of the individual's personal services performed during the year are performed in the real property trades or businesses in which the individual materially participates.
      ii) The individual performs more than 750 hours of service in the real property trades or businesses in which the individual materially participates.
   c) This provision also applies to a closely held C corporation if 50% of gross receipts for the tax year are from real property trades or businesses in which the corporation materially participated.
   d) Any deduction allowed under this rule is not taken into consideration in determining the taxpayer's AGI for purposes of the phaseout of the $25,000 deduction.
   e) If 50% or less of the personal services performed are in real property trades or businesses, the individual will be subject to the passive activity limitation rules.

EXAMPLE 8-10   PAL Limitation -- Active Participation

Lynne, a single taxpayer, has $70,000 in wages, $15,000 income from a limited partnership, and a $26,000 loss from rental real estate activities in which she actively participated and is not subject to the modified adjusted gross income phaseout rule. She can use $15,000 of her $26,000 loss to offset her $15,000 passive income from the partnership. She actively participated in her rental real estate activities, so she can use the remaining $11,000 rental real estate loss to offset $11,000 of her nonpassive income (wages).

---

f. **Suspension**

   1) A PAL not allowable in the current tax year is carried forward indefinitely and treated as a deduction in subsequent tax years.

g. PALs continue to be treated as PALs even after the activity ceases to be passive in a subsequent tax year, except that it may also be deducted against income from that activity.

h. Disposition of a Passive Activity

   1) Suspended (and current-year) losses from a passive activity become deductible in full in the year the taxpayer completely disposes of all interest in the passive activity.
   2) The loss is deductible first against net income or gain from the taxpayer's other passive activities. The remainder of the loss, if any, is then treated as nonpassive.

7. Excess Business Loss

a. After passing the at-risk limit and the passive activity loss rule, non-C corporate business losses are subject to the excess business loss limit. C corporations are excluded from this limitation and allowed to offset pass-through losses received from pass-through entities against nonbusiness income (e.g., capital gains).

b. Excess business loss is calculated as follows:

$$\frac{\text{Gross income or gain from trades or businesses} + \$262{,}000\ (\$524{,}000\ \text{MFJ})\ \text{floor}}{\text{Limitation}} - \frac{\text{All deductions from trades or businesses}}{\text{Limitation}} = \underline{\underline{\text{Excess business loss}}}$$

c. The excess business loss is carried forward as an NOL. In carryover years, NOL is limited to 80% of the future year's taxable income.

STOP & REVIEW

You have completed the outline for this subunit.
Study multiple-choice questions 9 through 20 beginning on page 218.

SU 8: Credits and Losses 215

QUESTIONS

8.1 Tax Credits

1. Karen, filing as head of household, and her son James and daughter Julia are all in graduate school. James and Julia are not dependents on Karen's return, although they live with her and she pays all of their education expenses. Karen paid $6,000 in qualified tuition expenses for herself in January 2021 for the term starting in January 2021. She also paid $2,500 in qualified tuition expenses for James and another $2,500 for Julia in July 2021 for the terms starting in July 2021. Her adjusted gross income is $70,000. Which of the following is true for tax year 2021?

A. Karen may claim no American Opportunity Credit and $2,000 Lifetime Learning Credit.

B. Karen may claim $5,000 American Opportunity Credit and $1,000 Lifetime Learning Credit.

C. Karen may claim neither the American Opportunity nor the Lifetime Learning Credit.

D. Karen may claim no American Opportunity Credit and $1,000 Lifetime Learning Credit.

Answer (C) is correct.
REQUIRED: The amount of American Opportunity Credit and Lifetime Learning Credit a taxpayer may claim.
DISCUSSION: The American Opportunity Credit and Lifetime Learning Credit may not be claimed at the same time. The American Opportunity Credit is available during a student's first 4 years in college. Since Karen is in graduate school, she does not qualify for the American Opportunity Credit. The Lifetime Learning Credit is available in years that the American Opportunity Credit is not taken (for example, graduate school). However, the Lifetime Learning Credit phases out for single filers whose AGI is between $59,000 and $69,000 in 2021. Since Karen's AGI is $70,000, the Lifetime Learning Credit is completely phased out.

2. Which of the following credits is a combination of several tax credits to provide uniform rules for the current and carryback-carryover years?

A. General Business Credit.
B. Foreign Tax Credit.
C. Minimum Tax Credit.
D. Research Credit.

Answer (A) is correct.
REQUIRED: The credit that is actually a combination of several credits.
DISCUSSION: The General Business Credit is a set of several credits commonly available to businesses, including credits for investment, research, and work opportunity jobs, among others.
Answer (B) is incorrect. The Foreign Tax Credit is a specific, individual credit. Answer (C) is incorrect. The Minimum Tax Credit is a specific, individual credit. Answer (D) is incorrect. The Research Credit is a specific, individual credit.

3. Which of the following credits can result in a refund even if the individual had **no** income tax liability?

A. Foreign Tax Credit.
B. Elderly and Permanently and Totally Disabled Credit.
C. Earned Income Credit.
D. Child and Dependent Care Credit.

Answer (C) is correct.
REQUIRED: The credit that is refundable.
DISCUSSION: A refundable credit is payable as a refund to the extent the credit amount exceeds tax otherwise due. Some of the refundable credits are credits for taxes withheld, overpayments of income tax, and the Earned Income Credit.
Answer (A) is incorrect. The credit for foreign taxes paid is not refundable. Answer (B) is incorrect. The Elderly and Disabled Credit is not refundable. Answer (D) is incorrect. The Child and Dependent Care Credit is not refundable.

4. To qualify for the Child Care Credit on a joint return, at least one spouse must

	Have an Adjusted Gross Income of $15,000 or Less	Be Gainfully Employed when Related Expenses Are Incurred
A.	Yes	Yes
B.	No	No
C.	Yes	No
D.	No	Yes

Answer (B) is correct.
REQUIRED: The requirement(s) to qualify for the Child Care Credit on a joint return.
DISCUSSION: The IRC allows a nonrefundable credit to a provider of care to dependents for a limited portion of expenses necessary to enable gainful employment. The credit claimant must have qualified child care expenses when the claimant is employed or actively seeking gainful employment. The credit amount is not eliminated when AGI exceeds $15,000, only phased down from 35% to 20% in increments of 1% for each $2,000 AGI exceeds $15,000.
Answer (A) is incorrect. Qualifying expenses may be incurred when the claimant is actively seeking gainful employment, and the credit is not eliminated by reference to AGI. The credit is phased from 35% to 20%. **Answer (C) is incorrect.** The credit is not eliminated when AGI exceeds a cap amount. The credit is phased from 35% to 20%. **Answer (D) is incorrect.** Qualifying expenses may be incurred when the claimant is actively seeking gainful employment.

5. Which of the following disqualifies an individual from the Earned Income Credit?

A. The taxpayer's qualifying child is a 17-year-old grandchild.
B. The taxpayer has earned income of $5,000.
C. The taxpayer's 5-year-old child lived in the taxpayer's home for only 8 months.
D. The taxpayer has a filing status of married filing separately.

Answer (D) is correct.
REQUIRED: The situation that disqualifies an individual from the EIC.
DISCUSSION: The Earned Income Credit is unavailable to taxpayers filing married filing separately.
Answer (A) is incorrect. The child must be under age 19 at the close of the tax year, or 24 if a student. **Answer (B) is incorrect.** The phaseout thresholds for the EIC vary depending on number of children and filing status. However, all thresholds exceed $5,000. **Answer (C) is incorrect.** The child needs only to live with the taxpayer for more than 6 months.

6. Which of the following statements about the Child and Dependent Care Credit is correct?

A. The credit is nonrefundable.
B. The child must be under the age of 18 years.
C. The child must be a direct descendant of the taxpayer.
D. The maximum credit is $600.

Answer (A) is correct.
REQUIRED: The true statement about the Child and Dependent Care Credit.
DISCUSSION: A nonrefundable tax credit is allowed for child and dependent care expenses incurred to enable the taxpayer to be gainfully employed. To qualify, the taxpayer must provide more than half the cost of maintaining a household for a dependent under age 13 or an incapacitated spouse or dependent. The maximum credit is equal to 35% of up to $3,000 of child and dependent care expenses for one qualifying individual ($6,000 for two or more individuals).
Answer (B) is incorrect. A child who is not incapacitated must be under the age of 13. Dependents who are incapacitated do not have an age restriction. **Answer (C) is incorrect.** Direct "descendant" is not a requirement (e.g., incapacitated spouse). **Answer (D) is incorrect.** The maximum credit is $1,050 ($3,000 expense limit × 35%) for one qualifying individual and $2,100 ($6,000 expense limit × 35%) for two or more qualifying individuals.

7. All of the following qualify as work-related expenses for computing the Child and Dependent Care Credit **except**

A. The parent-employer's portion of Social Security tax paid on wages for a person to take care of dependent children while the parents work.

B. Payments to a nursery school for the care of dependent children while the parents work.

C. The cost of meals for a housekeeper who provides necessary care for a dependent child while the parents work.

D. Payments to a housekeeper who provides dependent care while the parent is off from work because of illness.

Answer (D) is correct.
    REQUIRED: The child or dependent care expense that does not qualify as employment-related.
    DISCUSSION: Employment-related expenses are paid for household services and for the care of a qualifying individual. Expenses are classified as work-related only if they are incurred to enable the taxpayer to be gainfully employed. An expense is not considered to be work-related merely because it is incurred while the taxpayer is gainfully employed.
    Answer (A) is incorrect. The parent-employer's portion of Social Security tax paid on wages for a person to take care of dependent children while the parents work is an expense incurred to enable the taxpayer to be gainfully employed. **Answer (B) is incorrect.** Payments to a nursery school for the care of dependent children while the parents work is an expense incurred to enable the taxpayer to be gainfully employed. **Answer (C) is incorrect.** The cost of meals for a housekeeper who provides necessary care for a dependent child while the parents work is an expense incurred to enable the taxpayer to be gainfully employed.

8. For the current year, for purposes of the Earned Income Credit, all of the following amounts qualify as earned income **except**

A. Earnings from self-employment.

B. Excluded combat-zone pay.

C. Unemployment compensation.

D. Wages from employment.

Answer (C) is correct.
    REQUIRED: The item that does not qualify as earned income for purposes of the Earned Income Credit.
    DISCUSSION: Earned income includes all wages, salaries, tips, and other employee compensation (including union strike benefits), plus the amount of the taxpayer's net earnings from self-employment. For purposes of the Earned Income Credit, earned income also includes nontaxable compensation such as the basic quarters and subsistence allowances for the military, parsonage allowances, the value of meals and lodging furnished for the convenience of the employer, and excludable employer-provided dependent care benefits. Earned income does not include interest and dividends, welfare benefits, veterans' benefits, pensions or annuities, alimony, Social Security benefits, workers' compensation, unemployment compensation, or taxable scholarships or fellowships.

8.2 Losses and Limits

9. Lee qualified as head of a household for 2021 tax purposes. Lee's 2021 taxable income was $100,000, exclusive of capital gains and losses. Lee had a net long-term capital loss of $8,000 in 2021. What amount of this capital loss can Lee offset against 2021 ordinary income?

A. $0
B. $3,000
C. $4,000
D. $8,000

Answer (B) is correct.
REQUIRED: The deductible amount of a net capital loss.
DISCUSSION: Capital losses offset capital gains. Excess of capital losses over capital gains (net capital loss) is deductible against ordinary income, but only up to $3,000 in the current tax year.
Answer (A) is incorrect. Lee may offset part of the capital loss. Answer (C) is incorrect. The offset is limited to $3,000. Answer (D) is incorrect. The whole amount of the loss may not be offset in the current year.

10. Don Wolf became a general partner in Gata Associates on January 1, 2021, with a 5% interest in Gata's profits, losses, and capital. Gata is a distributor of auto parts. Wolf does not materially participate in the partnership business. For the year ended December 31, 2021, Gata had an operating loss of $100,000. In addition, Gata earned interest of $20,000 on a temporary investment while awaiting delivery of equipment that is presently on order. The principal will be used to pay for this equipment. Wolf's passive loss (before any limitation) for 2021 is

A. $0
B. $4,000
C. $5,000
D. $6,000

Answer (C) is correct.
REQUIRED: The amount treated as a passive loss.
DISCUSSION: In general, losses arising from one passive activity may be used to offset income from other passive activities but may not be used to offset active or portfolio income. Wolf's $5,000 operating loss ($100,000 × 5%) may not be used to offset his $1,000 portfolio income ($20,000 × 5%); i.e., interest and dividends are portfolio income. Therefore, his passive loss for 2021 is his $5,000 operating loss. The losses may be carried forward indefinitely or until the entire interest is disposed of.
Answer (A) is incorrect. The operating losses are passive since Wolf does not materially participate. Answer (B) is incorrect. The interest income is classified as portfolio income and is not offset by passive losses. Answer (D) is incorrect. The $1,000 interest constitutes income, not loss.

11. In computing an individual's net operating loss, which of the following is **not** considered business income or deduction(s)?

A. Wages.
B. Personal casualty loss.
C. Gain on sale of investment property.
D. Gain on sale of business property.

Answer (C) is correct.
REQUIRED: The item not considered business income or deductions in computing an individual's NOL.
DISCUSSION: Business and nonbusiness income and deductions need to be distinguished because nonbusiness deductions are deductible in computing a NOL only to the extent of nonbusiness income. Nonbusiness deductions and income are those that are not attributable to, or derived from, a taxpayer's trade or business. Also, capital losses are only deductible to the extent of capital gains. A gain on the sale of investment property is a capital gain and not business income.
Answer (A) is incorrect. Employment is considered a trade or business; therefore, wages are business income. Answer (B) is incorrect. A personal casualty loss is treated as a business deduction. Answer (D) is incorrect. A gain on the sale of business property is considered business income.

12.
Which of the following statements is **false** regarding individual taxpayers and allowed losses?

A. Net capital loss deductions are limited by ordinary income and $3,000 maximum ($1,500 if married filing separately).

B. A disaster loss may be taken on the prior year's return but still subject to current year AGI limitations.

C. Loss deductions are limited to the amount a person has at risk in the activity.

D. A person who actively participates in rental real estate activity is entitled to deduct up to $25,000 of losses from the passive activity from active income.

Answer (B) is correct.
REQUIRED: The false statement regarding allowed losses.
DISCUSSION: Taxpayers have the option of deducting a disaster loss on the return for the year in which the loss actually occurred or the preceding year's return. The AGI limitation is based on the AGI of the return year. In this case, it would be the AGI of the prior year.
Answer (A) is incorrect. Capital losses are deductible in excess of capital gains, but this excess is limited to the lesser of ordinary income or $3,000 ($1,500 if married filing separately). **Answer (C) is incorrect.** The at-risk rules limit the amount of a deductible loss to the amount a person has at risk in the activity. **Answer (D) is incorrect.** All rental activity is passive. A person who actively participates in rental real estate activity is entitled to deduct up to $25,000 of losses from the passive activity from other than passive income. This is often referred to as the "small landlord" exception or "mom and pop" exception.

13.
If an individual taxpayer's passive losses and credits relating to rental real estate activities **cannot** be used in the current year, then they may be carried

A. Back 2 years, but they cannot be carried forward.

B. Forward up to a maximum period of 20 years, but they cannot be carried back.

C. Back 2 years or forward up to 20 years, at the taxpayer's election.

D. Forward indefinitely or until the property is disposed of in a taxable transaction.

Answer (D) is correct.
REQUIRED: The correct statement concerning the carryover or carryback of unused passive losses and credits.
DISCUSSION: Disallowed passive activity losses (and credits) are carried forward and used to offset passive activity income (and taxes) in later years. This applies to passive losses and credits from rental real estate activities or from any other passive activity. The carryover is accomplished by treating the disallowed loss from each activity as a deduction for the activity in the following year. In this manner, the carryforward is indefinite. If the entire interest in a passive activity is disposed of in a taxable transaction in a later year, the passive loss may be used at that time.

14. Which of the following statements about losses in federally declared disaster areas is **false**?

A. The taxpayer has the option of deducting the loss on the return for the year immediately preceding the year in which the disaster actually occurred.
B. Any AGI limitations are based on the AGI of the year the loss is reported.
C. Disaster area loss deductions are subject to a per-event and AGI floor.
D. Once made, the election to deduct the loss on the prior-year return cannot be revoked.

Answer (D) is correct.
REQUIRED: The false statement about losses in federally declared disaster areas.
DISCUSSION: If a taxpayer sustains a loss from a disaster in an area subsequently designated as a federal disaster area, a special rule may help the taxpayer to cushion his or her loss. The taxpayer has the option of deducting the loss on his or her return for the year in which the loss occurred or on the return for the previous year. Revocation of the election to deduct the loss on the preceding year's tax return may be made before the expiration of time for filing the return for the year of loss. The calculation of the deduction for a disaster loss follows the same rules as those for nonbusiness casualty losses. The AGI floor is based on the AGI of the return year the loss is reported (e.g., current or preceding).
Answer (A) is incorrect. It is a true statement about losses in federally declared disaster areas. **Answer (B) is incorrect.** It is a true statement about losses in federally declared disaster areas. **Answer (C) is incorrect.** It is a true statement about losses in federally declared disaster areas.

15. The at-risk rules

A. Limit a taxpayer's deductible losses from investment activities.
B. Limit the type of deductions in income-producing activities.
C. Apply to business and income-producing activities on a combined basis.
D. Apply at the entity level for partnerships and S corporations.

Answer (A) is correct.
REQUIRED: The correct statement concerning the at-risk rules.
DISCUSSION: The at-risk rules limit a taxpayer's deductible losses from each business and income-producing activity to the amount for which the taxpayer is at risk with respect to that activity.
Answer (B) is incorrect. The losses from each activity, not the type of deductions, are limited. **Answer (C) is incorrect.** The at-risk rules apply to each business and income-producing activity separately. **Answer (D) is incorrect.** The at-risk rules apply at the partner or shareholder level for these pass-through entities.

16. Which of the following is **not** subject to the excess business loss limit?

A. Sole proprietor.
B. Partner.
C. S corporation shareholder.
D. C corporation.

Answer (D) is correct.
REQUIRED: The business type not subject to the excess business loss limit.
DISCUSSION: After application of the basis, the at-risk limit, and the passive activity loss rule, non-C corporation taxpayers' business losses are now subject to the excess business loss limit. C corporations are excluded from this limitation and allowed to offset pass-through losses received from pass-through entities against non-business income (e.g., capital gains).
Answer (A) is incorrect. Sole proprietors receive pass-through income/losses and are subject to the excess business loss limit. **Answer (B) is incorrect.** Partners receive pass-through income/losses and are subject to the excess business loss limit. **Answer (C) is incorrect.** S corporation shareholders receive pass-through income/losses and are subject to the excess business loss limit.

SU 8: Credits and Losses

17. What is the tax treatment of net operating losses (NOLs) arising in tax year 2021 and later?

A. They can be carried back 2 years and carried forward 20 years.

B. They can be carried back 5 years and carried forward indefinitely.

C. They cannot be carried back, but they can be carried forward indefinitely.

D. They cannot be carried back or carried forward to other tax years.

Answer (C) is correct.
REQUIRED: The carryover treatment of NOLs.
DISCUSSION: NOLs generated in 2021 and later cannot be carried back, but they can be carried forward indefinitely. However, they can only offset up to 80% of taxable income in the future year.
Answer (A) is incorrect. This is the rule for NOLs arising in 2017 and earlier. **Answer (B) is incorrect.** This is the rule for NOLs arising in 2018, 2019, and 2020. **Answer (D) is incorrect.** NOLs arising in 2021 and later can be carried forward.

18. Annie and Bobby are married taxpayers filing a joint return. In 2021, the couple sold stock in Acme, Inc., resulting in a capital loss of $5,000. The couple had no other capital gains or losses during the year. Their ordinary income for the year is $95,000. How much of the $5,000 loss can the couple deduct on their joint tax return?

A. $6,000

B. $5,000

C. $3,000

D. $1,500

Answer (C) is correct.
REQUIRED: The deductible capital loss.
DISCUSSION: Individual taxpayers can deduct up to $3,000 of net capital losses on their tax returns ($1,500 is the limit if married filing separately).

19. Which of the following is a true statement concerning losses from passive activities?

A. Losses from each passive activity are not deductible, regardless of income earned in other passive activities.

B. The losses may offset passive income, such as interest and dividends, but not business income or earned income.

C. The rules apply to losses but not credits.

D. Losses from one passive activity may offset income from another passive activity.

Answer (D) is correct.
REQUIRED: The true statement concerning losses from passive activities.
DISCUSSION: In general, losses from passive activities may not offset nonpassive income, such as salary, interest, dividends, or active business income (Sec. 469). However, deductions from one passive activity may offset income from the same passive activity, and losses from one passive activity may generally offset income from another passive activity.
Answer (A) is incorrect. Losses from a passive activity are deductible to the extent of income from other passive activities. **Answer (B) is incorrect.** Losses from passive activities may not offset income, such as interest and dividends, which are considered portfolio income. **Answer (C) is incorrect.** The passive loss rules apply to credits as well as losses.

20. Dr. J has adjusted gross income for the current year of $130,000 before the deduction for a $2,000 contribution to his IRA and before any potential deduction for $40,000 of losses from rental real estate activities in which he actively participates. How much of the rental losses may he deduct if the rental real estate activities were acquired in the current year?

A. $0
B. $10,000
C. $11,000
D. $25,000

Answer (B) is correct.
REQUIRED: The amount a taxpayer may deduct for losses from active participation in rental real estate activities when adjusted gross income is in excess of $100,000.
DISCUSSION: The $25,000 allowance of losses from active participation in rental real estate activities against nonpassive income is reduced by 50% of the amount by which adjusted gross income (determined without regard to Social Security benefits, IRA contributions, and passive losses) exceeds $100,000 [Sec. 469(i)(3)]. Dr. J's adjusted gross income exceeds $100,000 by $30,000. Therefore, the $25,000 allowance is reduced by $15,000 ($30,000 × 50%). This leaves $10,000 of losses that can be deducted.
Answer (A) is incorrect. A portion of rental losses may be deducted. **Answer (C) is incorrect.** The phase-out amount was based on AGI after claiming the deduction for the contribution to an IRA ($128,000). **Answer (D) is incorrect.** AGI exceeds $100,000, so the $25,000 loss allowance must be phased out.

Access the **Gleim CPA Premium Review System** featuring our SmartAdapt technology from your Gleim Personal Classroom to continue your studies. You will experience a personalized study environment with exam-emulating multiple-choice questions.

STUDY UNIT NINE
PROPERTY TRANSACTIONS: BASIS AND GAINS

(29 pages of outline)

9.1	Basis	224
9.2	Depreciation and Amortization	233
9.3	Capital Gains and Losses	244

The tax treatment of property transactions is integrated with that of other transactions on the CPA Exam. Visualize the following steps to analyze the income tax consequences of property transactions.

1) Determine gain or loss realized.
2) Apply capital loss rules.
3) Apply other loss limits.

   a) At-risk rules
   b) Passive activity loss rules
   c) Excess business loss rules
   d) Net operating loss rules

4) Report gross income, claim deductions, and compute taxable income and tax liability in accordance with other rules. For example,

   a) Apply installment sales rules.
   b) Deduct allowable capital losses.
   c) Separate capital gains from other income.
   d) Apply tax rates separately to capital gains and other income.

The sale of a business requires special attention. When more than one asset of a business is transferred in bulk (total consideration exchanged for assets in combination), including all the assets of a sole proprietorship, gain or loss must be accounted for separately for each asset transferred. Allocation among assets of consideration paid or to be paid is by agreement of parties, by relative FMV of assets, or by the residual method. Also note the following:

1) Capital gain or loss might arise from assets that have no fixed or determinable useful life, such as goodwill that was not amortized (self-created goodwill) under Sec. 197 or an exclusive franchise.

2) Ordinary income or loss might arise from the following assets:

   a) Inventory
   b) Accounts receivable
   c) Covenants not to compete (all ordinary)
   d) Section 1231 property, e.g., land and depreciable trade or business property held for greater than 1 year, which includes

      i) Section 1245 property, e.g., equipment
      ii) Section 1250 property, i.e., depreciable realty

Some candidates find it helpful to have the entire tax form side-by-side with our Knowledge Transfer Outline when studying, and others may prefer to see the final draft of a form when it is released. The full versions of the most up-to-date forms are easily accessible at www.gleim.com/taxforms. These forms and the form excerpts used in our outline are periodically updated as the latest versions are released by the IRS.

9.1 BASIS

1. **Overview**
   a. When a taxpayer acquires property, his or her basis in the property is initially cost, transferred, or exchanged basis.
      1) **Cost basis** is the sum of capitalized acquisition costs.
         a) Cost basis includes the fair market value of property given up. If it is not determinable with reasonable certainty, use FMV of property received.
         b) A rebate to the purchaser is treated as a reduction of the purchase price. It is not included in gross income.
         c) Amounts included in gross income increase cost basis.
      2) **Transferred basis** is computed by reference to basis in the property in the hands of another. This is also commonly referred to as a carryover basis.
      3) **Exchanged basis** is computed by reference to basis in other property previously held.
         a) The basis of property converted into business use is the lesser of the FMV of the property at the conversion date or the adjusted basis at conversion. This prevents personal losses from being converted into business losses.
      4) Stepped-up (or down) basis occurs when property is acquired through inheritance and basis reflects FMV at the time of death.

2. **Unit of Property**
   a. The determination of whether tangible property costs are deducted or capitalized is determined by examining the unit of property. The unit of property is a group of functionally interdependent components and can either be an asset, group of assets, or a defined portion of an asset.
      1) Non-building property generally remains subject to the functional interdependence test.
         a) In the case of personal or real property other than a building, all the components that are functionally interdependent comprise a single unit of property.
         b) Components of property are functionally interdependent if the placing in service of one component by the taxpayer is dependent on the placing in service of the other component by the taxpayer. The following are included in this classification of unit of property:
            i) Personal and other real property,
            ii) Improvements to a unit of property,
            iii) Components with different property classes,
            iv) Plant property, and
            v) Network assets.
   b. Taxpayers must further divide the identified units of property into major components and substantial structural parts. Absent an available exception, costs to replace a major component or substantial structural part must be capitalized.

3. **Capitalized Costs**
   a. Initial basis in purchased property is the cost of acquiring it. Only capital costs are included.
      1) Capital expenditures may be made by cash, by cash equivalent, in property, with liability, or by services.
   b. An improvement expenditure must be capitalized if it (1) results in a betterment to the unit of property, (2) adapts the unit of property to a new or different use, or (3) results in a restoration of the unit of property.
      1) An expenditure is a **betterment** if it ameliorates a condition or defect that existed before acquisition of the property or arose during the production of the property; is for a material addition to the property; or increases the property's productivity, efficiency, strength, etc.
      2) An expenditure is an **adaptation** to a new or different use if it adapts the unit of property to a use inconsistent with the taxpayer's intended ordinary use at the time the taxpayer originally placed the property into service.
      3) An expenditure is a **restoration** if it
         a) Restores a basis that has been taken into account,
         b) Returns the unit of property to working order from a state of nonfunctional disrepair,
         c) Results in a rebuilding of the unit of property to a like-new condition after the end of the property's alternative depreciation system class life, or
         d) Replaces a major component or substantial structural part of the unit of property.

Common Capitalized Costs (for Sec. 1012)

Purchase Price (Stated)	Miscellaneous Costs
Liability to which property is subject NOTE: Not unstated interest	Appraisal fees Freight Installation Testing
Closing Costs	**Major Improvements**
Brokerage commissions Pre-purchase taxes Sales tax on purchase Excise taxes Title transfer taxes Title insurance Recording fees Attorney fees Document review, preparation	New roof New gutters Extending water line to property Demolition costs and losses New electrical wiring

---

EXAMPLE 9-1   Tax Basis -- Building with a Mortgage

If an individual buys a building for $20,000 cash and assumes a mortgage of $80,000 on it, his or her basis is $100,000.

---

      4) In the case of repainting a building's exterior, the basic rules are
         a) If painting is the only thing being done, the painting costs are expensed.
         b) If painting is part of a larger project that includes capital improvements to the building's structure, the painting costs are capitalized.

c. A taxpayer must capitalize amounts paid to **facilitate** the acquisition of real or personal property. This treatment applies when the amount is paid in the process of investigating or otherwise pursuing the acquisition.

1) Some examples of facilitative costs include appraisal fees, transportation costs, inspection costs, sales and transfer taxes, finders' fees, and title registration costs.
2) Facilitative (i.e., capitalized) costs do not include amounts paid to determine whether to acquire real property or which real property to acquire. Such amounts are current deductions.
3) Amounts paid for employee compensation and overhead are treated as amounts that do not facilitate the acquisition of real or personal property.

EXAMPLE 9-2   Facilitative Cost

Susan is a manager of a family-owned grocery store and is assigned to determine where to open a second location. The compensation for Susan's time is deducted, not capitalized, by the grocery store as a facilitative cost. If the work had been performed by a real estate professional and paid as commission, the amount would have to be capitalized because it was paid to facilitate the acquisition of real property.

---

d. **Expenses not properly chargeable to a capital account.** Costs of maintaining and operating property are not added to basis.

4. **Uniform Capitalization Rules**

    a. Costs for construction (manufacture) of real or tangible personal property to be used in trade or business and costs of producing or acquiring property for sale to customers (retail) are capitalized.

    1) Capitalize all costs necessary to prepare it for its intended use, both direct and most allocable indirect costs, e.g., engineering, permit, material, storage, and equipment rent.

        a) Costs and losses associated with demolishing a structure are allocated to the **land**. The basis of any new building constructed on the land is its original cost (not FMV).

    2) Construction period interest and taxes must be capitalized as part of building cost.
    3) Indirect costs not capitalized include, among others, marketing, selling, advertising, distribution, research, experimental, Sec. 179, strike, warranty, unsuccessful bid, and deductible service costs.

    b. Uniform capitalization rules do not apply to producers and resellers if the company's average annual gross receipts (for the past 3 years) do not exceed $26 million.

5. De Minimis Expense

a. Taxpayers can make an election to deduct a de minimis amount for each transaction relating to tangible property with an economic useful life of at least 12 months.

   1) A **de minimis amount** is a cost that is so small that it is not worth tracking. Taxpayers may expense any purchased assets with a cost of less than $2,500 (per invoice or per item) provided they also use this policy for financial accounting purposes.

      a) If the taxpayer has audited or other approved financial statements, assets up to $5,000 (per invoice or per item) may be expensed.

      b) The determination of the value of an asset includes all capitalized costs, but the limit is applied on a per unit basis.

EXAMPLE 9-3   De Minimis Expense

Henry, a business owner who does not have his financial statements audited, purchases 2 computers for $3,000 and pays $500 to have them installed. The cost per computer is $1,750 [($3,000 + $500) ÷ 2], which allows the computers to be expensed as a de minimis expense.

---

6. Lump-Sum Assets

a. When more than one asset is purchased for a lump sum, the basis of each is computed pro rata by apportioning the total cost based on the relative FMV of each asset.

$$\text{Allocable cost (basis)} = \frac{\text{FMV of asset}}{\text{FMV of all assets purchased}} \times \text{Lump sum purchase price}$$

b. Alternatively, the transferor and transferee may agree in writing as to the allocation of consideration or the FMV of any assets. The agreement is binding unless the IRS deems it improper.

c. The residual method must be used for any transfers of a group of assets that constitutes a trade or business and for which the buyer's basis is determined only by the amount paid for the assets.

d. The **residual method** allocates purchase price for both transferor and transferee to asset categories up to FMV in the following order:

   1) Cash and cash equivalents
   2) Near-cash items, such as CDs, U.S. government securities, foreign currency, and other marketable securities
   3) Accounts receivable, mortgages, and credit card receivables acquired in the ordinary course of business
   4) Property held primarily for sale to customers in the ordinary course of a trade or business or stocks included in dealer inventory
   5) Assets not listed in 1) through 4) above
   6) Section 197 intangibles, such as patents and covenants not to compete except goodwill and going-concern value
   7) Goodwill and going-concern value

   NOTE: When the purchase price is lower than the aggregate FMV of the assets other than goodwill/going-concern value, the price is allocated first to the face amount of cash and then to assets 2) through 6) above, according to relative FMVs.

EXAMPLE 9-4   Lump-Sum Assets -- Price < FMV

Bennett Industries just purchased Beard Nation, Inc., for $450,000. All of the liabilities were paid off at the date of purchase. The assets of Beard Nation are as follows:

Cash	$ 50,000
Marketable securities	150,000
Accounts receivable	125,000
Inventory	100,000
Equipment	75,000
Land	50,000
FMV of all assets	$550,000

The basis of cash is the face value of $50,000, which reduces the outstanding basis to $400,000. Next, the fair market value is assigned to Class 2 assets, so the basis for marketable securities is $150,000, which reduces the remaining basis to $250,000. Accounts receivable are Class 3 assets and are assigned the fair market value of $125,000, reducing the remaining basis to $125,000. Inventory is a Class 4 asset and receives the fair market value of $100,000, reducing the remaining allocable basis to $25,000. The land and equipment are both Class 5 assets, but the fair market value of these assets is less than the remaining basis. The basis needs to be allocated between these two assets based upon the relative fair market values. The equipment receives a basis of $15,000 ($25,000 × $75,000 ÷ $125,000), and the land receives a $10,000 basis ($25,000 × $50,000 ÷ $125,000).

EXAMPLE 9-5   Lump-Sum Assets -- Price > FMV

Use the information from Example 9-4, except Bennett Industries purchases Beard Nation, Inc., for $650,000.

The basis of the assets acquired from Beard Nation are their FMVs because the purchase price exceeds the FMV of all assets. The remaining $100,000 ($650,000 purchase price – $550,000 FMV of all assets) is classified as goodwill and going concern value.

7. **Property for Services**

    a. The FMV of property received in exchange for services is income (compensation) to the provider when it is not subject to a substantial risk of forfeiture and not restricted as to transfer. The property acquired has a tax cost basis equal to the FMV of the property (i.e., the amount included in income).

EXAMPLE 9-6   Tax Basis -- Property Received for Services

Jim's neighbor needs his fence painted and offers to give Jim a rare baseball card if Jim paints his fence. The baseball card has a fair market value of $500. If Jim paints the fence, he has $500 in gross income and a $500 basis in the baseball card.

    b. Sale of restricted stock to an employee is treated as gross income to the extent the FMV exceeds the price paid. This amount is included in gross income in the first taxable year in which the property is unrestricted.

SU 9: Property Transactions: Basis and Gains

8. **Gifts**

   a. The donee's basis in property acquired by gift is the donor's basis (transferred basis), increased for any gift tax paid attributable to appreciation. The donee's basis is increased by

   $$\text{Gift tax paid} \times \left[\frac{\text{FMV (at time of gift)} - \text{Donor's basis}}{\text{FMV (at time of gift)} - \text{Annual exclusion}} \right]$$

   NOTE: The 2021 annual exclusion for gift tax purposes is $15,000 per person [i.e., a donor can give a donee $15,000 each year without paying gift tax or using a portion of their lifetime exemption (gift tax exclusions are covered in more detail in Study Unit 10)].

   b. If the FMV on the date of the gift is less than the donor's basis, the donee has a dual basis for the property, which minimizes the gain (loss) recognized on a subsequent transfer.

      1) **Loss basis.** The FMV at the date of the gift is used if the property is later transferred at a loss.
      2) **Gain basis.** The donor's basis is used if the property is later transferred at a gain.
      3) If the property is later transferred for more than FMV at the date of the gift but for less than the donor's basis at the date of the gift, no gain (loss) is recognized.

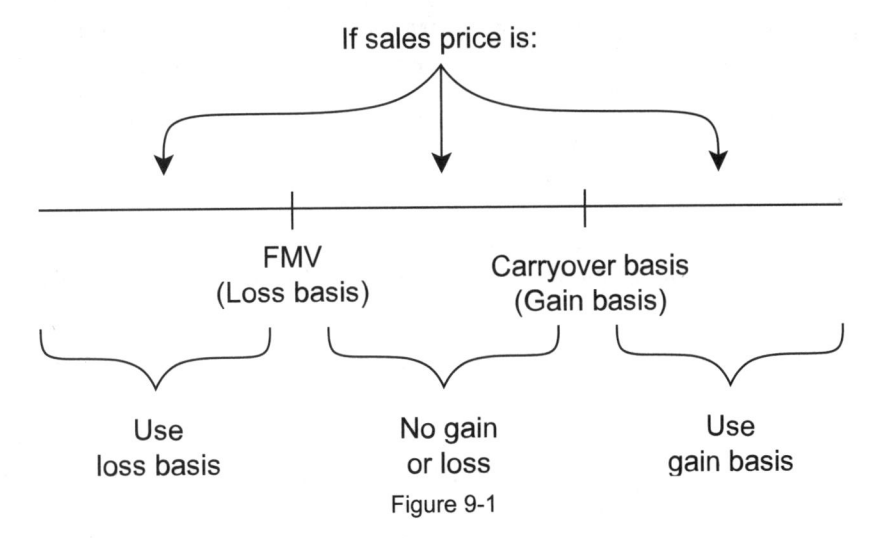

   Figure 9-1

   c. Depreciable basis is transferred basis adjusted for gift taxes paid. If converted from personal to business use, it is the lesser of FMV on the date of conversion or the transferor's adjusted basis.

EXAMPLE 9-7   Sale of Gift Property

Bobby received a house as a gift from his father. At the time of the gift, the house had a FMV of $80,000 and the father's adjusted basis was $100,000. If no events occurred that changed the basis and Bobby sells the house for $120,000, Bobby will have a $20,000 gain because he must use the father's adjusted basis ($100,000) at the time of the gift to figure his gain. If he sells the house for $70,000, he will have a $10,000 loss because he must use the FMV ($80,000) at the time of the gift to figure his loss.

If the sale was between $80,000 and $100,000, Bobby would not recognize a gain or a loss.

---

   d. When property other than money is contributed by a nonshareholder (e.g., government), the transferred basis is $0.

9. **Inherited Property**

   a. Basis is the FMV on the date of death or 6 months after if the executor elects the alternate valuation date for the estate tax return. The FMV basis rule also applies to the following property:

      1) Property received prior to death without full and adequate consideration (if a life estate was retained in it) or subject to a right of revocation. Basis is reduced by the depreciation deductions allowed to the donee.
      2) One-half of community property interests.
      3) Property acquired by form of ownership, e.g., by right of survivorship, except if consideration was paid to acquire the property from a nonspouse.

EXAMPLE 9-8   Basis of Inherited Property

A purchased 10 shares of ABC, Inc., in 1980 for $200. When A dies in the current year, she leaves the stock to her grandson, B, in her will. At the date of A's death, the stock has a FMV of $1,000. The estate has not elected an alternative valuation date. B's basis in the stock is $1,000.

EXAMPLE 9-9   Alternate Valuation Date

A purchased 10 shares of XYC, Inc., in 1980 for $200. When A dies on February 1 of the current year, she leaves the stock to her grandson, B, in her will. At the date of A's death, the stock has a FMV of $1,000. The FMV of the stock remains unchanged until October 1 of the current year, when the FMV of the stock declined to $980. The estate has elected the alternate valuation date. B's basis in the stock is $1,000 (the FMV of the stock on August 1, 6 months after A's death).

---

10. **Adjusted Basis**

    a. Initial basis is adjusted consistent with tax-relevant events. Adjustments include the following:

       1) Certain expenditures subsequent to acquisition are property costs, and they increase basis, e.g., legal fees to defend title or title insurance premiums.
       2) Basis must be increased for expenditures that prolong the life of the property by at least 1 year or materially increase its value, i.e., improve the unit of property. Assessments/improvements that increase the value of property should be capitalized.

          a) Examples include major improvements (e.g., new roof, addition to building, etc.) and zoning changes.

EXAMPLE 9-10   Adjusted Basis

In order to save money on their utility bills, Mr. and Mrs. Thrifty paid to replace their old roof with a new one with better insulation. The new roof materially increased the value of the house, so the cost of the roof should be added to the basis of the house.

3) Generally, repairs and maintenance expenses are considered a current-period deduction. However, certain repairs may be classified as an improvement, which must be capitalized. There are multiple safe harbors that allow repairs and maintenance to always be classified as a current-period expense instead of capitalized.

   a) Taxpayers who have elected to use the de minimis expense treatment must expense all repairs up to the de minimis amount (i.e., $2,500, or $5,000 for taxpayers with audited or other approved financial statements).

   b) The costs of performing certain routine maintenance activities for property may result in an improvement to the unit of property, i.e., capitalized costs. However, a safe harbor allows routine repairs and maintenance to be expensed. This safe harbor applies to actions that maintain the asset and is reasonably expected to be performed more than once for the asset's class life under the alternative depreciation system.

4) Basis must be reduced by the larger of the amount of depreciation allowed or allowable (even if not claimed). Unimproved land is not depreciated.

5) A shareholder does not recognize gain on the voluntary contribution of capital to a corporation. The shareholder's stock basis equals his or her basis in the contributed property. The corporation has a transferred basis in the property.

   a) A return of capital distribution reduces basis and becomes a capital gain when the shareholder's basis in the stock reaches zero.

6) The basis of stock acquired in a nontaxable distribution (e.g., stock rights) is allocated a portion of the basis of the stock upon which the distribution was made.

   a) If the new shares and old shares are not identical, the basis is allocated in proportion to the FMV of the original stock and the distribution as of the date of distribution.

   b) If the new and old shares are identical (e.g., stock splits) the old basis is simply divided among the new total of shares.

   c) If the FMV of the stock rights is less than 15% of the FMV of the stock upon which it was issued, the rights have a basis of zero (unless an election is made to allocate basis).

7) Basis adjustment is required for certain specific items that represent a tax benefit. Three examples follow:
   a) Casualty losses reduce basis by the amount of the loss, by any amounts recovered by insurance, and by any amounts for which no tax benefit was received, e.g., $100 floor for individuals with losses only attributed to a federally declared disaster and losses to the extent of casualty gains are deductible.
   b) Debt discharge. Specific exclusion from gross income is allowed to certain insolvent persons for debt discharged. Taxpayers may elect to reduce basis in depreciable assets by the amount of the exclusion. If an election is not made, they must reduce certain tax attributes.
   c) Credit for building rehabilitation. The full amount of the credit must be deducted from the basis.

Common Examples of Decreases to Basis

Exclusion from income of subsidies for energy conservation measures
Casualty or theft loss deductions (losses only attributed to a federally declared disaster and losses to the extent of casualty gains are deductible) and insurance reimbursements
Certain vehicle credits
Section 179 deduction
Deductions previously allowed (or allowable) for amortization, depreciation, and depletion
Depreciation
Nontaxable corporate distributions
Rebates treated as adjustments to the sales price

STOP & REVIEW

You have completed the outline for this subunit.
Study multiple-choice questions 1 through 7 beginning on page 252.

SU 9: Property Transactions: Basis and Gains

9.2 DEPRECIATION AND AMORTIZATION

SUCCESS TIP: Candidates should expect to be tested on capital cost recovery for corporations, including depreciation, Sec. 179 expense, and amortization.

1. **General Information**

   From Form 4562

   | 16 Other depreciation (including ACRS) . . . . | 16 | |

   a. Tax accounting methods of depreciation that allow a deduction in excess of the estimated current year's decline in economic value are accelerated cost recovery methods.

   b. Property subject to the allowance for depreciation is tangible property used in trade, in business, or for production of income and has a determinable, limited useful life.

   c. The amount of a current depreciation deduction is computed by applying a rate to depreciable basis.

   > **BACKGROUND 9-1 Accelerated Depreciation**
   >
   > Accelerated depreciation is a tax relief measure highly desired by businesses. Quickly expensing the cost of investment in plant and equipment for tax purposes allows businesses to significantly reduce their tax liability and thus reduce the cost of capital investment. However, it is important to note that the benefit provided by accelerated depreciation is based on the time value of money (i.e., a deduction today is better than a deduction tomorrow).

   d. The IRS has published a list of acceptable useful life ranges by types of asset: the **asset depreciation range (ADR)**.

   e. Straight-line (SL) depreciation. The annual amount allowable is the depreciable basis reduced for salvage value (SV) and divided by the useful life of the asset.

   $$(\text{Basis} - \text{SV}) \div \text{Useful life}$$

   f. 150% declining balance (DB). Basis (not reduced by SV) minus previously allowable deductions, which is adjusted basis (AB), is multiplied by 150% of the straight-line rate.

   $$\text{AB} \times (150\% \div \text{Useful life})$$

   1) The rate is constant. It is applied to declining basis. It is generally applicable to used property with a useful life of at least 3 years and used depreciable real property.

   g. 200% declining balance. The constant rate is 200% of the straight-line rate.

   $$\text{AB} \times (200\% \div \text{Useful life})$$

   1) It is generally allowable for property with a useful life of at least 3 years and new residential rental property.

   h. Unit of Production Method

   $$(\text{Basis} - \text{SV}) \times \left(\frac{\text{\# of units produced during tax year}}{\text{Estimated total of units asset will produce}}\right)$$

   i. Operating Days Method

   $$(\text{Basis} - \text{SV}) \times \left(\frac{\text{\# of days used during tax year}}{\text{Estimated total of days asset can be used}}\right)$$

2. Modified Accelerated Cost Recovery System (MACRS)

From Form 4562

Part III — MACRS Depreciation (Don't include listed property. See instructions.)

Section A

17 MACRS deductions for assets placed in service in tax years beginning before [Year] . . . . **17** _____

18 If you are electing to group any assets placed in service during the tax year into one or more general asset accounts, check here . . . . ▶ ☐

Section B—Assets Placed in Service During [Year] Tax Year Using the General Depreciation System

(a) Classification of property	(b) Month and year placed in service	(c) Basis for depreciation (business/investment use only—see instructions)	(d) Recovery period	(e) Convention	(f) Method	(g) Depreciation deduction
19a 3-year property						
b 5-year property						
c 7-year property						
d 10-year property						
e 15-year property						
f 20-year property						
g 25-year property			25 yrs.		S/L	
h Residential rental property			27.5 yrs.	MM	S/L	
			27.5 yrs.	MM	S/L	
i Nonresidential real property			39 yrs.	MM	S/L	
				MM	S/L	

Section C—Assets Placed in Service During [Year] Tax Year Using the Alternative Depreciation System

20a Class life					S/L	
b 12-year			12 yrs.		S/L	
c 30-year			30 yrs.	MM	S/L	
d 40-year			40 yrs.	MM	S/L	

a. The Modified Accelerated Cost Recovery System (MACRS) is used to recover the basis of most business and investment property placed in service after 1986.

b. MACRS consists of two depreciation systems, the **General Depreciation System (GDS)** and the **Alternative Depreciation System (ADS)**. Generally, GDS must be used unless the taxpayer is specifically required by law to use ADS or the taxpayer elects to use ADS. Election must be made by the due date, including extensions, for the tax return of the year in which the property was placed in service.

1) A switch is made to straight-line on adjusted (reduced for allowable depreciation) basis when it yields a higher amount. However, the current year's depreciation cannot exceed the item's adjusted basis.

2) Real property costs are recovered using a straight-line rate on unadjusted basis.

3) Salvage value is ignored.

4) The 200%-declining-balance method is used for MACRS recovery periods of 3, 5, 7, and 10 years.

5) 150% is used for 15- and 20-year property.

6) ADS utilizes a straight-line rate based on longer recovery periods. Examples of ADS recovery periods follow:

# of Years	Items
5	Cars, light trucks, certain technological equipment
12	Personal property with no class life
15	Agricultural structures (single-purpose)
30	Residential rental
40	Nonresidential real estate

c. Mid-year (personal property), which is also commonly referred to as half-year, and mid-month (real property) conventions apply.

   1) Under the mid-year convention, each asset is treated as placed into service at the midpoint of the year in which it was actually placed into service.
   2) Under the mid-month convention, each asset is treated as placed into service at the midpoint of the month in which it was actually placed into service.
   3) A mid-quarter convention applies when asset acquisition is bunched at year end.

      a) Each asset is treated as placed in service at the midpoint of the quarter in which it actually was placed in service.
      b) The convention is applied to all depreciable property acquired during the tax year when the sum of the bases of all depreciable personal property placed in service during the last quarter of the year exceeds 40% of those placed in service during the entire year.
      c) The first year depreciation is calculated by multiplying the full-year amount by the following percentages based on the quarter placed in service:

         87.5% for the first quarter
         62.5% for the second quarter
         37.5% for the third quarter
         12.5% for the fourth quarter

EXAMPLE 9-11	Mid-Quarter Convention

The formula for 3-year property placed in service in the third quarter is AB × (200% ÷ Useful life) × 37.5%.

d. IRS tables provide rates to be applied to the unadjusted basis (except for Sec. 179 expense) for each year of service. The rate incorporates applicable methods, applicable recovery periods, and conventions.

e. Depreciation is allowed during a disposition year. However, no depreciation is allowed if an asset is placed in service and disposed of during the same year.

f. Personal property is assigned a recovery period of either 3, 5, 7, 10, 15, or 20 years. The half-year or mid-quarter convention is applied.

MACRS Recovery Periods (Personal Property)

MACRS Recovery Period (# of Years)	DB Rate Applicable Percent	Examples
3	200	Special tools, e.g., for rubber manufacturing
5	200	Computers, office machinery (e.g., copier) Cars, trucks R&E equipment
7	200	Most machinery Office furniture and equipment Property without ADR midpoint & not otherwise classified
10	200	Water vessels, e.g., barge Petroleum processing equipment Food & tobacco manufacturing Agricultural structures (single-purpose)
15	150	Data communication plants, e.g., for phone Sewage treatment plants Billboards
20	150	Utilities, e.g., municipal sewers Not real property with ADR midpoint 27.5 years

g. Real property. The straight-line method and the mid-month convention apply.

1) Residential rental property. The straight-line rate is based on a 27 1/2-year recovery period.

   a) It is real property with at least 80% of gross rents coming from dwelling units. Partial use by the owner is included. Transient use of more than half the units excludes the property, e.g., a motel.

2) Nonresidential real estate is assigned a 39-year recovery period.

   a) It is real property that is not residential rental property.

3) Some realty has a recovery period less than 27 1/2 years, e.g., specified farm buildings.

Property Expensing and Disposition

	Personal Property	Real Property Residential	Real Property Nonresidential
Depreciation method	MACRS	Straight-line	Straight-line
Recovery period	Normally 5 and 7 years	27.5 years	39 years
Convention	Mid-year Mid-quarter (40% rule)	Mid-month	Mid-month
Disposition	Same as the convention of the property No cost recovery if placed in service and disposed of in the same year		

Depreciation Methods

Method		Type of Property	Benefit
GDS	200% DB	• Nonfarm 3-, 5-, 7-, and 10-year property • Farm 3-, 5-, 7-, and 10-year property placed in service after 2017, in tax years ending after 2017	• Provides a greater deduction during the earlier recovery years • Changes to SL when that method provides an equal or greater deduction
	150% DB	• Farm 3-, 5-, 7-, or 10-year property placed in service before 2018 • All 15- and 20-year property • Nonfarm 3-, 5-, 7-, or 10-year property • Farm 3-, 5-, 7-, or 10-year property placed in service after 2017	• Provides a greater deduction during the earlier recovery years • Changes to SL when that method provides an equal or greater deduction
	SL	• Nonresidential real property • Residential rental property • Trees or vines bearing fruit or nuts • Water utility property • All 3-, 5-, 7-, 10-, 15-, and 20-year property • Property for which you elected Sec. 168(k)(4) of the Internal Revenue Code for a tax year beginning before January 1, 2018 • Qualified improvement property [as defined in Sec. 168(e)(6) of the Internal Revenue Code] placed in service after 2017	• Provides for equal yearly deductions (except for the first and last years)
ADS	SL	• Listed property used 50% or less for business • Property used predominantly outside the U.S. • Tax-exempt property • Tax-exempt bond-financed property • Farm property used when an election not to apply the uniform capitalization rules is in effect • Imported property • Any property for which you elect to use this method • Any nonresidential real property, residential rental property, or qualified improvement property held by an electing real property trade or business [as defined in Sec. 163(j)(7)(B) of the Internal Revenue Code] • Any property that has a recovery period of 10 years or more under the GDS that is held by an electing farming business [as defined in Sec. 163(j)(7)(C) of the Internal Revenue Code]	• Provides for equal yearly deductions (except for the first and last years)

h. **Qualified Improvement Property (QIP)** means any improvement to an interior portion of a building which is nonresidential real property if such improvement is placed in service after the date such building was first placed in service.

   1) QIP does not include any improvement for which the expenditure is attributable to the enlargement of the building, any elevator or escalator, or the internal structural framework of the building.

   2) QIP is 15-year property under MACRS (20-year property under ADS). QIP qualifies for Sec. 179 and is eligible for 100% bonus depreciation.

i. The ADS recovery period of residential rental property is reduced from 40 years to 30 years for acquisitions placed in service after December 31, 2017.

j. The cost recovery period is revised from 7 to 5 years for any machinery or equipment (other than any grain bin, cotton ginning asset, fence, or other land improvement used in a farming business, the original use of which commences with the taxpayer after December 31, 2017).

3. **Section 179 Expense**

From Form 4562

Part I — Election To Expense Certain Property Under Section 179
Note: If you have any listed property, complete Part V before you complete Part I.

1	Maximum amount (see instructions)	1
2	Total cost of section 179 property placed in service (see instructions)	2
3	Threshold cost of section 179 property before reduction in limitation (see instructions)	3
4	Reduction in limitation. Subtract line 3 from line 2. If zero or less, enter -0-	4
5	Dollar limitation for tax year. Subtract line 4 from line 1. If zero or less, enter -0-. If married filing separately, see instructions	5

6	(a) Description of property	(b) Cost (business use only)	(c) Elected cost

7	Listed property. Enter the amount from line 29 7	
8	Total elected cost of section 179 property. Add amounts in column (c), lines 6 and 7	8
9	Tentative deduction. Enter the **smaller** of line 5 or line 8	9
10	Carryover of disallowed deduction from line 13 of your [prior year] Form 4562	10
11	Business income limitation. Enter the smaller of business income (not less than zero) or line 5 (see instructions)	11
12	Section 179 expense deduction. Add lines 9 and 10, but don't enter more than line 11	12
13	Carryover of disallowed deduction to [next year]. Add lines 9 and 10, less line 12 ▶ 13	

Note: Don't use Part II or Part III below for listed property. Instead, use Part V.

a. A person may elect to deduct all or part of the cost of Sec. 179 property acquired during the year as an expense rather than a capital expenditure.

   1) Section 179 expense is treated as depreciation.

      a) It must be elected by the taxpayer.

      b) It reduces basis in the property (but not below zero) prior to computation of any other depreciation deduction allowable for the first year.

      c) It is subject to depreciation recapture under Sec. 1245.

b. Section 179 property is depreciable personal property and qualified real property used in the active conduct of a trade or business.

   1) Section 179 property must be acquired by purchase from an unrelated party.

c. Section 179 property also includes qualified real property to include any of the following improvements to nonresidential real property placed in service after the date such property was first placed in service:
   1) Roofs
   2) Security systems
   3) Fire protection and alarm systems
   4) Heating, ventilation, and air-conditioning property
      a) Qualified energy-efficient-heating-and-air-conditioning property means any Sec. 1250 property
         i) With respect to which depreciation (or amortization in lieu of depreciation) is allowable;
         ii) Which is installed as part of a building's heating, cooling, ventilation, or hot water system; and
         iii) Which is within the scope of Standard 90.1-2007 or any successor standard.
d. For 2021, a deduction may be for no more than either
   1) The amount of $1,050,000 minus the excess of Sec. 179 eligible asset acquisitions for the year over $2.62 million (no Sec. 179 deduction if total purchase cost is above $3.67 million) or
   2) Taxable income (TI) from the active conduct of any trade or business during the tax year.
      a) Current-year excess over TI may be carried forward and treated as Sec. 179 cost in a subsequent year subject to the overall limitation.

EXAMPLE 9-12   Maximum Sec. 179 Deduction

In 2021, Diana's Corner Stores upgraded various equipment and computers at a total cost of $2,920,000. All assets purchased are eligible for Sec. 179 treatment. The Sec. 179 deduction is phased out dollar for dollar once the minimum threshold for purchases is exceeded. Therefore, the maximum Sec. 179 deduction Diana's Corner Stores can take is $750,000 [$1,050,000 maximum deduction − ($2,920,000 purchases − $2,620,000 phaseout)].

---

e. Apply the following limits in the order presented:
   1) Pass-through entities. Apply each limit on Sec. 179 expense first at the entity level and then at the partner/shareholder level.
   2) Trusts and estates may not claim a Sec. 179 deduction.
   3) Only the business-use portion of the cost of Sec. 179 property may be expensed.
   4) Cost of Sec. 179 property does not include the basis determined by reference to other property held by the taxpayer.
   5) No more than the statutory amount may be deducted as depreciation on cars and certain luxury items. Excess over the limit may not be expensed under Sec. 179.
   6) The limit described in item d. above.

f. Recapture. Section 179 property need not be used to elect the deduction. The amount of allowed Sec. 179 deduction may be allocated to Sec. 179 property as desired. But if Sec. 179 property is disposed of prior to the end of the MACRS recovery period, gross income includes any

1) Excess of Sec. 179 deduction over
2) MACRS deductions allowable, notwithstanding Sec. 179.

NOTE: Recapture also applies when the business use of the Sec. 179 property changes to less than 50% of total use.

4. **100% Expensing (Bonus Depreciation)**

From Form 4562

Part II	Special Depreciation Allowance and Other Depreciation (Don't include listed property. See instructions.)
14 Special depreciation allowance for qualified property (other than listed property) placed in service during the tax year. See instructions	14

a. There is additional first-year bonus depreciation of 100% for qualified property (including certain planted or grafted plants bearing fruits and nuts) acquired and placed in service after September 27, 2017, and before January 1, 2023.

1) For certain property with longer production periods, the acquisition and placed-in-service period is after September 27, 2017, and before January 1, 2024.
2) The property is eligible for the additional depreciation if it is the taxpayer's first use. This allows for the property to be new or used.
3) Qualified property would not include any property used by a regulated public utility company or any property used in a real property trade or business.
4) Qualifying property must be new or used MACRS property with a 20-year-or-less recovery period and must be placed into service before January 1, 2027 (before January 1, 2028, for certain property with longer production periods).
5) Qualifying property includes leasehold improvements.
6) The property cannot be acquired from a related party.

b. Any deduction for bonus depreciation is taken before the regular depreciation is recalculated.

c. The bonus depreciation rate is phased down in subsequent years as follows:

1) 80% -- property placed in service after December 31, 2022, and before January 1, 2024.
2) 60% -- property placed in service after December 31, 2023, and before January 1, 2025.
3) 40% -- property placed in service after December 31, 2024, and before January 1, 2026.
4) 20% -- property placed in service after December 31, 2025, and before January 1, 2027.

NOTE: For certain property with longer production periods, the dates above are increased by 1 year. For instance, 80% per property placed in service after December 31, 2023, and before January 1, 2025.

5. **Amortization**

From Form 4562

Part VI	Amortization				
(a) Description of costs	(b) Date amortization begins	(c) Amortizable amount	(d) Code section	(e) Amortization period or percentage	(f) Amortization for this year
42 Amortization of costs that begins during your [Year] tax year (see instructions):					
43 Amortization of costs that began before your [Year] tax year				43	
44 **Total.** Add amounts in column (f). See the instructions for where to report				44	

a. Amortization accounts for recovery of capital (e.g., intangible assets, Sec. 197) in a similar manner as straight-line depreciation. Intangible assets make up the majority of amortizable assets and are recovered over the asset's useful life or, in the case of Sec. 197 intangibles, 15 years. Other items are amortized over a period specified for that item.

b. Any start-up costs or organizational expenses after the allowed $5,000 immediate deduction (each) are amortized over 15 years. The $5,000 deduction is reduced by the amount of the total costs exceeding $50,000. Amortization starts with the month the active trade or business begins.

c. Costs of acquiring a lease are amortized over the lease term.

   1) Renewal options are included in the term if less than 75% of the cost is attributable to the period prior to renewal. Allocate the cost over the original and renewal term, unless the contract (reasonably) specifies otherwise.

   2) Improvements by the lessee are deducted under the MACRS method.

      a) For a lease entered into before September 26, 1985, the lessee could elect to recover the costs over the remaining lease term.

d. Intangibles. The cost of certain intangibles acquired (not created) in connection with the conduct of a trade or business or income-producing activity is amortized over a 15-year period, beginning with the later of the month in which the intangible is acquired or business begins.

   1) Qualified intangibles do not include intangibles that result from the taxpayer's own efforts, unless in connection with the acquisition of a trade or business.

   2) Qualified intangibles include the following:

      a) Acquired goodwill and going-concern value
      b) The work force, information base, patent, copyright, know-how, customers, suppliers, or similar items
      c) Licenses, permits, or other rights granted by governmental units
      d) Covenants not to compete
      e) Any franchise, trademark, or trade name

3) Excluded from intangible amortization treatment are the following:
   a) Interests in corporations, partnerships, trusts, estates
   b) Interests in land
   c) Most financial instruments and contracts
   d) Leases of intangible personal property
   e) Professional sports franchises

EXAMPLE 9-13   Amortization of Intangible Assets

EMEN Corp. purchased all the assets of a sole proprietorship, including the following intangible assets:

Goodwill	$98,000
Copyright	71,000
Interest in land	12,000
Covenant not to compete	13,000

The cost of certain intangibles acquired (not created) in connection with the conduct of a trade or business or income-producing activity is amortized over a 15-year period. Qualified intangibles include acquired goodwill, copyrights, and covenants not to compete. Therefore, EMEN should amortize $182,000 ($98,000 goodwill + $71,000 copyright + $13,000 covenant not to compete) over the 15-year period.

---

4) Loss realized on disposition of a qualified intangible is disallowed if the taxpayer retains other qualified intangibles acquired in the same (set of) transaction(s). The amount disallowed is added to the basis of the intangibles retained.

e. Reforestation costs not immediately deductible are amortized over 7 years. Amortization starts the sixth month of the year costs are incurred.

f. The cost of geological and geophysical expenses related to domestic oil and gas exploration or development are amortized over 2 years. Like reforestation cost, amortization begins on the mid-point of the year costs are paid or incurred.

g. Pollution control facility costs are amortized over 5 years, with an exception of 7 years for atmospheric facilities.

h. Research and experimentation costs have a 5-year amortization period.

SU 9: Property Transactions: Basis and Gains

6. **Depletion**

    From Form 1040 Schedule E

    | 18 | Depreciation expense or depletion ...... | 18 | | | |

    a. Depletion accounts for recovery of investment in natural resources property.
    b. Only a person who has an economic interest in a (mineral) property is entitled to deductions for depletion.
        1) A person has an economic interest if (s)he
            a) Acquires by investment an interest in the mineral in place
            b) Derives income from extraction of the mineral
            c) Looks to the extracted mineral for return of capital
        2) Investment need not be in cash and could be in, for example,
            a) Land that ensures control over access to the mineral
            b) Stationary equipment used to extract and produce the mineral
    c. Cost depletion is computed as follows:

    $$\frac{\text{Adjusted basis in mineral property}}{\text{Estimated mineral units available at year's start}} \times \text{Mineral units sold during year}$$

    NOTE: The total deductions are limited to unrecovered capital investment.

    d. Percentage depletion allows deduction in excess of capital investment and is the lower of
        1) 50% of the person's TI before depletion (100% for oil and gas property) or
        2) A percentage (specified by statute) of gross income from the property less related rents or royalties paid or incurred.

STOP & REVIEW

You have completed the outline for this subunit.
Study multiple-choice questions 8 through 13 beginning on page 255.

9.3 CAPITAL GAINS AND LOSSES

1. **Capital Assets**

    a. All property is characterized as a capital asset, unless expressly excluded.

    b. The following types of property are not capital assets:

    1) Inventory (or stock in trade) -- property held primarily for sale to customers in the ordinary course of a trade or business
    2) Real or depreciable property used in a trade or business
    3) Accounts or notes receivable acquired in the ordinary course of trade or business for services rendered or for 1) or 2) above
    4) Copyrights and artistic compositions held by the person who composed them
    5) Certain U.S. government publications acquired at reduced cost

    c. Property held either for personal use or for the production of income is a capital asset, but dealer property (i.e., property held primarily for sale to customers in the ordinary course of trade or business) is not.

    1) Stocks, bonds, commodities, and the like are capital assets unless they are dealer property.
    2) Land held primarily for investment (capital asset), which is then subdivided, may be treated as converted to property held for sale in a trade or business.

    d. Goodwill is a capital asset when generated within the business. If a business sells its assets and receives more than the FMV of those assets, the remainder is considered a capital gain from the sale of goodwill.

2. **Gain (Loss) Realized and Recognized**

    a. Generally, all gains (losses) are realized on the sale or other disposition of property. This includes sales or exchanges that are required in characterizing a realized gain or loss as capital. For capital assets that become wholly worthless during the year, the sale or disposition date is considered to be the last day of the year.

    1) For real property, a sale or exchange occurs on the earlier of the date of conveyance or the date that the burdens of ownership pass to the buyer.
    2) Also, liquidating distributions and losses on worthless securities are treated as sales or exchanges.
    3) The transfer of a franchise is not treated as a sale or exchange of a capital asset if the transferor retains significant power, rights, or continuing interest with respect to the franchise.

    b. The following formula shows computation of gain or loss realized:

        Money received (or to be received)
    + FMV of other property received[1]
    + Liability relief[2]
    − Money or other property given up
    − Selling expenses[3]
    − Liabilities assumed[2]
    = **Amount realized**

        Amount realized
    − Adjusted basis
    = **Gain (loss) realized**

    [1] If FMV of other property received is not determinable with reasonable certainty, FMV of the property given up is used.
    [2] Whether recourse or nonrecourse.
    [3] Selling expenses are subtracted from gross receivables to yield the amount realized.

SU 9: Property Transactions: Basis and Gains

> **EXAMPLE 9-14**   **Realized Gain**
>
> The purchase price of a building was $400,000 ($100,000 cash + $300,000 mortgage). Two years later, improvements of $80,000 were made to the building. The building sold for $700,000 ($600,000 cash + $100,000 mortgage balance). A total of $180,000 depreciation had been taken as of the date sold. The adjusted basis is $300,000 ($400,000 original basis + $80,000 improvements – $180,000 depreciation taken). The realized gain is $400,000 ($700,000 cash and liability relief – $300,000 adjusted basis).

    c. All realized gains must be recognized unless the IRC expressly provides otherwise. Conversely, no deduction is allowed for a realized loss unless the IRC expressly provides for it.

    NOTE: Though personal-use property is a capital asset and gains from such property are recognized, a loss is not deductible.

3. **Holding Period**

    a. The holding period of an asset is measured in calendar months, beginning on the day after acquisition and including the disposal date.

Acquisition by or of	Holding Period -- Starts or by reference to
Sale or exchange	Acquisition[1]
Gift: For gain	Donor's acquisition
For loss	Acquisition
Inheritance	Automatic LT
Nontaxable exchanges	
Like-kind (Sec. 1031)	Include HP of exchanged asset[2]
Corporate stock (Sec. 351)	Include HP of contributed asset
Property in entity	Include transferor's HP
Partnership interest (Sec. 721)	Include HP of contributed asset[2]
Property in entity	Include transferor's HP[2]
Ordinary income property	Exchange
Involuntary conversion (Sec. 1033)	Include HP of converted asset
Residence (Sec. 1034)	Include HP of old home
Use conversion (T/B & personal)	Include period of prior use
Optioned property	Exclude option period
Securities	Trading date
Short sales (Ss)	Earlier of Ss closing or property sale date
Commodity futures	LT after 6-month HP

[1] Always start computation using day after date of applicable acquisition.
[2] If capital asset or Sec. 1231 property; otherwise, the holding period starts the day after date of exchange.

    b. Long-term capital gain or loss (LTCG or LTCL) is realized from a capital asset held for more than 1 year. Short-term capital gain or loss (STCG or STCL) is realized if the asset was held 1 year or less.

    c. For individuals, net capital gain (NCG) is the excess of net LTCG over net STCL. Net STCG is not included in NCG. Do not confuse it with capital gain net income.

    d. Net STCG is treated as ordinary income for individuals. Net capital gain rates do not apply to net STCG.

        1) Net STCG = STCG – STCL
        2) But net STCG may be offset by net LTCL.

4. **Taxation**
   a. For individuals, net short-term capital gain is taxed as ordinary income.
   b. For individuals, capital transactions involving **long-term holding periods** (assets held for over 12 months) are grouped by tax rates. The maximum capital gains rates are 0%, 15%, 20%, 25%, or 28%.
      1) The thresholds for the application of the capital gains rates are adjusted for inflation. The 2021 thresholds are listed below.

Filing Status	0% Breakpoint	15% Breakpoint	20% Breakpoint
Married Filing Jointly	Under $80,800	$80,800	$501,600
Head of Household	Under 54,100	54,100	473,750
Single	Under 40,400	40,400	445,850
Married Filing Separately	Under 40,400	40,400	250,800
Estates and Trusts	Under 2,700	2,700	13,250

   c. The capital gains rate is **25%** on unrecaptured Sec. 1250 gains (discussed further in Study Unit 10, Subunit 4).
   d. The maximum capital gains rate is **28%** on gains and losses from the sale of collectibles and the taxable portion of gains from qualified Sec. 1202 stock (i.e., gains from certain small business stock after the 50% or 75% exclusion is applied).

   NOTE: The 0%, 15%, 20%, 25%, and 28% capital gains rate outline content above will be referenced as "baskets" in the following outline content for simplicity.

   e. After gains and losses are classified in the appropriate baskets, losses for each long-term basket are used to offset any gains within that basket.
   f. If a long-term basket has a net loss, the loss will be used to offset net gain for the highest long-term rate basket, then to offset the next highest rate basket and so on.

EXAMPLE 9-15   Capital Gains (Losses) and Grouping by Tax Rates

A taxpayer realizes a $10,000 net loss in the 15% basket, a $5,000 net gain in the 25% basket, and an $8,000 net gain in the 28% basket. The taxpayer will first apply the net loss against the gain in the 28% basket, reducing the gain in this basket to zero. Then, the remaining $2,000 loss is applied against the gain in the 25% basket, leaving a $3,000 net capital gain in the 25% basket.

SU 9: Property Transactions: Basis and Gains

g. A carryover of a net long-term capital loss from a prior year is used first to offset any net gain in the 28% basket, then to offset any net gain in the 20% basket, and finally to offset any net gain in the 15% basket. Likewise, net STCL is also used first to offset net gain for the highest long-term basket and so on.

EXAMPLE 9-16 — Long-Term Capital Loss Carryover and Net STCL

A taxpayer has a $1,000 long-term capital loss carryover, a net short-term capital loss of $2,000, a $1,000 net gain in the 28% basket, and a $5,000 net gain in the 15% basket. Both losses are first applied to offset the 28% rate gain, using the $1,000 loss carryover first until completely exhausted. Since no gain exists in the 28% basket after applying the carryover, the net STCL is then applied against the next highest gain in the 15% basket. As a result, only a $3,000 net capital gain remains in the 15% basket.

---

h. An individual may deduct a net capital loss in the current year up to the lesser of $3,000 ($1,500 if MFS) or ordinary income.

1) An individual may carry forward any excess CLs indefinitely.
2) The carryforward is treated as a CL incurred in the subsequent year.
3) Net STCL is treated as having been deductible in the preceding year before net LTCL.
4) No carryover is allowed from a decedent to his or her estate.

i. Schedule D (Form 1040) is used to compute and summarize capital gains and/or losses on the sale or disposition of capital assets listed on Form 8949, and the summary combines the long-term gains (losses) with the short-term gains (losses). When these capital gains and losses all net to a gain, it is called capital gain net income.

j. For corporations, all capital gain is taxed at the corporation's regular tax rate.

k. A corporation may use CLs only to offset CGs each year. A corporation must carry the excess CL back 3 years and forward 5 years and characterize all carryovers as STCLs (regardless of character).

EXAMPLE 9-17 — Excess Capital Loss

ABC, Inc., a C corporation, has $500 in capital gains and $600 in capital losses. Only $500 of the capital losses can offset the capital gains. The remaining $100 of capital loss is nondeductible in the current year and is carried back 3 years and forward 5 years.

5. **Return of Capital**

    a. The amount of a distribution is a dividend to the extent of earnings and profits. Dividends do not reduce the shareholder's basis in the stock.

    b. A shareholder treats the amount of a distribution in excess of earnings and profits (E&P) as tax-exempt return of capital to the extent of his or her basis. A distribution in excess of basis is a capital gain.

6. **Wash Sales**

    a. To prevent abusive transactions in which a taxpayer sells property at a loss but quickly repurchases the property, leaving the taxpayer in the position of still having the property but with the benefit of recognizing a loss, a current loss realized on a wash sale of securities is not recognized. A wash sale occurs when substantially the same securities are purchased within 30 days before or after being sold at a loss.

        1) The disallowed loss is added to the basis of the stock purchased in the wash sale.
        2) The holding period includes that of the originally purchased stock.
        3) Spouses are treated as one person.

EXAMPLE 9-18   Wash Sales -- Same Number of Shares

Taxpayer sells 100 shares of ABC stock for $400, at a loss of $200. Within 30 days, Taxpayer purchases an identical 100 shares of ABC for $500 and sells all 100 shares two months later for $900. Taxpayer recognizes no loss on the first sale and only a $200 gain ($900 sale price − $500 cost − $200 basis adjustment due to loss) on the subsequent sale of stock.

EXAMPLE 9-19   Wash Sales -- Repurchase Fewer Shares

Taxpayer sells 100 shares of ABC stock for $400, at a loss of $200. Within 30 days, Taxpayer purchases an identical 40 shares of ABC for $200 and sells all 40 shares two months later for $320. Taxpayer recognizes a loss of $120 [$200 loss × (60 ÷ 100) proportion of shares not repurchased] on the first sale and a gain on the subsequent sale of stock of $40 ($320 sale price − $200 cost − $80 basis adjustment due to loss).

EXAMPLE 9-20   Wash Sales -- Repurchase More Shares

Taxpayer sells 100 shares of ABC stock for $400, at a loss of $200. Within 30 days, Taxpayer purchases an identical 120 shares of ABC for $600 and sells all 120 shares two months later for $1,080. Taxpayer recognizes no loss on the first sale and a gain on the subsequent sale of stock of $280 ($1,080 sale price − $600 cost − $200 basis adjustment due to loss).

7. **Small Business Stock Losses**

    a. Section 1244 stock is stock (common or preferred, voting or nonvoting) of a small business corporation held since its issuance (e.g., not acquired by gift) and issued for money or other property (not stock or securities).

    b. Up to $50,000 ($100,000 if MFJ) of loss realized on disposition or worthlessness of Sec. 1244 stock is treated as an ordinary loss.

    1) The limit applies to Sec. 1244 stock held in all corporations.
    2) The limit is applied at a partner level, if applicable.
    3) The loss is considered to be from a trade or business for NOL purposes.

    c. To be classified as a small business corporation, the aggregate amount of money and property received by the corporation for stock cannot exceed $1 million.

    1) Even if the contributions exceed $1 million, part of the stock (up to $1 million) may be designated by the corporation as qualifying for Sec. 1244 ordinary loss treatment.

    d. If the basis of property contributed in exchange for Sec. 1244 stock exceeds its FMV, the excess is treated as capital loss before any other realized loss may be treated as ordinary.

    1) Basis in the stock is equal to the property's basis in the hands of the transferor when contributed.

    e. Additional investment without issuance of additional shares of Sec. 1244 stock increases original basis; however, any resulting loss must be apportioned between the qualifying Sec. 1244 stock and the nonqualifying additional capital interest.

8. **Small Business Stock Exclusion**

    a. Under Sec. 1202, taxpayers may exclude 50% of the gain from the sale or exchange of small business stock. The stock must have been issued after August 10, 1993, and held for more than 5 years. The exclusion increases to 75% for stock acquired after February 17, 2009, and before September 28, 2010. The exclusion increases to 100% for stock acquired after September 27, 2010.

    b. The exclusion is limited to the greater of $10 million ($5 million MFS) or 10 times the taxpayer's adjusted basis in the stock.

SUCCESS TIP: Capital gains and losses has been a heavily tested topic on the CPA Exam, with both conceptual and calculation questions being used to test this area.

9. **Nonbusiness Bad Debt**

    a. A business bad debt is deductible to arrive at AGI (above-the-line) as ordinary loss. A nonbusiness bad debt is treated as a STCL.

10. **Business Start-Up Costs**

    a. Capitalized amounts not yet amortized upon disposition of the business are treated as a capital loss.

11. **Short Sales**

    a. A short sale occurs when a taxpayer sells property the taxpayer does not own (or owns but does not wish to sell). The sale is made in two steps.

        1) The taxpayer borrows property and delivers it to a buyer.
        2) At a later date, the taxpayer either buys substantially identical property and delivers it to the lender or makes delivery out of property the taxpayer held at the time of the sale.

            a) The taxpayer does not recognize gain or loss until delivery of property to close the short sale.
            b) The character of the gain or loss is dependent upon the character of the property used to close the sale.

    b. The holding period of the property used in the short sale runs from the date the seller originally purchased the property to the date the property is delivered to close out the sale (i.e., when the borrowed shares are returned).

        1) If, prior to the short sale, the taxpayer owns identical property (e.g., stock-for-stock sale), then the holding period ends on the date of the short sale.

EXAMPLE 9-21   Short Sale without Prior Ownership

On 1/3/Year 2, Mary agrees to sell 500 shares of ABC Corp. to John. Because Mary does not own any of ABC's shares, she borrows the 500 shares from her broker and delivers them to John. Mary is obligated to return the shares to her broker by 1/10/Year 3. What are the holding period and character of gain or loss in the following scenarios?

(1) Mary buys 500 shares from the market on 1/4/Year 3 and delivers them to her broker on 1/10/Year 3.

(2) Mary buys 500 shares from the market on 1/10/Year 3 and immediately delivers them to her broker.

(3) Mary buys 500 shares from the market on 1/4/Year 2 and delivers them to her broker on 1/10/Year 3.

Scenario	Holding Period	Character
1	6 days (1/4/Year 3-1/10/Year 3)	Short-term capital gain/loss
2	< 1 day (1/10/Year 3-1/10/Year 3)	Short-term capital gain/loss
3	> 1 year (1/4/Year 2-1/10/Year 3)	Long-term capital gain/loss

Since Mary does not own any identical property (ABC's shares) prior to the short sale, the holding period of the short-sold shares runs from the date she purchased the property from the market to the date the shares are delivered to close out the sale (1/10/Year 3). The gains or losses will be recognized on 1/10/Year 3, and they will be classified as capital gains or losses because the property used to close the short sale is a capital asset.

> **EXAMPLE 9-22**   **Short Sale with Owned Property**
>
> On 1/3/Year 2, Mary agrees to sell 500 shares of ABC Corp. to John. Because Mary does not wish to sell the ABC shares she already possesses, which were purchased in Year 1, she borrows the 500 shares from her broker and delivers them to John. Mary is obligated to, and does, return the shares to her broker by 1/10/Year 3. What are the holding period and character of gain or loss in the following scenarios?
>
> (1) Mary's shares on hand were purchased on 6/15/Year 1.
>
> (2) Mary's shares on hand were purchased on 1/1/Year 1.
>
> | Scenario | Holding Period | Character |
> |---|---|---|
> | 1 | < 1 year (6/15/Year 1-1/3/Year 2) | Short-term capital gain/loss |
> | 2 | > 1 year (1/1/Year 1-1/3/Year 2) | Long-term capital gain/loss |
>
> Since Mary owns identical property (ABC's shares) prior to the short sale, the holding period of the short-sold shares runs from the date she originally purchased the property to the date of the short sale. The gains or losses will be recognized on 1/10/Year 3, and they will be classified as capital gains or losses because the property used to close the short sale is a capital asset.

12. **Casualties**

    a. Casualty losses on personal-use capital assets are itemized deductions.

       1) The deduction for personal casualty and theft losses is suspended for the tax years 2018 through 2025. However, losses attributed to a federally declared disaster and losses to the extent of casualty gains are deductible.

13. **Market Discount Bonds**

    a. Gain on sale is treated as ordinary income to the extent the market discount could have accrued as interest.

$$\text{Taxable accrued market discount} = \text{Market discount} \times \frac{\text{\# of days security held}}{\text{\# of days from acquisition to maturity}}$$

> **EXAMPLE 9-23**   **Sale of Market Discount Bonds**
>
> John purchases a $100, 360-day bond for $90. The market discount equals $10. If John sells the bond 180 days later, he must recognize $5 (half of the discount) as ordinary income (interest).

14. **Bond Premium Treatment**

    a. The bondholder may either (1) elect to amortize the premium until bond maturity and reduce the basis or (2) elect not to amortize and treat the premium as bond basis.

STOP & REVIEW

You have completed the outline for this subunit.
Study multiple-choice questions 14 through 20 beginning on page 257.

QUESTIONS

9.1 Basis

1. Bluff purchased equipment for business use for $35,000 and made $1,000 of improvements to the equipment. After deducting depreciation of $5,000, Bluff gave the equipment to Russett for business use. At the time the gift was made, the equipment had a fair market value of $32,000. Ignoring gift tax consequences, what is Russett's basis in the equipment?

A. $31,000
B. $32,000
C. $35,000
D. $36,000

Answer (A) is correct.
REQUIRED: The basis of an asset that was received as a gift.
DISCUSSION: According to IRS Publication 551, if the FMV of the property is equal to or greater than the donor's adjusted basis, the donee's basis is the donor's adjusted basis at the time the donee received the gift. The fair market value at the date of the gift is $32,000, while the donor's adjusted basis is $31,000 ($35,000 cost + $1,000 improvements – $5,000 depreciation). Thus, Russett's basis is equal to Bluff's adjusted basis of $31,000.
Answer (B) is incorrect. The FMV at the date of the gift is $32,000. The FMV is used only if the FMV is less than the donor's basis and the property is later sold for a loss. Answer (C) is incorrect. A basis of $35,000 ignores the $1,000 improvement that should be capitalized and the $5,000 of depreciation that reduces Bluff's adjusted basis in the equipment. Answer (D) is incorrect. A basis of $36,000 ignores the $5,000 of depreciation that reduces Bluff's adjusted basis in the equipment.

2. Which of the following is subject to the Uniform Capitalization Rules of Code 263A?

A. Editorial costs incurred by a freelance writer.
B. Research and experimental expenditures.
C. Mine development and exploration costs.
D. Warehousing costs incurred by a manufacturing company with $28 million in average annual gross receipts.

Answer (D) is correct.
REQUIRED: The uniform capitalization rules.
DISCUSSION: The uniform capitalization rules require the costs for construction (manufacture) of real or tangible personal property to be used in trade or business and costs of producing or acquiring property for sale to customers (retail) to be capitalized. The uniform capitalization rules do not apply to producers and resellers if the company's average annual gross receipts for the past 3 years do not exceed $26 million. Both direct and most allocable indirect costs necessary to prepare the inventory for its intended use must be capitalized. The warehousing costs are direct costs that must be capitalized, and the manufacturing company has average annual gross receipts of $28 million, so the exemption does not apply.
Answer (A) is incorrect. The editorial costs incurred by a freelance writer are not manufacturing or acquisition costs. Answer (B) is incorrect. The research and experimental expenditures are not manufacturing or acquisition costs. Answer (C) is incorrect. Mine development and exploration costs are not manufacturing or acquisition costs.

SU 9: Property Transactions: Basis and Gains

3. Fred Berk bought a plot of land with a cash payment of $40,000 and a $50,000 mortgage. In addition, Berk paid $200 for a title insurance policy. Berk's basis in this land is

A. $40,000
B. $40,200
C. $90,000
D. $90,200

Answer (D) is correct.
REQUIRED: The basis of the property acquired.
DISCUSSION: The basis of property is its cost. Cost includes cash paid and any debt to which the property is subject, regardless of whether the debt is recourse or nonrecourse. In addition, basis includes expenditures for major improvements and costs to acquire title.
Answer (A) is incorrect. Basis includes acquisition debt and costs. **Answer (B) is incorrect.** Basis includes acquisition debt to which the property is subject. **Answer (C) is incorrect.** The cost to acquire property, such as title insurance, is part of its cost basis.

4. In January Year 1, Joan Hill bought one share of Orban Corp. stock for $300. On March 1, Year 3, Orban distributed one share of preferred stock for each share of common stock held. This distribution was nontaxable. On March 1, Year 3, Joan's one share of common stock had a fair market value of $450, while the preferred stock had a fair market value of $150. After the distribution of the preferred stock, Joan's bases for her Orban stocks are

	Common	Preferred
A.	$300	$0
B.	$225	$75
C.	$200	$100
D.	$150	$150

Answer (B) is correct.
REQUIRED: The bases of common stock and preferred stock received as a nontaxable dividend.
DISCUSSION: Since the preferred stock dividend was nontaxable, the original basis of the common stock is allocated between the common stock and the preferred stock based on the relative fair market value of each on the date of the stock dividend. Joan's tax basis in the common stock after the receipt of the dividend is ($450 ÷ $600) × $300 = $225. Joan's tax basis in the preferred stock is ($150 ÷ $600) × $300 = $75.
Answer (A) is incorrect. It fails to account for the stock dividend. **Answer (C) is incorrect.** Basis of the common stock is allocated between the common stock and the preferred stock based on the relative fair market value of each on the date of the stock dividend. **Answer (D) is incorrect.** Basis of the common stock and the preferred stock are not weighted equally.

5. Lewis Brown bought four lots of land for $100,000. On the date of purchase, the lots had the following fair market values:

Lot #1	$25,000
Lot #2	$31,250
Lot #3	$20,625
Lot #4	$48,125

What is the basis to Lewis of Lot #3?

A. $31,250
B. $25,000
C. $20,625
D. $16,500

Answer (D) is correct.
REQUIRED: The basis of an asset purchased for a lump sum.
DISCUSSION: When more than one asset is purchased for a lump sum, the basis of each is computed by apportioning the total cost based on the relative FMV of each asset. Lot #3 has a FMV that is 16.5% of the FMV of all of the lots purchased [$20,625 ÷ ($25,000 + $31,250 + $20,625 + $48,125)]. Thus, the basis of Lot #3 is $16,500 ($100,000 × 16.5%).
Answer (A) is incorrect. The amount of $31,250 is obtained by equally apportioning the FMV of all of the lots to each lot ($125,000 ÷ 4). **Answer (B) is incorrect.** The amount of $25,000 is obtained by equally apportioning the lump-sum cost of all of the lots to each lot ($100,000 ÷ 4). **Answer (C) is incorrect.** The basis of an asset purchased for a lump sum is computed by apportioning the total cost based on the relative FMV of each asset.

6. A beneficiary acquired property from a decedent. The fair market value at the date of the decedent's death was $100,000. The decedent had paid $130,000 for the property. Estate taxes attributed to the property were $2,000. The beneficiary sold the property 2 years after receipt from the estate. What is the basis of the property for the beneficiary?

A. $100,000
B. $102,000
C. $130,000
D. $132,000

Answer (A) is correct.
REQUIRED: The calculation of basis on inherited property.
DISCUSSION: Basis is the FMV on the date of death or 6 months after if the executor elects the alternate valuation date for the estate tax return.
Answer (B) is incorrect. The amount of $102,000 includes estate taxes attributed to the property.
Answer (C) is incorrect. The amount of $130,000 is the historical cost for the decedent. **Answer (D) is incorrect.** The amount of $132,000 is the historical cost for the decedent plus estate taxes.

7. Which of the following types of costs are required to be capitalized under the Uniform Capitalization Rules of Code Sec. 263A?

A. Marketing.
B. Distribution.
C. Warehousing.
D. Office maintenance.

Answer (C) is correct.
REQUIRED: The expense required to be capitalized for UNICAP.
DISCUSSION: UNICAP rules require the capitalization of all expenses necessary to bring the asset to its intended use. Storage of an asset prior to its intended use would qualify as a cost incurred to bring it to its full use and should be capitalized under UNICAP.
Answer (A) is incorrect. UNICAP rules require the capitalization of all expenses necessary to bring the asset to its intended use. Marketing expenses would be an expense incurred in the sale of goods or services, not in the implementation of the asset. **Answer (B) is incorrect.** UNICAP rules require the capitalization of all expenses necessary to bring the asset to its intended use. Distribution costs would be attributable to the sale of goods and services, not to the acquisition and implementation of an asset. **Answer (D) is incorrect.** UNICAP rules require the capitalization of all expenses necessary to bring the asset to its intended use. Office maintenance is an indirect expense allocable to all of the operations of the business equally, not a particular asset.

9.2 Depreciation and Amortization

8. On August 1 of the current year, Graham purchased and placed into service an office building costing $264,000, including $30,000 for the land. What was Graham's MACRS deduction for the office building in the current year?

A. $9,600
B. $6,000
C. $3,600
D. $2,250

Answer (D) is correct.
REQUIRED: The amount of MACRS depreciation deduction.
DISCUSSION: Under MACRS, an office building is nonresidential real estate having a 39-year recovery period and is depreciated using the straight-line depreciation method. The land is not depreciable. The cost of the office building ($234,000) is divided by 39 years to yield $6,000. Because of the mid-month convention, 4.5 months of depreciation, or $2,250, is deductible in the year of purchase.
Answer (A) is incorrect. The $30,000 attributable to the land is not depreciable; nonresidential real property uses a 39-year, not a 27.5-year, recovery period; and only 4.5 months of depreciation can be expensed in the year of purchase. Answer (B) is incorrect. Only 4.5 months of depreciation can be expensed in the year of purchase. Answer (C) is incorrect. The $30,000 attributable to the land is not depreciable, and nonresidential real property uses a 39-year, not a 27.5-year, recovery period.

9. Which of the following conditions must be satisfied for a taxpayer to expense, in the year of purchase, under Internal Revenue Code Sec. 179, the cost of new or used tangible depreciable personal property?

I. The property must be purchased for use in the taxpayer's active trade or business.
II. The property must be purchased from an unrelated party.

A. I only.
B. II only.
C. Both I and II.
D. Neither I nor II.

Answer (C) is correct.
REQUIRED: The conditions that must be satisfied under Sec. 179 to expense property.
DISCUSSION: In order for a property to be expensed under Sec. 179, it must be both purchased for use in the taxpayer's active trade or business as well as be purchased from an unrelated party.
Answer (A) is incorrect. The property must also be purchased from an unrelated party. Answer (B) is incorrect. The property must also be purchased for use in the taxpayer's active trade or business. Answer (D) is incorrect. At least one of the conditions must be satisfied.

10. All of the following statements are correct regarding bonus depreciation **except**

A. Only new property is eligible for bonus depreciation.
B. Qualified property would not include any property used by a regulated public utility company or any property used in a real property trade or business.
C. First-year bonus depreciation is 100% for qualified property.
D. The property cannot be acquired from a related party.

Answer (A) is correct.
REQUIRED: The incorrect statement about 100% expensing (bonus depreciation).
DISCUSSION: The TCJA expanded the property that is eligible for bonus depreciation by repealing the requirement that the original use of the property begin with the taxpayer. Instead, the property is eligible for the additional depreciation if it is the taxpayer's first use.
Answer (B) is incorrect. Qualified property would not include any property used by a regulated public utility company or any property used in a real property trade or business. Answer (C) is incorrect. The TCJA increased the 50% first-year bonus depreciation to 100% for qualified property. Answer (D) is incorrect. Property acquired from a related party does not qualify for bonus depreciation.

11. George wants to take bonus depreciation on equipment he placed in service in 2021. What percentage of the cost of equipment can George deduct in 2021 as bonus depreciation?

A. 80%
B. 40%
C. 60%
D. 100%

Answer (D) is correct.
REQUIRED: The bonus depreciation rate for each depreciable period.
DISCUSSION: The 50% first-year bonus depreciation increased to 100% for qualified property acquired and placed in service after September 27, 2017, and before January 1, 2023. For certain properties with longer production periods, the acquisition and placed-in-service period is after September 27, 2017, and before January 1, 2024.
Answer (A) is incorrect. The percentage for property with shorter production periods placed in service after December 31, 2022, and before January 1, 2024, is 80%. Answer (B) is incorrect. The percentage for property with shorter production periods placed in service after December 31, 2024, and before January 1, 2026, is 40%. Answer (C) is incorrect. The percentage for property with shorter production periods placed in service after December 31, 2023, and before January 1, 2025, is 60%.

12. Browne, a self-employed taxpayer, had 2021 business taxable income of $1,040,000 prior to any expense deduction for equipment purchases. In 2021, Browne purchased and placed into service, for business use, office machinery costing $1,045,000. This was Browne's only 2021 capital expenditure. Browne's business establishment was not in an economically distressed area. Browne made a proper and timely expense election to deduct the maximum amount. Browne was not a member of any pass-through entity. What is Browne's deduction under the election?

A. $1,040,000
B. $1,045,000
C. $1,050,000
D. $2,620,000

Answer (A) is correct.
REQUIRED: The maximum amount of Sec. 179 deduction in 2021.
DISCUSSION: Tangible and depreciable personal property can be expensed by up to $1,050,000 in 2021, the year of acquisition. This amount is reduced when the amount of Sec. 179 property placed in service in a given year exceeds $2,620,000. Since this limit does not apply, the maximum deduction would be $1,050,000; however, there are other limits. Section 179(b)(3)(A) limits the deduction to taxable income derived from the active conduct of any trade or business. In this case, the maximum deduction is $1,040,000.
Answer (B) is incorrect. The Sec. 179 deduction is limited to taxable income. Answer (C) is incorrect. The maximum Sec. 179 deduction of $1,050,000 for 2021 ignores the taxable income limit. Answer (D) is incorrect. The amount of $2,620,000 is the threshold at which the deduction is reduced dollar-for-dollar, ignoring the taxable income limit in this case.

13. In 2021, Micro Corp. purchased a machine to be used in its business. The machine qualifies as Sec. 179 property. The cost of the machine is $3,050,000. What is the amount of Sec. 179 deduction that Micro Corp. may take in 2021?

A. $0
B. $620,000
C. $610,000
D. $1,050,000

Answer (B) is correct.
REQUIRED: The amount of Sec. 179 deduction allowed.
DISCUSSION: The maximum dollar amount that may be deducted under Sec. 179 is $1,050,000 in 2021 for the cost of qualifying depreciable tangible property placed in service in the year 2021. The phase-out threshold for eligible property placed in service is $2,620,000 in 2021. Thus, the $1,050,000 maximum Sec. 179 deduction is reduced (but not below zero) by the amount that the cost of qualifying property placed in service during the year exceeds $2,620,000. Thus, the Sec. 179 deduction is $620,000 [$1,050,000 – ($3,050,000 – $2,620,000)].
Answer (A) is incorrect. A Sec. 179 deduction may be taken. Answer (C) is incorrect. Using the $1,040,000 limit from last year results in $610,000. Answer (D) is incorrect. The amount of $1,050,000 does not reduce the deduction by the phase-out.

9.3 Capital Gains and Losses

14. Joe Hall owns a limousine for use in his personal service business of transporting passengers to airports. The limousine's adjusted basis is $40,000. In addition, Hall owns his personal residence and furnishings, which together cost him $280,000. Hall's capital assets amount to

A. $320,000
B. $280,000
C. $40,000
D. $0

Answer (B) is correct.
REQUIRED: The amount of capital assets.
DISCUSSION: Capital assets include all property held by a taxpayer unless excluded by the IRC, such as property used in a trade or business. Personal-use property, such as a residence, is a capital asset.
Answer (A) is incorrect. The limousine is depreciable business property and not a capital asset. **Answer (C) is incorrect.** Personal-use properties are capital assets. The limousine is depreciable business property and not a capital asset. **Answer (D) is incorrect.** The personal residence and furnishings are capital assets.

15. Which of the following is a capital asset?

A. Inventory held primarily for sale to customers.
B. Accounts receivable.
C. A computer system used by the taxpayer in a personal accounting business.
D. Land held as an investment.

Answer (D) is correct.
REQUIRED: The property classified as a capital asset.
DISCUSSION: All property is classified as a capital asset unless specifically excluded. Accounts receivable, inventory, and depreciable property or real estate used in a business are not capital assets. Land held as an investment, however, is a capital asset unless it is held by a dealer (the general rule and not an exception is being tested).
Answer (A) is incorrect. Inventory held primarily for sale to customers is not included in the capital assets classification. **Answer (B) is incorrect.** Accounts receivable are specifically excluded as capital assets. **Answer (C) is incorrect.** A computer system is amortized over its useful life (i.e., depreciable property used in a trade or business) and is not considered a capital asset.

16. In the current year, Susan sold an antique that she bought 6 years ago to display in her home. Susan paid $800 for the antique and sold it for $1,400. Susan chose to use the proceeds to pay a court-ordered judgment. The $600 gain that Susan realized on the sale of the antique should be treated as

A. Ordinary income.
B. Long-term capital gain.
C. An involuntary conversion.
D. A nontaxable transaction.

Answer (B) is correct.
REQUIRED: The treatment of gain on a property sale.
DISCUSSION: The antique is a capital asset. A capital asset must be held for more than 1 year for gain or loss on its sale or exchange to be treated as long-term.
Answer (A) is incorrect. The facts do not indicate that Susan held the asset as a dealer. Unless an exception applies, sale of a capital asset gives rise to capital gain or loss. **Answer (C) is incorrect.** How proceeds of an asset sale are used defines neither an involuntary conversion nor a capital asset. **Answer (D) is incorrect.** The IRC contains no provision excepting from recognition gain realized on this transaction.

17. Sand purchased 100 shares of Eastern Corp. stock for $18,000 on April 1 of the prior year. On February 1 of the current year, Sand sold 50 shares of Eastern for $7,000. Fifteen days later, Sand purchased 25 shares of Eastern for $3,750. What is the amount of Sand's recognized gain or loss?

A. $0
B. $500
C. $1,000
D. $2,000

Answer (C) is correct.
REQUIRED: The recognized gain or loss on a wash sale of stock.
DISCUSSION: A current loss realized on a wash sale of securities is not recognized. A wash sale occurs when substantially the same securities are purchased within 30 days before or after being sold at a loss. Although Sand sold 50 shares of Eastern on February 1, it reacquired 25 more shares of Eastern less than 30 days later. Thus, the 25 shares that Sand reacquired 15 days later do not contribute to the recognized loss on February 1. If the total realized loss on February 1 is $2,000 ($9,000 basis of shares sold − $7,000 sales price), only half is recognized because only half is not subsequently reacquired.
Answer (A) is incorrect. Sand may recognize a $1,000 loss equal to the shares of stock sold on February 1 not subsequently reacquired 15 days later. **Answer (B) is incorrect.** The realized loss on February 1 is related to 50 shares. If 25 shares are subsequently reacquired, half the loss must not be recognized, not 75% of it. **Answer (D) is incorrect.** Half of the shares sold on February 1 are reacquired within the 30-day wash sale period. Thus, the realized loss of $2,000 must be reduced by the 25 shares reacquired 15 days later.

18. During the current year, all of the following events occurred: On June 1, Ben Rork sold 500 shares of Kul Corp. stock. Rork had received this stock on May 1 as a bequest from the estate of his uncle, who died on March 1. Rork's basis was determined by reference to the stock's fair market value on March 1. Rork's holding period for this stock was

A. Short-term.
B. Long-term.
C. Short-term if sold at a gain; long-term if sold at a loss.
D. Long-term if sold at a gain; short-term if sold at a loss.

Answer (B) is correct.
REQUIRED: The holding period for property acquired from a decedent.
DISCUSSION: Under Sec. 1223(11), if property acquired from a decedent is sold or otherwise disposed of by the recipient within 12 months of the decedent's death, then the property is considered to have been held for more than 12 months. Therefore, under Sec. 1223(3), it is long-term and subject to the maximum tax rate of the applicable ordinary income breakpoint.

SU 9: Property Transactions: Basis and Gains

19. On March 10, Year 6, James Rogers sold 300 shares of Red Company common stock for $4,200. Rogers had acquired the stock in Year 1 at a cost of $5,000. On April 4, Year 6, he repurchased 300 shares of Red Company common stock for $3,600 and held them until July 18, Year 6, when he sold them for $6,000. How should Rogers report the above transactions for Year 6?

A. A long-term capital loss of $800.
B. A long-term capital gain of $2,400.
C. A long-term capital gain of $1,600.
D. A long-term capital loss of $800 and a short-term capital gain of $2,400.

Answer (C) is correct.
REQUIRED: The amount and character of capital gain after stocks purchased in a wash sale are sold.
DISCUSSION: The sale of stock on March 10 was a wash sale because identical stock was repurchased within 30 days. The $800 loss realized in March will not be recognized for tax purposes. The disallowed loss is added to the basis of the stock that is subsequently purchased in April. The basis in the stock purchased in April is $4,400 ($3,600 cost + $800 disallowed loss), and a gain of $1,600 is recognized when the stock is sold for $6,000 on July 18. The gain is long-term because the holding period of stock acquired in a wash sale includes the holding period of the originally purchased stock.

20. For 2021, Mr. G has a short-term capital loss of $4,000, a short-term capital gain of $1,900, a short-term capital loss carryover from 2019 of $700, a long-term capital gain of $800 from property held for 3 years, and a long-term capital loss of $1,500 from property held for 4 years. Mr. G is in the 15% breakpoint basket. What is Mr. G's deductible loss in 2021?

A. $0
B. $2,800
C. $3,000
D. $3,500

Answer (C) is correct.
REQUIRED: The amount of deductible capital loss.
DISCUSSION: Short-term capital gains and losses and long-term capital gains and losses are first netted to determine the capital loss deduction. The carryover from 2019 retains its character as a short-term capital loss and is netted with the other short-term transactions.

Short-term: ($1,900 – $4,000 – $700)	$(2,800)
Long-term (15% basket): ($800 – $1,500)	(700)
Capital loss	$(3,500)

Since the loss computed above exceeds $3,000, the amount deductible is limited to the lesser of $3,000 or taxable income (Sec. 1211). Long-term capital losses of $500 are carried forward to the 28% basket.
Answer (A) is incorrect. Some capital losses may be deducted. **Answer (B) is incorrect.** The total capital loss without considering the two carryovers is $2,800. **Answer (D) is incorrect.** The total capital loss is $3,500.

Access the **Gleim CPA Premium Review System** featuring our SmartAdapt technology from your Gleim Personal Classroom to continue your studies. You will experience a personalized study environment with exam-emulating multiple-choice questions.

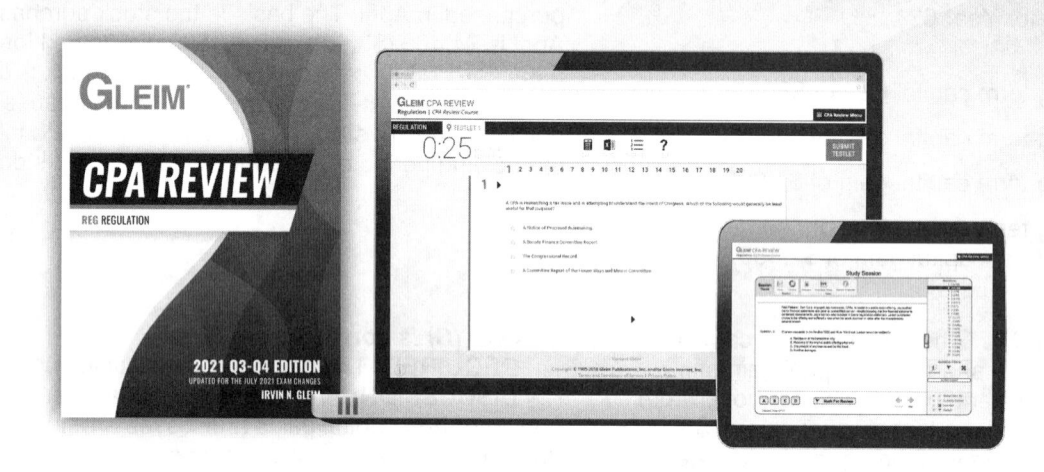

STUDY UNIT TEN
PROPERTY TRANSACTIONS: SPECIAL TOPICS

(25 pages of outline)

10.1	Related Party Sales	262
10.2	Installment Sales	264
10.3	Nonrecognition Transactions	267
10.4	Business Property Recharacterization	275
10.5	Gift Tax	283

The tax treatment of property transactions is integrated with that of other transactions on the CPA Exam. Visualize the following steps to analyze the income tax consequences of property transactions.

1) Apply related party sales rules.
2) Apply nonrecognition rules.
3) Apply Sec. 1245 and 1250 recapturing rules.
4) Characterize gains and losses under Sec. 1231.

The fifth subunit introduces the gift tax, which is a tax on the transfer of assets from one person to another. It is not an income tax. The donor, not the recipient, must generally pay the tax. The exam scope of this subunit has been significantly reduced, and this outline reflects that change.

Some candidates find it helpful to have the entire tax form side-by-side with our Knowledge Transfer Outline when studying, and others may prefer to see the final draft of a form when it is released. The full versions of the most up-to-date forms are easily accessible at www.gleim.com/taxforms. These forms and the form excerpts used in our outline are periodically updated as the latest versions are released by the IRS.

10.1 RELATED PARTY SALES

1. **Limited Tax Avoidance**
    a. These rules limit tax avoidance between related parties.
    b. Gain recognized on an asset transfer to a related person in whose hands the asset is depreciable is ordinary income (OI).
    c. The Internal Revenue Code imputes interest for property sales transactions when the related party extends credit with less than sufficient stated interest.
        1) The lender is treated as having made a gift of the imputed interest to the borrower each year the loan is outstanding.
    d. Loss realized on sale or exchange of property to a related person is not deductible. The transferee takes a cost basis. There is no adding of holding periods.
        1) Gain realized on a subsequent sale to an unrelated party is recognized only to the extent it exceeds the previously disallowed loss.
            a) If the gain realized on the sale to an unrelated third party is less than the amount of disallowed loss, no gain is recognized.

EXAMPLE 10-1   Limited Tax Avoidance

Taxpayer A sells stock with a basis of $100,000 to a related person, Taxpayer B, for $80,000, creating a $20,000 disallowed loss for Taxpayer A. If Taxpayer B then sells the stock to an unrelated party for $130,000, the realized gain will be $50,000 ($130,000 sale price – $80,000 basis) and Taxpayer B will recognize a $30,000 gain ($50,000 realized gain – $20,000 disallowed loss from original transaction between A and B).

However, if the sale to an unrelated party were for $90,000, the resulting $10,000 gain ($90,000 sale price – $80,000 basis) would not be recognized. The $10,000 gain is offset by $10,000 of the $20,000 disallowed loss.

Finally, if the unrelated sale had been for $65,000 (creating an additional $15,000 loss), Taxpayer B could only recognize a $15,000 loss, not a $35,000 loss ($20,000 disallowed loss + $15,000 unrelated-sale loss).

---

        2) Loss realized on a subsequent sale to a third party is recognized, but the previously disallowed loss is not added to it.
    e. For property purchased on or after January 1, 2016, a new rule precludes the above recognition of the disallowed loss when later sold to an unrelated party if the original transferor (e.g., Taxpayer A in Example 10-1) is a tax-indifferent party.
        1) Tax-indifferent parties are those not subject to federal income tax or to whom an item would have no substantial impact on its income tax. Examples include non-U.S. persons, tax-exempt organizations, and government entities.

EXAMPLE 10-2   Limited Tax Avoidance -- Tax-Indifferent Party

If we use the details from Example 10-1 but change Taxpayer A to a tax-indifferent party, the disallowed loss will still be $20,000 when the stock sells for $80,000 to Taxpayer B; however, on the sale from Taxpayer B to an unrelated party for $130,000, the realized and recognized gain is $50,000 ($130,000 – $80,000). The $50,000 gain is not offset by the disallowed loss.

---

    f. For purposes of these provisions, related parties generally include
        1) Ancestors (parents, grandparents, etc.), descendants (children, grandchildren, etc.), spouses, and siblings
        2) Trusts and beneficiaries of trusts
        3) Controlled entities (greater than 50% ownership)

        NOTE: Constructive ownership rules between family members apply.

SU 10: Property Transactions: Special Topics

- g. Loss on sale or exchange of property between a partnership and a person owning more than 50% of the capital or profit interests in the partnership is not deductible.

2. **Constructive Ownership -- Corporation Stock**
   a. Generally, an individual is considered to own the stock owned by his or her brothers and sisters (whole or half blood), spouse, ancestors, and lineal descendants.
      1) An individual owning any stock in a corporation proportionately owns any stock the corporation owns in another entity (i.e., corporation, partnership, etc.).
   b. **Stock Redemptions**
      1) The (redeemed) shareholder is treated as owning shares owned by certain related parties. The following ownership types are considered constructively owned by the shareholder through related parties:
         a) Stock owned directly or indirectly by or for the shareholder's spouse, children, grandchildren, or parents

---

EXAMPLE 10-3   Constructive Ownership

A corporation has 100 shares outstanding. A husband, wife, child, and grandchild (the child's child) each own 25 shares. The husband, wife, and child are each considered to own 100 shares. The grandchild is considered to own only 50 shares (25 shares of the grandchild + 25 shares of the child).

---

   b) Stock owned directly or indirectly by or for a partnership (or S corporation) in which the shareholder is a partner
      i) The reverse also applies (i.e., a partnership owns stock owned by a partner).
   c) Stock owned directly or indirectly by an estate or trust in which the shareholder is treated as a beneficiary or an owner
   d) Stock owned directly or indirectly by or for a corporation (other than an S corporation) in which the shareholder owns directly or indirectly at least 50% of the value of the stock
   e) Stock on which the shareholder holds an option to buy

3. **Constructive Ownership -- Partnership Interest**
   a. Generally, an individual is treated as owning the interest owned by his or her spouse, brothers and sisters, children, grandchildren, and parents.
      1) An interest directly or indirectly owned by or for a corporation, partnership, estate, or trust is considered to be owned proportionately by or for its shareholders, partners, or beneficiaries. In the case of a C corporation, attribution only occurs if such a shareholder (directly or indirectly) owns 5% or more of the corporation.
   b. A **family partnership** is one consisting of a taxpayer and his or her spouse, ancestors, lineal descendants, or trusts for the primary benefit of any of them.
      1) Siblings are not treated as members of the taxpayer's family for these purposes.

STOP & REVIEW

You have completed the outline for this subunit.
Study multiple-choice questions 1 through 5 beginning on page 286.

10.2 INSTALLMENT SALES

1. **Overview**

   a. An installment sale is a disposition of property in which at least one payment is to be received after the close of the tax year of the disposition.

   b. The installment method must be used to report installment sales unless election is made not to apply the method.

   > **EXAMPLE 10-4 Installment Sale**
   >
   > Harold sold his house to Jennifer in January Year 2 for $200,000. Jennifer paid a $50,000 down payment, and the remainder is owner-financed by Harold with a 3% interest rate. Jennifer must make 18 equal monthly payments beginning in February Year 2. Harold considers the sale of his home an installment sale because the payments continue beyond Year 2.

2. **Excluded Dispositions**

   a. Installment sales do not apply to the following dispositions:

      1) Inventory personal property sales
      2) Revolving credit personal property sales
      3) Dealer dispositions, including dispositions of
         a) Personal property of a type regularly sold by the person on the installment plan
         b) Real property held for sale to customers in the ordinary course of trade or business
      4) Securities, generally, if publicly traded
      5) Sales on agreement to establish an irrevocable escrow account

3. **Specific Dispositions Not Excluded**

   a. Not excluded from installment sale deferral are certain sales of residential lots or timeshares subject to interest on the deferred tax and property used or produced in a farming business.

4. **Recognized Gain**

   a. The amount of realized gain to be recognized in a tax year is equal to the gross profit multiplied by the ratio of payments received in the current year divided by the total contract price.

   b. Recognize, as income, payments received multiplied by the gross profit percentage.

      Recognized gain = Gross profit percentage × Payments received

      1) A payment is considered paid in full if the balance is placed into an irrevocable escrow account (i.e., amounts that cannot revert to the purchaser) at a later date.

c. The gross profit is the sales price minus selling expenses (including debt forgiveness) and adjusted basis (AB).
   1) The sales price is the sum of any cash received, liability relief, and installment notes from the buyer. It does not include imputed interest.
d. The total contract price is the sales price minus liabilities assumed by the buyer (that does not exceed the seller's basis in the property).
   1) Contract price includes the excess of liability assumed over AB and selling expenses.
      a) When the liability exceeds AB and selling expenses, the gross profit percentage is 100%.
e. The gross profit percentage is the ratio of the gross profit to the total contract price.

$$\text{Gross profit percentage} = \frac{\text{Gross profit}}{\text{Contract price}} = \frac{\text{Selling price} - \text{Selling expenses} - \text{Adjusted basis}}{\text{Amount to be collected}}$$

   1) When the selling price is reduced in a future year, the gross profit on the sale also will be reduced. Therefore, the gross profit percentage must be recalculated for the remaining periods by using the reduced sales price and subtracting the gross profit already recognized.

EXAMPLE 10-5   Installment Sale -- Gross Profit Percentage

In 2021, Drew sold 40 acres of land for $200,000 to be collected over 10 years. The land was purchased in 1990 for $80,000. Drew's gross profit is $120,000 ($200,000 – $80,000). The contract price is $200,000, the amount received. The gross profit percentage is 60% ($120,000 gross profit ÷ $200,000 contract price). In 2021, Drew received $50,000 as a down payment and includes $30,000 as a capital gain ($50,000 received × 60% gross profit percentage).

EXAMPLE 10-6   Installment Sale -- Mortgage Assumed by Buyer

Taylor sold a piece of property for $105,000. The property had a basis of $40,000 with a $55,000 mortgage attached that was assumed by the buyer. The buyer paid a $6,000 down payment and financed $44,000 through Taylor. The selling expenses were $5,000. The gross profit is $60,000 ($105,000 selling price – $40,000 basis – $5,000 selling expenses). The contract price is $60,000 ($6,000 down payment + $44,000 mortgage + $15,000 excess of mortgage assumed over basis – $5,000 selling expenses). Because the $55,000 mortgage is greater than the $50,000 collection, the excess of liabilities over AB and selling expenses is added to the amount collected. The gross profit percentage is 100% ($60,000 gross profit ÷ $60,000 contract price). The amount collected in the first year is $16,000 ($6,000 cash + $15,000 excess mortgage – $5,000 selling expenses).

---

5. **Repossession**
   a. The seller recognizes as gain or loss any difference between the FMV of repossessed personal property and the AB of an installment sale obligation satisfied by the repossession. If real property, recognize the lesser of
      1) Cash and other property (FMV) received in excess of gain already recognized or
      2) Gross profit in remaining installments less repossession costs.

b. Interest is imposed on deferred tax on obligations from nondealer installment sales (of more than $150,000) outstanding at the close of the tax year. This interest is applied if the taxpayer has nondealer installment receivables of over $5 million at the close of the tax year from installment sales of over $150,000 that occurred during the year.

   1) This interest is not applied to the following:
      a) Personal-use property
      b) Residential lots and time shares
      c) Property produced or used in the farming business

EXAMPLE 10-7   Interest on Installment Sale

Hans sold his construction company for $10 million to be paid in 25 annual payments of $400,000. Because (1) the installment receivables are more than $5 million and (2) there are annual payments of more than $150,000, Hans needs to report interest income on the installment sale.

---

6. **Disposition of Installment Obligations**

   a. Excess of the FMV over the AB of an installment obligation is generally recognized if it is transferred. FMV is generally the amount realized. If a gift, use the face amount of the obligation.

   b. **Exceptions.** Disposition of obligations by the following events can result in the transferee treating payments as the transferor would have:

      1) Transfers to a controlled corporation
      2) Corporate reorganizations and liquidations
      3) Contributions to capital of, or distributions from, partnerships
      4) Transfer between spouses incident to divorce
      5) Transfer upon death of the obligee

   c. The date the installment payment is received determines the capital gains rate to be applied rather than the date the asset was sold under an installment sales contract.

7. **Character**

   a. Character of gain recognized depends on the nature of the property in the transferor's hands.

   b. The full amount of Secs. 1245 and 1250 ordinary gain ("depreciation recapture") must be recognized in the year of sale, even if it is more than payments received. Any remaining gain that is not recaptured is taken into account using the installment method.

   c. An anti-avoidance rule applies to an installment sale of property to a related party. On a second disposition (by the related party transferee in the first sale), payments received must be treated as a payment received by the person who made the first (installment) sale to a related party.

      1) A second disposition by gift is included. The FMV is treated as the payment.
      2) Death of the first disposition seller or buyer does not accelerate recognition.

STOP & REVIEW

You have completed the outline for this subunit.
Study multiple-choice questions 6 through 9 beginning on page 288.

10.3 NONRECOGNITION TRANSACTIONS

1. **General Rule**
   a. The general rule is to recognize all gain realized during the tax year. This topic discusses some transactions for which the IRC requires or permits exclusion or deferral of all or part of the gain realized in the current tax year.

2. **Like-Kind Exchanges (LKE)**
   a. Section 1031 defers recognizing gain or loss to the extent that real property productively used in a trade or business or held for the production of income (investment) is exchanged for property of like kind.
      1) Only real property qualifies for like-kind treatment for transfers. Real property located within the United States is like-kind with all other real property in the U.S. Foreign real estate is like-kind with other foreign real estate. But U.S. real estate and foreign real estate are not like-kind.
         a) Properties are of like kind without regard to differences in use (e.g., business or investment), improvements (e.g., bare land or house), location (e.g., city or rural), or proximity.
            i) Examples of like-kind exchanges are an unimproved farm property for an office building, a store building for a parking lot, and investment real property for business real property. A lease of real property for 30 or more years is treated as real property.

LKE – Boot

3. Boot is all nonqualified property transferred in an exchange transaction.
   a. Gain is recognized equal to the lesser of gain realized or boot received.
   b. Boot received includes cash, net liability relief, and other nonqualified property (its FMV).

EXAMPLE 10-8	Like-Kind Exchange with Boot

Scott owned a parcel of real estate that he was holding for investment. It had an adjusted basis of $50,000. Scott exchanged the real estate for a piece of land with a fair market value of $60,000, a boat for personal use that had a fair market value of $3,000, and $2,000 cash. Scott's basis in the land received is equal to the adjusted basis of the real estate transferred ($50,000), less the boot received of the boat ($3,000) and the cash ($2,000), plus the gain recognized on the transaction. Gain is recognized to the extent of boot received. Here, the boat and the cash are boot; therefore, a gain of $5,000 must be recognized. This recognized gain increases basis of the land to $50,000.

EXAMPLE 10-9	Like-Kind Exchange

Real property with an adjusted basis of $50,000 is exchanged for $20,000 cash and like-kind property with a FMV of $40,000. The recognized gain is $10,000 ($40,000 + $20,000 – $50,000), the lesser of the gain realized ($10,000) and the boot received ($20,000).

EXAMPLE 10-10	Like-Kind Qualified Property

Alan exchanged real property with a basis of $60,000 plus $5,000 cash for like-kind property with a FMV of $63,000. Alan's $2,000 loss [$63,000 – ($60,000 + $5,000)] is not deductible.

LKE – Liabilities

4. Liabilities are treated as money paid or received.

    a. If each party assumes a liability of the other, only the net liability given or received is treated as boot.

    b. Liabilities include mortgages on property.

LKE – Basis

5. Qualified property received in a like-kind exchange has an exchanged basis adjusted for boot and gain recognized.

    $$\begin{array}{rl} & \text{AB of property given} \\ + & \text{Gain recognized} \\ + & \text{Boot given (cash, liability incurred, other property)} \\ - & \text{Boot received (cash, liability relief, other property) + Exchange fees incurred} \\ - & \text{Loss recognized (boot given)} \\ \hline = & \text{Basis in acquired property} \end{array}$$

NOTE: The IRS has ruled that exchange expenses can be deducted to compute gain or loss realized, offset against cash payments received in determining recognized gain, or included in the basis of the property received.

LKE – Realized Gain

6. Under Sec. 1031, realized gain is usually recognized only to the extent of boot received (Cash + FMV of other property + Net liability relief).

    a. **Section 1245** ordinary income is limited to the sum of the following:

        1) Gain recognized and

        2) FMV of property acquired that is not Sec. 1245 property and is not included in computing the recognized gain.

    b. **Section 1250** ordinary income is limited to the greater of the following:

        1) Recognized gain or

        2) Excess of the potential Sec. 1250 ordinary income over the FMV of Sec. 1250 property received.

    c. Basis in property acquired is increased for gain recognized.

LKE – Loss

7. If some qualified property is exchanged, loss realized with respect to qualified property is not recognized, but loss on boot given may be recognized.

SU 10: Property Transactions: Special Topics   269

LKE – Qualified Exchange Accommodation Arrangement or Agreement

8. With a qualified exchange accommodation agreement, the property given up or the replacement property is transferred to a qualified intermediary (QI), also referred to as exchange accommodation titleholder (EAT) or facilitator. The QI is considered the beneficial owner of the property.

    a. This arrangement allows a transfer in which a taxpayer acquires replacement property before transferring relinquished property to qualify as a tax-free exchange.
    b. The following requirements must be met:
        1) Time limits for identifying and transferring the property are satisfied.
        2) A written agreement exists.
        3) The exchange accommodation titleholder has the qualified indications of ownership of the property.

LKE – Exchange Expenses

9. Any exchange expenses are subtracted from the total of the following (but not below zero):

    a. Any cash paid to the taxpayer by the other party;
    b. The FMV of other (not like-kind) property received by the taxpayer, if any; and
    c. Net liabilities assumed by the other party–the excess, if any, of liabilities (including mortgages) assumed by the other party over the total of (1) any liabilities assumed, (2) cash paid by the taxpayer to the other party, and (3) the FMV of the other (not like-kind) property given up by the taxpayer. If the exchange expenses exceed (1), (2), and (3), the excess is added to the basis of the like-kind property.

Like-Kind Exchange Process Flowchart

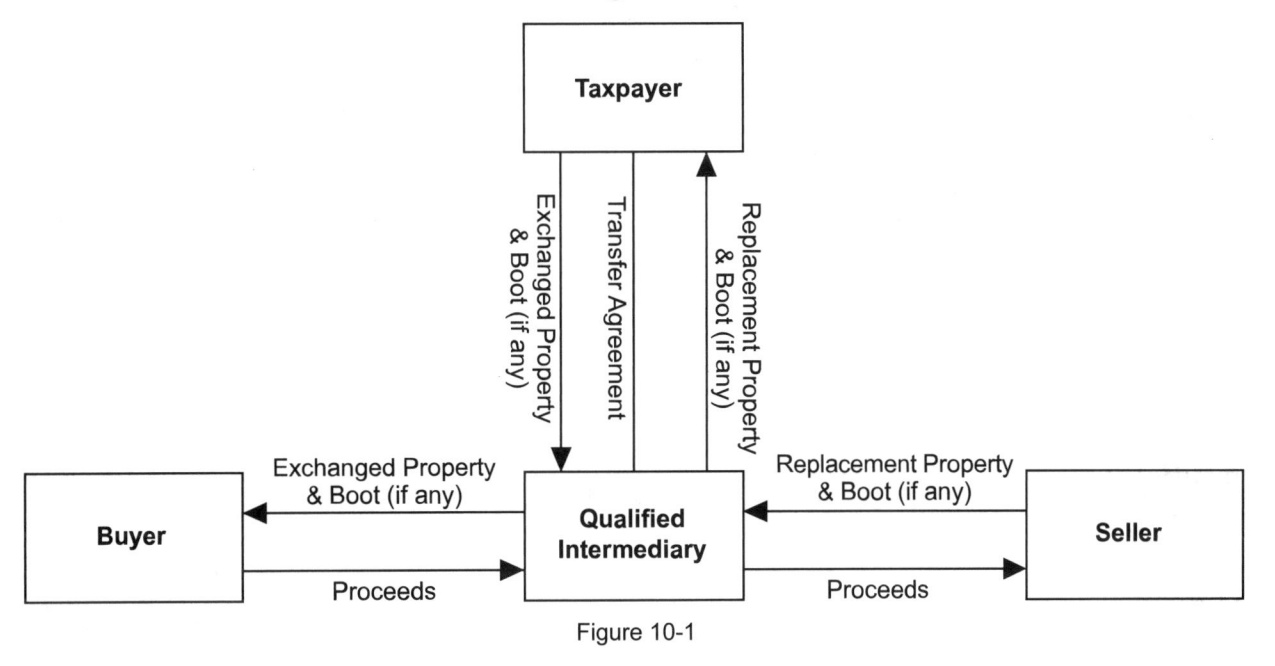

Figure 10-1

Realized Gain or (Loss), Recognized Gain, and Basis of Like-Kind Property Received

Not Like-Kind Property

1. Fair market value (FMV) of other property given up $XXX,XXX
2. **Less:** Adjusted basis of other property given up   (XX,XXX)
3.   **Gain or (loss) recognized on other property given up** $XX,XXX

Realized Gain or (Loss)

4. Boot Received: Cash received, FMV of other property received, plus net liabilities assumed by other party, reduced (but not below zero) by any exchange expenses $ XX,XXX
5. **Plus:** FMV of acquired like-kind property   XX,XXX
6. **Less:** Adjusted basis of like-kind property given up, net amounts paid to other party, plus any exchange expenses not used above   (XX,XXX)
7.   **Realized gain or (loss)**   XX,XXX

Recognized Gain

8. Lesser of boot received or realized gain or (loss), but not less than zero $ XX,XXX
9. **Less:** Ordinary income under recapture rules   (XX,XXX)
10. Subtract line 9 from line 8 (if zero or less, enter -0-)   X,XXX
11.   **Recognized gain** (add lines 9 and 10)   XX,XXX

Deferred Gain or (Loss)

12. Subtract line 11 from line 7 $XX,XXX

Basis of Acquired Like-Kind Property

13. Subtract line 4 from the sum of lines 6 and 11 $XX,XXX

SU 10: Property Transactions: Special Topics

10. **Involuntary Conversions**

    a. A taxpayer may elect to defer recognition of gain if property is involuntarily converted into money or property that is similar or related in service or use under Sec. 1033.

        1) An involuntary conversion of property results from destruction, theft, seizure, requisition, condemnation, or the threat of imminent requisition or condemnation.
        2) Section 1033 does not apply to any realized losses.
            a) Loss from condemnation or requisition of a personal-use asset is not deductible. But certain casualty losses are deductible.
            b) When loss is realized, basis is determined independently of Sec. 1033.
        3) Involuntary conversions are **not limited to** real property.

EXAMPLE 10-11	Involuntary Conversion

    Jennifer's office building is requisitioned by the city government under eminent domain to expand a road. Jennifer is paid $500,000 for the office, which had an adjusted basis of $200,000 for the building and $125,000 for the land. Jennifer uses the $500,000 to purchase a $600,000 office building within 6 months. Involuntary conversion rules allow Jennifer to defer recognition of the $175,000 realized gain.

    b. Similar or related in service or use means that the property has the qualities outlined in items 1) and 2) below:

        1) For an **owner-user**, functional similarity, i.e., meets a functional use test that requires that the property
            a) Have similar physical characteristics
            b) Be used for the same purpose
        2) For an **owner-investor**, a close relationship to the service or use the previous property had to the investor, such that the owner-investor's
            a) Risks, management activities, services performed, etc., continue without substantial change.
        3) Generally, if property held for investment or for productive use in a trade or business is involuntarily converted due to a **federally declared disaster**, the tangible replacement property will be deemed similar or related in service or use.

c. **Direct conversion.** Conversion into property similar or related in service or use to the converted property.
   1) Nonrecognition is mandatory, not elective, on direct conversion to the extent of any amount realized in the form of qualified replacement property.
   2) Basis in the proceeds (property) is exchanged, i.e., equal to the basis in the converted property.
d. **Indirect conversion.** Acquiring control of a corporation that owns similar or related-in-service-or-use property is treated as acquiring qualified property. Control is ownership of at least 80% of the voting stock and 80% of any other stock.
   1) Recognized gain is limited to any excess of any amount realized over any cost of qualified property.
e. When property is converted involuntarily into nonqualified proceeds and qualified property is purchased within the replacement period, an election may be made to defer realized gain.
   1) The deferral is limited to the extent that the amount realized is reinvested in qualified replacement property.
   2) Basis in the qualified replacement property is the cost of such property decreased by the amount of any unrecognized gain.
f. The replacement period begins on the earlier of the date of disposition or the threat of condemnation and ends 2 years after the close of the first tax year in which any part of the gain is realized.
   1) If real property used in business or held for investment (not inventory, dealer property, or personal-use property) is converted by condemnation or requisition, or threat thereof, 3 years is allowed.
   2) Construction of qualified property must be complete before the end of the replacement period for its cost to be included.
g. For real property used in business or held for investment (not inventory, dealer property, personal-use property, etc.), if conversion is by condemnation, like-kind property qualifies as replacement. This standard is less stringent.
   1) Conversion must be direct. There is no indirect ownership allowance.
h. To recap, on a Sec. 1033 involuntary conversion, realized gain is generally recognized only to the extent that any amount realized exceeds the cost of the similar or related-in-service property.
   1) The gain recognized is classified as ordinary income under Sec. 1245 or Sec. 1250.
i. The following is a summary of like-kind exchange and involuntary conversions:
   1) Like-kind exchange:

   Recognized gain = Lesser of gain realized or boot received

   Basis of acquired property = FMV (acquired property) − Deferred gain + Deferred loss

   2) Involuntary conversion:

   Recognized gain = Lesser of gain realized or reimbursement not reinvested

   Basis of acquired property = FMV (acquired property) − Deferred gain

11. **Sale of Principal Residence**

    a. Section 121 provides an exclusion upon the sale of a principal residence. No loss may be recognized on the sale of a personal residence.

    b. A taxpayer may exclude up to $250,000 ($500,000 for married taxpayers filing jointly) of realized gain on the sale of a principal residence.

    c. The individual must have owned and used the residence for an aggregate of 2 of the 5 prior years.

        1) For married taxpayers, the $500,000 exclusion is available if

            a) Either spouse meets the ownership requirement
            b) Both spouses meet the use requirement
            c) Neither spouse is ineligible for the exclusion by virtue of a sale or an exchange of a residence within the last 2 years

        2) However, if one spouse fails to meet these requirements, the other qualifying spouse is not prevented from claiming a $250,000 exclusion.

EXAMPLE 10-12	Sale of Principal Residence Exclusion

Harry, who is eligible for the exclusion, marries Sally, who used her exclusion last year. Harry can still claim the $250,000 exclusion even though Sally used her exclusion last year. However, the couple is not entitled to the full $500,000 exclusion available to married taxpayers who both meet the requirements for the exclusion.

    d. The exclusion may be used only once every 2 years.

    e. The exclusion amount may be prorated if the use and ownership tests are not met. The exclusion is based on the ratio of months used to 24 months and is a proportion of the total exclusion.

        1) The pro rata exclusion is allowed if the sale is due to a change in the place of employment, health, or unforeseen circumstances.

EXAMPLE 10-13	Sale of Principal Residence Exclusion

Alex purchased a home on January 1, 2021, for $200,000. He used the home as his personal residence until he sold it for $475,000 on July 1, 2022. He sold it because of a change of employment. His exclusion is limited to $187,500 [$250,000 × (18 months ÷ 24 months)].

    f. The gain on the sale of the residence must be prorated between qualified and nonqualified use.

        1) Nonqualified use includes periods on or after January 1, 2009, that the residence was not used as the principal residence of the taxpayer. However, periods when the residence was not used as a principal residence occurring after the last date the property was used as a principal residence are not counted as nonqualified use.

            a) This rule is designed to prevent a landlord from moving into rental property for 2 years and then making the gain on the sale of that property eligible for the principal residence exclusion. Conversely, by not counting periods after the last use as a principal residence as nonqualified, the provision does not penalize a taxpayer who moves out of the principal residence and then rents it short-term prior to selling.

> **EXAMPLE 10-14   Sale of Principal Residence Exclusion**
>
> Sharon purchased a rental house on January 1, 2016. She used the house as her personal residence for 3 years and then rented the house for 2 years before selling it on January 1, 2021. The time the residence was not used as a principal residence is not considered nonqualified use because it occurred after the last date the property was used as a principal residence. Thus, Sharon is eligible for the full exclusion.

> **EXAMPLE 10-15   Sale of Principal Residence Exclusion**
>
> Mary purchased a rental house on January 1, 2016. She rented the house for 3 years and then made it her principal residence for 2 years before selling it on January 1, 2021. The time the residence was not used as a principal residence before the last date the property was used as a principal residence is nonqualified use and reduces the amount of gain eligible for exclusion. Thus, only 40% (2 years ÷ 5 years) of the gain is eligible for the exclusion.

    g.   Gain must be recognized to the extent of any depreciation adjustments with respect to the rental or business use of a principal residence after May 6, 1997.

    h.   Basis in a new home is its cost.

12. **Section 1202 Qualified Small Business Stock**

    a. When a taxpayer sells or exchanges Sec. 1202 small business stock that the taxpayer has held for more than 5 years, a portion of the gain may be excluded from the taxpayer's gross income. The amount of excludable gain depends on the date the stock was acquired.

Acquisition Date	Exclusion Percentage
After August 10, 1993, and before February 18, 2009	50%
After February 17, 2009, and before September 28, 2010	75%
After September 27, 2010	100%

    b. The general requirements for stock to be treated as Sec. 1202 qualified small business stock are as follows:

    1) The stock is received after August 10, 1993.
    2) The issuing corporation is a domestic C corporation.
    3) The seller is the original owner of the stock.
    4) The corporation's gross assets do not exceed $50 million at the time the stock was issued.

STOP & REVIEW

You have completed the outline for this subunit.
Study multiple-choice questions 10 through 13 beginning on page 290.

10.4 BUSINESS PROPERTY RECHARACTERIZATION

Author's note: Because the concepts in this subunit are challenging, we have included Examples 10-20 to 10-23, beginning on page 281, to provide additional context. Read through the outline and be sure to pay close attention to the examples in order to see the rules in practice.

1. **Overview**

    a. Sections 1231, 1245, and 1250 recharacterize gain or loss.

    NOTE: Remember that while these Sections may change the character of gain or loss, they will not change the amount of any gain or loss.

Overview of Business Property Recharacterization

(i.e., depreciation recapture)

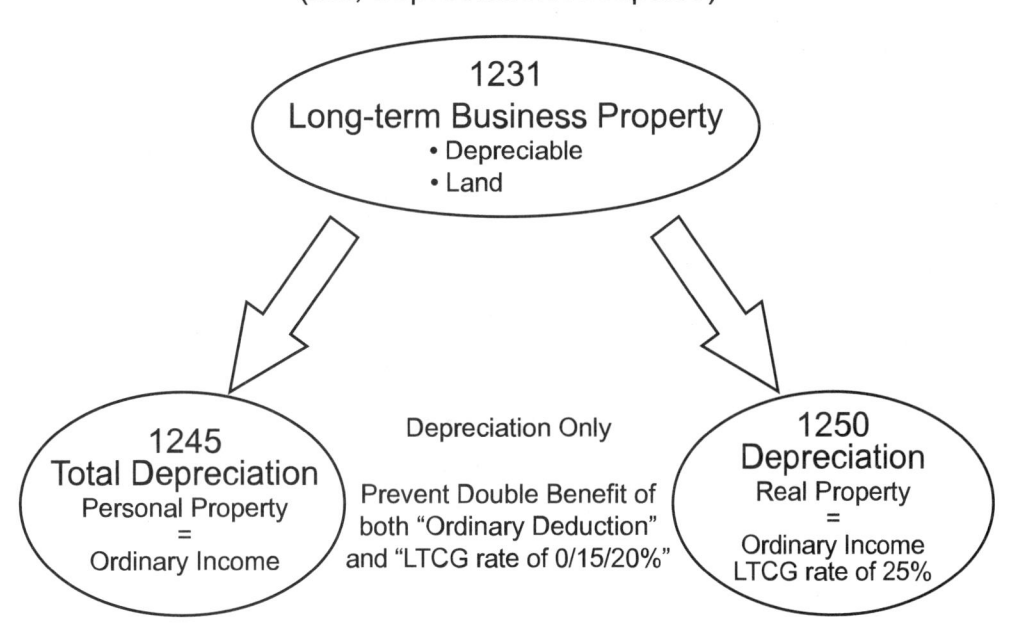

```
               1231
        Long-term Business Property
              • Depreciable
              • Land
           /                    \
          /                      \
         v                        v
    ┌─────────────┐          ┌─────────────┐
    │    1245     │          │    1250     │
    │   Total     │  Depreciation Only    │ Depreciation│
    │ Depreciation│                       │Real Property│
    │  Personal   │ Prevent Double Benefit│      =      │
    │  Property   │ of both "Ordinary     │  Ordinary   │
    │     =       │ Deduction" and        │   Income    │
    │  Ordinary   │ "LTCG rate of         │ LTCG rate   │
    │   Income    │  0/15/20%"            │   of 25%    │
    └─────────────┘                       └─────────────┘
```

Figure 10-2

2. **Section 1231 Property**

> **BACKGROUND 10-1**   **Special Treatment for Capital Gains**
>
> Before 1938, productive assets used in business were treated as capital property. As the Great Depression dragged on, however, it became clear that relief was needed. Businesses struggling to sell their outmoded equipment found themselves subject to the limitations on recognizing capital losses. Thus, the Revenue Act of 1938 carved out an exception to capital gain-and-loss treatment for business property. By 1942, however, another change was called for, since the treatment needed during a depression was not appropriate for a wartime economy. Firms making large profits selling to the government needed lower rates on capital gains, so Sec. 117 (forerunner of the current Sec. 1231) was modified once again to provide special treatment for capital gains.

    a. Section 1231 property is property held for more than 1 year and includes

        1) All real or depreciable property used in a trade or business

        2) Involuntarily converted capital assets held in connection with a trade or business or in a transaction entered into for a profit

    b. Examples of Sec. 1231 property include land, apartment buildings, parking lots, manufacturing equipment, and involuntarily converted investment artwork.

        1) Land is not depreciable. Thus, it does not fall within Sec. 1245 or Sec. 1250. Land is referred to as pure Sec. 1231 property if used for trade or business and held for more than 1 year.

    c. Examples of property that are not Sec. 1231 property include personal-use property and inventory.

Overview of Business Property Gains & Losses

(i.e., beyond depreciation recapture)

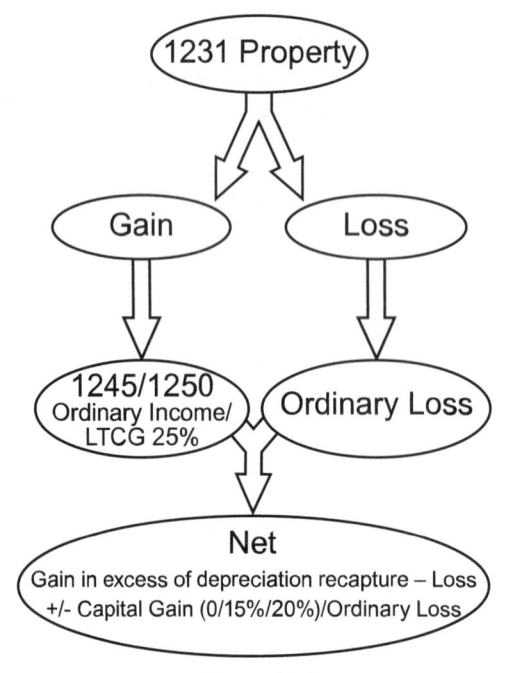

```
            ( 1231 Property )
               /         \
              ↓           ↓
           (Gain)       (Loss)
              ↓           ↓
       ( 1245/1250 )  ( Ordinary Loss )
       Ordinary Income/
         LTCG 25%
              \         /
               ↓       ↓
              (   Net   )
       Gain in excess of depreciation recapture – Loss
       +/- Capital Gain (0/15%/20%)/Ordinary Loss
```

Figure 10-3

- d. Section 1231 is beneficial to the taxpayer. When Sec. 1231 property gains exceed losses (a net Sec. 1231 gain), each gain or loss is treated as being from the sale of a long-term capital asset. However, if Sec. 1231 property losses exceed gains (a net Sec. 1231 loss), each gain or loss is considered ordinary. Section 1231 has a two-step test.
    1) Step 1: Determine net gain or loss from all casualties or thefts of Sec. 1231 property for the tax year. Gain or loss from involuntary conversions by other than casualty or theft is included in Step 2 but not Step 1.
        a) If the result is a net loss, each gain or loss is treated as ordinary income or loss.
        b) If the result is a net gain, each gain or loss is included in Step 2.
    2) Step 2: Determine net gain or loss from all dispositions of Sec. 1231 property for the year, including the property included in Step 1 only if Step 1 resulted in a net gain.
        a) If the result is a net loss, each gain or loss is treated as ordinary income or loss.
        b) If the result is a net gain, each gain or loss is treated as a long-term capital gain or loss.
- e. Recapture. To discourage clustering losses in 1 year and gains in another, net gain on Sec. 1231 property is treated as ordinary income to the extent of unrecaptured net Sec. 1231 losses from preceding tax years (i.e., the lookback rule).
    1) Unrecaptured net Sec. 1231 losses are the total of net Sec. 1231 losses for the last 5 tax years, reduced by net Sec. 1231 gains characterized as ordinary income under Sec. 1231(c).
    2) Sections 1245 and 1250 recapture is computed before Sec. 1231 recapture, but Sec. 1231 recapture is computed before Steps 1 and 2 above.

NOTE: The use of the term "recapture" in reference to recapturing current-year gain as ordinary income to the extent of prior-year loss as ordinary income under Sec. 1231 is not to be confused with the recapture of depreciation as ordinary income under Secs. 1245 and 1250.

- f. The installment method can apply to Sec. 1231 property. Section 1231 merely characterizes gain or loss. Any Sec. 1231 gain that is recharacterized as capital gain will first consist of 25% gain, then 0/15/20% gain.
- g. Allocation is required when Sec. 1245 or Sec. 1250 property is also Sec. 1231 property and only a portion of gain recognized is Sec. 1245 or Sec. 1250 OI.
- h. Sections 1245 and 1250 only involve gains. If disposition of business property results in a loss, it is a Sec. 1231 loss.

EXAMPLE 10-16   Section 1231 Recapture (Lookback Rule)

A taxpayer recognizes the following Sec. 1231 gains and losses:

Year	Section 1231 gain (loss)
1	$(5,000)
2	1,000
3	(3,000)
4	2,500
5	500
6	500
7	4,000

Section 1231 gains in Years 2, 4, 5, and 6 total $4,500 and are recaptured as ordinary income by the Sec. 1231 loss in Year 1. The remaining $500 loss in Year 1 is not applied to Year 7. In Year 7, $3,000 of the $4,000 gain is recaptured as ordinary income by the Sec. 1231 loss in Year 3. The remaining $1,000 ($4,000 – $3,000) gain in Year 7 is a Sec. 1231 gain.

3. **Section 1245 Ordinary Income**

   a. Section 1245 property generally is depreciable personal property (tangible/intangible) used in a trade or business for over 12 months.

   b. Gain on the disposition of Sec. 1245 property is ordinary income to the extent of the lesser of all depreciation taken (including amounts expensed under Sec. 179) or gain recognized.

      1) If gain realized is not recognized (like-kind exchanges, involuntary conversions, etc.), Sec. 1245 ordinary income is limited to the sum of the following:

         a) Gain recognized
         b) FMV of property acquired that is not Sec. 1245 property and is not included in computing the recognized gain

      2) The recognized gain in excess of the depreciation taken may be treated as a gain from the sale or exchange of Sec. 1231 property.

   c. The following is a summary of Sec. 1245:

   Ordinary income = Lesser of recognized gain or accumulated depreciation

   Section 1231 gain = Recognized gain – Ordinary income recaptured

   ---
   EXAMPLE 10-17   Section 1245 Ordinary Income

   Stewart purchased a machine for $20,000. He took $14,000 in depreciation before selling the asset for $9,000. The basis on the machine is $6,000 ($20,000 cost basis – $14,000 depreciation), so he has a $3,000 gain ($9,000 selling price – $6,000 basis). The $3,000 is ordinary income (the lesser of the gain or depreciation taken).

   EXAMPLE 10-18   Section 1245 Ordinary Income and Section 1231 Gain

   Assume the same information from Example 10-17 except Stewart sells the machine for $25,000. The realized gain is $19,000 ($25,000 – $6,000 basis). This gain has both Sec. 1245 gain and Sec. 1231 gain. The $14,000 of depreciation taken on the equipment is a Sec. 1245 gain (the lesser of the gain or depreciation taken), and the remaining gain of $5,000 is a Sec. 1231 gain.

   ---

   d. Examples of intangible amortizable personal Sec. 1245 property include

      1) Leaseholds of Sec. 1245 property
      2) Professional athletic contracts, e.g., baseball
      3) Patents
      4) Goodwill acquired in connection with the acquisition of a trade or business
      5) Covenants not to compete

4. **Section 1250 Ordinary Income**

   a. Section 1250 property is all depreciable real property, such as a building or its structural components.

      1) Examples of Sec. 1250 property include shopping malls, an apartment or office building, low-income housing, rented portions of residences, and escalators or elevators.

      2) Land is not Sec. 1250 property, but leases of land are Sec. 1250 intangible properties. Certain improvements to land may be treated as land, e.g., dams and irrigation systems.

SU 10: Property Transactions: Special Topics

    b. Section 1250 property is subject to its own recapture rules. For the three items listed below, the aggregate gain recognized on the sale or disposition of Sec. 1250 property is ordinary income.

        1) The excess of accelerated depreciation taken over S-L depreciation is ordinary income to the extent of gain recognized. However, because most Sec. 1250 property (e.g., 39-year nonresidential real property and 27.5-year residential real property) has been depreciated using straight-line since 1987, it is relatively uncommon to encounter Sec. 1250 recapture.

        2) For property held less than 1 year, the remaining depreciation is recaptured.

        NOTE: Partial reduction of excess depreciation is provided for under Sec. 1250 for low-income housing and rehabilitated structures.

        3) For corporations, the gain must be computed under both Sec. 1245 and 1250. If Sec. 1245 gain is larger than Sec. 1250 gain, 20% of the difference is characterized as ordinary income.

    c. If gain realized is not recognized (like-kind exchanges, involuntary conversions, etc.), Sec. 1250 ordinary income is limited to the greater of the following:

        1) Recognized gain

        2) Excess of the potential Sec. 1250 ordinary income over the FMV of Sec. 1250 property received

5. **Section 1250 Unrecaptured Gain**

    a. For corporate and noncorporate taxpayers, any gain from the disposition of Sec. 1250 property that is not recaptured as ordinary income will qualify as Sec. 1231 gain. However, for individual taxpayers, any portion of that gain that is attributable to straight-line depreciation will be subject to a maximum capital gains rate of 25% (as opposed to 0/15/20%).

EXAMPLE 10-19   **Section 1250 Unrecaptured Gain Taxed as Section 1231 Gain**

Annie sold a building used in her trade or business for $110,000. Annie purchased the building several years ago for $100,000. At the time of the sale, the building has accumulated depreciation of $20,000. Because the building was acquired after 1986, it has been depreciated using the straight-line method; therefore, Sec. 1250 recapture does not apply, and Annie has a Sec. 1231 gain of $30,000 ($110,000 amount realized – $80,000 adjusted basis). Of the $30,000 gain, $20,000 is attributable to straight-line depreciation and is classified as Sec. 1250 unrecaptured gain, which is subject to a maximum rate of 25%. The remaining $10,000 gain is taxed at a maximum rate of 0/15/20%.

---

    b. The following is a summary of Sec. 1250 recapture:

        1) C corporations:

        Ordinary income = 20% × Lesser of recognized gain or accumulated depreciation

            Section 1231 gain = Recognized gain – Ordinary income recaptured

        2) Noncorporate taxpayers:

    Ordinary gain = MACRS accumulated depreciation – Straight-line accumulated depreciation

        25% gain = Lesser of recognized gain or straight-line accumulated depreciation

            Section 1231 gain = Recognized gain – Ordinary gain – 25% gain

6. **Gift Property**
    a. Neither Sec. 1245 nor Sec. 1250 applies to a gift disposition.
    b. Any gain realized by the donee upon a subsequent taxable disposition is subject to Sec. 1245 and Sec. 1250 characterization up to the sum of
        1) Potential Sec. 1245 and Sec. 1250 OI at the time of the gift
        2) Potential Sec. 1245 and Sec. 1250 OI arising between gift and subsequent disposition

7. **Inherited Property**
    a. Neither Sec. 1245 nor Sec. 1250 applies to a disposition by bequest, devise, or intestate succession.
    b. Exceptions: Sec. 1245 and Sec. 1250 OI are recognized for a transfer at death to the extent of any income in respect of a decedent (IRD). Section 1245 OI potential also results from depreciation allowed to a decedent because the depreciation does not carry over to the transferee.

8. **Installment Sales**
    a. All gain realized and recharacterized as ordinary income from a disposal of recaptured Sec. 1245 or Sec. 1250 property in an installment sale must be recognized in the period of sale.
        1) Any excess gain over Sec. 1245 or Sec. 1250 OI is accounted for by the installment method.

9. **Income for Multiple Assets**
    a. Income received or accrued for more than one asset is allocated to each asset by agreement, by FMV, or by the residual method.
        1) To compute Sec. 1245 and Sec. 1250 ordinary income, an amount realized allocable to an asset must be further allocated to each use of a mixed use asset for each tax year.

10. **Section 351 Exchange for Stock**
    a. Generally, no gain is recognized upon an exchange of property for all the stock of a newly formed corporation.
    b. Section 1245 and Sec. 1250 OI is limited to any amount of gain recognized in a Sec. 351 transaction.

SUCCESS TIP

The topic of business property gain (loss) recharacterization often intimidates CPA candidates as they study for the exam due to the different rules applied under Secs. 1231, 1245, and 1250. Because the AICPA has tested this area relatively often, you should have a solid understanding of these rules. Take the time necessary to understand the outline and answer the multiple-choice questions to reinforce your knowledge of this area.

SU 10: Property Transactions: Special Topics

> **EXAMPLE 10-20   Section 1245 Recapture**
>
> On January 17, Year 1, Relief Corp. purchased and placed into service 7-year MACRS tangible property costing $100,000. On December 21, Year 4, Relief Corp. sold the property for $105,000 after taking $60,000 in MACRS depreciation deductions.
>
> The adjusted basis of the property is $40,000 ($100,000 historical cost – $60,000 depreciation); therefore, Relief will recognize a gain of $65,000 ($105,000 selling price 1 – $40,000 adjusted basis). Since this property qualifies for Sec. 1245 recapture, the gain will be recaptured as ordinary income to the extent of the lesser of all depreciation taken or gain realized. Thus, Relief will have $60,000 of Sec. 1245 (ordinary) gain. The remaining $5,000 of gain is Sec. 1231 (capital) gain.

> **EXAMPLE 10-21   Section 1245 Recapture**
>
> The facts from Example 10-20 apply, except Relief sold the property for $95,000.
>
> Relief recognizes a gain of $55,000 ($95,000 selling price – $40,000 adjusted basis). Since this property qualifies for Sec. 1245 recapture, the gain is recaptured as ordinary income to the extent of the lesser of all depreciation taken or gain realized. Thus, Relief has $55,000 of Sec. 1245 gain.
>
> **Sec. 1245 Depreciation Recapture: Examples 10-20 and 10-21**
>
> Figure 10-4

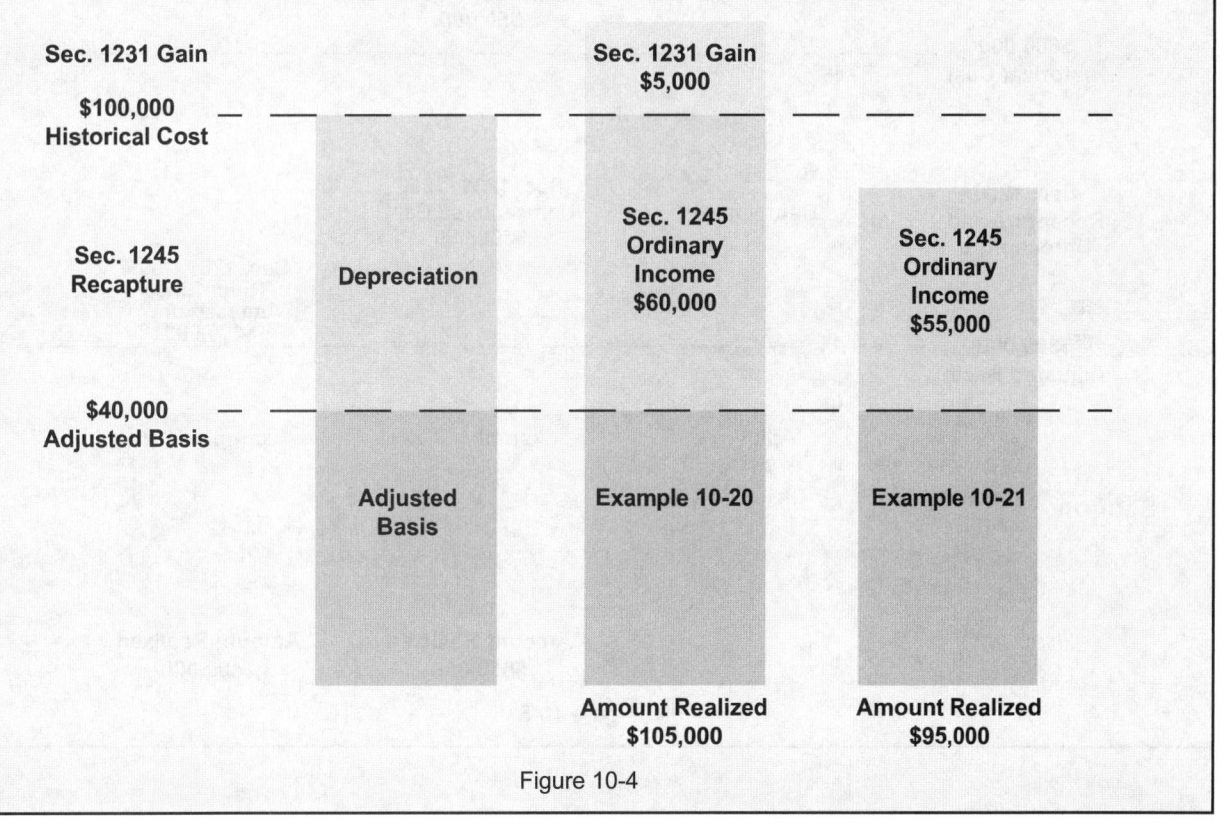

EXAMPLE 10-22   Section 1250 Unrecapture

Martha purchased and placed into service Sec. 1250 property costing $600,000. After 5 years, the property was sold for $650,000 after having taken $300,000 in straight-line depreciation deductions.

The adjusted basis of the property is $300,000 ($600,000 historical cost – $300,000 depreciation); therefore, Martha recognizes a gain of $350,000 ($650,000 selling price – $300,000 adjusted basis). Because the property was depreciated using straight-line depreciation, Sec. 1250 recapture will not apply. Thus, Martha will have $350,000 of Sec. 1231 (capital) gain, $300,000 of which is Sec. 1250 unrecaptured gain taxed at a maximum rate of 25%.

EXAMPLE 10-23   Section 1250 Unrecapture

The facts from Example 10-22 apply, except Martha sold the property for $400,000.

Martha recognizes a gain of $100,000 ($400,000 selling price – $300,000 adjusted basis). Since all of the gain is attributable to straight-line depreciation, Martha has $100,000 of Sec. 1250 unrecaptured gain.

Sec. 1250 Depreciation Recapture: Examples 10-22 and 10-23

Figure 10-5

STOP & REVIEW

You have completed the outline for this subunit.
Study multiple-choice questions 14 through 19 beginning on page 292.

10.5 GIFT TAX

1. **Definition of Gift Tax**

    a. The gift tax is a tax of the transfer imposed on the donor. Below is the basic tax formula modified for the gift tax.

    ```
           GIFT AMOUNT
              FMV on date of gift, for
                 All gifts in the calendar year
         − Exclusions
              Annual exclusion
                 $15,000 per donee
              Paid (directly) on behalf of another for
                 Medical care
                 Education tuition
         − Deductions
              Marital
              Charitable
         = TAXABLE GIFTS FOR CURRENT YEAR
         + Taxable gifts for prior years
         = TAXABLE GIFTS TO DATE
         × Tax Rate
         = TENTATIVE GIFT TAX
         − (Prior year's gifts × Current tax rates)
         − Applicable credit amount
         = GIFT TAX LIABILITY
    ```

2. **Amount of Gift**

    a. Any excess of FMV of transferred property over the FMV of consideration for it is a gift.

    ```
         FMV of transferred property: Given
         − FMV of consideration (property, money,
              etc.): Received
         = Gift amount
    ```

    b. A gift is complete when the giver has given over dominion and control such that (s)he is without legal power to change its disposition.

EXAMPLE 10-24   Joint Bank Account -- Completion of Gift

R opens a joint bank account with A, I, and H, with R the only depositor to the account. R, A, I, and H may each withdraw money. A gift is complete only when A, I, or H withdraws money.

c. Gifts completed when the donor is alive **(inter vivos gifts)** are the only ones subject to gift tax. Transfers made in trusts are included.
d. Property passing by will or inheritance is not included (although the estate tax may apply).
e. To the extent credit is extended with less than sufficient stated interest, the Code imputes that interest is charged. If the parties are related, the lender is treated as having made a gift of the imputed interest to the borrower each year the loan is outstanding.
   1) Gift loans are excluded if the aggregate outstanding principal is not more than $10,000.
f. Basis in a gift is basis in the hands of the donor plus gift tax attributable to appreciation.

EXAMPLE 10-25   Basis of a Gift of Land

Amanda made a gift to her daughter of a piece of land with a FMV of $95,000. The land had a basis to Amanda of $60,000. She paid a taxable gift of $80,000 ($95,000 FMV – $15,000 annual exclusion) and a gift tax of $32,000 ($80,000 × 40%). The basis of the land to the daughter is carryover basis of $60,000 plus the gift tax attributable to the appreciation.

$$\$60{,}000 + \frac{\$35{,}000 \text{ increase in value}}{\$80{,}000 \text{ taxable gift}} \times \$32{,}000 = \$74{,}000$$

SUCCESS TIP: The AICPA has historically tested candidates' knowledge on the various aspects of gift tax, specifically the annual exclusion, medical or tuition costs, and marital deductions.

3. **Annual Exclusion**
   a. The first $15,000 of gifts of present interest to each donee is excluded from taxable gift amounts. The annual exclusion is indexed to reflect inflation.
   b. The $15,000 exclusion applies only to gifts of present interests.
   c. A present interest in property includes an unrestricted right to the immediate possession or enjoyment of property or the income from property (such as a life estate or a term for years). Gifts of future interests in property (such as remainders or reversions) do not qualify for the annual exclusion.

EXAMPLE 10-26   Gift of a Present Interest and a Future Interest

Edward sets up a trust with the income going to his daughter for her life and the remainder to his granddaughter. Edward has made a gift of a present interest to his daughter and a future interest to his granddaughter.

---

4. **Medical or Tuition Costs**
   a. Excluded from taxable gifts are amounts paid on behalf of another individual such as tuition to an educational organization or for medical care.
   b. The payment must be made directly to the third party, i.e., the medical provider or the educational organization.
   c. Amounts paid for room, board, and books are not excluded.

5. **Marital Deduction**
   a. The amount of a gift transfer to a spouse is deducted in computing taxable gifts. Donor and donee must be married at the time of the gift, and the donee must be a U.S. citizen for the unlimited amount. For noncitizen spouses, the deduction is limited to $159,000 in 2021.
   b. The deduction may not exceed the amount includible as taxable gifts.
   c. Otherwise, the amount of the deduction is not limited.

   > **EXAMPLE 10-27   Marital Deduction**
   > Sid Smith gave his wife, Mary, a diamond ring valued at $20,000 and cash gifts of $30,000 during 2021. Sid is entitled to a $15,000 exclusion with respect to the gifts to Mary. The marital deduction allows Sid to exclude an additional $35,000 ($20,000 + $30,000 − $15,000).

6. **Charitable Deduction**
   a. The FMV of property donated to a qualified charitable organization is deductible. Like the marital deduction, the amount of the deduction is the amount of the gift reduced by the $15,000 exclusion with respect to the donee.

7. **Spousal Support**
   a. Transfers that represent support are not gifts.

8. **Political Contributions**
   a. Political contributions are not subject to gift tax.

9. **Computing the Gift Tax**
   a. Tentative tax is the sum of taxable gifts to each person for the current year and for each preceding year times the rate. Taxable gifts to a person is the total of gift amounts (FMV) in excess of exclusions and the marital and charitable deductions for a calendar year.
   b. The unified transfer tax rates are used.
      1) Current-year applicable rates are applied to both current and preceding years' taxable gifts.
      2) The rate is 18% for taxable gifts up to $10,000.
      3) The rates increase in small steps (e.g., 2%, 3%) over numerous brackets.
      4) The maximum rate is 40% on cumulative gifts in excess of $1 million in 2021.

STOP & REVIEW

You have completed the outline for this subunit.
Study multiple-choice questions 20 through 22 on page 294.

QUESTIONS

10.1 Related Party Sales

1. Gibson purchased stock with a fair market value of $14,000 from Gibson's adult child for $12,000. The child's cost basis in the stock at the date of sale was $16,000. Gibson sold the same stock to an unrelated party for $18,000. What is Gibson's recognized gain from the sale?

A. $0
B. $2,000
C. $4,000
D. $6,000

Answer (B) is correct.
REQUIRED: The amount of gain recognized when stock acquired from a related party is sold to an unrelated third party.
DISCUSSION: Under Sec. 267, losses are not allowed on sales or exchanges of property between related parties. Gibson's adult child realized a $4,000 loss ($16,000 – $12,000) on the sale but may not deduct it. On the subsequent sale, Gibson realized a $6,000 gain ($18,000 sales price – $12,000 basis). However, he only recognizes a gain of $2,000 ($18,000 – $16,000) because the Sec. 267(d) disallowed loss is used to offset the subsequent gain on the sale of the property.
Answer (A) is incorrect. There is a recognized gain from the sale. Answer (C) is incorrect. The fair market value at date of related party sale is irrelevant. Answer (D) is incorrect. The realized gain is recognized to the extent it exceeds the previously disallowed loss.

2. Among which of the following related parties are losses from sales and exchanges **not** recognized for tax purposes?

A. Father-in-law and son-in-law.
B. Brother-in-law and sister-in-law.
C. Grandfather and granddaughter.
D. Ancestors, lineal descendants, and all in-laws.

Answer (C) is correct.
REQUIRED: The identification of the related party.
DISCUSSION: Losses are not allowed on sales or exchanges of property between related parties. Related parties include ancestors (grandfather), descendants (granddaughter), spouses, and siblings.

3. Bank Corp.'s voting stock is owned by the following individuals: Farber, 25%; Farber's mother, 15%; Farber's father, 40%; and Grosset, an unrelated person, 20%. Farber's sister sold equipment to Bank at a loss. For the purposes of determining whether the sister's loss is deductible under the related party rules, what percentage of Bank's stock, if any, does the sister constructively own?

A. 0%
B. 25%
C. 55%
D. 80%

Answer (D) is correct.
REQUIRED: The limited tax avoidance rules on related party sales.
DISCUSSION: Tax avoidance is limited on related party sales. For purposes of these provisions, related parties generally include ancestors (parents, grandparents, etc.), descendants (children, grandchildren, etc.), spouses, siblings, trusts and beneficiaries of trusts, and controlled entities (50% ownership). Therefore, Farber's sister constructively owns 80% (25% Farber + 15% Farber's mother + 40% Farber's father).
Answer (A) is incorrect. Constructive ownership rules between family members apply. Answer (B) is incorrect. The amount of 25% is attributable to Farber only. Farber's sister constructively owns stock owned by all related parties, which also includes Farber's mother and father. Answer (C) is incorrect. The amount of 55% is attributable to Farber's mother and father. Farber's sister constructively owns stock owned by all related parties, which also includes Farber.

4. On July 1, Daniel Wright owned stock (held for investment) purchased 2 years earlier at a cost of $10,000 and having a fair market value of $7,000. On this date, he sold the stock to his son, William, for $7,000. William sold the stock for $6,000 to an unrelated person on November 1 of the same year. How should William report the stock sale (before any deduction) on his tax return?

A. As a short-term capital loss of $1,000.
B. As a long-term capital loss of $1,000.
C. As a short-term capital loss of $4,000.
D. As a long-term capital loss of $4,000.

Answer (A) is correct.
REQUIRED: The treatment of a loss on the sale of stock acquired from a related party in a loss transaction.
DISCUSSION: Losses are not allowed on sales or exchanges of property between related parties. A father and son are related parties for this purpose. Thus, Daniel's loss of $3,000 on the sale of the stock to William is disallowed. William takes as his basis for the stock the cost of $7,000. Since William's stock basis is determined by his cost (not by reference to Daniel's cost), there is no carryover of Daniel's holding period to William. Therefore, upon the sale of the stock to an unrelated party for $6,000, William realizes a short-term capital loss of $1,000.
Answer (B) is incorrect. The $1,000 loss is short-term because William does not take a carryover holding period and only held the stock for 4 months. **Answer (C) is incorrect.** A $4,000 short-term capital loss results from a calculation using the $10,000 as a carryover basis for William's stock. **Answer (D) is incorrect.** A $4,000 long-term capital loss results from a calculation using the $10,000 as a carryover basis with a carryover holding period for William's stock.

5. Justin Justice owns 55% of the outstanding stock of Rego Corporation. During the current year, Rego sold a trailer to Justin for $10,000. The trailer had an adjusted tax basis of $12,000 and had been owned by Rego for 3 years. In its current-year income tax return, what is the allowable loss that Rego can claim on the sale of this trailer?

A. $0.
B. $2,000 ordinary loss.
C. $2,000 Sec. 1231 loss.
D. $2,000 Sec. 1245 loss.

Answer (A) is correct.
REQUIRED: The amount and character of loss on the sale of property by a corporation to a 55% shareholder.
DISCUSSION: Rego realized a $2,000 loss ($10,000 realized – $12,000 adjusted basis). A loss from the sale or exchange of property between related parties is not deductible. Related parties include a corporation and an individual who owns more than 50% of the stock. Since Justin owns more than 50% of the Rego stock, the loss is not deductible.

10.2 Installment Sales

6. For the current year, the installment method may **not** be used for

A. Sales of personal property (except farm property) by dealers who regularly sell this type of personal property on an installment plan.
B. Sales of real property (except farm property and certain sales of residential lots or timeshares) held by a dealer for sale in the ordinary course of business.
C. Publicly traded equity securities.
D. All of the answers are correct.

Answer (D) is correct.
REQUIRED: The transactions for which the installment method of accounting is disallowed.
DISCUSSION: Under current law, use of the installment method is usually disallowed for dispositions of property by dealers [Sec. 453(b)(2)]. This includes any disposition of (1) personal property, if the person regularly sells such personal property on the installment plan, and (2) real property held by the taxpayer for sale to customers in the ordinary course of his or her trade or business. Exceptions are made for property used or produced in the trade or business of farming, and, if so elected, sales of residential lots or timeshares, subject to interest payments on the deferred tax [Sec. 453(l)]. Additionally, in general, installment sales do not apply to publicly traded securities.
Answer (A) is incorrect. The installment method may not be used for sales of personal property (except farm property) by dealers who regularly sell this type of personal property on an installment plan. **Answer (B) is incorrect.** The installment method may not be used for sales of real property (except farm property and certain sales of residential lots or timeshares) held by a dealer for sale in the ordinary course of business. **Answer (C) is incorrect.** In general, installment sales do not apply to publicly traded securities.

7. With respect to the disposition of an installment obligation, which of the following is **false**?

A. No gain or loss is recognized on the transfer of an installment obligation between a husband and wife if incident to a divorce.
B. If the obligation is sold, the gain or loss is the difference between the basis in the obligation and the amount realized.
C. A gift of an installment obligation is considered a disposition.
D. If an installment obligation is canceled, it is not treated as a disposition.

Answer (D) is correct.
REQUIRED: The incorrect statement with respect to the disposition of an installment obligation.
DISCUSSION: Section 453B provides that, when an installment obligation is disposed of, gain or loss is recognized to the extent of the difference between the basis of the obligation and the amount realized (or the fair market value of the obligation if disposed of other than by sale or exchange). The main purpose of Sec. 453B is to prevent the shifting of income between taxpayers. Section 453B(a) expressly requires recognition whether the obligation is sold or otherwise disposed of. Cancellation of an installment obligation is a disposition of the obligation.
Answer (A) is incorrect. Section 453B(g) excludes from the definition of a disposition a transfer between husband and wife incident to a divorce. The same tax treatment with respect to the obligation that would have applied to the transferor then applies to the transferee. **Answer (B) is incorrect.** The gain or loss on sale of an installment obligation is the difference between the amount realized and the basis in the obligation. **Answer (C) is incorrect.** A gift is a disposition for purposes of Sec. 453B.

SU 10: Property Transactions: Special Topics

8. In Year 1, Ray sold land with a basis of $40,000 for $100,000. He received a $20,000 down payment and the buyer's note for $80,000. In Year 2, he received the first of four annual payments of $20,000 each, plus 12% interest. What is the gain to be reported in Year 1?

A. None.
B. $8,000
C. $12,000
D. $20,000

Answer (C) is correct.
REQUIRED: The amount of gain reported on an installment sale.
DISCUSSION: The transaction qualifies for treatment as an installment sale. The amount of gain is the proportion of the payments received in the year that the gross profit bears to the total contract price. The contract price is the total amount the seller will ultimately collect from the buyer. Ray's gross profit is $60,000 ($100,000 sales price − $40,000 adjusted basis). Since $20,000 was received in Year 1, the gain is $12,000.

$$\frac{\$60,000 \text{ gross profit}}{\$100,000 \text{ contract price}} \times \$20,000 = \$12,000$$

Answer (A) is incorrect. A gain must be reported on the sale. **Answer (B) is incorrect.** The amount of the payment that is considered a return of capital is $8,000. **Answer (D) is incorrect.** Only the portion that is not a return of capital must be reported as a gain. This portion is determined by calculating the gross profit percentage.

9. In an installment sale, if the buyer assumes a mortgage that is greater than the installment sale basis of the property sold,

A. There is never a profit or a loss.
B. The transaction is disqualified as an installment sale.
C. The gross profit percentage is always 100%.
D. The gain is treated as short-term capital gain.

Answer (C) is correct.
REQUIRED: The statement that applies when a buyer assumes a mortgage greater than the installment sale basis of the property sold.
DISCUSSION: In an installment sale when the buyer assumes a mortgage that is greater than the basis of the asset, the seller is required to recognize the excess mortgage as a payment in year of sale and also increase the contract price by the amount of the excess. If the contract price were not increased, the gross profit percentage would be greater than 100%. The amount of increase in the contract price will make the contract price equal to the gross profit, thus giving a gross profit percentage of 100%.
Answer (A) is incorrect. The installment sale may give rise to a profit or loss. **Answer (B) is incorrect.** The presented circumstance does not prevent the sale from qualifying as an installment sale. **Answer (D) is incorrect.** Any gain realized from a disposal of recaptured property in an installment sale is characterized as ordinary income by Secs. 1245 and 1250.

10.3 Nonrecognition Transactions

10. Joan Reed exchanged commercial real estate that she owned for other commercial real estate plus cash of $50,000. The following additional information pertains to this transaction:

Property given up by Reed
Fair market value $500,000
Adjusted basis 300,000

Property received by Reed
Fair market value 450,000

What amount of gain should be recognized in Reed's income tax return?

A. $200,000
B. $150,000
C. $50,000
D. $0

Answer (C) is correct.
REQUIRED: The recognized gain or loss on an exchange of like-kind property with boot.
DISCUSSION: Neither gain nor loss is recognized on an exchange of like-kind property held for productive use in a trade or business or for investment. When boot (cash) is received, gain or loss is recognized to the extent of the boot. Reed recognizes a $50,000 gain.
Answer (A) is incorrect. The amount of $200,000 is the realized gain. Answer (B) is incorrect. The amount of $150,000 results from subtracting the adjusted basis of the property given up from the fair market value of the property received by Reed. Answer (D) is incorrect. In a like-kind exchange, realized gain must be recognized to the extent of boot received ($50,000).

11. Mr. Baker sold his home on November 1, Year 15 (the current year) for $355,000. He owned and lived in the home for 15 years, and it had an adjusted basis of $75,000. He purchased a new home for $200,000. What amount of gain may Mr. Baker exclude on this transaction?

A. $0
B. $250,000
C. $280,000
D. $355,000

Answer (B) is correct.
REQUIRED: The amount of gain recognized on the sale of a principal residence.
DISCUSSION: Mr. Baker will realize a $280,000 ($355,000 – $75,000) gain on the sale of the home. Mr. Baker is allowed to exclude up to $250,000 of gain on this sale. Therefore, he recognizes a gain of $30,000.

SU 10: Property Transactions: Special Topics

12. On October 1, 2021, Donald Anderson exchanged an apartment building, having an adjusted basis of $375,000 and subject to a mortgage of $100,000, for $25,000 cash and another apartment building with a fair market value of $550,000 and subject to a mortgage of $125,000. The property transfers were made subject to the outstanding mortgages. What amount of gain should Anderson recognize in his tax return for 2021?

A. $0
B. $25,000
C. $125,000
D. $175,000

Answer (B) is correct.
REQUIRED: The gain recognized in a like-kind exchange of properties subject to mortgages.
DISCUSSION: Anderson's realized gain is

Fair market value of building received		$ 550,000
Mortgage on old building		100,000
Cash received		25,000
Total amount realized		$ 675,000
Less: Basis of old building	$375,000	
Mortgage on new building	125,000	(500,000)
Realized gain (only $25,000 recognized)		$ 175,000

Under Reg. 1.1031(d)-2, excess mortgage incurred cannot be netted against cash received to reduce the amount of boot received.

Answer (A) is incorrect. The $25,000 cash boot received by Anderson is recognized gain. **Answer (C) is incorrect.** The mortgages are netted. Thus, Anderson is considered to have given $25,000 boot by taking the larger mortgage and not to have received another $100,000 boot. **Answer (D) is incorrect.** Gain realized is recognized only to the extent of boot received in a like-kind exchange.

13. Gwen owned a duplex and lived in one-half. The other half was rental property. The cost of the property was $80,000, of which $70,000 was allocated to the building and $10,000 to the land. During the current year, the property was condemned by the city. Up to that time, she had allowed/allowable depreciation of $23,000. The city paid Gwen $70,000. She bought another duplex for $85,000. Gwen lived in one-half, and the other half is a rental. What is the basis of the replacement property?

A. $62,000
B. $67,000
C. $72,000
D. $85,000

Answer (B) is correct.
REQUIRED: The basis of the replacement property.
DISCUSSION: Gwen has two assets, one for rental and one for personal use. Each asset must be computed separately. The basis of the rental building before the sale was $17,000 ($40,000 purchase price – $23,000 depreciation taken). That portion of the building was sold for $35,000, leaving a gain of $18,000. The gain is deferred, leaving a basis for the replacement property of $24,500 ($42,500 – $18,000). The personal-use building has a $5,000 loss ($35,000 selling price – $40,000 basis). That loss is a nondeductible personal loss. The replacement portion has a basis of $42,500, the purchase price. The total basis is $67,000 ($24,500 rental portion + $42,500 personal-use portion).

Answer (A) is incorrect. The loss does not reduce the basis. **Answer (C) is incorrect.** The loss is not deferred. **Answer (D) is incorrect.** The deferred gain reduces the basis of the new asset.

10.4 Business Property Recharacterization

14. On January 2, Year 1, Bates Corp. purchased and placed into service 7-year MACRS tangible property costing $100,000. On December 31, Year 3, Bates sold the property for $102,000, after having taken $47,525 in MACRS depreciation deductions. What amount of the gain should Bates recapture as ordinary income?

A. $0
B. $2,000
C. $47,525
D. $49,525

Answer (C) is correct.
REQUIRED: The amount of gain recaptured as ordinary income in Sec. 1245.
DISCUSSION: Depreciable tangible property used in a trade or business is Sec. 1245 property. Section 1245 states that gain realized on the disposition of this property is recaptured as ordinary income to the extent of the lesser of depreciation taken or realized gain.
Answer (A) is incorrect. Section 1245 recaptures as ordinary income the realized gain to the extent of the depreciation taken. Answer (B) is incorrect. The amount of Sec. 1231 gain is $2,000. Answer (D) is incorrect. The realized gain is $49,525. Section 1245 states that realized gain up to the amount of depreciation taken is reclassified as ordinary income.

15. Mary Brown purchased an apartment building on January 1, 2011, for $200,000. The building was depreciated using the straight-line method. On December 31, 2021, the building was sold for $210,000 when the asset basis net of accumulated depreciation was $160,000. On her 2021 tax return, Brown should report

A. Section 1231 gain of $10,000 and ordinary income of $40,000.
B. Section 1231 gain of $40,000 and ordinary income of $10,000.
C. Ordinary income of $50,000.
D. Section 1231 gain of $50,000.

Answer (D) is correct.
REQUIRED: The amount and character of gain that should be recognized.
DISCUSSION: When depreciable property used in a trade or business is sold at a gain, first Sec. 1245 and Sec. 1250 are applied; then the balance of the gain not recaptured as ordinary income is Sec. 1231 gain. In this case, Sec. 1245 does not apply, and Sec. 1250 recapture is limited to the excess of accelerated depreciation over straight-line depreciation. Since the building was depreciated using the straight-line method, the entire $50,000 gain ($210,000 – $160,000) is Sec. 1231 gain, $40,000 of which is attributable to straight-line depreciation and taxed at the maximum Sec. 1250 unrecaptured gains rate of 25%.

16. Four years ago, a self-employed taxpayer purchased office furniture for $30,000. During the current tax year, the taxpayer sold the furniture for $37,000. At the time of the sale, the taxpayer's depreciation deductions totaled $20,700. What part of the gain is taxed as long-term capital gain?

A. $0
B. $7,000
C. $20,700
D. $27,700

Answer (B) is correct.
REQUIRED: The long-term capital gain portion from disposal of Sec. 1245 property.
DISCUSSION: Section 1245 property is depreciable personal property held for greater than 1 year and used in a trade or business (e.g., office furniture). Gain on the disposition of Sec. 1245 property is ordinary income to the extent of the lesser of all depreciation taken or gain realized. The realized gain in excess of the depreciation taken may be treated as a gain from the sale or exchange of Sec. 1231 property. If the net result of all Sec. 1231 gains and losses is a gain, the gain is taxed as a long-term capital gain. The realized gain of $27,700 is greater than the depreciation taken ($20,700) by $7,000. All Sec. 1245 and 1231 property is long term.
Answer (A) is incorrect. The realized gain is greater than the depreciation taken. Answer (C) is incorrect. The depreciation recapture is ordinary income. Answer (D) is incorrect. The Sec. 1231 gain is the excess gain over ordinary income.

17. Platt owns land that is operated as a parking lot. A shed was erected on the lot for the related transactions with customers. With regard to capital assets and Sec. 1231 assets, how should these assets be classified?

	Land	Shed
A.	Capital	Capital
B.	Sec. 1231	Capital
C.	Capital	Sec. 1231
D.	Sec. 1231	Sec. 1231

Answer (D) is correct.
REQUIRED: The classification of property as a Sec. 1231 or capital asset.
DISCUSSION: Capital assets are any property not excluded by IRC definition. Real property used in a trade or business is excluded. Section 1231 property includes all real or depreciable property used in the taxpayer's trade or business and held more than 1 year.

18. Which of the following is Sec. 1250 property?

A. Land held for investment.
B. Irrigation system.
C. Lease on land.
D. Dams.

Answer (C) is correct.
REQUIRED: The qualification of Sec. 1250 intangible property.
DISCUSSION: Land is not Sec. 1250 property, but leases are Sec. 1250 intangible properties. Certain improvements to land may be treated as land, e.g., dams and irrigation systems. Section 1250 property includes depreciable real property acquired after 1986.
Answer (A) is incorrect. Land is not Sec. 1250 property, but leases of land are Sec. 1250 intangible properties. **Answer (B) is incorrect.** Irrigation systems may be treated as land and are not Sec. 1250 property, but leases of land are Sec. 1250 intangible properties. **Answer (D) is incorrect.** Dams may be treated as land and are not Sec. 1250 property, but leases of land are Sec. 1250 intangible properties.

19. Which of the following items qualifies for treatment under Sec. 1231 (Property Used in the Trade or Business and Involuntary Conversions)?

A. Copyright used in the business, held for 10 years.
B. Building used in the business, held for 6 months.
C. Machinery used in the business, held for 11 months.
D. Computer used in the business, held for 4 years.

Answer (D) is correct.
REQUIRED: The proper identification of Sec. 1231 property.
DISCUSSION: Section 1231 property is property held for more than 1 year and includes all real or depreciable property used in a trade or business. A computer used in the business that was held for 4 years meets this definition.
Answer (A) is incorrect. Copyrights are explicitly excluded from Sec. 1231 treatment. **Answer (B) is incorrect.** Section 1231 property must be held for more than 1 year. **Answer (C) is incorrect.** Section 1231 property must be held for more than 1 year.

10.5 Gift Tax

20. Which of the following payments would require the donor to file a gift tax return?

A. $30,000 to a university for a spouse's tuition.

B. $40,000 to a university for a cousin's room and board.

C. $50,000 to a hospital for a parent's medical expenses.

D. $80,000 to a physician for a friend's surgery.

Answer (B) is correct.
REQUIRED: The payment requiring a gift tax return.
DISCUSSION: Although tuition is an amount excluded as a taxable gift, room and board does not qualify. It must be reported on the gift tax return.
Answer (A) is incorrect. A payment for tuition or to a medical organization may be excluded from gift tax assuming it is paid directly to the third party. Answer (C) is incorrect. Medical expenses are excluded as taxable gifts pending payment directly to the third party providing the medical care. Answer (D) is incorrect. Excluded from taxable gifts are amounts paid on behalf of another individual for medical care. The payment must be directly to the medical provider.

21. If an individual donor makes a gift of future interest in which the donee is to receive possession of the gift at some future time, the annual exclusion for gift tax purposes is

A. $0

B. $3,000

C. $5,000

D. $15,000

Answer (A) is correct.
REQUIRED: The annual exclusion for a gift of a future interest.
DISCUSSION: A donor is allowed an annual exclusion of $15,000 for gifts to each donee. The exclusion is specifically limited to gifts of present interest.
Answer (B) is incorrect. The amount of $3,000 does not qualify for the exclusion. Answer (C) is incorrect. The amount of $5,000 does not qualify for the exclusion. Answer (D) is incorrect. The amount of $15,000 does not qualify for the exclusion.

22. In 2021, Sayer, who is single, gave an outright gift of $53,000 to a friend, Johnson, who needed the money to pay medical expenses. In filing the 2021 gift tax return, Sayer was entitled to a maximum exclusion of

A. $0

B. $3,000

C. $15,000

D. $30,000

Answer (C) is correct.
REQUIRED: The maximum exclusion for a gift used to pay medical expenses.
DISCUSSION: An unlimited exclusion is available for amounts paid on behalf of the donee as medical care. The transfer for medical care must be made directly to the person who provides it (not the donee). Therefore, this unlimited exclusion is not available for Sayer. However, the annual exclusion of $15,000 is allowed.
Answer (A) is incorrect. Sayer may take an exclusion. Answer (B) is incorrect. Sayer may exclude the maximum amount. Answer (D) is incorrect. The maximum exclusion is $15,000 per year per donee.

STUDY UNIT ELEVEN
CORPORATE TAXABLE INCOME

(23 pages of outline)

11.1	Definition and Accounting	296
11.2	Formation	298
11.3	Gross Income of a Corporation	302
11.4	Deductions of a Corporation	303
11.5	Losses of a Corporation	316

Entities that are classified as C corporations for federal tax purposes are subject to an entity-level income tax. In addition, when a C corporation distributes its profits to its owners as dividends, the owners are subject to income taxation on the dividend income they receive. This "double" taxation is the hallmark of C corporation status.

The computation of taxable income for C corporations is similar to that of individuals. Gross income is broadly conceived (unless excluded by a code section) and then taxpayers are allowed various deductions before arriving at the taxable income upon which the income tax is computed. From the total tax liability, a taxpayer can subtract their prepayments and tax credits before arriving at their amount due or refund due. And, like an individual, a corporation must make estimated tax payments throughout the year.

However, C corporation tax calculations have several important differences. First, properties held by C corporations are guided by special rules upon formation and are treated differently than property of individuals. Second, C corporations do not use the concept of adjusted gross income (AGI); therefore, there are no below-the-line or above-the-line deductions. Third, C corporations are not allowed credits or deductions of a personal nature (e.g., the standard deduction or the Child Tax Credit). Also, unlike the progressive tax rate schedules used for individuals, C corporations are taxed at a flat rate of 21%. A C corporation tax return is made on Form 1120, *U.S. Corporation Income Tax Return*.

In addition to a corporate-level income tax, corporations may also be subject to the AET (accumulated earnings tax) and the PHC (personal holding company) tax for failing to distribute sufficient earnings to shareholders.

Some candidates find it helpful to have the entire tax form side-by-side with our Knowledge Transfer Outline when studying, and others may prefer to see the final draft of a form when it is released. The full versions of the most up-to-date forms are easily accessible at www.gleim.com/taxforms. These forms and the form excerpts used in our outline are periodically updated as the latest versions are released by the IRS.

11.1 DEFINITION AND ACCOUNTING

1. **Double Taxation**

    a. C corporations are subject to a 21% entity-level flat tax on corporate income. In addition, shareholders must include any dividends received from a C corporation in their own gross incomes. This results in corporate income being taxed twice, once at the corporate level and once at the shareholder level.

> **EXAMPLE 11-1   Double Taxation**
>
> Peter and Paul each own 50% of AZY Company. Assume AZY has taxable income of $500,000. If AZY is a C corporation, AZY will file Form 1120 and pay tax at a rate of 21%. So, AZY will pay $105,000 in corporate income taxes and have net income after taxes of $395,000. If AZY chooses to distribute this income to its shareholders ($197,500 each), the income will be included on Peter and Paul's individual tax returns as dividend income and will be taxed once again. Assuming Peter and Paul qualify for a 15% tax rate on dividends, they will each incur an additional $29,625 in tax. Due to this double taxation, the total tax levied on the $500,000 of corporate income is $164,250 ($105,000 + $29,625 + $29,625).

2. **General Entity Classification**

    a. **Default classification.** By default, noncorporate entities (e.g., LLCs, LLPs, etc.) with two or more owners are classified as partnerships for federal tax purposes. Noncorporate entities with only one owner (e.g., a single-member LLC) are classified as disregarded entities. Disregarded entities are included in the tax return of their owner.

        1) **Limited liability company (LLC).** Normally, an LLC would elect partnership status to avoid being taxed as a corporation. This election allows for limited liability of the owners while at the same time retaining the single taxation. The owners are allowed to participate in the operations of the business, and there are no restrictions on the type of owners. If corporate status is chosen, the election is made between S corporation and C corporation status.

    b. **Check-the-box regulations.** For most noncorporate entities other than trusts, an election can be made under the check-the-box regulations to change an entity's status from the default classification (e.g., partnership, disregarded entity) to being taxed as a C corporation. The effect of the flexibility provided by the check-the-box regulations is to make tax factors secondary to non-tax factors in a choice of entity decision where the options are noncorporate entities (e.g., LLC vs. LLP).

        1) Once an entity has elected to be taxed as a C corporation, a separate election to be taxed as an S corporation is available if the entity meets the criteria for S corporation status (no more than 100 shareholders, one class of stock, etc.).

        2) An S corporation is a pass-through entity that is generally not subject to an entity-level income tax. Instead, income, deductions, and credits pass through to shareholders similar to a partnership.

> **EXAMPLE 11-2   Check-the-Box**
>
> ABC, LLP, a limited liability partnership, is taxed as a partnership for federal tax by default because it has two or more owners (recall that a partnership must have at least two owners). However, ABC can elect under the check-the-box regulations to be taxed as a C corporation. Note that the check-the-box election does not change ABC's entity type under state law; instead, only ABC's classification for federal tax has changed. And, once ABC is a C corporation, if eligible, it can make an S election to be taxed as an S corporation.

SU 11: Corporate Taxable Income   297

c. In contrast to the great flexibility afforded to noncorporate entities under check-the-box regulations, entities organized as corporations under state law cannot make an election under check-the-box. These entities are known as "per se" corporations. A per se corporation is taxed as a C corporation. These entities' only option is to make an S election if eligible. Thus, tax factors remain very important in the choice of entity decision when deciding whether to incorporate.

   1) Other entities required to be taxed as corporations include associations (foreign LLC entities are by default associations), joint stock companies, insurance companies, certain banks, state-owned organizations, certain foreign organizations, and publicly traded partnerships.

   2) A professional association (PA) is an association of professionals (e.g., accountants, doctors, or lawyers) and is treated as a corporation for tax purposes if it is both organized under a state's professional association act and operated as a corporation.

   3) A personal service corporation's (PSC) principal activity is performing personal services, substantially by employee-owners. An employee-owner owns more than 10% of the stock. The IRS may allocate income, deductions, credits, exclusion, and other allowances between a PSC and its employee-owners if substantially all of the PSC's services are performed for one other corporation, partnership, or entity, and the principal purpose of the PSC is tax avoidance.

Summary of Check-the-Box Classifications

Entity Type	Default Classification	Check-the-Box Election
Noncorporate, single-owner entity (e.g., single-member LLC)	Disregarded entity (included as part of owner's tax return)	Taxed as a corporation (Form 1120)
Noncorporate, multiple-owner entity (e.g., partnership or multimember LLC)	Partnership (Form 1065)	Taxed as a corporation (Form 1120)
Incorporated entity	Taxed as a corporation (Form 1120)	Not available

3. **Tax Year**

   a. Generally, a corporation may elect either a calendar or fiscal tax year.

      1) A PSC is required to use a calendar tax year.

         a) An exception exists for a valid business purpose or a PSC that makes "minimum distributions."

      2) A C corporation's tax return is due on or before the 15th day of the 4th month following the close of the tax year (e.g., April 15 for a calendar-year corporation).

         a) A corporation that files Form 7004 and pays its estimated unpaid tax liability is allowed an extension of up to 6 months for calendar-year and fiscal-year C corporations other than June 30 fiscal-year C corporations.

         b) C corporations with a June 30 fiscal year will continue to have a due date of the 15th day of the 3rd month following the close of the tax year. This will continue until tax years beginning after December 31, 2025. The extension date is April 15, resulting in a 7-month extension until tax year 2026.

4. **Accounting Method**
    a. No formal election is required for the accounting method of a newly incorporated C corporation. Any method allowed by the C corporation may be "elected" simply by using that method on its initial return. For example, a newly formed C corporation that chooses to use the accrual method must only use this method on its initial return in order to elect the method.
    b. The cash method may be used only by PSCs, S corporations, certain farming corporations, and C corporations that have average annual gross receipts of no more than $26 million in the 3 preceding tax years. Tax shelters may not use the cash method.

5. **Corporation Income Tax Formula**

	Gross income
−	Deductions
=	**Taxable income before special deductions**
−	Dividends-received deduction
−	Net operating losses
=	**Taxable income**
×	Tax rate
=	**Tax liability**
−	Credits
−	Prepayments
=	**Tax due or refund receivable**

STOP & REVIEW

You have completed the outline for this subunit. Study multiple-choice questions 1 through 3 beginning on page 318.

11.2 FORMATION

1. **Overview**
    a. Without Sec. 351, any gain realized on the transfer of property to a corporation in exchange for stock of the corporation would be recognized.

EXAMPLE 11-3   Transfer of Property for Stock

A taxpayer transfers property with a basis of $10,000 and a FMV of $20,000 for a corporation's stock with a FMV of $20,000. The taxpayer realizes and recognizes a $10,000 gain ($20,000 FMV − $10,000 basis).

---

    b. Section 351 requires that no gain or loss be recognized if property (e.g., cash, tangible property, intangible property) is transferred to a corporation by one or more persons solely in exchange for stock in the corporation and, immediately after the exchange, such person or persons control the corporation. This nonrecognition treatment is mandatory, not elective.

        1) Section 351 generally applies to S corporations as it does to C corporations.

SU 11: Corporate Taxable Income   299

2. **Section 351**
   a. **Control** is ownership of 80% or more of the voting power of stock and 80% or more of the shares of each class of nonvoting stock of the corporation.
      1) Stock exchanged for services is not counted toward the 80%.
         a) The FMV of the stock is gross income to the shareholder.
         b) The shareholder's basis in the stock exchanged for services is its FMV.
      2) Nonqualified preferred stock is treated as boot received and is not counted as stock toward the 80%-ownership test.
   b. **Solely for stock.** To the extent the **shareholder** receives the corporation's stock in exchange for property, nonrecognition is required. This is true even if the shareholder receives some boot (money or other property) in the exchange.

> **EXAMPLE 11-4   Transfer of Asset in a Sec. 351 Exchange**
>
> Taxpayer transfers an asset to the corporation in a Sec. 351 exchange. The asset has a basis of $10,000. Taxpayer receives $3,000 in cash and stock worth $15,000. Taxpayer has a realized gain of $8,000 and a recognized gain of $3,000.

      1) **Disparate value.** Inequality of FMV of the stock and property exchanged is not relevant in itself.
         a) The shareholder may have gross income if the disparity represents an (unstated) additional transaction, e.g., payment of compensation, a constructive dividend.
      2) Section 351 may apply to an exchange after formation.
      3) Section 351 can apply to contributions of property even if the corporation issues no stock in the exchange, e.g., a capital contribution by a sole shareholder who receives no stock in exchange for the contribution.
      4) Section 351 may also apply when the corporation exchanges treasury stock.
   c. **Boot.** The shareholder recognizes gain realized to the extent of money and the FMV of other property (except the stock of the corporation) received in the exchange.
      1) FMV of property given up is used if FMV of property received cannot be ascertained.
      2) Character of the gain depends on the property contributed.
      3) No loss is recognized on the receipt of boot.
   d. **Liabilities.** Section 351 applies even if the corporation assumes the shareholder's liability or takes property subject to a liability in the exchange, and liabilities are generally not treated as boot.
      1) The amount of the liabilities is treated as recognized gain from the sale or exchange of an asset only to the extent it exceeds the AB of all property contributed by the shareholder.

> **EXAMPLE 11-5   Liability Transfer under Sec. 351**
>
> A taxpayer transfers an asset with a basis of $60,000 and a FMV of $100,000 to a corporation for all of its stock. The asset has a liability attached of $70,000. The taxpayer must recognize $10,000 of income, the excess of the liability ($70,000) over the basis of the asset ($60,000).

      2) If tax avoidance was a purpose or if no business purpose was present for the assumption or transfer, the liability is treated as boot and would trigger gain recognition.

e. The **corporation** recognizes no gain on exchange of its stock for property (including money).

1) Treasury stock is included.
2) The corporation recognizes gain on exchanging other property (neither money nor its stock), even with a shareholder, unless an exception applies.

3. **Basis of Shareholder in Stock**

   a. A control group shareholder's basis in the stock of the corporation is the adjusted basis (AB) in contributed property adjusted for the boot received and the gain recognized.

       Cash and AB in contributed property
       − Boot received
           Money, including
           Property received FMV (other than above and the corporation's stock)
       − Liability relief (corporation assumes or takes subject to)
       + Gain recognized by shareholder
       = **Basis in stock of issuing corporation**

   b. Holding period is generally tacked, i.e., the holding period of the property exchanged for stock is added to the holding period of the stock.

4. **Basis of Shareholder in Boot**

   a. Boot generally has a basis equal to fair market value.

5. **Basis of Corporation in Property**

   a. The corporation's initial carryover basis in property exchanged by a control group shareholder for its stock is an adjusted carryover basis.

       AB in property to shareholder
       + Gain recognized by shareholder
       = **Basis in property to corporation**

   b. This basis also applies when the shareholder receives nothing in return.
   c. This basis is also the corporation's initial depreciable basis in the property.
      1) Allowable depreciation is apportioned based on the number of months the corporation owned the asset.
   d. When the shareholder's AB in the property exceeds the FMV (i.e., when a built-in loss exists), the basis is limited to the FMV.
   e. Holding period is tacked.

EXAMPLE 11-6   FMV < AB (Built-in Loss)

Becky formed a corporation by contributing a machine with an AB of $65,000 and a FMV of $50,000. Since there is a built-in loss in the contributed property (AB > FMV), the corporation's basis in the machine is limited to the FMV of $50,000.

EXAMPLE 11-7 — Corporate Formation

A, B, C, D, and E formed XYZ Corporation by contributing the following:

Shareholder	Contribution	Receipt
A	Legal services worth $100,000	20% of XYZ's stock
B	Equipment with AB of $50,000 and FMV of $100,000	20% of XYZ's stock
C	Office building with AB of $70,000 and FMV of $130,000; the office building is subject to a mortgage of $30,000	20% of XYZ's stock
D	Building with AB of $40,000 and FMV of $160,000; the building is subject to a mortgage of $60,000	20% of XYZ's stock
E	Warehouse with AB of $65,000 and FMV of $120,000	20% of XYZ's stock plus $20,000 cash

Immediately after the contribution, the five shareholders control the corporation (80%; stock exchanged for services is not counted).

Shareholder A: A recognizes gross income of $100,000, the FMV of the legal services provided. XYZ recognizes an expense of $100,000. A's basis in the stock is $100,000 (gain recognized), the FMV of the legal services.

Shareholder B: B realizes a gain of $50,000 ($100,000 FMV − $50,000 AB). B recognizes no gain as no boot is received. XYZ does not recognize any gain or loss. B's basis in the stock is $50,000 ($50,000 AB in property, no boot received or liability relieved). XYZ's basis in the property is $50,000 ($50,000 AB in property + $0 gain recognized by B).

Shareholder C: C realizes a gain of $60,000 ($130,000 FMV − $70,000 AB). Recognized gain is zero as no boot is received. XYZ does not recognize any gain or loss. C's basis in the stock is $40,000 ($70,000 AB in property − $30,000 liability relieved). XYZ's basis in the property is $70,000 ($70,000 property + $0 gain recognized by C).

Shareholder D: D recognizes a gain of $20,000 ($60,000 liability relieved − $40,000 AB of property). XYZ does not recognize any gain or loss. D's basis in the stock is $0 ($40,000 AB in property − $60,000 liability relieved + $20,000 gain recognized). XYZ's basis in the property is $60,000 ($40,000 AB in property + $20,000 gain recognized by D).

Shareholder E: E realizes a gain of $55,000 ($120,000 FMV − $65,000 AB). Recognized gain is limited to boot received of $20,000. Thus, E recognizes $20,000 gain. XYZ does not recognize any gain or loss. E's basis in the stock is $65,000 ($65,000 AB in property − $20,000 boot received + $20,000 gain recognized). XYZ's basis in the property is $85,000 ($65,000 AB in property + $20,000 gain recognized by E).

STOP & REVIEW

You have completed the outline for this subunit.
Study multiple-choice questions 4 through 6 beginning on page 319.

11.3 GROSS INCOME OF A CORPORATION

1. **Scope**
   a. Gross income of a corporation, similar to individual taxation, is all income from whatever source derived unless specifically excluded. Reconciling book and taxable income (i.e., book-to-tax differences) is covered in Study Unit 16, Subunit 4.

2. **Excluded Items**
   a. **Capital contributions** are excluded from a corporation's gross income.
      1) **Gifts from a nonshareholder.** Property other than money gifted from a nonshareholder has a zero basis. When money is contributed instead of property, it is given a basis equal to the value of the money and the basis of other property is reduced. First, reduce basis in property acquired within 1 year after the gift, then in all depreciable property, if any, and then in any remaining property, in proportion to the relative basis of any property in each of these categories.
         a) **Exceptions to capital contributions exclusion.** Nonshareholder contributions from customers or potential customers are included in gross income of a corporation. The other exceptions to the general exclusion of contributions by nonshareholders are contributions by governments or civic groups.
      2) Pro rata contributions by shareholders, whether voluntary or by assessment, are not deductible by the shareholders. Instead, their individual basis in the stock is increased. The corporation may take a transferred basis in the property.
   b. **Treasury stock.** No gain or loss is recognized by a corporation on the sale or exchange of its own stock (including treasury stock).

3. **Included Items**
   a. **Life insurance income.** Proceeds received due to the death of the insured are generally excluded from gross income.
      1) If an employer purchases a policy that covers an employee and is issued after August 17, 2006, the proceeds from the policy are taxable to the extent proceeds exceed premiums paid.
         a) An exception is made for key employees, for whom the full amount of life insurance proceeds is excluded from gross income.
      2) Proceeds received under a policy transferred for consideration (e.g., secured debt) are income to the recipient only to the extent that the proceeds exceed the consideration.
   b. **Discharge of debt.** Except in stock-for-debt exchanges, income from cancellation of a corporation's debt at less than the outstanding carrying amount is excluded to the extent the corporation is insolvent. When the exclusion applies, the following tax attributes of the corporation must be reduced (dollar for dollar) in the order listed:
      1) NOLs and NOL carryovers
      2) The general business credit
      3) Capital loss carryovers
      4) Basis in property of the corporation
      5) Foreign tax credit carryovers

      NOTE: An election to first reduce basis is available.

SU 11: Corporate Taxable Income

c. **Bond repurchase.** A corporation's income includes the issue price of its own bond minus the repurchase price and any premium it has already recognized. Item 15. in Subunit 11.4 discusses repurchase at a premium.
d. **Sinking-fund income.** Interest or other income from property (including money) in a sinking fund to satisfy an obligation is income (even if in the hands of a trustee).
e. **Unrestrained claim.** Both cash- and accrual-basis taxpayers must include in gross income, in the year of receipt, amounts actually or constructively received if the taxpayer has an unrestrained claim to the amounts (e.g., prepaid rent).
f. **Refunds.** As with individuals, a refund of state taxes deducted for a prior year is included in income for the current year, to the extent that the deduction in the prior year generated a tax benefit. If the deduction generated no tax benefit, the refund is not included.

> **STOP & REVIEW**
> You have completed the outline for this subunit.
> Study multiple-choice questions 7 through 9 on page 321.

11.4 DEDUCTIONS OF A CORPORATION

> **SUCCESS TIP**
> Deductions of a corporation have been regularly tested on the CPA Exam. You should be familiar with calculating both corporate book income and corporate taxable income. In a question testing corporate deductions, you may be given corporate book income, along with other information, and asked to calculate corporate taxable income.

NOTE: This subunit covers deductions with special rules. Ordinary deductions without restrictions (e.g., utilities) are not specifically addressed. Reconciling book and taxable income (i.e., book-to-tax differences) is covered in Study Unit 16, Subunit 4.

1. **Overview**
    a. Theoretically, all corporate expenditures have a business objective. Deductions from corporate gross income for ordinary and necessary business expenses are allowed. Differences from deductions for individuals are discussed below.
        1) Organizational expenditures are allowed an immediate expense and amortization of balance.
        2) Deduction is allowed for dividends received from corporations.
        3) Interest on a corporation's own debt is generally deductible.
        4) AGI and limits based on it do not apply to a corporation.
        5) Personal deductions, e.g., the standard deduction, are not allowed.
        6) Passive activity loss rules do not apply to C corporations.
    b. In general, expenses for excludible (i.e., tax exempt) income are not deductible.

2. **Organizational Expense and Start-Up Costs**
   a. Costs of organizing a corporation are properly chargeable to a capital account. They generally are not deductible as a current expense because they benefit more than one tax period.
      1) However, a corporation may elect to expense up to $5,000 of qualified organizational expenses and $5,000 of start-up costs in the taxable year in which the business begins.
         a) The amount expensed is reduced dollar for dollar by the costs exceeding $50,000. The phaseout is computed separately for both start-up and organizational costs.
         b) The remaining balance is amortized over a 15-year (180-month) period beginning with the month business began.
         c) Only expenditures incurred before the end of the tax year in which the corporation commences business may be expensed (amortized). When they are paid is irrelevant.
         d) The election is irrevocable and deemed to be automatically made by taxpayers.
   b. **Qualifying organizational expenditures** are ones incurred incidental to formation of the corporation and are distinct from start-up costs.
      1) Examples are legal fees for drafting the charter, incorporation fees, expenses for temporary directors, and organizational meeting costs.
   c. Organizational expenditures that are not qualified are costs related to the transfer of assets to the corporation or the issuance and sale of stock.
      1) Examples are printing stock certificates; professional fees for issuing stock; and costs incurred in the marketing, advertising, or promoting of stock issuances.
   d. Examples of start-up costs are costs incurred to prepare to enter into the trade or business, to secure suppliers and customers, and to obtain certain supplies and equipment.

EXAMPLE 11-8   Start-Up and Organizational Costs

ABC Corporation has incurred $52,000 in start-up costs and $4,000 in organizational costs. Because ABC's start-up costs exceed $50,000, their $5,000 deduction phases-out dollar for dollar, resulting in a $3,000 deduction ($5,000 − $2,000 phase-out). Because ABC's organizational costs do not exceed $50,000, ABC can deduct up to $5,000 in organizational costs, making the full $4,000 incurred deductible. The $49,000 of start-up costs that cannot be immediately deducted are amortized over 180 months, beginning with the month business begins.

Start-Up Costs and Organizational Costs: Expense or Capitalize?

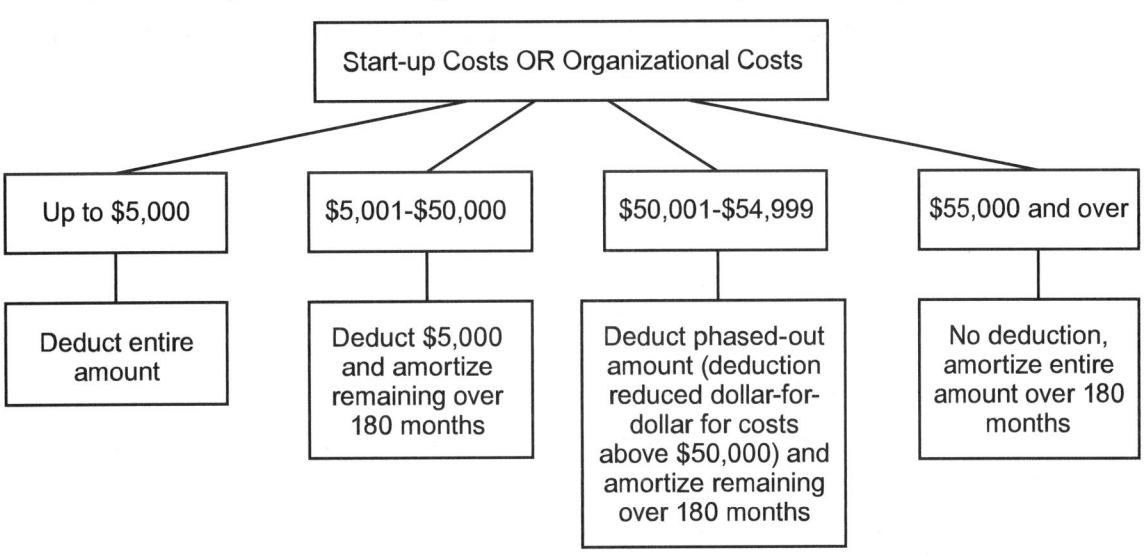

```
                    Start-up Costs OR Organizational Costs
                    ┌──────────┬──────────────┬──────────────┐
                    │          │              │              │
              Up to $5,000  $5,001-$50,000  $50,001-$54,999  $55,000 and over
                    │          │              │              │
              Deduct entire  Deduct $5,000  Deduct phased-out  No deduction,
                 amount      and amortize   amount (deduction  amortize entire
                             remaining over  reduced dollar-for-  amount over 180
                             180 months     dollar for costs      months
                                            above $50,000) and
                                            amortize remaining
                                            over 180 months
```

Figure 11-1

3. **Charitable Contributions**

   a. A corporation's charitable contribution is deductible only if it is made to a qualified organization.

   b. Deductible amounts must be paid during the tax year. An accrual method corporation may elect to deduct an amount authorized by the board during the current tax year and paid not later than 3 1/2 months after the close of the tax year.

   c. A corporation may deduct the adjusted basis of inventory and other ordinary income property contributed.

   d. A corporation is allowed a deduction for the donation of qualified food and book inventory.

      1) The deduction is equal to basis plus one-half of the gain that would have been recognized if the asset were sold at FMV.

      2) The deduction may not exceed two times the asset's basis.

EXAMPLE 11-9   Charitable Contribution

Corcory's Bakery only sells food prepared within the last 2 days to ensure customers receive products at peak freshness. However, the food is edible for a full week, so the bakery donates the unsold food to the local food bank, which qualifies as a donation of inventory to the needy. If, on a given day, Corcory donates food that would have sold for $100 and cost $50 to make, Corcory could take a deduction of $75 [$50 + .5 × ($100 − $50)] for the inventory plus any additional costs to provide the food to the food bank.

e. In general, the deduction for the contribution of capital gain property is the property's FMV.
f. The property must be used in a manner related to the organization's exempt purpose. It must not be disposed of for value.
g. Under the CARES Act, deductions in tax year 2021 are limited to 25% of taxable income (TI) before any

1) Charitable contributions
2) Dividends-received deduction
3) Capital loss carryback
4) Deduction allowed under IRC Sec. 249 for bond premium

NOTE: For all other tax years, the limitation is 10% of TI. The 25% limitation of TI only applies to tax years 2020 and 2021.

h. Contributions paid in cash for relief efforts in qualified disaster areas (excluding COVID-19) are deductible up to 100% of taxable income.
i. Excess over the TI limit is deductible during the succeeding 5 tax years.

1) No carryback is allowed.
2) Current-year contributions are deducted first.
3) FIFO treatment applies to carryforwards.

4. **Dividends-Received Deduction (DRD)**

a. A special corporate deduction for dividends received from domestic taxable corporations is allowed.
b. Amounts deductible vary with the percentage of the stock of the distributing corporation (by voting and value) owned by the recipient.

Percent of Ownership	Percent of Dividends Deductible	Limit: Percent of TI of Recipient
< 20%	50%	50%
≥ 20%, < 80%	65%	65%
≥ 80% & affiliated	100%	N/A

c. To be eligible for the DRD, a corporation must hold the stock at least 46 days during the 91-day period that begins 45 days before the stock becomes ex-dividend with respect to the dividend.
d. A corporation cannot take a DRD if it holds a short position in substantially similar or related property.
e. The DRD may be reduced when the investment company receives substantial amounts of income from sources other than dividends from domestic corporations eligible for the DRD.
f. The 50% and 65% DRD is limited by the recipient corporation's adjusted taxable income. The TI limit does not apply to dividends eligible for a 100% DRD.

1) To compute the limit, use TI before the following most common adjustments:

   a) Dividends-received deduction
   b) NOL deduction
   c) Capital loss carryback

2) First, compute the limit with respect to 20%-and-more-owned corporate dividends.
3) The TI limit does not apply if a current NOL exists or an NOL results from the DRD.

SU 11: Corporate Taxable Income

> **EXAMPLE 11-10   DRD**
>
> Alpha Corporation owns 10% of Beta Corporation. Alpha Corporation has $200,000 of ordinary income plus $100,000 in dividend income from Beta Corporation. Alpha Corporation has a $50,000 ($100,000 dividend × 50%) dividends-received deduction. This is less than 50% of TI before the DRD (i.e., $300,000 × 50% = $150,000); therefore, the TI limit does not apply.

> **EXAMPLE 11-11   DRD -- NOL**
>
> A corporation has taxable income of $1,000, including $10,000 in dividends received from a less-than-20%-owned domestic taxable corporation before the DRD. The DRD before applying the TI limit is $5,000 ($10,000 × 50%). Because the DRD produces an NOL, it is not limited to 50% of taxable income before the deduction, i.e., $500 ($1,000 × 50%).

    g.   The DRD is allowable for dividends received from foreign corporations if the following are met:

        1) The distributing foreign corporation is at least 10% owned by the recipient domestic corporation,

        2) The foreign corporation is subject to U.S. federal income tax,

        3) The foreign corporation has income effectively connected with a trade or business in the U.S., and

        4) The foreign corporation is not a foreign personal holding company.

    h.   The DRD is allowable only on the portion of the dividends attributable to the effectively connected income.

    i.   Credit for foreign taxes deemed paid by the corporation on the dividend producing earnings and profit (E&P) may be allowable.

    j.   An S corporation may not claim the DRD.

    k.   Disqualified dividends. No deduction is allowed, or it is further restricted, for dividends received from the following:

        1) Mutual savings banks (they are like interest)
        2) Real estate investment trusts
        3) Domestic international sales corporations, generally
        4) Public utilities, on preferred stock
        5) A corporation exempt from tax during the distribution year

5. **Gifts**

    a.   Gifts are distinguished from charitable contributions, which are made to qualified organizations. A deduction for business gifts is allowable only to the extent of $25 per donee per year. The following are not treated as gifts for this limit:

        1) Signs or promotional materials used on the recipient's business premises
        2) An item costing less than $4 having a permanent imprint of the donor's name

6. **Compensation**
    a. Compensation, e.g., salary, wages, or bonuses, is a deductible business expense unless the services are capital in nature.
    b. Unreasonable compensation to a shareholder is generally treated as a distribution, characterized as a dividend, to the extent of earnings and profits.
    c. Compensation by an accrual taxpayer (corporation) to a related party cash-basis taxpayer (e.g., a PSC employee-owner, regardless of the ownership percentage) is not deductible by the corporation until the period in which the cash-basis taxpayer receives the payment and recognizes the income.
    d. Payments made 2 1/2 months after year end (March 15 for a calendar-year corporation) may be accrued and expensed in a prior year if related to services rendered in that prior year.
    e. Deduction is disallowed to a publicly held corporation for compensation in excess of $1 million paid in any tax year to certain employees.
        1) The limit applies to compensation paid to the principal executive officer (commonly referred to as the CEO), the principal financial officer, and to the three other highest-compensated officers (i.e., those whose compensation must be reported to shareholders under the Securities Exchange Act of 1934).
            a) Any employee subject to the limit in a preceding year remains subject to the limit for the current year.
            b) No amount of a "parachute payment" made to an officer, shareholder, or highly compensated person is deductible.
        2) The following forms of remuneration are not included in the $1 million limit:
            a) Income from pension plans, annuity plans, and specified employer trusts
            b) Benefits that are tax-free under the Code
            c) Compensation paid before being publicly held
        3) The disallowance of the deduction for the compensation payment does not change the employee's reporting of the compensation for income tax purposes.
            a) The $1 million and any excess is generally compensation gross income.
            b) The salary, bonus, or other payment is not required to be treated as a dividend.
            c) Dividend reporting for compensation may be required if part or all of the compensation is unreasonable.

EXAMPLE 11-12   Deductibility of Corporate Compensation

David Davidson is the Chief Executive Officer (CEO) for publicly held Davidson & Sons, Inc. David is paid a $3 million cash salary, $500,000 in bonuses tied to performance, and $10,000 in tax-free fringe benefits that are accessible to all employees. David includes $3.5 million in income ($3,000,000 salary + $500,000 bonuses). Davidson & Sons can deduct $1,010,000 ($1,000,000 maximum deductible salary + $10,000 fringe benefits).

f. Stock. FMV of property received for services is gross income (to the employee) when it is not subject to a substantial risk of forfeiture and its value can be ascertained with reasonable certainty. Deduction of the compensation (by the employer/corporation) is allowed when the amount is included as gross income (by the employee) but only if federal income tax on the compensation is withheld.

EXAMPLE 11-13	Stock Compensation

Employee purchases stock (FMV = $1,000) in Year 1 for $500. In Year 8, when its FMV is $2,000, Employee's rights in it are no longer subject to a substantial risk of forfeiture. Employee includes $1,500 in gross income in Year 8. Employer may deduct $1,500 in Year 8.

1) Sale prior to vesting in a non-arm's-length transaction results in gross income computed from the current FMV of the property. Further, gross income is includible upon a subsequent arm's-length sale.

EXAMPLE 11-14	Stock Compensation

Employee from Example 11-13 sold the stock to Spouse in Year 2 for $750 when its FMV was $1,500. The sale in Year 8 was by Spouse. Employee includes and Employer deducts $1,000 in Year 2 and $500 in Year 8.

g. Education. An employer's expenditures for employee education are deductible as a business expense. An individual, in contrast, may not deduct educational expenses.

7. **Meals**

    a. Travel and meals are deductible business expenses. Meals purchased while traveling or served on the business premises are deductible by 50% of the amount incurred if not provided by a restaurant.

        1) For a meal to be 50% deductible, the meal expense must be an ordinary and necessary expense and either the taxpayer or an employee of the taxpayer must be present.

        2) Generally, expenses for **entertainment** that are ordinary and necessary to the business are no longer deductible.

        3) For events that combine entertainment and meals, 50% of the meal expense is deductible only if the costs for food and beverages are invoiced separately from the entertainment costs.

            a) Events primarily for the benefit of employees (e.g., a company picnic or office holiday) are not subject to the meals and entertainment limitations and are 100% deductible.

310   SU 11: Corporate Taxable Income

> **EXAMPLE 11-15   Deductibility of Meals and Entertainment**
>
> Joe is an employee of ARC. He invited several of ARC's top clients to a presentation on new product lines. ARC often uses these presentations to entice clients to place orders. After the presentation, Joe took the clients out to dinner and a show at a cost of $1,000 ($800 show + $200 meal). If not separated into entertainment and meal expenses, none of the $1,000 is deductible. If, however, the amounts are separately stated, 50% of the meal is deductible. ARC would then deduct $100 of this expense ($200 meal × 50%) since the amount paid is ordinary, necessary, and associated with the active conduct of trade or business.

   b. Limitation of deduction. If the employee's meal expenses are reimbursed by his or her employer and the reimbursement is not treated as compensation, the employer's deduction is limited to 50% of the expenses.

      1) Employers are not subject to the 50% limit to the extent they treat the reimbursement as compensation to employees.

8. **Insuring an Employee**

   a. Reasonable amounts of expenditures to promote employee health, goodwill, and welfare are deductible. Reasonable amounts paid or incurred for employee life insurance are included.

   b. Key employee. Premiums for life insurance covering an officer or employee are not deductible if the corporation is a direct or indirect beneficiary.

   c. A deduction is denied for interest expense incurred with respect to corporate-owned life insurance policies, or endowment or annuity contracts.

9. **R&E Expenditures**

   a. Qualified research and experimental expenditures may be capitalized, amortized, or currently deducted.

      1) Generally, costs incidental to development of a model, process, or similar property are included.

      2) Not included are costs of market research, sociological research, or development of art.

      3) Purchase of equipment and land receives its regular treatment and may not be deducted immediately.

10. **Fines**

    a. Fines and penalties paid to a governmental entity generally are not deductible.

11. **Bad Debts**

    a. For cash-basis taxpayers, income is only recognized when actually received. Therefore, any bad debt will not be included as part of income since the cash is never received. Accrual-basis taxpayers, however, do recognize the income and are allowed a bad debt deduction.

b. The allowance method is not allowed (except for financial institutions).

1) A corporation must use the direct charge-off method or the nonaccrual-experience method.

2) The nonaccrual-experience method is a procedure for not recognizing income if it is expected to be uncollectible. This is similar to treatment by cash-basis taxpayers in that the income is never recognized and therefore there is no need for a deduction.

12. **Worthless Securities**

a. Loss incurred when a security becomes worthless is generally treated as a capital loss subject to the capital loss limitations. Loss incurred when a security of an affiliated corporation becomes worthless may be treated as an ordinary loss.

13. **Stock Redemptions**

a. Generally, deduction of amounts paid or incurred with respect to a stock redemption or the redemption of the stock of any related person is not allowed. An exception to the general rule is the allowance for deductions for interest paid or accrued within the tax year on indebtedness.

14. **Original Issue Discount (OID)**

a. OID is treated as deductible interest expense.

b. Constant yield method. OID is deductible as interest, using the yield method to amortize the discount.

1) Constant yield to maturity is computed and applied to adjusted issue price (AIP) to compute deductible interest.

2) The OID portion does not include cash interest payments made to the holder during the period.

3) AIP is the original issue price adjusted for OID previously taken into account.

4) Yield to maturity is determined on the basis of compounding at the end of each (typically 6-month) accrual period.

a) Daily portions of OID must be computed. It is the ratable daily portion of the excess of AIP multiplied by yield to maturity over cash interest payable for the bond year.

EXAMPLE 11-16   OID -- Yield Method of Amortization

Consider a 5-year 10% bond issued on June 30, Year 1, with a $10,000 face, a $9,250 original issue price, and 12% yield.

Year 1 amortization of interest: $9,250 price × 12% yield × $\frac{6 \text{ months}}{12 \text{ months}}$

= $555 − $500 ($10,000 face × 10% × $\frac{6 \text{ months}}{12 \text{ months}}$) cash paid

= $55 interest

Year 2 amortization of interest: ($9,250 price + $55 interest) × 12% yield

= $1,116.60 − $1,000 ($10,000 face × 10%) cash paid

= $116.60 interest

15. **Repurchase at Premium**

    a. A corporation that repurchases its own bonds may deduct as interest expense the excess of the repurchase price over the issue price.

        1) Issue price is adjusted for OID deducted.

        2) No more than the normal call premium on nonconvertible debt is allowable, unless the corporation can show that the excess is not attributed to a conversion feature.

        3) A call premium not exceeding 1 year's interest at the rate stated in the bond is considered normal.

16. **Interest Expense**

    a. Interest expense incurred in a trade or business is generally deductible from gross income.

    b. The business interest deduction is limited to the sum of business interest income, 30% of the business's adjusted taxable income, and floor plan financing interest. Disallowed business interest may be carried forward indefinitely. For S corporations and partnerships, the limitation is generally applied at the corporate or partnership level. Any business interest deduction is taken into account in determining the non-separately stated taxable income or loss of the S corporation and partnership.

        1) The adjusted taxable income is computed without regard to

            a) Any item of income, gain, deduction, or loss that is not properly allocable to a trade or business

            b) Business interest expense or business interest income

            c) Net operating loss deduction

            d) Qualified business income deduction (QBID)

            e) Any deductions allowable for depreciation, amortization, or depletion

        2) Floor plan financing interest refers to interest paid or accrued on debt used to finance the acquisition of a motor vehicle held for sale or lease and secured by the inventory.

        3) The deduction limitation does not apply to small businesses with average gross receipts of $26 million or less.

        4) For S corporations and partnerships, the deduction may also be applied at the shareholder and partner level.

            a) But the adjusted taxable income of the shareholder and partner is determined without regard to the shareholder's and partner's distributive share of any items of income, gain, deduction, or loss of the S corporation or partnership.

5) Any excess taxable income (the S corporation's and partnership's unused business interest deduction due to the limitation) is passed through to shareholders and partners.

   a) Each shareholder's and partner's deduction limit is increased by his or her distributive share of the S corporation and the partnership's excess taxable income.

EXAMPLE 11-17 **Business Interest Expense**

ABC Corp.'s current-year taxable income before any interest expense deduction is $300,000, including $100,000 of interest income. During the current year, ABC incurred interest expense of $180,000. The deductible interest expense is the sum of the interest income of $100,000 plus 30% of its adjusted taxable income of $200,000 ($300,000 – $100,000). Therefore, the deductible interest expense is $160,000 [$100,000 + ($200,000 × 30%)].

---

c. Interest expense incurred on borrowings used to repurchase stock is deductible in the period in which it is paid or incurred. However, other expenses related to a stock purchase on reorganization are generally not deductible.

17. **Casualty Losses**

    a. Casualty losses are deductible. When business property is partially destroyed, the deductible amount is the lesser of the decline in FMV or the property's adjusted basis (prior to the loss).

       1) When business property is completely destroyed, the deductible amount is the property's adjusted basis (prior to the loss).

18. **Taxes**

    a. State income taxes based on gross income are deductible. However, federal income taxes are not.

19. **Political Contributions and Lobbying Expenses**

    a. Contributions to a political party or candidate and, generally, lobbying expenses are not deductible.

    b. De minimis exception

       1) In-house lobbying expenses (e.g., travel expenses incurred for a company representative to offer testimony against proposed legislation) that do not exceed $2,000 are deductible. However, once total costs exceed $2,000, all costs become nondeductible.

Form 1120 pages 1 and 2 are reproduced on the following pages to illustrate the sections of the tax return used to report income and deduction items.

314 SU 11: Corporate Taxable Income

Form 1120 — U.S. Corporation Income Tax Return
Department of the Treasury
Internal Revenue Service
For calendar year [Year] or tax year beginning _____, [Year], ending _____, 20 ____
▶ Go to *www.irs.gov/Form1120* for instructions and the latest information.
OMB No. 1545-0123
[Year]

A Check if:
1a Consolidated return (attach Form 851) ☐
b Life/nonlife consolidated return ☐
2 Personal holding co. (attach Sch. PH) ☐
3 Personal service corp. (see instructions) ☐
4 Schedule M-3 attached ☐

TYPE OR PRINT
Name
Number, street, and room or suite no. If a P.O. box, see instructions.
City or town, state or province, country, and ZIP or foreign postal code

B Employer identification number
C Date incorporated
D Total assets (see instructions) $

E Check if: (1) ☐ Initial return (2) ☐ Final return (3) ☐ Name change (4) ☐ Address change

Income

1a	Gross receipts or sales 1a	
b	Returns and allowances 1b	
c	Balance. Subtract line 1b from line 1a	1c
2	Cost of goods sold (attach Form 1125-A)	2
3	Gross profit. Subtract line 2 from line 1c	3
4	Dividends and inclusions (Schedule C, line 23)	4
5	Interest	5
6	Gross rents	6
7	Gross royalties	7
8	Capital gain net income (attach Schedule D (Form 1120))	8
9	Net gain or (loss) from Form 4797, Part II, line 17 (attach Form 4797)	9
10	Other income (see instructions—attach statement)	10
11	**Total income.** Add lines 3 through 10 . . . . ▶	11

Deductions (See instructions for limitations on deductions.)

12	Compensation of officers (see instructions—attach Form 1125-E) . . . . ▶	12
13	Salaries and wages (less employment credits)	13
14	Repairs and maintenance	14
15	Bad debts	15
16	Rents	16
17	Taxes and licenses	17
18	Interest (see instructions)	18
19	Charitable contributions	19
20	Depreciation from Form 4562 not claimed on Form 1125-A or elsewhere on return (attach Form 4562) . . .	20
21	Depletion	21
22	Advertising	22
23	Pension, profit-sharing, etc., plans	23
24	Employee benefit programs	24
25	Reserved for future use	25
26	Other deductions (attach statement)	26
27	**Total deductions.** Add lines 12 through 26 . . . . ▶	27
28	Taxable income before net operating loss deduction and special deductions. Subtract line 27 from line 11.	28
29a	Net operating loss deduction (see instructions) 29a	
b	Special deductions (Schedule C, line 24) 29b	
c	Add lines 29a and 29b	29c

Tax, Refundable Credits, and Payments

30	**Taxable income.** Subtract line 29c from line 28. See instructions	30
31	Total tax (Schedule J, Part I, line 11)	31
32	[Year] net 965 tax liability paid (Schedule J, Part II, line 12)	32
33	Total payments, credits, and section 965 net tax liability (Schedule J, Part III, line 23) . . .	33
34	Estimated tax penalty. See instructions. Check if Form 2220 is attached . . . . ▶ ☐	34
35	**Amount owed.** If line 33 is smaller than the total of lines 31, 32, and 34, enter amount owed . . .	35
36	**Overpayment.** If line 33 is larger than the total of lines 31, 32, and 34, enter amount overpaid . . .	36
37	Enter amount from line 36 you want: **Credited to [Next Year] estimated tax** ▶ _____ **Refunded** ▶	37

Sign Here
Under penalties of perjury, I declare that I have examined this return, including accompanying schedules and statements, and to the best of my knowledge and belief, it is true, correct, and complete. Declaration of preparer (other than taxpayer) is based on all information of which preparer has any knowledge.

▶ Signature of officer _____ Date _____ Title _____

May the IRS discuss this return with the preparer shown below? See instructions. ☐ Yes ☐ No

Paid Preparer Use Only

Print/Type preparer's name	Preparer's signature	Date	Check ☐ if self-employed	PTIN
Firm's name ▶			Firm's EIN ▶	
Firm's address ▶			Phone no.	

For Paperwork Reduction Act Notice, see separate instructions.   Cat. No. 11450Q   Form **1120** [Year]

Form 1120 [Year] — Page 2

Schedule C — Dividends, Inclusions, and Special Deductions (see instructions)

#	Description	(a) Dividends and inclusions	(b) %	(c) Special deductions (a) × (b)
1	Dividends from less-than-20%-owned domestic corporations (other than debt-financed stock)		50	
2	Dividends from 20%-or-more-owned domestic corporations (other than debt-financed stock)		65	
3	Dividends on certain debt-financed stock of domestic and foreign corporations		see instructions	
4	Dividends on certain preferred stock of less-than-20%-owned public utilities		23.3	
5	Dividends on certain preferred stock of 20%-or-more-owned public utilities		26.7	
6	Dividends from less-than-20%-owned foreign corporations and certain FSCs		50	
7	Dividends from 20%-or-more-owned foreign corporations and certain FSCs		65	
8	Dividends from wholly owned foreign subsidiaries		100	
9	**Subtotal.** Add lines 1 through 8. See instructions for limitations		see instructions	
10	Dividends from domestic corporations received by a small business investment company operating under the Small Business Investment Act of 1958		100	
11	Dividends from affiliated group members		100	
12	Dividends from certain FSCs		100	
13	Foreign-source portion of dividends received from a specified 10%-owned foreign corporation (excluding hybrid dividends) (see instructions)		100	
14	Dividends from foreign corporations not included on line 3, 6, 7, 8, 11, 12, or 13 (including any hybrid dividends)			
15	Section 965(a) inclusion		see instructions	
16a	Subpart F inclusions derived from the sale by a controlled foreign corporation (CFC) of the stock of a lower-tier foreign corporation treated as a dividend (attach Form(s) 5471) (see instructions)		100	
b	Subpart F inclusions derived from hybrid dividends of tiered corporations (attach Form(s) 5471) (see instructions)			
c	Other inclusions from CFCs under subpart F not included on line 15, 16a, 16b, or 17 (attach Form(s) 5471) (see instructions)			
17	Global Intangible Low-Taxed Income (GILTI) (attach Form(s) 5471 and Form 8992)			
18	Gross-up for foreign taxes deemed paid			
19	IC-DISC and former DISC dividends not included on line 1, 2, or 3			
20	Other dividends			
21	Deduction for dividends paid on certain preferred stock of public utilities			
22	Section 250 deduction (attach Form 8993)			
23	**Total dividends and inclusions.** Add column (a), lines 9 through 20. Enter here and on page 1, line 4			
24	**Total special deductions.** Add column (c), lines 9 through 22. Enter here and on page 1, line 29b			

Form 1120 [Year]

STOP & REVIEW

You have completed the outline for this subunit.
Study multiple-choice questions 10 through 17 beginning on page 322.

11.5 LOSSES OF A CORPORATION

1. The following rules apply only for corporations, not individuals.
2. **Net Operating Loss (NOL)**
   a. An NOL is any excess of deductions over gross income.
   b. Modified deductions for some items are used in computing an NOL.
      1) An NOL carried over from other tax years is not allowed in computing a current NOL.
      2) A dividends-received deduction (DRD) may produce or increase an NOL.
         a) A corporation is entitled to disregard the limitations on a DRD when calculating an NOL. The DRD would increase the NOL.
      3) Deductions for foreign-derived intangible income (FDII) and QBI are not allowed in computing a current NOL.
      4) Charitable contributions are not allowed in computing a current NOL.
   c. The treatment of an NOL in the current year depends on the year in which the NOL originally arose (i.e., the year the loss was incurred).
      1) NOLs that arose prior to 2018 can be carried back 2 years and carried forward for 20 years. The usage of the NOL is not limited by taxable income. Any excess carries over to future years until the NOL is exhausted or expires after 20 years.
      2) Under the CARES Act, NOLs for tax years 2018, 2019, and 2020 may be carried back 5 years and carried forward indefinitely. The carryback or carryforward period may offset the taxpayer's entire taxable income until 2021.
      3) NOLs that arise in 2021 and later may be carried forward indefinitely, but no carryback is allowed. The carryover is limited to 80% of taxable income for the year it is carried to. Any excess continues to carry over to future years until exhausted.

      NOTE: If the CARES Act had not been passed, the elimination of the carryback and the 80% offset limit would have applied to tax years 2018, 2019, and 2020.

      4) When utilizing NOLs, the earliest year is used first.

3. **Capital Gains and Losses**
   a. Unlike individuals, corporations do not receive a preferential tax rate on long-term capital gains (LTCGs). Instead, LTCGs, or net capital gains (NCGs), are taxed at the same 21% tax rate as other corporate income.

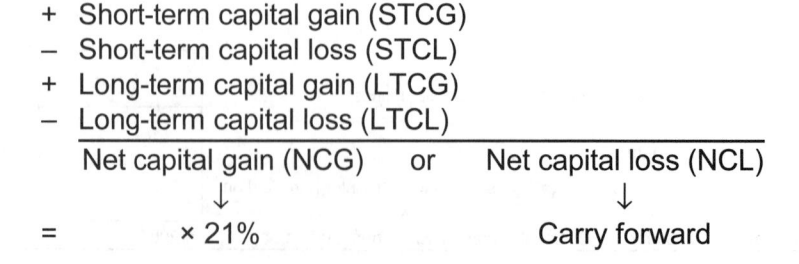

```
    + Short-term capital gain (STCG)
    − Short-term capital loss (STCL)
    + Long-term capital gain (LTCG)
    − Long-term capital loss (LTCL)
    ─────────────────────────────────────────────
      Net capital gain (NCG)   or   Net capital loss (NCL)
              ↓                            ↓
    =       × 21%                     Carry forward
```

b. Also unlike individuals, who can deduct up to a $3,000 NCL, corporations cannot take a net capital loss deduction. Instead, capital losses can only offset capital gains. Capital losses in excess of capital gains are nondeductible in the current year.

c. Nondeductible net capital losses can be carried back 3 years and forward 5 years.

   1) A corporation cannot carry a capital loss from or to a year that it is an S corporation.
   2) No election to forgo the carryback is available.
   3) The capital loss carryback/carryover must be used to the extent possible in the earliest applicable tax year.
   4) When utilizing a capital loss carryback/carryover, the oldest loss is used first.
   5) The NCL is treated as an STCL in a carryover tax year. It offsets only a net capital gain before the carryover, but it may not produce or increase a current-year NCL or an NOL.

	Capital Losses	
	Personal	**Business**
Capital loss deduction	100% capital gain + $3,000 ($1,500 MFS)	100% capital gain
Carryover	No carryback Carry forward indefinitely	Carry back 3 years Carry forward 5 years

4. **Passive Activity Loss (PAL)**

   a. The passive activity loss limitation rules explained in Study Unit 8, Subunit 2, apply to individuals, estates, and trusts (other than grantor trusts). Special PAL rules apply to closely held corporations and personal service corporations.

      1) Even though the PAL rules do not apply to grantor trusts, partnerships, and S corporations directly, they do apply to the owners of these entities.

STOP & REVIEW

You have completed the outline for this subunit.
Study multiple-choice questions 18 through 20 beginning on page 325.

QUESTIONS

11.1 Definition and Accounting

1. In Year 1, Brun Corp. properly accrued $10,000 for an income item on the basis of a reasonable estimate. In Year 2, Brun determined that the exact amount was $12,000. Which of the following statements is true?

A. Brun is required to file an amended return to report the additional $2,000 of income.
B. Brun is required to notify the IRS within 30 days of the determination of the exact amount of the item.
C. The $2,000 difference is includible in Brun's Year 2 income tax return.
D. The $2,000 difference of income must be included when the reasonable estimate amount is determined.

Answer (C) is correct.
   REQUIRED: The true statement about accrual of a reasonable estimate when the exact amount is greater than the estimate.
   DISCUSSION: Under the accrual method of accounting, income is includible in gross income when all the events have occurred that fix the right to receive the income and the amount can be determined with reasonable accuracy. If an amount of income is properly accrued on the basis of a reasonable estimate and the exact amount is subsequently determined, the difference, if any, shall be taken into account for the taxable year in which such determination is made.
   Answer (A) is incorrect. The excess is reported as gross income in the tax year in which the exact amount is determined, in this case, in Year 2. **Answer (B) is incorrect.** Notification is not necessary. **Answer (D) is incorrect.** The taxpayer cannot include an amount (s)he is not aware of. The additional amount of $12,000 was determined later.

2. An S corporation engaged in manufacturing has a year end of June 30. Revenue consistently has been more than $30 million under both cash and accrual basis of accounting. The stockholders would like to change the tax status of the corporation to a C corporation using the cash basis with the same year end. Which of the following statements is correct if it changes to a C corporation?

A. The year end will be December 31, using the cash basis of accounting.
B. The year end will be December 31, using the accrual basis of accounting.
C. The year end will be June 30, using the accrual basis of accounting.
D. The year end will be June 30, using the cash basis of accounting.

Answer (C) is correct.
   REQUIRED: The appropriate year end for a C corporation.
   DISCUSSION: C corporations that are not personal service corporations, S corporations, or small C corporations (less than an average of $26 million in revenues per year over the past 3 years) must use the accrual basis of accounting. A corporation can use a fiscal year end; June 30 is therefore allowed.
   Answer (A) is incorrect. C corporations that are not personal service corporations, S corporations, or small C corporations (less than an average of $26 million in revenues per year over the past 3 years) must use the accrual basis of accounting. A corporation is not required to use a calendar year end; it can use a fiscal year end. **Answer (B) is incorrect.** The corporation does not need to change its tax year to a calendar year end. The C corporation can keep the fiscal year end of June 30. **Answer (D) is incorrect.** C corporations that are not personal service corporations or small C corporations must use the accrual basis of accounting.

3. Which of the following entities may adopt any tax year end?

A. C corporation.
B. S corporation.
C. Partnership.
D. Trust.

Answer (A) is correct.
REQUIRED: The allowable tax years for C corporations, S corporations, partnerships, and trusts.
DISCUSSION: A corporation, generally, may elect either a calendar or fiscal tax year. A personal service corporation (PSC) is required to use a calendar tax year. An exception exists for a valid business purpose or a PSC that makes "minimum distributions." Each subsidiary included in a consolidated return must adopt the parent's tax year. Though exceptions exists for the other answer selections, C corporations are the best answer and CPA candidates are expected to make similar decisions during the exam.
Answer (B) is incorrect. An S corporation, generally, must adopt a calendar tax year. **Answer (C) is incorrect.** Barring an exception approved by the IRS, partnerships are obligated to use a required tax year. The required tax year is the first of the following to apply:

1) Majority interest tax year
2) Principal partners' tax year
3) Least aggregate deferral tax year

Answer (D) is incorrect. Generally, a trust must adopt a calendar tax year. Only tax-exempt and wholly charitable trusts may qualify to use a fiscal tax year.

11.2 Formation

4. Ames and Roth form Homerun, a C corporation. Ames contributes several autographed baseballs to Homerun. Ames purchased the baseballs for $500, and they have a total fair market value of $1,000. Roth contributes several autographed baseball bats to Homerun. Roth purchased the bats for $5,000, and they have a fair market value of $7,000. What is Homerun's basis in the contributed bats and balls?

A. $0
B. $5,500
C. $6,000
D. $8,000

Answer (B) is correct.
REQUIRED: The basis in property contributed to a corporation.
DISCUSSION: The basis of property acquired by a corporation in connection with a Sec. 351 transaction is the same as the basis in the hands of the transferor (shareholder), increased by the amount of gain recognized by the transferor on such transfer. Since neither shareholder received any boot, no gain was recognized. Thus, the corporation's total basis in the transferred assets is the same as that in the shareholder's hands, or $5,500 ($500 + $5,000).
Answer (A) is incorrect. The basis of property acquired by a corporation in connection with a Sec. 351 transaction is the same as the basis in the hands of the transferor (shareholder), increased by the amount of gain recognized by the transferor on such transfer. **Answer (C) is incorrect.** The $6,000 takes a basis equal to the fair market value of Ames's contribution and the adjusted basis of Roth's contribution. The basis of property acquired by a corporation in connection with a Sec. 351 transaction is the same as the basis in the hands of the transferor (shareholder), increased by the amount of gain recognized by the transferor on such transfer. **Answer (D) is incorrect.** A basis of $8,000 is equal to the fair market value of each of the contributions. The basis of property acquired by a corporation in connection with a Sec. 351 transaction is the same as the basis in the hands of the transferor (shareholder), increased by the amount of gain recognized by the transferor on such transfer.

5. On July 1 of the current year, Rich, sole proprietor of Kee Nail, transferred all of Kee's assets to Merit, Inc., a new corporation, solely for a certain percentage of Merit's stock. Dee, who is not related to Rich, also bought some of Merit's stock on July 1. Merit's outstanding capital stock consisted of 1,000 shares of common stock with a par value of $100 per share. For the transfer of Kee Nail's assets to be tax-free, what is the minimum number of shares of Merit's stock that must be owned by Rich and Dee immediately after the exchange?

A. 500
B. 501
C. 800
D. 801

Answer (C) is correct.
REQUIRED: The minimum number of shares of stock that must be owned by two transferors immediately after the exchange for the transfer to be tax-free.
DISCUSSION: A transfer of assets for stock of a corporation is tax-free if the transferors are in control of the corporation immediately after the exchange. A person who transfers appreciated property will receive the benefit if another transferor transfers property and together they meet the control test. Property includes money. Control is ownership of stock possessing at least 80% of the total combined voting power of all classes of stock entitled to vote and at least 80% of the total number of shares of all other classes of stock of the corporation. At a minimum, Rich and Dee must own 800 shares (1,000 shares × 80%).
Answer (A) is incorrect. The number 500 results from multiplying the 1,000 shares of common stock by 50%. **Answer (B) is incorrect.** The number 501 results from a greater than 50% ownership. Transferors must own a minimum of 80% of the common shares. **Answer (D) is incorrect.** A total of 801 shares is greater than the 80% minimum number of shares of ownership to receive tax-free treatment.

6. In April, A and B formed X Corp. A contributed $50,000 cash, and B contributed land worth $70,000 (with an adjusted basis of $40,000). B also received $20,000 cash from the corporation. A and B each receive 50% of the corporation's stock. What is the tax basis of the land to X Corp.?

A. $40,000
B. $50,000
C. $60,000
D. $70,000

Answer (C) is correct.
REQUIRED: The tax basis of land transferred to X Corp.
DISCUSSION: The basis of land to X Corp. is the adjusted basis to B ($40,000) increased by B's recognized gain ($20,000). B's realized gain is $30,000. Recognized gain is the lesser of boot received ($20,000) and realized gain.
Answer (A) is incorrect. A $40,000 basis would be the applicable tax basis to X Corp. if B did not recognize any gain on the transfer. **Answer (B) is incorrect.** Neither the use of the FMV of the property nor a reduction equal to the boot received is how X Corp. calculates the basis of the land ($50,000 is the FMV of the property transferred to X Corp. reduced by the boot received by B). **Answer (D) is incorrect.** The inclusion of gain realized in the basis of the land is limited to the boot received by B.

11.3 Gross Income of a Corporation

7. The following information pertains to treasury stock sold by Lee Corporation to an unrelated broker in the current year:

Proceeds received	$50,000
Cost	30,000
Par value	9,000

What amount of capital gain should Lee recognize in the current year on the sale of this treasury stock?

A. $0
B. $20,000
C. $21,000
D. $41,000

Answer (A) is correct.
REQUIRED: The gain a corporation should report as a result of the sale of treasury stock.
DISCUSSION: A corporation does not recognize gain or loss on the receipt of money or other property in exchange for its stock, including treasury stock. Therefore, no gain or loss is recognized by Lee as a result of the treasury stock sale.

8. For the year ended December 31, 2021, Kell Corp.'s book income, before income taxes, was $70,000. Included in the computation of this $70,000 was $10,000 of proceeds of a life insurance policy, representing a lump-sum payment in full as a result of the death of Kell's controller. Kell was the owner and beneficiary of this policy since 2005. In its income tax return for 2021, Kell should report taxable life insurance proceeds of

A. $10,000
B. $8,000
C. $5,000
D. $0

Answer (D) is correct.
REQUIRED: The extent to which proceeds of a life insurance policy constitute gross income.
DISCUSSION: For employer-owned policies issued prior to August 17, 2006, proceeds of a life insurance policy paid by reason of death of the insured are excluded by the beneficiary. Since no part of the $10,000 represents interest on proceeds retained by the insurance company, no part of it is reported as gross income.

9. Sanders Corporation purchased a $1 million 10-year debenture for $1.2 million on January 1, 2014. In 2021, how much amortization of bond premium must Sanders report on its 2021 income tax return from purchase of this bond?

A. $240,000
B. $200,000
C. $20,000
D. $0

Answer (C) is correct.
REQUIRED: The income reported from the issuance of a 10-year debenture.
DISCUSSION: In the case of a bond, the amount of amortizable bond premium for the taxable year shall be allowed as a reduction of interest income. The amount is amortized over the life of the bond. Thus, Sanders must report $20,000 [($1,200,000 − $1,000,000) ÷ 10].
Answer (A) is incorrect. Incorrectly amortizing the issue price over 5 years results in $240,000. **Answer (B) is incorrect.** The total premium is $200,000. **Answer (D) is incorrect.** The premium may be amortized over the life of the bond.

11.4 Deductions of a Corporation

10. If a corporation's charitable contributions exceed the limitation for deductibility in a particular year, the excess

  A. Is not deductible in any future or prior year.
  B. May be carried back or forward for 1 year at the corporation's election.
  C. May be carried forward to a maximum of 5 succeeding years.
  D. May be carried back to the preceding year.

Answer (C) is correct.
REQUIRED: The treatment of a corporation's excess charitable contributions.
DISCUSSION: A corporation may carry unused charitable contributions forward for 5 years. Current contributions are deducted before carryovers. Carryovers are applied on a FIFO basis. Carrybacks of excess charitable contributions are not permitted.

11. Placebo Corp. is an accrual-basis, calendar-year corporation. On December 13, 2021, the board of directors declared a 2%-of-profits bonus to all employees for services rendered during 2021 and notified them in writing. None of the employees own stock in Placebo. The amount represents reasonable compensation for services rendered and was paid on March 13, 2022. Placebo's bonus expense may

  A. Not be deducted on Placebo's 2021 tax return because the per-share employee amount cannot be determined with reasonable accuracy at the time of the declaration of the bonus.
  B. Be deducted on Placebo's 2021 tax return.
  C. Be deducted on Placebo's 2022 tax return.
  D. Not be deducted on Placebo's tax return because payment is a disguised dividend.

Answer (B) is correct.
REQUIRED: The treatment of bonus compensation.
DISCUSSION: Under Sec. 404, certain contributions paid by an employer are subject to being treated as deferred compensation and are deductible in the year of payment. This limitation is applicable if the deduction would otherwise be allowed under Sec. 162(a). The deduction is required in the payment year unless distributed within 2 1/2 months after year end (i.e., March 15 for a calendar-year corporation). Because the present amount was paid on March 13, the time of receipt was within the allocated period of time, and the compensation can be deducted as a business expense under Sec. 162 in 2020.
Answer (A) is incorrect. This determination is not required by Sec. 404. **Answer (C) is incorrect.** Section 404 is not applicable due to the timely payment of the bonus. **Answer (D) is incorrect.** The facts of the problem provide that the amount of the bonus represents reasonable compensation and not a disguised dividend.

12. Which of the following costs are amortizable organizational expenditures?

  A. Professional fees to issue the corporate stock.
  B. Printing costs to issue the corporate stock.
  C. Legal fees for drafting the corporate charter.
  D. Commissions paid by the corporation to an underwriter.

Answer (C) is correct.
REQUIRED: The costs amortizable as organizational expenditures.
DISCUSSION: A corporation is deemed to elect to deduct up to $5,000 (subject to a phase-out) of qualified organizational expenses. Any remaining amount is amortized over a period of 180 months. Expenditures associated with the formation of the corporation, including legal fees for drafting the corporate charter, are amortizable.

13. In 2021, Kara Corp. incurred the following expenditures in connection with the repurchase of its stock from shareholders:

Interest on borrowings used to repurchase stock	$100,000
Legal and accounting fees in connection with the repurchase	400,000

The total of the above expenditures deductible in 2021 is

A. $0
B. $100,000
C. $400,000
D. $500,000

Answer (B) is correct.
REQUIRED: The amount that a corporation may deduct for expenses related to the repurchase of its stock.
DISCUSSION: Interest expense incurred on business borrowings is deductible in the period in which it is paid or accrued. However, other expenses related to a stock repurchase or reorganization are not deductible.
Answer (A) is incorrect. Interest expense incurred on business borrowings is deductible. Answer (C) is incorrect. Amounts paid or incurred in connection with a stock redemption are not deductible. Answer (D) is incorrect. The interest is deductible, but the costs associated with the repurchase are not.

14. John Budd is the sole shareholder of Ral Corp., an accrual-basis taxpayer engaged in wholesaling operations. Ral's retained earnings at January 1, 2021, amounted to $1 million. For the year ended December 31, 2021, Ral's book income, before federal income tax, was $300,000. Included in the computation of this $300,000 were the following:

Key employee insurance premiums paid on Budd's life (Ral is the beneficiary of this policy.)	$3,000
Group term insurance premiums paid on $10,000 life insurance policies for each of Ral's four employees (The employees' spouses are the beneficiaries.)	4,000

What amount should Ral deduct for key employee and group life insurance premiums in computing taxable income for 2021?

A. $0
B. $3,000
C. $4,000
D. $7,000

Answer (C) is correct.
REQUIRED: The amount that a corporation may deduct for payment of life insurance premiums.
DISCUSSION: Ral Corp. may deduct the premiums paid for group term life insurance. However, no deduction is allowed for premiums paid for life insurance for which the corporation is the beneficiary.
Answer (A) is incorrect. Premiums paid for group term life insurance are deductible. Answer (B) is incorrect. Premiums paid for life insurance for which the corporation is the beneficiary are not deductible. Answer (D) is incorrect. The group term life premiums are deductible, but the key employee insurance premiums are not.

15. Pope, a C corporation, owns 15% of Arden Corporation. Arden paid a $3,000 cash dividend to Pope. What is the amount of Pope's dividends-received deduction?

A. $3,000
B. $1,950
C. $1,500
D. $0

Answer (C) is correct.
REQUIRED: The dividends-received deduction for a 15% owner.
DISCUSSION: The dividends-received deduction is available only to corporations. The deduction is based on the distributee corporation's percentage ownership of the distributing corporation and may be limited to taxable income. The deduction percentage is 50% for corporations with less than 20% ownership in the distributing corporation. Pope's deduction is $1,500 ($3,000 dividend × 50%).
Answer (A) is incorrect. The deduction is limited based on Pope's ownership percentage of Arden. Pope must own 80% or more of Arden to take a 100% dividends-received deduction. **Answer (B) is incorrect.** A 65% deduction requires an ownership of the distributing corporation that is at least 20% but less than 80%. **Answer (D) is incorrect.** Corporations are allowed a deduction based on ownership. The minimum deduction is 50%.

16. The costs of organizing a corporation in 2021

A. May be deducted in full in the year in which these costs are incurred even if paid in later years.
B. May be deducted only in the year in which these costs are paid.
C. May be amortized over a period of 180 months, even if these costs are capitalized on the company's books.
D. Are nondeductible capital expenditures.

Answer (C) is correct.
REQUIRED: The deductibility of a corporation's organization costs.
DISCUSSION: A corporation is deemed to elect to deduct $5,000 of organizational expenses (subject to a phase-out) and amortize the remaining expenditures over a period of 180 months, beginning with the month in which the corporation starts business.

17. In 2021, Pine Corporation had losses of $20,000 from operations. It received $180,000 in dividends from a 25%-owned domestic corporation. Pine's taxable income is $160,000 before the dividends-received deduction. What is the amount of Pine's dividends-received deduction?

A. $0
B. $117,000
C. $104,000
D. $180,000

Answer (C) is correct.
REQUIRED: The dividends-received deduction of a corporation.
DISCUSSION: A corporate deduction for dividends received from domestic taxable corporations is allowed. Pine Corporation may deduct 65% of dividends received from a domestic corporation in which Pine owned between 20% and 80% of the stock. This dividends-received deduction is limited to 65% of taxable income. Without regard to the limitation, Pine could deduct $117,000 ($180,000 × 65%). Pine, however, is limited to a $104,000 deduction ($160,000 taxable income × 65%). Thus, Pine's dividends-received deduction is $104,000.
Answer (A) is incorrect. Pine is entitled to a dividends-received deduction. **Answer (B) is incorrect.** Pine's dividends-received deduction is limited to 65% of taxable income. **Answer (D) is incorrect.** Pine may not deduct all of the dividends received.

11.5 Losses of a Corporation

18. In 2021, Geyer, Inc., a calendar-year corporation, had net income (loss) per books of $(60,000). Included in Geyer's gross revenues were taxable dividends of $20,000 received from an unrelated 20%-owned domestic corporation. What is Geyer's NOL that may be carried forward to 2022?

A. $80,000
B. $70,000
C. $60,000
D. $73,000

Answer (D) is correct.
REQUIRED: The net operating loss (NOL) carryover.
DISCUSSION: An NOL generated in 2018 and later may be carried forward indefinitely to the succeeding taxable years. In computing the NOL, the dividends-received deduction (DRD) is computed without regard to the 65%-of-taxable-income limitation.

Net loss per books	$(60,000)
Allowable DRD ($20,000 × 65%)	(13,000)
NOL carryover	$(73,000)

Answer (A) is incorrect. The DRD for a 20%-owned corporation is 65%. **Answer (B) is incorrect.** The DRD for a 20%-owned corporation is 65%. **Answer (C) is incorrect.** In computing the NOL, the dividends-received deduction is computed without regard to the 65%-of-taxable-income limitation.

19. A C corporation has gross receipts of $150,000, $35,000 of other income, and deductible expenses of $95,000. In addition, the corporation incurred a net long-term capital loss of $25,000 in the current year. What is the corporation's taxable income?

A. $65,000
B. $87,000
C. $90,000
D. $115,000

Answer (C) is correct.
REQUIRED: The correct calculation of corporate taxable income.
DISCUSSION: Net capital gains (NCGs) constitute gross income. However, a corporation's capital losses are deductible only to the extent of capital gains, whether they are short- or long-term. Therefore, a net capital loss is not deductible in the tax year incurred. The corporation has taxable income of $90,000 ($150,000 + $35,000 – $95,000).

Answer (A) is incorrect. Capital losses are deductible only to the extent of capital gains; therefore, a net capital loss is not deductible in the tax year incurred. **Answer (B) is incorrect.** Only individuals (not corporations) are allowed to deduct up to $3,000 of net capital losses in the current year. Corporations may only deduct capital losses up to the amount of capital gains. **Answer (D) is incorrect.** Both gross receipts and other income are additions (increases) to taxable income. In addition, there are other reductions to taxable income to consider in this problem.

20. Wonder, Inc., had 2021 taxable income of $200,000 exclusive of the following:

Gain on sale of land used in business (held greater than 1 year)	$25,000
Loss on sale of machinery used in business (held greater than 1 year)	(13,000)
Loss on sale of securities held 3 years	(4,000)
Loss on sale of securities held 3 months	(3,000)

On what amount of taxable income should Wonder compute tax?

A. $200,000
B. $202,500
C. $205,000
D. $212,000

Answer (C) is correct.
REQUIRED: The taxable income of a corporation with both capital and Sec. 1231 gains and losses.
DISCUSSION: The sale of the land and the sale of machinery used in the business are Sec. 1231 transactions, if held more than 1 year. Since the gain and loss net to a gain of $12,000, they are a long-term capital gain and loss. The capital losses on the securities are fully deductible because they do not exceed the $12,000 net Sec. 1231 gain.
Answer (A) is incorrect. Net capital gain constitutes taxable income. **Answer (B) is incorrect.** The Code allows no deduction for net capital gains. **Answer (D) is incorrect.** The net Sec. 1231 gain is treated as capital gain and can be offset by capital losses.

STUDY UNIT TWELVE
CORPORATE TAX COMPUTATIONS

(21 pages of outline)

12.1	Regular Income Tax and Credits	328
12.2	Consolidated Returns	330
12.3	Controlled Groups	333
12.4	Estimated Tax	336
12.5	Earnings and Profits	338
12.6	Distributions	339
12.7	Accumulated Earnings Tax (AET)	345
12.8	Personal Holding Company (PHC) Tax	347

The only credit explained in the corporate tax study unit is the Foreign Tax Credit. This credit also applies to individuals. The subject matter appears here because it has been tested most commonly in the corporate context. Candidates should also review the General Business Credit and its limits discussed in Study Unit 8, Subunit 1, which also apply to corporations.

Some candidates find it helpful to have the entire tax form side-by-side with our Knowledge Transfer Outline when studying, and others may prefer to see the final draft of a form when it is released. The full versions of the most up-to-date forms are easily accessible at www.gleim.com/taxforms. These forms and the form excerpts used in our outline are periodically updated as the latest versions are released by the IRS.

12.1 REGULAR INCOME TAX AND CREDITS

1. **Tax Rate**

   a. Section 11 imposes tax on the taxable income of corporations using a flat 21% rate. This rate applies to ordinary income, capital gains, personal service corporations, and any controlled group of corporations.

   > **EXAMPLE 12-1**   **Corporate Tax Rate**
   >
   > Little Corporation had $175,000 of taxable income in the ordinary course of business that does not include a $30,000 capital gain. The tax on the taxable income is $36,750 ($175,000 × 21%) and the tax on the capital gain is $6,300 ($30,000 × 21%). Little Corporation's total regular federal income tax is $43,050 ($36,750 + $6,300).

2. **Disallowed Corporate Credits**

   a. Most tax credits are allowable to corporations. However, the following are not permitted:
      1) Earned Income Credit
      2) Child and Dependent Care Credit
      3) Elderly and Disabled Credit
      4) Child and Other Dependents Tax Credit
      5) Adoption Credit
      6) American Opportunity Credit
      7) Lifetime Learning Credit

3. **Foreign Tax Credit (FTC)**

   a. A taxpayer may elect either a credit or a deduction for taxes paid to other countries or U.S. possessions on foreign-sourced income subject to U.S. tax.

   b. Generally, the FTC is applied against gross tax liability before all other credits.

   c. The FTC is not creditable against the **accumulated earnings tax (AET)** or the **personal holding company (PHC) tax**.

   d. **Pass-through entities** apportion the foreign taxes among the partners, shareholders (of an S corporation), or beneficiaries (of an estate). The individuals elect and compute a credit or deduction on their personal returns.

   e. For a **non-U.S. taxpayer**, the FTC is allowed only for foreign taxes paid on income effectively connected with conduct of a trade or business in the U.S. and against U.S. tax on the effectively connected income.

   f. **Qualified foreign taxes (QFTs)** include foreign taxes on income, war profits, and excess profits.

      1) QFTs must be analogous to the U.S. income tax. They must be based on a form of net annual income, including gain. Concepts such as realization should be incorporated into the tax structure.
      2) Foreign taxes paid on foreign earned income or housing costs excluded as excessive may neither be credited nor deducted.

g. The maximum amount of tax that may be credited is computed using the following formula:

$$\text{FTC limit} = \text{U.S. income tax before FTC} \times \frac{\text{Foreign source taxable income}}{\text{Worldwide taxable income}}$$

1) The limit must be applied separately to passive income, foreign branch income, global intangible low-taxed income (GILTI), and general income (these are known as "baskets"). A branch and GILTI are explained in Study Unit 13.
2) The amount used for TI in the numerator and denominator is regular TI with adjustments.
3) The current allowance of FTC is the lesser of (a) foreign tax paid or (b) maximum amount of tax allowed **(FTC limit)**. However, the FTC for the GILTI basket is limited to 80% of the otherwise allowable FTC.

h. Foreign tax paid in excess of the FTC limit may be carried back 1 year and forward 10 years in chronological order. However, there is no carryover for the GILTI basket.

1) The carryover is treated as foreign tax paid subject to the FTC limit.
2) The carryover may not be applied in any year when a deduction for foreign taxes is taken (in lieu of the FTC).

EXAMPLE 12-2   FTC

A client paid $400,000 in qualified foreign taxes. The corporation had $1,000,000 in foreign source taxable income and $10,000,000 in worldwide taxable income (all general basket). If the corporation had a $2,100,000 U.S. income tax liability before the FTC, its FTC limit would be calculated as follows:

$$\text{FTC limit} = \$2,100,000 \times (\$1,000,000 \div \$10,000,000)$$
$$= \$210,000$$

Thus, the client's FTC is $210,000, the lesser of foreign taxes paid and the FTC limit. The client may carry the remaining $190,000 ($400,000 in foreign taxes paid − $210,000 allowed credit) FTC back 1 year, and any unused amount is then carried forward for up to 10 years.

STOP & REVIEW

You have completed the outline for this subunit.
Study multiple-choice questions 1 and 2 on page 348.

12.2 CONSOLIDATED RETURNS

1. **Overview**

    a. A single federal income tax return may be filed by two or more includible corporations that are members of an affiliated group.

2. **Includible corporations** are all corporations **except** the following:

    a. Tax-exempt corporations
    b. S corporations
    c. FSCs (foreign sales corporations)
    d. Insurance corporations
    e. REITs (real estate investment trusts)
    f. Regulated investment companies
    g. DISCs (domestic international sales corporations)

3. **Affiliated Groups**

    a. An affiliated group includes each corporation in a chain of corporations under the following conditions:

        1) The other group members must directly own stock in the corporation that represents both

            a) 80% or more of total voting power **and**
            b) 80% or more of total value outstanding.

        2) A parent corporation must directly own stock as outlined in 1) above (80% voting and value) of at least one includible corporation.

4. **Election**

    a. Election to file a consolidated return is made by the act of filing a consolidated return.
    b. Consent of each included corporation is required.
    c. Consolidated financial statements or IRS approval is not required to file a consolidated return.
    d. Consent of the IRS is required to terminate an election.
    e. Controlled group restrictions (mandatory rules for certain related companies) apply without regard to some of its members filing a consolidated return.

5. **Tax Year**

    a. Each subsidiary included in a consolidated return must adopt the parent's tax year.

6. **Accounting Methods**

    a. One or more members of a controlled group filing a consolidated return may use the cash method, and one or more others may use the accrual method.

SU 12: Corporate Tax Computations

7. **Consolidation**
   a. Consolidated taxable income is calculated by computing the taxable income of each member of the group and computing certain consolidated amounts.
   b. **Certain consolidated amounts** include the following:
      1) Charitable contribution deductions
      2) Dividends received and paid deductions
      3) Percentage depletion of mineral properties
      4) NOL deductions
      5) Section 1231 gains and losses
      6) Capital gains and losses

8. **Dividends on a Consolidated Return**
   a. A dividend distributed by one consolidated corporation to another is eliminated.
   b. The dividends-received deduction (DRD) is not allowed for such dividends (because the dividend is not included in income).
   c. A deduction for dividends received from corporations outside the consolidating group is computed on a consolidated basis.

9. **Losses**

          TI (Separate net TI)
   + Net capital gain
   − Section 1231 net loss
   − Charitable contribution deduction
   − Dividends-received deduction
   − Dividends-paid deduction
   = **Consolidated NOL**

   a. Losses of one consolidating corporation may offset TI of another. Consolidated NOL is computed using consolidated items (aggregate of consolidating corporations' separate items) as shown above.
   b. In general, a pre-consolidation NOL carryforward from a company that joins a consolidated group can only offset that company's taxable income (not another company's income in the consolidated group).

10. **Intercompany Transactions**

    a. An intercompany transaction is a transaction between corporations that are members of the same consolidated group. In the consolidated tax return, realizing any gain or loss is postponed until the next transaction outside the consolidated group. This treatment is referred to as the single-entity approach.

    b. For consolidation purposes, the buyer in the intercompany transaction assumes the same basis and holding period as the selling member. The consolidated gain or loss is recognized upon the happening of an event such as

        1) The acquiring corporation claiming depreciation
        2) One of the members leaving the consolidated group
        3) Disposition of the property outside of the consolidated group

    c. The character of the recognized gain or loss is determined with reference to the consolidated group member holding the property immediately before the recognition event.

EXAMPLE 12-3   Character of Gain or Loss -- Sale Outside Consolidated Entity

P and S are two affiliated corporations that file consolidated tax returns. P sells an asset held for investment (i.e., a capital asset) to S at a gain of $10,000. S holds the property as inventory and sells to an unrelated party at an additional gain of $5,000. Under the single-entity approach, the consolidated entity recognizes $15,000 of ordinary income upon the sale to the outside party.

If the gain on the sale to the unrelated party were $2,000 less than the intercompany gain of $10,000, the recognized gain of the consolidated entity would be only $8,000.

---

    d. In certain other intercompany transactions, the income and expense items net each other out.

SUCCESS TIP

The AICPA has tested candidates' knowledge of the rules and regulations for filing consolidated returns. Most of the released AICPA questions test the theory and do not require calculations.

STOP & REVIEW

You have completed the outline for this subunit.
Study multiple-choice questions 3 through 5 on page 349.

12.3 CONTROLLED GROUPS

1. **Definition**
   a. A controlled group of corporations includes corporations with a specified degree of relationship by stock ownership.

2. **Parent-Subsidiary Controlled Group**
   a. This type of controlled group consists of
      1) Two corporations if one of the corporations owns stock that represents
         a) 80% or more of total voting power **or**
         b) 80% or more of total value outstanding of the stock of the other
      2) Any other corporation that meets the requirements in 1) above (if the two corporations discussed above and others in the group own stock in it)
   b. A member of a controlled group need not use a parent's tax year.

> **EXAMPLE 12-4 Parent-Subsidiary Controlled Group**
>
> Each corporation has a single class of stock. P owns 80% of S stock. P and S each own 40% of O stock. P, S, and O each own 30% of T stock. P, S, O, and T are a controlled group.

3. **Brother-Sister Controlled Group**
   a. Any two or more corporations are considered a brother-sister controlled group if the stock of each is owned by the same five or fewer persons (only individuals, trusts, or estates)
      1) Represents either
         a) 80% or more of voting power of all classes or
         b) 80% or more of value of all classes and
      2) Represents either (counting for each person only the smallest amount owned by that person in any of the corporations)
         a) More than 50% of voting power of all classes or
         b) More than 50% of value of all classes.

> **EXAMPLE 12-5 Brother-Sister Controlled Group**
>
> Alpha, Bravo, and Charley Corporations, each with one class of stock, have the following ownership:
>
> | | 80% Test | | | |
> | | Alpha | Bravo | Charley | 50% Test |
> | Shareholders | | | | |
> |---|---|---|---|---|
> | Mike | 45% | 5% | 30% | 5% |
> | Sierra | 30% | 65% | 10% | 10% |
> | Oscar | 25% | 30% | 60% | 25% |
> | | 100% | 100% | 100% | 40% |
>
> Alpha, Bravo, and Charley passed the 80% test but not the 50% test and therefore are not a controlled brother-sister group.

4. **Constructive Ownership**

    a. Stock both actually and constructively owned is counted. Generally, for purposes of determining whether a control group exists, a person constructively owns stock owned by a

        1) Family member [spouse (not legally separated), child, grandchild, parent, or grandparent] and
        2) Corporation, partnership, estate, or trust

            a) In which (s)he has a 5% or more interest
            b) In proportion to that interest.

    b. Any person who has an option (i.e., rights) to acquire stock is considered the owner of that stock.

5. **Limit on Tax Benefits**

    a. Each of the following is an example of tax benefit items of which only one must be shared by the members of a controlled group:

        1) Section 179 expensing maximum of $1.05 million
        2) General business credit $25,000 offset
        3) AET $250,000 presumed deduction base

    NOTE: A controlled group generally may choose any method to allocate the amounts among themselves. By default, an item is divided equally among members.

EXAMPLE 12-6   Brother-Sister Corporation -- Allocation of Tax Benefit

Brother Bill, Inc., and Sister Suzie, Inc., are brother-sister corporations. Controlled groups must split the $1.05 million Sec. 179 amount among the members. By default, both corporations receive a $525,000 Sec. 179 amount. However, Brother Bill and Sister Suzie may allocate the available Sec. 179 election in any manner that is agreed upon.

6. **Intergroup Transactions**
    a. Anti-avoidance rules apply to transactions between members of a controlled group.
    b. Loss is not recognized when property is sold by one member of a controlled group to another.
        1) The loss may be recognized on a subsequent sale to an unrelated third party.
    c. Expenditure to a controlled group member is not deductible before being included in the income of the payee.
    d. Gain on sale or exchange of property by a controlled group member to a member in whose hands the property is depreciable is treated as ordinary income.
    e. The IRS is authorized to redetermine the price for property transferred between members of a controlled group.
        1) To reflect income clearly or to prevent tax evasion, the price may be redetermined to reflect an arm's-length price.
        2) Three methods to determine an arm's-length price are by reference to
            a) Comparable uncontrolled prices
            b) Resale prices
            c) Cost plus return

STOP & REVIEW

You have completed the outline for this subunit.
Study multiple-choice questions 6 and 7 beginning on page 350.
Note that these are questions on consolidated returns as well as controlled groups.

12.4 ESTIMATED TAX

1. **Due Dates**

   a. A corporation is required to make estimated tax payments on the 15th day of the 4th, 6th, 9th, and 12th months of the tax year.

   b. Any difference between the estimated tax and actual tax is due with the return by the 15th day of the 4th month following the end of the tax year (April 15 for calendar-year C corporations).

   c. An extension of time to file the tax return does not provide an extension of time to pay the tax liability without incurring interest and/or penalty.

2. **Estimated Payments**

   a. Tax includes the regular income tax, net of credits and payments.

   b. Each quarterly estimated tax payment required is 25% of the lesser of

      1) 100% of the prior year's tax (provided a tax liability existed and the preceding tax year was 12 months) or

      2) 100% of the current year's tax.

      NOTE: Any increase in estimated tax during the year should be reconciled and paid on the next estimated payment.

   c. A corporation with uneven income flows can make its estimated tax payments by annualizing its income.

      1) A corporation has the option of annualizing income and paying its estimated taxes accordingly.

      2) If income in later quarters is greater than in prior quarters, the estimated tax payments must be increased so that 100% of the shortfall is covered.

   d. Paying 100% of the prior year's tax is not an option for a large corporation.

      1) A large corporation may make its first quarter estimated tax payment based on the preceding year's tax liability and make up any difference in its second quarter payment.

         a) A large corporation is one with taxable income of $1 million or more during any of the 3 preceding years.

3. **Penalty**

    a. A penalty is imposed in the amount by which any required installment exceeds estimated tax paid multiplied by the federal short-term rate plus 3% (5% for underpayments in excess of $100,000).

    b. The penalty accrues from the installment due date until the underpayment is paid or, if earlier, the due date for filing the tax return.

    c. The penalty is not allowed as an interest deduction.

    d. If any underpayment of estimated tax is indicated by the tax return, Form 2220 should be submitted with the return.

EXAMPLE 12-7   Underpayment of Estimated Tax

Fad Corporation paid $4 million in taxes in Year 1, causing it to be considered a large corporation. In Year 2, Fad had a tax liability of $10 million. Incorrectly relying on its Year 1 tax liability, Fad paid the Year 2 quarterly estimated taxes of $1 million on April 15, June 15, September 15, and December 15, Year 2. Assuming income was not seasonal, each payment fell short by $1.5 million [($10 million ÷ 4 quarters) – $1 million]. Assuming a 0.5% short-term federal interest rate, interest of 5.5% accrues from each of the payment dates until Fad pays the outstanding taxes on March 31, Year 3. To have avoided the penalty, Fad should have made an adjustment following the first quarter, paying the difference in the second quarter.

---

    e. **No** estimated tax penalty is imposed if

        1) Tax liability shown on the return for the tax year is less than $500
        2) The IRS waives all or part of the penalty for good cause
        3) An erroneous IRS notice to a large corporation is withdrawn by the IRS

4. **Refund**

    a. A corporation may obtain a quick refund of estimated tax paid, but adjustment is allowed only if the overpayment is both ≥ $500 and ≥ 10% of the corporation's estimate of its tax liability.

    b. Application is filed (Form 4466) after the close of the tax year but before the return due date (without extensions).

STOP & REVIEW

You have completed the outline for this subunit.
Study multiple-choice questions 8 through 10 on page 352.

12.5 EARNINGS AND PROFITS

1. **Definition**
   a. The term "earnings and profits" (E&P) is the federal tax accounting version of financial accounting's retained earnings. Though similar in purpose, they are not the same amount. E&P determines whether corporate distributions are taxable dividends.
      1) There are two types of E&P: current and accumulated. A corporation first determines its current E&P, which is the E&P for the current year. Then any excess current E&P after making distributions is added to the accumulated E&P balance, and any distributions in excess of current E&P reduce the accumulated E&P balance.

>   Current E&P
>   – Dividend distributions
>   = **Increase (decrease) to accumulated E&P**

2. **Calculation**
   a. Calculating current E&P starts with the current-year taxable income or loss and then makes various positive and negative adjustments.
      1) The positive adjustments include some exempt income, deductions, and deferred income. Examples include interest from municipal bonds, injury compensation, life insurance proceeds, DRD, capital and NOL carryover, depreciation in excess of straight-line, income per completed-contract method, and deferred income from an installment sale.
      2) The negative adjustments include some nondeductible items for taxable income and recognized deferred income. Examples include life insurance premiums, penalties, fines, municipal bond expense, excessive compensation, federal income taxes, generally 50% of meals and 100% of entertainment, charitable contributions in excess of the percentage of AGI limit, and prior-year(s) installment sales.
      3) Transactions excluded from both E&P and taxable income do not require any adjustment. Examples include unrealized gains and losses, gifts, state tax refunds, and contributions to capital.

EXAMPLE 12-8   Current E&P

NEEM Co. had taxable income of $20,000 that included the following unadjusted items:

Meals	$ 400
Capital loss carried over from prior year	5,000

Current E&P is the current-year taxable income adjusted for specific items. Positive adjustments include loss carryovers, as they were negative adjustments in the year they occurred. Negative adjustments include the nondeductible portion of meals. Corporations are allowed to deduct 50% of qualifying meals expenses. The corporation's current E&P is $24,800 [$20,000 + $5,000 – ($400 × 50%)].

STOP & REVIEW

You have completed the outline for this subunit.
Study multiple-choice questions 11 through 13 on page 353.

12.6 DISTRIBUTIONS

1. **Definition**

    a. A **distribution** is any transfer of property by a corporation to any of its shareholders with respect to the shareholder's shares in the corporation. Property is defined as money, bonds or other obligations, stock in other corporations, and other property, including receivables.

2. **Distribution Amount**

	Money
+	Obligations (FMV), e.g., a bond
+	Property (FMV), other
−	Related liabilities, recourse or not
=	Distribution amount

3. **Corporate Treatment**

    a. A corporation is required to file a Form 1099-DIV no later than February 28 of the following year (due date is March 31 if filed electronically) for each shareholder if the corporation did any of the following at the shareholder level:

    1) Paid gross dividends of $10 or more during the calendar year
    2) Withheld any federal income taxes under the backup withholding rules
    3) Made payments of $600 or more as part of a liquidation

    b. **Corporate loss unrecognized.** No loss realized on an ordinary distribution of property (AB > FMV) may be recognized. The shareholder takes a FMV basis in the property.

    1) Loss on a sale to a more-than-50% shareholder is not recognized.

        a) Stock owned by related parties is attributed to the shareholder.
        b) The shareholder takes a FMV basis in the property.
        c) Gain realized on a subsequent taxable disposition to an unrelated party is recognized only to the extent it exceeds the previously disallowed loss.

    c. **Corporate gain recognized.** Gain realized on distributed property must be recognized by the corporation as if the property were sold to the distributee at its FMV. But no gain is recognized to the corporation on distribution of money or obligations it issues, e.g., bonds.

EXAMPLE 12-9   Corporate Gain on Distributed Property

Kyle Corp. owned 200 shares of Honey Corp. stock that it bought 19 years ago for $10 per share. This year, when the fair market value of the Honey stock was $14 per share, Kyle distributed this stock to a noncorporate shareholder. Because a corporation must recognize gains realized on distributions of property and the stock involved is not issued by Kyle, Kyle must recognize a gain of $800 ($2,800 FMV − $2,000 basis) on this distribution.

---

1) Liabilities. FMV is conclusively presumed to be no less than liabilities related to the property subject to which the shareholder assumes or takes the property, whether with recourse or not.

2) The character of recognized gain is determined by treating the distribution as a sale to the shareholder.

    a) Gain recognized on depreciable property in the hands of a more-than-50% shareholder distributee is ordinary income (OI).

3) Earnings and profits (E&P). Recognized gains increase E&P. Tax on the gain and FMV reduce E&P.

4. Shareholder Treatment

> **SUCCESS TIP**
>
> The CPA Exam has often contained questions regarding shareholder treatment of corporate distributions. A common question format has asked for the distribution amount that is taxable as dividend income to the shareholder.

a. **Dividend.** The amount of a distribution is a dividend to the extent, first, of any current E&P and then of any accumulated E&P (AE&P).

   1) When distributions during the year exceed current E&P, pro rata portions of each distribution are deemed to be from current E&P.

      a) If the current E&P balance is positive, the positive balance is computed as of the close of the taxable year, without regard to the amount of E&P at the time of the distribution.

      b) If the current E&P balance is negative, prorate the negative balance to the date of each distribution made during the year.

   2) Treatment of a distribution is determined by reference to AE&P only after any current E&P have been accounted for.

      a) AE&P constitute the remaining balance of E&P from prior tax years.

      b) Deficit in AE&P never results from a distribution. It results from any aggregate excess of current E&P deficits over unused positive AE&P. Deficit in AE&P does not offset current E&P.

      c) Current E&P are added to AE&P after determining treatment of distributions.

   3) Distributions > AE&P. When distributions exceed both current E&P and AE&P, allocate AE&P to distributions in their chronological order.

   4) Distributions from current E&P are first allocated to preferred stock, and any excess is then allocated to common stock.

EXAMPLE 12-10   Recipient Shareholders' Reporting

Impartial, Inc., has a zero balance in AE&P but $25,000 in current E&P. Impartial makes a distribution of $20,000 to its preferred shareholders and a distribution of $10,000 to its common shareholders. The preferred shareholders will report the $20,000 as dividend income. The common shareholders will report $5,000 as dividend income and $5,000 as a return of capital.

---

   5) To determine E&P from taxable income, adjustments similar to those used to reconcile income per books with taxable income must be made. For example, tax-exempt interest would be added to taxable income because, although it is excluded from gross income, it represents earnings available for distribution as dividends.

      a) Gain recognized on distribution of appreciated property increases E&P.

      b) E&P are determined at the end of the tax year.

         i) They are then reduced for money and the greater of FMV or AB of other property (net of liabilities) distributed during the year.

         ii) If E&P remain for the current year, they increase a positive AE&P balance or reduce a negative AE&P balance.

6) **Constructive dividends** are treated the same as other distributions.

   a) Constructive dividends are undeclared distributions to shareholders.

      i) Examples include the use of corporate vehicles or money borrowed from the corporation to purchase personal items.

   b) Like other distributions, constructive dividends may not be deducted by the company, potentially creating double taxation of that income (corporate level and shareholder level).

   c) To the extent the distribution exceeds current and accumulated earnings and profits, it is treated as a return of capital to the shareholder.

      i) Once the basis of the stock has been reduced to zero, any distributions received are treated as a gain from the sale of the stock.

      ii) In other words, constructive dividends are only dividends to the extent of E&P. So, if no E&P exists, a constructive dividend is not taxed like a dividend (it is a nondividend distribution instead).

b. **Capital recovery.** A shareholder treats the amount of a distribution in excess of dividends as tax-exempt return of capital to the extent of his or her basis.

   1) Basis in the stock is reduced (but not below zero).
   2) Apportion the distribution among the shares if they have different bases.

c. **Gain on sale.** Any excess of the amount of a distribution over E&P and basis is treated as gain on the sale of the stock (e.g., the $2,000 in Example 12-11 below).

   1) Character of the gain is determined by the nature of the property in the hands of the shareholder (e.g., a capital asset or dealer property).
   2) Loss may be recognized only if the stock becomes worthless or is redeemed.

EXAMPLE 12-11   Capital Recovery

Corporation distributes $90,000 when E&P are $60,000. Shareholder N receives $30,000 of the distribution, of which $20,000 is a dividend (2/3).

	# of Shares	Basis	Dividend	Capital Recovery	Gain
Block 1	1,000	$ 3,000	$10,000	$3,000	$2,000
Block 2	1,000	15,000	10,000	5,000	0

EXAMPLE 12-12   C Corporation Nonliquidating Distribution

Aaron is the sole shareholder in Alpha Corp., a C corporation. Aaron has a tax basis of $90,000 in the stock of Alpha. At the end of current year, Alpha distributed to Aaron equipment it had been using for 5 years with an AB of $300,000 and a FMV of $360,000. Alpha had AE&P of $450,000 at the beginning of the current year and E&P of $(250,000) for the current year before considering the distribution.

Alpha recognizes a gain of $60,000 from the equipment as if it were sold to a third party. This amount is added to the current E&P. Current E&P is therefore $(190,000) [$(250,000) current E&P before distribution + $60,000 ($360,000 FMV − $300,000 AB) gain recognized]. The amount of the distribution taxable as dividends is the sum of the AE&P and the current E&P, or $260,000 [$450,000 AE&P + $(190,000) current E&P]. Of the $360,000 distribution, $260,000 is taxed as dividends, while the remaining $100,000 reduces Aaron's tax basis of $90,000 (not below zero). This $90,000 is a tax-exempt return of capital. The remaining $10,000 ($100,000 − $90,000 tax basis) is a capital gain to Aaron.

d. **Basis in distributed property.** The shareholder's basis in property received in a nonliquidating distribution is generally its FMV at the time of the distribution.
   1) The FMV is used for obligations of the distributing corporation.
   2) If liabilities assumed or liabilities of property taken are
      a) < FMV, then the shareholder's basis in the property is its FMV.
      b) > FMV and the distributee shareholder assumes personal liability, then the shareholder's basis should equal the liability.

EXAMPLE 12-13   Shareholder Basis in Distributed Land

Gabrielle, the sole shareholder in Kleen, a C corporation, has a tax basis of $71,000. Kleen has $50,000 of accumulated positive earnings and profits at the beginning of the year and $9,000 of current positive earnings and profits for the current year. At year end, Kleen distributed land with an adjusted basis of $28,000 and a fair market value (FMV) of $46,000 to Gabrielle. The land has an outstanding mortgage of $10,000 that Gabrielle must assume.

Because the distribution is nonliquidating and the assumed liability is less than the FMV of the land, Gabrielle's basis in the land is equal to the $46,000 FMV. Had the liability assumed exceeded the FMV, then the basis would be the amount of the liability.

---

5. **Extraordinary Dividend**
   a. Additional gain may be recognized by a shareholder who sells stock on which an extraordinary dividend was received.
   b. An extraordinary dividend is a dividend on stock held 2 years or less that exceeds 10% (5% for preferred stock) of the adjusted basis in the stock.
   c. Basis in the stock is reduced by the nontaxed portion of the extraordinary dividend, i.e., the amount of a DRD (dividends-received deduction).
   d. If the nontaxed portion of the dividend exceeds the stock's basis, the excess is treated as a gain from the sale or exchange of such stock in the year the extraordinary dividend is received.

6. Stock Distributions

a. A corporation recognizes no gain or loss on distribution of its own stock. Generally, a shareholder does not include a distribution of stock or rights to acquire stock in gross income unless it is a

1) Distribution in lieu of money (i.e., the shareholder had the option to take cash instead of the stock)
2) Disproportionate distribution
3) Distribution on preferred stock
4) Distribution of convertible preferred stock
5) Distribution of common and preferred stock, resulting in receipt of preferred stock by some shareholders and common stock by other shareholders

b. A **proportionate distribution** of stock issued by the corporation is generally not gross income to the shareholders.

1) A shareholder allocates the aggregate basis (AB) in the old stock to the old stock and new stock in proportion to the FMV of the old and new stock.

a) Basis is apportioned by relative FMV to different types (e.g., common, preferred) of stock if applicable.

> **EXAMPLE 12-14   Basis Allocation -- Proportionate Distribution of Stock**
>
> Company A distributed two shares of preferred stock for each share of its common stock in a nontaxable distribution. On the day of distribution, Company B had 100 shares of Company A common stock. The FMV of common stock on the day of distribution was $80 per share, and the value of the preferred stock was $60 per share. Company B would therefore allocate 3/5 of the basis in Company A common stock to the 200 shares (100 shares of common stock × 2) of distributed preferred stock, calculated as follows:
>
> (200 preferred × $60 FMV) ÷ [(200 preferred × $60 FMV) + (100 common × $80 FMV)] = 0.6 or 3/5
>
> The remaining 2/5 would stay allocated to the common stock.

2) The holding period of the distributed stock includes that of the old stock.
3) E&P are not altered for a tax-free stock dividend.

c. **Stock rights.** Treat a distribution of stock rights as a distribution of the stock.

1) Basis is allocated based on the FMV of the rights.

a) Basis in the stock rights is zero if their aggregate FMV is less than 15% of the FMV of the stock on which they were distributed, unless the shareholder elects to allocate.

2) Basis in the stock, if the right is exercised, is any basis allocated to the right, plus the exercise price.
3) Holding period of the stock begins on the exercise date.
4) No deduction is allowed for basis allocated to stock rights that lapse. Basis otherwise allocated remains in the underlying stock.

7. **Taxable Stock Distribution**
    a. Distributions of stock described in items 1) through 6) below are subject to tax. Unless otherwise stated in 1) through 6) below, the amount of a distribution subject to tax is the FMV of distributed stock or stock rights.
        1) Any shareholder has an option to choose between a distribution of stock or a distribution of other property. The amount of the distribution is the greater of
            a) The FMV of stock or
            b) The cash or FMV of other property.
        2) Some shareholders receive property, and other shareholders receive an increase in their proportionate interests.
        3) Some common shareholders receive common stock; others receive preferred stock.
        4) Distribution is on preferred stock.
        5) Convertible preferred stock is distributed, and the effect is to change the shareholder's proportionate stock ownership.
        6) Constructive stock distributions change proportionate interests resulting from, e.g., a change in conversion ratio or redemption price.
    b. E&P are reduced by the FMV of stock and stock rights distributed.
    c. Basis in the underlying stock does not change. Basis in the new stock or stock rights is their FMV.
    d. The holding period for the new stock begins on the day after the distribution date.
    e. If a distribution of a stock dividend or stock right is taxable when received, the basis is the FMV on the date of acquisition.
        1) When the dividend is taxable, there is no tacking on of the holding period for the underlying stock.
        2) The holding period begins the day following the acquisition date.

8. **Stock Split**
    a. A stock split is not a distribution.
    b. Basis in the old stock is also "split" and allocated to the new stock.
    c. The holding period of the new stock includes that of the old stock.

STOP & REVIEW

You have completed the outline for this subunit.
Study multiple-choice questions 14 through 16 on page 354.

12.7 ACCUMULATED EARNINGS TAX (AET)

1. **Definition**
   a. The AET is a penalty tax imposed on C corporations that, for the purpose of avoiding income tax at the shareholder level, allow current-year earnings to accumulate instead of distributing them to shareholders. The tax equals 20% of accumulated (undistributed) taxable income (ATI). This tax is in addition to the corporate income tax.
      1) AET liability is determined by the IRS only during an audit. A corporation does not file a form to compute AET with its annual income tax return.
   b. A corporation is liable for the AET when it accumulates (does not distribute) earnings beyond the accumulated earnings credit (AEC) of $250,000 or its (reasonable) business needs, whichever is greater.
      1) The AEC is reduced to $150,000 for certain service corporations (e.g., health, law, engineering, accounting).
   c. The AET is only a tax on ATI (undistributed current-year earnings less dividends-paid deduction in excess of the AEC). However, undistributed prior-year earnings still factor into the calculation of whether total accumulated earnings exceed the accumulated earnings credit or reasonable business needs.

	Taxable income
+/–	Adjustments
	Current E&P (i.e., undistributed current-year earnings)
–	Dividends paid
–	AEC
	ATI
×	20%
	AET

   d. No offsetting credit or deduction is allowed for either the corporation or its shareholders, not even upon subsequent distribution of the earnings.

2. **Reasonable Needs of the Business**

    a. Reasonable needs of a business include only those items required to meet future needs and for which there are specific, foreseeable plans for use.

    NOTE: Most businesses are able to avoid the AET by documenting reasonable needs of the business periodically.

    b. Reasonable needs might include the following:

        1) Raw materials purchase
        2) Equipment update
        3) Expansion of production facilities
        4) Retirement of business debt
        5) Redeeming stock in gross estate of a shareholder
        6) Product liability loss reserves
        7) Realistic business contingencies
        8) Acquiring a related business
        9) Investments or loans to suppliers or customers
        10) Working capital

    c. The following are **not** considered reasonable needs of a business:

        1) Funding plans to declare a stock dividend or redeem stock of a shareholder
        2) Unrealistic business hazard protection
        3) Investment property unrelated to business activities of the corporation
        4) Loans to shareholders

3. **Exempt Entities**

    a. No AET liability is incurred by the following:

        1) S corporations
        2) Tax-exempt corporations
        3) PHCs (personal holding companies)
        4) FPHCs (foreign personal holding companies)
        5) PFICs (passive foreign investment companies)

EXAMPLE 12-15   Accumulated Earnings Credit

ABC Corporation, a C corporation, has $200,000 in current-year accumulated (undistributed) taxable income before inclusion of the credit. In addition, ABC has $100,000 in accumulated (undistributed) prior-year earnings. With the $250,000 accumulated earnings credit, ABC will be subject to an AET of $10,000 [($300,000 total accumulated earnings − $250,000 credit) × 20% tax rate]. To avoid the AET entirely, ABC would require a reasonable business need for the entire $300,000 accumulation.

You have completed the outline for this subunit.
Study multiple-choice questions 17 and 18 on page 355.

STOP & REVIEW

12.8 PERSONAL HOLDING COMPANY (PHC) TAX

1. **Definition**
   a. The PHC tax is a 20% penalty tax imposed on the undistributed income of personal holding companies. The tax is designed to deter passive investors from using a C corporation to avoid higher individual rates.
      1) The penalty tax is in addition to the regular corporate income tax.
      2) A corporation cannot be subject to the PHC tax and the AET in the same year.
   b. Self-assessment of PHC tax liability is required. Schedule PH is filed with Form 1120 by a PHC. There is a 6-year statute of limitations if the schedule is not filed.
   c. If a corporation determines that it is liable for the PHC tax, it can reduce or eliminate the tax by paying a deficiency dividend within 90 days.

2. **Entities Subject to the PHC Tax**
   a. Every corporation that is not exempt and meets two objective tests (with respect to stock ownership distribution and the nature of its income) is a PHC subject to PHC tax.
      1) **Stock ownership test.** More than 50% by value of the corporation's shares are owned, directly or indirectly, by five or fewer shareholders at any time during the last half of the year.
      2) **Nature of income test.** Sixty percent or more of adjusted ordinary gross income (AOGI) of the corporation is personal holding company income (PHCI).
         a) PHCI consists of specifically defined types of passive income (taxable interest, dividends from domestic unrelated corporations, royalties, net rental income, personal services income by a 25%-or-more owner).
         b) AOGI is gross income (GI) for regular tax reduced by capital gains from asset dispositions and further reduced by certain deductions, such as those allowed against rental and royalty income.

3. **Exempt Entities**
   a. No PHC tax liability is incurred by the following:
      1) S corporations
      2) Tax-exempt corporations
      3) FPHCs (foreign personal holding companies)
      4) Banks
      5) Insurance companies

SUCCESS TIP

The AICPA has tested candidates' knowledge of the personal holding company tax. Remember that one income amount, personal holding company income, is used to determine whether or not a corporation meets the nature of income test in determining if it is a PHC. If the corporation is a personal holding company, then another income amount, undistributed personal holding company income, is used to calculate the amount of personal holding company tax owed by the corporation. Be careful not to confuse these two amounts.

STOP & REVIEW

You have completed the outline for this subunit.
Study multiple-choice questions 19 and 20 on page 356.

QUESTIONS

12.1 Regular Income Tax and Credits

1. Jackson Corp.'s taxable income for 2021 from all of its global operations was $500,000. Taxable income from foreign sources was $125,000 during 2021. Jackson, a domestic corporation, calculated its 2021 tax liability before consideration of the Foreign Tax Credit to be $50,000, due with its 2021 tax return on March 1, 2022. What is the amount of Jackson's Foreign Tax Credit limitation for 2021?

A. $200,000
B. $125,000
C. $50,000
D. $12,500

Answer (D) is correct.
REQUIRED: The amount of the Foreign Tax Credit limitation.
DISCUSSION: The maximum amount of foreign taxes that may be credited is the proportion of the taxpayer's tentative U.S. income tax (before consideration of the Foreign Tax Credit) that the taxpayer's foreign taxable income bears to the taxpayer's worldwide taxable income for the year. The proportion of Jackson's foreign income to its worldwide income is $125,000 ÷ $500,000. Therefore, Jackson's allowable Foreign Tax Credit for 2021 is limited to $50,000 × ($125,000 ÷ $500,000), or $12,500.
Answer (A) is incorrect. Using $500,000 in the numerator of the fraction and $125,000 in the denominator results in $200,000. **Answer (B) is incorrect.** The total amount of foreign source income is $125,000. **Answer (C) is incorrect.** The total amount of U.S. taxes due before consideration of the Foreign Tax Credit is $50,000.

2. Sunex Co. is an accrual-basis, calendar-year domestic C corporation. In the current year, Sunex's U.S. tax liability on its domestic and foreign source income is $60,000, and no prior-year foreign income taxes have been carried forward. Which factor(s) may affect the amount of Sunex's Foreign Tax Credit available in its current-year corporate income tax return?

	Income Source	The Foreign Tax Rate
A.	Yes	Yes
B.	Yes	No
C.	No	Yes
D.	No	No

Answer (A) is correct.
REQUIRED: The factor(s) that may affect the amount of the Foreign Tax Credit.
DISCUSSION: The Foreign Income Tax Credit is equal to the lesser of the actual foreign tax paid or the Foreign Tax Credit limit. The Foreign Tax Credit limit is the proportion of the taxpayer's tentative income tax (before the Foreign Tax Credit) that the taxpayer's foreign source taxable income bears to his or her worldwide taxable income for the year.
Answer (B) is incorrect. The Foreign Income Tax Credit is equal to the lesser of the actual foreign tax paid or the Foreign Tax Credit limit. **Answer (C) is incorrect.** The Foreign Tax Credit limit is the proportion of the taxpayer's tentative income tax (before the Foreign Tax Credit) that the taxpayer's foreign source taxable income bears to his or her worldwide taxable income for the year. **Answer (D) is incorrect.** The Foreign Income Tax Credit is equal to the lesser of the actual foreign tax paid or the Foreign Tax Credit limit. The Foreign Tax Credit limit is the proportion of the taxpayer's tentative income tax (before the Foreign Tax Credit) that the taxpayer's foreign source taxable income bears to his or her worldwide taxable income for the year.

12.2 Consolidated Returns

3. With regard to consolidated tax returns, which of the following statements is true?

A. Operating losses of one group member may be used to offset operating profits of the other members included in the consolidated return.

B. Only corporations that issue their audited financial statements on a consolidated basis may file consolidated returns.

C. Of all intercompany dividends paid by the subsidiaries to the parent, 70% are excludable from taxable income on the consolidated return.

D. The common parent must directly own 51% or more of the total voting power of all corporations included in the consolidated return.

Answer (A) is correct.
REQUIRED: The true statement regarding consolidated tax returns.
DISCUSSION: Operating losses of one group member must be used to offset current-year operating profits of other group members before a net operating loss carryforward can occur.
Answer (B) is incorrect. There is no such requirement. **Answer (C) is incorrect.** A dividend distributed by one member of a group filing a consolidated tax return to another member of that same group is completely eliminated. There is no dividends-received deduction. **Answer (D) is incorrect.** A corporation must own 80% of the total voting power and 80% of the total value of the stock in order to file a consolidated return.

4. Tech Corp. files a consolidated return with its wholly owned subsidiary, Dow Corp. During 2021, Dow paid a cash dividend of $20,000 to Tech. What amount of this dividend is taxable on the 2021 consolidated return?

A. $20,000
B. $14,000
C. $6,000
D. $0

Answer (D) is correct.
REQUIRED: The taxable amount of a dividend distributed by a wholly owned subsidiary to its parent when a consolidated return is filed.
DISCUSSION: A dividend distributed by one member of a group filing a consolidated tax return to another member of that group is eliminated. The recipient of the dividend makes an adjustment to its separate taxable income that eliminates the dividend from the affiliated group's consolidated taxable income. Note that the dividends-received deduction (DRD) does not apply to intergroup dividends of affiliated groups that file a consolidated tax return.

5. Potter Corp. and Sly Corp. file consolidated tax returns. In January of Year 1, Potter sold land, with a basis of $60,000 and a fair value of $75,000, to Sly for $100,000. Sly sold the land in December of Year 2 for $125,000. In the consolidated group's Year 1 and Year 2 tax returns, what amount of gain should be reported for these transactions in the consolidated return?

	Year 2	Year 1
A.	$25,000	$40,000
B.	$50,000	$0
C.	$50,000	$25,000
D.	$65,000	$0

Answer (D) is correct.
REQUIRED: The amount of gain on the sale of land to be reported in the consolidated returns.
DISCUSSION: A sale or exchange of property between members of the consolidated group is a deferred intercompany transaction. In the case of nondepreciable property (e.g., land) not sold on the installment basis, the gain is not reported until the property is sold outside the group. Therefore, Potter should report no income in the consolidated return for Year 1 as a result of the sale. For Year 2, however, Potter should recognize the full amount of the $65,000 gain ($125,000 – $60,000).
Answer (A) is incorrect. The Year 1 sale is a deferred intercompany transaction between members of a consolidated group. The gain realized is reported when the property is sold outside the group. **Answer (B) is incorrect.** The deferred intercompany gain of $15,000 is recognized when the property is sold outside the group. **Answer (C) is incorrect.** The gain is reported when the property is sold outside the group.

12.3 Controlled Groups

6. Which one of the following statements about a controlled group of corporations is **false**?

A. Any controlled group may elect to file consolidated federal income tax returns.

B. A parent corporation and its 80%-owned subsidiary make up a controlled group.

C. All members of a controlled group need not use the parent's tax year.

D. Members of a controlled group are entitled to only one accumulated earnings tax credit.

Answer (A) is correct.
REQUIRED: The false statement concerning a controlled group of corporations.
DISCUSSION: Under Sec. 1563(a), a controlled group of corporations may be a parent-subsidiary controlled group, a brother-sister controlled group, or a combined group. Either a parent-subsidiary controlled group or the parent-subsidiary portion of a combined group may file a consolidated tax return because there is a common parent corporation and the includible corporations are all 80%-owned. However, a brother-sister controlled group exists when two or more corporations are owned by five or fewer persons who own at least 80% of the voting stock or 80% of the value of the outstanding stock. There is no common parent corporation, so a consolidated tax return could not be filed. The affiliated group definition requires ownership of 80% of the voting stock and 80% of the value of the controlled corporation. The controlled group definition is an "or" test, and some controlled groups may meet one, but not both, of the tests and not be able to file a consolidated return.
Answer (B) is incorrect. It describes a parent-subsidiary controlled group. **Answer (C) is incorrect.** There is no requirement that members of a controlled group use the parent's tax year. However, the members of the parent-subsidiary controlled group must use the parent's tax year once a consolidated tax return election has been made. **Answer (D) is incorrect.** One of the purposes of ascertaining whether a controlled group exists is to allocate to the group various tax benefits that can be claimed once by the group and not by each of the individual members. These benefits include the accumulated earnings tax credit, the Sec. 179 expensing maximum of $1.05 million, and the general business credit ($25,000) offset.

7. The only class of outstanding stock of Corporations L, M, N, O, and P is owned by the following unrelated individuals:

Individual	Corporations/Percent of Stock Owned				
	L	M	N	O	P
G	30%	40%	50%	50%	5%
H	10%	5%	10%	20%	5%
I	30%	40%	30%	10%	5%
J	30%	15%	10%	20%	5%
K	-0-	-0-	-0-	-0-	5%

Which of the following corporations are members of a brother-sister controlled group?

A. Only L, M, N, and O.
B. Only M, N, O, and P.
C. Only L, M, O, and P.
D. Only L, M, and N.

Answer (A) is correct.
REQUIRED: The corporations that are members of a brother-sister controlled group.
DISCUSSION: The significance of a controlled group is that members are not allowed many of the benefits of separate corporations; e.g., all members must share the Accumulated Earnings Credit, 100% General Business Tax Credit offset, etc., as one corporation. Under Sec. 1563(a), a brother-sister controlled group means two or more corporations of which five or fewer persons who are individuals, estates, or trusts own at least 80% of the voting power or value of each corporation, and more than 50% of the voting power or value of the stock of each corporation counting only identical ownership interests (i.e., the smallest amount owned by each person in any of the corporations is all that is counted in the other corporations for the 50% test). Individual K's ownership is not counted because (s)he does not own stock in each corporation. Corporation P does not pass the 80% test and so is not included in the 50% test. The 50% test is met for L, M, N, and O.

Total Percent of Each Corporation Owned by G, H, I, and J	
Corporation L	100%
Corporation M	100%
Corporation N	100%
Corporation O	100%
Corporation P	20%

Identical Percent Owned in Each of L, M, N, O	
Individual G	30%
Individual H	5%
Individual I	10%
Individual J	10%
Total	55%

Answer (B) is incorrect. L is a member of a brother-sister controlled group, while P is not. **Answer (C) is incorrect.** N is a member of a brother-sister controlled group. P is not a member because only 20% of P's stock is owned by G, H, I, and J, and the 50% common ownership requirement is also not met. **Answer (D) is incorrect.** O is also a member of a brother-sister controlled group.

12.4 Estimated Tax

8. Blink Corp., an accrual-basis, calendar-year corporation, has zero tax liability for the tax year ended December 31, Year 1. Blink's gross revenues have been under $500,000 since inception. Blink expects to have profits for the tax year ending December 31, Year 2. Which method(s) of estimated tax payment can Blink use for its quarterly payments during the Year 2 tax year to avoid underpayment of federal estimated taxes?

I. 100%-of-the-preceding-tax-year method
II. Annualized income method

A. I only.
B. Both I and II.
C. II only.
D. Neither I nor II.

Answer (C) is correct.
REQUIRED: The acceptable method(s) of estimating quarterly tax payments.
DISCUSSION: Blink Corp. qualifies as a small corporation because it has not had taxable income exceeding $1 million during any of the 3 preceding years. However, it must have shown a tax liability in the previous year in order to use the 100%-of-the-preceding-tax-year method. Since the previous year had zero tax liability, this method cannot be used. The annualized income method is available in this situation.
Answer (A) is incorrect. The 100%-of-the-preceding-tax-year method cannot be used since the preceding tax year had zero tax liability. **Answer (B) is incorrect.** The 100%-of-the-preceding-tax-year method cannot be used since the preceding tax year had zero tax liability. However, the annualized income method is available in this situation. **Answer (D) is incorrect.** The annualized income method is available in this situation.

9. Finbury Corporation's taxable income for the year ended December 31, 2020, was $2 million. For Finbury to escape the estimated tax underpayment penalty for the year ending December 31, 2021, its total 2021 estimated tax payments must equal at least

A. 100% of the 2020 tax liability.
B. 80% of the 2021 tax liability.
C. 90% of the 2021 tax liability.
D. 100% of its 2021 tax liability.

Answer (D) is correct.
REQUIRED: The minimum amount of estimated tax payments to avoid the underpayment penalty.
DISCUSSION: A large corporation will not be considered to have underpaid its income tax if it pays 100% of the tax shown on the return for the tax year. A large corporation is one having $1 million or more taxable income during any of its 3 preceding tax years. Large corporations are not able to avoid underpaying their taxes by relying on the 100% of the tax shown on the return for the preceding year exception.

10. Maple Corporation, a calendar-year corporation, estimated its income tax for 2021 will be $20,000. Its 2020 tax liability was $100,000. Maple deposited the first two estimated tax installments on April 15 and June 15, 2021, in the amount of $5,000 each (25% of $20,000). On July 1, 2021, Maple estimated its tax will be $40,000. What are the amounts of the estimated tax payments that Maple Corporation should pay on September 15, 2021, and December 15, 2021?

	Sept. 15, 2021	Dec. 15, 2021
A.	$15,000	$15,000
B.	$20,000	$10,000
C.	$10,000	$20,000
D.	$ 5,000	$ 5,000

Answer (B) is correct.
REQUIRED: The estimated tax payments for the third and fourth installments.
DISCUSSION: Under Sec. 6655(d), the minimum installment is 25% of the required annual payment (the lesser of 100% of current tax or 100% of preceding year's tax). Although Maple correctly estimated its first two tax payments, the amount of estimated tax for the year increased. Since Maple already paid $10,000 ($5,000 × 2) in taxes, it still owes $30,000 ($40,000 – $10,000). Seventy-five percent of $40,000 should be paid by the third installment, so Maple would have to pay $20,000 to get the total of $30,000. The final installment would be $10,000, which should finish its estimated payments.
Answer (A) is incorrect. Maple must catch up with the third quarter payment. Allocating the remaining tax equally between the third and fourth payment is not allowed. **Answer (C) is incorrect.** The amount of taxes that need to be paid if an equal amount is paid each quarter is $10,000. **Answer (D) is incorrect.** The amount paid on each of the first two installments is $5,000.
NOTE: Annualization of the estimated tax payments is not possible due to a lack of information provided in the original IRS question.

12.5 Earnings and Profits

11. What is the current earnings and profits (E&P) of a corporation with taxable income of $10,000 that included the following unadjusted items:

Meals	$ 200
Capital loss carried over from prior year	3,000

- A. $7,100
- B. $10,000
- C. $12,800
- D. $12,900

Answer (D) is correct.
   REQUIRED: The current E&P of the corporation.
   DISCUSSION: Current E&P is the current-year taxable income adjusted for specific items. Positive adjustments include loss carryovers, as they were negative adjustments in the year they occurred. Negative adjustments include the nondeductible portion of meals. Corporations are allowed to deduct 50% of qualifying meal expenses. The corporation's current E&P is $12,900 [$10,000 + $3,000 − ($200 × 50%)].
   Answer (A) is incorrect. The loss carryover is a positive adjustment, and the excess portion of deductible meals is a negative adjustment. **Answer (B) is incorrect.** Taxable income is only the starting point for calculating current E&P. Both positive and negative adjustments must be made in order to arrive at current E&P. **Answer (C) is incorrect.** Only the nondeductible portion of meals for taxable income is adjusted for current E&P.

12. Which of the following is a positive adjustment for calculating current earnings and profits (E&P)?

- A. Recognized gain from prior year installment sales.
- B. Deferred gain on installment sales.
- C. Life insurance premiums when the corporation is the beneficiary.
- D. Federal income tax.

Answer (B) is correct.
   REQUIRED: The positive adjustment required for calculating current E&P.
   DISCUSSION: Current E&P is the current year taxable income adjusted for specific items. Some adjustments are positive and some are negative. Deferred gain on installment sales for taxable income is recognized in the year of sale (i.e., the current year) for E&P.
   Answer (A) is incorrect. The recognition of gain from a prior year installment sale is a negative adjustment because the income was already recognized, for E&P, in the year of sale. **Answer (C) is incorrect.** Because life insurance premiums are not deductible for taxable income when the corporation is the beneficiary, a negative adjustment has to be made for E&P because the payment reduced profits. **Answer (D) is incorrect.** Though not deductible for taxable income, payment of federal income taxes reduces profits.

13. Which of the following items is excluded from both E&P and taxable income and does **not** require an adjustment in calculating current E&P?

- A. Injury compensation.
- B. Federal income taxes.
- C. Unrealized gain.
- D. Municipal bond interest.

Answer (C) is correct.
   REQUIRED: The item excluded from both E&P and taxable income.
   DISCUSSION: Transactions excluded from both E&P and taxable income do not require any adjustment. Examples include unrealized gains and losses, gifts, state tax refunds, and contributions to capital.
   Answer (A) is incorrect. Positive adjustments to taxable income to arrive at E&P include items of exempt income, such as injury compensation. **Answer (B) is incorrect.** Negative adjustments to taxable income to arrive at E&P include nondeductible items for taxable income, such as income taxes, meals, and entertainment. **Answer (D) is incorrect.** Positive adjustments to taxable income to arrive at E&P include items of exempt income, such as interest from municipal bonds.

12.6 Distributions

14. Nyle Corp. owned 100 shares of Beta Corp. stock that it bought 16 years ago for $9 per share. This year, when the fair market value of the Beta stock was $20 per share, Nyle distributed this stock to a noncorporate shareholder. Nyle's recognized gain on this distribution was

A. $2,000
B. $1,100
C. $900
D. $0

Answer (B) is correct.
REQUIRED: The amount of gain recognized by a corporation on distribution of stock.
DISCUSSION: A corporation must recognize gain realized on distributions of property. The definition of property excludes stock, but only if issued by the corporation. Thus, Nyle Corp. must recognize gain of $1,100 ($2,000 FMV – $900 basis).
Answer (A) is incorrect. The FMV of the stock is $2,000. Answer (C) is incorrect. The basis of the stock is $900. Answer (D) is incorrect. A corporation recognizes gain or loss on distribution of stock that is not issued by the corporation.

15. Brisk Corp. is an accrual-basis, calendar-year C corporation with one individual shareholder. At year end, Brisk had $600,000 accumulated and current earnings and profits as it prepared to make its only dividend distribution for the year to its shareholder. Brisk could distribute either cash of $200,000 or land with an adjusted tax basis of $75,000 and a fair market value of $200,000. How would the taxable incomes of both Brisk and the shareholder change if land were distributed instead of cash?

	Brisk's taxable income	Shareholder's taxable income
A.	No change	No change
B.	Increase	No change
C.	No change	Decrease
D.	Increase	Decrease

Answer (B) is correct.
REQUIRED: The effect of a property distribution on a corporation's and shareholder's taxable income.
DISCUSSION: The shareholder will include the cash or the FMV of the property in their income regardless of the two distributions. Each will also be dividend income because Brisk has sufficient E&P. Brisk's taxable income will increase, based on the gain from the property's excess FMV over its adjusted basis.
Answer (A) is incorrect. Even though the shareholder's taxable income will not change based on the cash or property distribution, Brisk's taxable income will increase as a result of the property distribution gain. Answer (C) is incorrect. Brisk's taxable income should increase as a result of the property distribution, and the shareholder's taxable income will not change if property is distributed. Answer (D) is incorrect. Brisk's taxable income will increase, yet the shareholder's taxable income will not decrease. The shareholder will include the FMV of the property in income, not the corporation's adjusted basis.

16. On January 1, Year 1, Kee Corp., a C corporation, had a $50,000 deficit in E&P. For Year 1, Kee had current E&P of $10,000 and made a $30,000 cash distribution to its shareholders. What amount of the distribution is taxable as dividend income to Kee's shareholders?

A. $30,000
B. $20,000
C. $10,000
D. $0

Answer (C) is correct.
REQUIRED: The amount of the distribution taxable as dividend income to the shareholders.
DISCUSSION: Treatment of a distribution is determined by reference to accumulated E&P only after any current E&P have been accounted for. To the extent current E&P are sufficient to cover a distribution, the distribution is treated as a taxable dividend, even if there is a deficit in the accumulated E&P. Thus, the current E&P of $10,000 results in ordinary dividend income to Kee's shareholders of $10,000.
Answer (A) is incorrect. The amount treated as ordinary dividend income cannot exceed the amount of positive current and accumulated E&P. Answer (B) is incorrect. It exceeds current and accumulated E&P. Answer (D) is incorrect. Distributions are treated as coming out of current E&P first without regard to accumulated E&P.

12.7 Accumulated Earnings Tax (AET)

17. In determining whether a corporation is subject to the accumulated earnings tax, which of the following items is **not** a subtraction in arriving at accumulated taxable income?

A. Federal income tax.
B. Capital loss carryback.
C. Dividends-paid deduction.
D. Accumulated Earnings Credit.

Answer (B) is correct.
REQUIRED: The item that does not reduce accumulated taxable income.
DISCUSSION: The accumulated earnings tax is applied to accumulated taxable income, which is taxable income, subject to certain adjustments. Capital loss carrybacks and carryforwards are not allowed. Instead, capital losses are deductible in full in the year incurred (but must be reduced by prior net capital gain deductions).
Answer (A) is incorrect. Federal income taxes are deducted as an adjustment to taxable income. **Answer (C) is incorrect.** The dividends-paid deduction is subtracted from adjusted taxable income. **Answer (D) is incorrect.** The Accumulated Earnings Credit is subtracted from adjusted taxable income.

18. The accumulated earnings tax

A. Should be self-assessed by filing a separate schedule along with the regular tax return.
B. Applies only to closely held corporations.
C. Can be imposed on S corporations that do not regularly distribute their earnings.
D. Cannot be imposed on a corporation that has undistributed earnings and profits of less than $150,000.

Answer (D) is correct.
REQUIRED: The entities subject to, the limits on, and the procedural characteristics of the AET.
DISCUSSION: The Accumulated Earnings Credit (AEC) is deducted from taxable income (TI) to determine accumulated taxable income (ATI), the AET base. The minimum credit base is $250,000. However, the minimum credit base is $150,000 for certain personal service corporations. When undistributed (current and accumulated) earnings and profits do not exceed $150,000, the ATI will be equal to zero in all circumstances and no accumulated earnings tax will be imposed.
Answer (A) is incorrect. AET is not self-assessed. It is assessed, if at all, on an IRS audit. Filing a separate return reporting AET is not required. **Answer (B) is incorrect.** AET can apply to publicly held corporations. **Answer (C) is incorrect.** An S corporation is expressly exempt from AET. Its shareholders are currently subject to tax on its earnings.

12.8 Personal Holding Company (PHC) Tax

19. Edge Corp. met the stock ownership requirements of a personal holding company. What sources of income must Edge consider to determine if the income requirements for a personal holding company have been met?

I. Interest earned on tax-exempt obligations
II. Dividends received from an unrelated domestic corporation

A. I only.
B. II only.
C. Both I and II.
D. Neither I nor II.

Answer (B) is correct.
REQUIRED: The items included in personal holding company income.
DISCUSSION: A personal holding company tax is assessed on the undistributed personal holding company income (PHCI) of many C corporations. This tax is self-assessed when more than 50% of the value of the corporation's shares are owned by five or fewer shareholders at any time during the last half of the fiscal year, and 60% or more of AGI is PHCI. PHCI includes taxable interest and dividends received from an unrelated domestic corporation but not tax-exempt interest.
Answer (A) is incorrect. Tax-exempt interest is not a type of PHCI since it is exempt from gross income. **Answer (C) is incorrect.** Only one option is a type of PHCI. **Answer (D) is incorrect.** Dividends received from unrelated domestic corporations are included in PHCI.

20. Benson, a singer, owns 100% of the outstanding capital stock of Lund Corporation. Lund contracted with Benson, specifying that Benson was to perform personal services for Magda Productions, Inc., in consideration of which Benson was to receive $50,000 a year from Lund. Lund contracted with Magda, specifying that Benson was to perform personal services for Magda, in consideration of which Magda was to pay Lund $1 million a year. Personal holding company income will be attributable to

A. Benson only.
B. Lund only.
C. Magda only.
D. All three contracting parties.

Answer (B) is correct.
REQUIRED: The corporation to which the personal holding company income will be attributed.
DISCUSSION: Amounts received by corporations under personal service contracts involving a 25%-or-more shareholder are personal holding company income if the contract designates specifically that only the shareholder will provide the services. As such, Lund has personal service income of $1 million a year.
Answer (A) is incorrect. Benson is an individual, and personal holding company income applies only to corporations. **Answer (C) is incorrect.** Magda is paying the income, not receiving it. **Answer (D) is incorrect.** Not all parties will have personal holding company income.

Access the Gleim CPA Premium Review System featuring our SmartAdapt technology from your Gleim Personal Classroom to continue your studies. You will experience a personalized study environment with exam-emulating multiple-choice questions.

STUDY UNIT THIRTEEN
CORPORATE TAX SPECIAL TOPICS

(24 pages of outline)

13.1	Redemptions	357
13.2	Complete Liquidation	361
13.3	Partial Liquidation	363
13.4	Subsidiary Liquidation	364
13.5	Reorganizations	365
13.6	Multiple Jurisdictions	368

This study unit addresses the federal income tax aspects of utilizing the corporate structure. This study unit will help develop an understanding of the tax treatments for the different kinds of liquidation and nonrecognition by parties to a reorganization.

Corporations have tax procedures that are specific to that type of entity.

Taxpayers who operate or otherwise have a presence in more than one tax jurisdiction are subject to tax laws that are distinct for each jurisdiction and subject to U.S. treatment of foreign operations.

Some candidates find it helpful to have the entire tax form side-by-side with our Knowledge Transfer Outline when studying, and others may prefer to see the final draft of a form when it is released. The full versions of the most up-to-date forms are easily accessible at www.gleim.com/taxforms. These forms and the form excerpts used in our outline are periodically updated as the latest versions are released by the IRS.

13.1 REDEMPTIONS

1. **Overview**

    a. Stock is redeemed when a corporation acquires its own stock from a shareholder in exchange for property, regardless of redeemed stock being canceled, retired, or held as treasury stock.

    b. A shareholder is required to treat amounts realized on a redemption (not in liquidation) either as a distribution (a corporate dividend) or as a sale of stock redeemed.

2. **Dividend or Sale Treatment**

    a. Redemptions of stock by a corporation are treated as distributions unless certain conditions are met. If any of the following conditions are met, the exchange is treated as a sale, and the gains or losses are capital gains and losses.

       1) The redemption is not essentially equivalent to a dividend.
       2) The redemption is substantially disproportionate.
       3) The distribution is in complete redemption of all of a shareholder's stock.
       4) The distribution is to a noncorporate shareholder in partial liquidation.
       5) The distribution is received by an estate.

3. **Gain Recognition**

    a. A **corporation** recognizes gain realized on a distribution

       1) As if the property distributed were sold at FMV to the distributee immediately prior to the distribution
       2) Even if stock is redeemed by the distribution

4. **Loss Recognition**
    a. No recognition of loss realized is allowed by the corporation, unless the redemption is
        1) In complete liquidation of the corporation or
        2) Of stock held by an estate (to pay death taxes).

5. **Recognition of Depreciated Property Distribution**
    a. A corporation recognizes ordinary income on the distribution of depreciated property to the extent of depreciation or amount realized, whichever is less.

6. **Shareholder Treatment**
    a. A **shareholder** treats a nonqualifying redemption in the same manner as a regular distribution. The amount is a dividend to the extent of E&P. Any unrecovered basis in the redeemed stock is added to the shareholder's basis in stock retained.

EXAMPLE 13-1   Shareholder Treatment -- Nonqualifying Redemption of Stock

Since 2015, Paige has owned all 1,010 outstanding shares of E and E Corporation's stock. Paige's basis for the stock is $10,100. In 2021, E and E has earnings and profits of $110,000. The corporation redeemed 450 shares of Paige's stock for $98,000 in 2021. Because Paige owns 100% of the stock before and after the redemption, the transaction is a dividend to the extent that E and E has earnings and profits. Because the distribution ($98,000) is less than earnings and profits ($110,000), the entire amount is taxable as a dividend.

NOTE: Do not confuse this with noncorporate shareholder treatment of a partial liquidation. (Details of partial liquidation requirements are covered in Subunit 13.3.)

---

7. **Stock Reacquisition**
    a. The expenses incurred in connection with any reacquisition by a corporation of its own stock or the stock of a related person (50% relationship test) are not deductible. An exception exists for any cost allocable to an indebtedness and amortized over the life of the indebtedness (e.g., financial advisory costs).

8. **Sale Treatment**
    a. The shareholder treats qualifying redemptions as if the shares redeemed were sold to a third party.
    b. Gain or loss is any spread between AB of the shares and the FMV of property received.
    c. The character of gain or loss depends on the nature of the stock in the shareholder's hands.
    d. The basis in distributed property is its FMV.
    e. The holding period for the property starts the day after the redemption exchange.
    f. This treatment applies only to redemptions that
        1) Terminate a shareholder's interest
        2) Are substantially disproportionate between shareholders
        3) Are not essentially equivalent to a dividend
        4) Are received by an estate
        5) Are from a shareholder, other than a corporation, in partial liquidation
    g. Treatment of a redemption as a sale is determined separately for each shareholder.

SU 13: Corporate Tax Special Topics

9. **Termination of Interest**

    a. Termination of a shareholder's interest must be complete to qualify. All the corporation's stock owned by the shareholder must be redeemed in the exchange for the property.

        1) Family attribution rules apply but may be waived if the following three requirements are met:

            a) The shareholder may not retain any interest (e.g., an employee, officer, director, or shareholder), except as a creditor, in the corporation (i.e., the family attribution rules can only be waived in a complete termination).

            b) The shareholder may not acquire any interest, except by bequest or inheritance, for 10 years.

            c) A written agreement must be filed with the IRS stating that the IRS will be notified if a prohibited interest is acquired.

10. **Substantially Disproportionate**

    a. Substantially disproportionate means that the amount received by shareholders is not in the same proportion as their stock holdings.

    b. It is tested by determining the shareholders' applicable ownership percentages (including constructive ownership) both before and after redemption.

    c. A redemption is substantially disproportionate with respect to a shareholder if, immediately after the redemption, the shareholder owns

        1) Less than 50% of the voting power of outstanding stock and

        2) Less than 80% each of the interest in the (a) voting stock owned before the redemption and (b) common stock owned before the redemption.

EXAMPLE 13-2   Substantially Disproportionate Redemption

Carol, an individual shareholder, owns 275 shares of Allegiance Corporation. Allegiance has 1,000 shares of common stock outstanding and redeems 200 shares of common stock from its shareholders. The least number of Carol's shares that will need to be redeemed in order for the redemption to be substantially disproportionate to Carol is determined as follows:

Carol owned 27.5% of Allegiance Corporation before the redemption (275 shares ÷ 1,000 shares). Carol must reduce her interest to below 22% for the redemption to be substantially disproportionate (80% × 27.5%). Carol needs to own less than 176 shares after the redemption [22% × (1,000 shares – 200 shares)]. Thus, more than 99 shares (275 shares – 176 shares) need to be redeemed to reduce Carol's interest below 22%. Accordingly, Carol needs to have a minimum of 100 shares redeemed for the redemption to be substantially disproportionate.

11. **Not Essentially Equivalent to a Dividend**
    a. Not essentially equivalent to a dividend means that there is a meaningful reduction in the shareholder's proportionate interest in the corporation. Reduction in voting power is generally required for a redemption. Shareholders in control of a corporation must generally lose control to qualify as not essentially equivalent to a dividend.

EXAMPLE 13-3	Not Essentially Equivalent to a Dividend
A shareholder who goes from owning 53% of a corporation to 51% in a redemption would not qualify for sale or exchange treatment as "not essentially equivalent to a dividend." But a shareholder going from 51% (in control) to 49% (out of control) would qualify as not essentially equivalent to a dividend.	

12. **Estate**
    a. An estate may treat a qualifying redemption (e.g., to pay death taxes) as a sale.
        1) Redeemed stock must be valued at more than 35% of the gross estate net of deductions allowed.
        2) Deductions allowed are administration expenses, funeral expenses, claims against the estate (including death taxes), and unpaid mortgages.

13. **Partial Liquidations**
    a. Partial liquidations to a noncorporate shareholder are one type of redemption. A genuine contraction of the corporate business and a plan of partial liquidation are required. The distribution must occur in the year of the plan or the year after.

14. **Constructive Ownership**
    a. The (redeemed) shareholder is treated as owning shares owned by certain related parties, e.g., family members (excluding siblings and grandparents).

STOP & REVIEW

You have completed the outline for this subunit.
Study multiple-choice questions 1 through 4 beginning on page 381.

13.2 COMPLETE LIQUIDATION

1. **Defined**
   a. Under a plan of complete liquidation, a corporation redeems all of its stock in a series of distributions.

2. **Corporate Gains**
   a. A corporation recognizes any gain or loss realized on distributions in complete liquidation as if the property were sold at its FMV to the shareholder immediately before its distribution.
   b. Gain or loss is computed on an asset-by-asset basis.
   c. FMV of distributed property is treated as not less than the related liabilities that the shareholder assumes or to which the property is subject.
   d. The character of amounts recognized depends on the nature of the asset in the hands of the distributing corporation, e.g., Secs. 1245 and 1250.

> **EXAMPLE 13-4   Complete Liquidation -- Corporate Gains**
>
> Under a plan of complete liquidation, Zaige Corporation distributed land having an adjusted basis to Zaige of $19,000 to its sole shareholder. The land was subject to a liability of $98,000, which the shareholder assumed for legitimate business purposes. The FMV of the land on the date of distribution was $71,000.
>
> Generally, the FMV of $71,000 would be used to determine any gain; however, because the liability relief of $98,000 is greater than the FMV, Zaige's recognized gain is $79,000 ($98,000 liability relief − $19,000 AB).

3. **Corporate Losses**
   a. A corporation generally recognizes any losses realized on liquidating distributions.
   b. Certain realized losses are not recognized when the distributee shareholder is related to the corporation. A more-than-50% shareholder, actually or constructively, is a typical related distributee.
      1) Applicable distributions are of assets non-pro rata or acquired within 5 years by a contribution to capital or a Sec. 351 exchange.
      2) Permanent disallowance results, even if the decline in value occurred post-contribution.
   c. Precontribution loss. The amount of a loss inherent on a contribution reduces loss recognized on distribution.
      1) Applicable dispositions are of assets a liquidating corporation distributes, sells, or exchanges that were acquired by a contribution to capital or by a Sec. 351 exchange when its AB exceeded FMV for the principal purpose of recognizing the loss on liquidation.
      2) The loss limit operates by requiring that basis for computing the amount of loss be reduced by loss inherent on contribution.
   d. Carryovers. Unused, unexpired NOLs, capital losses, and charitable contribution carryover amounts are lost.

4. **Shareholder Treatment**

    a. A shareholder treats amounts distributed in complete liquidation as realized in exchange for stock.
    b. Capital recovery to the extent of basis is permitted before recognizing gain or loss.
    c. The holding period will not include that of the liquidated corporation.
    d. Amounts realized include money and the FMV of other distributed property received.
        1) Liabilities to which property is subject reduce the amount realized.
        2) Allocation of amounts realized to each block of stock is required.

EXAMPLE 13-5   Liquidating Distribution to Shareholder

Consider a single liquidating distribution to Shareholder S on February 1, 2021, of $70 cash and a car ($25 = FMV) subject to a liability of $15. S's amount realized is $80 [$70 + ($25 − $15)].

Block	Shares	Acquired	Basis	Amount Realized	Gain (Loss) Realized
A	1	5/16	$10	$20	$10
B	3	10/17	90	60	(30)

---

   e. Character of recognized gain or loss depends on the nature of each block of the stock in the hands of the shareholder.

EXAMPLE 13-6   Character of Recognized Gain or Loss

If S in Example 13-5 held the stock for investment, S would recognize LTCG on Block A and STCL on Block B.

---

   f. Basis in distributed property is its FMV, but only after gain or loss on its receipt has been recognized.

5. **Reporting**

    a. A corporation must file an information return (Form 966, *Corporate Dissolution or Liquidation*) reporting adoption of a plan or resolution for its dissolution, or partial or complete liquidation, within 30 days of adoption.
        1) The IRS requires a corporation to file Form 1099-DIV for each calendar year it makes partial distribution(s) of $600 or more under a plan of complete liquidation.
        2) Liquidation expenses incurred are deductible by the dissolved corporation.

STOP & REVIEW

You have completed the outline for this subunit.
Study multiple-choice questions 5 through 7 on page 383.

13.3 PARTIAL LIQUIDATION

1. **Noncorporate Shareholder**

    a. A noncorporate shareholder treats a distribution as a sale to the extent it is (in redemption) in partial liquidation of the corporation.

2. **Corporate Distributor**

    a. The corporation making the distribution recognizes gain but not loss.

3. **Corporate Distributee**

    a. A corporation that receives a distribution in redemption for partial liquidation of another corporation treats the distribution as a dividend to the extent of E&P of the distributing corporation. The distributee corporation is eligible for the dividends-received deduction.

4. **Contraction of the Corporation**

    a. Partial liquidation refers to contraction of the corporation. Focus is not on the shareholders but on genuine reduction in size of the corporation.

    b. Partial liquidation must be pursuant to a plan. The partial liquidation must be complete within either the tax year of plan adoption or the succeeding tax year.

    c. Pro rata distributions do not preclude partial liquidation sale treatment, and shareholders are not required to surrender stock to the corporation.

    d. Safe harbor. Noncorporate shareholders apply partial liquidation sale treatment to distributions received if the following conditions are satisfied:

    1) The distribution is attributable to the corporation ceasing to conduct a trade or business that it actively conducted for at least 5 years ending with the date of the distribution.

    2) Immediately after the distribution, the corporation continues to conduct at least one active trade or business it has conducted for 5 years.

STOP & REVIEW

You have completed the outline for this subunit.
Study multiple-choice question 8 through 10 on page 384.

13.4 SUBSIDIARY LIQUIDATION

1. **Nonrecognition**
   a. Neither the parent corporation nor a controlled subsidiary recognizes gain or loss on a liquidating distribution to the parent.

2. **Control**
   a. Control means the parent owns 80% or more of both the voting power and total value of the stock of the liquidating corporation.

3. **Basis**
   a. Basis in property distributed to the parent is transferred to the parent, and basis in stock in the subsidiary disappears.

4. **Liabilities**
   a. No gain is recognized on distributions that satisfy obligations of the subsidiary to the parent.

5. **Tax Attributes**
   a. Tax attributes of the subsidiary, such as NOLs and capital losses, carry over to the parent. The holding period will include that of the subsidiary.

6. **Minority Shareholders**
   a. Complete liquidation rules apply to distributions made to shareholders other than the parent. The subsidiary recognizes gains but not losses. The shareholder recognizes gain or loss and takes FMV basis in the property.

You have completed the outline for this subunit.
Study multiple-choice questions 11 through 13 on page 385.

STOP & REVIEW

13.5 REORGANIZATIONS

1. **Overview**

   a. For federal tax purposes, a qualified reorganization of one or more corporations is considered a mere change in form of investment rather than a disposition of assets. For this reason, a general rule of nonrecognition applies to qualifying reorganizations. However, gain is recognized to the extent of boot received.

   b. Generally, the rules apply to S corporations as they do to C corporations.

2. **Shareholders**

   a. In a reorganization, a shareholder recognizes no gain or loss on an exchange of stock or securities solely for stock or securities in the same or another corporation that is a party to the reorganization.

   b. **Boot.** Gain on nonqualifying property (generally, property other than stock or securities in a corporation that is a party to the reorganization) is recognized.

      1) The amount recognized is the lesser of gain realized or FMV of nonqualifying property.

      2) Securities received when none are surrendered are nonqualifying property.

         a) The FMV of any excess of face value received over that given up is boot.

      3) **Character.** The shareholder is deemed to have received only stock and then to have redeemed the stock for cash.

         a) Gain is treated as a dividend (OI) to the extent of E&P, if the exchange has the effect of a dividend distribution.

   c. Loss. No loss is recognized.

   d. Basis in stock or qualified securities received is exchanged.

      1) Basis in boot is (tax) cost.

3. **Transferor Corporation (Acquired or Purchased)**

   a. A corporation that is a party to a reorganization generally recognizes no gain or loss on exchange of property solely for stock or securities of another corporate party.

   b. Gain is recognized only on boot not distributed (by the transferee). Liability relief is not boot unless it was for a nonbusiness or tax-avoidance purpose.

   c. The transferor (acquired) corporation recognizes gain realized if it distributes property other than stock or securities of another corporate party.

      1) The amount of liability in excess of basis is treated as the FMV of the property.
      2) No loss is recognized unless distribution is to a creditor.

   d. The transferor (acquired) corporation, finally, recognizes no gain or loss on distribution (even if the distribution is to a creditor) of

      1) Stock or securities it received from a party to the reorganization
      2) Boot received, except for post-acquisition gain realized

4. **Transferee Corporation (Acquiring or Purchasing)**

   a. The transferee corporation recognizes gain only on appreciated property (but not its own stock or securities) exchanged.

   b. Basis in property acquired from the transferor is transferred, i.e., the basis of the property

      1) In the hands of the transferor corporation, plus
      2) Gain recognized by the transferor corporation.

   > **SUCCESS TIP**
   > The CPA Exam has required candidates to determine from a series of facts whether a qualified reorganization has occurred. It also has tested candidates on the basic characteristics of the types of reorganizations.

5. **Reorganization Types**

   a. Nonrecognition treatment applies only if the change in corporate structure fits within the definition of one of the following specific reorganization types.

      1) **Type A: Statutory merger or consolidation.** Under state law, two corporations merge into one. Stock in the non-surviving corporation is canceled. In exchange, its shareholders receive stock in the surviving corporation.

         a) Merger. One of the corporations remains, while the other is no longer in existence.
         b) Consolidation. Existing corporations are combined into a newly formed corporation.

      2) **Type B: Stock-for-stock.** Shareholders acquire stock of a corporation solely for part or all of the voting stock of the acquiring corporation or its parent.

         a) No boot is allowed.
         b) The acquiring corporation must control the acquired corporation after the exchange; i.e., it must own 80% of the stock (voting and all other).

      3) **Type C: Stock-for-assets.** One corporation acquires substantially all the assets of another in exchange for its voting stock (or its parent's). The transferor (sale of assets) corporation must liquidate.

         a) Only 20% of the assets acquired may be exchanged for other than voting stock of the acquiring corporation. Limited amounts of boot are thus allowable.
         b) "Substantially all assets" means ≥ 90% of the FMV of net assets and ≥ 70% of gross assets.

4) **Type D: Division**
    a) A corporation transfers all or part of its assets to another in exchange for the other's stock.
    b) The transferor or its shareholders must control the transferee after the exchange. Control means owning 80% of voting power and 80% of each class of nonvoting stock.
    c) The stock or securities of the controlled corporation must be distributed to shareholders of the corporation that transferred assets to the controlled corporation.
    d) Distribution of the stock need not be pro rata among the shareholders of the corporation that transferred assets to the controlled corporation. Thus, division of the original corporation may result.
5) **Type E: Recapitalization.** The capital structure of the corporation is modified by exchanges of stock and securities between the corporation and its shareholders.
6) **Type F: Reincorporation.** Stock and securities are exchanged upon a mere change in the name, form, or place of incorporation.
7) **Type G: Bankruptcy reorganization.** Stock, securities, and property are exchanged pursuant to a court-supervised bankruptcy proceeding.

6. **Nonrecognition Requirements**
    a. Nonrecognition applies only to the extent each of several statutory and judicially sourced requirements are met.
        1) The reorganization must be pursuant to a plan, a copy of which is filed with the tax return of each participating corporation.
        2) Nonrecognition treatment applies only with respect to distributions in exchange for stock or securities of a corporation that is a party to the reorganization.
        3) Business purpose, other than tax avoidance, must be present.
        4) Owners of the reorganized enterprise(s) must retain an interest in the continuing enterprise. At least 40% continuity of equity interest by value is a benchmark.
        5) Continuity of business enterprise. The acquiring corporation must continue either operating the historic business of the acquired corporation or using a significant portion of the acquired corporation's historic business assets. Continuing a significant line of business is sufficient if there was more than one.

You have completed the outline for this subunit.
Study multiple-choice questions 14 through 16 beginning on page 386.

STOP & REVIEW

13.6 MULTIPLE JURISDICTIONS

1. **Multijurisdictional Issues for State Taxes**

    a. A tax jurisdiction is a geographic area with its own distinct set of tax rules and regulations, e.g., a municipality, county, state, or country. When a taxable transaction has occurred across multiple jurisdictions, authoritative guidance must be established in order to reconcile or override the distinct sets of tax rules that may apply.

        1) The Foreign Tax Credit presented in Study Unit 8, Subunit 1, is an example of a multijurisdictional issue.

    b. This subunit explains two of the longest-standing rules for interstate taxation: Public Law (PL) 86-272 and the Uniform Division of Income for Tax Purposes Act (UDITPA). Although the applicable taxes are state (not federal) taxes, these rules are tested as federal taxation by the AICPA because they are established at the federal level.

2. **Cross-Boundary Taxation**

    a. In general, a **nexus** (also called sufficient physical presence) is a connection. In tax law, a "foreign" entity (not a citizen of a given tax jurisdiction, e.g., city, county, state, nation) is required to have a nexus to the tax jurisdiction before a sales tax or income tax may be imposed on the activities of that entity.

        1) For example, Internet sales by online retailers resulted in no sales or income taxes being paid on sales made within the borders of many taxing authorities. For a long time, states have been trying to capture revenue from online sales made inside their states, and states recently won a major victory. The threshold for substantive physical presence within a state has decreased, so businesses now face sales tax collection in more states than previously. Foreign companies have also tried to recapture sales, income, and value-added taxes.

3. **Sales Tax**

    a. In 1967 and 1992, the U.S. Supreme Court ruled that states cannot collect sales taxes on retailers unless there is a physical presence (nexus) within the state. In 2018, the U.S. Supreme Court reversed direction and ruled in the Wayfair case that the physical presence test of the prior cases was unsound and incorrect. This has resulted in almost every state adopting an economic nexus threshold, which emphasizes sales activities within the state.

    b. For sales taxes, a business might have nexus if it has

        1) A physical location in the state,
        2) Resident employees working in the state,
        3) Real or intangible property (owned or rented) within the state,
        4) Employees who regularly solicit business within the state, or
        5) Significant sales or transactions within the state.

    c. Forwarding services in states without sales taxes (e.g., Oregon) have been used to avoid the sales tax; however, if that occurs, the sale may be traced back up the distribution chain.

    d. An entity is generally allowed to offset taxes paid to another jurisdiction either by a direct tax credit for U.S. taxes or a deduction of the foreign taxes paid.

        1) For the tax credit, the payer must not receive a specific benefit from paying the tax. The right to engage in business is not considered a benefit for this purpose.

SU 13: Corporate Tax Special Topics 369

4. **Income Tax**

   a. The form of organization may influence how cross-border events and transactions are taxed.

   1) A **branch** is not a separate legal entity of the parent company, but is a legal extension of the head office. The parent company is subject to taxes on all income, not just branch income.

   2) A **subsidiary** is a separate legal entity owned by a parent company. The most common are single-member limited liability corporations (LLCs), which are pass-through entities in which the owner pays the income tax. However, a subsidiary may be set up so the income does not pass through to the owner.

5. **Public Law 86-272 (Interstate Act of 1959)**

   a. Before a state can tax a nonresident (e.g., a resident of another state), a minimum presence in the taxing state by the nonresident must be established. As mentioned on the previous page, sufficient presence to tax the nonresident is nexus.

   b. Public Law 86-272 limits the state's ability to tax the net income of nonresidents by establishing the following nexus rules:

   1) Nexus is not established if

      a) Activity is limited to solicitation of orders for tangible personal property,
      b) The orders are sent out of state for approval or rejection, and
      c) The orders are filled by shipment or delivery from a point outside the state if approved.

   c. The Multistate Tax Commission's (MTC's) "Statement of Information Concerning Practices of Multistate Tax Commission and Signatory States Under Public Law 86-272" lists the following as **protected in-state activities** (i.e., they will not establish nexus for income tax):

   1) Soliciting orders for sales by any type of advertising
   2) Soliciting of orders by an in-state resident with only an "in-home" office
   3) Carrying free samples and promotional materials for display or distribution
   4) Furnishing display racks and advising customers of the products without charge
   5) Providing automobiles for conducting protected activities
   6) Passing orders, inquiries, and complaints on to the home office
   7) Missionary sales activities

      a) For example, a manufacturer's solicitation of retailers to buy the manufacturer's goods from the manufacturer's wholesale customers

   8) Coordinating shipment/delivery and providing related information without charge
   9) Checking customers' inventories (e.g., reorder, but not quality control)
   10) Maintaining a sample/display room at one location for less than 14 days during the tax year
   11) Recruiting, training, and evaluating sales personnel
   12) Mediating customer complaints solely for ingratiating the sales personnel with the customer and facilitating order request
   13) Owning, leasing, using, or maintaining personal property for use in the employee's "in-home" office or automobile that is solely limited to the conducting of protected activities

d. The MTC's statement lists the following as **unprotected in-state activities** (i.e., they create nexus):
   1) Making repairs to or performing maintenance or service on the property sold or to be sold
   2) Collecting on accounts
   3) Investigating creditworthiness
   4) Installing a product at or after shipment or delivery
   5) Conducting training courses, seminars, or lectures for non-soliciting personnel
   6) Providing technical assistance or service for purposes other than the facilitation of the solicitation of orders
      a) For example, engineering assistance or design service
   7) Investigating, handling, or otherwise assisting in resolving customer complaints, other than mediating direct customer complaints with the sole purpose of ingratiating the sales personnel with the customer
   8) Approving or accepting orders
   9) Repossessing property
   10) Securing deposits on sales
   11) Picking up or replacing damaged or returned property
   12) Hiring, training, or supervising personnel (other than personnel involved only in solicitation)
   13) Using agency stock checks or any other instrument or process by which sales are made within the home state by sales personnel
   14) Maintaining a sample or display room at any one location in excess of 14 days during the tax year
   15) Carrying samples for sale, exchange, or distribution in any manner for consideration or other value

16) Owning, leasing, using, or maintaining any of the following facilities or property in-state:
    a) Repair shop
    b) Parts department
    c) Office other than "in-home" office
    d) Warehouse
    e) Meeting place for directors, officers, or employees
    f) Stocks of goods other than samples
    g) Telephone-answering service publicly attributed to the company/representative
    h) Mobile stores
    i) Real property or fixtures to real property of any kind

17) Consigning stock of goods or other tangible personal property for sale

18) Maintaining, by the employee or other representative, an office or place of business of any kind other than a qualified "in-home" office

NOTE: Generally, telephone or other public listings indicating company/employee contact at a specific location creates nexus; however, normal distribution of business cards/stationery does not create nexus.

19) Entering into or disposing of a franchise or licensing agreement or transferring related tangible personal property

20) Conducting any activity not listed as protected that is not entirely ancillary to requests for orders, even if such activity helps to increase purchases

e. The MTC's uniformity committee has issued a whitepaper on the Wayfair Implementation, but this topic is still evolving.

6. **The Uniform Division of Income for Tax Purposes Act (UDITPA)**

   a. The UDITPA was drafted by the National Conference of Commissioners on Uniform State Laws and is recommended for enactment in all states. Each state decides whether or not to adopt the act.

   b. Once nexus is established, net income must be accurately allocated or apportioned among the various jurisdictions. The UDITPA provides a uniform method for allocating and apportioning a business's income. The rules for the business's nonbusiness income are different than those for the business's business income.

   c. **Allocation** is used to identify nonbusiness income to a specific state or local taxing authority for income derived solely from assets held for investment purposes.

d. **Apportionment** uses the formula below to calculate the average amount of business income a company brings in by conducting operations within the taxing state.

$$\frac{\text{Property factor + Payroll factor + Sales factor}}{3}$$

NOTE: Most states use only the single sales factor.

1) The property factor determines the in-state use of real and tangible personal business property.

$$\frac{\text{Average value of in-state real and tangible personal property used}}{\text{Average value of all real and tangible personal property used}}$$

 a) Property owned by the taxpayer is valued at its original cost, not the AB (i.e., no depreciation reduction).
 b) Property rented by the taxpayer is valued at eight times the net annual rental rate (rate paid minus rate received from sub-rentals).

2) The payroll factor uses amounts determined by the accounting methods of the business so that accruals are treated as paid.

$$\frac{\text{In-state compensation paid}}{\text{Total compensation paid}}$$

 a) Payroll attributed to management or maintenance or otherwise allocable to nonbusiness property should be excluded from the formula.

3) The sales factor is only for business income. Capital gains are nonbusiness income and are allocated, not apportioned.

$$\frac{\text{In-state sales}}{\text{Total sales}}$$

 a) Sales means net sales after discounts and returns.
 b) Sales shipped to a state with no taxation of the taxpayer (i.e., no nexus) may be thrown back and taxed by the shipped-from state. If neither state taxes the taxpayer, the state in which the order was taken may be apportioned the sale.

e. Nonbusiness income is all income other than business income. It is allocated, not apportioned. Specific rules apply to nonbusiness income from rents, royalties, capital gains, interest, dividends, patents, and copyrights as follows:

Property Type		Allocation Based On
Net Rents & Royalties	Real	Location of property
	Tangible Personal	Proportional use[1] or commercial domicile[2]
Capital Gains & Losses	Real	Location of property
	Tangible Personal	Location of property[3] or commercial domicile[4]
	Intangible Personal	Commercial domicile
Interest & Dividends		Commercial domicile
Patent & Copyright Royalties		Proportional use[1] or commercial domicile[2]

[1] Proportional use within the taxing state
[2] The taxpayer's commercial domicile (i.e., home state) if the taxpayer is not organized or taxed in the state the property is used
[3] Location of property at time of sale
[4] The taxpayer's commercial domicile if the taxpayer is not taxed in the state the property is located at time of sale

f. If the allocation and apportionment provisions do not fairly represent the taxpayer's in-state activity, the taxpayer may request or the state may require
   1) Separate accounting (typically costly and difficult to carry out),
   2) The exclusion of any one or more factors,
   3) The inclusion of one or more additional factors, or
   4) The employment of any other method to equitably allocate and apportion the income.

EXAMPLE 13-7   Apportionment of Business Income (All Factors Weighted Singly)

ABC Corporation, with headquarters in Kansas, has operations in Kansas, Montana, and Oklahoma. In the current year, ABC generates business income of $375,000. ABC has the following property, payroll, and sales in the states where it operates:

State	Average Property	Average Payroll	Average Sales	Nonbusiness Income
Kansas	$250,000	$ 60,000	$500,000	$ 60,000
Montana	100,000	20,000	200,000	20,000
Oklahoma	50,000	20,000	100,000	20,000
	$400,000	$100,000	$800,000	$100,000

For Kansas,

Property factor is 62.5% ($250,000 ÷ $400,000)
Payroll factor is 60% ($60,000 ÷ $100,000)
Sales factor is 62.5% ($500,000 ÷ $800,000)
Weighted factor = 61.667%
Apportioned income = $231,250 ($375,000 × 61.667%)

For Montana,

Property factor is 25% ($100,000 ÷ $400,000)
Payroll factor is 20% ($20,000 ÷ $100,000)
Sales factor is 25% ($200,000 ÷ $800,000)
Weighted factor = 23.3333%
Apportioned income = $87,500 ($375,000 × 23.3333%)

For Oklahoma,

Property factor is 12.5% ($50,000 ÷ $400,000)
Payroll factor is 20% ($20,000 ÷ $100,000)
Sales factor is 12.5% ($100,000 ÷ $800,000)
Weighted factor = 15%
Apportioned income = $56,250 ($375,000 × 15%)

State	Apportioned Income	Allocated Income	Taxable Income
Kansas	$231,250	$60,000	$291,250
Montana	87,500	20,000	107,500
Oklahoma	56,250	20,000	76,250

7. Multijurisdictional Issues for Multinational Transactions

a. Noncorporate U.S. taxpayers are subject to tax on worldwide income. This may result in the income being subject to double-taxation. In an effort to mitigate double-taxation, various allowances have been made (e.g., foreign earned income exclusion, Foreign Tax Credit). These allowances, to varying degrees, give up U.S. jurisdiction over foreign income.

b. However, corporate taxpayers have moved from a worldwide system of taxation to a quasi-territorial system of taxation. The result is that the foreign-sourced income of foreign corporations at least 10% owned by U.S. corporations is not subject to U.S. taxation (the participation exemption) with some notable and significant exceptions (e.g., Subpart F, GILTI).

   1) Nonresident aliens are usually only subject to U.S. income tax on U.S. source income. The table below shows the general rules for determining U.S. source income of nonresident aliens.

General Rules for Income Source

Item of Income	Factor Determining Source
Salaries, wages, other compensation	Where services performed

Business Income:
  Personal services
  Sale of inventory – purchased
  Sale of inventory – produced
	
	Where services performed
	Where sold
	Where produced (Allocation may be necessary)

Interest	Residence of payer
Dividends	Whether a U.S. or foreign corporation*
Rents	Location of property

Royalties:
  Natural resources
  Patents, copyrights, etc.
	
	Location of property
	Where property is used

Sale of real property	Location of property
Sale of personal property	Generally seller's tax home
Pension distributions attributable to contributions	Where services were performed that earned the pension
Investment earnings on pension contributions	Location of pension trust
Sale of natural resources	Allocation based on fair market value of product at export terminal
Scholarships Fellowships	Generally, the residence of the payer
*Exceptions include Part of a dividend paid by a foreign corporation is U.S. source income if at least 25% of the corporation's gross income for the preceding 3 tax years before the year in which the dividends are declared is effectively connected with a U.S. trade or business.	

- c. U.S. tax law attempts to reclaim some of the lost income due to the surrendering of jurisdiction, especially when the taxpayer's accounting practices are perceived as simply a means to avoid U.S. tax law or for certain types of income (e.g., Subpart F income, which is covered in item 11.h. in Study Unit 4, Subunit 1).
- d. Transfer pricing is an accounting practice used to determine proper tax treatment of transactions between related entities, one of which is domestic and the other foreign.
    1) The taxpayer's goal in the allocation of income and deductions is to minimize global tax liabilities. Since the foreign parent corporations do not normally do business in the U.S., their income is free from U.S. tax.
    2) To prevent improper avoidance, the IRS may attempt to reallocate items affecting taxable income as if the transactions were conducted in an arm's-length transaction between uncontrolled parties.

8. **Base-Erosion and Anti-Abuse Tax (BEAT)**
   - a. The Tax Cuts and Jobs Act added Sec. 59A, *Payments of Taxpayers With Substantial Gross Receipts*, which imposes on each applicable taxpayer a tax equal to the base erosion minimum tax amount for the taxable year.
       1) Section 59A applies to base erosion payments to related foreign persons paid or accrued in taxable years beginning after December 31, 2017.
           a) A **base erosion payment** is any amount paid or accrued for which a deduction is allowable by an applicable taxpayer to a foreign person that is a related party with respect to which a deduction is allowable.
           b) Generally, a related person is
               i) Any 25% owner of (a) the total voting power of all classes of stock of the applicable taxpayer entitled to vote or (b) the total value of all classes of stock of such applicable taxpayer
               ii) Any person who is related to the applicable taxpayer within the meaning of Sec. 267(b) or Sec. 482 or any 25% owner of the applicable taxpayer
   - b. An applicable taxpayer is, with respect to any tax year, a taxpayer who meets all of the following three criteria:
       1) The taxpayer is a corporation other than a regulated investment company, a real estate investment trust, or an S corporation.
       2) The taxpayer has average annual gross receipts for the 3-tax-year period ending with the preceding taxable year that are at least $500 million (the **"gross receipts test"**).
       3) The taxpayer has a base erosion percentage for the tax year of 3% or higher or 2% or higher for a taxpayer who is a member of an affiliated group, including a bank or a registered securities dealer as defined in Sec. 59A(b)(3)(B) (the **"base erosion percentage test"**).
           a) A **base erosion tax benefit** is generally any deduction that is allowed for the tax year for any base erosion payment.
           b) The **base erosion percentage** is the aggregate amount of base erosion tax benefits of the taxpayer for the tax year divided by all allowable deductions.
   - c. The **base erosion minimum tax** amount for the tax year is the excess of 10% of the modified taxable income of the applicable taxpayer for the tax year over the applicable taxpayer's regular tax liability reduced by certain specified tax credits.

9. **Global Intangible Low-Taxed Income (GILTI)**

From Form 8992

Part I — Net Controlled Foreign Corporation (CFC) Tested Income

1. Sum of Pro Rata Share of Net Tested Income

   If the U.S. shareholder is not a member of a U.S. consolidated group, enter the total from Form 8992, Schedule A, line 1, column (e).

   If the U.S. shareholder is a member of a U.S. consolidated group, enter the amount from Schedule B (Form 8992), Part II, column (c), that pertains to the U.S. shareholder. **1**

2. Sum of Pro Rata Share of Net Tested Loss

   If the U.S. shareholder is not a member of a U.S. consolidated group, enter the total from Form 8992, Schedule A, line 1, column (f).

   If the U.S. shareholder is a member of a U.S. consolidated group, enter the amount from Schedule B (Form 8992), Part II, column (f), that pertains to the U.S. shareholder. ..... **2** ( )

3. Net CFC Tested Income. Combine lines 1 and 2. If zero or less, stop here **3**

Part II — Calculation of Global Intangible Low-Taxed Income (GILTI)

1. Net CFC Tested Income. Enter amount from Part I, line 3 ..... **1**

2. Deemed Tangible Income Return (DTIR)

   If the U.S. shareholder is not a member of a U.S. consolidated group, multiply the total from Form 8992, Schedule A, line 1, column (g), by 10% (0.10).

   If the U.S. shareholder is a member of a U.S. consolidated group, enter the amount from Schedule B (Form 8992), Part II, column (i), that pertains to the U.S. shareholder. **2**

3a. Sum of Pro Rata Share of Tested Interest Expense

   If the U.S. shareholder is not a member of a U.S. consolidated group, enter the total from Form 8992, Schedule A, line 1, column (j).

   If the U.S. shareholder is a member of a U.S. consolidated group, leave line 3a blank. **3a**

b. Sum of Pro Rata Share of Tested Interest Income

   If the U.S. shareholder is not a member of a U.S. consolidated group, enter the total from Form 8992, Schedule A, line 1, column (i).

   If the U.S. shareholder is a member of a U.S. consolidated group, leave line 3b blank. **3b**

c. Specified Interest Expense

   If the U.S. shareholder is not a member of a U.S. consolidated group, subtract line 3b from line 3a. If zero or less, enter -0-.

   If the U.S. shareholder is a member of a U.S. consolidated group, enter the amount from Schedule B (Form 8992), Part II, column (m), that pertains to the U.S. shareholder. **3c**

4. Net DTIR. Subtract line 3c from line 2. If zero or less, enter -0- **4**

5. GILTI. Subtract line 4 from line 1 ..... **5**

Schedule A — Schedule A for U.S. Shareholder Calculation of Global Intangible Low-Taxed Income (GILTI)

Name of person filing this form | **A** Identifying number

Name of U.S. shareholder | **B** Identifying number

(a) Name of CFC	(b) EIN or Reference ID	Calculations for Net Tested Income (see instructions)									GILTI Allocated to Tested Income CFCs (see instructions)	
		(c) Tested Income	(d) Tested Loss	(e) Pro Rata Share of Tested Income	(f) Pro Rata Share of Tested Loss	(g) Pro Rata Share of Qualified Business Asset Investment (QBAI)	(h) Pro Rata Share of QBAI Amount	(i) Pro Rata Share of Tested Loss Income	(j) Pro Rata Share of Tested Interest Expense	(k) GILTI Allocation Ratio (Divide Col. (e) by Col. (e), Line 1 Total)	(l) GILTI Allocated to Tested Income CFCs (Multiply Form 8992, Part II, Line 5, by Col. (k))
			( )		( )		( )				

a. In an attempt to encourage the return of intangible property to the U.S., new provisions have been created to move U.S. taxation to a more territorial system than the historical taxation on worldwide income discussed in item 7., beginning on page 374.

   1) These provisions are for GILTI (a penalty) and foreign-derived intangible income (FDII) (an incentive).

      a) GILTI income is certain foreign-sourced income that is included in U.S. corporate income. But a 50% deduction is allowed for GILTI income.

      b) This means that GILTI is effectively a 10.5% minimum tax on certain global income. The 10.5% is derived from 21% corporate tax rate less the 50% GILTI deduction.

b. A domestic taxpayer (e.g., individual, corporation, partnership, trust, or estate) who owns at least 10% of the value or voting rights in one or more controlled foreign corporations (CFCs) will be required to include its GILTI as currently taxable income, regardless of whether any amount is distributed to the shareholder.

c. The basic calculation and components are illustrated and defined as follows:

   1) Part I of Form 8992: Net CFC tested income = Sum of pro rata share CFC tested income − Sum of pro rata share CFC tested loss

      a) Tested income/loss = Gross income (less exclusions) − Deductions (including taxes) allocable to the income

   2) **Qualified Business Asset Investment (QBAI)** basically includes the adjusted basis of tangible property used in the business and depreciable property. In essence, if a corporation earns a return in excess of 10% of their QBAI, they will face a GILTI inclusion of the excess return.

   3) **Specified interest expense** is the amount of interest expense taken into account in determining the net CFC tested income for the taxable year to the extent the interest income attributable to that expense is not taken into account in determining the net CFC tested income.

   4) Accordingly, the following is the formula for calculating GILTI:

   GILTI = Net CFC tested income − [(10% × QBAI) − Specified interest expense]

   where [(10% × QBAI) − Specified interest expense] is the Net deemed tangible income return.

d. Taxpayers can use the Foreign Tax Credit to offset GILTI with two important limitations. First usage of a GILTI FTC is limited to 80% of the otherwise allowable FTC. Second, there is no carryover of an unused GILTI FTC.

10. Foreign-Derived Intangible Income (FDII)

a. To encourage the placement of intangible assets in the U.S., the FDII provision allows a 37.5% deduction for certain qualifying income, in effect providing a 13.125% tax rate for FDII income [21% – (1 – .375)].

b. For the domestic C corporate deduction of intangible income, there are several factors that qualify income as FDII. The following questions help determine if the income qualifies:

1) Is the income deduction-eligible income?

   a) This is gross income less exceptions and allocable deductions. A fraction of the intangible portion of this amount will make up the FDII. The intangible portion is calculated similar to GILTI by subtracting 10% of QBAI from the deduction-eligible income. The gross income amount does not include

      i) Subpart F income
      ii) GILTI
      iii) Finance service income
      iv) CFC dividends received
      v) Domestic oil and gas extraction income
      vi) Foreign branch income

2) Is the income foreign-derived deduction-eligible income?

   a) This question is answered by the answers to the following questions:

      i) Was the property sold to a non-U.S. person or the service provided outside the U.S., and in the case of property sold, was it for use, consumption, or disposition not within the U.S.?

      ii) Was the property sold or service provided to an unrelated domestic intermediary? If so, the income is not foreign even if it is subsequently sold to or provided for a foreign use.

      iii) Was the property sold to a non-U.S. person or the service provided outside the U.S. to a related party, as defined in item 3. in Study Unit 12, Subunit 2, except with a 50% threshold instead of 80%, who is not a U.S. person? If so, the subsequent sale or service to an unrelated party must be foreign as well, i.e., not sold or provided to a U.S. person.

c. The calculation for FDII is as follows:

$$\text{FDII} = \text{Deemed intangible income} \times \frac{\text{Foreign-derived deduction-eligible income}}{\text{Deduction-eligible income}}$$

Deemed intangible income = Deduction-eligible income – (10% × QBAI)
$\qquad\qquad\qquad\qquad\qquad\qquad\qquad\qquad\qquad\underbrace{\qquad\qquad\qquad\qquad}_{\text{Deemed tangible income return}}$

Deduction-eligible income = Gross income – Exceptions – Allocable deductions

SU 13: Corporate Tax Special Topics

11. Federal Filing Requirements for Cross-Border Business Investments

a. A tax return must be filed if a foreign corporation is engaged in a trade or business in the U.S.

b. U.S. citizens and residents are taxed on world-wide income regardless of where they live. The income that needs to be reported on a U.S. tax return includes, but is not limited to, earned and unearned income, such as wages, salary and tips, interest, dividends, capital gains, pensions, rents, and royalties. This is true even if the income is nontaxable under Internal Revenue Code or treaty.

c. Nonresident aliens are generally subject to U.S. income taxes only on their U.S.-source income. Passive income (e.g., interest, dividends, rents, and royalties) is generally taxed at a flat rate of 30% unless a tax treaty specifies a lower rate. Nonpassive income "effectively connected" to a U.S. trade or business is taxed at the same rates as citizens and residents.

d. Another significant filing requirement is the reporting of foreign financial accounts and specified foreign assets. Generally, any U.S. citizen, resident, or person doing business in the United States who has an ownership interest in or signatory authority or other authority over any number of financial accounts in a foreign country with an aggregate value in excess of $10,000 at any time during the calendar year must file a Form FinCEN Report 114, *Report of Foreign Bank and Financial Accounts* (commonly referred to as an FBAR), reporting certain information with respect to those accounts by April 15 of the subsequent year or the extension due date of October 15, if applicable.

   1) Failure to file an FBAR is subject to both civil and criminal penalties. A related form is Part III of Form 1040 Schedule B. This is presented below and assists taxpayers in making sure they comply with foreign account reporting rules.

From Form 1040 Schedule B

Part III	You must complete this part if you (a) had over $1,500 of taxable interest or ordinary dividends; (b) had a foreign account; or (c) received a distribution from, or were a grantor of, or a transferor to, a foreign trust.	Yes	No
Foreign Accounts and Trusts	**7a** At any time during [Year], did you have a financial interest in or signature authority over a financial account (such as a bank account, securities account, or brokerage account) located in a foreign country? See instructions		
Caution: If required, failure to file FinCEN Form 114 may result in substantial penalties. See instructions.	If "Yes," are you required to file FinCEN Form 114, Report of Foreign Bank and Financial Accounts (FBAR), to report that financial interest or signature authority? See FinCEN Form 114 and its instructions for filing requirements and exceptions to those requirements		
	b If you are required to file FinCEN Form 114, enter the name of the foreign country where the financial account is located ▶		
	8 During [Year], did you receive a distribution from, or were you the grantor of, or transferor to, a foreign trust? If "Yes," you may have to file Form 3520. See instructions		

For Paperwork Reduction Act Notice, see your tax return instructions.   Cat. No. 17146N   Schedule B (Form 1040) [Year]

2) Individuals must use Form 8938 to report specified foreign financial assets with an aggregate value that exceeds $50,000 on the last day of the year or exceeds $75,000 at any time during the tax year (this threshold is doubled for married individuals filing jointly).

   a) Form 8938 is required to be filed with an individual's annual income tax return. Individuals not required to file an annual income tax return are not required to file Form 8938.

3) The purposes of Form 8938 and the FBAR are similar, and there is significant overlap. Yet, filing Form 8938 does not relieve an individual of the requirement to file an FBAR. Many individuals will be required to file both Form 8938 and an FBAR to report substantially the same information.

   a) Despite the similarities, there are some differences between Form 8938 and the FBAR. The FBAR is not filed with an individual's federal income tax return to the IRS, but is instead filed electronically through the Bank Secrecy Act (BSA) e-file system with the Treasury's Financial Crimes Enforcement Network (FinCEN).

12. **Tax Withholding in the U.S.**

    a. Three types of tax withholding are imposed in the U.S., depending on the payment source:

       1) Wages earned, e.g., income tax, Social Security, and Medicare.

       2) Generally, payments (mainly of passive income) to foreign persons, including nonresident aliens, foreign corporations, foreign partnerships, and foreign partners in U.S. partnerships. The withholding rate for these payments is generally 30%.

       3) Backup withholding on dividends and interest if

          a) A person fails to provide a tax identification number to the payer or
          b) The IRS has notified the payer that the payer must withhold taxes.

    b. The payer must send the withheld amounts to the IRS, and excess withholding is refunded to the payee after an annual tax return has been filed.

You have completed the outline for this subunit.
Study multiple-choice questions 17 through 20 beginning on page 387.

STOP & REVIEW

QUESTIONS

13.1 Redemptions

1. Elm Corp. is an accrual-basis, calendar-year C corporation with 100,000 shares of voting common stock issued and outstanding as of December 30, Year 1. On December 31, Year 1, Hall surrendered 2,000 shares of Elm stock to Elm in exchange for $33,000 cash. Hall had no direct or indirect interest in Elm after the stock surrender. Additional information follows:

Hall's adjusted basis in 2,000 shares of Elm on December 31, Year 1 ($8 per share)	$16,000
Elm's accumulated earnings and profits at January 1, Year 1	25,000
Elm's Year 1 net operating loss	(7,000)

What amount of income did Hall recognize from the stock surrender?

A. $33,000 dividend.
B. $25,000 dividend.
C. $18,000 capital gain.
D. $17,000 capital gain.

Answer (D) is correct.
REQUIRED: The income recognized from a stock redemption.
DISCUSSION: In the case of a stock redemption in complete liquidation of a shareholder's interest, the redemption is treated as a sale or exchange of a capital asset. Therefore, Hall's income from the redemption is a $17,000 capital gain ($33,000 – $16,000 basis).
Answer (A) is incorrect. The amount of cash exchanged for the Elm stock is $33,000. **Answer (B) is incorrect.** The amount of Elm's accumulated earnings and profits at January 1, Year 1, is $25,000. **Answer (C) is incorrect.** The difference between Elm's accumulated earnings and profits and Elm's Year 1 net operating loss is $18,000.

2. Zeb, an individual shareholder, owned 25% of Towne Corporation stock. Pursuant to a series of stock redemptions, Towne redeemed 10% of the shares of stock Zeb owned in exchange for land having a fair market value of $30,000 and an adjusted basis of $10,000. Zeb's basis for all of his Towne stock was $200,000. Zeb reported the redemption transaction as if it were a dividend. Zeb's basis in the land and his Towne stock (immediately after the redemption) is

A. Land, $30,000; stock, $200,000.
B. Land, $30,000; stock, $180,000.
C. Land, $10,000; stock, $200,000.
D. Land, $20,000; stock, $200,000.

Answer (A) is correct.
REQUIRED: The basis in land received in a redemption of stock treated as a dividend, and the basis in the stock after the redemption.
DISCUSSION: If a redemption of shares does not qualify as a sale or exchange, it is treated as a dividend. The amount of a dividend distribution is the amount of money received plus the fair market value of the property received. Zeb has a $30,000 dividend. The basis of property received in a distribution is the FMV of such property. Therefore, Zeb's basis in the land is $30,000. A dividend distribution does not affect the basis in a shareholder's stock, so Zeb's stock basis remains $200,000.

3. All of the following statements regarding stock redemptions are true **except**

A. A redemption occurs when a corporation reacquires its stock in exchange for property.
B. The term property includes money, securities, and any other property except stock in the distributing corporation.
C. The stock that is redeemed by a corporation may not be held as treasury stock.
D. Redemptions that are not complete or partial liquidations can be distributions in part or full payment for the stock surrendered.

Answer (C) is correct.
REQUIRED: The statement regarding stock redemptions that is false.
DISCUSSION: Section 317(b) states that stock is treated as redeemed by a corporation if the corporation acquires its stock from a shareholder in exchange for property, whether or not the acquired stock is canceled, retired, or held as treasury stock.
Answer (A) is incorrect. The statement is true, since Sec. 317(b) provides that stock is treated as redeemed when a corporation acquires its own stock from a shareholder in exchange for property. Answer (B) is incorrect. The statement is true, since property, as defined by Sec. 317(a), includes anything distributed by a corporation except its own stock or rights to acquire its own stock. Answer (D) is incorrect. The statement is true, since, under Sec. 302, several types of redemptions are treated as part or full payment for the stock even though there is no partial or complete liquidation of the corporation.

4. Corporation H has 1,000 shares of stock issued and outstanding. Mr. K, the founder, owns 40% of the stock, his wife owns 10%, his son owns 20%, and the balance is owned by unrelated parties. Under the constructive ownership rules of the stock redemption provisions, what percentage of stock is Mr. K considered to own?

A. 50%
B. 60%
C. 70%
D. 100%

Answer (C) is correct.
REQUIRED: The percentage of stock a taxpayer is considered to own under the constructive ownership rules for a stock redemption.
DISCUSSION: The stock redemption provisions found in Sec. 302 use the constructive ownership (attribution) rules of Sec. 318. Under the Sec. 318(a)(1) rules, an individual is considered to own the stock owned by members of his or her family including his or her spouse, children, grandchildren, and parents. Therefore, Mr. K owns 40% of the stock directly, and he indirectly owns the stock owned by his wife and son. Mr. K has direct and indirect ownership of 70% (40% + 20% + 10%) of Corporation H. For that matter, so do his wife and son.
Answer (A) is incorrect. His son's ownership of 20% should be included as part of his constructive ownership. Answer (B) is incorrect. His wife's ownership of 10% should be included as part of his constructive ownership. Answer (D) is incorrect. An individual is treated as owning stock owned by family members under Sec. 318. They include spouse, parents, grandchildren, and children.

13.2 Complete Liquidation

5. Krol Corporation distributed marketable securities in redemption of its stock in a complete liquidation. On the date of distribution, these securities had a basis of $100,000 and a fair market value of $150,000. What gain does Krol have as a result of the distribution?

A. $0
B. $50,000 capital gain.
C. $50,000 Sec. 1231 gain.
D. $50,000 ordinary gain.

Answer (B) is correct.
REQUIRED: The gain to a corporation on distribution of property in redemption of its stock in a complete liquidation.
DISCUSSION: Gain or loss is recognized when a corporation distributes property as part of a complete liquidation. Krol recognizes a $50,000 gain ($150,000 FMV – $100,000 AB). It is a capital gain because the marketable securities are a capital asset.
Answer (A) is incorrect. A corporation must recognize any gain it realizes on distribution of property in redemption of its stock in a complete liquidation. Answer (C) is incorrect. Marketable securities are usually not used in trade or business and are thus not Sec. 1231 properties. Answer (D) is incorrect. Marketable securities are capital assets.

6. A corporation was completely liquidated and dissolved during the current year. The filing fees, professional fees, and other expenditures incurred in connection with the liquidation and dissolution are

A. Deductible in full by the dissolved corporation.
B. Deductible by the shareholders and not by the corporation.
C. Treated as capital losses by the corporation.
D. Not deductible by either the corporation or the shareholders.

Answer (A) is correct.
REQUIRED: The tax treatment for expenses incurred in connection with a corporate liquidation.
DISCUSSION: The filing fees, professional fees, and other liquidation-related expenses are deductible in the final tax return of the corporation.
Answer (B) is incorrect. The expense is not incurred by the shareholders. Therefore, the shareholders cannot deduct them. Answer (C) is incorrect. The expenses are deductible as trade or business expenses. Answer (D) is incorrect. The expenses are deductible by the corporation.

7. As part of a complete liquidation, a C corporation distributed the following assets to unrelated individual shareholders:

	Basis	FMV
Investment land	$500,000	$540,000
Inventory	130,000	150,000
Marketable securities	70,000	20,000

What is the amount of capital gain?

A. $10,000 net capital loss.
B. $40,000 capital gain.
C. $10,000 net capital gain.
D. No capital gain or loss.

Answer (A) is correct.
REQUIRED: The corporate gains on complete liquidation.
DISCUSSION: A corporation recognizes any gain or loss on distributions in complete liquidation as if the property were sold at its FMV to the shareholder immediately before the distribution. The character of amounts recognized depends on the nature of the asset in the hands of the distributing corporation. The $10,000 net capital loss is calculated as the $40,000 capital gain (FMV of the land less basis) – $50,000 capital loss (FMV of the marketable securities less basis). The inventory's $20,000 gain (FMV of the inventory less basis) retains its ordinary income character; thus, the gain on inventory is recognized as ordinary income and not as capital gain.
Answer (B) is incorrect. A capital gain of $40,000 omits marketable securities from the calculation. Answer (C) is incorrect. A $10,000 net capital gain includes the ordinary income recognized on the inventory. Answer (D) is incorrect. The transaction results in a capital loss.

13.3 Partial Liquidation

8. How does a noncorporate shareholder treat the gain on a redemption of stock that qualifies as a partial liquidation of the distributing corporation?

A. Entirely as capital gain.
B. Entirely as a dividend.
C. Partly as capital gain and partly as a dividend.
D. As a tax-free transaction.

Answer (A) is correct.
REQUIRED: The treatment of a partially liquidating distribution received by a noncorporate shareholder.
DISCUSSION: A redemption made in partial liquidation of an interest held by a noncorporate shareholder is treated as a distribution in exchange for the stock, i.e., a sale. The shareholder will treat any gain on the redemption as a capital gain. The amount of the distribution is the FMV of the property.

9. Ivana Dolla received property with a fair market value of $60,000 and an adjusted basis of $33,000 from Candid Corporation in partial liquidation. Candid's earnings and profits for the year prior to the distribution were $250,000. Ms. Dolla's basis in the stock she exchanged was $44,000. What is the amount of Ms. Dolla's recognized gain?

A. $11,000
B. $16,000
C. $27,000
D. $60,000

Answer (B) is correct.
REQUIRED: The amount of gain recognized by a noncorporate shareholder in a partial liquidation.
DISCUSSION: Under Sec. 302(b)(4), a redemption of an interest held by a noncorporate shareholder made in partial liquidation of the corporation is treated as a distribution in exchange for the stock. The shareholder will treat any gain on the redemption as a capital gain. The amount of the gain is computed under Sec. 1001. Under Sec. 301(b)(1), the amount of the distribution is the fair market value of the property. Ms. Dolla will recognize a gain of $16,000 on the distribution ($60,000 fair market value of the distributed property − $44,000 basis in the stock).
Answer (A) is incorrect. The gain is not the difference between the adjusted basis of the stock and the adjusted basis of the property. **Answer (C) is incorrect.** The gain is not the difference between the fair market value of the property and the adjusted basis of the property. **Answer (D) is incorrect.** The gain does not equal the fair market value of the property.

10. With respect to a partial liquidation under Sec. 302(b)(4), which of the following statements are **false**?

1. The redemption must be part of a plan.
2. The shareholder may be a corporation.
3. The redemption may be pro rata.
4. The distribution may not be made in the year after the plan was adopted.

A. 1 and 2.
B. 1 and 3.
C. 2 and 4.
D. 3 and 4.

Answer (C) is correct.
REQUIRED: The false statements regarding the partial liquidation of a corporation.
DISCUSSION: The redemption must be part of a plan, and the redemption may be pro rata. However, a shareholder that is a corporation does not qualify for partial liquidation treatment. Furthermore, a distribution may be made in the year the plan is adopted or in the succeeding tax year.
Answer (A) is incorrect. The redemption must be part of a plan. Also, the distribution can be made in the year after the plan was adopted. **Answer (B) is incorrect.** The distribution can be made in the year after the plan was adopted and that the shareholder may be a corporation. It is true that the redemption must be part of a plan and that the redemption may be pro rata. **Answer (D) is incorrect.** It is not true that the shareholder may be a corporation, but it is true that the redemption may be pro rata.

13.4 Subsidiary Liquidation

11. Forrest Corp. owned 100% of both the voting stock and total value of Diamond Corp. Both corporations were C corporations. Forrest's basis in the Diamond stock was $200,000 when it received a lump sum liquidating distribution of property as a result of the redemption of all of Diamond stock. The property had an adjusted basis of $270,000 and a fair market value of $500,000. What amount of gain did Forrest recognize on the distribution?

A. $0
B. $70,000
C. $270,000
D. $500,000

Answer (A) is correct.
REQUIRED: The recognized gain of a liquidating distribution to a parent corporation.
DISCUSSION: Neither the parent corporation nor a controlled subsidiary recognizes gain or loss on a liquidating distribution to the parent. Control means the parent owns 80% or more of both the voting power and total value of the stock of the liquidating corporation. Forrest controls Diamond because it owns 100% of the voting stock and total value of Diamond. Thus, Forrest does not recognize any gain on the liquidating distribution.
Answer (B) is incorrect. The amount of $70,000 uses the AB to calculate a gain. Special rules apply to complete liquidations between parent and controlled corporations. **Answer (C) is incorrect.** The amount of $270,000 is the AB of the distribution; however, in a complete liquidation, the amount realized is the FMV. In addition, special rules apply to complete liquidations between parent and controlled corporations. **Answer (D) is incorrect.** The amount of $500,000 is the realized gain (not recognized gain) in a complete liquidation between noncontrolling corporations. Special rules apply to complete liquidations between parent and controlled corporations.

12. When a parent corporation completely liquidates its 80%-owned subsidiary, the parent (as shareholder) will ordinarily

A. Be subject to capital gains tax on 80% of the long-term gain.
B. Be subject to capital gains tax on 100% of the long-term gain.
C. Have to report any gain on liquidation as ordinary income.
D. Not recognize gain or loss on the liquidating distribution(s).

Answer (D) is correct.
REQUIRED: The correct statement about a complete liquidation of a subsidiary.
DISCUSSION: When a subsidiary corporation is liquidated into the parent corporation, no gain or loss is recognized on the liquidation.
Answer (A) is incorrect. The parent corporation will not be subject to capital gains tax on 80% of the long-term gain. **Answer (B) is incorrect.** The parent corporation will not be subject to capital gains tax on 100% of the long-term gain. **Answer (C) is incorrect.** The parent corporation will not have to report any gain on liquidations as ordinary income.

13. Borasco Corp. owns land with a fair market value of $200,000. Borasco purchased the land 10 years ago for $65,000 and owes a liability of $50,000 as of August 2 of the current year. Alvo Corp. owns 100% of Borasco. Borasco is completely liquidated on August 2 of the current year, according to a plan adopted on June 18 of the current year. As a result, the land is transferred to Alvo in complete cancellation of Borasco's stock. What basis does Alvo have in the land it receives?

A. $15,000
B. $65,000
C. $150,000
D. $200,000

Answer (B) is correct.
REQUIRED: The amount of basis in assets received in a subsidiary liquidation.
DISCUSSION: When a subsidiary is liquidated into its parent pursuant to a plan of reorganization, no gain or loss is recognized on distribution of assets. As no gain or loss is recognized, the basis remains the same in the hands of the parent as it was in the subsidiary. Therefore, basis is $65,000.
Answer (A) is incorrect. Basis in the land is not affected by the liability. **Answer (C) is incorrect.** Basis is not equal to the fair market value less the liability. **Answer (D) is incorrect.** Basis is not equal to fair market value.

13.5 Reorganizations

14. Jaxson Corp. has 200,000 shares of voting common stock issued and outstanding. King Corp. has decided to acquire 90% of Jaxson's voting common stock solely in exchange for 50% of its voting common stock and retain Jaxson as a subsidiary after the transaction. Which of the following statements is true?

A. King must acquire 100% of Jaxson stock for the transaction to be a tax-free reorganization.

B. The transaction will qualify as a tax-free reorganization.

C. King must issue at least 60% of its voting common stock for the transaction to qualify as a tax-free reorganization.

D. Jaxson must surrender assets for the transaction to qualify as a tax-free reorganization.

Answer (B) is correct.
REQUIRED: The requirements of a stock-for-stock acquisition.
DISCUSSION: A Type B, or stock-for-stock, acquisition qualifies as a tax-free reorganization if the shareholders of one company acquire the stock of the target company solely in exchange for stock of their company. The acquiring company must control at least 80% of the stock of the target company after the exchange.
Answer (A) is incorrect. Only 80% or more of the target company's stock must be acquired. **Answer (C) is incorrect.** There is no such requirement for a stock-for-stock reorganization. **Answer (D) is incorrect.** Assets need not be surrendered for qualification as a tax-free reorganization.

15. Pursuant to a plan of corporate reorganization adopted in July Year 1, Gow exchanged 500 shares of Lad Corp. common stock that he had bought in January Year 1 at a cost of $5,000 for 100 shares of Rook Corp. common stock having a FMV of $6,000. Gow's recognized gain on this exchange was

A. $1,000 long-term capital gain.

B. $1,000 short-term capital gain.

C. $1,000 ordinary income.

D. $0.

Answer (D) is correct.
REQUIRED: The amount of gain recognized in a corporate reorganization.
DISCUSSION: The exchange of stock for stock in obtaining control of a corporation qualifies as a reorganization. No gain or loss is recognized in a reorganization if stock or securities are exchanged solely for stock or securities in the same corporation or in another corporation that was a party to the reorganization. For Gow, since no boot was received, no gain is recognized.
Answer (A) is incorrect. The amount of $1,000 is the difference between the $6,000 of Rook Corp. common stock and $5,000 of Lad Corp. common stock. No capital gain is recognized. Long-term capital gain occurs for capital property held longer than 1 year.
Answer (B) is incorrect. The amount of $1,000 is the difference between the $6,000 of Rook Corp. common stock and $5,000 of Lad Corp. common stock. This transaction is tax-free, and no gain is recognized.
Answer (C) is incorrect. The amount of $1,000 is the difference between the $6,000 of Rook Corp. common stock and $5,000 of Lad Corp. common stock. No gain is recognized because the transaction is a stock-for-stock reorganization.

16. Ace Corp. and Bate Corp. combine in a qualifying reorganization and form Carr Corp., the only surviving corporation. This reorganization is tax-free to the

	Shareholders	Corporation
A.	Yes	Yes
B.	Yes	No
C.	No	Yes
D.	No	No

Answer (A) is correct.
REQUIRED: The taxability of reorganization.
DISCUSSION: This exchange represents a Type A statutory consolidation wherein neither the shareholders nor the corporations involved will recognize income, provided no boot is exchanged.

13.6 Multiple Jurisdictions

17. What is the general term for a single geographic area that has its own distinct set of tax rules and regulations?

A. Municipality.
B. Interstate commerce.
C. Tax jurisdiction.
D. Multijurisdictional.

Answer (C) is correct.
REQUIRED: The general term for an area with its own tax rules.
DISCUSSION: A tax jurisdiction is a geographic area that has its own distinct set of tax rules and regulations. Specific examples of tax jurisdictions include a municipality, county, state, or country.
Answer (A) is incorrect. A municipality is a specific example of a tax jurisdiction. **Answer (B) is incorrect.** Interstate commerce is commercial activity involving multiple states, each with its own distinct set of tax rules and regulations. A state is a specific example of a tax jurisdiction. **Answer (D) is incorrect.** Multijurisdictional describes issues involving more than one jurisdiction.

18. In accordance with the UDITPA, which of the following is correct for allocating interest and dividends?

A. Allocate based on the location of the property.
B. Allocate based on the commercial domicile of the taxpayer.
C. Allocate based on proportional use within the taxing state.
D. Not allocated, but apportioned with other business income.

Answer (B) is correct.
REQUIRED: The correct statement regarding allocation of interest and dividends.
DISCUSSION: Nonbusiness income means all income other than business income. It is allocated, not apportioned. Specific rules apply to nonbusiness income from rents, royalties, capital gains, interest, dividends, patents, and copyrights. Interest and dividends are allocated based on the taxpayer's commercial domicile; i.e., they are taxed by the company's "home state."
Answer (A) is incorrect. There is no physical location for interest and dividends. **Answer (C) is incorrect.** Proportional use applies to tangible personal property. Interest and dividends do not have physical characteristics to be used in any particular location. **Answer (D) is incorrect.** The UDITPA specifically classifies interest and dividends as nonbusiness property and subject to allocation.

19. Which of the following may qualify as Foreign-Derived Intangible Income (FDII)?

A. Property sold within the U.S.
B. Property sold outside the U.S. to a related party.
C. Subpart F income.
D. Finance service income.

Answer (B) is correct.
REQUIRED: The qualifying factor for FDII.
DISCUSSION: Multiple factors can affect whether income qualifies as FDII. Among those is the location where the property was sold and the relationship to the buyer. Property sold outside the U.S. to a related party may qualify, though the subsequent unrelated party sale will still need to be for foreign use.
Answer (A) is incorrect. Property must be sold outside of the U.S. to qualify as FDII. **Answer (C) is incorrect.** The gross income of the deduction-eligible income does not include Subpart F income. **Answer (D) is incorrect.** The gross income of the deduction-eligible income does not include finance service income.

20. Which of the following statements is correct regarding Base-Erosion and Anti-Abuse Tax (BEAT)?

A. The base erosion minimum tax rate is 21% for 2021.
B. The base erosion minimum tax rate is 5% for 2021.
C. The base erosion minimum tax rate is 10% for 2021.
D. The base erosion minimum tax rate is 3% for 2021.

Answer (C) is correct.
REQUIRED: The correct statement about Base-Erosion and Anti-Abuse Tax (BEAT).
DISCUSSION: The base erosion minimum tax amount for the tax year is the excess of 10% of the modified taxable income of the applicable taxpayer for the tax year over the applicable taxpayer's regular tax liability reduced by certain specified tax credits.
Answer (A) is incorrect. The tax rate of 21% represents the income tax rate for corporations. **Answer (B) is incorrect.** The base erosion minimum tax rate was 5% in the case of a tax year beginning back in 2018. It is increased to 10% for 2019 to 2025 and to 12.5% starting from 2026. **Answer (D) is incorrect.** The base erosion percentage test minimum threshold for nonaffiliated groups is 3%.

GLEIM — **GO TO ONLINE COURSE**

Access the **Gleim CPA Premium Review System** featuring our SmartAdapt technology from your Gleim Personal Classroom to continue your studies. You will experience a personalized study environment with exam-emulating multiple-choice questions.

STUDY UNIT FOURTEEN
S CORPORATIONS

(18 pages of outline)

14.1	Eligibility and Election	390
14.2	Operations	394
14.3	Distributions	402
14.4	Special Taxes	405

An S corporation is generally not subject to a federal tax on its income. Its items of income, loss, deduction, and credit are passed through to its shareholders on a per-day and per-share basis. Each shareholder is taxed on his or her share of the S corporation's income as it is earned (the qualified business income deduction is discussed in Study Unit 7, Subunit 3). Distributions of cash or property generally are not income to its shareholders.

Some candidates find it helpful to have the entire tax form side-by-side with our Knowledge Transfer Outline when studying, and others may prefer to see the final draft of a form when it is released. The full versions of the most up-to-date forms are easily accessible at www.gleim.com/taxforms. These forms and the form excerpts used in our outline are periodically updated as the latest versions are released by the IRS.

14.1 ELIGIBILITY AND ELECTION

1. **Overview**
    a. A corporation is treated as an S corporation only for those days for which each specific eligibility requirement is met and the required election is effective.

2. **Eligibility**
    a. Eligibility depends on the nature of the corporation, its shareholders, and its stock.
    b. An S corporation must have only one class of stock.
        1) Variation in voting rights of that one class of stock is permitted.
        2) Rights to profits and assets on liquidation must be identical.
        3) Debt may be treated as a disqualifying second class of stock.
    c. Issuance of debt does not disqualify S corporation status. A conversion feature or some other provision that would entitle the debtholder to control of the corporation is generally needed to disqualify S corporation status.
    d. The number of shareholders may not exceed 100.
        1) A husband and wife are considered a single shareholder for this purpose.
        2) Family members in a six-generation range are considered one shareholder.
        3) A nonresident alien (NRA) may not own any shares.
        4) Each shareholder must be either an individual (including an individual owner of a single-member LLC), an estate, or a qualified trust.
            a) Certain small business trusts and tax-exempt organizations (e.g., qualified retirement plans) can be shareholders.
            b) Partnerships, Charitable Remainder Unitrusts, and Charitable Remainder Annuity Trusts may not be shareholders.
        5) The following is a list of qualified trusts that are allowed as shareholders of an S corporation:
            a) A trust, all of which is treated as owned by an individual who is a citizen or resident of the United States.
            b) A trust described in item a) immediately before the death of the deemed owner that continues in existence after such death.
                i) This provision lasts for 2 years, beginning on the day of the deemed owner's death.
            c) A trust that receives a stock transfer pursuant to the terms of a will.
                i) This provision lasts for 2 years, beginning on the day of the stock transfer.
            d) A trust created primarily to exercise the voting power of stock transferred to it. This does not apply to any foreign trust.
    e. Certain entities cannot elect S status. These include some insurance companies, possession corporations, domestic international sales corporations (DISC) and former DISCs, and some institutions using the reserve method of accounting for bad debts.
        1) However, domestic building and loan associations, mutual savings banks, and a cooperative bank–without capital stock organized and operated for mutual purposes and without profit–are all able to elect S status.

- f. The corporation must be domestic and eligible.
    1) Ineligible corporations include financial institutions, such as banks (that use the allowance method of accounting) and insurance companies.
- g. S corporations can own C corporations or Qualified Subchapter S Subsidiaries (QSSS).
    1) A QSSS is an electing domestic corporation that qualifies as an S corporation and is 100% owned by an S corporation parent. The operations of a QSSS are included in the parent's tax return.

3. **Election**
   a. An eligible corporation must make the election for S corporation status by filing Form 2553.
   b. All shareholders at the time the election is made must file a consent.
       1) Each person who was a shareholder at any time during the part of the tax year before the election is made must also consent.
       2) If any former shareholders do not consent, the election is considered made for the following year.
   c. For an election to be effective from the first day of the same tax year, the election must be made within the first 2 1/2 months of the beginning of the corporation's tax year.
   d. Election made after the first 2 1/2 months of the corporation's tax year will become effective on the first day of the following tax year.
   e. The IRS can treat a late-filed election as timely filed if it determines that reasonable cause existed for failing to file the election in a timely manner.
   f. After revocation or termination of an election, a new election cannot be effectively made for 5 years without the consent of the IRS.
   g. The IRS can waive the effect of an invalid election resulting from failure to qualify as an S corporation and/or failing to obtain the necessary shareholder consents.

4. **Termination**
   a. Upon the occurrence of a terminating event, an S corporation becomes a C corporation.
       1) The IRS may waive termination.
           a) The terminating event must be inadvertent and corrected within a reasonable time.
   b. An S corporation election is terminated by any of the following:
       1) An effective revocation. A majority of the shareholders (voting and nonvoting) must consent.
       2) Any eligibility requirement not being satisfied on any day (e.g., a partnership or corporation becomes a shareholder).
       3) Passive investment income (PII) termination.
   c. The termination is effective as of the date the disqualifying event, other than a PII termination, occurs.

d. **PII termination** occurs when, for 3 consecutive tax years, the corporation has both Subchapter C E&P on the last day and PII that is greater than 25% of gross receipts.
   1) An S corporation does not have E&P unless it was formerly a C corporation or acquired E&P in a tax-free reorganization, e.g., a merger.
   2) Gross receipts are gross receipts of the S corporation for the tax year.
      a) This amount is reduced by capital losses (other than on stock and securities) to the extent of capital gains.
   3) PII consists of gross receipts from dividends, interest, royalties, rents, and annuities, reduced by
      a) Interest on accounts receivable (notes) for inventory sold in the ordinary course of trade or business
      b) Rents from a lease under which significant services are rendered to the lessee (those not customarily rendered)
   4) Interest includes tax-exempt interest.
   5) Receipts from sales and exchanges of stock and securities are not considered PII.
   6) Termination is effective at the beginning of the following tax year.

> **SUCCESS TIP**
> The AICPA has used theoretical questions to test candidates' knowledge of requirements for S corporation eligibility, election, and termination.

5. **Accounting Method**
   a. An S corporation is not required to use the accrual method, regardless of gross receipts. However, if inventory sales are a material part of the S corporation's operations, the accrual method must be used to calculate gross profit.
   b. Accounting method election is generally made by the S corporation.
   c. Shareholders, however, personally elect
      1) Credit or a deduction for foreign income taxes
      2) Percentage or cost depletion for oil and gas properties
      3) Treatment of mining exploration expenditures

6. **Tax Year**
   a. An S corporation generally must adopt a calendar tax year.
   b. With IRS consent, it may adopt a fiscal year, if it establishes a valid business purpose for doing so, that coincides with a natural business year.
      1) A natural business year may end with or after the end of a peak or seasonal period of a cyclical business (e.g., a ski resort closing at the end of snow season).
      2) A natural business year also exists if greater than 25% of gross receipts occur in the last 2 months of the proposed year over a 3-year period.

EXAMPLE 14-1   Fiscal Year Natural Business Year

Acme, Inc., an S corporation, provides tax preparation services. Normally its required tax year would be a calendar year. However, because greater than 25% of Acme's gross receipts have occurred in March and April over the past 3 years, Acme has a business purpose for a fiscal year ending on April 30.

c. An S corporation that deposits the equivalent amount of the deferred tax may elect a fiscal year (Sec. 444 election).
   1) A new S corporation is limited to no more than 3 months' deferral of income to its shareholders.
   2) An existing S corporation may continue to use the fiscal year previously adopted.

EXAMPLE 14-2	Fiscal Year Sec. 444 Election

Ace, Inc., a newly formed S corporation, has a required tax year ending on December 31 (i.e., a calendar year). However, Ace can make a Sec. 444 election to change its tax year so that it provides no more than 3 months of deferral. This means that Ace can elect a September 30 year end (3 months of deferral), an October 31 year end (2 months of deferral), or a November 30 year end (1 month of deferral). In order to make the election, Ace will have to make a noninterest-bearing deposit with the IRS (the deposit eliminates the time value of money savings provided by deferral).

d. To make a Sec. 444 election, an S corporation should file Form 8716 by the earlier of the 15th day of the 5th month following the 1st month of the tax year for which the election will be effective or the original due date of the tax return for the tax year resulting from the Sec. 444 election.
e. To change its tax year other than by a Sec. 444 election, an S corporation should file Form 1128 by the 15th day of the 3rd month of the new tax year.
f. When S status is terminated, creating a short year, nonseparately computed income is allocated on a pro rata basis unless certain exceptions apply or an election is made.

7. **Administration**
   a. The tax treatment of S corporation items of income, loss, deduction, and credit is determined at the corporate level.
   b. The S corporation files a tax return (Form 1120-S). The due date is the 15th day of the 3rd month following the close of the tax year (e.g., March 15 for calendar-year taxpayers).
   c. Each shareholder must report a pro rata share of income and expenses on his or her personal tax return.
      1) The shareholder's reporting must be consistent with the corporate return.
         a) An exception applies if the shareholder notifies the IRS of the inconsistency.
      2) A shareholder's pro rata share of items is reported on his or her tax return for his or her tax year in which the S corporation tax year ends.

EXAMPLE 14-3	Time of Reporting S Corporation Items

Compliance Corporation is a calendar-year S corporation. Compliance has two shareholders: Shelly, with a year end of June 30 of the current year, and Julie, with a year end of December 31 of the current year. Because Julie is a calendar-year taxpayer, she will report any current-year income from Compliance on her current-year return. Shelly, on the other hand, will report any current-year income from Compliance on her return for the following year.

d. Administrative and judicial proceedings to determine proper treatment of items are unified at the level of the S corporation.

STOP & REVIEW

You have completed the outline for this subunit.
Study multiple-choice questions 1 through 5 beginning on page 407.

14.2 OPERATIONS

1. **Exempt Taxes**

   a. Provisions that govern taxation of C corporations also govern taxation of S corporations unless a specific exception applies. S corporations are expressly exempt from the following taxes:

      1) Corporate income tax
      2) AET (accumulated earnings tax)
      3) PHC (personal holding company) tax

2. **Reported Items**

   a. The items of income, deduction (including losses), and credit of an S corporation are reported by the corporation.

From Form 1120-S

Income	1a	Gross receipts or sales	1a	
	b	Returns and allowances	1b	
	c	Balance. Subtract line 1b from line 1a		1c
	2	Cost of goods sold (attach Form 1125-A)		2
	3	Gross profit. Subtract line 2 from line 1c		3
	4	Net gain (loss) from Form 4797, line 17 (attach Form 4797)		4
	5	Other income (loss) (see instructions—attach statement)		5
	6	**Total income (loss).** Add lines 3 through 5 ▶		6
Deductions (see instructions for limitations)	7	Compensation of officers (see instructions—attach Form 1125-E)		7
	8	Salaries and wages (less employment credits)		8
	9	Repairs and maintenance		9
	10	Bad debts		10
	11	Rents		11
	12	Taxes and licenses		12
	13	Interest (see instructions)		13
	14	Depreciation not claimed on Form 1125-A or elsewhere on return (attach Form 4562)		14
	15	Depletion **(Do not deduct oil and gas depletion.)**		15
	16	Advertising		16
	17	Pension, profit-sharing, etc., plans		17
	18	Employee benefit programs		18
	19	Other deductions (attach statement)		19
	20	**Total deductions.** Add lines 7 through 19 ▶		20
	21	**Ordinary business income (loss).** Subtract line 20 from line 6		21
Tax and Payments	22a	Excess net passive income or LIFO recapture tax (see instructions)	22a	
	b	Tax from Schedule D (Form 1120-S)	22b	
	c	Add lines 22a and 22b (see instructions for additional taxes)		22c
	23a	[Year] estimated tax payments and [Year] overpayment credited to [Year]	23a	
	b	Tax deposited with Form 7004	23b	
	c	Credit for federal tax paid on fuels (attach Form 4136)	23c	
	d	Reserved for future use	23d	
	e	Add lines 23a through 23d		23e
	24	Estimated tax penalty (see instructions). Check if Form 2220 is attached ▶ ☐		24
	25	**Amount owed.** If line 23e is smaller than the total of lines 22c and 24, enter amount owed		25
	26	**Overpayment.** If line 23e is larger than the total of lines 22c and 24, enter amount overpaid		26
	27	Enter amount from line 26: Credited to [Year] estimated tax ▶ Refunded ▶		27

b. A shareholder computes taxable income by taking into account the pro rata share of items passed through from the S corporation. The shareholder reports his or her pro rata share in the tax year within which the tax year of the S corporation ended.

EXAMPLE 14-4	Shareholder Inclusion of S Corporation Items

Super, Inc., an S corporation, properly reported nonseparately stated net income from operations of $100,000 for its tax year ending November 30, Year 1. Sheldon, a calendar-year taxpayer who owns 5% of the shares of Super, Inc., must include $5,000 of ordinary income in his tax return for Year 1, which is due on or before April 15, Year 2.

3. **S Corporation Income and Deductions**

    a. An S corporation's ordinary income minus its ordinary deductions results in the S corporation's ordinary business income (loss). However, S corporation items of income, deduction, and credit, which could affect the tax liability of shareholders if taken into account by them on their personal returns, are required to be stated and passed through separately. **Separately stated items** include

        1) Section 1231 gains and losses
        2) Net short-term capital gains and losses
        3) Net long-term capital gains and losses
        4) Dividends
        5) Charitable contributions
        6) Taxes paid to a foreign country or to a U.S. possession
        7) Tax-exempt interest and related expense
        8) Investment income and related expense
        9) Amounts previously deducted (e.g., bad debts)
        10) Real estate activities
        11) Section 179 deduction (immediate expensing of new business equipment)
        12) Credits
        13) Other deductions whose separate treatment could affect a shareholder's tax liability

EXAMPLE 14-5	Separately Stated Items

ABC Corp., an S corporation, has a Sec. 1231 gain. But, because the ultimate treatment of Sec. 1231 gains depends on whether a taxpayer has a net Sec. 1231 gain or loss, the treatment of ABC's Sec. 1231 gain could vary at the shareholder level and must be separately stated. For example, for a shareholder with Sec. 1231 losses, a Sec. 1231 gain from ABC will reduce the Sec. 1231 loss amount that can offset ordinary income. Conversely, the share of ABC's Sec. 1231 gain for a shareholder with a net Sec. 1231 gain will be taxed at preferential long-term capital gains rates.

Form 1120-S (Year), Page 3

Schedule K — Shareholders' Pro Rata Share Items

Income (Loss)

1	Ordinary business income (loss) (page 1, line 21)	1
2	Net rental real estate income (loss) (attach Form 8825)	2
3a	Other gross rental income (loss) 3a	
b	Expenses from other rental activities (attach statement) . . . 3b	
c	Other net rental income (loss). Subtract line 3b from line 3a	3c
4	Interest income	4
5	Dividends: a Ordinary dividends	5a
	b Qualified dividends 5b	
6	Royalties	6
7	Net short-term capital gain (loss) (attach Schedule D (Form 1120-S))	7
8a	Net long-term capital gain (loss) (attach Schedule D (Form 1120-S))	8a
b	Collectibles (28%) gain (loss) 8b	
c	Unrecaptured section 1250 gain (attach statement) . . . 8c	
9	Net section 1231 gain (loss) (attach Form 4797)	9
10	Other income (loss) (see instructions) . . . Type ▶	10

Deductions

11	Section 179 deduction (attach Form 4562)	11
12a	Charitable contributions	12a
b	Investment interest expense	12b
c	Section 59(e)(2) expenditures . . . Type ▶	12c
d	Other deductions (see instructions) . . Type ▶	12d

Credits

13a	Low-income housing credit (section 42(j)(5))	13a
b	Low-income housing credit (other)	13b
c	Qualified rehabilitation expenditures (rental real estate) (attach Form 3468, if applicable)	13c
d	Other rental real estate credits (see instructions) Type ▶	13d
e	Other rental credits (see instructions) . . Type ▶	13e
f	Biofuel producer credit (attach Form 6478)	13f
g	Other credits (see instructions) . . . Type ▶	13g

Foreign Transactions

14a	Name of country or U.S. possession ▶	
b	Gross income from all sources	14b
c	Gross income sourced at shareholder level	14c
	Foreign gross income sourced at corporate level	
d	Reserved for future use	14d
e	Foreign branch category	14e
f	Passive category	14f
g	General category	14g
h	Other (attach statement)	14h
	Deductions allocated and apportioned at shareholder level	
i	Interest expense	14i
j	Other	14j
	Deductions allocated and apportioned at corporate level to foreign source income	
k	Reserved for future use	14k
l	Foreign branch category	14l
m	Passive category	14m
n	General category	14n
o	Other (attach statement)	14o
	Other information	
p	Total foreign taxes (check one): ☐ Paid ☐ Accrued ▶	14p
q	Reduction in taxes available for credit (attach statement)	14q
r	Other foreign tax information (attach statement)	

Form 1120-S (Year), Page 4

Schedule K — Shareholders' Pro Rata Share Items (continued)

Alternative Minimum Tax (AMT) Items

15a	Post-1986 depreciation adjustment	15a
b	Adjusted gain or loss	15b
c	Depletion (other than oil and gas)	15c
d	Oil, gas, and geothermal properties—gross income	15d
e	Oil, gas, and geothermal properties—deductions	15e
f	Other AMT items (attach statement)	15f

Items Affecting Shareholder Basis

16a	Tax-exempt interest income	16a
b	Other tax-exempt income	16b
c	Nondeductible expenses	16c
d	Distributions (attach statement if required) (see instructions)	16d
e	Repayment of loans from shareholders	16e

Other Information

17a	Investment income	17a
b	Investment expenses	17b
c	Dividend distributions paid from accumulated earnings and profits	17c
d	Other items and amounts (attach statement)	

Reconciliation

18	**Income (loss) reconciliation.** Combine the amounts on lines 1 through 10 in the far right column. From the result, subtract the sum of the amounts on lines 11 through 12d and 14p	18

4. **Corporate-Level Items**

    a. Items not required to be separately stated, such as organizational costs, utilities, noninvestment interest expense, and other ordinary items of income and expense, are combined at the corporate level, and the net amount of ordinary income or loss is passed through to shareholders.

5. **Amortizable Items**

    a. Shareholders (who are individuals) may elect to deduct ratably the expenses incurred during the tax year for

    1) Research and experimentation costs (over a 10-year period)
    2) Mining exploration and development costs (over a 10-year period)
    3) Increasing the circulation of a periodical (over a 3-year period)
    4) Intangible drilling costs (over a 5-year period)

6. **Allocation**

    a. The amount of each item that each shareholder takes into account is computed on a per-day and then a per-share basis. A shareholder's holding period does not include the date of acquisition but does include the date of disposition. All allocations are made on a per-share, per-day basis.

EXAMPLE 14-6   Allocation of Items Per Share and Per Day

Abel transfers 100 shares of GHI Corp., an S corporation, to fellow shareholder Duff on March 14. Therefore, Abel is allotted 73 days of ownership (January 1 – March 14) amounting to 20% (73 days ÷ 365 days) of net income from the 100 shares. Duff will receive the other 80% (292 days ÷ 365 days) of net income from the 100 shares.

---

    1) Upon a termination of a shareholder's interest during the tax year, an election is available to allocate items according to the books and records of the corporation (its accounting methods) instead of by daily proration.

7. **IRS Reallocation**

    a. Pro rata shares of S corporation items passed through may be reallocated by the IRS among shareholders who are members of the same family.

    b. Distributive shares must reflect reasonable compensation for services or capital furnished to the corporation by family members.

    c. The IRS may disregard a stock transfer (by gift or sale) motivated primarily by tax avoidance.

8. **Character**

    a. The shareholder characterizes each item as the corporation would.

9. **Carryovers**

    a. C corporation NOL carryovers do not transfer over to S corporations as a result of an S corporation election.

    1) NOLs generated by S corporations flow through to shareholders; therefore, NOLs are not utilized at the entity level.

    NOTE: Do not confuse this rule with the carryover rules for built-in gains tax explained in Subunit 14.4.

10. **Employee Fringe Benefits**
    a. A person who directly or by attribution owns more than 2% of the stock of an S corporation (voting power or amount) on any day during its tax year is not considered an employee entitled to employee benefits (i.e., they are employee-owners, not employees). Thus, 2% shareholders are subject to special rules.
    b. The S corporation must treat an amount paid for most fringe benefits to more-than-2% shareholders as deductible compensation (as opposed to a deductible fringe benefit), and the more-than-2% shareholders must include the amount in gross income.
    c. This rule does not apply to pension and profit-sharing plans.
    d. The following benefits are not excludable from the wages of more-than-2% shareholders:
        1) Payments to accident and health plans
        2) Group-term life insurance coverage up to $50,000
        3) Medical reimbursement plans and disability plans
        4) Meals and lodging furnished for the convenience of the employer
        5) Cafeteria plans
        6) Qualified transportation benefits
        7) Personal use of employer-provided property or services
        8) Adoption assistance program
        9) Employment achievement award
    e. Fringe benefits available to 2% shareholders include the following:
        1) Dependent care assistance program
        2) Educational assistance program
        3) Compensation for injury and sickness
        4) No additional-cost service
        5) Qualified employee discount
        6) Working condition fringe
        7) De minimis fringe
        8) On-premises athletic facilities
    f. Accident and health insurance premiums paid by an S corporation are considered for services rendered.
        1) The premiums are deductible by the S corporation and includible in the shareholder's W-2.
        2) The premiums are excludable for Social Security and Medicare if the payments are made under a "qualified plan," such as a cafeteria plan.
        3) Qualified plans are those that treat all employees uniformly and do not give preferential treatment to key employees.
    g. The medical insurance deduction is available for 2% shareholders of S corporations for amounts paid by their corporation for health insurance on their behalf.
        1) The premiums must be included in income by the 2% shareholder.
            a) A deduction is allowed above-the-line on Form 1040 if the taxpayer has self-employment earnings at least equal to the deduction.

11. **Stock and Debt Basis**
    a. An individual is considered as owning the stock directly by or for
        1) The individual's spouse (other than a legally separated spouse)
        2) The individual's children, grandchildren, and parents

- b. Generally, if a shareholder purchases stock, the shareholder's original basis in the stock is its cost.
    1) If a shareholder receives stock in exchange for property in a nontaxable exchange (i.e., Sec. 351 as discussed in Study Unit 11), the basis is usually the same as the property's basis.
    2) If a shareholder lends money to the S corporation, a separately tracked type of basis called **debt basis** is created. The basis is usually the amount of the loan.
    3) If a shareholder guarantees a third-party loan to an S corporation, the loan does not increase the shareholder's basis. Two exceptions apply:
        a) The shareholder makes payments on the loan.
        b) The shareholder is the primary signer on the note, and the S corporation is the guarantor.
- c. The adjusted basis of the shareholder's stock is calculated at year end with increases for the shareholder's pro rata share of the following:
    1) All income items of the S corporation, including tax-exempt income, that are separately stated
    2) Any nonseparately stated income of the S corporation
    3) The amount of the deduction for depletion (other than oil and gas) that is more than the basis of the property being depleted

---

EXAMPLE 14-7   **Adjusted Basis of Shareholder's Stock -- Increases**

The taxpayer's basis in the S corporation is $12,000 at the beginning of the year. The corporation has ordinary income of $6,000, tax-exempt interest of $2,000, and a long-term capital gain of $1,500. The taxpayer's basis will be increased by $9,500 ($6,000 + $2,000 + $1,500) to $21,500 at the end of the year.

- d. The adjusted basis of the shareholder's stock must also be decreased by the shareholder's pro rata share of the following:
    1) Distributions by the S corporation that were not included in income (done before determining the allowable loss deduction)
    2) All separately stated loss and deduction items
    3) Any nonseparately stated loss of the S corporation
    4) Any expenses of the S corporation that are not deductible in figuring its taxable income or are not properly capitalized
        a) A nondeductible expense decreases stock basis so that the nondeductible expense does not result in less gain recognized upon disposition of the stock (i.e., through a higher basis).
    5) The shareholder's deduction for depletion of oil and gas property held by the S corporation to the extent it is not more than the shareholder's share of the adjusted basis of the property

---

EXAMPLE 14-8   **Adjusted Basis of Shareholder's Stock -- Decreases**

The taxpayer's basis at the beginning of the year is $22,000. The taxpayer withdraws $16,000 during the year, and the corporation has an ordinary loss of $9,000. Basis in the corporation is first reduced by the $16,000 distribution to $6,000. Only $6,000 of the loss is deductible by the shareholder, limited to basis.

e. After basis in the shareholder's S corporation stock has been reduced to zero, the shareholder's basis in debt of the S corporation to that shareholder is reduced (but not below zero) by his or her share of items of loss and deduction.

   1) In a subsequent tax year, items passed through must restore the basis in the debt before basis in the stock.
   2) **Limit.** A shareholder's share of loss and deduction items in excess of basis in the debt is not deductible.
      a) The excess is suspended and carried over indefinitely.
      b) It may be deducted in a subsequent tax year in which basis is restored to debt or to stock.

EXAMPLE 14-9   **Adjusted Basis of Stock and Debt**

The taxpayer's basis in the corporation is made up of $19,500 stock basis and $2,500 debt basis. The stock basis is first reduced by the $16,000 distribution to $3,500. Then, the stock basis is reduced to zero by the loss passthrough. Next, the debt basis is reduced to zero by the loss passthrough, with $3,000 of the loss carried forward ($9,000 − $3,500 − $2,500).

---

12. **At-Risk Rules**
    a. At-risk rules are applied at the shareholder level.
       1) If the shareholder's pro rata share of passed-through losses exceeds his or her amount at risk at the close of his or her tax year, the excess is not deductible.
          a) The excess is suspended and carried forward indefinitely.
          b) It is deductible when the shareholder's amount at risk has increased.
    b. Each shareholder's at-risk amount equals, basically, the sum of the following:
       1) Money and the adjusted basis of property contributed to the corporation
       2) Amounts borrowed and lent to the corporation to the extent the shareholder has personal liability for repayment (recourse debt) or (s)he has pledged as security for repayment property not used in the activity (of the corporation)
          a) However, it does not include other debts of the corporation to third parties (nonrecourse debt), even if the repayment is guaranteed by the shareholder.
       3) The shareholder's amount at risk is increased or decreased by the shareholder's pro rata share of passed-through income and deduction (tax-exempt related also) and by distributions to the shareholder.
    c. The shareholder's basis in his or her stock and debt of the corporation is reduced (subject to prior application of the basis loss limitation), even if current deductibility of the loss is prohibited by the at-risk rules.

13. **Passive Activity Loss Rules**
    a. Current deductibility of any passive activity losses passed through is limited, at the shareholder level, to passive activity income.
        1) Passive activity includes rental activity or any activity of the corporation in which the shareholder does not materially participate.
            a) Material participation by the S corporation is not sufficient.
    b. A shareholder's amount at risk must be reduced by the full amount allowable as a current deduction after application of the at-risk rules, even if part of it must be suspended by the passive loss rules.

14. **Failure to File Penalty**
    a. The penalty base amount (regardless of any tax amount owed) is imposed in the amount of the number of persons who were shareholders during any part of the year, multiplied by $210 (for 2021 tax returns filed in 2022) for each of up to 12 months (including a portion of one) that the return was late or incomplete.

EXAMPLE 14-10   Failure to File Penalty

An S corporation has 5 shareholders, and the tax return is filed 1 1/4 months late. The penalty is calculated by multiplying $210 by the 5 shareholders, and then multiplying by 2 (1 1/4 months rounded to 2). Thus, the total penalty is $2,100.

---

   b. **If tax is due**, the penalty is the amount stated above plus 5% of the unpaid tax for each month or part of a month the return is late, up to a maximum of 25% of the unpaid tax. The minimum penalty for a return that is more than 60 days late is the smaller of the tax due or $435.

EXAMPLE 14-11   Failure to File Penalty -- Tax Due

Expand Example 14-10 to include a $10,000 tax liability. The penalty is calculated by multiplying the $10,000 by 10% (5% × 2 months) and then adding $2,100, which equals a $3,100 failure to file penalty.

---

15. **Excess Business Loss**
    a. When total losses from all trades or businesses exceed all gross income and gains from all sources, only $262,000 of the net loss is deductible on an individual return ($524,000 in the case of MFJ).
        1) Any nondeductible loss is treated as a net operating loss (covered in Study Unit 8).

SUCCESS TIP: Past CPA Exams have contained questions asking for calculations of both a shareholder's adjusted basis in S corporation stock and a shareholder's share of net income from the S corporation.

STOP & REVIEW: You have completed the outline for this subunit. Study multiple-choice questions 6 through 14 beginning on page 408.

14.3 DISTRIBUTIONS

1. **Overview**

   a. Distributions include nonliquidating and liquidating distributions of money or other property but not of the S corporation's own stock or obligations. The amount of a particular distribution is the sum of any money plus the FMV of property distributed.

2. **Shareholder Accounts**

   a. S corporations are required to maintain records, with respect to each shareholder, called

      1) Accumulated adjustments account (AAA)
      2) Other adjustments account (OAA)

      These records, along with the shareholder's basis in his or her stock and any Subchapter C E&P (i.e., AE&P), are used to determine the shareholder's tax treatment of distributions.

   b. Distributions from an S corporation are funded in the following source order:

      1) AAA
      2) AE&P
      3) OAA
      4) Stock basis

   c. Note that the AAA and OAA records and information are needed by S corporations only for purposes of helping shareholders determine taxability of distributions when the S corporation has E&P.

   d. Subchapter C E&P. An S corporation does not have E&P unless it was formerly a C corporation or acquired E&P in a tax-free reorganization, e.g., a merger.

   e. The AAA represents the current cumulative balance of the S corporation.

      1) It is recommended that the AAA be maintained by all S corporations.
      2) It is calculated without regard to any net negative adjustments (excess of losses and deductions over income and gains).
      3) The AAA is not affected by any transactions related to when it was a C corporation (e.g., federal income taxes).
      4) Nondeductible expenditures by the S corporation decrease basis in stock and the AAA.
      5) Adjustment is not made to the AAA for tax-exempt income (which increases basis) or related nondeductible expenses (which reduce basis). These adjustments are made to the OAA.
      6) The AAA balance can be reduced below zero by the corporation's operations (e.g., losses). (Basis may not.) However, distributions do not reduce AAA below zero.

   f. The OAA represents a cumulative balance of tax-exempt interest earned and life insurance proceeds, reduced by expenses incurred in earning it.

3. **Distributions of Property**

   a. An S corporation recognizes gain realized on the distribution of appreciated property (FMV > basis).

   b. The amount and character of the gain and its treatment are determined as if the distributed property were sold to the shareholder at its FMV.

      1) Ordinary income results if the property is depreciable in the hands of a more-than-50% shareholder.

   c. The gain is passed through pro rata to each shareholder.

      1) The shareholder's basis in his or her stock and the AAA is increased by his or her shares as if the S corporation had sold the property.

      2) The distributee (recipient) shareholder must determine the proper treatment of the distribution.

EXAMPLE 14-12	Gain on Property Distribution

   The S corporation sells an investment asset with a basis of $15,000 for $23,000. The corporation reports an $8,000 gain, which flows through to the shareholders.

   d. When loss property (basis > FMV) is distributed, no loss may be recognized by the S corporation.

      1) The loss is passed through to the shareholders and is nondeductible.

         a) Each shareholder must reduce the basis in his or her stock in the S corporation and take a FMV basis in the property distributed.

         b) The distributee (recipient) shareholder must determine the proper treatment of the distribution.

      2) Sale instead of distribution results in pass-through of loss.

EXAMPLE 14-13	Loss on Property Distribution

   The S corporation has a capital asset with a basis of $7,000 and a FMV of $5,000, which it distributes to the sole shareholder. The corporation has a nondeductible loss of $2,000. The shareholder reduces basis by $7,000 and has a $5,000 basis in the asset. If the corporation sold the asset and distributed the proceeds, the shareholder would have a $2,000 deductible loss.

   e. An S corporation is not required to recognize gain on the liquidating distributions of certain installment obligations.

      1) The shareholder treats each payment as a passed-through item.

4. **Shareholder Treatment of Distributions**

   a. Shareholder treatment of distributions from the S corporation is determined at the end of the S corporation's tax year.

      1) The AAA, OAA, basis in shareholders' stock, and basis in corporate-shareholder debt must be adjusted for the S corporation's items of income, deduction, etc., before each shareholder determines the proper treatment of his or her distributions.

b. **No E&P.** Shareholder treatment of distributions is straightforward when the S corporation has no Subchapter C E&P.
   1) That portion of distributions that does not exceed the basis in the shareholder's stock is treated as tax-free return of capital.
   2) Excess over basis is treated as gain on sale of the stock.
      a) The character depends on the nature of the stock in the hands of the shareholder and his or her holding period.
c. If there are Subchapter C E&P, the distribution is first treated as return of capital (tax-free) to the extent of the shareholder's AAA balance (up to any basis in the shareholder's stock).
   1) Excess distribution beyond the AAA is dividend income to the extent of Subchapter C E&P in the corporation.
   2) Excess distribution beyond Subchapter C E&P is return of capital to the extent of the OAA.
   3) Excess distribution beyond the OAA is return of capital to the extent of any remaining basis in the stock.
   4) Any excess distribution over remaining basis distributed is treated as gain from the sale of the stock.

S Corporation without Subchapter C E&P

Shareholder Distribution	Tax Result
To extent of basis in stock	Not subject to tax; reduces basis in stock
In excess of basis of stock	Taxed as capital gain

S Corporation with Subchapter C E&P

Shareholder Distribution	Tax Result
To extent of AAA	Not subject to tax; reduces AAA and basis in stock
To extent of C corporation E&P	Taxed as a dividend; reduces E&P, but not basis in stock
To extent of OAA	Not subject to tax; reduces OAA and basis in stock
To extent of basis in stock	Not subject to tax; reduces basis in stock
In excess of basis	Taxed as capital gain

NOTE: In the above determination of shareholder treatment of distributions, any amount to be treated as tax-free return of capital reduces the shareholder's basis in his or her stock.

EXAMPLE 14-14   Shareholder Treatment of Distributions

A single-owner S corporation has an AAA of $12,000 and E&P of $8,000. The shareholder's basis is $25,000. The first $12,000 of any distribution reduces AAA to $0 ($12,000 AAA – $12,000 of distribution) and shareholder basis by $12,000 to $13,000 ($25,000 basis – $12,000 of distribution) and is nontaxable. The next $8,000 of distributions is classified as dividend income and reduces E&P to $0 ($8,000 E&P – $8,000 of distribution). The next $13,000 (i.e., the balance of basis calculated previously) of distributions is a tax-free reduction of basis and is classified as return of capital. Any distributions above $33,000 ($25,000 basis + $8,000 E&P) will be taxed as capital gain income.

---

d. An election may be made to treat distributions as coming first from Subchapter C E&P.
   1) This results in ordinary dividend income to the distributee (recipient) to the extent of the E&P.
   2) Any excess distribution is treated as in 4.b. above.

e. Cash distributions within a relatively short transition period subsequent to termination of an S election are treated as a return of capital to the extent of the AAA.

1) Basis in shareholder stock is reduced.

f. Form 1099-DIV is used to report any distribution that is in excess of the accumulated adjustments account and that is treated as a dividend to the extent of accumulated earnings and profits.

From Form 1120-S

Schedule M-2	Analysis of Accumulated Adjustments Account, Shareholders' Undistributed Taxable Income Previously Taxed, Accumulated Earnings and Profits, and Other Adjustments Account (see instructions)				
		(a) Accumulated adjustments account	(b) Shareholders' undistributed taxable income previously taxed	(c) Accumulated earnings and profits	(d) Other adjustments account
1	Balance at beginning of tax year				
2	Ordinary income from page 1, line 21				
3	Other additions				
4	Loss from page 1, line 21	( )			
5	Other reductions	( )			( )
6	Combine lines 1 through 5				
7	Distributions				
8	Balance at end of tax year. Subtract line 7 from line 6				

Form **1120-S** [Year]

5. **Qualified Business Income Deduction**

   a. Study Unit 7, Subunit 3, covers the qualified business income deduction.

STOP & REVIEW

You have completed the outline for this subunit.
Study multiple-choice questions 15 through 17 on page 412.

14.4 SPECIAL TAXES

1. **Overview**

   a. Although S corporations are not generally subject to income tax, the following four special taxes are imposed on S corporations.

   b. **Passive Investment Income (PII) Tax**

      1) An S corporation with Subchapter C E&P at the close of its tax year and PII of more than 25% of its gross receipts is subject to a tax of 21% of excess net passive income.

      2) Gross receipts (GR) and PII are defined in item 4.d. of Subunit 14.1.

      3) Net passive income (NPI) is PII reduced by expenses directly attributable to its production.

      4) PII tax liability is allocated to the PII items and reduces the amount of the item passed through to shareholders.

      5) S corporations are required to make estimated payments of PII tax.

c. **Built-In Gains (BIG) Tax**
   1) To avoid circumvention of a taxable liquidation, an S corporation that, upon conversion from C to S status, had net appreciation inherent in its assets is subject to tax of 21% on net gain recognized (up to the amount of built-in gain on conversion) during the recognition period.
   2) The recognition period is the 5-year period beginning on the date the S election became effective.
      a) Thus, for a conversion effective January 1, 2016, the BIG tax will apply through December 31, 2020, allowing 2021 disposals to avoid the tax.
   3) The tax liability is passed through, as a loss, pro rata to its shareholders.
      a) It reduces basis in each shareholder's stock and any AAA balance.
      b) Subchapter C E&P are not reduced by BIG tax liability.
   4) S corporations are required to make estimated payments of BIG tax.
   5) Any net operating or capital loss carryover arising in a tax year in which the S corporation was a C corporation can offset the built-in gain for the tax year.

d. **LIFO Recapture**
   1) Any excess of the FIFO inventory value over the LIFO inventory value at the close of the last tax year of C corporation status is gross income to a corporation that used the LIFO method to inventory goods.
   2) Basis of the inventory is increased by the amount on which the recapture tax is imposed.
   3) The tax associated with the recapture income is spread over 4 years: the last C corporation year and the first 3 years of the S corporation.

> **EXAMPLE 14-15   LIFO Recapture**
>
> Mile, Inc., switched from a C corporation to an S corporation at the beginning of the current year. Mile had used the LIFO inventory valuation method during its existence as a C corporation. Mile's inventory for the previous year was $2,750,000, and if it used the FIFO method, its inventory would be valued at $3,000,000. Therefore, for the previous year's tax return, Mile must include an additional $250,000 of gross income due to the LIFO recapture, and the tax associated with this additional gross income will be paid over four equal annual installments beginning with the previous year.

e. **General Business Credit Recapture**
   1) An S corporation remains liable for any recapture attributable to credits during C corporation tax years.

STOP & REVIEW

You have completed the outline for this subunit.
Study multiple-choice questions 18 through 20 on page 413.

QUESTIONS

14.1 Eligibility and Election

1. Bristol Corp. was formed as a C corporation on January 1, 1985, and elected S corporation status on January 1, 1991. At the time of the election, Bristol had accumulated C corporation earnings and profits that have not been distributed. Bristol has had the same 25 shareholders throughout its existence. In 2021, Bristol's S election will terminate if it

A. Increases the number of shareholders to 50.
B. Adds a decedent's estate as a shareholder to the existing shareholders.
C. Takes a charitable contribution deduction.
D. Has passive investment income exceeding 90% of gross receipts in each of the 3 consecutive years ending December 31, 2021.

Answer (D) is correct.
REQUIRED: The S corporation termination event.
DISCUSSION: An S corporation's status will terminate if (1) it has C corporation earnings and profits at the close of 3 consecutive years, and (2) during those 3 years, over 25% of the gross receipts of the S corporation was due to passive investment income. First, the existence of the undistributed earnings and profits satisfies the first test. Second, with 90% passive investment income within the gross receipts, the termination is effective.
Answer (A) is incorrect. An S corporation is limited to a maximum of 100 shareholders. **Answer (B) is incorrect.** An estate is an eligible shareholder. **Answer (C) is incorrect.** A charitable contribution deduction will not terminate the election.

2. On February 10, 2021, Ace Corp., a calendar-year corporation, elected S corporation status, and all shareholders consented to the election. There was no change in shareholders in 2021. Ace met all eligibility requirements for S status during the pre-election portion of the year. What is the earliest date on which Ace can be recognized as an S corporation?

A. February 10, 2021.
B. February 10, 2022.
C. January 1, 2022.
D. January 1, 2021.

Answer (D) is correct.
REQUIRED: The effective date of an S corporation election.
DISCUSSION: The S corporation election can be effective for the current tax year if it is made on or before March 15 for calendar-year corporations, subject to certain exceptions relating to ineligibility and complete consent. Since this election was made on February 10 and no exceptions applied, the election can be effective for the entire taxable year in which it was made.

3. An S corporation has 30,000 shares of voting common stock and 20,000 shares of nonvoting common stock issued and outstanding. The S election can be revoked voluntarily with the consent of the shareholders holding, on the day of the revocation,

	Shares of Voting Stock	Shares of Nonvoting Stock
A.	0	20,000
B.	7,500	5,000
C.	10,000	16,000
D.	20,000	0

Answer (C) is correct.
REQUIRED: The number of shares required to consent to a voluntary revocation of an S election.
DISCUSSION: An S corporation election may be terminated by revocation. A revocation may be made only with the consent of shareholders who, at the time the revocation is made, hold more than one-half of the number of issued and outstanding shares of stock (including both voting and nonvoting stock) of the corporation.

4. Which of the following conditions will prevent a corporation from qualifying as an S corporation?

A. The corporation has both common and preferred stock.
B. The corporation has one class of stock with different voting rights.
C. One shareholder is an estate.
D. One shareholder is a grantor trust.

Answer (A) is correct.
REQUIRED: The condition that will prevent a corporation from qualifying as an S corporation.
DISCUSSION: An S corporation may have only one class of stock.
Answer (B) is incorrect. An S corporation may have only one class of (common) stock, but shares of that class may have different voting rights. Answer (C) is incorrect. A decedent's estate may be a shareholder. Answer (D) is incorrect. A grantor trust may be a shareholder for a 2-year period following the death of a grantor.

5. Lindal Corporation, organized in 2021, immediately filed an election for S corporation status under the rules of Subchapter S. What is the maximum amount of passive investment income that Lindal will be allowed to earn and still qualify as an S corporation?

A. 80% of gross receipts.
B. 50% of gross receipts.
C. 20% of gross receipts.
D. No limit on passive investment income.

Answer (D) is correct.
REQUIRED: The maximum amount of passive investment income allowable to an S corporation.
DISCUSSION: There is no limit on the amount of passive investment income that a corporation can earn and still qualify as an S corporation. S corporation status is terminated if the corporation has had passive investment income in excess of 25% of gross receipts for 3 consecutive taxable years and has had Subchapter C earnings and profits at the end of each of those taxable years. Subchapter C earnings and profits are those accumulated during a taxable year for which a Subchapter S election was not in effect. Lindal filed an S election immediately after formation, which prevents C corporation earnings and profits.

14.2 Operations

6. Bern Corp., an S corporation, had an ordinary loss of $36,500 for the year ended December 31, 2021. On January 1, 2021, Meyer owned 50% of Bern's stock. Meyer held the stock for 40 days in 2021 before selling the entire 50% interest to an unrelated third party. Meyer's basis for the stock was $10,000. Meyer was a full-time employee of Bern until the stock was sold. Meyer's share of Bern's 2021 loss was

A. $0
B. $2,000
C. $10,000
D. $18,250

Answer (B) is correct.
REQUIRED: The allocable share of an S corporation item when a shareholder's interest changes during the tax year.
DISCUSSION: The amount of each S corporation item, which each shareholder takes into account, is computed on a per-day and per-share basis. The portion of the loss passed through to Meyer is

$$\$36{,}500 \times 50\% \times \frac{40}{365} = \$2{,}000$$

Answer (A) is incorrect. Each shareholder's allocable portion is determined on a per-day and a per-share basis. Answer (C) is incorrect. Each shareholder's allocable portion is determined on a per-day and a per-share basis. Meyer's basis in Bern Corp. was $10,000 before the sale. Answer (D) is incorrect. Each shareholder's allocable portion is determined on a per-day and a per-share basis. The amount of $18,250 represents 50% of the loss and is not allocated between the two owners.

7. Bob and Sally, unmarried taxpayers, each owned 50% of Lostalot, Inc., an S corporation. The corporation had a $50,000 operating loss for the tax year ending December 31, 2021. As of December 31, 2020, Bob's basis in his stock was $15,000 and Sally's was $5,000. During the 2021 tax year, Sally mortgaged her home for $25,000 and loaned the money to the corporation. Although not personally liable, Bob told her not to worry and that if anything happened, he would help pay the mortgage debt. Calculate the amount of allowable loss deduction each shareholder would be able to recognize on their individual 2021 tax returns.

A. Bob: $25,000, and Sally: $25,000.
B. Bob: $15,000, and Sally: $5,000.
C. Bob: $15,000, and Sally: $30,000.
D. Bob: $15,000, and Sally: $25,000.

Answer (D) is correct.
REQUIRED: The loss deduction that may be recognized on a shareholder's individual return.
DISCUSSION: Bob and Sally's share of the loss is $25,000 each. However, the deduction for each is limited to their basis in the S corporation. Bob's deduction is limited to his $15,000 basis in the stock. Sally's basis consists of her $5,000 stock basis and her $25,000 debt basis. Sally has enough basis to cover her share of the loss. Bob receives no debt basis from the mortgage debt because he is not personally liable.
Answer (A) is incorrect. Bob's basis is not large enough to cover the $25,000 share of the loss. **Answer (B) is incorrect.** Sally's basis is larger than $5,000. **Answer (C) is incorrect.** Sally's share of the loss is not $30,000.

8. Graphite Corp. has been a calendar-year S corporation since its inception on January 2, 2014. On January 1, 2021, Smith and Tyler each owned 50% of the Graphite stock in which their respective bases were $12,000 and $9,000. For the year ended December 31, 2021, Graphite had $80,000 in ordinary business income and $6,000 in tax-exempt income. Graphite made a $53,000 cash distribution to each shareholder on December 31, 2021. What total amount of income from Graphite is includible in Smith's 2021 adjusted gross income?

A. $96,000
B. $93,000
C. $43,000
D. $40,000

Answer (D) is correct.
REQUIRED: The amount of income a shareholder should recognize from an S corporation.
DISCUSSION: All of an S corporation's income is taxed to the shareholders each year, whether distributed or not. Each shareholder's basis is increased by his or her share of income, including tax-exempt income. Distributions in general then reduce the shareholder's basis, and any distribution that is not in excess of basis is treated as a tax-free return of capital. Therefore, Smith will recognize $40,000 of ordinary income ($80,000 × 50% interest). The tax-exempt income is not included in a shareholder's income. The distribution does not affect Smith's gross income because it does not exceed his basis ($12,000 basis + $43,000 income).

9. Bow, Inc., an S corporation, has three equal shareholders. For the year ended December 31, 2021, Bow had taxable income of $300,000. Bow made cash distributions totaling $120,000 during 2021. For 2021, what amount from Bow should be included in each shareholder's gross income?

A. $140,000
B. $100,000
C. $60,000
D. $40,000

Answer (B) is correct.
REQUIRED: The gross income of a shareholder of an S corporation with current earnings that made distributions.
DISCUSSION: Each shareholder includes in his or her personal gross income his or her share of ordinary income and separately stated items of the S corporation on a per-day and per-share basis. Each shareholder's share is 1/3 of $300,000. Shareholder inclusion will be $100,000 each. Excess distributions are treated as tax-free return of capital.

10. Which of the following items is **not** a separately stated item for Form 1120-S shareholders?

A. Charitable contributions made by the corporation.
B. Section 179 deduction.
C. Depreciation.
D. Tax-exempt interest.

Answer (C) is correct.
REQUIRED: The item that is not a separately stated item for Form 1120-S shareholders.
DISCUSSION: An S corporation passes a pro rata share of its total income (loss) through to the individual shareholders except for items that require separate treatment by the shareholder. Charitable contributions made by the corporation, Sec. 179 deduction, and tax-exempt interest must be separately stated. Depreciation, however, is combined with other nonseparately stated income or loss.
Answer (A) is incorrect. Charitable contributions made by the corporation are separately stated for Form 1120-S shareholders. **Answer (B) is incorrect.** A Sec. 179 deduction is an item that is separately stated for Form 1120-S shareholders. **Answer (D) is incorrect.** Tax-exempt interest is an item that is separately stated for Form 1120-S shareholders.

11. As of January 1, 2021, Kane owned all 100 issued shares of Manning Corp., a calendar-year S corporation. On the 40th day of 2021, Kane sold 25 of the Manning shares to Rodgers. For the year ended December 31, 2021 (a 365-day calendar year), Manning had $73,000 in nonseparately stated income and made no distributions to its shareholders. What amount of nonseparately stated income from Manning should be reported on Kane's 2021 tax return?

A. $56,750
B. $54,750
C. $16,250
D. $0

Answer (A) is correct.
REQUIRED: The shareholder's income from an S corporation when shares are transferred during the year.
DISCUSSION: Each shareholder shall include in gross income the pro rata share of the S corporation's income. The pro rata share is the taxpayer's share of the corporation's income after assigning an equal portion of the income to each day of the taxable year and then dividing that portion pro rata among the shares outstanding on each day. Therefore, each day of the year will be assigned $200 of income ($73,000 ÷ 365). Kane's share will be $56,750 [$8,000 (40 days × $200 × 100% ownership) plus $48,750 (325 days × $200 × 75% ownership)].
Answer (B) is incorrect. The amount of $54,750 applies Kane's end-of-year ownership percentage to the entire year's income instead of on a pro rata basis for the shares outstanding on each day. **Answer (C) is incorrect.** The amount of $16,250 is Rodgers's pro rata share. **Answer (D) is incorrect.** Each shareholder must include in taxable income the pro rata share of the S corporation's income.

12. A shareholder's basis in the stock of an S corporation is increased by the shareholder's pro rata share of income from

	Tax-Exempt Interest	Taxable Interest
A.	No	No
B.	No	Yes
C.	Yes	No
D.	Yes	Yes

Answer (D) is correct.
REQUIRED: The item(s) that increase(s) a shareholder's basis in S corporation stock.
DISCUSSION: Interest income received by an S corporation, whether taxable or nontaxable, increases the basis of an S corporation shareholder's stock.

13. Tap, a calendar-year S corporation, reported the following items of income and expense in the current year:

Revenue	$44,000
Operating expenses	20,000
Long-term capital loss	6,000
Charitable contributions	1,000
Interest expense	4,000

What is the amount of Tap's ordinary income?

A. $13,000
B. $19,000
C. $20,000
D. $24,000

Answer (C) is correct.
REQUIRED: The amount of Tap's ordinary income.
DISCUSSION: The items of income, deduction, and credit of an S corporation are reported by the corporation; however, an S corporation is not allowed deductions for items that must be separately stated, which include long-term capital losses and charitable contributions. Therefore, Tap's ordinary income equals $20,000 ($44,000 revenue − $20,000 operating expenses − $4,000 interest expense).
Answer (A) is incorrect. The long-term capital loss and charitable contribution must be stated separately and are therefore not deductible by the S corporation. Answer (B) is incorrect. The charitable contribution must be stated separately and is therefore not deductible in the computation of ordinary business income by the S corporation. Answer (D) is incorrect. The S corporation may deduct the $4,000 of interest expense.

14. Sandy is the sole shareholder of Swallow, an S corporation. Sandy's adjusted basis in Swallow stock is $60,000 at the beginning of Year 1. During the year, Swallow reports the following income items:

Ordinary income	$30,000
Tax-exempt income	5,000
Capital gains	10,000

In addition, Swallow makes a nontaxable distribution to Sandy of $20,000 during Year 1. What is Sandy's adjusted basis in the Swallow stock at the end of Year 1?

A. $60,000
B. $70,000
C. $80,000
D. $85,000

Answer (D) is correct.
REQUIRED: The shareholder's adjusted basis in the stock of an S corporation.
DISCUSSION: The adjusted basis of the shareholder's stock is figured at year end with increases for the shareholder's pro rata share of all income items, including tax-exempt income, that are separately stated and any nonseparately stated income. Also, all separately and nonseparately stated losses, distributions, and deduction items decrease the basis of the shareholder's stock on a pro rata basis. Sandy's stock basis on January 1, Year 1, is $60,000.

Original basis	$60,000
Ordinary income	30,000
Tax-exempt income	5,000
Capital gains	10,000
Nontaxable distribution	(20,000)
Adjusted basis	$85,000

Answer (A) is incorrect. A $60,000 adjusted basis ignores the effects of the income items and the nontaxable distribution. Answer (B) is incorrect. A $70,000 adjusted basis excludes the effects of the tax-exempt income and the capital gains. Answer (C) is incorrect. An $80,000 adjusted basis does not include the effects of the tax-exempt income.

14.3 Distributions

15. If an S corporation has no accumulated earnings and profits, the amount distributed to a shareholder

A. Must be returned to the S corporation.
B. Increases the shareholder's basis in the stock.
C. Decreases the shareholder's basis in the stock.
D. Has no effect on the shareholder's basis in the stock.

Answer (C) is correct.
REQUIRED: The true statement regarding a distribution by an S corporation that has no accumulated earnings and profits.
DISCUSSION: Distribution from an S corporation with no Subchapter C earnings and profits is treated as a tax-free return of capital to the extent of a shareholder's basis in his or her stock of the corporation, decreasing the stock's basis. Excess is treated as gain or loss on the sale of the stock.

16. Packer Corp., an accrual-basis, calendar-year S corporation, has been an S corporation since its inception. Starr was a 50% shareholder in Packer throughout the current year and had a $10,000 tax basis in Packer stock on January 1. During the current year, Packer had a $1,000 net business loss and made an $8,000 cash distribution to each shareholder. What amount of the distribution was includible in Starr's gross income?

A. $8,000
B. $7,500
C. $4,000
D. $0

Answer (D) is correct.
REQUIRED: The amount includible in Starr's income from the distribution.
DISCUSSION: S corporations (without E&P from previously being a C corporation) may make tax-free distributions to shareholders to the extent of basis. Once the stock basis is reduced to zero, any further distributions are treated as a capital gain. Therefore, the cash distribution received by Starr reduces his basis in the stock of the S corporation, and he is not required to include the cash distribution in gross income because the distribution does not exceed his basis.
Answer (A) is incorrect. There were no earnings and profits to pay the $8,000 cash distribution, and it is not included in gross income. **Answer (B) is incorrect.** The business loss is not used to offset the cash distribution received from Starr in determining the amount of gross income. **Answer (C) is incorrect.** Starr received an $8,000 cash distribution, and it was not included in gross income because there are not earnings and profits in the S corporation because it was not a C corporation.

17. Jenny Corporation (an S corporation) is owned entirely by Craig. At the beginning of 2021, Craig's adjusted basis in his Jenny Corporation stock was $20,000. Jenny reported ordinary income of $5,000 and a capital loss of $10,000. Craig received a cash distribution of $35,000 in November 2021. What is Craig's gain from the distribution?

A. $0
B. $10,000
C. $20,000
D. $35,000

Answer (B) is correct.
REQUIRED: The sole shareholder's gain from the distribution of an S corporation.
DISCUSSION: The basis is increased by the ordinary income to $25,000. The $35,000 distribution is taken next and, since it exceeds the basis, there is a $10,000 gain. The capital loss is nondeductible because there is no basis left after the deduction from the distribution for Craig and it is carried over.
Answer (A) is incorrect. If the distribution is greater than the basis, the excess is taxable as a sale or an exchange of property (a taxable capital gain). **Answer (C) is incorrect.** The distribution is taken before the deduction for the capital loss. **Answer (D) is incorrect.** The entire distribution is not taxable, only the difference between the distribution and the basis.

14.4 Special Taxes

18. Tax Corp. converted from C to S status in 2021. The net appreciation inherent in its assets is subject to a tax on net gain recognized

A. At the time of the conversion.
B. During a recognition period of 2 years.
C. With no effect on any shareholder's basis in the stock.
D. Up to the amount of built-in gain on conversion.

Answer (D) is correct.
REQUIRED: The true statement about the built-in gains tax.
DISCUSSION: An S corporation that, upon conversion from C to S status, has net appreciation inherent in its assets is subject to a tax of 21% on net gain recognized (up to the amount of built-in gain on conversion) during the recognition period.
Answer (A) is incorrect. The net appreciation inherent in its assets is subject to a tax on net gain recognized during the recognition period. **Answer (B) is incorrect.** The recognition period is a 5-year period beginning on the date the S election became effective. **Answer (C) is incorrect.** The tax liability is passed through, as a loss, pro rata to its shareholders, and it reduces each shareholder's basis in the stock.

19. Invest, Inc., is an S corporation that is liable for the special tax on its excess net passive income (ENPI) for the current tax year. Invest, Inc., has $100,000 of ENPI for the current tax year. What is the amount of the tax?

A. $37,000
B. $21,000
C. $35,000
D. $15,000

Answer (B) is correct.
REQUIRED: The amount of tax on excess net passive income of an S corporation.
DISCUSSION: The tax on the excess net passive income (ENPI) of an S corporation is the ENPI times the highest corporate tax rate (21%). Thus, the tax is $21,000 ($100,000 × 21%).

20. Magic Corp., a regular C corporation, elected S corporation status at the beginning of the current calendar year. It had an asset with a basis of $40,000 and a fair market value (FMV) of $85,000 on January 1. The asset was sold during the year for $95,000. What was Magic's tax liability as a result of the sale?

A. $0
B. $2,100
C. $9,450
D. $11,550

Answer (C) is correct.
REQUIRED: The gain on a sale reported by a C corporation that elected to be an S corporation.
DISCUSSION: An S corporation that, upon conversion from C to S status, had net appreciation inherent in its assets is subject to a built-in gains tax of 21% on net gain recognized (up to the amount of built-in gain on conversion) during the recognition period. Magic had $45,000 ($85,000 FMV in January 1 – $40,000 basis) of built-in gains at the time that Magic elected to be an S corporation. The tax on the $45,000 is $9,450 ($45,000 × 21%).
Answer (A) is incorrect. A gain on the sale is recognized by Magic. **Answer (B) is incorrect.** The amount of $2,100 is the corporate tax on the gain that occurred after the S corporation election. **Answer (D) is incorrect.** The amount of $11,550 is the corporate tax on the entire gain of $55,000 ($95,000 amount realized – $40,000 basis).

STUDY UNIT FIFTEEN
PARTNERSHIPS: FORMATION AND INCOME

(16 pages of outline)

15.1	Partnership Formation and Tax Year	416
15.2	Partner's Taxable Income	421

    A partnership is a business organization other than a corporation, trust, estate, or qualified joint venture co-owned by two or more persons and operated for a profit. The partnership, as an untaxed flow-through entity, reports taxable income or loss and separately stated items. For the computation of personal income tax liability, each partner considers his or her distributive share of the partnership's taxable income or loss and each of the partnership's separately stated items, whether or not any distributions are made from the partnership to the partner. Federal income tax rules for partnerships are similar to those for S corporations. Nonseparately and separately stated partnership items are currently taxed to the partners, but distributions (Study Unit 16) are generally received tax free. The qualified business income deduction (QBID) is discussed in Study Unit 7, Subunit 3, and Study Unit 15 multiple-choice questions and simulations exclude QBID ramifications.

    Some candidates find it helpful to have the entire tax form side-by-side with our Knowledge Transfer Outline when studying, and others may prefer to see the final draft of a form when it is released. The full versions of the most up-to-date forms are easily accessible at www.gleim.com/taxforms. These forms and the form excerpts used in our outline are periodically updated as the latest versions are released by the IRS.

15.1 PARTNERSHIP FORMATION AND TAX YEAR

1. **Overview**

    a. Realized gain or loss is not generally recognized by a partner when a partnership interest is received in exchange for property contributed to the partnership.

    b. There is no boot in a Sec. 721 exchange. Instead, if property in addition to a partnership interest is received in exchange for contributed property, the transaction will be split into a part tax-free contribution and part sale.

    > **EXAMPLE 15-1   Simultaneous Transfers as a Sale**
    >
    > Alex transfers property to a partnership in exchange for a partnership interest and cash. In this situation, Alex is considered to have sold a portion of the property in a taxable sale and to have contributed a portion of the property tax-free in a Sec. 721 exchange. The basis of the property will be allocated between the two transactions to determine gain or loss on the sale and Alex's carryover basis in the partnership interest received.

    c. Types of partnership interest. A partner has two distinct interests in a partnership.

    1) Capital interest. A capital interest is the partner's share of the assets currently owned by the partnership. In other words, what would the partner receive if the partnership were to liquidate and distribute the proceeds?

    2) Profits interest. A profits interest is the partner's share of future income and losses of the partnership.

2. **Contributed Property**

    a. A **partner's basis** in contributed items is exchanged for basis in the partnership interest received, adjusted for gain recognized and liabilities. The formula to calculate basis in a partnership is as follows:

    >   Cash contributed
    >   + Adjusted basis (AB) of property contributed
    >   + Any gain recognized on contributed
    >   property or services
    >   + Share of partnership liabilities
    >   − Partner's liability assumed by partnership
    >   = **Basis in partnership interest**

    1) A partner's basis in a partnership interest is known as "outside basis."

    b. When a partner contributes **property subject to a liability** or the partnership assumes a liability of the contributing partner, the partner is treated as receiving a distribution of money from the partnership in the amount of the liability. A distribution reduces the partner's basis in the partnership interest.

    c. **Recognized gain.** To the extent liabilities assumed by the partnership exceed the partner's aggregate AB in all property contributed, the partner recognizes gain, and basis in the partnership interest is zero.

    1) Note that a partner still bears responsibility for his or her share of the liabilities assumed by the partnership. Basis of other partners also increases by their share of assumed liability.

SU 15: Partnerships: Formation and Income 417

2) The gain recognized may be characterized as ordinary income by Secs. 1245 and 1250.

   a) Ordinary income recapture potential in excess of the amount of gain recognized remains with the property in the hands of the partnership.

EXAMPLE 15-2   Gain -- Liability Assumed by the Partnership

In 2021, Albert acquired a 20% interest in a partnership by contributing a parcel of land and $10,000 in cash. At the time of Albert's contribution, the land had a fair market value of $50,000, an adjusted basis to Albert of $20,000, and was subject to a mortgage of $70,000. Albert's relinquished liability is a gain. When Albert became a 20% partner, he was relieved of 80% of the mortgage debt. Thus, 80% of his $70,000 mortgage, or $56,000, is a benefit to Albert because the other partners are assuming part of the mortgage obligation. Therefore, Albert has a gain of $26,000 ($56,000 benefit − $10,000 cash − $20,000 AB of property).

	Cash contributed	$ 10,000
+	AB of property contributed	20,000
+	Any gain recognized on contributed property or services	26,000
+	Share of partnership liabilities	14,000
−	Partner's liability assumed by partnership	(70,000)
=	**Basis in partnership interest**	$ 0

SUCCESS TIP: The AICPA has tested on the calculation of the initial basis of a partner's interest in a partnership. Questions have described the various items contributed by a partner and asked for the amount of the contributing partner's basis in the partnership.

3. **Contributed Services**

   a. A partner who receives a partnership capital interest in exchange for services recognizes compensation income equal to the FMV of the partnership capital interest.

      1) Gross income must be reported when an interest received is subject to neither substantial risk of forfeiture nor restrictions on transfer.
      2) The income reported is ordinary.

   b. However, there is generally no immediate income recognition upon receipt of a profits interest. Instead, future profits are taxed when earned by the partnership.

SUCCESS TIP: Some prior exam questions have neglected to identify an interest as capital or profits. In these cases, the interest was tested as capital. We suggest that if you see a question not indicating the type of interest, you should assume it is capital.

EXAMPLE 15-3   Basis in the Partnership -- Contribution of Services

In 2021, Albert provided services to Jim's Sole Proprietorship in exchange for a 20% share of the newly created partnership. If the FMV of the assets equals $500,000 and the liabilities equal $100,000, Albert recognizes $80,000 as compensation income ($400,000 × 20%), which is the FMV of the capital interest received. Albert's basis in the partnership is equal to the compensation income recognized; in this case, it is $80,000.

4. **Partnership's Gain**
    a. The partnership realizes neither gain nor loss when it receives contributions of money or property in exchange for partnership interests.

5. **Partnership's Basis in Contributed Property**
    a. The partnership's basis in contributed property is equal to the contributing partner's AB in the property immediately before contribution and is not adjusted for liabilities.
        1) A partnership's basis in property owned by the partnership is known as "inside basis."
        2) For investment partnerships, the partnership's basis is increased by any gain recognized by the partner on the contribution. An investment partnership is one that would be treated as an investment company if it were incorporated.

6. **Holding Periods**
    a. The holding period (HP) of the partner's interest includes the HP of contributed capital and Sec. 1231 assets.
        1) If the interest was received in exchange for ordinary income property or services, the HP starts the day following the exchange.
        2) The partnership's HP in contributed property includes the partner's HP even if the partner recognized gain.

7. **Partner-Purchased Interest**
    a. The basis in a partnership interest purchased from a partner is its cost, which is the sum of the purchase price and the partner's share of partnership liabilities.
    b. The partnership may elect to adjust the basis in its assets by the difference between the transferee's basis in his or her partnership interest and his or her proportionate share of the partnership's AB in its assets. This is referred to as a Sec. 754 election.
        1) The difference is allocated first to Sec. 1231 property and capital assets and then to other partnership property. Finally, allocation is made to assets within each of the two classes.
            a) For **upward adjustment**, allocation is on the basis of relative appreciation of classes and assets. No adjustment is made to a depreciated class or asset.
            b) For **downward adjustment**, allocation is on the basis of relative depreciation of classes and assets. No allocation is made to an appreciated class or asset.

8. **Partners' Capital Accounts**
    a. A capital account is maintained for each partner at the partnership level.
        1) A partner's initial capital account balance is the FMV of the assets (net of liabilities) (s)he contributed to the partnership (book capital account).
            a) The **tax capital account** represents the book capital account adjusted for tax code requirements.
        2) It is separate from the partner's AB in his or her partnership interest.

3) Capital accounts are used to ensure that a partnership's allocations for tax match their underlying economic agreement. (Item 4. in Subunit 15.2 discusses a partner's distributive share, to which capital accounts apply.)

EXAMPLE 15-4	Adjusted Basis of Contributed Property

Taxpayer contributes property that has an adjusted basis of $400 and a FMV of $1,000. Taxpayer's partner contributes $1,000 cash. While each has increased his or her capital account by $1,000, the adjusted basis of Taxpayer's partnership interest is only $400, and the adjusted basis of Taxpayer's partner's partnership interest is $1,000.

9. **Partnership Tax Year**

    a. The partnership's tax year is determined with respect to the partners' tax years.

        1) Unless an exception applies, the partnership must use a required tax year. A required tax year is the first of a), b), or c) below that applies.

            a) **Majority interest tax year.** It is the tax year of partners owning more than 50% of partnership capital and profits if they have the same year as determined on the first day of the partnership's tax year.

            b) **Principal partners' tax year.** It is the tax year of all principal partners, i.e., partners owning 5% or more of capital or profits, if they all have the same tax year.

            c) **Least aggregate deferral tax year.**

                i) Multiply each partner's ownership percentage by the number of months of income deferral for each possible partnership tax year.

                ii) Select the tax year that produces the smallest total tax deferral.

                iii) The deferral period begins with the possible partnership tax-year end date and extends to the partner's tax-year end date.

EXAMPLE 15-5	Least Aggregate Deferral Tax Year

Test 12/31	Year End	Ownership ×	Months Deferred =	Deferral
Tom Barnes	12/31	50%	0	0.0
Jerry Corp	11/30	50%	11	5.5
			Total Deferral	5.5

Test 11/30				
Tom Barnes	12/31	50%	1	0.5
Jerry Corp	11/30	50%	0	0.0
			Total Deferral	0.5

The least aggregate deferral tax year is 11/30.

    2) Any time there is a change in partners or a partner changes his or her tax year, the partnership may be required to change its tax year.

b. When each partner includes his or her pro rata share of partnership income depends on both the partnership tax year and the individual's tax year.
   1) If the partner's tax year coincides with the partnership's, the partner reports his or her distributive share of partnership items, including guaranteed payments, in that year.
   2) If the partner's tax year does not coincide with the partnership's, the partner reports his or her distributive share of partnership items, including guaranteed payments, in the tax year in which the partnership's tax year ends.

EXAMPLE 15-6   Partner's Tax Year Different from Partnership's

Annie, a calendar-year individual, is a partner in ABC Partnership. ABC has a fiscal year ending July 31. Annie will report ABC's activities from August 1, 2020, through July 31, 2021, on her 2021 tax return.

---

c. A year other than one required may be adopted for a business purpose, with IRS approval. Income deferral is not a business purpose.
   1) Natural business year. Accounting for a natural business year, e.g., in a seasonal line of business, can be an acceptable business purpose.
      a) The business is considered seasonal if, in any 12-month period, at least 25% of annual gross receipts were received during the last 2 months of the year in each of the preceding 3 years.
   2) Section 444 election (fiscal year). A partnership may elect a tax year that is neither the required year nor a natural business year.
      a) The year elected may result in no more than 3 months' deferral (between the end of a tax year elected and the end of the required tax year).
      b) The partnership must pay an amount approximating the amount of additional tax that would have resulted had the election not been made.

10. **Partnership Elections**
    a. **Elections** are generally made by the partnership.
       1) Partnership-level election examples are accounting methods, tax year, inventory methods, start-up costs, installment sales, and depreciation methods.
       2) Each partner makes certain elections for his or her distributive share, e.g., deduction (credit) for foreign tax expense of the partnership or the order of reducing tax attributes upon forgiveness of partnership debt.

STOP & REVIEW

You have completed the outline for this subunit.
Study multiple-choice questions 1 through 10 beginning on page 431.

15.2 PARTNER'S TAXABLE INCOME

1. **Overview**

   a. A partner's taxable income may be affected by his or her interest in a partnership in several ways, e.g., as a result of his or her distributive share of partnership taxable income and separately stated items, from sale of his or her partnership interest, and from dealings with the partnership.

   b. Partnership taxable income is determined in the same way as for individuals, except that certain deductions are not allowed for a partnership, other items are required to be separately stated, and business interest expense is limited the same way as for C and S corporations.

2. **Partnership's Income and Deductions**

   a. A partnership computes its net ordinary business income or loss; however, each partnership item of income, gain, deduction, loss, or credit that may vary the tax liability of any two partners differently must be **separately stated**. Items that must be separately stated include the following:

      1) Rental activities and related expenses
      2) Guaranteed payments
      3) Interest and dividend income
      4) Royalties
      5) Net short- and long-term capital gain or loss from the sale or exchange of capital assets
      6) Section 1231 gain and loss
      7) Other income: (a) portfolio income, (b) cancellation of debt, (c) recovery items (e.g., prior taxes, bad debts, etc.), and (d) investment income
      8) Section 179 deductions
      9) Other deductions: (a) charitable contributions, (b) investment expense, and (c) depletion on oil and gas wells
      10) Foreign income taxes paid or accrued
      11) Tax-exempt income and related expenses
      12) Distributions
      13) Qualified items of income, gain, and loss for the qualified business income deduction (QBID)

SUCCESS TIP: To better understand the need to separately state certain items, consider the following: The ability of individuals to deduct charitable contributions as itemized deductions is based on an AGI ceiling. Different individuals will have different AGIs. Moreover, C corporation partners can only deduct charitable contributions that do not exceed 25% of taxable income.

From Form 1065 Schedule K-1

	Part III Partner's Share of Current Year Income, Deductions, Credits, and Other Items		
1	Ordinary business income (loss)	15	Credits
2	Net rental real estate income (loss)		
3	Other net rental income (loss)	16	Foreign transactions
4a	Guaranteed payments for services		
4b	Guaranteed payments for capital		
4c	Total guaranteed payments		
5	Interest income		
6a	Ordinary dividends		
6b	Qualified dividends		
6c	Dividend equivalents	17	Alternative minimum tax (AMT) items
7	Royalties		
8	Net short-term capital gain (loss)		
9a	Net long-term capital gain (loss)	18	Tax-exempt income and nondeductible expenses
9b	Collectibles (28%) gain (loss)		
9c	Unrecaptured section 1250 gain		
10	Net section 1231 gain (loss)		
		19	Distributions
11	Other income (loss)		
		20	Other information
12	Section 179 deduction		
13	Other deductions		
14	Self-employment earnings (loss)		
21	☐ More than one activity for at-risk purposes*		
22	☐ More than one activity for passive activity purposes*		
*See attached statement for additional information.			

SU 15: Partnerships: Formation and Income

3. **Ordinary Business Income (Loss)**

    a. Generally, this includes taxable items of income, gain, loss, or deduction that are not separately stated.

       1) Ordinary business income is different from taxable income, which is the sum of all taxable items, including the separately stated items and the partnership ordinary business income or loss.

          a) Ordinary business income includes such items as gross profit, administrative expenses, and employee salaries.

          b) **Exception:** Guaranteed payments are subtracted as expenses for computing ordinary business income but are separately stated as income to the recipient partner.

From Form 1065

Income	1a	Gross receipts or sales	1a	
	b	Returns and allowances	1b	
	c	Balance. Subtract line 1b from line 1a	1c	
	2	Cost of goods sold (attach Form 1125-A)	2	
	3	Gross profit. Subtract line 2 from line 1c	3	
	4	Ordinary income (loss) from other partnerships, estates, and trusts (attach statement)	4	
	5	Net farm profit (loss) (attach Schedule F (Form 1040 or 1040-SR))	5	
	6	Net gain (loss) from Form 4797, Part II, line 17 (attach Form 4797)	6	
	7	Other income (loss) (attach statement)	7	
	8	**Total income (loss).** Combine lines 3 through 7	8	
Deductions (see instructions for limitations)	9	Salaries and wages (other than to partners) (less employment credits)	9	
	10	Guaranteed payments to partners	10	
	11	Repairs and maintenance	11	
	12	Bad debts	12	
	13	Rent	13	
	14	Taxes and licenses	14	
	15	Interest (see instructions)	15	
	16a	Depreciation (if required, attach Form 4562)	16a	
	b	Less depreciation reported on Form 1125-A and elsewhere on return .	16b	16c
	17	Depletion **(Do not deduct oil and gas depletion.)**	17	
	18	Retirement plans, etc.	18	
	19	Employee benefit programs	19	
	20	Other deductions (attach statement)	20	
	21	**Total deductions.** Add the amounts shown in the far right column for lines 9 through 20 . . .	21	
	22	**Ordinary business income (loss).** Subtract line 21 from line 8	22	

4. **Partner's Distributive Share**
    a. Each partner is taxed on his or her share of partnership income, whether or not it is distributed.
    b. If the partnership agreement does not allocate a partnership item or lacks substantial economic effect, the item must be allocated to partners according to their interests in the partnership.
        1) The economic effect is **substantial** if there is a reasonable possibility that the allocation will significantly affect the after-tax economic position of the partners.
    c. **Precontribution gain or loss.** To the extent of gain not recognized on contribution of property to the partnership, gain or loss subsequently recognized on the sale or exchange of an asset must be allocated to the contributing partner.
        1) Postcontribution gain or loss is allocated among partners as distributive shares, i.e., as any other gain or loss.

> **EXAMPLE 15-7**   **Postcontribution Gain or Loss**
>
> Tony and Mary form a partnership as equal partners. Tony contributes cash of $100,000, and Mary contributes an asset with a basis of $80,000 and a FMV of $100,000. Two years later, the partnership sells the asset for $110,000. The $30,000 gain ($110,000 selling price – $80,000 basis) is allocated, $25,000 to Mary [$20,000 precontribution gain + (50% partnership interest × $10,000 postcontribution gain)] and $5,000 to Tony (50% partnership interest × $10,000 postcontribution gain).

    2) Accounting for variation between the property's FMV and adjusted basis (AB) immediately before contribution also applies to related deductions. For example, depreciation must be apportioned and allocated.
    d. **Character.** The character of distributive shares of partnership items is generally determined at the partnership level.
        1) Any capital loss (FMV < AB) inherent at contribution is capital loss to the extent of any loss realized when the partnership disposes of the property. This applies for 5 years after contribution.
        2) Partnership gain or loss on contributed inventory and unrealized receivables is ordinary income. This treatment of the inventory disappears 5 years after contribution.
    e. If the size of a partner's interest in the partnership varies (e.g., by sale, purchase, exchange, liquidation) during a partnership tax year, the distributive shares of partnership items must be allocated between periods of varying ownership (the interim closing method). Alternatively, the partners can elect to apportion based on days (the proration method).
        1) The partnership may change profit and loss ratios up to the date of the return.
        2) The following items of a cash-basis partnership must be accounted for on an accrual basis but only for apportioning distributive shares: payments for services or the use of property, interest, and taxes.

5. **Adjustments to Basis**

   a. The basis of a partner's interest in a partnership is adjusted each year for subsequent contributions of capital, partnership taxable income (loss), separately stated items, variations in the partner's share of partnership liabilities, and distributions from the partnership to the partner.

	Initial basis
+	Subsequent contributions to capital
+/–	Distributive share of partnership ordinary business income (loss)
+	Separately stated taxable and nontaxable income
–	Separately stated deductible and nondeductible expenditures
+	Increase in allocable share of partnership liabilities
–	Decrease in allocable share of partnership liabilities
–	Current-year excess business interest expense
–	Share of the adjusted basis of charitable property contributions and foreign taxes paid or accrued
–	Distributions from partnership
=	**Adjusted basis in partnership interest**

   > **EXAMPLE 15-8   Year-End Adjusted Basis**
   >
   > The taxpayer's ownership and basis in the partnership are 50% and $15,000, respectively, at the beginning of the year. The partnership has ordinary business income of $8,000, made charitable contributions of $3,000, and made a $5,000 distribution to the taxpayer. The taxpayer's basis at the end of the year is $12,500 [$15,000 beginning basis + ($8,000 ordinary income × 50% ownership) – ($3,000 charitable contribution × 50% ownership) – $5,000 distribution].

   b. Basis is adjusted for variations in a partner's allocable share of partnership liabilities during the year, e.g., by payments on principal.

      1) Partner capital accounts are not adjusted for partnership liability variations.

   c. Basis is not reduced below zero.

   d. Basis is reduced without regard to losses suspended under passive activity loss rules and at-risk rules, or losses creating an NOL under the excess loss rules.

   e. No adjustment to basis is made for guaranteed payments received.

6. **Loss Limits**
    a. A partnership ordinary loss is a negative balance of taxable income.
    b. **Basis limit.** A partner is allowed to deduct the pro rata share of the partnership's ordinary loss only to the extent of his or her basis in the partnership.
        1) Excess loss is deductible in a subsequent year in which AB is greater than zero.
    c. **At-risk rules.** Each partner may deduct only a partnership ordinary loss to the extent (s)he is at risk with respect to the partnership.
        1) The at-risk limits also apply at the partnership level with respect to each partnership activity.
            a) The amount of a partnership loss currently deductible (up to an amount for which the partnership bears economic risk of loss with respect to each partnership activity) is allocated to partners as a deductible distributive share.
        2) A limited partner is at risk in the partnership to the extent of contributions and his or her share of qualified nonrecourse financing, that is, the amount the partner would lose if the partnership suddenly became worthless.
    d. Passive activity losses are deductible in the current year only to the extent of gains from passive activities (in the aggregate).
        1) Partnership ordinary loss is generally passive to a partner unless the partner materially participates in the partnership activity.

> **SUCCESS TIP:** Past CPA Exam questions have tested candidates' knowledge of calculating a partner's share of taxable income and the partner's adjusted basis in the partnership. Also, questions have asked for the calculation of the partnership's income.

    e. **Excess business loss.**
        1) When total losses from all trades or businesses exceed all gross income and gains from all sources, only $262,000 of the net loss is deductible on an individual return ($524,000 in the case of MFJ).
            a) Any nondeductible loss is treated as a net operating loss (covered in Study Unit 8, Subunit 2).

7. **Sale of a Partnership Interest**
    a. A sale or exchange of a partnership interest results in capital gain or loss, except that any gain realized attributable to unrealized receivables and inventory is ordinary income (OI).
    b. Gain or loss realized includes the selling partner's share of partnership liabilities.
    c. A long-term capital gain results if the partner held the interest more than 1 year.

d. Gain realized on the sale of a partnership is OI to the extent attributable to the partner's share of Sec. 751, or "hot" assets. These include unrealized receivables (URs) and inventory.

   1) URs are rights to payments to the extent not already included in income under the partnership's accounting method. The rights to payment may be for services or for goods other than capital assets.

      a) URs also include the OI potential (recapture) in Sec. 1245 and Sec. 1250 property and in franchises, trademarks, or trade names.
      b) Note that, to the extent that an accrual-method partnership has basis in an account receivable, the receivable is not unrealized.

   2) "Inventory" in this context includes not only inventory held for sale but also any partnership property characterized as other than Sec. 1231 property or a capital asset in the hands of the partnership, selling partner, or a distributee partner (e.g., copyrights, accounts receivable, unrealized receivables).

EXAMPLE 15-9	Sale of a Partnership Interest

S sells a 25% interest (AB = $100,000) in Partnership to B for $200,000. Partnership's assets are cash ($80,000), land (FMV = $300,000, AB = $160,000), and inventory (FMV = $400,000, AB = $280,000). Of S's realized gain of $100,000, at least $30,000 is ordinary income [($400,000 − $280,000) × 25%].

8. **Liability Relief**

   a. A partner's relief from partnership liabilities is treated as a distribution of money.

EXAMPLE 15-10	Relief from Partnership Liabilities

Tami sold her share of a partnership for $29,000. Her basis in the partnership is $24,000, including $10,000 of liabilities. The selling price is considered to be $39,000 ($29,000 cash received plus the $10,000 relief of liabilities). Thus, her gain on the sale of the partnership interest is $15,000 ($39,000 − $24,000).

9. **Gift of a Partnership Interest**

   a. Generally, no gain is recognized upon the gift. However, if partnership liabilities allocable to the gifted interest exceed the AB of the partnership interest, the donor must recognize gain. No loss is recognized on the gift.
   b. The donee's basis in the interest is the donor's basis after adjustment for the donor's distributive share of partnership items up to the date of the gift.
   c. For purposes of computing a loss on a subsequent sale of the interest by the donee, the FMV of the interest immediately prior to the gift is used if the FMV of the gifted partnership interest is lower than the basis at the time of the gift.
   d. Generally, partnership interest gifted to a related minor is attributed to others (e.g., parents).

      1) There are limits on the amount of partnership income that can be allocated to a related minor.

10. **Inheritance**
    a. The tax year of a partnership closes with respect to a partner whose entire interest in the partnership terminates, whether by death, liquidation, or otherwise.
    b. The successor has a FMV basis in the interest.
    c. The partnership tax year does not close with respect to the other partners.

11. **Family Partnerships**
    a. A family partnership is one consisting of a taxpayer and his or her spouse, ancestors, lineal descendants, or trusts for the primary benefit of any of them. Siblings are not treated as members of the taxpayer's family for these purposes.
    b. **Services.** A services partnership is one in which capital is not a material income-producing factor.
        1) In a family partnership, a family member is treated as a services partner only to the extent (s)he provides services that are substantial or vital to the partnership.
    c. **Capital.** A family member is treated as a partner in a partnership in which capital is a material income-producing factor, whether the interest is acquired by gift or purchase.
        1) The partnership agreement is disregarded to the extent a partner receives less than reasonable compensation for services.

EXAMPLE 15-11   Family Partnership -- Gift to Child

R gives Son a gift of $250,000. Son contributes it in exchange for a 50% interest in a newly formed partnership with R. R&S Partnership continues what was R's sole proprietorship. The reasonable value of R's services the following tax year is $75,000. Of R&S's gross income of $125,000, $75,000 must be allocated to R for his services. Son's distributive share attributable to his capital interest is no more than $25,000 [($125,000 − $75,000) × 50%].

---

    2) This rule applies to all partners, not just family members.
    d. Spouses filing a joint return may elect out of partnership treatment by choosing to be a qualified joint venture.
        1) The only members of the joint venture must be the spouses, and both must materially participate and make the election.
        2) Each spouse will be treated as a sole proprietor, allowing both to receive Social Security benefits.

EXAMPLE 15-12   Spousal Joint Venture

Paul has always wanted to open an Italian restaurant. When he married Denise, they decided to open the restaurant together. Denise, Paul, and Paul's brother Mark contributed equal amounts to form a partnership to build the restaurant. Paul and Mark run the restaurant, and Denise is a silent partner who is not involved in operations. The business is not eligible to be a qualified joint venture because the couple is not the only members of the business. Had Mark never been a member, the business still would not be a qualified joint venture because Denise does not materially participate in the business.

12. **Reporting Requirements**
    a. A partnership, as a conduit, is generally not subject to federal income tax. But it must report information including partnership items of income, loss, deduction, and credit to the IRS.
    b. A partnership is required to file an initial return for the first year in which it receives income or incurs expenditures treated as deductions for federal income tax purposes.
    c. Form 1065 is used for the partnership's information return.
    d. Any partnership item that may vary tax liability of any partner is separately stated on Schedule K.
    e. A Schedule K-1 is prepared for each partner and contains the partner's distributive share of partnership income and separately stated items to be reported on the partner's tax return.
    f. A partnership return is due (postmark date) on or before the 15th day of the 3rd month following the close of the partnership's tax year (March 15 for calendar-year partnerships). Partnership extension periods are, like most others, 6 months (September 15 for a calendar-year partnership).
    g. Signature by any partner is evidence that the partner was authorized to sign the return. Only one partner is required to sign the return.
    h. **Inadequate filing.** A penalty is imposed in the amount of the number of persons who were partners at any time during the year, multiplied by $210 (for 2021 tax returns filed in 2022) for each of up to 12 months (including a portion of one) that the return was late or incomplete.
    i. Each partner must report his or her share of items consistent with their treatment on the partnership return unless
        1) The partner identifies an inconsistency on a filed statement, or
        2) The partnership has no more than 10 partners, and no estate or nonresident alien is a partner.
    j. The IRC provides for designation of a partnership representative (PR) who has sole authority to commit the partnership to tax and litigation matters.

Operations Attributes Chart

Earnings Implications		Ownership & Basis Adjustments	
Income Characterization	Passed through to partners; character is the same as if a partner received it directly	Death – Basis Adjustments	Basis of partnership interest is generally FMV on the date of death; Sec. 754 election available at partnership level
Allocation of Income	Based on partnership agreement if it has substantial economic effect	Basis Increases from Operations	Increased by profits and additional contributions, and increase in partner's share of debts
Exempt Income (i.e., municipal bond interest)	Passed through to partners; retains character as exempt		
Capital Losses	Passed through to shareholders with normal limitations applying at partner level	Basis Decreases from Operations	Decreased by losses, deductions, distributions, and decreases in partner's share of debts
Charitable Contributions	Passed through to partner; normal limitations apply at partner level (e.g., AGI percentage limits for individuals and taxable income percentage limits for C corporations)	Transferability of Interest/Ownership	Can sell all or a portion of partnership interest
		Liquidating and Nonliquidating Distributions	Based on partnership agreement
Deductibility of Losses	Passed through to partners; normal limitations apply, basis, at risk, passive, excess loss		

Tax Implications

Pass-Through Tax Treatment	Yes
Double Taxation	No
Income Tax Brackets	Income tax brackets of the partner
Business Income Taxability	Business net income taxed as personal income to partners

STOP & REVIEW

You have completed the outline for this subunit.
Study multiple-choice questions 11 through 19 beginning on page 435.

15.1 Partnership Formation and Tax Year

1. Which one of the following statements regarding a partnership's tax year is true?

A. A partnership formed on July 1 is required to adopt a tax year ending on June 30.
B. A partnership may elect to have a tax year other than the generally required tax year if the deferral period for the tax year elected does not exceed 3 months.
C. A "valid business purpose" can no longer be claimed as a reason for adoption of a tax year other than the generally required tax year.
D. Within 30 days after a partnership has established a tax year, a form must be filed with the IRS as notification of the tax year adopted.

Answer (B) is correct.
   REQUIRED: The correct statement regarding a partnership tax year.
   DISCUSSION: A partnership may elect a fiscal year with no more than a 3-month deferral period; i.e., the number of months between the end of the tax year selected and the end of the required tax year.
   Answer (A) is incorrect. A partnership may elect any taxable year as long as it corresponds to that of its majority partner(s), all its principal partners, any taxable year given that its principal partners change to the same tax year, or a calendar year if all of its principal partners do not have the same tax year. **Answer (C) is incorrect.** Any fiscal year may be chosen if a business purpose is established and the IRS gives its consent. **Answer (D) is incorrect.** The partnership elects its tax year on its first return, which must be filed by the 15th day of the third month following the end of its tax year.

2. Strom acquired a 25% interest in Ace Partnership by contributing land having an adjusted basis of $16,000 and a fair market value of $50,000. The land was subject to a $24,000 recourse mortgage, which was assumed by Ace. No other liabilities existed at the time of the contribution. What was Strom's basis in Ace?

A. $0
B. $16,000
C. $26,000
D. $32,000

Answer (A) is correct.
   REQUIRED: The partner's basis after a contribution of property with a liability in excess of basis.
   DISCUSSION: A partner's basis in a partnership equals the adjusted basis of the property contributed plus the partner's share of all partnership liabilities minus any liability of the partner assumed by the partnership. A liability assumed by the partnership is treated as a distribution to the partner. The basis of this partnership interest is the basis of the contributed land ($16,000) reduced by the liability assumed by the partnership ($24,000) and increased by the partner's share of recourse partnership liabilities ($6,000 = $24,000 × 0.25) and recognized gain on contributed property ($2,000). Thus, the basis will be $0.
   Answer (B) is incorrect. The amount of $16,000 is the basis of the contributed property, which must be reduced by the liability assumed by the partnership and increased by the partner's share of partnership liabilities and recognized gain on contributed property. **Answer (C) is incorrect.** The amount of $26,000 is the FMV of the land reduced by the liability. The basis of the land, not the FMV, should be used to determine the partner's basis. Additionally, the partner's basis should be increased by his or her share of partnership liabilities and recognized gain on contributed property. **Answer (D) is incorrect.** The amount of $32,000 results from using the FMV of the land rather than the adjusted basis.

3. The holding period of a partnership interest acquired in exchange for a contributed capital asset begins on the date

A. The partner is admitted to the partnership.
B. The partner transfers the asset to the partnership.
C. The partner's holding period of the capital asset began.
D. The partner is first credited with the proportionate share of partnership capital.

Answer (C) is correct.
REQUIRED: The partner's holding period for a partnership interest acquired in exchange for a contributed capital asset.
DISCUSSION: The holding period of the partner's interest includes the holding period of contributed capital and Sec. 1231 assets. The holding period on an interest acquired in exchange for money, ordinary income property, or services begins the day after the exchange.

4. Nolan designed Timber Partnership's new building. Nolan received an interest in the partnership for the services. Nolan's normal billing for these services would be $80,000, and the fair market value of the partnership interest Nolan received is $120,000. What amount of income should Nolan report?

A. $0
B. $40,000
C. $80,000
D. $120,000

Answer (D) is correct.
REQUIRED: The recognized income from services in exchange for interest in a partnership.
DISCUSSION: A partner who receives a partnership capital interest in exchange for services recognizes compensation income equal to the FMV of the partnership capital interest. Gross income must be reported when an interest received is subject to neither substantial risk of forfeiture nor restrictions on transfer. The income reported is ordinary.
Answer (A) is incorrect. Income includes compensation for services. This is not a nonrecognition transaction. **Answer (B) is incorrect.** The value of service performed is also considered income. **Answer (C) is incorrect.** Income from services exchanged for partnership interest is not valued based on normal billing.

5. The following information pertains to Carr's admission to the Smith & Jones partnership on July 1, 2021:

Carr's contribution of capital: 800 shares of Ed Corporation stock bought in 2003 for $30,000; fair market value of $150,000 on July 1, 2021.

Carr's interest in capital and profits of Smith & Jones: 25%.

Fair market value of net assets of Smith & Jones on July 1, 2021, after Carr's admission: $600,000.

Carr's gain in 2021 on the exchange of the Ed stock for Carr's partnership interest was

A. $120,000 ordinary income.
B. $120,000 long-term capital gain.
C. $120,000 Sec. 1231 gain.
D. $0

Answer (D) is correct.
REQUIRED: The partner's gain recognized on the exchange of stock for a partnership interest.
DISCUSSION: No gain or loss is recognized by a partnership or its partners when property is contributed to the partnership in exchange for a partnership interest. Carr's realized gain of $120,000 (25% of the $600,000 value of the partnership minus his $30,000 basis in his contribution) is not recognized. The precontribution gain on the asset is allocated to the contributing partner when the partnership later sells the asset.
Note that stock does constitute property. However, if the partnership would be an investment company if it were incorporated, the gain will be recognized. For this purpose, an investment company is one in which the partner has diversified his or her interest in stocks and securities and in which 80% or more of the partnership's assets are marketable stocks or securities.

SU 15: Partnerships: Formation and Income

6. Which of the following should be used in computing the basis of a partner's interest acquired from another partner?

	Cash Paid by Transferee to Transferor	Transferee's Share of Partnership Liabilities
A.	No	Yes
B.	Yes	No
C.	No	No
D.	Yes	Yes

Answer (D) is correct.
REQUIRED: The basis in a partnership interest purchased from a partner.
DISCUSSION: The purchasing partner's basis in his or her partnership interest is its cost basis. It includes both cash paid the seller and the purchaser's allocable share of partnership liabilities. But the partnership's basis in partnership property is not adjusted when a partnership interest is transferred unless a Sec. 754 election is in effect.
Answer (A) is incorrect. The transferee's basis also includes any cash paid. **Answer (B) is incorrect.** The transferee's basis also includes the purchaser's allocable share of partnership liabilities. **Answer (C) is incorrect.** The transferee's basis includes both any cash paid the seller and the purchaser's allocable share of partnership liabilities.

7. Pert contributed land with a fair market value of $20,000 to a new partnership in exchange for a 50% partnership interest. The land had an adjusted basis to Pert of $12,000 and was subject to a $4,000 mortgage, which the partnership assumed. What is the adjusted basis of Pert's partnership interest?

A. $10,000
B. $12,000
C. $18,000
D. $20,000

Answer (A) is correct.
REQUIRED: The partner's basis in a partnership to which (s)he contributed property with a liability.
DISCUSSION: The basis of an interest in a partnership acquired by the contribution of property is the adjusted basis of such property to the contributing partner. A decrease in a partner's personal liabilities by reason of the assumption by the partnership of such liabilities is treated as a distribution of money to the partner, which in turn reduces the basis of the partner's interest (but not below zero). When Pert became a 50% partner, his net liability relief was 50% of the $4,000 mortgage. Pert's basis in his partnership interest is the $12,000 basis in the property contributed less the $2,000 of liability relief (limited to zero).

8. Under Sec. 444 of the Internal Revenue Code, certain partnerships can elect to use a tax year different from their required tax year. One of the conditions for eligibility to make a Sec. 444 election is that the partnership must

A. Be a limited partnership.
B. Be a member of a tiered structure.
C. Choose a tax year in which the deferral period is not longer than 3 months.
D. Have less than 75 partners.

Answer (C) is correct.
REQUIRED: The condition for eligibility to make a Sec. 444 election.
DISCUSSION: A partnership may elect, under Sec. 444, a fiscal year other than normally required and for which a business purpose does not exist. The fiscal year elected must be one with no more than a 3-month deferral period, i.e., the number of months between the beginning of the tax year selected and the end of the required tax year. For the election to be effective, a payment is required that approximates the tax the partners would have paid if the entity had used its required year.

9. On June 1, 2021, Kelly received a 10% interest in Rock Co., a partnership, for services contributed to the partnership. Rock's net assets at that date had a basis of $70,000 and a fair market value of $100,000. In Kelly's 2021 income tax return, what amount must Kelly include as income from transfer of partnership interest?

A. $7,000 ordinary income.
B. $7,000 capital gain.
C. $10,000 ordinary income.
D. $10,000 capital gain.

Answer (C) is correct.
REQUIRED: The income recognized when a partnership interest is received for services.
DISCUSSION: An individual recognizes compensation as ordinary income when a partnership interest is received in exchange for services (current or past) rendered. The receipt of a capital interest in a partnership for services is included in the year of receipt. Income recognized is the $10,000 (10% × $100,000) FMV of the partnership interest received unless the interest is nontransferable or subject to a substantial risk of forfeiture.

10. On January 2, Year 1, Black acquired a 50% interest in New Partnership by contributing property with an adjusted basis of $7,000 and a fair market value of $9,000, subject to a mortgage of $3,000. What was Black's basis in New at January 2, Year 1?

A. $3,500
B. $4,000
C. $5,500
D. $7,500

Answer (C) is correct.
REQUIRED: The partner's basis in a partnership when property subject to a liability is contributed.
DISCUSSION: The basis of an interest in a partnership acquired by the contribution of property is the adjusted basis of such property to the contributing partner. A decrease in a partner's individual liabilities by reason of the assumption by the partnership of such liabilities is treated as a distribution of money to the partner, which in turn reduces the basis of the partner's interest (but not below zero). When Black became a partner, he was relieved of 50% of the $3,000 liability, or $1,500. Thus, Black's basis in his or her interest in New is $5,500 ($7,000 – $1,500).
Answer (A) is incorrect. The amount of $3,500 incorrectly allocates Black's partnership interest to the adjusted basis of contributed property. **Answer (B) is incorrect.** The amount of $4,000 applies the entire mortgage against basis instead of the amount assumed by the partnership (100% – 50% interest). **Answer (D) is incorrect.** The amount of $7,500 incorrectly uses the FMV of the property contributed instead of the adjusted basis.

15.2 Partner's Taxable Income

11. On January 2, 2021, Arch and Bean contribute cash equally to form the JK Partnership. Arch and Bean share profits and losses in a ratio of 75% to 25%, respectively. For 2021, the partnership's ordinary income was $40,000. A distribution of $5,000 was made to Arch during 2021. What is Arch's share of taxable income for 2021?

A. $5,000
B. $10,000
C. $20,000
D. $30,000

Answer (D) is correct.
REQUIRED: The partner's share of partnership taxable income.
DISCUSSION: Arch's 75% share of the partnership's $40,000 ordinary income, or $30,000, is Arch's share of taxable income for 2021 even if not distributed. Distributions are received free of tax by the partner, provided (s)he has adequate basis in the partnership, i.e., at least as much basis as the distribution. A partner's basis is increased by his or her share of partnership income and decreased by distributions.
Answer (A) is incorrect. The amount of $5,000 is the distribution to the partner. The partner is taxed on his or her distributive share of partnership taxable income. Answer (B) is incorrect. Arch's profit share is 75%, not 25%. Answer (C) is incorrect. Arch's profit share is 75%, not 50%.

12. Molloy contributed $40,000 in cash in exchange for a one-third interest in the RST Partnership. In the first year of partnership operations, RST had taxable income of $60,000. In addition, Molloy received a $5,000 distribution of cash and, at the end of the partnership year, had a one-third share in the $18,000 of partnership recourse liabilities. What was Molloy's basis in RST at year end?

A. $55,000
B. $61,000
C. $71,000
D. $101,000

Answer (B) is correct.
REQUIRED: The taxpayer's adjusted basis in partnership.
DISCUSSION: A partner's initial basis in the partnership interest received is equal to any cash contribution made. The basis of a partner's interest in a partnership is adjusted up for allocable share of partnership taxable income and increases in the partner's share of partnership liabilities and adjusted down for distributions from the partnership to the partner. Molloy's basis at year end is $61,000 ($40,000 initial basis + $20,000 taxable income – $5,000 distribution + $6,000 liability assumed).
Answer (A) is incorrect. Basis is adjusted for a partner's share of assumed liability. Answer (C) is incorrect. Basis is adjusted down for distributions made during the year. Answer (D) is incorrect. Taxable income of the partnership is allocated to each partner according to the partner's share of interest in the partnership.

13. Lee inherited a partnership interest from Dale. The adjusted basis of Dale's partnership interest was $50,000, and its fair market value on the date of Dale's death (the estate valuation date) was $70,000. What was Lee's original basis for the partnership interest?

A. $70,000
B. $50,000
C. $20,000
D. $0

Answer (A) is correct.
REQUIRED: The basis in an inherited partnership interest.
DISCUSSION: The original basis in a partnership interest of a person who acquired it by inheritance is the fair market value of the interest on the date of death (if the estate does not elect the alternate valuation date).
Answer (B) is incorrect. A partnership interest acquired by inheritance does not use the decedent's adjusted basis as basis in the hands of the inheritor. Answer (C) is incorrect. The original basis of a partnership interest acquired by inheritance is not the difference between it FMV and adjusted basis at date of the grantor's death. Answer (D) is incorrect. The original basis of a partnership interest acquired by inheritance is its FMV.

14. Evan, a 25% partner in Vista Partnership, received a $20,000 guaranteed payment in 2021 for deductible services rendered to the partnership. Guaranteed payments were not made to any other partner. Vista's 2021 partnership income consisted of

Net business income before guaranteed payments	$80,000
Net long-term capital gains	10,000

What amount of income should Evan report from Vista Partnership on her 2021 tax return?

A. $37,500
B. $27,500
C. $22,500
D. $20,000

Answer (A) is correct.
REQUIRED: The amount of partner income.
DISCUSSION: A partner will report the ownership portion of the partnership income. Partnership income is the balance of the taxable income of a partnership that is not required to be separately stated. Capital gains and losses are generally segregated from ordinary net income and carried into the income of the individual partners. Any guaranteed payment (GP), while deductible for the partnership, is included in gross income of the receiving partner. Reportable income is calculated as follows:

Business income pre-GP	$80,000
Less: GP	(20,000)
Reportable partnership income	$60,000
25% interest	$15,000
Guaranteed payment	20,000
25% capital gain	2,500
Total	$37,500

Answer (B) is incorrect. The amount of $27,500 results from not deducting the guaranteed payment from net business income and adding only 25% of the guaranteed payment in the income calculation. **Answer (C) is incorrect.** The amount of $22,500 ignores the partner's share of partnership ordinary income. **Answer (D) is incorrect.** The amount of $20,000 ignores the business income and net capital gains.

15. Last year, Jim, one of two equal partners, contributed land with a basis to him of $15,000 and a fair market value of $10,000 to the partnership of which he was a member. His capital account was credited for $10,000. The land was later sold for $8,000. As a result of this sale, Jim must report on his personal income tax return

A. $1,000 loss.
B. $3,500 loss.
C. $5,000 loss.
D. $6,000 loss.

Answer (D) is correct.
REQUIRED: The tax effect of a sale of contributed property.
DISCUSSION: Generally, neither the partnership nor any partner recognizes gain or loss when property is contributed in exchange for a partnership interest. The partnership's basis in the property is $15,000 (the contributing partner's basis at the time of contribution). The sale of the property by the partnership resulted in a $7,000 loss ($8,000 proceeds less $15,000 AB). Precontribution loss must be allocated to the contributing partner. Jim must recognize all of the precontribution loss of $5,000 ($15,000 basis – $10,000 FMV contribution) plus his $1,000 share of postcontribution loss [($10,000 FMV of contribution – $8,000 sales price) × 1/2].
Answer (A) is incorrect. The loss recognized must be allocated to Jim to the extent of the built-in loss unrecognized on contribution. **Answer (B) is incorrect.** The entire initial $5,000 loss is allocated to Jim, but only half the $2,000 partnership loss is allocated to him. **Answer (C) is incorrect.** Jim's $1,000 distributive share of the post-contribution loss recognized is also gross income to Jim.

16. The method used to depreciate partnership property is an election made by

A. The partnership and must be the same method used by the principal partner.
B. The partnership and may be any method approved by the IRS.
C. The principal partner.
D. Each individual partner.

Answer (B) is correct.
REQUIRED: The correct statement about election of the method used to depreciate partnership property.
DISCUSSION: The partnership, although a conduit, is an entity distinct from the partners for certain tax purposes. Elections available with respect to the treatment of partnership items are generally made by the partnership. Accounting method and depreciation method elections, for example, are made by the partnership.

17. Which of the following limitations will apply in determining a partner's deduction for that partner's share of partnership losses if the partner is an individual?

	At-Risk	Passive Loss
A.	Yes	No
B.	No	Yes
C.	Yes	Yes
D.	No	No

Answer (C) is correct.
REQUIRED: The applicability of at-risk and passive activity loss rules to a partner's distributive share of partnership losses.
DISCUSSION: Each partner may deduct no more of his or her distributive share of partnership loss than the amount for which (s)he is at risk in the partnership. Each partner's share is passive unless the partner materially (or actively) participates in the partnership activity. Thus, each partner must apply passive limits to his or her distributive share. These rules do not apply to partners who are widely held corporations.
Answer (A) is incorrect. The passive activity loss rules apply to each partner. **Answer (B) is incorrect.** The at-risk rules apply to each partner. **Answer (D) is incorrect.** Both the at-risk and passive activity loss rules apply to each partner.

18. Partners Ann, Bob, and Carol of ABC, a calendar-year partnership, share partnership profits and losses in a ratio of 5:3:2, respectively. All three materially participate in the partnership business. Each partner's adjusted basis in the partnership as of December 31, 2021, was as follows:

Ann	$19,000
Bob	22,000
Carol	9,000

The partnership incurred an operating loss of $50,000 in 2021. What are Ann's, Bob's, and Carol's shares of the loss deductible on their 2021 individual income tax returns?

	Ann	Bob	Carol
A.	$19,000	$15,000	$9,000
B.	$19,000	$15,000	$10,000
C.	$19,000	$22,000	$9,000
D.	$25,000	$15,000	$10,000

Answer (A) is correct.
REQUIRED: The partners' individual shares of the loss of a partnership.
DISCUSSION: In determining his or her income tax, a partner must separately consider his or her distributive share of the partnership's income, gain, loss, deduction, or credit. A partner's distributive share of partnership loss is allowed only to the extent of the adjusted basis of such partner's interest in the partnership. Thus, Ann may recognize loss only up to her basis of $19,000, Bob can recognize his entire share ($15,000) of the loss, and Carol can recognize the loss up to her basis of $9,000.
Answer (B) is incorrect. Carol can recognize the loss only up to the amount of her basis. **Answer (C) is incorrect.** Bob's share of the loss is only $15,000; $22,000 is his basis. **Answer (D) is incorrect.** Ann and Carol can recognize the loss only up to the amount of their bases.

19. Which of the following entities must pay taxes for federal income tax purposes?

A. General partnership.
B. Limited partnership.
C. Joint venture.
D. C corporation.

Answer (D) is correct.
REQUIRED: The entity that must pay taxes for federal income tax purposes.
DISCUSSION: Corporate taxable income computations generally parallel those for individuals. General tax is determined by applying applicable tax rates to taxable income. Shareholders are then subject to federal income tax on distributions out of corporate earnings and profits. In addition to regular income tax, a C corporation may also be subject to the AMT. Partnerships and joint ventures are all pass-through entities, which are taxed at the individual level, not the partnership level.
Answer (A) is incorrect. A partnership, as a conduit, is not subject to federal income tax; however, it must report information including partnership items of income, loss, deduction, and credit to the IRS. **Answer (B) is incorrect.** A partnership, as a conduit, is not subject to federal income tax; however, it must report information including partnership items of income, loss, deduction, and credit to the IRS. **Answer (C) is incorrect.** A joint venture is an easily formed business structure allowing MFJ taxpayers to elect out of partnership treatment, which permits both to receive Social Security benefits. A joint venture is like a partnership and is not subject to federal income tax.

Access the **Gleim CPA Premium Review System** featuring our SmartAdapt technology from your Gleim Personal Classroom to continue your studies. You will experience a personalized study environment with exam-emulating multiple-choice questions.

STUDY UNIT SIXTEEN
PARTNERSHIP TRANSACTIONS AND BOOK-TO-TAX DIFFERENCES

(20 pages of outline)

16.1	Partners Dealing with Own Partnership	440
16.2	Treatment of Partnership Liabilities	443
16.3	Distribution of Partnership Assets	445
16.4	Reconciling Book and Taxable Income	451

Partnerships are collaborative ventures governed by the partnership agreement. Ownership interest in a partnership is determined by contributions to the partnership and the operations of the partnership, including assumption of liability. Candidates should be prepared to identify a payment to a partner as a guaranteed payment, as a distributive share, or in a nonpartner capacity, and the effect of the classification, e.g., a deduction to the partnership passed through ratably to all partners. Partnership liability fluctuations have special significance because they vary the partners' bases in their partnership interests and affect treatment of distributions. Book-to-tax differences exist due to differences between generally accepted accounting principles, the Internal Revenue Code, and applicable regulations. The qualified business income deduction (QBID) is discussed in Study Unit 7, Subunit 3, and Study Unit 16 multiple-choice questions and simulations exclude QBID ramifications.

Some candidates find it helpful to have the entire tax form side-by-side with our Knowledge Transfer Outline when studying, and others may prefer to see the final draft of a form when it is released. The full versions of the most up-to-date forms are easily accessible at www.gleim.com/taxforms. These forms and the form excerpts used in our outline are periodically updated as the latest versions are released by the IRS.

16.1 PARTNERS DEALING WITH OWN PARTNERSHIP

1. **Overview**

   a. The Code recognizes that a partner can engage in property, services, and loan transactions with the partnership in a capacity other than as a partner, i.e., as an independent, outside third party. The tax result, in general, is as if the transaction took place between two unrelated persons after arm's-length negotiations.

2. **Customary Partner Services**

   a. When a partner performs services for the partnership that are customarily performed by a partner, the partner's return is generally his or her share of profits of the partnership business.

      1) It is gross income, not as compensation, but as a distributive share of partnership income.
      2) The value of the services is not deductible by the partnership.

3. **Guaranteed Payments**

   a. A guaranteed payment (GP) is a payment to a partner for services rendered or capital used that is determined without regard to the income of the partnership.

      1) It is used to distinguish payments that are a function of partnership income and payments connected with partners acting in a nonpartner capacity.

   b. **Services.** The services must be a customary function of a partner. They are normal activities of a partner in conducting partnership business.

   c. **Use of capital.** The payment may be stated to be interest on the partner's capital account or to be rent on contributed property.

   d. **Fixed amount stated.** If the partnership agreement provides for a GP in a fixed amount, e.g., annual salary amount, the GP amount is the stated amount.

   e. **Stated minimum amount.** The partnership agreement may allocate a share of partnership income to the partner. Any excess over the partner's pro rata share is considered GP.

      GP = Stated minimum amount − Partner's share of partnership income

   f. For purposes of determining the partner's gross income, the GP is treated as if made to a nonpartner.

      1) The partner separately states the GP from any distributive share.
      2) The payment is ordinary income to the partner.
      3) The payment is reported in the tax year in which the partnership makes the GP.
      4) Receipt of a GP does not directly affect the partner's AB in his or her partnership interest.

g. For purposes of determining deductibility by the partnership, a GP is treated as if made to a nonpartner.

   1) The payment is deductible if it would have been deductible if made to a nonpartner.
   2) Usually, deductible GPs are for a general business expenditure that need not be separately stated.
   3) Investment interest expense is an exception. It should be separately stated even if it is GP and even if it is deductible by a partner.

   NOTE: If the GP exceeds the partnership's ordinary income, the resulting ordinary loss is allocated among the partners (including the partner who receives the GP).

EXAMPLE 16-1   Guaranteed Payment to a Partner

Under a partnership agreement, Meena is to receive 30% of the partnership income, but not less than $13,000. The partnership has net income of $30,000. Meena's share, without regard to the minimum guarantee, is $9,000 (30% × $30,000). The guaranteed payment that can be deducted by the partnership is $4,000 ($13,000 – $9,000). Meena's income from the partnership is $13,000, and the remaining $17,000 of partnership income will be reported by the other partners in proportion to their shares under the partnership agreement.

If the partnership net income had been $50,000, there would have been no guaranteed payment since Meena's share, without regard to the guarantee, would have been greater than the guarantee.

---

h. For all other purposes, the GP is treated as if made to a partner in his or her capacity as a partner. A partner is not an employee of the partnership. The GP is self-employment income to the receiving partner. Partnership contributions to a self-employment retirement plan are not deductible by the partnership.

SUCCESS TIP: A GP is reported in three places: (1) as a deduction used to compute ordinary business income or loss, which is shared among all partners, taken on Form 1065, page 1, line 10; (2) as a separately stated item on Schedule K, line 4, which is allocated to the receiving partner; and (3) on the receiving partner's Schedule K-1.

4. **Nonpartner Capacity**

   a. Payments to a partner without regard to income of the partnership for property or for services not customarily performed by a partner are generally treated as if the transaction took place between two unrelated persons after arm's-length negotiations.
   b. **Loans.** Interest paid to a partner on a (true) loan is all gross income to the partner and a deductible partnership item.
   c. **Services.** Payments to the partner for services rendered (of a nature not normally performed by a partner) to or for the partnership are gross income to the partner and generally an ordinary deductible expense of the partnership.
   d. **Property.** A partner acting as a nonpartner (independent third party, outsider) can sell (or exchange) property to (or with) the partnership, and vice-versa. Gain or loss on the transaction is recognized, unless an exception applies.

EXAMPLE 16-2   Sale to Partner Acting as a Nonpartner

Partnership sells land to Partner. Partnership recognizes loss unless the sale is to a related party. The loss is a partnership item allocable to partners as distributive shares. Partner takes a cost basis in the property.

e. Character and loss limit rules.

1) **Applicability.** These character and loss limit rules apply to any transaction between the partnership and either

   a) A partner who owns more than 50% of the partnership or
   b) Another partnership, if more than 50% of the capital or profits interest of each is owned by the same persons.

2) **Character.** Any gain recognized is ordinary income if the property is held as other than a capital asset by the acquiring partner or partnership.

EXAMPLE 16-3   Sale of Capital Assets -- Change in Character

Dora has held a capital asset for several years. The asset has a basis of $16,000 and a FMV of $24,000. She sells the asset to a partnership in which she is more than a 50% owner. The partnership will hold the property as a depreciable asset. Her gain of $8,000 ($24,000 – $16,000) will be ordinary income since she sold a capital asset to a more than 50% owned partnership that is not a capital asset to the partnership. If the partnership were to hold the asset as a capital asset, her gain would be capital gain.

---

3) **Loss limit.** No deduction is allowed for realized losses.

   a) The acquiring party has a cost basis.
   b) A subsequent taxable disposition event results in gain recognition limited to the previously unrecognized gain.
   c) Expenditures are deductible when, and not before, the amount is includible in gross income by the payee even if the payor is an accrual-method taxpayer.

f. **Distribution for contribution.** When a partner contributes property to a partnership and immediately receives a distribution, the transaction is essentially a sale.

1) Gain realized is recognized to the extent the contributed property is deemed purchased by the other partners.

EXAMPLE 16-4   Recognized Gain -- Purchase by Other Partner

P and Q contributed land with FMVs of $250,000 and $500,000, respectively, each in exchange for a 50% interest in PQ Partnership. PQ mortgaged the land for $550,000 and distributed $250,000 of the proceeds to Q. Q recognizes any gain realized on 50% of the land she contributed. Fifty percent of the AB in the land is included in Q's basis in her partnership interest.

STOP & REVIEW

You have completed the outline for this subunit.
Study multiple-choice questions 1 through 5 beginning on page 459.

16.2 TREATMENT OF PARTNERSHIP LIABILITIES

1. **Overview**

    a. A partner's share of partnership liabilities affects the partner's basis in his or her partnership interest and can result in increased gain being recognized by the partner. Any increase in a partner's share of liabilities of the partnership increases the partner's basis. The opposite is true for a decrease in partnership liabilities.

2. **Recourse Liabilities**

    a. A liability is a recourse liability if the creditor has a claim against any partner for payment if the partnership defaults.

> **EXAMPLE 16-5**   **Recourse Liability**
>
> ABC Partnership, a general partnership, purchased a building for $100,000 with a $90,000 mortgage from XYZ Bank secured by the building. Later, the building is destroyed and becomes worthless. Because ABC is a general partnership, ABC's general partners are liable for the debts of the partnership in the event the partnership is unable to pay. If ABC defaults on the mortgage, XYZ can take legal action against the partners of ABC to pay the $90,000 debt. Thus, the loan is recourse to the partners of ABC (i.e., the partners bear the economic risk).

   b. Partners generally share recourse liabilities based on their ratio for sharing losses.

   1) However, regulations allocate a recourse liability to the partner(s) who would be liable for it if at the time all partnership debts were due, all partnership assets (including cash) had zero value and a hypothetical liquidation occurred.

   2) A partner who pays more than his or her proportionate share of a partnership debt that becomes uncollectible is permitted to take a bad debt deduction equal to the amount in excess of that partner's share of the debt.

   c. A limited partner cannot share in recourse debt in excess of any of his or her obligations to make additional contributions to the partnership and any additional amount(s) (s)he would actually lose if the partnership could not pay its debt.

   d. **General partner.** A general partner is a partner who is personally liable for partnership debts.

   1) A general partnership is an arrangement by which two or more persons agree to share in all assets, profits, and financial and legal liabilities of a business.

      a) Such partners have unlimited liability, which means their personal assets are liable to the partnership's obligations.

         i) Any partner can be sued for the entirety of a partnership's business debts.

3. **Nonrecourse Liabilities**
   a. The creditor has no claim against any partners. At most, the creditor has a claim against a particular secured item of partnership property.
   b. Generally, partners share in nonrecourse liabilities based on their ratio for sharing profits.

EXAMPLE 16-6	Nonrecourse Liabilities

ABC, LLP, purchased a building for $100,000 with a $90,000 mortgage from XYZ Bank. The loan was secured by the building itself and no partner made a personal guarantee on the loan. In the event that ABC defaults and is unable to pay the loan, XYZ's only option is to foreclose and sell the property. If the property's value has decreased and the sale proceeds are insufficient to recover the balance of the loan, XYZ has no other legal remedy. This is because ABC's partners have limited liability by being partners in an LLP and are not generally liable for the debts of the partnership. Thus, the loan is nonrecourse to the partners of ABC (i.e., the lender bears the economic risk, not the partners).

EXAMPLE 16-7	Recourse and Nonrecourse Liabilities

ABC Partnership is a limited partnership. A is a general partner, while B and C are limited partners. A, B, and C are equal partners. ABC purchased a building for $100,000 with a $90,000 mortgage from DEF Bank. The building is not secured by itself, so it is a recourse liability. Also, ABC purchased a warehouse for $70,000 with a $60,000 mortgage secured by the warehouse itself. The mortgage of the warehouse is thus a nonrecourse liability. ABC defaults on the two mortgages. The partners' bases on the mortgages are as follows:

A's basis = $110,000 [$90,000 recourse + ($60,000 ÷ 3) nonrecourse]

B's basis = $20,000 [($60,000 ÷ 3) nonrecourse]

C's basis = $20,000 [($60,000 ÷ 3) nonrecourse]

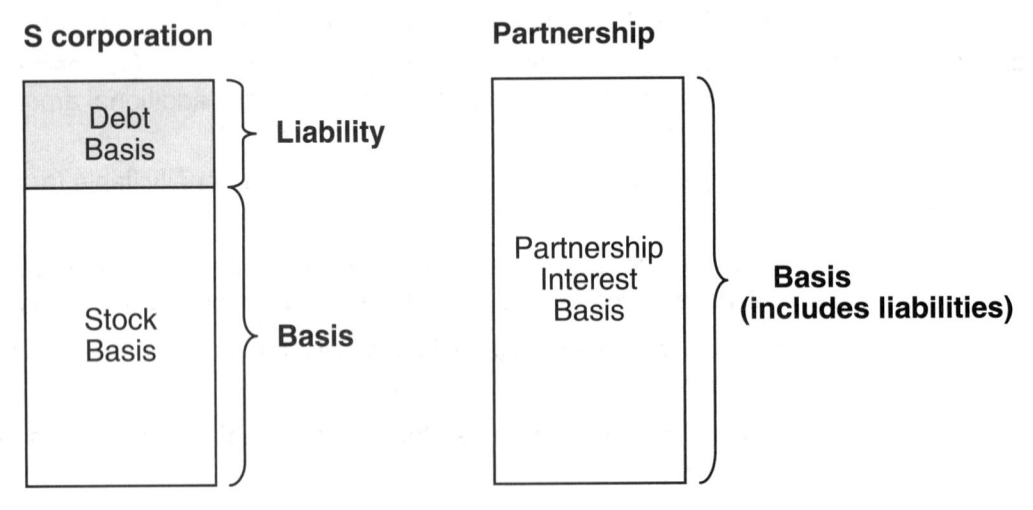

Figure 16-1

c. Recall that shareholders of S corporations have both the debt and stock basis. Bases used in the event of distribution and loss limitations by S corporation shareholders do not take into account the liabilities of the S corporation, while partnership basis affects the partners' bases in their partnership interests.

SUCCESS TIP: The CPA Exam often does not specify whether the liability is recourse or nonrecourse. Candidates should presume that the liabilities are recourse for exam purposes.

STOP & REVIEW: You have completed the outline for this subunit. Study multiple-choice questions 6 through 10 beginning on page 461.

16.3 DISTRIBUTION OF PARTNERSHIP ASSETS

1. **Overview**

    a. A distribution is a transfer of value from the partnership to a partner in reference to his or her interest in the partnership.

    1) A distribution may be in the form of money, liability relief, or other property.
    2) A draw is a distribution.

    b. Form 1065 Schedule M-2 is the section of the partnership tax return where distributions are required to be recorded.

From Form 1065 Schedule M-2

Schedule M-2	Analysis of Partners' Capital Accounts			
1	Balance at beginning of year . . .		6	Distributions: **a** Cash . . . . . .
2	Capital contributed: **a** Cash . . .			**b** Property . . . . .
	b Property . .		7	Other decreases (itemize): _____
3	Net income (loss) per books			
4	Other increases (itemize): _____		8	Add lines 6 and 7 . . . .
5	Add lines 1 through 4		9	Balance at end of year. Subtract line 8 from line 5

Form **1065** [Year]

2. **Current Distributions**
   a. A current (or operating) distribution reduces the partner's basis in the partnership interest.
      1) A decrease in a partner's allocable share of partnership liabilities is treated as a distribution of money.
   b. **Money distributions.** The partnership recognizes no gain.
      1) A partner recognizes gain only to the extent the distribution exceeds the AB in the partnership interest immediately before the distribution.
      2) Gain recognized is capital gain.
      3) Basis in the interest is decreased, but not below zero.
      4) Loss is not recognized.
   c. **Property Distributions**
      1) **Partnership.** Generally, no gain or loss is recognized by the partnership when it distributes property, including money. Sections 1245 and 1250 do not trigger recognition on the distribution.
         a) Precontribution gain or loss. If property is distributed to a noncontributing partner within 7 years of contribution, the partnership recognizes gain or loss to the extent of any unrealized gain or loss, respectively, that existed at the contribution date.
            i) Allocate this recognized gain (loss) to the contributing partner.
            ii) The contributing partner's basis in his or her partnership interest is increased.
            iii) Basis in the property is also increased.
            iv) The distributee has a transferred basis.
         b) Disproportionate distributions of unrealized receivables or substantially appreciated inventory (SAI) result in gain recognition.
            i) Inventory is considered substantially appreciated if its FMV exceeds 120% of the partnership's adjusted basis.
            ii) Gains from such distributions are taxed as ordinary income.
      2) **Partner.** The distributee partner generally recognizes gain only to the extent that money (including liability relief) exceeds his or her AB in his or her interest.
   d. The partner's basis in the distributed property is the partnership's AB in the property immediately before distribution, but it is limited to the distributee's AB in his or her partnership interest minus any money received in the distribution.
   e. When the limit in item d. above applies, allocate basis
      1) First to unrealized receivables and inventory, up to partnership AB in the partnership interest, and
      2) Second to other (noncash) property.

f. If the available basis is too small, the decrease (Partnership basis in assets – Basis in partnership interest) is allocated to the assets. The decrease is allocated by the following steps:

1) Assign each asset its partnership basis.
2) Calculate the decrease amount.
3) Allocate the decrease first to any assets that have declined in value.
4) Allocate any remaining decrease to the assets based on relative adjusted basis at this point in the calculation.

EXAMPLE 16-8   Allocation if Available Basis Is Inadequate

Karen has a $6,000 basis in the BK partnership immediately before receiving a current distribution (there is no remaining precontribution gain). The distribution consists of $5,000 cash, a computer with a FMV of $1,500 and a $4,000 basis to the partnership, and a desk with a FMV of $500 and a $1,500 basis to the partnership. Karen's basis in the distributed property is determined as follows:

Beginning basis in partnership interest	$6,000
Less: Money received	(5,000)
Remaining basis to allocate	$1,000

		Computer	Desk
Step 1 -- Allocate partnership basis to each asset	Partnership basis in assets	$4,000	$1,500
Step 2 -- Calculate decrease			
Total partnership basis $5,500			
Basis to allocate (1,000)			
Decrease amount $4,500			
Step 3 -- Allocate decrease to assets with a decline in FMV	Decline in FMV	(2,500)	(1,000)
	Relative adjusted basis	$1,500	$500
Step 4 -- Allocate remaining decrease of $1,000 ($4,500 – $2,500 – $1,000) based on relative adjusted basis	Remaining decrease	(750)*	(250)*
	Karen's basis in distributed property	$750	$250

* $750 = ($1,500 ÷ $2,000) × $1,000
$250 = ($500 ÷ $2,000) × $1,000

---

g. The partner's holding period in the distributed property includes that of the partnership.

h. The partner's basis in his or her ownership interest in the partnership is reduced by the amount of money and the AB of property received in the distribution.

3. **Disproportionate Distributions**
    a. Gain is recognized on a distribution of property that is disproportionate with respect to unrealized receivables (URs) or substantially appreciated inventory (SAI).
    b. The distribution will be recharacterized as if the URs or SAI were distributed.
4. **Liquidating Distributions**
    a. Distributions liquidating the entire interest of a partner may be due to partnership termination and/or the retirement or death of the partner. Sale to the partnership of a partner's entire interest is treated as a liquidating distribution.
    b. Payments to a retired partner that are determined by partnership income are treated as a distributive share of partnership income, regardless of the period over which they are paid. The income is characterized at the partnership level.
    c. Amounts received from the partnership in liquidation of a partnership interest are generally treated the same as other (nonliquidating) distributions.
        1) **Gain** is recognized to the extent money distributed exceeds the liquidating partner's AB in the partnership interest immediately before the distribution.
            a) Decrease of the partner's share of partnership liabilities is treated as a distribution of money.
            b) The gain is capital gain. However, precontribution gain or disproportionate distribution of SAI or URs could result in ordinary income.
        2) The liquidating partner is treated as a partner for tax purposes until all payments in complete liquidation have been made.
    d. **Loss.** A loss is realized when money and the FMV of property distributed are less than the AB of the partnership interest.
        1) No loss is recognized if any property other than money, URs, and inventory is distributed in liquidation of the interest.
        2) Loss recognized is limited to any excess of the AB in the partnership interest over the sum of money and the AB in the URs and inventory.
        3) Loss recognized is characterized as if from sale of a capital asset.

EXAMPLE 16-9	Loss from Liquidation

Amber has a basis in the partnership of $17,000. In complete liquidation of her interest, she received $11,000 in cash and receivables with a basis of $0. Amber will report a capital loss of $6,000 ($17,000 – $11,000 – $0) from the liquidation. The basis of the receivables will be $0 to her. If she had received a capital asset instead of the receivables, she would not qualify to take a loss, and the capital asset would have a basis to her of $6,000 ($17,000 – $11,000).

e. The distributee's basis in (noncash) property received in a distribution in liquidation is any excess of his or her AB in the partnership interest immediately before distribution over any amount of money received.

1) If the total partnership basis of assets distributed exceeds the partner's basis in the partnership interest, allocate the decrease in the same manner as for current distributions.

2) For liquidating distributions only, if the basis in the partnership interest exceeds the total partnership basis of distributed assets, allocate the increase by the following steps:

Beginning basis	a) Determine the amount of basis to be allocated (the calculation is to the left).
− Money received	
− Unrealized receivables and inventory	b) Allocate any appreciation to each asset.
= **Basis to allocate**	c) Allocate any remaining basis (Basis to allocate − Appreciation of distributed assets) to the assets based on FMV prior to the distribution.

EXAMPLE 16-10   Taxpayer Basis in Property after Liquidation

A taxpayer with a $75,000 basis in partnership interest liquidates the entire interest, receiving properties A and B. Neither property is inventory or unrealized receivables. On the date of liquidation, property A had an adjusted basis to the partnership of $35,000 and a FMV of $75,000. Property B had an adjusted basis to the partnership of $15,000 and a FMV of $25,000. The taxpayer's basis in each property after liquidation would be $55,000 for property A [($25,000 excess partnership basis over adjusted basis of both properties × 80% due to $40,000 appreciation) + $35,000 property A's adjusted basis] and $20,000 for property B [($25,000 excess partnership basis over adjusted basis of both properties × 20% due to $10,000 appreciation) + $15,000 property B's adjusted basis].

---

f. The distributee's holding period in the distributed property includes that of the partnership.

g. Gain on the sale of URs distributed by the partnership is ordinary income.

1) Gain or loss realized on inventory distributed depends on the nature of the property in the distributee's hands.

2) If the distributee sells or exchanges the inventory 5 years or more after distribution, capital gain treatment may be available.

5. **Termination of Partnership**
   a. **Overview**
      1) A partnership terminates for federal tax purposes only when operations of the partnership cease.
         a) The partnership's tax year ends on the date of termination.
      2) Sale or exchange termination is treated as a distribution of assets immediately followed by the contribution of those assets to a new partnership.
      3) A return must be filed for the short period, which is the period from the beginning of the tax year through the date of termination.
      4) The tax year of a partnership closes with respect to a partner whose entire interest in the partnership terminates by death, liquidation, or other means.
         a) A deceased partner's allocable share of partnership items up to the date of death will be taxed to the decedent on his or her final return.
         b) Any items allocated after the date of death will be the responsibility of the successor in interest.
         c) The partnership's tax year does not end.
   b. **Merger**
      1) The merging partnership's tax year is used if the partners of the merged firms own more than 50% of the resulting partnership. Otherwise, a new tax year is started.
   c. **Split**
      1) The old partnership's tax year continues; however, if partners owned less than 50% of the original partnership, a new tax year should be started.

EXAMPLE 16-11   Split of a Partnership

Tin-Pan-Alley-Cat Partnership is in the manufacturing and wholesaling business. Tin owns a 40% interest in the capital and profits of the partnership, while each of the other partners owns a 20% interest. All of the partners are calendar-year taxpayers. On November 3 of the current year, a decision is made to separate the manufacturing business from the wholesaling business, and two new partnerships are formed. Tin-Pan Partnership takes over the manufacturing business, and Alley-Cat Partnership takes over the wholesaling business. For tax purposes, Tin-Pan is considered to be a continuation of the Tin-Pan-Alley-Cat Partnership because Tin-Pan owned more than 50% of the original partnership. Alley-Cat Partnership will start a new tax year.

SUCCESS TIP

Be prepared to answer questions regarding basis and gain (loss) calculations resulting from both current and liquidating distributions of partnership assets.

STOP & REVIEW

You have completed the outline for this subunit.
Study multiple-choice questions 11 through 15 beginning on page 463.

16.4 RECONCILING BOOK AND TAXABLE INCOME

SUCCESS TIP: The reconciliation of book and taxable income applies to both corporations and partnerships. The presentation assumes knowledge of the information in Study Units 11-15 as well as Subunits 16.1-16.3.

1. **Overview**

    a. Corporations file federal returns using Form 1120. Reconciliation of income (loss) per books of the corporation with income (loss) per tax is reported on Schedule M-1.

    b. Schedule M-3 is required for corporations with total assets of $10 million or more.

    1) Schedule M-3 reconciles book net income (loss) for general financial reporting with taxable income (loss) for tax accounting, indicating temporary and permanent differences by category and dollar amount.

    NOTE: Carefully review the Form 1120 Schedule M-1 in Example 16-12 on page 454 and Schedule M-3 beginning on page 456.

    c. Income tax liability (if any) is reported by

    1) **Current** income tax liability or refund receivable calculated based on temporary and permanent book-to-tax differences

    2) **Deferred** income tax liability and/or asset for the future tax consequences of temporary differences (permanent differences are not considered) recognized currently in the financial statements or tax returns

2. **Temporary and Permanent Differences**

    a. Temporary differences are timing differences and occur because tax laws require the recognition of certain items of income and expense in different tax years than are required for book purposes.

    1) Temporary differences originate in 1 tax year and reverse or terminate in 1 or more subsequent tax years.

    2) Temporary differences can be derived from

        a) Cost recovery or income recognition methods (e.g., installment sale income and accelerated depreciation);

        b) Balance sheet perspectives, such as when book basis (e.g., Reserves: Bonus compensation) exceeds or is less than its corresponding tax basis; or

        c) Any other differences that do not involve balance sheet accounts (e.g., net operating loss carryover, net capital loss carryover, and charitable contribution carryover).

    b. Permanent differences result from transactions that will not be offset by any corresponding differences in later years.

Common Temporary Differences	Common Permanent Differences

Prepayments of income
Installment sale income
Accelerated depreciation (e.g., 100%-expensing, Sec. 179, MACRS, lease-type)
Amortization
Charitable contributions
Reserves:
   Credit losses/Bad debt
   Bonus compensation
Capitalized inventory costs (i.e., Sec. 263A)
Net operating loss carryover
Net capital loss carryover
	Tax-exempt interest income (and associated expenses)
	Life insurance proceeds (and associated expenses)
	Nondeductible penalties and fines
	Nondeductible meals (50%) and entertainment
	Dividends-received deduction
	Lobbying and political expenditures
	Club dues

3. **Calculation**

   a. **Current income tax.** To reconcile income (loss) per books with income (loss) per tax, the following adjustments are made to net income (loss) per books (similar to Schedule M-1):

         Net income (loss) per books
   - + Federal income tax
   - + Excess of capital losses over capital gains
   - + Income subject to tax not recorded on books
   - + Expenses recorded on books not deducted on the tax return
     (e.g., Book depreciation > Tax depreciation, penalties, and fines)
   - − Income recorded on books not subject to tax
     (e.g., municipal bond interest income, life insurance proceeds associated with key personnel)
   - − Deductions on this return not charged against book income
     (e.g., Tax depreciation > Book depreciation)
   - = **Taxable income before NOL and DRD**

   NOTE: Remember that M-1 adjustments occur before the DRD and NOLs. Thus, statements such as "book income and taxable income differ by the M-1 adjustments" are incorrect.

   b. **Deferred income tax expense or benefit.** Deferred tax expense or benefit is the net change during the year in an entity's deferred tax amounts.

      1) **Deferred tax liabilities (DTLs)** record the deferred tax consequences of taxable temporary differences (e.g., future income taxes payable).
      2) **Deferred tax assets (DTAs)** record the deferred tax consequences of deductible temporary differences and carryforwards (e.g., future income taxes refundable).

   c. **Taxable temporary differences** result in future taxable amounts and DTLs.

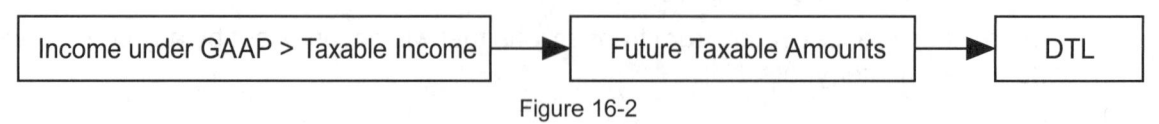

   | Income under GAAP > Taxable Income | → | Future Taxable Amounts | → | DTL |

                                            Figure 16-2

   d. **Deductible temporary differences** result in future deductible amounts and DTAs.

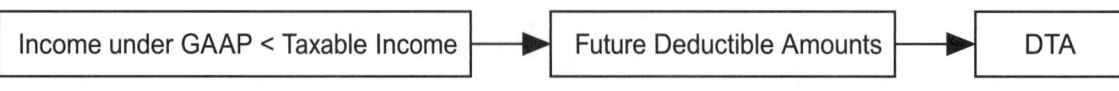

   | Income under GAAP < Taxable Income | → | Future Deductible Amounts | → | DTA |

                                            Figure 16-3

EXAMPLE 16-12 Schedule M-1 -- Reconciliation of Income (Loss)

The following information comes from MEEN Corporation's financial statements:

1. MEEN's net income per books **(before tax expenses)** is $51,007,500.

2. MEEN received $40,000 of interest income, of which $24,000 relates to municipal bonds and is tax exempt. Thus, a $24,000 adjustment is required to decrease taxable income.

3. MEEN received $200,000 in prepaid rent in the current year. The $200,000 prepaid rent collected in the current year is subject to tax and must be added to net income per books in order to arrive at taxable income.

4. MEEN's books showed a $40,000 short-term capital gain distribution from a mutual fund corporation and a $63,000 loss on the sale of Retro stock that was purchased 3 years ago. The stock was an investment in an unrelated corporation. There were no other gains or losses and no loss carryovers from prior years. Therefore, a $23,000 adjustment is required to increase taxable income (i.e., capital losses are limited to capital gains).

5. MEEN uses the allowance method for determining credit loss expense ($170,000) for book, and the specific write-off method is used for tax. The specific write-off method calculates $110,000 credit loss expense; thus, a $60,000 bad debt adjustment is required to increase taxable income.

6. Book depreciation on all fixed assets is $10,000,000. Tax depreciation is $20,000,000 for the fixed assets. Because tax depreciation is $10,000,000 greater than book, the adjustment is recorded on line 8a. If book depreciation were greater than tax, the amount would be recorded on line 5a.

7. MEEN's business meals of $200,500 meet the conditions for deductibility and are properly substantiated under an accountable plan. The reimbursement is not treated as employee compensation. Only 50% of business meals are deductible for tax purposes. Therefore, a $100,250 adjustment is required to increase taxable income.

8. MEEN expensed $19,000 for the term life insurance premiums on the corporation's officers. MEEN was the policy owner and the beneficiary. Key-person life insurance premiums paid by an employer are not deductible for tax purposes if the employer is a beneficiary under the policy. Thus, a $19,000 adjustment is required to increase taxable income.

9. MEEN has a $12,040,000 NOL carryforward from last year. The NOL is deductible when carried to a year in which there is taxable income. The amount applied in any carryover year is limited to 80% of that year's taxable income. Therefore, a $12,040,000 adjustment is required to decrease taxable income (100% of NOL carryover is utilized because it is less than 80% of taxable income).

10. MEEN owns 18% of EPM Industries, from which it received $48,000 in dividend income. A special corporate deduction for dividends received from domestic taxable corporations is allowed. Since MEEN owns less than 20% of EPM, a 50% deduction of $48,000 of dividend income is allowed, with a limitation of 50% of taxable income. Thus, a $24,000 adjustment is required to decrease taxable income.

The completed book-to-tax worksheet and M-1 on the next page show the reconciliation from book net income to taxable income. The explanations showing how each amount was determined are illustrated by number.

-- Continued on next page --

EXAMPLE 16-12 -- Continued

Income Statement for Current Year	Book Income	(T)emporary or (P)ermanent Differences	Book-to-Tax Differences (DR)	CR	Taxable Income
Sales revenue	$500,000,000				$500,000,000
Cost of goods sold	(410,000,000)				(410,000,000)
Gross profit	$ 90,000,000				$ 90,000,000
Other income:					
Interest income	$ 40,000	P	[2]$ (24,000)		$ 16,000
Dividend income	48,000				48,000
Rent income	0	T		[3]$200,000	200,000
Capital gains (losses)	(23,000)	T		[4] 23,000	0
Gross income	$ 90,065,000				$ 90,264,000
Expenses:					
Salaries and wages	$ (21,000,000)				$ (21,000,000)
Insurance	(900,000)				(900,000)
Licenses and permits	(250,000)				(250,000)
Credit loss expense	(170,000)	T		[5] 60,000	(110,000)
Communications	(1,400,000)				(1,400,000)
Information systems expenses	(1,600,000)				(1,600,000)
Depreciation	(10,000,000)	T	[6](10,000,000)		(20,000,000)
Advertising	(2,500,000)				(2,500,000)
Security expenses	(850,000)				(850,000)
Meals	(200,500)	P		[7] 100,250	(100,250)
Life insurance premiums	(89,000)	P		[8] 19,000	(70,000)
Other expenses	(98,000)				(98,000)
Total expenses before NOL and DRD	$ (39,057,500)				$ (48,878,250)
Income before NOL and DRD	$ 51,007,500				*$ 41,385,750
NOL carryforward from prior year	0	T	[9](12,040,000)		**(12,040,000)
Dividends-received deduction	0	P	[10] (24,000)		***(24,000)
Book/taxable income	[1]$ 51,007,500		$(22,064,000)	$402,250	$ 29,321,750
Tax rate					× 21%
			Current income tax payable	****$	6,157,568

*Sch. M-1 line 10; Form 1120 p.1, line 28
**Form 1120 p.1, line 29a
***Form 1120 p.1, line 29b
****Form 1120 p.1, line 30

NOTE: Items [9] (NOL carryforward) and [10] (DRD) do not appear on Schedule M-1.

Schedule M-1 Reconciliation of Income (Loss) per Books With Income per Return
Note: The corporation may be required to file Schedule M-3. See instructions.

1	Net income (loss) per books	[1] 51,007,500	7	Income recorded on books this year not included on this return (itemize):	
2	Federal income tax per books			Tax-exempt interest $ [2] 24,000	
3	Excess of capital losses over capital gains	[4] 23,000			24,000
4	Income subject to tax not recorded on books this year (itemize):				
	Rent Income	[3] 200,000	8	Deductions on this return not charged against book income this year (itemize):	
5	Expenses recorded on books this year not deducted on this return (itemize):		a	Depreciation $[6]10,000,000	
a	Depreciation $		b	Charitable contributions $	
b	Charitable contributions $				
c	Travel and entertainment $				10,000,000
	[5] Bad debt [7] Meals [8] Life Insurance	*179,250	9	Add lines 7 and 8	
6	Add lines 1 through 5	51,409,750	10	Income (page 1, line 28)—line 6 less line 9	41,385,750

*$60,000 (bad debt) + $100,250 (meals) + $19,000 (life insurance) = $179,250

EXAMPLE 16-13 — Deferred Tax Liability Calculation for Accumulated Depreciation Basis

Book: Change in accumulated depreciation basis	
Beginning of the year	$100,000,000
End of the year	110,000,000
Net change	**$ 10,000,000**
Tax: Change in accumulated depreciation basis	
Beginning of the year	$200,000,000
End of the year	220,000,000
Net change	**$ 20,000,000**
Beginning of the year book-tax fixed assets basis difference	
Tax basis	$200,000,000
Book basis	100,000,000
Basis difference	$100,000,000
Tax rate	× 21%
Beginning of the year deferred tax liability	**$ 21,000,000**
End of the year book-tax fixed assets basis difference	
Tax basis	$220,000,000
Book basis	110,000,000
Basis difference	$110,000,000
Tax rate	× 21%
End of the year deferred tax liability	**$ 23,100,000**
Beginning of the year deferred tax liability	$21,000,000
End of the year deferred tax liability	$23,100,000
Difference: Current year deferred tax expense	**$2,100,000**

STOP & REVIEW

You have completed the outline for this subunit.
Study multiple-choice questions 16 through 18 on page 466.

SCHEDULE M-3 (Form 1120) Department of the Treasury Internal Revenue Service	**Net Income (Loss) Reconciliation for Corporations With Total Assets of $10 Million or More** ▶ Attach to Form 1120 or 1120-C. ▶ Go to *www.irs.gov/Form1120* for instructions and the latest information.	OMB No. 1545-0123 **[Year]**

Name of corporation (common parent, if consolidated return) | **Employer identification number**

Check applicable box(es): (1) ☐ Non-consolidated return (2) ☐ Consolidated return (Form 1120 only)
(3) ☐ Mixed 1120/L/PC group (4) ☐ Dormant subsidiaries schedule attached

Part I   Financial Information and Net Income (Loss) Reconciliation (see instructions)

1a Did the corporation file SEC Form 10-K for its income statement period ending with or within this tax year?
    ☐ **Yes.** Skip lines 1b and 1c and complete lines 2a through 11 with respect to that SEC Form 10-K.
    ☐ **No.** Go to line 1b. See instructions if multiple non-tax-basis income statements are prepared.
b Did the corporation prepare a certified audited non-tax-basis income statement for that period?
    ☐ **Yes.** Skip line 1c and complete lines 2a through 11 with respect to that income statement.
    ☐ **No.** Go to line 1c.
c Did the corporation prepare a non-tax-basis income statement for that period?
    ☐ **Yes.** Complete lines 2a through 11 with respect to that income statement.
    ☐ **No.** Skip lines 2a through 3c and enter the corporation's net income (loss) per its books and records on line 4a.
2a Enter the income statement period: Beginning MM/DD/YYYY Ending MM/DD/YYYY
b Has the corporation's income statement been restated for the income statement period on line 2a?
    ☐ **Yes.** (If "Yes," attach an explanation and the amount of each item restated.)
    ☐ **No.**
c Has the corporation's income statement been restated for any of the five income statement periods immediately preceding the period on line 2a?
    ☐ **Yes.** (If "Yes," attach an explanation and the amount of each item restated.)
    ☐ **No.**
3a Is any of the corporation's voting common stock publicly traded?
    ☐ **Yes.**
    ☐ **No.** If "No," go to line 4a.
b Enter the symbol of the corporation's primary U.S. publicly traded voting common stock . . . .
c Enter the nine-digit CUSIP number of the corporation's primary publicly traded voting common stock . . . .

4a	Worldwide consolidated net income (loss) from income statement source identified in Part I, line 1 .	**4a**
b	Indicate accounting standard used for line 4a (see instructions): (1) ☐ GAAP (2) ☐ IFRS (3) ☐ Statutory (4) ☐ Tax-basis (5) ☐ Other (specify) _____	
5a	Net income from nonincludible foreign entities (attach statement)	**5a** ( )
b	Net loss from nonincludible foreign entities (attach statement and enter as a positive amount) . . .	**5b**
6a	Net income from nonincludible U.S. entities (attach statement)	**6a** ( )
b	Net loss from nonincludible U.S. entities (attach statement and enter as a positive amount)	**6b**
7a	Net income (loss) of other includible foreign disregarded entities (attach statement)	**7a**
b	Net income (loss) of other includible U.S. disregarded entities (attach statement)	**7b**
c	Net income (loss) of other includible entities (attach statement)	**7c**
8	Adjustment to eliminations of transactions between includible entities and nonincludible entities (attach statement)	**8**
9	Adjustment to reconcile income statement period to tax year (attach statement)	**9**
10a	Intercompany dividend adjustments to reconcile to line 11 (attach statement)	**10a**
b	Other statutory accounting adjustments to reconcile to line 11 (attach statement)	**10b**
c	Other adjustments to reconcile to amount on line 11 (attach statement)	**10c**
11	**Net income (loss) per income statement of includible corporations.** Combine lines 4 through 10 .	**11**
	Note: Part I, line 11, must equal Part II, line 30, column (a), or Schedule M-1, line 1 (see instructions).	

12 Enter the total amount (not just the corporation's share) of the assets and liabilities of all entities included or removed on the following lines.

		Total Assets	Total Liabilities
a	Included on Part I, line 4 . . . . ▶		
b	Removed on Part I, line 5 . . . . ▶		
c	Removed on Part I, line 6 . . . . ▶		
d	Included on Part I, line 7 . . . . ▶		

For Paperwork Reduction Act Notice, see the Instructions for Form 1120.   Cat. No. 37961C   Schedule M-3 (Form 1120) [Year]

Schedule M-3 (Form 1120) [Year]				Page **2**
Name of corporation (common parent, if consolidated return)				**Employer identification number**

Check applicable box(es): **(1)** ☐ Consolidated group **(2)** ☐ Parent corp **(3)** ☐ Consolidated eliminations **(4)** ☐ Subsidiary corp **(5)** ☐ Mixed 1120/L/PC group
Check if a sub-consolidated: **(6)** ☐ 1120 group **(7)** ☐ 1120 eliminations

Name of subsidiary (if consolidated return)	Employer identification number

Part II — Reconciliation of Net Income (Loss) per Income Statement of Includible Corporations With Taxable Income per Return (see instructions)

	Income (Loss) Items (Attach statements for lines 1 through 12)	(a) Income (Loss) per Income Statement	(b) Temporary Difference	(c) Permanent Difference	(d) Income (Loss) per Tax Return
1	Income (loss) from equity method foreign corporations				
2	Gross foreign dividends not previously taxed				
3	Subpart F, QEF, and similar income inclusions				
4	Gross-up for foreign taxes deemed paid				
5	Gross foreign distributions previously taxed				
6	Income (loss) from equity method U.S. corporations				
7	U.S. dividends not eliminated in tax consolidation				
8	Minority interest for includible corporations				
9	Income (loss) from U.S. partnerships				
10	Income (loss) from foreign partnerships				
11	Income (loss) from other pass-through entities				
12	Items relating to reportable transactions				
13	Interest income (see instructions)				
14	Total accrual to cash adjustment				
15	Hedging transactions				
16	Mark-to-market income (loss)				
17	Cost of goods sold (see instructions)	( )			( )
18	Sale versus lease (for sellers and/or lessors)				
19	Section 481(a) adjustments				
20	Unearned/deferred revenue				
21	Income recognition from long-term contracts				
22	Original issue discount and other imputed interest				
23a	Income statement gain/loss on sale, exchange, abandonment, worthlessness, or other disposition of assets other than inventory and pass-through entities				
b	Gross capital gains from Schedule D, excluding amounts from pass-through entities				
c	Gross capital losses from Schedule D, excluding amounts from pass-through entities, abandonment losses, and worthless stock losses				
d	Net gain/loss reported on Form 4797, line 17, excluding amounts from pass-through entities, abandonment losses, and worthless stock losses				
e	Abandonment losses				
f	Worthless stock losses (attach statement)				
g	Other gain/loss on disposition of assets other than inventory				
24	Capital loss limitation and carryforward used				
25	Other income (loss) items with differences (attach statement)				
26	**Total income (loss) items.** Combine lines 1 through 25				
27	**Total expense/deduction items** (from Part III, line 39)				
28	Other items with no differences				
29a	Mixed groups, see instructions. All others, combine lines 26 through 28				
b	PC insurance subgroup reconciliation totals				
c	Life insurance subgroup reconciliation totals				
30	**Reconciliation totals.** Combine lines 29a through 29c				

Note: Line 30, column (a), must equal Part I, line 11, and column (d) must equal Form 1120, page 1, line 28.

Schedule M-3 (Form 1120) [Year]

Schedule M-3 (Form 1120) [Year] — Page 3

Name of corporation (common parent, if consolidated return) | Employer identification number

Check applicable box(es): (1) ☐ Consolidated group (2) ☐ Parent corp (3) ☐ Consolidated eliminations (4) ☐ Subsidiary corp (5) ☐ Mixed 1120/L/PC group
Check if a sub-consolidated: (6) ☐ 1120 group (7) ☐ 1120 eliminations

Name of subsidiary (if consolidated return) | Employer identification number

Part III — Reconciliation of Net Income (Loss) per Income Statement of Includible Corporations With Taxable Income per Return—Expense/Deduction Items (see instructions)

Expense/Deduction Items	(a) Expense per Income Statement	(b) Temporary Difference	(c) Permanent Difference	(d) Deduction per Tax Return
1 U.S. current income tax expense				
2 U.S. deferred income tax expense				
3 State and local current income tax expense				
4 State and local deferred income tax expense				
5 Foreign current income tax expense (other than foreign withholding taxes)				
6 Foreign deferred income tax expense				
7 Foreign withholding taxes				
8 Interest expense (see instructions)				
9 Stock option expense				
10 Other equity-based compensation				
11 Meals and entertainment				
12 Fines and penalties				
13 Judgments, damages, awards, and similar costs				
14 Parachute payments				
15 Compensation with section 162(m) limitation				
16 Pension and profit-sharing				
17 Other post-retirement benefits				
18 Deferred compensation				
19 Charitable contribution of cash and tangible property				
20 Charitable contribution of intangible property				
21 Charitable contribution limitation/carryforward				
22 Domestic production activities deduction (see instructions)				
23 Current year acquisition or reorganization investment banking fees				
24 Current year acquisition or reorganization legal and accounting fees				
25 Current year acquisition/reorganization other costs				
26 Amortization/impairment of goodwill				
27 Amortization of acquisition, reorganization, and start-up costs				
28 Other amortization or impairment write-offs				
29 Reserved				
30 Depletion				
31 Depreciation				
32 Bad debt expense				
33 Corporate owned life insurance premiums				
34 Purchase versus lease (for purchasers and/or lessees)				
35 Research and development costs				
36 Section 118 exclusion (attach statement)				
37 Section 162(r)—FDIC premiums paid by certain large financial institutions (see instructions)				
38 Other expense/deduction items with differences (attach statement)				
39 **Total expense/deduction items.** Combine lines 1 through 38. Enter here and on Part II, line 27, reporting positive amounts as negative and negative amounts as positive				

QUESTIONS

16.1 Partners Dealing with Own Partnership

1. Sara is a member of a four-person, equal partnership. Sara is unrelated to the other partners. In 2021, Sara sold 100 shares of a listed stock to the partnership for the stock's fair market value of $20,000. Sara's basis for this stock, which was purchased in 2010, was $14,000. Sara's recognized gain on the sale of this stock was

A. $0
B. $1,500
C. $4,500
D. $6,000

Answer (D) is correct.
REQUIRED: The partner's recognized gain on the sale of stock to the partnership.
DISCUSSION: When a partner engages in a transaction with the partnership not in a capacity as a partner, the transaction is considered to occur between the partnership and a nonpartner. Sara recognizes a $6,000 long-term capital gain ($20,000 proceeds less $14,000 AB). If Sara had owned more than 50% of the capital or profit interest of the partnership, a gain could still have been recognized, but a loss on a sale to the partnership would not.
Answer (A) is incorrect. Sara is treated as having sold the stock to an independent third party, and the full amount of realized gain is recognized. Answer (B) is incorrect. The full amount of realized gain is recognized. Answer (C) is incorrect. When a partner engages in a transaction with the partnership not in a capacity as a partner, the transaction is considered to occur between the partnership and a nonpartner.

2. Freeman, a single individual, reported the following income in the current year:

Guaranteed payment from services rendered to a partnership	$50,000
Ordinary income from an S corporation	20,000

What amount of Freeman's income is subject to self-employment tax?

A. $0
B. $20,000
C. $50,000
D. $70,000

Answer (C) is correct.
REQUIRED: The amount of income subject to self-employment tax.
DISCUSSION: Amounts received as guaranteed payments from services rendered to a partnership are subject to self-employment tax [Reg. Sec. 1.707-1(c)]. The amount is deemed to be similar to a salary to the partner. Ordinary income from an S corporation is simply considered a distribution that passes through to the shareholders and is therefore not subject to the self-employment tax. Therefore, Freeman's income subject to self-employment tax is $50,000.
Answer (A) is incorrect. The guaranteed payment is subject to the tax. Answer (B) is incorrect. The S corporation ordinary income is not subject to the self-employment tax, while the guaranteed payment is. Answer (D) is incorrect. The ordinary income is not subject to the tax.

460 SU 16: Partnership Transactions and Book-to-Tax Differences

3. Peterson has a one-third interest in the Spano Partnership. During 2021, Peterson received a $16,000 guaranteed payment, which was deductible by the partnership, for services rendered to Spano. Spano reported a 2021 operating loss of $70,000 before the guaranteed payment. What, if any, are the net effects of the guaranteed payment?

I. The guaranteed payment increases Peterson's tax basis in Spano by $16,000.

II. The guaranteed payment increases Peterson's ordinary income by $16,000.

A. I only.
B. II only.
C. Both I and II.
D. Neither I nor II.

Answer (B) is correct.
REQUIRED: The income from a partnership to be reported by a partner who receives a guaranteed payment.
DISCUSSION: For purposes of determining the partner's gross income, the guaranteed payment (GP) is treated as made to a nonpartner. The partner separately states the GP from any distributive share. The payment is ordinary income to the partner.
Answer (A) is incorrect. Receipt of the GP does not directly affect Peterson's tax basis in his partnership interest. Answer (C) is incorrect. The payment is ordinary income to the partner. Answer (D) is incorrect. For purposes of determining the partner's gross income, the guaranteed payment is treated as made to a nonpartner. The partner separately states the GP from any distributive share. The payment is ordinary income to the partner.

4. Under the Internal Revenue Code sections pertaining to partnerships, guaranteed payments are payments to partners for

A. Payments of principal on secured notes honored at maturity.
B. Timely payments of periodic interest on bona fide loans that are not treated as partners' capital.
C. Services or the use of capital without regard to partnership income.
D. Sales of partners' assets to the partnership at guaranteed amounts regardless of market values.

Answer (C) is correct.
REQUIRED: The definition of guaranteed payments.
DISCUSSION: Guaranteed payments are payments to a partner for services or for the use of capital which are determined without regard to the income of the partnership.
Answer (A) is incorrect. Payments of principal on secured notes honored at maturity are not guaranteed payments. Answer (B) is incorrect. Timely payments of periodic interest on bona fide loans that are not treated as partners' capital are not guaranteed payments. Answer (D) is incorrect. Sales of partners' assets to the partnership at guaranteed amounts regardless of market values are not guaranteed payments.

5. Guaranteed payments made by a partnership to partners for services rendered to the partnership that are deductible business expenses under the Internal Revenue Code are

I. Deductible expenses on the *U.S. Partnership Return of Income*, Form 1065, in order to arrive at partnership income (loss).

II. Included on Schedule K-1 to be taxed as ordinary income to the partners.

A. I only.
B. II only.
C. Both I and II.
D. Neither I nor II.

Answer (C) is correct.
REQUIRED: The proper reporting of guaranteed payments.
DISCUSSION: Guaranteed payments are considered as ordinary and necessary business expenses, like salary expenses, so they are deductible by the partnership and reported on line 10 of Form 1065. The recipient partner also includes the full guaranteed payment, reported on line 4 of Schedule K-1, as ordinary income.
Answer (A) is incorrect. Guaranteed payments are included on Schedule K-1 as ordinary income to the partner. Answer (B) is incorrect. Guaranteed payments are deductible expenses by the partnership on Form 1065. Answer (D) is incorrect. Guaranteed payments are deductible expenses by the partnership on Form 1065 and are included on Schedule K-1 as ordinary income to the partner.

16.2 Treatment of Partnership Liabilities

6. A $100,000 increase in partnership liabilities is treated in which of the following ways?

A. Increases each partner's basis in the partnership by $100,000.
B. Increases the partners' bases only if the liability is nonrecourse.
C. Increases each partner's basis in proportion to their ownership.
D. Does not change any partner's basis in the partnership regardless of whether the liabilities are recourse or nonrecourse.

Answer (C) is correct.
REQUIRED: The correct treatment of an increase in partnership liabilities.
DISCUSSION: A partner's share of a partnership liability is treated as if the partner contributed an equivalent amount of money to the partnership. The deemed contribution increases the partner's basis in his or her partnership interest. Normally, general partners share liabilities based on their ratio for sharing economic losses (recourse liability).
Answer (A) is incorrect. Each partner's share increases based on his or her ratio for sharing economic losses (recourse liability) or partnership profits (nonrecourse liability). **Answer (B) is incorrect.** A recourse liability also increases a partner's share, but does so based on his or her ratio for sharing losses. **Answer (D) is incorrect.** The increase in partnership liabilities does affect the partner's basis in his or her partnership interest.

7. On January 4, 2021, Smith and White contributed $4,000 and $6,000 in cash, respectively, and formed the Macro General Partnership. The partnership agreement allocated profits and losses 40% to Smith and 60% to White. In 2021, Macro purchased property from an unrelated seller for $10,000 cash and a $40,000 mortgage note that was the general liability of the partnership. Macro's liability

A. Increases Smith's partnership basis by $16,000.
B. Increases Smith's partnership basis by $20,000.
C. Increases Smith's partnership basis by $24,000.
D. Has no effect on Smith's partnership basis.

Answer (A) is correct.
REQUIRED: The effect of an increase in liability on a partner's basis.
DISCUSSION: A partner's share of a partnership liability is treated as if the partner contributed an equivalent amount of money to the partnership. The deemed contribution increases the partner's basis in the partnership interest. Smith's partnership basis will increase by $16,000 ($40,000 × 40%). The cash payment (exchange) for the property has a net zero effect on partner basis.

8. Beck and Nilo are equal partners in B&N Associates, a general partnership. B&N borrowed $10,000 from a bank on an unsecured note, thereby increasing each partner's share of partnership liabilities. As a result of this loan, the basis of each partner's interest in B&N was

A. Increased.
B. Decreased.
C. Unaffected.
D. Dependent on each partner's ability to meet the obligation if called upon to do so.

Answer (A) is correct.
REQUIRED: The effect of an increase in partnership nonrecourse liability.
DISCUSSION: A partner's share of a partnership liability is treated as if the partner contributed an equivalent amount of money to the partnership. The deemed contribution increases the partner's basis in his or her partnership interest. Normally, general partners share liabilities based on their ratio for sharing economic losses (recourse liability) or partnership profits (nonrecourse liability).
Answer (B) is incorrect. The increase in partnership liabilities results in an increase in the partners' basis in their respective partnership interests. **Answer (C) is incorrect.** The increase in partnership liabilities does affect the partners' basis in their respective partnership interests. **Answer (D) is incorrect.** The increase in partnership liabilities is treated as if the partner contributed an equivalent amount of money to the partnership. It also results in an increase in the partners' basis in their respective partnership interests.

9. Ted and Jane form a cash-basis general partnership with cash contributions of $20,000 each. They share all partnership profits and losses equally. They borrow $60,000 and purchase depreciable business equipment. Jane, however, is required to pay the creditor if the partnership defaults. Which of the following is true?

A. Ted and Jane each have a basis of $80,000 in the partnership.
B. Ted has a basis of $50,000 and Jane has a basis of $80,000.
C. Ted and Jane each have a basis of $50,000 in the partnership.
D. Ted has a basis of $20,000 and Jane has a basis of $80,000 in the partnership.

Answer (D) is correct.
REQUIRED: The partners' bases in the partnership.
DISCUSSION: A partner receives a basis in a partnership equal to the basis of the property contributed to the partnership. An increase in a partner's share of liabilities is treated as a contribution of money by such partner, which increases the partner's basis. Jane's basis increases by $60,000, the amount of the liabilities, because she is the guarantor of the loan and her share of liabilities has increased.
Answer (A) is incorrect. Only Jane's basis will be increased by the liability. **Answer (B) is incorrect.** Ted's basis is unaffected by Jane's guarantee of the loan. **Answer (C) is incorrect.** Ted's basis is unaffected by Jane's guarantee of the loan. Further, Jane's basis will be increased by the entire amount of the liability.

SU 16: Partnership Transactions and Book-to-Tax Differences

10. At the beginning of 2021, Paul owned a 25% interest in Associates Partnership. During the year, a new partner was admitted, and Paul's interest was reduced to 20%. The partnership liabilities at January 1, 2021, were $150,000 but decreased to $100,000 at December 31, 2021. Paul's and the other partners' capital accounts are in proportion to their respective interests. Disregarding any income, loss, or drawings for 2021, the basis of Paul's partnership interest at December 31, 2021, compared to the basis of his interest at January 1, 2021, was

  A. Decreased by $37,500.
  B. Increased by $20,000.
  C. Decreased by $17,500.
  D. Decreased by $5,000.

Answer (C) is correct.
REQUIRED: The change in basis of a partner's interest in the partnership.
DISCUSSION: A decrease in a partner's share of partnership liabilities is treated as a distribution of money to the partner. At the beginning of the year, Paul's 25% share of the $150,000 of partnership liabilities was $37,500. At the end of the year, Paul's 20% share of the $100,000 of partnership liabilities was $20,000. Thus, Paul's share of partnership liabilities decreased by $17,500 ($37,500 – $20,000), and his basis was reduced by the same amount.
Answer (A) is incorrect. The beginning balance of Paul's share of partnership liabilities is $37,500. **Answer (B) is incorrect.** The ending balance of Paul's share of partnership liabilities is $20,000. **Answer (D) is incorrect.** A decrease in $5,000 only uses the $100,000 ending amount for partnership liabilities for calculating partner basis.

16.3 Distribution of Partnership Assets

11. Baker is a partner in BDT with a partnership basis of $60,000. BDT made a liquidating distribution of land with an adjusted basis of $75,000 and a fair market value of $40,000 to Baker. What amount of gain or loss should Baker report?

  A. $35,000 loss.
  B. $20,000 loss.
  C. $0.
  D. $15,000 gain.

Answer (C) is correct.
REQUIRED: The partner's gain or loss from a liquidating distribution.
DISCUSSION: A partner recognizes gain only to the extent a money distribution exceeds the AB in the partnership interest immediately before the distribution. In the case of capital property distributions, there is no gain or loss; instead, the partner's basis in the property is adjusted for any variance between the partner's partnership basis and the partnership's AB in the property distributed. Therefore, Baker has a $0 gain (loss).
Answer (A) is incorrect. The amount of $35,000 represents a loss by the partnership; however, no gain or loss is recognized by the partnership when it distributes property, including money. **Answer (B) is incorrect.** A gain can only be recognized when cash is distributed. Losses are never recognized. In addition, the value of distributed property is determined by the partnership's adjusted basis (not the FMV). **Answer (D) is incorrect.** Gains are only recognized when cash in excess of partnership interest is distributed (not property).

12. Fern received $30,000 in cash and an automobile with an adjusted basis and market value of $20,000 in a proportionate liquidating distribution from EF Partnership. Fern's basis in the partnership interest was $60,000 before the distribution. What is Fern's basis in the automobile received in the liquidation?

A. $0
B. $10,000
C. $20,000
D. $30,000

Answer (D) is correct.
REQUIRED: The distributee's basis in noncash property from liquidating distribution.
DISCUSSION: The distributee's basis in (noncash) property received in a distribution in liquidation is any excess of his or her AB in the partnership interest immediately before distribution over any amount of money received. Therefore, Fern's basis in the automobile is $30,000 ($60,000 basis – $30,000 cash received in distribution).
Answer (A) is incorrect. The cash distributed was only $30,000 and not $60,000 (i.e., equal to Fern's basis in the partnership interest). **Answer (B) is incorrect.** The amount of $10,000 would be the basis if the distribution included $50,000 in cash. In addition, the basis in the automobile is not equal to the difference between the cash received and the value of the automobile nor the difference between the distribution and the basis in the partnership interest. **Answer (C) is incorrect.** Carryover basis of capital assets from the partnership is adjusted for any difference in the total distribution and the partner's basis in the partnership interest.

13. Owen's tax basis in Regal Partnership was $18,000 at the time Owen received a nonliquidating distribution of $3,000 cash and land with an adjusted basis of $7,000 to Regal and a fair market value of $9,000. Regal did not have unrealized receivables, appreciated inventory, or properties that had been contributed by its partners. Disregarding any income, loss, or any other partnership distribution for the year, what was Owen's tax basis in Regal after the distribution?

A. $9,000
B. $8,000
C. $7,000
D. $6,000

Answer (B) is correct.
REQUIRED: The basis of distributive property in the partnership.
DISCUSSION: A current distribution reduces the partner's basis in the partnership. The partner's basis in his or her ownership interest in the partnership is reduced by the amount of money and the adjusted basis of property received in the distribution. Therefore, Owen's basis in Regal is

Basis of the partnership interest	$18,000
Less: Cash received	(3,000)
Less: Adjusted basis of the property received	(7,000)
Basis in the partnership	$ 8,000

Answer (A) is incorrect. Owen's basis in the partnership is reduced by the cash received and the adjusted basis (not the FMV) of property received. **Answer (C) is incorrect.** The amount of $7,000 is the adjusted basis of the land, not the partnership. **Answer (D) is incorrect.** Owen's basis in the partnership is reduced by the adjusted basis (not the FMV) of the property received.

14. The adjusted basis of Stan's partnership interest is $15,000. He receives a distribution of cash of $6,000 and property with an adjusted basis to the partnership of $11,000. (This was not a distribution in liquidation.) What is the basis of the distributed property in Stan's hands?

A. $9,000
B. $11,000
C. $5,000
D. $17,000

Answer (A) is correct.
REQUIRED: The basis of distributive property in the partnership.
DISCUSSION: The basis of property distributed to a partner is the property's adjusted basis to the partnership immediately before such distribution. This basis, however, cannot exceed the adjusted basis of the partner's interest in the partnership less any money received in the same distribution. Stan's basis in the property distributed is

Basis of partnership interest	$15,000
Less: Cash received	(6,000)
Basis in distributed property	$ 9,000

Answer (B) is incorrect. The basis of the distributed property cannot exceed the adjusted basis of the partner's interest in the partnership. **Answer (C) is incorrect.** The basis of the distributed property will not be equal to the difference between the amount of cash received and the partnership's basis in the property. **Answer (D) is incorrect.** The amount of $17,000 does not take into account Stan's original partnership interest.

15. The adjusted basis of Vance's partnership interest in Lex Associates was $180,000 immediately before receiving the following distribution in complete liquidation of Lex:

	Basis to Lex	Fair Market Value
Cash	$100,000	$100,000
Real estate	70,000	96,000

What is Vance's basis in the real estate?

A. $96,000
B. $83,000
C. $80,000
D. $70,000

Answer (C) is correct.
REQUIRED: The basis of property received in liquidation of a partnership interest.
DISCUSSION: In a liquidating distribution, a partner's basis for his or her partnership interest is reduced by the amount of money received. Any remaining basis is then allocated to other property received ($180,000 basis – $100,000 cash).
Answer (A) is incorrect. The basis of distributed property is not the fair market value. **Answer (B) is incorrect.** The basis is first reduced by the full amount of cash distributed. **Answer (D) is incorrect.** The basis of distributed property is the adjusted basis of the partner's interest less any money received in the same transaction.

16.4 Reconciling Book and Taxable Income

16. Would the following expense items be reported on Schedule M-1 of the corporation income tax return showing the reconciliation of income per books with income per return?

	Interest Incurred on Loan to Carry U.S. Obligations	Current State Corporation Income Tax Expense
A.	Yes	Yes
B.	No	No
C.	Yes	No
D.	No	Yes

Answer (B) is correct.
REQUIRED: The item reported on Schedule M-1.
DISCUSSION: Items treated differently in computing income per books and taxable income are reported and reconciled on Schedule M-1. Items treated the same for financial and tax purposes are not reported on the schedule. Both interest to carry U.S. obligations and state income tax are deducted in computing book income and taxable income.

17. In the current year, Starke Corp., an accrual-basis, calendar-year corporation, reported book income of $380,000. Included in that amount was $50,000 municipal bond interest income, $170,000 for federal income tax expense, and $2,000 interest expense on the debt incurred to carry the municipal bonds. What amount should Starke's taxable income be as reconciled on Starke's Schedule M-1 of Form 1120, *U.S. Corporation Income Tax Return*?

A. $330,000
B. $500,000
C. $502,000
D. $550,000

Answer (C) is correct.
REQUIRED: The corporation's taxable income given book income and some of its components.
DISCUSSION: The municipal bond income and the related interest expenses are not considered for tax purposes. The federal tax expense is not deductible for federal income tax purposes. Therefore, the net Schedule M-1 adjustment of $122,000 ($2,000 + $170,000 – $50,000) results in taxable income of $502,000 ($380,000 + $122,000).
Answer (A) is incorrect. The $170,000 income tax expense and the $2,000 interest expense on the municipal bonds are positive adjustments to book income. Answer (B) is incorrect. Interest expense on tax-exempt investments is not deductible. Answer (D) is incorrect. The $50,000 of municipal bond interest is a negative adjustment, and $2,000 of related interest expense is a positive adjustment.

18. In the reconciliation of income per books with income per return,

A. Only temporary differences are considered.
B. Only permanent differences are considered.
C. Both temporary and permanent differences are considered.
D. Neither temporary nor permanent differences are considered.

Answer (C) is correct.
REQUIRED: The differences included in the reconciliation of income per books with income per return.
DISCUSSION: Reconciling income per books with income per return considers both temporary differences (i.e., differences expected to be eliminated in the future, such as an accelerated method of depreciation for tax purposes and a straight-line method for financial reporting purposes) and permanent differences (i.e., differences not expected to be eliminated in the future, such as that caused by the deduction of federal income tax for financial reporting purposes).
Answer (A) is incorrect. Permanent differences must be reconciled. Answer (B) is incorrect. Temporary differences must be reconciled. Answer (D) is incorrect. Both temporary and permanent differences must be reconciled.

STUDY UNIT SEVENTEEN
BUSINESS ORGANIZATIONS

(23 pages of outline)

17.1	General Partnerships	467
17.2	Limited Partnerships	474
17.3	Limited Liability Companies (LLCs)	476
17.4	Corporate Formation	479
17.5	Corporate Operation, Financing, and Distributions	481
17.6	Shareholders' Rights	483
17.7	Directors and Officers: Authority, Duties, and Liability	484
17.8	Mergers and Termination	487
17.9	Advantages and Disadvantages of Corporations	488

This study unit addresses certain basic business structures. They should be contrasted with the **sole proprietorship**, the most basic and common structure. It consists of an individual engaged in any business who (1) has unlimited personal liability, (2) is taxed directly on the profits, (3) makes all operating decisions, and (4) provides all capital. It is created at the proprietor's will with no formalities and is terminated at the proprietor's discretion or by death.

A **partnership** is an association of two or more persons carrying on a business as co-owners for profit. This study unit covers (1) the form of partnership that may be created without statutory formalities (the **general partnership**), (2) partnerships created only by statute (the **limited partnership**), and (3) the **limited liability company** (a hybrid of the corporation and the partnership).

A **corporation** differs from other business organizations because, for all purposes, it is a **separate legal entity** that may exist in perpetuity. Unlike a sole proprietorship or a general partnership, its rights and obligations are separate from those of its owners or managers.

17.1 GENERAL PARTNERSHIPS

1. **Formation**

   > **BACKGROUND 17-1   Uniform Acts**
   >
   > In the U.S., partnership law was codified in the Uniform Partnership Act of 1914 (UPA) and updated in the Revised Uniform Partnership Act (RUPA) in 1994. The revised act was amended in 1997 to include provisions for limited liability partnerships (LLPs). These changes conform the law of partnership to modern business practice while retaining many features of the original act.

   a. The **Revised Uniform Partnership Act (RUPA)** defines a **partnership** as "an association of two or more persons to carry on as co-owners a business for profit."
      1) A business is any trade, occupation, or profession.
      2) A partnership is a legal entity distinct from its owners.
   b. An advantage of the general partnership is that it can exist without any formalities. No filings are required, and a partnership may be created without an explicit agreement (oral or written) or even an intent to form a partnership.
      1) Under the **Statute of Frauds**, a contract (e.g., a partnership agreement), the performance of which cannot be performed within 1 year of its making, must be in writing or proper electronic form to be valid.
         a) For example, a contract to create a partnership for a specified 2-year period must be in writing.

2) Fictitious name statutes have been enacted in most states to protect creditors.

   a) Registration permits creditors to discover the persons liable for the entity's debts.

3) Although an intent to form a partnership is not required, the co-owners must **intend** to make a profit even if no profit is earned.

   a) A person who receives a share of the profit is assumed to be a partner. But this assumption is overcome if the amounts received are as payments for debts, principal or interests, rent, wages, etc.

   b) Not-for-profit entities are not partnerships.

4) If the elements of a partnership are present, it is formed even if the parties do not intend to be partners.

EXAMPLE 17-1   Partnership Formation

Jim is doing business as Harvin Shoes, a sole proprietorship. In the past year, Jim has regularly joined with Stewart in the marketing of sport accessories. Jim and Stewart have formed a partnership if they intend to make a profit.

---

5) A **partnership by estoppel** may be recognized when an actual partnership does not exist to prevent injustice. The duties and liabilities of a partner sometimes may be imposed on a nonpartner (a purported partner).

   a) A **purported partner** has represented that (s)he is a partner or has consented to such a representation.

   b) A third party who has reasonably relied on the representation and suffered harm as a result may assert the existence of a partnership.

EXAMPLE 17-2   Partnership by Estoppel

Lawyer A falsely represented to Client that Lawyer A and Lawyer B were partners. Client, in reasonable reliance on this statement, sought legal services from Lawyer B. Because these services were performed without due care, Client suffered harm. Lawyer A (as well as Lawyer B) is liable as a partner despite the absence of an actual partnership.

---

2. **Capitalization**

   a. A general partnership cannot raise equity by selling shares.

3. **Profits, Losses, and Distributions**

   a. The RUPA provides that partners share (1) profits equally and (2) losses in the same proportion as profits. But the partners may agree otherwise.

      1) A major disadvantage of a general partnership is that each partner has **unlimited personal liability** for all losses and debts of the business.

   b. A partner also has the right to distributions. A **distribution** is a transfer of partnership property from the partnership to a partner for profits, payment for services, or reimbursements.

   c. Unless otherwise agreed, the right to compensation for services is generally a right to receive a share of the profits, not to be paid for services.

SU 17: Business Organizations

4. **Partnership Interest**
    a. A partner's **transferable interest** consists only of (1) a partner's share of partnership profits and losses and (2) the right to receive distributions as defined in 3.b. on the previous page.
        1) Transfer (assignment) of a partner's interest does not by itself result in (a) loss of rights (other than to the transferable interest) or (b) excuse the performance of the duties and obligations of a partner. It also does not result in dissociation or dissolution of the partnership.
            a) The assignee (or the estate of a deceased partner) does not receive the rights or incur the liabilities of a partner. The assignee is entitled only to the profits and distributions the assignor normally would receive. The assignee does **not** automatically become a partner and cannot act as an agent of the partnership.
        2) Partners and their creditors, assignees, and heirs have no interest in any **specific partnership property**. Thus, no creditor can proceed against specific partnership property. This property is not assignable by the partner or subject to attachment by the partner's creditors. Instead, creditors can proceed only against the partner's interest.
            a) Property is partnership property when acquired with **partnership assets**.
        3) When a partner dies, his or her partnership interest is personal property that may be **inherited** according to a valid will. The heirs are assignees, not partners.
            a) The estate does not become a partner.
            b) The death of a partner causes dissociation, not dissolution.
                i) The remaining partners may choose to continue the partnership.
            c) The estate is responsible for the partner's allocated share of any partnership liabilities.
        4) A judgment creditor of a general or limited partner may attach the partner's transferable interest only by securing a **charging order** (a lien on the interest) from a court.

> **SUCCESS TIP**
> The AICPA often tests sharing of profits, losses, and distributions in partnerships. Candidates should understand that sharing is determined by the RUPA's equal distribution default rule only when the partners have not agreed otherwise.

5. **Taxation**
    a. An advantage of a partnership (general or limited) is that it is a tax reporting, **not** a tax paying, entity.
    b. Profit or loss is passed through to the partners.

6. **Rights of Partners**
    a. The rights, powers, duties, and liabilities of partners are largely defined by the **law of agency**.
        1) However, partners may agree to limit their rights.

- b. Each partner has a right to **equal participation in management** of the partnership.
    1) The general rule for ordinary matters is majority rule.
    2) A unanimous vote is required to
        a) Amend a partnership agreement,
        b) Admit a new partner, and
        c) Determine other nonroutine matters.
- c. A partner's right of **access to partnership information** is the right to inspect and copy the partnership books and records.
    1) A reasonable demand for other partnership information also must be honored.
- d. The right to **use or possess partnership property** may be exercised only on behalf of the partnership.
- e. The right to **choose associates** means that admission as a partner requires the consent of **all** partners. Unanimous consent vests in the new partner all the rights, duties, and powers of a partner.
    1) A transfer of a partner's interest does not make the transferee a partner. The transferee is entitled only to receive the share of profits and distributions allocated to the interest acquired. The transferee has no management rights.

7. **Powers of Partners**
    - a. Each partner consents to being both a **principal and an agent** of the partnership.
        1) Thus, a general partnership and the other general partners are bound by a contract made by a partner acting within the scope of his or her actual or apparent authority.
    - b. A majority of partners may decide ordinary matters and therefore bind the other partners. But a nonroutine matter requires a unanimous vote.
    - c. **Apparent authority** to act as an agent of the partnership results from words or actions of the principal (the partnership) that reasonably induce a third party to rely on the agent's (partner's) authority.
        1) The scope of apparent authority is limited to carrying on in the ordinary course the partnership business or business of the kind carried on by the partnership.
        2) If a partner acts without actual or apparent authority, the partnership and the other partners are **not** bound unless the other partners **ratify**.
        3) The RUPA provides for filing a **statement of partnership authority** that gives notice of any limitations on the authority of a partner.

8. **Duties of Partners**
    - a. Duties imposed upon partners include the **fiduciary** duties of loyalty and care. The duty of **loyalty** is limited to
        1) Not competing with the partnership,
        2) Not acting as a party with an adverse interest, and
        3) Not exploiting a partnership opportunity or secretly using partnership assets.
    - b. The duty of **care** is not to engage in
        1) Knowing violations of the law,
        2) Intentional wrongdoing, or
        3) Gross negligence.
    - c. A partner also has an obligation of **good faith and fair dealing**.

9. **Liabilities of Partners**

   a. Partners are **jointly and severally liable** (individually and as a partnership) for the full amount of any partnership obligations. These include the **torts** (e.g., negligence) committed by another partner who acted (1) within the ordinary course and scope of the partnership business or (2) with the authorization of the other partners.

      1) A plaintiff may sue one partner or the partnership. But only a partner who is a judgment debtor is personally liable.

   b. A partner may obligate the partnership and partners by contract when acting with actual or apparent authority.

   c. **Admission** into an existing partnership results in liability for partnership obligations incurred prior to admission to the extent of the investment.

   d. A **withdrawing** partner remains liable for partnership debts incurred before withdrawal unless the creditors contractually agree otherwise.

10. **Termination**

    a. The partners may choose to limit the duration of the partnership to a definite term or the completion of a specific undertaking.

       1) The partnership also may be **at will**. A partnership at will is **not** limited to "a definite term or the completion of a specific undertaking."

    b. **Dissociation** is a partner's ceasing to be associated in carrying on the business of the partnership. A partner can dissociate at any time, subject to payment of damages if the dissociation is wrongful.

       1) For example, dissociation results from the following:

          a) Notice to the partnership of a partner's express will to withdraw
          b) An event specified in the agreement
          c) Expulsion under the partnership agreement
          d) Incapacity or death
          e) Bankruptcy or insolvency

       2) Upon dissociation, management rights (except winding up) terminate.

       3) After dissociation, the partnership may continue, but the dissociated partner's interest must be **purchased**. If the partnership does not continue, dissolution begins.

          a) The agreement of the remaining partners to hold a dissociating partner harmless for partnership debts does not affect liability to third parties.

       4) The partnership is **not** necessarily dissolved by dissociation of a partner unless it occurs by the partner's notice of an **express will** to leave the partnership.

       5) A **statement of dissociation** may be filed by the partnership or a dissociated partner. It is deemed to provide notice of dissociation **90 days** after filing.

          a) Such notice terminates the partner's apparent authority and his or her liability for the partnership's post-dissociation obligations.
          b) A dissociated partner (or the estate of a deceased partner) has apparent authority for **2 years** to bind the partnership to contracts with third parties.
          c) A dissociated partner (or the estate of a deceased partner) remains liable to creditors for obligations incurred prior to dissociation.

c. **Dissolution and winding up** occur only after certain events. But dissolution may occur without winding up.

   1) Dissolution may be by **operation of law**, for example, because of an event that makes the partnership's business illegal.

      a) Moreover, a **court** may order dissolution, for example, because the economic purpose of the partnership cannot be achieved.

   2) **Actual** authority of a partner to act on behalf of the partnership terminates upon dissolution except as necessary to wind up partnership affairs.

   3) **Apparent** authority of a partner may continue to exist throughout the winding up process unless notice of the dissolution has been communicated to the other party to the transaction.

   4) A partner's liability for the partnership's obligations continues after dissolution.

   5) Most fiduciary duties of the partners also remain in effect.

   6) A **statement of dissolution** may be filed by any partner who has not wrongfully dissociated to give nonpartners 90 days' notice after filing.

d. A partnership may **continue after dissolution** if all parties (including any dissociating partner who has not wrongfully dissociated) waive the right to winding up and termination.

e. **Winding up** is the administrative process of settling partnership affairs, including the use of partnership assets and any required contributions by partners to pay creditors.

   1) **Creditors** are paid in full before any distributions are made to partners. However, partners who are creditors share equally with nonpartner creditors under the RUPA.

   2) After payment of creditors, any surplus is paid in cash to the partners.

      a) A partner has no right to a distribution **in kind (of noncash assets)** and need not accept a distribution in kind.

EXAMPLE 17-3   Allocation of Profit after Liquidation

Zoe and Zed are the only partners in a general partnership. Zoe contributes $10,000 in cash, and Zed contributes services only. No partnership agreement states how partnership profits and losses are to be allocated. When the partnership dissolves, Zoe and Zed liquidate its assets. The net receipts are $60,000 in cash. If creditors are owed $45,000, the following is the determination of profit:

Cash	$60,000
Payments to creditors	(45,000)
Available cash	$15,000
Zoe's contribution	(10,000)
Profit	$ 5,000

Zoe and Zed did not agree on the allocation of profit. It therefore is shared equally ($5,000 ÷ 2 = $2,500 to each partner). Zoe receives $12,500 ($10,000 contribution + $2,500), and Zed receives $2,500 ($0 contribution + $2,500).

---

   3) If a partner's account has a negative (debit) balance, the partner is liable to contribute the amount of the balance.

      a) If a partner does not make a required contribution, the other partners must pay the difference in the same proportion in which they share losses.

> **EXAMPLE 17-4** Allocation of Loss after Liquidation
>
> In Example 17-3, assume that the net receipts after liquidation of assets equaled $50,000. The following is the determination of the loss:
>
> | | |
> |---|---:|
> | Cash | $50,000 |
> | Payments to creditors | (45,000) |
> | Available cash | $ 5,000 |
> | Zoe's contribution | (10,000) |
> | Loss | $ (5,000) |
>
> Zoe and Zed did not agree on the allocation of loss. It therefore is shared equally [$(5,000) ÷ 2 = $(2,500) to each partner]. Zoe receives $7,500 [$10,000 contribution + $(2,500) share of loss], and Zed is liable for $2,500.

SUCCESS TIP: The AICPA has tested candidates' knowledge of how general partnerships terminate, especially the effects of a partner's death on the partnership and the rights of the deceased partner's heirs.

11. **Limited Liability Partnership (LLP)**

    a. An LLP is a general partnership with limited liability. It is a favorable form of organization for professionals who have not incorporated. In many states, this form is restricted to use by professionals.

        1) An LLP must file a **statement of qualification** with the secretary of state and maintain professional liability insurance.

        2) All partners are general partners who have limited liability for the acts of other parties. In most states, liability is limited for all partnership obligations, including those resulting from contracts. Thus, a **full shield** statute imposes liability only to the extent of the LLP's assets, with certain exceptions.

            a) For example, a partner remains liable for obligations s(he) personally guaranteed or incurred and for wrongful acts.

            b) A partner who is an immediate **supervisor** also is liable for the wrongs committed within the scope of employment by an employee.

12. **Joint Ventures**

    a. A joint venture is an easily formed business structure common in international commerce. It is an association of persons who as co-owners engage in a specific undertaking for profit.

        1) A joint venture is treated as a partnership in most cases.

STOP & REVIEW: You have completed the outline for this subunit. Study multiple-choice questions 1 through 4 beginning on page 490.

17.2 LIMITED PARTNERSHIPS

1. **Limited Partnership**
    a. Most statutes are based on the **Revised Uniform Limited Partnership Act (RULPA)**. A limited partnership has one or more general partners and one or more limited partners. A business entity may be a partner.
        1) At least one **general partner** must manage the partnership and have full personal liability for debts of the partnership.
            a) A person may be both a general partner and a limited partner with the rights and liabilities of each.
        2) A **limited partner** is an investor and generally by default not a manager or agent. Exceptions to the general or default prohibition to agency can be allowed by including such powers in the partnership agreement. A limited partner's contribution may be cash, services, or other property. Limited partnership interests are securities that must be registered with the SEC unless an exemption applies.
            a) A limited partner does **not** (1) manage the limited partnership or (2) have a fiduciary duty to the limited partnership.
            b) The limited partnership interest is intangible personal property because the limited partner has no right to specific partnership property.
    b. **Formation**
        1) A written **certificate of limited partnership** must be filed in the state where it is organized to give creditors notice of the limited liability of the limited partners. Without a filing, the entity is treated as a general partnership.
    c. **Operation**
        1) The operation of a limited partnership is similar to that of a general partnership.
        2) One exception is that, without a contrary agreement, profits and losses are shared on the basis of the value of contributions actually made by each partner.
    d. **Partner Rights and Liabilities**
        1) Unless the partnership agreement states otherwise, a **general partner** in a limited partnership has the same rights and powers and the same duties as a partner in a general partnership.
            a) General partners cannot unilaterally admit additional general or limited partners without the **unanimous** written consent of all partners.
                i) But a general or limited partner may assign the interest to creditors or others without dissolving the partnership.
        2) Among other things, a **limited partner** has the right to
            a) Propose and vote on partnership affairs that do not directly control partnership operations, e.g., admission or removal of a general partner.
            b) Withdraw upon 6 months' notice or according to the partnership agreement.
                i) A limited partner may not withdraw the capital contribution if the effect is to impair creditors' rights.
            c) Do business with the partnership, e.g., become a creditor (secured or unsecured) by lending it money.

- d) Have reasonable access to partnership records, including tax returns, and to inspect and copy partnership records.
- e) Assign the limited partnership interest. But the assignee does not become a substituted limited partner.
    - i) If the limited partner is insolvent, a creditor may obtain a charging order from a court that acts as an involuntary assignment.
- f) Apply for dissolution of the partnership.
- g) Obtain an accounting of partnership affairs.

3) A limited partner is liable for
- a) Partnership liabilities only to the extent of his or her capital contribution.
    - i) (S)he has **no** right to participate in control of the business. **Control** is participation in day-to-day management decisions.
- b) Knowingly permitting his or her name to be used in the partnership name and held out as a participant in management. But liability is incurred only to persons who reasonably believe the limited partner is a general partner.

e. **Termination**

1) A limited partnership is **dissolved** by an event (time) specified in the partnership agreement, a unanimous decision of the partners, or a court order.
   - a) An event of withdrawal of a **general partner**, e.g., death or retirement, also causes dissolution. But the agreement may provide that the business may be carried on by the remaining general partners (if any).
      - i) If no general partner remains, the limited partners may agree to continue the business and appoint a new general partner(s).
2) The limited partnership is **not** dissolved by the bankruptcy, incapacity, or death of a limited partner or by the transfer of a limited partner's interest.
   - a) The personal representative of a decedent's estate has the rights and liabilities of a limited partner solely for the purpose of settling the estate.
3) After dissolution, **winding up** is done by a general partner who has not caused the dissolution. If no general partner exists, it may be performed by the **limited partners** or by a court designee.
4) Remaining assets, if any, are distributed to
   - a) Creditors, including creditors who are partners
   - b) Present partners and former partners for unpaid distributions
   - c) The partners as a return of their contributions
   - d) The partners according to the limited partnership agreement in the proportions in which they share distributions

STOP & REVIEW

You have completed the outline for this subunit.
Study multiple-choice questions 5 through 7 on page 492.

17.3 LIMITED LIABILITY COMPANIES (LLCs)

1. **Overview**
    a. An LLC is a noncorporate hybrid business structure that combines the limited liability of the corporation and the limited partnership with the tax advantages of the general partnership and the limited partnership.
    b. An LLC is a legal entity separate from its owner-investors (called **members**). Individuals and any corporate and noncorporate business entities may be members.

2. **Formation**
    a. An LLC may be formed for any lawful purpose under a state statute.
        1) An LLC is formed by one or more persons when articles of organization are filed with the appropriate secretary of state (or the equivalent).
    b. The **articles of organization** should state at a minimum (1) the LLC's name; (2) the address of the principal place of business or registered office; (3) the name and street address of the initial agent for service of process; and (4) whether managers, who may not be members, will manage the LLC.
    c. The members' contract or **operating agreement** ordinarily is **not** legally required. It also may be oral but should be written.
        1) Unless the agreement states otherwise, it may be amended only by a unanimous resolution of the members.
        2) The operating agreement may address such matters as the following:
            a) Sharing of profits and losses
            b) Voting rights
            c) The circumstances causing dissolution
    d. The LLC must at all times maintain a registered **agent** for service of process and a registered **office** in the state.

3. **Capitalization**
    a. Funding of an LLC is from members' **contributions**. Without an agreement to the contrary, it may consist of tangible and intangible property and services, including obligations to contribute cash or property or to perform services.
    b. A disadvantage is that LLC interests may be considered securities subject to federal and state regulation.

4. **Profits, Losses, and Distributions**
    a. Without a contrary agreement, statutes most often provide for profits, losses, and distributions to be shared based on the values of members' **contributions**.

5. **LLC Interest**
   a. A member may transfer (assign) his or her distributional interest without dissolving the LLC. This interest is personal property.

6. **Taxation**
   a. Members may elect to be taxed as partners in a partnership (a pass-through entity). But single-member LLCs (called "disregarded entities" for tax purposes) are taxed as sole proprietorships.
   b. Taxation as a corporation (a taxable entity) may be advantageous if reinvestment in the LLC is desired, and corporate rates are lower than personal rates.

7. **Management**
   a. An LLC is deemed to be member-managed unless the articles provide otherwise.
   b. In a **member-managed LLC**, all members have a right to participate, and most business matters are decided by the majority.
   c. In a **manager-managed LLC**, each manager, who need not be a member, has equal rights, and most business matters are decided by the manager or by a majority of the managers.

8. **Liability of Members and Managers**
   a. Member-managers have limited liability.

9. **Termination**
   a. An LLC is dissolved upon
      1) Expiration of a specified time period or occurrence of a specified event.
      2) Consent of a number or percentage of members provided in their agreement.
      3) Death of a member if noted in the articles.
      4) Judicial determination of the following:
         a) Frustration of purpose
         b) Impracticability of continuing (e.g., because of a member's conduct)
         c) Inappropriate behavior
         d) The equitability of liquidation

Characteristics of Noncorporate Business Entities

	Formation	Capitalization	Operation	Liability	Transferability	Taxation	Termination
General Partnership	No formalities. No filings. Formed based on written or oral agreement.	Resources of general partners.	Each partner has right to equal participation in management. Can restrict management rights to one or more partners.	Partners are jointly and severally liable for any partnership obligation.	Partner may transfer financial interest without loss of rights, duties, and liabilities as partner.	Tax reporting entity only. Partners subject to tax.	Dissociation followed by dissolution and winding up.
Limited Partnership	Formalities. Must file written certificate of limited partnership with state.	Resources of general and limited partners.	General partner has full management rights. Limited partner has no management rights.	General partner has unlimited liability for partnership obligations. Limited partner liable only to extent of capital contribution.	General partner may transfer financial interest without loss of rights, duties, and liabilities as partner. Limited partner may assign interest.	Tax reporting entity only. Partners subject to tax.	Event of withdrawal of a general partner.
Limited Liability Partnership	Formalities. Must file with secretary of state and maintain professional liability insurance.	Resources of partners.	Favorable form of organization for professionals (e.g., lawyers, CPAs, etc.). All partners are general partners with limited liability.	Not personally liable for partnership obligations except to extent of LLP's assets. Partners remain personally liable for their own malpractice.	Partner may transfer financial interest without loss of rights, duties, and liabilities as partner.	Tax reporting entity only. Partners subject to tax.	Dissociation followed by dissolution and winding up.
Limited Liability Company	Formalities. Must file articles of organization with secretary of state.	Contributions of members.	Unless provided otherwise, all members have equal management rights.	Owners who participate in management have limited liability.	A member can transfer his or her distributional interest. This interest is personal property.	May elect flow-through taxation or be taxed as an entity.	Dissolution followed by liquidation.

STOP & REVIEW

You have completed the outline for this subunit.
Study multiple-choice questions 8 and 9 on page 493.

17.4 CORPORATE FORMATION

> **BACKGROUND 17-2   MBCA**
>
> Corporations are established under state law. To provide guidance for state lawmakers, the American Bar Association issued the **Model Business Corporation Act (MBCA)**. The MBCA has been adopted at least in part by every state. The **Revised Model Business Corporation Act of 1984 (RMBCA)** applies to publicly held and closely held corporations. This outline is based on the RMBCA.

1. **Overview**

    a. A corporation is a separate legal entity created under a **state statute** by filing its organizational document (articles of incorporation) with the proper state authority.

     1) The corporation ordinarily is treated as a **legal person** with rights and obligations separate from its owners and managers.

    b. Corporations are owned by **shareholders** (owners) who elect a board of directors and approve fundamental changes in the corporate structure.

    c. A **close (closely held) corporation**

     1) Is owned by relatively few shareholders,
     2) Does not sell its stock to the public,
     3) Is commonly owned by its officers and directors, and
     4) Has shareholder-managers.

    d. A **foreign** corporation is one that does business in any state other than the one in which it is incorporated. A **certificate of authority** is required to **do business** within the borders of another state.

    e. An **S corporation** has elected under federal law to be taxed similarly to a partnership. Thus, it usually does not pay corporate income tax, so tax liabilities flow through to its shareholders. (A **C corporation** is taxed at the corporate income tax rate.)

     1) Study Unit 14 covers S corporations.

    f. **Professional corporations** (professional service associations) give accountants, lawyers, and other professionals the benefits of incorporation. Statutes typically restrict stock ownership to specific professionals licensed within that state.

2. **Preincorporation Contracts**

    a. A **promoter** arranges for the formation of the corporation. (S)he provides for the financing of the corporation and for compliance with any relevant securities law.

    b. **Prior to incorporation**, the promoter enters into ordinary and necessary contracts required for initial operation.

     1) Promoters generally are personally liable on their contracts.
     2) The corporation is not liable because a promoter cannot be an agent of a nonexistent entity.

c. A corporation may **not ratify** a preincorporation contract because no principal existed at the time of contracting. However, **adoption** of the contract is a legal substitute for ratification. It may be implied from accepting the benefits of the contract.

   1) Adoption is an assignment of rights and delegation of duties from the promoter to the corporation. But it is not retroactive and does not release the promoter from liability.
   2) If the promoter, the third party, and the corporation enter into a **novation** substituting the corporation for the promoter, only the corporation is liable, and the promoter is released.

d. The promoter secures potential investors using **preincorporation subscription agreements**. Each subscriber agrees to purchase a certain amount of shares at a specified price, payable at an agreed future time.

   1) A **preincorporation subscription agreement** is irrevocable for 6 months, unless otherwise provided in the agreement, or all subscribers consent to revocation. Many state statutes require the agreement to be written.

3. **Incorporation**

   a. Incorporation may be in any state. **Articles of incorporation** (the corporate charter) must be filed with the secretary of state or another designated official.
   b. **Incorporators** sign the articles. Only one incorporator is required.
   c. **Articles of incorporation** must include the following:
      1) Corporation's name
      2) Number of authorized shares
      3) Name and street address of the corporation's registered agent
      4) Name and street address of each incorporator
   d. The articles also may contain **optional provisions**.
   e. After filing, the incorporators elect the members of the **initial board of directors** if they have not been named in the articles. The incorporators then resign.
   f. The board of directors holds an **organizational meeting** to take all steps needed to complete the organizational structure. The new board
      1) Adopts **bylaws** if they were not adopted by the incorporators.
         a) Bylaws govern the internal structure and operation of the corporation. They may contain any provision for managing the business as long as it does not conflict with the law or the articles.
      2) Elects officers.

STOP & REVIEW

You have completed the outline for this subunit.
Study multiple-choice questions 10 and 11 beginning on page 493.

17.5 CORPORATE OPERATION, FINANCING, AND DISTRIBUTIONS

1. **Corporate Powers**

    a. A corporation may do any lawful act to further its business.

    b. A corporation may be held liable for the actions of its employees.

    1) Under the law of agency (**respondeat superior**, or "let the master answer"), a corporate principal may be liable for an agent's **torts** (civil wrongs not resulting from contracts) committed within the scope of employment.

    c. Under the doctrine of **ultra vires**, a corporation may not act beyond its implied or express powers.

    1) But a corporate action generally may not be challenged on the ground that the corporation lacked power to act. A corporation essentially has the same powers as an individual.

    2) Moreover, the ultra vires doctrine has been eliminated as a defense by either party in a suit involving a corporation.

    3) However, the RMBCA provides a cause of action in three instances in which the power to act may be questioned:

        a) A shareholder can seek an injunction,
        b) Corporations can proceed against directors or officers, and
        c) The state attorney general can proceed against the corporation.

2. **Piercing the Corporate Veil**

    a. Courts disregard the corporate form (and thus shareholders are personally liable for corporate acts) when it is used merely to

    1) Commit wrongdoing,
    2) Shield its shareholders from liability for fraud, or
    3) Otherwise circumvent the law.

    b. A court might disregard a corporate entity if it finds the shareholders have not conducted the business on a corporate basis, for example, if

    1) Assets of the corporation and the shareholder(s) are commingled,
    2) The corporation was established for a sham purpose,
    3) Corporate formalities are ignored, or
    4) The corporation is inadequately capitalized to carry on its intended business.

EXAMPLE 17-5	Piercing the Corporate Veil

Jennifer organizes a corporation with capital of only $500, intending to buy goods (inventory) worth $1,000,000 on credit. Jennifer expects to pay for the goods from profits generated from sales. If the business is not successful, she expects not to be personally liable because the purchase was made in the corporation's name. Because the corporation is undercapitalized, creditors may be successful in piercing the corporate veil and Jennifer could be held personally liable for the debt.

3. **Financing**
    a. **Debt** financing increases the corporation's **risk** because it must be repaid at fixed times even if the corporation is not profitable (versus dividends on equity securities, which are discretionary).
    b. **Equity** financing in the form of voting shares (common shares) transfers ownership interests. Thus, shareholders are **not** creditors.
        1) In bankruptcy, creditors have **priority** in remaining assets.
4. **Dividends and Other Distributions**
    a. The board has discretion to determine the time and amount of distributions. A distribution ordinarily is a transfer of money or other property.
    b. Generally, two prerequisites are used to determine whether the board is likely to distribute dividends.
        1) First, the corporation should not be insolvent after the distribution. Profitability is **not** a legal condition of a distribution. However, a distribution is illegal if the corporation is insolvent or payment would cause insolvency. A dividend also is illegal if not paid from the funds **statutorily** designated to be available for payment.
        2) Second, the board must authorize the distribution. **Directors** must declare a distribution by resolution.
    c. **Shareholders** have the status of unsecured creditors once a dividend is declared.
5. **Types of Dividends**
    a. Dividends are returns on capital paid in cash, shares, or other property.
        1) **Preferred shareholders** are entitled to a fixed amount that must be paid **before common shareholders** are paid.
            a) If the preferred shares are **cumulative**, any dividends not paid in preceding years (dividends in arrears) are carried forward and must be paid before the common shareholders receive anything.
        2) **Liquidating dividends** are a return of, not a return on, a shareholder's capital.
    b. **Stock (share) dividends** are payable in the shares of the corporation as a percentage of the shares outstanding.
        1) When a stock dividend is declared, the corporation transfers the legally required amount from earned surplus (retained earnings) to stated capital (common stock). Total equity is not changed.
    c. **Stock (share) split** is an issuance of shares to reduce the unit value of each share. A stock split does not increase a shareholder's proportionate ownership. It merely increases the number of shares outstanding.

STOP & REVIEW

You have completed the outline for this subunit.
Study multiple-choice questions 12 and 13 beginning on page 494.

17.6 SHAREHOLDERS' RIGHTS

1. **Shareholders**

    a. A shareholder is an owner but has no direct rights, for example, to manage the corporation.

    b. The shareholders' primary participation is by **meeting annually and electing directors**. Directors are elected by a **plurality** of the votes (the most votes, not a majority) cast by the shares entitled to vote at a meeting at which a quorum is present. A quorum is the minimum number of shareholders necessary to conduct the meeting.

    1) Shareholders must approve **fundamental corporate changes**, including

        a) Mergers and share exchanges other than short-form mergers.
        b) A sale of or a disposition of substantially all assets that leave the corporation with **no significant continuing business activity**.
        c) Dissolutions.
        d) Amendments to the articles that materially and adversely affect shareholders' rights.

    2) Shareholders may amend or repeal the articles of incorporation and the **bylaws**.

    c. A shareholder has no right to receive dividends unless they have been declared.

2. **Voting Rights**

    a. The **articles** may establish the voting rights per share.

3. **Preemptive Rights**

    a. These are important to owners of a closely held corporation. They give a shareholder an option to subscribe to a new issuance of shares in proportion to their current interest in the corporation. Thus, they limit dilution of equity.

4. **Inspection Rights**

    a. Shareholders and their agents have a fundamental **right** to a reasonable inspection of books and records of the corporation, including the articles, bylaws, minutes of shareholder meetings, and the annual report.

    b. Inspection must be in good faith and for a **proper purpose** that relates to the shareholders' interest in the corporation.

    c. An **improper purpose** does not relate to the shareholders' interest in the corporation, e.g., to benefit a personal business. Improper purposes include

    1) Discovery of trade secrets,
    2) Gaining a competitive advantage for another company, and
    3) Development of a mailing list for sale or similar use.

5. **Dissenters' (Appraisal) Rights**

   a. Shareholders who disagree with fundamental corporate changes may be paid the **fair value** of their shares in cash.

   b. For example, dissenters' rights might arise from

      1) A disposition of assets that leaves the corporation without a significant continuing business activity.

      2) Certain mergers and share exchanges. Shareholder awareness of dissenters' rights is especially important in a **short-form merger** because notice of the merger is not required to be given to shareholders of the parent.

6. **Shareholder Suits**

   a. **Direct suits** by shareholders are lawsuits filed on their own behalf, either individually or as members of a class.

   b. A **shareholder derivative suit** is to recover for wrongs done to the corporation. The action is for the benefit of the corporation, and any recovery belongs to it, not to the shareholder. The corporation is the true plaintiff. An example is a suit to recover damages from management for an **ultra vires** act (actions outside the corporation's authority).

You have completed the outline for this subunit.
Study multiple-choice questions 14 and 15 on page 495.

STOP & REVIEW

17.7 DIRECTORS AND OFFICERS: AUTHORITY, DUTIES, AND LIABILITY

1. **Composition of the Board**

   a. Each state has a specific requirement with respect to the **number of directors** elected to sit on the board. Many states require a minimum of three. Under the RMBCA, a minimum of one director is required. However, the RMBCA also permits a corporation to dispense with a board by unanimous shareholder agreement.

EXAMPLE 17-6	Number of Directors

   X Corp. has only one shareholder. It is incorporated in a state that requires at least three directors. But if the entity has fewer than three shareholders, the number of directors may equal the number of shareholders. X Corp. is permitted by statute to have one director.

   b. The **initial board** is usually appointed by the incorporators or named in the articles, and this board serves until the first meeting of the shareholders.

   c. In most states, shareholders have a right to remove, **with or without cause**, any director or the entire board by a majority vote.

2. **Authority of the Board**

   a. Directors formulate overall policy for the corporation, but they are **neither trustees nor agents** of the corporation. A director **cannot** act individually to bind the corporation.

3. **Directors' Fiduciary Duty**

    a. Directors owe a **fiduciary duty** to the corporation to (1) act in its best interests, (2) be loyal, (3) use due diligence in discharging responsibilities, (4) be informed about information relevant to the corporation, and (5) disclose conflicts of interest. **Controlling or majority shareholders** owe similar duties.

    b. A **director's duty of care** is tested objectively.

        1) A director must discharge his or her duties

            a) In good faith,
            b) In a manner (s)he reasonably believes to be in the best interests of the corporation, and
            c) With the care that a person in a similar position would reasonably believe appropriate under similar circumstances.

        2) **Reliance on others.** In exercising reasonable care, a director may rely on information, reports, opinions, and statements prepared or presented by persons (an appropriate officer, employee, or specialist) whom the director **reasonably believes** to be competent in the matters presented.

    c. Directors owe a **duty of loyalty** to the corporation.

        1) **Conflicting-interest transactions.** To protect the corporation against self-dealing, a director is required to make **full disclosure** of any financial interest (s)he may have in any transaction to which both the director and the corporation may be a party. A director must not make a secret profit.

            a) A transaction is **not** improper merely on the grounds of a director's conflict of interest. If the transaction (1) is fair to the corporation or (2) has been approved by a majority of informed, disinterested directors or shareholders, it is not voidable even if the director profits.

        2) Directors may not usurp any **corporate opportunity**. A director must give the corporation the right of first refusal.

EXAMPLE 17-7   Usurpation of a Corporate Opportunity

Skip, a director of The Fishing Corp., learns in his corporate capacity that a state-of-the-art, deep-sea hydroplane fishing vessel is available for a bargain price. The purchase of this unique hydroplane may be a business opportunity from which the corporation could benefit. If Skip purchases the hydroplane for himself without giving the corporation the right of first refusal, he is usurping a corporate opportunity.

---

4. **Officers**

    a. Officers are elected or appointed by the **board**. Generally, officers manage the operations of the corporation. The board may not remove without cause an officer elected or employed by the shareholders.

    b. The usual officers are a president, vice president, secretary, and treasurer. Moreover, an officer may serve as a director.

    c. Unlike directors, officers are **agents** of the corporation and manage the corporation.

        1) Officers have **express authority** conferred by the bylaws or the board.
        2) Officers have **implied authority** to do things that are reasonably necessary to accomplish their express duties.

    d. Officers, like directors, owe **fiduciary duties** to the corporation.

        1) Officers are subject to the same duties of care and loyalty as directors.

5. **Liability and the Business Judgment Rule**
   a. Courts avoid substituting their business judgment for that of **officers or directors**.
   b. The rule protects an officer or a director from **personal liability** for honest errors of judgment if (s)he
      1) Acted in good faith;
      2) Was not motivated by fraud, conflict of interest, or illegality; and
      3) Was not grossly negligent.
   c. To avoid personal liability, directors and officers must
      1) Make informed decisions (educate themselves about the issues),
      2) Be free from conflicts of interest, and
      3) Have a rational basis to support their position.
   d. Most states permit corporations to **indemnify** directors and officers for expenses of litigation involving business judgments, subject to some exceptions.
      1) The RMBCA permits the **articles** to limit the liability of directors to the corporation or shareholders. However, the limitation applies only to **money damages**. The articles may not limit liability for the wrongful acts of a director.
      2) Usually, an officer or director who is liable to the corporation for **negligent** performance is not entitled to indemnification as a matter of public policy.
         a) However, a **court** may order indemnification of an officer or director (even though found negligent) if the court determines (s)he is fairly and reasonably entitled to it in view of all the relevant circumstances.

SUCCESS TIP

Directors' and officers' fiduciary duty and the duties of care and loyalty owed to their corporations have been highly publicized because of the major scandals involving improper practices. You most likely will see questions covering these topics on your exam.

STOP & REVIEW

You have completed the outline for this subunit.
Study multiple-choice questions 16 and 17 on page 496.

17.8 MERGERS AND TERMINATION

1. **Mergers**
    a. A **merger** combines two or more corporations. One corporation is absorbed by the other and ceases to exist.
        1) The surviving corporation succeeds to the legal rights and duties, liabilities to creditors, and assets of the merged corporation.
        2) In contrast, a corporation can purchase solely the assets of a corporation and then it does not assume the corporation's liabilities.
    b. In a **consolidation**, a new corporation is formed, and the two or more consolidating corporations cease operating as separate entities. Otherwise, the requirements and effects of the combination are similar to those for a merger.
    c. The shareholders of a merged corporation may receive shares or other securities issued by the surviving corporation.
        1) Shares of the merged (acquired) corporation are canceled.
    d. A merger requires the approval of (1) each board and (2) shareholders entitled to vote for each corporation. Approval is generally by a majority vote unless state law or the articles require a supermajority. After appropriate notice, shareholder approval must be given at a **special meeting**.
        1) Shareholders of each corporation must be provided a copy of the **plan of merger**.
        2) Shareholders of **each corporation** have appraisal rights.
        3) The sale of substantially all of the corporation's assets outside the regular course of business requires the approval of shareholders.
    e. The purchase or lease of substantially all of the **assets** of another corporation or an acquisition of another corporation's **shares** that allows the acquirer a controlling interest is not a merger. The acquiree is legally a separate entity.
        1) These transactions do **not** require shareholder approval.

2. **Tender Offers**
    a. An acquirer may bypass board approval of a business combination by extending a tender offer of cash or shares, usually at a higher-than-market price, directly to shareholders to purchase a certain number of the outstanding shares.
    b. Managements of target corporations have implemented diverse strategies to counter hostile tender offers. The following are examples of antitakeover strategies:
        1) **Issuing stock.** The target significantly increases its outstanding stock.
        2) **Self-tender.** The target borrows to tender an offer to repurchase its shares.
        3) **Legal action.** A target may challenge one or more aspects of a tender offer. A resulting delay increases costs for the raider and enables further defensive action.

3. **Dissolution**

    a. A corporation that has issued stock and commenced business may be **voluntarily dissolved** by

       1) Unanimous written consent of all shareholders or
       2) A majority shareholder vote at a special meeting called for the purpose if the directors have adopted a resolution of dissolution. A majority of the shares entitled to vote must be represented at the special meeting.

    b. Shareholders may seek a **judicial dissolution** when a deadlock of the board is harmful to the corporation, or the directors' actions are contrary to the best interests of the corporation.

> **STOP & REVIEW**
>
> You have completed the outline for this subunit.
> Study multiple-choice questions 18 and 19 on page 497.

17.9 ADVANTAGES AND DISADVANTAGES OF CORPORATIONS

1. **Advantages**

    a. **Limited liability.** A shareholder's exposure to corporate liabilities is limited to the investment.
    b. **Separation of ownership from management.** Shareholders have no inherent right to participate in management.
    c. **Free transferability of interests.** Without contractual or legal restriction, shares may be freely transferred, e.g., by sale, gift, pledge, or inheritance.

       1) A shareholder has no interest in specific property.

    d. **Perpetual life.** A corporation has perpetual existence unless the articles provide for a shorter life, or it is dissolved by the state.
    e. **Ease of raising capital.** A corporation raises capital (to start or expand the business) by selling stock or issuing bonds.
    f. **Constitutional rights.** A corporation is considered a **person** for most purposes under the **U.S. Constitution**. Thus, it has the right to equal protection, due process, freedom from unreasonable searches and seizures, and freedom of speech. It also has the right to make nearly unlimited contributions of money for political purposes.
    g. **Transfers of property to a controlled corporation.** A transfer of assets for shares of any corporation is **tax-free** if the transferors gain control immediately after the exchange. Two or more transferors of appreciated property receive the benefit if together they meet the control test. Property includes money.

SU 17: Business Organizations

2. **Disadvantages**

   a. Reduced individual control of a business operated by managers, not owners
   b. Payment of taxes on corporate income and payment by the shareholders of taxes on distributions received from the corporation
   c. Substantial costs of meeting the requirements of corporate formation and operation
   d. State and federal regulation of securities transactions
   e. Hostile takeover of a publicly traded corporation
   f. Sale or other transfer of unrestricted shares in a close corporation
   g. An inability of a minority shareholder in a close corporation to liquidate his or her interest or to influence the conduct of the business

3. **Summary of Corporate Entities**

	Formation	Capitalization	Operation	Liability	Transferability	Taxation	Termination
S corporation	Formalities. Files articles of incorporation with state. Elects S corporation status.	Members and shareholders (number of shareholders may not exceed 100).	Shareholder-elected board appoints officers to manage daily operations.	Shareholders generally are liable only to the extent of their investment.	Shareholders generally may transfer their interests to qualifying shareholders.	Flow-through taxation on a per-day and per-share basis.	If entity ceases to qualify as an S corporation, it becomes a C corporation.
C corporation	Formalities. Files articles of incorporation with state.	May sell common and preferred stock. May issue debt.	Shareholder-elected board appoints officers to manage daily operations.	Shareholders generally are liable only to the extent of their investment.	Shareholders generally are free to transfer their interests.	Income taxed at corporate level. Shareholders pay tax on dividends received.	Perpetual existence. A shareholder's death, bankruptcy, or withdrawal does not terminate corporation.

STOP & REVIEW

You have completed the outline for this subunit.
Study multiple-choice question 20 on page 498.

QUESTIONS

17.1 General Partnerships

1. Cobb, Inc., a partner in TLC Partnership, assigns its partnership interest to Bean, who is not made a partner. After the assignment, Bean may assert the rights to

I. Participation in the management of TLC
II. Cobb's share of TLC's partnership profits

A. I only.
B. II only.
C. I and II.
D. Neither I nor II.

Answer (B) is correct.
REQUIRED: The right(s), if any, of an assignee of a partnership interest.
DISCUSSION: Partnership rights may be assigned without the dissolution of the partnership. The assignee is entitled only to the profits the assignor would normally receive. The assignee does not automatically become a partner and would not have the right to participate in managing the business or to inspect the books and records of the partnership. The assigning partner remains a partner with all the duties and other rights of a partner.

2. Eller, Fort, and Owens do business as Venture Associates, a general partnership. Trent Corp. brought a breach of contract suit against Venture and Eller individually. Trent won the suit and filed a judgment against both Venture and Eller. Venture then entered bankruptcy. Under the RUPA, Trent will generally be able to collect the judgment in full from

A. Partnership assets but not partner personal assets.
B. The personal assets of Eller, Fort, and Owens.
C. Eller's personal assets only after partnership assets are exhausted.
D. Eller's personal assets.

Answer (D) is correct.
REQUIRED: The assets from which a judgment against a partnership and a specific partner may be collected.
DISCUSSION: The RUPA provides that partners are jointly and severally liable for all obligations of the partnership, including those arising out of a contract. The keys to the question are that (1) Trent sued both the partnership and one partner, (2) that partner can be held individually liable for the entire amount of a partnership obligation (joint and several liability), and (3) only parties who are judgment debtors can be held liable. Because Trent won the lawsuit against Venture and Eller, either Venture or Eller or both are liable for the judgment amount. In this scenario, the partnership is in bankruptcy. A plaintiff with a judgment against a defendant in bankruptcy typically collects very little, if any, of the judgment. The judgment against the partnership will be subordinated to the claims of secured creditors and creditors with priority. As a result, Trent will likely seek to recover the full judgment from Eller's personal assets, given that Eller was a co-defendant in the lawsuit. Furthermore, because Venture is in bankruptcy, the RUPA provides that Trent need not seek a writ of execution against (compel collection of the judgment amount from) Venture before proceeding against Eller's personal assets.
Answer (A) is incorrect. Trent may collect in full from Eller. **Answer (B) is incorrect.** Fort and Owens must be judgment debtors to be held liable by Trent. **Answer (C) is incorrect.** Trent need not exhaust the partnership assets. Venture is in bankruptcy.

3. Wind, who has been a partner in the PLW general partnership for 4 years, decides to withdraw from the partnership despite a written partnership agreement that states, "No partner may withdraw for a period of 5 years." Under the Revised Uniform Partnership Act (RUPA), what is the result of Wind's withdrawal?

A. Wind's withdrawal causes a dissolution of the partnership by operation of law.
B. Wind's withdrawal has no bearing on the continued operation of the partnership by the remaining partners.
C. Wind's withdrawal is not effective until Wind obtains a court-ordered decree of dissolution.
D. Wind's withdrawal causes dissociation from the partnership despite being in violation of the partnership agreement.

Answer (D) is correct.
REQUIRED: The result of an early withdrawal from a partnership.
DISCUSSION: Under the RUPA, a partnership is considered an entity substantially separate from its partners. A partner has the power (if not the right) to dissociate at any time. However, if the partner wrongfully dissociates from the partnership, (s)he is liable for any resulting damages to the other partners. After dissociation, the business either continues after purchase of the dissociated partner's interest or dissolution begins.
Answer (A) is incorrect. A partnership is not dissolved by operation of law under RUPA when a partner withdraws. Such a dissolution results from such events as the illegality of the business and certain judicial determinations. **Answer (B) is incorrect.** Wind will remain liable to creditors for predissociation obligations and any post-dissociation contracts for up to 2 years unless (s)he files a statement of dissociation. **Answer (C) is incorrect.** A court-ordered decree is not needed for the withdrawal to be effective. The partner may withdraw by notice to the partnership of an express will to withdraw.

4. Gillie, Taft, and Dall are partners in an architectural firm. The partnership agreement is silent about the payment of salaries and the division of profits and losses. Gillie works full-time in the firm, and Taft and Dall each work half-time. Taft invested $120,000 in the firm, and Gillie and Dall invested $60,000 each. Dall is responsible for bringing in 50% of the business, and Gillie and Taft 25% each. How should profits of $120,000 for the year be divided?

	Gillie	Taft	Dall
A.	$60,000	$30,000	$30,000
B.	$40,000	$40,000	$40,000
C.	$30,000	$60,000	$30,000
D.	$30,000	$30,000	$60,000

Answer (B) is correct.
REQUIRED: The division of partnership profits when the partnership agreement is silent about salaries and the division of profits and losses.
DISCUSSION: Partners are not entitled to compensation for their actions, skill, and time applied on behalf of the partnership, except when such an arrangement is explicitly provided for in the partnership agreement. The partnership agreement is silent on this point, so salaries are not paid to the partners. Profits and losses may be divided among the partners according to any formula stated in the partnership agreement. Without a contrary agreement, partners share equally in the profits. Thus, each partner will receive $40,000.

17.2 Limited Partnerships

5. Marshall formed a limited partnership for the purpose of engaging in the export-import business. Marshall obtained additional working capital from Franklin and Lee by selling them each a limited partnership interest. Under these circumstances, the limited partnership

A. Will usually be treated as a taxable entity for federal income tax purposes.
B. Will lose its status as a limited partnership if it has more than one general partner.
C. Can limit the liability of all partners.
D. Can exist as such only if it is formed under the authority of a state statute.

Answer (D) is correct.
REQUIRED: The true statement regarding a limited partnership.
DISCUSSION: The limited partnership is not available as a form of business organization under the common law. An organization purporting to be a limited partnership but formed in a state with no statutory authority for such a form of business organization will very likely be treated as a general partnership.
Answer (A) is incorrect. A partnership is not a taxable entity for federal income tax purposes. Partnerships are required to file informational returns only. **Answer (B) is incorrect.** A limited partnership may have more than one general partner. The minimum is at least one limited and one general partner. **Answer (C) is incorrect.** At least one general partner must have unlimited personal liability.

6. Wichita Properties is a limited partnership created in accordance with the provisions of the Uniform Limited Partnership Act. The partners have voted to dissolve and settle the partnership's accounts. Which of the following will be the last to be paid?

A. General partners for unpaid distributions.
B. Limited partners in respect to capital.
C. Limited and general partners in respect to their undistributed profits.
D. General partners in respect to capital.

Answer (C) is correct.
REQUIRED: The lowest priority of distribution upon liquidation of a limited partnership.
DISCUSSION: Under the RULPA, limited and general partners are treated equally. Unless the partnership agreement provides otherwise, assets are distributed as follows:

1) Creditors (including all partner-creditors)
2) Partners for unpaid distributions (i.e., declared but not paid)
3) Partners for the return of their contributions
4) Partners for remaining assets (i.e., undistributed profits) in the proportions in which they share distributions

7. Absent any contrary provisions in the agreement, under which of the following circumstances will a limited partnership be dissolved?

A. A limited partner dies and his or her estate is insolvent.
B. A personal creditor of a general partner obtains a judgment against the general partner's interest in the limited partnership.
C. A general partner retires and all the remaining general partners do not consent to continue.
D. A limited partner assigns his or her partnership interest to an outsider and the purchaser becomes a substituted limited partner.

Answer (C) is correct.
REQUIRED: The circumstance in which a limited partnership is dissolved.
DISCUSSION: Retirement of a general partner generally dissolves a limited partnership or a general partnership. However, dissolution can be avoided if the business is continued by the remaining general partners either with the consent of all partners or pursuant to a stipulation in the partnership agreement.
Answer (A) is incorrect. The death of a limited partner, regardless of the solvency of the estate, does not dissolve the partnership. **Answer (B) is incorrect.** A judgment against the interest of a general partner is similar to an assignment of that interest, which does not dissolve the partnership. **Answer (D) is incorrect.** The assignment of a limited partnership interest does not dissolve the partnership. It makes no difference whether the assignee becomes a substituted limited partner.

17.3 Limited Liability Companies (LLCs)

8. Which of the following parties generally has the most management rights?

A. Minority shareholder in a corporation listed on a national stock exchange.
B. Limited partner in a general partnership.
C. Member of a limited liability company.
D. Limited partner in a limited partnership.

Answer (C) is correct.
REQUIRED: The party that generally has the most management rights.
DISCUSSION: In a member-managed LLC, all members have a right to participate, and most business matters are decided by the majority. In a manager-managed LLC, each manager has equal rights, but managers are selected or removed by a majority vote of the members. An LLC is deemed to be member-managed unless the articles of organization state otherwise.
Answer (A) is incorrect. A minority shareholder in a public corporation generally has few or no management rights. **Answer (B) is incorrect.** A general partnership has no limited partners. **Answer (D) is incorrect.** In a limited partnership, a limited partner has no authority to participate in management and control of the business.

9. The advantage of a limited liability company is

A. Informal organizational procedures.
B. Unlimited liability only for members that actively participate in management.
C. Each member's receipt of an equal share of profits.
D. Tax status as a pass-through entity.

Answer (D) is correct.
REQUIRED: The advantage of an LLC.
DISCUSSION: An LLC may elect to be taxed as if it were a general partnership.
Answer (A) is incorrect. An LLC is formed only by filing articles of organizations with the appropriate state authority. **Answer (B) is incorrect.** A great advantage of an LLC is that creditors ordinarily have no claim on the personal assets of members or managers. **Answer (C) is incorrect.** The members' operating agreement determines how profits and losses are distributed. Without an agreement, state statutes often provide for sharing in proportion to members' contributions.

17.4 Corporate Formation

10. Which of the following statements is true with respect to the general structure of a corporation?

A. The corporation is treated as a legal person with rights and obligations jointly shared with its owners and managers.
B. Shareholders establish corporate policies and elect or appoint corporate officers.
C. A corporation is governed by shareholders who elect a board of directors and approve fundamental changes in its structure.
D. The board of directors is responsible for carrying out the corporate policies in the day-to-day management of the organizations.

Answer (C) is correct.
REQUIRED: The general structure of a corporation.
DISCUSSION: A corporation is an entity formed under state law that is treated as a legal person with rights and obligations separate from its owners. Shareholders hold the voting power of a corporation. This power gives them the ability to elect a board of directors and to approve fundamental changes in the corporate structure. Thus, the shareholders have the power to govern the corporation.
Answer (A) is incorrect. A corporation is a legal entity with rights and obligations separate from its owners and managers. **Answer (B) is incorrect.** Directors establish corporate policies and elect or appoint corporate officers, not shareholders. **Answer (D) is incorrect.** Corporate officers are responsible for the day-to-day management of the organization.

11. Case Corp. is incorporated in State A. Under the Revised Model Business Corporation Act, which of the following activities engaged in by Case requires that Case obtain a certificate of authority to do business in State B?

A. Maintaining bank accounts in State B.
B. Collecting corporate debts in State B.
C. Hiring employees who are residents of State B.
D. Maintaining an office in State B to conduct intrastate business.

Answer (D) is correct.
REQUIRED: The interstate business activity that requires a certificate of authority.
DISCUSSION: A state may exercise authority over a foreign corporation if the corporation has at least minimum contacts with the state. The minimum contacts consist of activities that (1) are not isolated and (2) either are purposefully directed toward the state or place a product in the stream of interstate commerce with an expectation or intent that it will be used in the state. Maintaining an office in State B to conduct intrastate business creates minimum contacts with State B under this test.
Answer (A) is incorrect. Maintaining bank accounts in State B is an isolated activity that does not meet the minimum contacts test. **Answer (B) is incorrect.** The collection of debts in State B does not by itself constitute minimum contacts in State B. For example, the debts may not have arisen from activities that involved State B. **Answer (C) is incorrect.** Hiring employees who reside in State B is not an activity that is purposefully directed toward the state or that places a product in interstate commerce with the expectation or intent that it will be used in the state.

17.5 Corporate Operation, Financing, and Distributions

12. Which of the following statements is correct regarding both debt and common shares of a corporation?

A. Common shares represent an ownership interest in the corporation, but debt holders do not have an ownership interest.
B. Common shareholders and debt holders have an ownership interest in the corporation.
C. Common shares typically have a fixed maturity date, but debt does not.
D. Common shares have a higher priority on liquidation than debt.

Answer (A) is correct.
REQUIRED: The true statement about debt and common shares.
DISCUSSION: Common shares are equity securities. Thus, they are ownership interests. In contrast, debt holders do not have ownership interests. Rather, debt holders have claims on the corporation's assets. In the event of a liquidation, the debt holders' claims must be satisfied before any distribution to common shareholders.
Answer (B) is incorrect. Debt holders do not have an ownership interest in the corporation. **Answer (C) is incorrect.** Debt securities typically have a fixed maturity date, but common shares do not. **Answer (D) is incorrect.** In the event of bankruptcy or liquidation, creditors, including bondholders, have first claim on corporate assets.

SU 17: Business Organizations   495

13. Under modern statutes, the two general prerequisites to the declaration of a dividend are

I. Corporate solvency.
II. A resolution by the directors to declare a dividend.

A. I only.
B. II only.
C. Both I and II.
D. Neither I nor II.

Answer (C) is correct.
REQUIRED: The general prerequisites to the declaration of a dividend.
DISCUSSION: The board has discretion to determine the time and amount of dividends and other distributions. However, two general prerequisites are used to determine whether the board is likely to distribute dividends. Those prerequisites are corporate profitability or solvency and a resolution by the directors to declare a dividend.

17.6 Shareholders' Rights

14. A shareholder's fundamental right to inspect books and records of a corporation will be properly denied if the purpose of the inspection is to

A. Commence a shareholder's derivative suit.
B. Obtain shareholder names for a retail mailing list.
C. Solicit shareholders to vote for a change in the board of directors.
D. Investigate possible management misconduct.

Answer (B) is correct.
REQUIRED: The improper purpose of shareholder inspection of corporate books and records.
DISCUSSION: The fundamental right of a shareholder to inspect the corporation's books and records may be exercised only in good faith for a proper purpose. A proper purpose relates to the shareholder's interest in the corporation, not his or her personal interests, and is not contrary to the corporation's interests. Obtaining a shareholder mailing list is not in itself improper unless it is to further the shareholder's personal interests.

15. A corporate shareholder is entitled to which of the following rights?

A. Elect officers.
B. Receive annual dividends.
C. Approve dissolution.
D. Prevent corporate borrowing.

Answer (C) is correct.
REQUIRED: The right of a shareholder.
DISCUSSION: Shareholders do not have the right to manage the corporation or its business. Shareholder participation in policy and management is through exercising the right to elect directors. Shareholders also have the right to approve charter amendments, disposition of all or substantially all of the corporation's assets, mergers and consolidations, and dissolutions.
Answer (A) is incorrect. The board elects officers. **Answer (B) is incorrect.** A shareholder does not have a general right to receive dividends. The board determines dividend policy. **Answer (D) is incorrect.** Determining capital structure and whether the corporation should borrow are policy and management determinations to be made according to the board's business judgment.

17.7 Directors and Officers: Authority, Duties, and Liability

16. Which of the following corporate actions is subject to shareholder approval?

A. Election of officers.
B. Removal of officers.
C. Declaration of cash dividends.
D. Removal of directors.

Answer (D) is correct.
REQUIRED: The action that must be approved by the shareholders.
DISCUSSION: A corporation is governed by shareholders (owners) who elect the directors on the corporation's board and who approve fundamental changes in the corporate structure. Directors establish corporate policies and elect or appoint corporate officers who carry out the policies in the day-to-day management of the organization. In most states, the shareholders may remove any director or the entire board by a majority vote, with or without cause.
Answer (A) is incorrect. The officers are elected by the directors. Answer (B) is incorrect. Officers are removed by the directors. Answer (C) is incorrect. The board of directors has the discretion to determine the nature, timing, and amount of dividends and other distributions.

17. Seymore was recently invited to become a director of Buckley Industries, Inc. If Seymore accepts and becomes a director, Seymore, along with the other directors, will **not** be personally liable for

A. Lack of reasonable care.
B. Honest errors of judgment.
C. Declaration of a dividend that the directors know will impair legal capital.
D. Diversion of corporate opportunities to themselves.

Answer (B) is correct.
REQUIRED: The action for which a director is not personally liable.
DISCUSSION: The directors of a corporation owe a fiduciary duty to the corporation and the shareholders. They also are expected to exercise reasonable business judgment. The law does recognize human fallibility and allows for directors to be safe from liability for honest errors of judgment.
Answer (A) is incorrect. Directors must discharge their duties with the care that a person in a similar position would reasonably believe appropriate under similar circumstances. Answer (C) is incorrect. Directors are prohibited from declaring dividends that would violate a state statute establishing a minimum legal capital. Answer (D) is incorrect. Directors may not usurp any corporate opportunity presented to them in their capacity as directors. The corporation must be given the right of first refusal.

17.8 Mergers and Termination

18. Generally, a merger of two corporations requires

A. That a special meeting notice and a copy of the merger plan be given to all shareholders of both corporations.
B. Unanimous approval of the merger plan by the shareholders of both corporations.
C. Unanimous approval of the merger plan by the boards of both corporations.
D. That all liabilities owed by the absorbed corporation be paid before the merger.

Answer (A) is correct.
　　REQUIRED: The prerequisite to a merger.
　　DISCUSSION: A corporation is merged into another when shareholders of the target corporation receive cash or shares of the surviving corporation in exchange for their target corporation shares. The target shares are canceled, and it ceases to exist. State law generally requires approval by a majority of the board and of shares of each corporation. A special shareholder meeting notice (purpose is stated) and a copy of the merger plan must be provided to shareholders of each corporation to enable informed voting.
　　Answer (B) is incorrect. Unless a state statute or the charter imposes a supermajority requirement, majority approval is generally required. **Answer (C) is incorrect.** Unless a state statute or the charter imposes a supermajority requirement, majority approval is generally required. **Answer (D) is incorrect.** Rights and liabilities of the absorbed company generally become those of the surviving corporation.

19. Which of the following actions may be taken by a corporation's board of directors without shareholder approval?

A. Purchasing substantially all of the assets of another corporation.
B. Selling substantially all of the corporation's assets not in the regular course of business.
C. Dissolving the corporation.
D. Amending the articles of incorporation.

Answer (A) is correct.
　　REQUIRED: The action by a corporation's board not requiring shareholder approval.
　　DISCUSSION: The board of directors directly controls a corporation by establishing overall corporate policy and overseeing its implementation. In exercising their powers, directors must maintain high standards of care and loyalty but need not obtain shareholder approval except for fundamental corporate changes. Purchasing substantially all of the assets (or stock) of another corporation is a policy decision properly made by the directors, not a fundamental change. It does not require shareholder approval in the absence of a bylaw or special provision in the articles of incorporation.
　　Answer (B) is incorrect. Selling substantially all of the corporation's assets not in the regular course of business is a transfer that must be approved by the shareholders. **Answer (C) is incorrect.** Dissolving the corporation must be approved by the shareholders. **Answer (D) is incorrect.** Amending the articles of incorporation ordinarily must be approved by the shareholders.

17.9 Advantages and Disadvantages of Corporations

20. Which of the following statements best describes an advantage of the corporate form of doing business?

A. Day-to-day management is strictly the responsibility of the directors.

B. Ownership is contractually restricted and is not transferable.

C. The operation of the business may continue indefinitely.

D. The business is free from state regulation.

Answer (C) is correct.
REQUIRED: The advantage of the corporate form.
DISCUSSION: A corporation has perpetual existence unless it is given a shorter life under the articles of incorporation or is dissolved by the state. Death, withdrawal, or addition of a shareholder, director, or officer does not terminate its existence.
Answer (A) is incorrect. Officers run day-to-day operations. **Answer (B) is incorrect.** Absent a specific contractual restriction, shares are freely transferable, e.g., by gift, sale, pledge, or inheritance. **Answer (D) is incorrect.** A corporation can be created only under state law.

Access the **Gleim CPA Premium Review System** featuring our SmartAdapt technology from your Gleim Personal Classroom to continue your studies. You will experience a personalized study environment with exam-emulating multiple-choice questions.

STUDY UNIT EIGHTEEN
CONTRACTS

(23 pages of outline)

18.1	Nature and Classification of Contracts	499
18.2	Mutual Assent (Offer and Acceptance)	501
18.3	Consideration	504
18.4	Capacity	506
18.5	Legality	507
18.6	Lack of Genuine Assent	508
18.7	Statute of Frauds	510
18.8	Parol Evidence Rule	512
18.9	Performance, Discharge, and Breach	513
18.10	Remedies	516
18.11	Contract Beneficiaries	517
18.12	Assignment and Delegation	518

This study unit covers the general concepts of contract law.

18.1 NATURE AND CLASSIFICATION OF CONTRACTS

1. **Formation**

    a. A contract is formed when its elements (mutual assent, consideration, capacity, and legality) are present. But a writing is **not** required to form a contract.

    1) A contract may be oral.

    b. If a valid, enforceable contract is formed, the law provides **remedies** if an obligation under the contract is breached.

    1) The law applies an objective standard (a reasonable person standard) to determine whether a contract was formed or breached.

2. **Express and Implied Contracts**

    a. The terms of an **express contract** are stated, either in writing or orally.

    b. The terms of an **implied contract** are wholly or partially inferred from conduct and circumstances but not from written or spoken words.

    1) A contract is **implied in fact** when the facts indicate a contract was formed.

EXAMPLE 18-1	Implied in Fact Contract

Kelly makes an appointment with a hairdresser. Kelly keeps the appointment and permits the hairdresser to cut her hair. Kelly has promised through her actions to pay for the haircut. A court will infer from Kelly's conduct that an implied contract was formed and a duty to pay was understood and agreed to.

3. **Unilateral and Bilateral Contracts**
    a. In a **unilateral contract**, only one party makes a promise. The other party is an actor, not a promisor. If (s)he performs a defined action (an acceptance), the promisor is obligated to keep the promise.

EXAMPLE 18-2	Unilateral Contract

Amy tells Bill, "I'll pay you $10 to polish my car." This offer is for a unilateral contract. Amy (the promisor) expects Bill (the actor) to accept by the act of polishing her car, not by making a return promise.

    b. In a **bilateral contract**, both parties make promises.

EXAMPLE 18-3	Bilateral Contract

Amanda tells Bob that she will provide him lodging in September if he agrees to pay her $200. This is an offer for a bilateral contract. If Bob accepts and promises to pay the $200, a bilateral contract is formed.

4. **Other Classifications**
    a. A **valid** contract has all the elements of a contract, and the law provides a remedy if breached. A valid contract is legally binding on both parties.
    b. An **unenforceable** contract is a valid contract because it has all the elements of a contract. But the law will not enforce the contract because it does not comply with another legal requirement.

EXAMPLE 18-4	Unenforceable Contract

Jane enters into an oral contract to sell land to Emily. To be enforceable, a contract for the sale of land must be in writing. Because the real estate contract was not written, it is not enforceable.

    c. A party may choose to either enforce or nullify a **voidable** contract.

EXAMPLE 18-5	Voidable Contract

Adam was induced to enter into a contract by Ben's intentional deception (i.e., fraud). Adam can choose to either enforce the contract or void the contract since it was fraudulently induced. Adam can also collect damages against Ben for any loss sustained due to fraud.

    d. A **void** contract is not binding and is considered void since its inception. A void contract cannot be ratified and enforced.

EXAMPLE 18-6	Void Contract

A contract requiring the commission of a crime is void. It is not recognizable as a contract, and there is no remedy provided by law to enforce it.

STOP & REVIEW

You have completed the outline for this subunit.
Study multiple-choice questions 1 and 2 on page 522.

18.2 MUTUAL ASSENT (OFFER AND ACCEPTANCE)

1. **Offer**

    a. A contract is formed when a party accepts an offer.

    1) An offer is a statement or other communication by which the offeror grants the offeree the power to accept a condition and form a contract.

    b. An offer must

    1) Be communicated to an offeree,
    2) Be in a communication authorized by the offeror,
    3) **Indicate an objective intent** to enter into a contract as determined in accordance with a reasonable-person standard, and
    4) Be sufficiently definite and certain.

    c. No specific manner of communication of the offer is required. An offer need not take any particular form. For example, **nonverbal** communication may be appropriate.

    d. Invitations to negotiate and preliminary negotiations do not constitute an offer. Invitations to negotiate include phrases, such as, "Are you interested in. . ." or "I'll probably take. . ." They differ from the language of an offer, which indicates commitment and intent to contract.

    1) Advertisements usually are **not** offers but invitations to submit offers.

        a) However, an advertisement can constitute an offer if it uses clear, definite, and explicit language that leaves nothing open for negotiation.

    e. Generally, a contract must be reasonably **definite** as to material terms and clearly state the rights and duties of the parties. Essential terms include

    1) **Names** of the parties,
    2) **Subject matter** involved,
    3) **Price and quantity**, and
    4) **Time and place** of performance.

    f. If a term is missing, it can be implied by the court (with the exception of a quantity term, which must be supplied by the parties). The presumption is that the parties intended to include a **reasonable** term.

    1) A quantity term is sufficiently definite if it is defined by the buyer's reasonable **requirements** or the seller's reasonable **output**.

        a) The buyer or seller must act in good faith and not vary substantially from an estimated or normal quantity.

    2) The law requires definiteness of the price term and generally will not imply the price (e.g., of real estate).

    g. Under the Uniform Commercial Code (UCC), a merchant's written, signed **firm offer** to sell **goods** that is to be held open for a stated or a reasonable period (not greater than 3 months) is irrevocable.

2. **Termination of Offer**
    a. **Lapse of time.** If no time is stated in the offer, the offer terminates after a reasonable period.
    b. **Death or incompetence** of either the offeror or the offeree generally terminates the power of acceptance, whether or not the other party had notice.
        1) Incompetence is a lack of legally required qualifications or physical or psychological fitness to bind oneself by contract.
        2) Death or incompetence generally does not terminate an existing contract, including an offer in a valid option contract. The offeree has already given consideration.
    c. **Destruction** or loss of the specific subject matter terminates an offer.
    d. **Illegality** of a proposed contract or performance terminates the offer.
    e. **Revocation.** The offeror may revoke an offer at any time prior to acceptance.
        1) Revocation must be communicated to the offeree prior to the offeree's acceptance.
            a) Revocation is **effective when received** by the offeree.
        2) Notice may be communicated by any reasonable means, either directly or indirectly.
            a) For example, an offeree may receive indirect notice of revocation if given actual notice of sale of the subject matter to another party.
            b) The offeree's knowledge that a third party has offered to buy the subject matter of the offer is not a revocation.
        3) An offer stating it will remain open may be terminated by notice that it has been revoked. But if consideration is given for an option or a firm offer is made, the offer is not revocable.
    f. **Rejection** terminates the offer. It implies an intent not to accept the offer. It may be expressed or implied by words or conduct.
        1) Rejection is **effective when received** by the offeror.
            a) After rejection is effective, later attempted acceptance becomes a new offer.
        2) A **counteroffer** is rejection of an offer and a new offer from the original offeree.
            a) In contrast, a mere inquiry about the proposed terms of an offer is tentative and does not indicate intent to reject the offer.

EXAMPLE 18-7	Inquiry about Proposed Terms

The statement "Would you consider shipping by air instead of by truck?" is not a counteroffer. It indicates no intent to reject or accept the offer but seeks additional information.

3. **Acceptance**
    a. The offeree has an exclusive power of acceptance, but neither the offeror nor the offeree is obligated until acceptance.
        1) The offeror may expressly limit what constitutes acceptance.
    b. An acceptance must relate to the terms of the offer and be positive, unequivocal, and unconditional. The acceptance may not vary the offer in any way.
        1) This principle is the **mirror image rule**.
        2) If a **conditional acceptance** requires the offeror's agreement to additional or different terms, it is a **counteroffer**, not an acceptance.

SU 18: Contracts

  c. Acceptance **must be communicated** to the offeror by any words or actions that a reasonable person would understand as an acceptance.

    1) However, an offeror generally cannot require the offeree to respond to avoid being contractually bound.

  d. If an offeror specifies a means of acceptance, it must be used.

    1) Generally, acceptance by an unauthorized means is effective upon receipt by the offeror, assuming the offer has not expired or been revoked.

  e. The offeror may waive compliance with particular terms of an offer regarding acceptance. For example, a deficient or late acceptance may be a new offer that the original offeror chooses to accept.

SUCCESS TIP

The AICPA has consistently tested candidates on the mailbox rule, including when an offeror attempts revocation after an acceptance has been dispatched.

---

4. **Mailbox Rule**

  a. The offer may state that acceptance is effective **on receipt**. If it does **not**, the law applies the mailbox rule to determine when the offer is accepted.

  b. Under the mailbox rule, acceptance is effective at the **moment of dispatch** if (1) the offeree has used an **authorized** means of acceptance to communicate to the offeror and (2) the offer is still open. Acceptance is effective even if the offeror attempts revocation while it is in transit.

EXAMPLE 18-8	**Medium of Acceptance Not Specified**

An offer is sent by mail. It does not specify a particular medium for acceptance. A letter of acceptance is deposited in the mail. If it was properly addressed and had proper postage affixed, the acceptance is considered legally effective even if it never reaches the offeror.

    1) An acceptance **following prior dispatch of a rejection** is effective only if received by the offeror before receipt of the rejection.

EXAMPLE 18-9	**Negating the Mailbox Rule**

The offeror mailed a revocation on July 15. It arrived on July 17, after the offeree had mailed an acceptance on July 16. The revocation is invalid because the acceptance was in transit before the offeree had notice of the revocation and a contract was formed. This outcome is avoided if the offeror explicitly states that the "acceptance must be received to be effective." The first item received by the offeror controls whether a contract is formed.

STOP & REVIEW

You have completed the outline for this subunit.
Study multiple-choice questions 3 and 4 on page 523.

18.3 CONSIDERATION

1. **Definition**

    a. Consideration is something of value given in a bargained-for exchange. It is the **promise, act, or forbearance** to do or not do something that parties agree to as part of their agreement.

    > **EXAMPLE 18-10   Consideration**
    >
    > Amanda tells Bob that she will provide him lodging in September if he agrees to pay her $200. Amanda's consideration is the promise of an obligatory future action. Bob's consideration is the act of paying $200. Both parties have provided consideration that was not legally required of them before the contract was created.

    b. The elements of consideration are

       1) Legal sufficiency and
       2) A bargained-for exchange (mutuality of consideration).

2. **Legal Sufficiency**

    a. Consideration is legally sufficient to render a promise enforceable if the promisee (1) incurs a legal detriment or (2) the promisor receives a legal benefit.

       1) To incur a legal detriment, the promisee must

          a) Do something (s)he is not legally obligated to do or
          b) Forebear to do something (s)he has a legal right to do.

       2) Almost any legal detriment is legally sufficient. Parity of value is **not** required.

          a) But extreme inadequacy or inequality of consideration may be evidence of fraud, a mistake, or a gift.

       3) In a **bilateral contract**, one promise is consideration for the other.
       4) Consideration may be legally sufficient without a simultaneous exchange and despite the form of the consideration.

3. **Bargained-For Exchange**

    a. A bargained-for exchange occurs when one party makes a promise or performance in exchange for a return promise or performance by the other party.

4. **Items Not Sufficient Consideration**

    a. **Past consideration** cannot be bargained for. Such acts have already happened, and the acting party cannot effectively promise to incur any legal detriment.

    > **EXAMPLE 18-11   Past Consideration**
    >
    > Father said to Daughter, "If you graduate, I promise to pay you $10,000 at the end of next month." If Daughter had already graduated at the time of the promise, Father is not obligated. Daughter incurred no legal detriment to support his promise.

b. **Pre-existing legal duty.** Consideration does not exist if
   1) An existing duty was imposed by law, or
   2) A person is already under contract to render a specified performance.

EXAMPLE 18-12	Pre-Existing Legal Duty

A contractor tells a homeowner that, unless she pays him an extra $500, he will leave her roof half repaired. Because the contractor has a pre-existing duty to repair the entire roof, he has not incurred any new consideration.

c. **Part payment of an undisputed (liquidated) debt** is not consideration for a promise by the creditor to accept the part payment in full satisfaction of the debt.
   1) A promise to pay part of a **disputed (unliquidated)** debt is consideration for the creditor's forgiveness of the remainder. But the dispute must be in good faith.

5. **Substitutes for Consideration**
   a. **Promissory estoppel** applies when
      1) A promise is given that the promisor should reasonably expect to induce action or forbearance by the promisee,
      2) The promise induces the action or forbearance, and
      3) Injustice can be avoided only by enforcing the promise.

EXAMPLE 18-13	Promissory Estoppel

John pledged $5 million to University. In reliance on the pledge, University began construction of a new building. If John retracts the pledge, a court will most likely enforce the promise. University has acted upon John's promise and likely incurred a significant debt to its detriment.

   b. A court finds that a **quasi-contract** (contract implied in law) exists when the parties make no promises and reach no agreement, one of the parties is substantially benefited at the expense of the other, and no legal remedy is adequate.
      1) To avoid **unjust enrichment** of the receiving party, the party who provided the benefit is entitled to the **reasonable** value (not the contract price) of the services rendered or property delivered.

EXAMPLE 18-14	Avoidance of Unjust Enrichment

A doctor found an unconscious person on the sidewalk and provided medical treatment. To avoid unjust enrichment, the patient must pay the doctor a reasonable fee even though the aid was unsolicited and no contract existed.

STOP & REVIEW

You have completed the outline for this subunit.
Study multiple-choice question 5 on page 524.

18.4 CAPACITY

1. **Overview**
   a. Parties to a contract must have the legal capacity to contract. Minors, persons lacking mental capacity, and intoxicated persons do not have legal capacity.
   b. The UCC adopts the common law in determining legal capacity to contract.

2. **Minors**
   a. Because a minor does not have legal capacity to enter contracts, a minor may **disaffirm** his or her contract. Thus, the contract is **voidable** by the minor.
      1) However, the minor is liable until disaffirmance. Moreover, regardless of disaffirmance, a minor is always liable based on a **quasi-contract** for the reasonable value, **not** the contract price, of **necessaries** (e.g., food, shelter, and clothing).
   b. Power to disaffirm continues until a **reasonable** time after the minor reaches the age of majority.
      1) Any unequivocal act that indicates an intent to disaffirm is sufficient. A written disaffirmance is not required.
         a) Performance is not a condition of disaffirmance.
      2) When the contract has been partially or wholly performed, the minor must, if possible, return any consideration received from the other party.
      3) A minor may disaffirm even if (s)he cannot return the consideration or the consideration is damaged.
   c. A contract entered into by a minor may be **ratified** by the minor orally or in writing **after** (s)he has reached the age of majority.
      1) Ratification may be either expressed or implied.
      2) A contract is ratified if the minor retains the consideration for an unreasonable time after (s)he reaches majority.
         a) Selling or donating property is ratification by the minor.
      3) Failure to disaffirm for a reasonable period after reaching majority is a ratification.

3. **Persons Lacking Mental Capacity**
   a. If a person was **judicially** determined to be insane or otherwise incompetent **before** contract formation, the contract is **void** and cannot be ratified.
      1) Judicial determination of incompetence **after** the formation of a contract renders the contract merely **voidable**.

4. **Intoxicated Persons**
   a. If mental capacity is lacking due to intoxication, the contract is **voidable** at the option of the intoxicated person.
      1) But the other party must have had reason to know that the intoxicated person (a) did not understand the nature and consequences of his or her actions or (b) was unable to act reasonably.

You have completed the outline for this subunit.
Study multiple-choice question 6 on page 524.

STOP & REVIEW

18.5 LEGALITY

1. **Overview**

    a. A promise to commit, or induce the commission of, a tort or crime is void on grounds of public policy.

        1) Agreements not to press criminal charges are **not** enforceable. They interfere with the state's duty to protect society by prosecuting criminals.

2. **Statutory Violations**

    a. A contract that cannot be performed without violating a statute is void.

    b. Commission of an illegal act during performance of a contract does not make the contract illegal. If the formation of the contract violated no law and the contract could be performed without violating any law, the contract is enforceable.

    c. A party who agrees to supply goods or services while unaware that such goods or services will be used for an unlawful purpose can enforce the contract.

        1) However, a person who intends to accomplish an unlawful purpose may not enforce a contract made for that purpose.

3. **Licensing Statutes**

    a. A **regulatory** statute is enacted for the protection of the public against unqualified or incompetent persons.

        1) If a licensing statute is regulatory, a person cannot recover for services unless (s)he holds the required license, regardless of whether the statute so states.

4. **Contracts in Restraint of Trade**

    a. A contract in restraint of trade restricts competition or otherwise interferes with the normal flow of goods or services. Thus, courts are reluctant to enforce them and they are narrowly construed.

    b. A typical restraint on trade is a **covenant not to compete**. It is an agreement not to engage in a particular trade, profession, or business. This restraint may be valid if

        1) The purpose is to protect a property interest of the promisee and

        2) The restraint is no more extensive in scope and duration than is reasonably necessary to protect that property or legitimate business interest.

    c. An **employment contract** may include a covenant not to compete during or after the period of employment.

        1) Restrictions on future employment tend to be more strictly scrutinized than covenants not to compete in agreements to sell a business. A restraint that is unreasonable, e.g., because of its effect on the ability to find other employment, may be voided or revised by the court to an acceptable form.

STOP & REVIEW

You have completed the outline for this subunit.
Study multiple-choice question 7 on page 524.

18.6 LACK OF GENUINE ASSENT

1. **Fraud**
    a. A contract induced by an intentional misrepresentation or the omission of a material fact is considered procured by fraud and is therefore **voidable**.
    b. The following are the **elements of fraud**:
        1) An actual or implied false representation (or concealment) of a material fact,
        2) Intent to misrepresent (scienter),
            a) The intent element is satisfied if the defendant (1) knew the representation was false or (2) **recklessly disregarded** its truth of falsity.
        3) Intent to induce reliance,
        4) Justifiable actual reliance by the innocent party based on the misrepresentation, and
        5) Damage (loss) suffered by the innocent party.
    c. A statement of opinion or a prediction is not usually the basis of a fraud claim. A fact is objective and verifiable, but an opinion or prediction is generally subject to debate.
    d. **Fraud in the inducement** occurs when the defrauded party is aware of entering into a contract and intends to do so, but the contract is procured by fraud.
        1) (S)he is intentionally deceived about a material fact to the contract (e.g., the nature or value of the goods or services).
        2) Thus, the contract is **voidable**.
    e. **Fraud in the execution** occurs when the signature of a party is obtained by a fraudulent misrepresentation that directly relates to the signing of a contract.
        1) The purported contract is **void**.
    f. A **duty to disclose facts** exists if any of the conditions listed below are met. Failure to do so constitutes actual fraud in these circumstances.
        1) The parties have a fiduciary relationship, creating a duty to disclose.
        2) One party knows a material fact and the other could not reasonably discover it.
        3) An important fact is misstated. It must be corrected as soon as possible.
    g. The remedy in cases of fraudulent representation is either a claim for damages or rescission of the entire contract.
        1) For a tort claim based on fraud, the injury sustained must have been caused by the misrepresentation.

2. **Negligent Misrepresentation**
    a. Negligent misrepresentation is a false representation of a material fact intended to be reasonably relied upon. It is made by a party that has **no knowledge** of its falsity but has acted **without due care**.
    b. The remedy to the injured party for negligent misrepresentation is a claim for damages. Only actual losses are recoverable.

3. **Innocent Misrepresentation**
   a. Innocent misrepresentation is a false representation of a material fact that is intended to be relied upon and that is reasonably relied on.
      1) The party that makes the misrepresentation has **no knowledge** of its falsity, believes the statement to be true, and has acted **with due care**.
      2) The remedy for innocent misrepresentation generally is rescission and occasionally damages (reliance damages only).
4. **Mistake**
   a. A **mutual mistake** occurs when both parties to a contract are mistaken about the same material **fact** but not value or quality. A mutual mistake of material fact is
      1) A basis for rescission or
      2) A sufficient defense for failure to perform the contract.

> **EXAMPLE 18-15   Mutual Mistake**
> Katie has a truck she uses for business. Curt offers to buy Katie's truck. She agrees to sell. Curt accepts her price and pays Katie. However, without the knowledge of either party, the truck was actually destroyed by fire a few hours before their contract was formed. Given that neither party was aware that the truck had been destroyed, a mutual mistake has occurred, and rescission is available to either party.

   b. A **unilateral mistake** occurs when only one party to a contract acts on the basis of a mistaken belief or assumption. The party is generally not relieved of the contractual obligation. However, the remedy of **rescission** by the mistaken party is available in limited circumstances when the mistake is **material** and
      1) The other party knew or should have known of the mistake;
      2) Enforcement would result in extreme hardship constituting injustice;
      3) The error was due to a mathematical mistake or omission of items in computing the cost of the contract; or
      4) The mistake was due to fraud, duress, or undue influence.
5. **Duress**
   a. One form of duress occurs when one party, by means of an **improper threat** that instills fear in a second party, effectively denies the second party's exercise of free will.
      1) The improper threat must have **sufficient coercive effect** so that it actually induces the particular person to agree to the contract.
         a) A threat based on a legal right and not constituting a tort or a crime may be improper if made in bad faith and with an ulterior motive.
      2) The contract entered into is **voidable** by the innocent party.
   b. **Economic duress** may arise when one party exerts extreme economic pressure that leaves the threatened party with no reasonable alternative but to comply.
      1) Merely taking advantage of another's financial difficulty is not duress.
      2) Inadequacy of consideration is not an element of duress.
   c. A threat of criminal prosecution is improper. Although a person has a legal right to report a crime to the police, (s)he may not do so for private gain.
      1) A threat of a civil suit is not improper unless it is made in bad faith, that is, when such an action has no legal basis.
   d. **Physical compulsion** with threats of personal violence renders the contract **void**.

6. **Undue Influence**

    a. Undue influence occurs when a dominant party (e.g., a trusted lawyer, physician, or guardian) wrongly exploits a confidential relationship to persuade a second party to enter into an unfavorable contract.

        1) A contract is **voidable** as a result of undue influence.

> **STOP & REVIEW**
>
> You have completed the outline for this subunit. Study multiple-choice questions 8 and 9 on page 525.

18.7 STATUTE OF FRAUDS

1. **Contracts Covered by the Statute**

    a. An oral contract is usually enforceable. However, the statute of frauds requires certain contracts to be in writing and signed by the defendant. The statute of frauds relates to enforcement, not formation, of contracts.

        1) **Agreements that cannot be performed within 1 year of the making of the contract.** If performance, however difficult or improbable, is possible within 1 year, the agreement is **not** covered by the statute of frauds.

            a) The day the contract is made is excluded, and the 1-year period expires at the close of the contract's express termination date.

EXAMPLE 18-16   Agreement Not Performable within 1 Year

John orally contracts to perform maintenance services on Mary's truck for as long as she owns it. The contract may be performed within 1 year if Mary decides to sell the truck within that time. Thus, the agreement is not required to be in writing. If John had contracted to maintain Mary's truck for the next 4 years, the contract would be unenforceable without a writing.

---

        2) **Agreements for the sale of an interest in land.** An interest may be a long-term lease (more than 1 year), mortgage, full ownership, or any other interest in land.

        3) **Agreements for the sale of goods for $500 or more.** An agreement for the sale of goods for $500 or more is not enforceable without a writing sufficient to indicate that a contract for sale has been made between the parties.

        4) **Agreements to answer for the debt of another.** A suretyship agreement must be in writing if the promise is secondary.

            a) **Main purpose rule.** A promise is **secondary** if its main purpose is to benefit the debtor.

EXAMPLE 18-17   Secondary Promise

Parent cosigns an educational loan for Child as a favor based on familial affection. Parent receives no economic benefit from the guarantee. Accordingly, the promise is secondary and must be in writing.

b) A promise is **primary** if its main purpose is to benefit the promisor (the surety, i.e., the party who agrees to pay if the debtor defaults).

EXAMPLE 18-18	Primary Promise

Company A agrees to buy inventory from Company B. B offers a favorable price if A will guarantee payment of a debt that B owes to a supplier. This promise is primary because its main purpose is to obtain an economic advantage for A, not to benefit B. Primary promises are enforceable even if not in writing.

      c) The statute of frauds does not apply to an oral promise made to the **debtor**.

   5) **Agreements made in contemplation of marriage.** A promise to marry must be made in writing with consideration other than mutual promises to marry.

2. **The Required Writing**

    a. A written memorandum complies with the statute if it contains the following:

        1) A reasonably certain description of the parties and the subject matter,
        2) The essential terms and conditions of the contract,
        3) A description of the consideration (no minimum or adequate amount is required), and
        4) The signatures of the parties against whom the writing is to be enforced.

    b. The agreement may consist of several writings if

        1) One is signed and
        2) The facts clearly indicate that they all relate to the same transaction.

3. **Alternatives to the Writing Requirement**

    a. The statute does **not** apply when both parties to an oral contract have fully performed.
    b. Lack of written evidence ordinarily does not prevent enforcement if one party has fully performed.
    c. **Part performance.** An oral contract for the sale of land may be enforced when the contract has been partially performed.

        1) The purchaser must have (a) taken action that is clearly based on the oral agreement and (b) reasonably relied on it to his or her substantial detriment.
        2) If part performance is established, a court may grant specific performance and force the transfer of the land.

STOP & REVIEW

You have completed the outline for this subunit.
Study multiple-choice questions 10 and 11 beginning on page 525.

18.8 PAROL EVIDENCE RULE

SUCCESS TIP: The AICPA often tests whether the parol evidence rule applies to terms in a contract.

1. **Definition**
   a. The parol evidence rule excludes any prior agreement or an oral agreement made at the time of the final writing that would tend to vary or contradict the terms of a written agreement intended to be complete.
      1) If the parties meant their written agreement to be entire, only terms incorporated directly or by reference are part of the contract as it existed at the time it was set forth in writing and signed.
   b. A writing apparently complete on its face is assumed to be completely integrated at the time of its making.
      1) Most contracts contain a merger or integration clause that states the writing constitutes the entire and final agreement between the parties.
      2) To determine the meaning of the contract, the parties must rely upon the wording in the document and cannot offer other evidence as to its meaning.

2. **Exceptions**
   a. Parol evidence is admissible to prove or explain the following:
      1) Circumstances that make the written contract void, voidable, or unenforceable. The following are examples:
         a) Illegality or lack of capacity to make a contract
         b) Fraud, mistake, duress, or undue influence
         c) Failure of a condition precedent
      2) The meaning of ambiguous terms in the contract explained or supplemented by (a) course of performance or dealing or (b) usage of trade
      3) Typographical or obvious drafting errors that clearly do not represent the intention of the parties
      4) A subsequent mutual modification or rescission

STOP & REVIEW: You have completed the outline for this subunit. Study multiple-choice question 12 on page 526.

18.9 PERFORMANCE, DISCHARGE, AND BREACH

1. **Discharge by Performance**
    a. **Strict performance.** A party discharges his or her contractual obligations by performing according to the terms of the contract.
    b. **Substantial performance** is a lesser standard of performance. It applies when duties are difficult to perform without some deviation from perfection.
        1) Substantial performance in good faith may be achieved even with an immaterial breach of contract.

> **EXAMPLE 18-19**   **Discharge by Substantial Performance**
>
> A contractor has just completed a mansion. Upon inspection, the homeowner finds that cheap water fixtures were used even though she explicitly required an expensive brand. Accordingly, she refuses to pay for or accept the home, attempting to void the contract. Because the breach is immaterial in relation to the total contract, the homeowner must pay for and accept the house. The contractor must pay damages for the repair or replacement of the fixtures.

        2) The doctrine is **not** applied if the party has intentionally committed this immaterial breach.
    c. **Good faith** is expected of the parties in performing contractual promises.
        1) Each party has a duty not to prevent another party from performing.

2. **Discharge by Agreement**
    a. **Mutual rescission** occurs when the parties to a contract agree to cancel it.
    b. Parties to a contract may make a new contract (an **accord**) in which the prior and the new contracts are to be discharged by performance **(satisfaction)** of the new contract. The implied promises not to sue provide the consideration.

> **EXAMPLE 18-20**   **Accord and Satisfaction**
>
> A general contractor and a homeowner contract for the construction of a deck on the back of the house. The contract specifies that the deck is to be constructed of pine, and the homeowner will pay $5,000. As construction is nearing completion, the homeowner discovers that pine has not been used in the deck and addresses this issue with the contractor. Both parties agree that the price of the deck construction will be lowered to $4,000 given the contractor's mistake. After the construction is completed, and the homeowner pays the contractor $4,000, neither party can sue successfully because of the inferior wood or decreased payment. The accord and satisfaction bars this legal action.

    c. In a **composition with creditors**, the participating creditors agree to extend time for payment, take lesser sums in satisfaction of the debts owed, or accept some other plan of financial adjustment.
        1) The consideration is provided by the mutual promises of the creditors to accept less than the amounts due.
    d. **Modification** of an existing contract's term(s) traditionally requires new consideration.
        1) However, the Restatement (Second) of Contracts does not require consideration if the contract is unperformed and the modification is fair given facts the parties did not anticipate when the contract was formed.
        2) Under the UCC, modifications involving a sale of **goods** do not require consideration if made in good faith.

e. A **substituted contract** is an agreement among all parties that cancels an existing contract. The new contract is supported by new consideration, which may include a promise made by a new party.

   1) A **novation** is a special form of substituted contract that replaces a party to the prior contract with another who was not originally a party. It completely releases the replaced party.

      a) The promise of the new party to perform in accordance with the novation is consideration for release of the replaced party.

f. **Release.** One party releases another of performance obligations without restoration to all parties' original positions. Releases are commonly used to settle differences if liability is contingent or disputed.

3. **Discharge by Operation of Law**

   a. **Illegality.** The nonperformance of a contractual duty may be excused if, after formation, the contract becomes objectively impossible to perform (e.g., the law changes, making the contract illegal).

   b. **Impossibility** is an exception to the general rule of strict performance.

      1) Circumstances must have changed so completely since the contract was formed that the parties could **not** reasonably have foreseen and expressly provided for the change.

         a) For example, an essential party to the performance of a contract dies or is incapacitated, an essential item or commodity is destroyed, or an intervening change of law makes performance illegal.

         b) However, the death, incapacity, or bankruptcy of a party who is to receive the performance does not discharge the duty.

      2) The impossibility must be **objective** in the sense that no one could perform the duty or duties specified in the contract.

   c. **Commercial impracticability** results from an **unforeseen** and unjust hardship. It is a less rigid doctrine than the impossibility exception.

      1) Impracticability results from occurrence of an event if its nonoccurrence was a basic assumption of the contract.

      2) An issue is whether the promisor assumed the risk of such an event.

   d. **Frustration of purpose** is a doctrine that permits discharge of parties even though performance is still possible. Frustration occurs when a contract becomes valueless, that is, when the purpose for which it was entered is no longer available because it has been destroyed by an intervening event that was not reasonably foreseeable.

4. **Conditions**
    a. Failure of a condition does not subject either party to liability because it is an event that must occur for the contract to continue.
    b. Conditions may be classified based on their timing.
        1) A condition **precedent** is an event that must occur before performance is due.
        2) A **concurrent** condition must occur or be performed simultaneously.
        3) A condition **subsequent** is an event that terminates one party's duty and another party's right to damages for breach of the duty. For example, a supplier has no contractual duty to deliver if the buyer ceases operations.
    c. Conditions also may be classified as express or implied.
        1) An **express** condition is explicitly stated, usually preceded by such terms as "on condition that" or "subject to."
        2) An **implied** condition is not expressly stated in the contract but inferred.
            a) **Implied-in-fact** conditions are understood by both parties to be part of the agreement.
            b) **Implied-in-law** conditions are imposed by law to promote fairness.

5. **Breach of Contract**
    a. A breach is the failure of a party to perform a duty required under a contract.
    b. A **material breach** is an unjustified failure to perform obligations arising from a contract, such that one party is deprived of what (s)he bargained for.
        1) A material breach discharges the nonbreaching party from any obligation to perform under the contract and entitles that party to sue for breach of contract.
    c. A **nonmaterial breach** is unintended, and the injured party receives substantially all of the benefits reasonably anticipated.
    d. An **anticipatory breach** occurs when one party **repudiates** the contract.
        1) An **anticipatory repudiation** is an express or implied indication that (s)he has no intention to perform the contract prior to the time set for performance.
    e. A **statute of limitations** is a law that designates a time period after which litigation may not be commenced. Expiration of the time period bars a judicial remedy.
        1) The statutory period begins to run for a breach of contract claim from the later of the date of the breach or the date when a party should reasonably have discovered the breach.

STOP & REVIEW

You have completed the outline for this subunit.
Study multiple-choice questions 13 and 14 on page 527.

18.10 REMEDIES

1. **Damages**
    a. The most common remedy for breach of contract is a judgment awarding an amount of money to compensate for damages.
        1) **Compensatory** (actual or general) damages are damages incurred from the wrongful conduct of the breaching party. Compensatory damages are intended to place the injured party in as good a position as if the breaching party had performed under the contract. The following are measures of compensatory damages:
            a) **Incidental** damages result directly from the breach.
            b) **Consequential** damages are not incidental damages. They are additional damages resulting from special circumstances that the defendant had reason to **foresee**.
        2) **Punitive** damages punish a breaching party and set a public policy example for others.
            a) A court awards punitive damages only when the breach is malicious, willful, or physically injurious to the nonbreaching party.
        3) **Liquidated** (undisputed) damages are agreed upon money damages in advance of an actual breach. Such a clause is enforceable if
            a) The clause is not intended as a penalty,
            b) It reasonably forecasts the probable loss due to the breach, and
            c) The loss is difficult to calculate.
    b. **Mitigation.** An injured party is required to take reasonable steps to mitigate damages (s)he may sustain as a result of the breach.

2. **Other Remedies**
    a. **Specific performance** is a nonmonetary judgment entered by the court requiring the breaching party to perform the duties specified in the contract.
        1) No other legal remedy is adequate.
            a) Monetary damages are not available or are not adequate.
            b) The subject matter of the contract is unique. For example, each parcel of land or each patent is deemed to be unique.
        2) Irreparable injury will result if specific performance is not granted.
        3) A judge will not order specific performance for a personal service contract.
    b. **Rescission** cancels a contract and returns the parties to the positions they would have been in if the contract had not been made. It results from mutual consent, conduct of the parties, or a court order.
    c. **Reformation.** When the parties' written agreement imperfectly expresses the parties' intent, it can be rewritten.
    d. **Replevin** is an action to recover personal property taken unlawfully.

SU 18: Contracts

e. An **injunction** is a court's order to do or not do some act.
f. **Restitution** is available when a party's performance conferred a recoverable benefit on the other party.

> **STOP & REVIEW**
> You have completed the outline for this subunit.
> Study multiple-choice questions 15 and 16 on page 528.

18.11 CONTRACT BENEFICIARIES

1. **Third-Party Beneficiaries**
    a. In a third-party beneficiary contract, at least one performance is intended for the direct benefit of a person not a party to the contract (not in **privity** of contract). This person is an **intended beneficiary**.
    b. Intended third-party beneficiaries have rights under the contract.

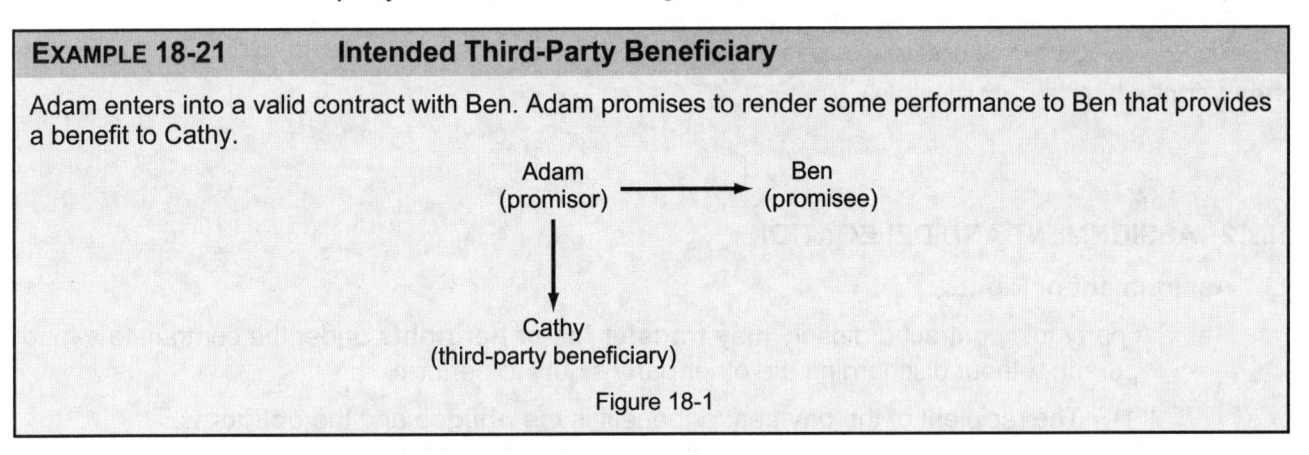

EXAMPLE 18-21   Intended Third-Party Beneficiary

Adam enters into a valid contract with Ben. Adam promises to render some performance to Ben that provides a benefit to Cathy.

```
Adam  ─────────▶  Ben
(promisor)       (promisee)
   │
   ▼
  Cathy
(third-party beneficiary)
```

Figure 18-1

---

   1) If a promisee's main purpose in entering the contract with promisor is to discharge a debt (s)he owes to a third party, the third party is an intended **creditor beneficiary**.
      a) If the contract in Example 18-21 above is breached, the creditor (Cathy) may sue the promisor (Adam) as a third-party beneficiary. But the creditor also may sue the original debtor (Ben).
   2) If a promisee's main purpose is to confer a benefit on a third party as a gift, the third party is a **donee beneficiary** (e.g., a beneficiary of life insurance).
    c. An intended third-party beneficiary's rights are derivative and therefore they are the same rights as the promisee's.
      1) The promisor may assert any defense against the beneficiary that the promisor could have asserted against the promisee.

d. An **incidental beneficiary** is a nonparty who might benefit if the contract is performed but whom the parties did not intend to benefit directly.

1) Because an incidental beneficiary is not an intended beneficiary, (s)he has no legal right to sue for performance of the contract.

EXAMPLE 18-22   Incidental Beneficiary

Adam enters into a valid contract to sell goods to Ben. Cathy will benefit unintentionally from performance of the contract because Ben purchases the goods from his wholesaler, Cathy. Because Cathy is an unintentional beneficiary, she has no legal rights to enforce.

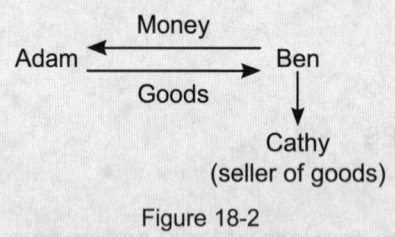

```
              Money
       Adam ◄──────── Ben
            ────────►
              Goods    │
                       ▼
                     Cathy
                (seller of goods)
```

Figure 18-2

STOP & REVIEW

You have completed the outline for this subunit.
Study multiple-choice questions 17 and 18 on page 529.

18.12 ASSIGNMENT AND DELEGATION

1. **Assignment of Rights**

    a. A party to a contract ordinarily **may transfer his or her rights** under the contract to a third person without discharging the other party's duty to perform.

    1) The recipient of the payment or benefit is the **obligee** and the **obligor** is contractually committed to provide the payment or benefit to the obligee.

    2) The right of the obligee is the obligor's performance (e.g., a payment).

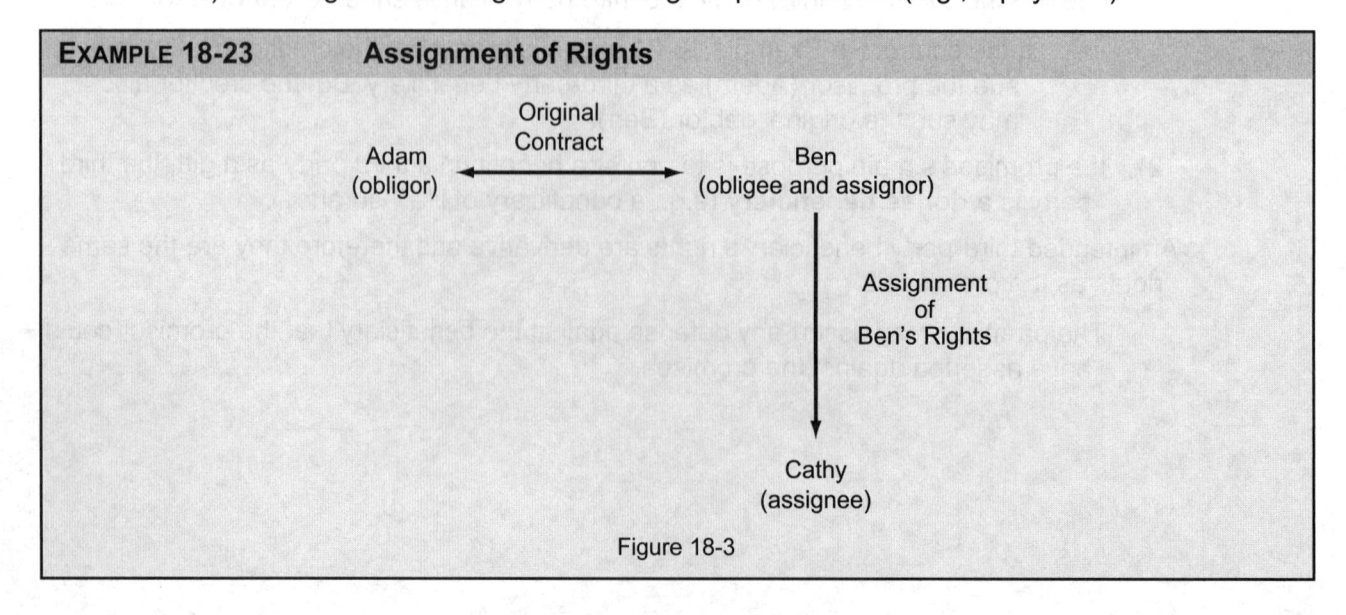

EXAMPLE 18-23   Assignment of Rights

```
                   Original
                   Contract
       Adam ◄─────────────────► Ben
     (obligor)              (obligee and assignor)
                                    │
                                    │ Assignment
                                    │    of
                                    │ Ben's Rights
                                    ▼
                                  Cathy
                                (assignee)
```

Figure 18-3

b. An assignment is a manifestation of the assignor's **intent** to transfer the right to the obligor's performance (due to the obligee) to a third party, the assignee.
   1) The party making the assignment is an **assignor**. The person to whom the assignment is made is an **assignee**.
   2) The assignor's right to the obligor's performance is extinguished in whole or in part if the assignment is **unconditional**.
   3) The assignment may be gratuitous (without consideration).
   4) An assignment need **not** be written unless required by statute.
   5) The obligor can assert the same defenses against the assignor and assignee.
   6) An assignment can be effective without notice to the obligor.
c. **Contract rights** generally are assignable without consent of the obligor and without a written document. But a signed assignment is required if the statute of frauds applies.
   1) An attempted assignment of a contract right is not effective if the contract expressly states that it is not assignable. Nevertheless, the following are assignable despite an agreement not to assign:
      a) A right to receive money
      b) Negotiable instruments
   2) A tenant may have the **right to assign or sublease** the premises without the consent of the landlord. The right may be restricted by the lease agreement.
      a) An **assignment** transfers the lessee's interest for the **entire unexpired term** of the original lease.
      b) A **sublease** is a **partial transfer** of the tenant's rights, and the sublessee is not in privity of estate or contract with the lessor.
      c) A lease term that prohibits assignment does not necessarily prohibit subleasing and vice versa.
      d) An assignment or sublease does not alter the legal relationship between the original lessee and lessor.
d. A right cannot be assigned without consent if the assignment would result in a material increase or alteration of the duties or risks of the obligor (e.g., insurance policies).
   1) Assignments of highly personal services contracts without consent are invalid. Examples are accounting, legal, medical, architectural, and artistic services.
e. A contract entered into in reliance by one party on the character or creditworthiness of the other party cannot be assigned without consent.

f. **Notice of assignment.** Between assignor and assignee, assignment is effective when made, even if no notice of assignment has been communicated to the obligor.
   1) Performance that the obligor renders to the assignor before receiving notice discharges the obligor's contract obligation to the assignee to the extent of the performance.
      a) The assignor is a trustee for the assignee of pre-notice or post-notice amounts received from the obligor after the assignment. The assignor must account to the assignee for these amounts.
   2) If the assignee does **not** give proper notice, (s)he cannot sue the obligor and force a repeat performance but instead must sue the assignor.
      a) After notice of the assignment is given, the assignee has the additional option of suing the obligor for payments made to the assignor.

> **EXAMPLE 18-24   Obligor Not Notified by Assignee before Payment**
>
> Jayhawk Corp. has $70,000 of outstanding accounts receivable. On March 10, Jayhawk assigned a $30,000 account receivable due from Tiger, one of Jayhawk's customers, to Clemons Bank for value. On March 30, Tiger paid Jayhawk the $30,000. On April 5, Clemons notified Tiger of the March 10 assignment from Jayhawk to Clemons. Clemons is entitled to collect $30,000 from Jayhawk only.

g. **Revocability of Assignments**
   1) An assignment given for consideration is irrevocable.
   2) A gratuitous assignment is usually revocable by the assignor. The following are means of revocation:
      a) Notice of revocation communicated by the assignor to the assignee or obligor
      b) Assignor's receipt of performance directly from the obligor
      c) Assignor's subsequent assignment of the same right to another assignee
      d) Bankruptcy of the assignor
      e) Death or insanity of the assignor
   3) However, an effective **delivery** of the gratuitous assignment to the assignee by the assignor prevents revocation. An example is a physical delivery of a signed, written assignment of the right.
   4) Revocation also is ineffective if the assignee has (a) collected from the obligor and (b) made a further assignment for consideration.

h. **Assignor's Warranties**
   1) If assignment is for consideration, the assignor impliedly warrants
      a) (S)he will do nothing to impair the value of the assignment and has no knowledge of any fact that would;
      b) The right assigned exists and is not subject to any limitations or defense against the assignor, except any that are stated or apparent; and
      c) Any writing shown to the assignee as evidence of the right is genuine.

i. If an assignee releases the obligor, the assignor also is released.

j. **Assignee's rights.** The assignee acquires all of the assignor's rights. The assignee stands in the shoes of the assignor.

2. **Delegation of Performance**

   a. Delegation means that a person under a duty to perform authorizes another person to render the performance.

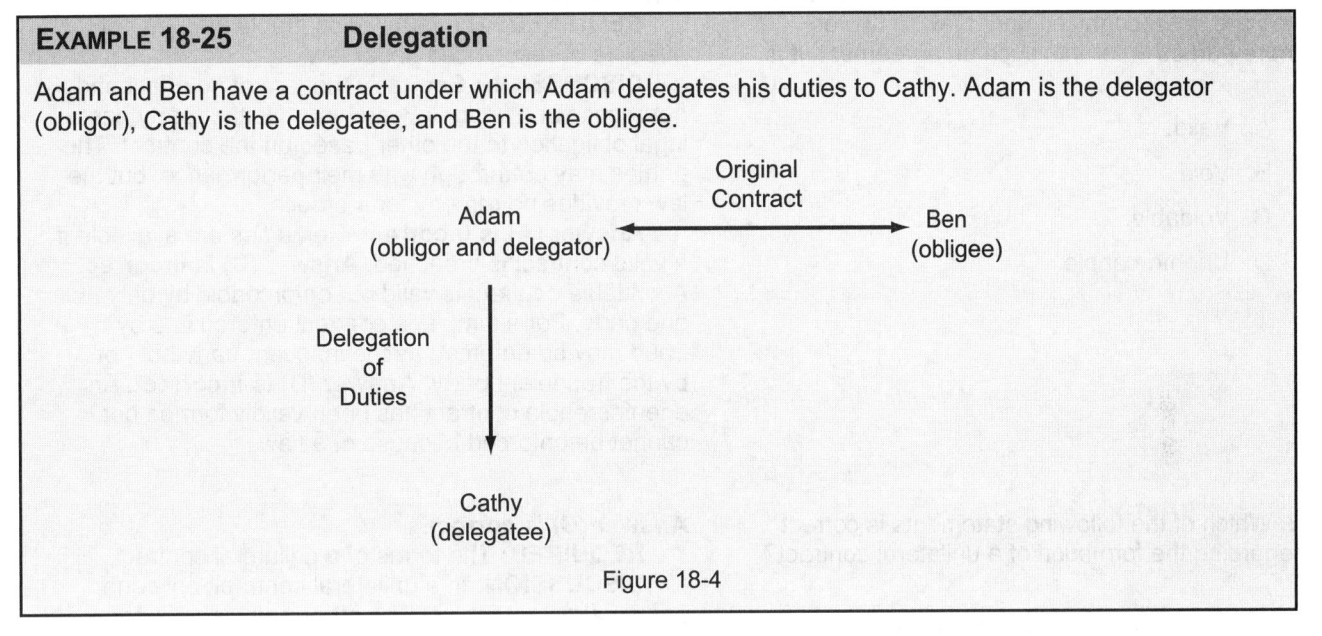

   EXAMPLE 18-25   **Delegation**

   Adam and Ben have a contract under which Adam delegates his duties to Cathy. Adam is the delegator (obligor), Cathy is the delegatee, and Ben is the obligee.

   ```
                  Adam  ←——Original Contract——→  Ben
         (obligor and delegator)                (obligee)
                   |
            Delegation
                of
              Duties
                   ↓
                 Cathy
              (delegatee)
   ```

   Figure 18-4

   ---

   b. A delegator may delegate performance if the delegatee's performance will be substantially similar to the delegator's (e.g., paying money, manufacturing ordinary goods, building according to a set of plans and specifications, or delivering standard merchandise).

      1) But highly personal services contracts generally are **not** delegable. The obligee has a strong interest in having the delegator perform. For example, a CPA firm cannot delegate performance of an audit.

   c. General language, such as "I hereby assign the contract," is a delegation of performance as well as an assignment of rights.

3. **Liability after Delegation**

   a. Delegation of performance does not relieve the obligor of liability even if notice is given to the obligee (unless the contract provides otherwise).

      1) The obligee may sue the delegatee, the obligor, or both after a breach.

STOP & REVIEW

You have completed the outline for this subunit.
Study multiple-choice questions 19 and 20 on page 530.

QUESTIONS

18.1 Nature and Classification of Contracts

1. Certain contracts have absolutely no effect and are not recognized under law. If two or more parties enter into such an agreement, it is

- A. Valid.
- B. Void.
- C. Voidable.
- D. Unenforceable.

Answer (B) is correct.
REQUIRED: The term for contracts that are not effective or recognized under law.
DISCUSSION: Contracts that are of no effect and not recognized under law are void. Neither party has a legal obligation to the other based on the contract. The parties may go through with their performance, but the law provides no remedy for a breach.
Answer (A) is incorrect. Remedies are available if a valid contract is breached. **Answer (C) is incorrect.** A voidable contract is valid but enforceable by only one party. For example, a contract entered into by fraud may be enforced by the innocent party but not by the fraudulent party. **Answer (D) is incorrect.** An unenforceable contract has been validly formed but cannot be enforced because of a flaw.

2. Which of the following statements is correct regarding the formation of a unilateral contract?

- A. A unilateral contract may be formed without consideration.
- B. A unilateral contract does **not** require performance.
- C. Only one party to a unilateral contract makes a promise.
- D. Only one party to a unilateral contract receives a benefit or suffers a detriment.

Answer (C) is correct.
REQUIRED: The terms of a unilateral contract.
DISCUSSION: In a unilateral contract, only one party makes a promise. The other party is an actor, not a promisor. If (s)he performs a defined action (an acceptance), the promisor is obligated to keep the promise.
Answer (A) is incorrect. Consideration is required for a unilateral contract to be formed. **Answer (B) is incorrect.** At least one party must perform a defined action for a unilateral contract to be formed. **Answer (D) is incorrect.** In a unilateral contract, one party makes a promise in exchange for the other party's act. Thus, a unilateral contract involves only one promise.

18.2 Mutual Assent (Offer and Acceptance)

3. On September 10, Harrin, Inc., a new car dealer, placed a newspaper advertisement stating that Harrin would sell 10 cars at its showroom for a special discount only on September 12, 13, and 14. On September 12, King called Harrin and expressed an interest in buying one of the advertised cars. King was told that five of the cars had been sold and that King should come to the showroom as soon as possible. On September 13, Harrin made a televised announcement that the sale would end at 10:00 p.m. that night. King went to Harrin's showroom on September 14 and demanded the right to buy a car at the special discount. Harrin had sold the 10 cars and refused King's demand. King sued Harrin for breach of contract. Harrin's best defense to King's suit would be that Harrin's

A. Offer was unenforceable.
B. Advertisement was not an offer.
C. Television announcement revoked the offer.
D. Offer had not been accepted.

Answer (B) is correct.
REQUIRED: The legal effect of a newspaper advertisement quoting sales prices.
DISCUSSION: Newspaper advertisements that merely cite prices on items in stock are invitations to negotiate, not offers. In rare instances, an advertisement may be so definite and indicate such clear intent that it constitutes an offer and not a solicitation of offers, e.g., a promise to give one mink stole for $1 to the first person requesting it on April 5.
Answer (A) is incorrect. If an offer had existed, and King's telephone call was an acceptance, the resulting agreement would have been enforceable. **Answer (C) is incorrect.** No offer existed that could have been revoked. **Answer (D) is incorrect.** If the newspaper advertisement constituted an offer, King might argue that the offer was accepted on September 12.

4. Ann Mayer wrote Tom Jackson and offered to sell Jackson a building for $200,000. The offer stated it would expire 30 days from July 1. Mayer changed her mind and does not wish to be bound by the offer. If a legal dispute arises between the parties regarding whether there has been a valid acceptance of the offer, which of the following is true?

A. The offer cannot be legally withdrawn for the stated period of time.
B. The offer will not expire prior to the 30 days even if Mayer sells the property to a third person and notifies Jackson.
C. If Jackson phoned Mayer on August 1 and unequivocally accepted the offer, a contract would be formed, provided Jackson had no notice of withdrawal of the offer.
D. If Jackson categorically rejects the offer on July 10, Jackson cannot validly accept within the remaining stated period of time.

Answer (D) is correct.
REQUIRED: The true statement about termination of an offer.
DISCUSSION: Rejection of an offer terminates it. An offeree cannot accept an offer after rejection is effective. An attempted acceptance after rejection is a new offer.
Answer (A) is incorrect. The offer may be legally withdrawn at any time prior to acceptance, even though it states it will be held open for a specified period. An offer for sale of a building is not a firm offer under the UCC because it is not for a sale of goods. **Answer (B) is incorrect.** Notice to the offeree of sale of the property to a third person has the effect of terminating the offer. **Answer (C) is incorrect.** Acceptance on August 1 would be ineffective. The time provided for acceptance expires on July 31.

18.3 Consideration

5. For there to be consideration for a contract, there must be

- A. A bargained-for detriment to the promisor(ee) or a benefit to the promisee(or).
- B. A manifestation of mutual assent.
- C. Genuineness of assent.
- D. Substantially equal economic benefits to both parties.

Answer (A) is correct.
REQUIRED: The element that is necessary for consideration.
DISCUSSION: The consideration provided by one party (the promisee) to support the enforceability of the other party's (the promisor's) promise may be a bargained-for legal detriment to the promisee or a legal benefit to the promisor. Consideration is always in the form of a promise, act, or forbearance.
Answer (B) is incorrect. A manifestation of assent is an element of a contract distinct from consideration.
Answer (C) is incorrect. Genuineness of assent is a contractual element distinct from consideration.
Answer (D) is incorrect. Courts rarely question adequacy or equality of consideration.

18.4 Capacity

6. Green was adjudicated incompetent by a court having proper jurisdiction. Which of the following statements is true regarding contracts subsequently entered into by Green?

- A. All contracts are voidable.
- B. All contracts are valid.
- C. All contracts are void.
- D. All contracts are enforceable.

Answer (C) is correct.
REQUIRED: The consequence of an adjudication of mental incompetence.
DISCUSSION: An incompetent person is one whose mental capacity is such that (s)he is unable to understand the nature and consequences of his or her acts. If a person is adjudicated insane or otherwise incompetent before a contract is entered into, the contract is void and cannot be ratified (even after the person is later adjudged competent).

18.5 Legality

7. West, an Indiana real estate broker, misrepresented to Zimmer that West was licensed in Kansas under the Kansas statute that regulates real estate brokers and requires all brokers to be licensed. Zimmer signed a contract agreeing to pay West a 5% commission for selling Zimmer's home in Kansas. West did not sign the contract. West sold Zimmer's home. If West sued Zimmer for nonpayment of commission, Zimmer would be

- A. Liable to West only for the value of services rendered.
- B. Liable to West for the full commission.
- C. Not liable to West for any amount because West did not sign the contract.
- D. Not liable to West for any amount because West violated the Kansas licensing requirements.

Answer (D) is correct.
REQUIRED: The recovery for services rendered in violation of a regulatory statute.
DISCUSSION: A person who performs services without obtaining a statutorily required license may recover only if the statute is solely a revenue measure. If the legislative intent was to protect the public from incompetent work by unqualified persons, the statute is regulatory and the contract is unenforceable, even if the defendant was benefited and the work performed was satisfactory.
Answer (A) is incorrect. A court will not give any remedy to a party who violates a regulatory statute. West will not recover in quasi-contract although Zimmer was unjustly enriched. **Answer (B) is incorrect.** A violator of a regulatory statute is not permitted any recovery. **Answer (C) is incorrect.** The contract is not subject to the statute of frauds. (It is not a contract to sell real property.) If it were, failure of West to sign would not relieve Zimmer of liability.

18.6 Lack of Genuine Assent

8. The intent, or scienter, element necessary to establish a cause of action for fraud will be met if the plaintiff can show that the

- A. Defendant made a misrepresentation with a reckless disregard for the truth.
- B. Defendant made a false representation of fact.
- C. Plaintiff actually relied on the defendant's misrepresentation.
- D. Plaintiff justifiably relied on the defendant's misrepresentation.

Answer (A) is correct.
REQUIRED: The proof of intent to defraud.
DISCUSSION: The essence of fraud is that one party intentionally deceives to take advantage of another. The scienter, or intent, element of a fraud action is satisfied if the defendant knew of the falsity of a representation, or (s)he made it with reckless disregard for whether it was true. The defendant must have intended that the other party rely on the representation.

9. A building subcontractor submitted a bid for construction of a portion of a high-rise office building. The bid contained material computational errors. The general contractor accepted the bid with knowledge of the errors. Which of the following statements best represents the subcontractor's liability?

- A. Not liable because the contractor knew of the errors.
- B. Not liable because the errors were a result of gross negligence.
- C. Liable because the errors were unilateral.
- D. Liable because the errors were material.

Answer (A) is correct.
REQUIRED: The effect of a material unilateral mistake.
DISCUSSION: Generally, a unilateral mistake in fact does not invalidate a contract except in limited circumstances. In this case, the subcontractor is not liable. The mistake was an obvious mathematical error, and the general contractor was aware of the mistake and was not acting in good faith. The contract is voidable at the subcontractor's option.
Answer (B) is incorrect. The subcontractor would be liable under the contract if the error were the result of gross negligence. **Answer (C) is incorrect.** The other contracting party knew of the mistake and was acting unfairly. **Answer (D) is incorrect.** Only if the unilateral mistake was material to formation would it be voidable by the mistaken party in limited circumstances.

18.7 Statute of Frauds

10. Which of the following statements is true with regard to the statute of frauds?

- A. All contracts involving consideration of $500 or more must be in writing.
- B. The written contract must be signed by all parties.
- C. The statute of frauds applies to contracts that can be fully performed within 1 year from the date they are made.
- D. The contract terms may be stated in more than one document.

Answer (D) is correct.
REQUIRED: The true statement about the statute of frauds.
DISCUSSION: If a contract is within the statute of frauds, it is not enforceable at law unless requirements of the statute are satisfied. There must be a sufficient written memorandum of the contract. It may be stated in more than one document if evidence shows they are all related. One of them must be signed by the party against whom enforcement is sought.
Answer (A) is incorrect. Under the UCC, contracts for the sale of goods for $500 or more must be in writing. All contracts for $500 or more are not within the general statute of frauds. **Answer (B) is incorrect.** A party who signs a sufficient writing may be bound to performance, even if the other parties do not sign. **Answer (C) is incorrect.** The statute of frauds applies to a contract that cannot be performed within a year of its making.

11. Kram sent Fargo, a real estate broker, a signed offer to sell a specified parcel of land to Fargo for $250,000. Kram, an engineer, had inherited the land. On the same day that Kram's letter was received, Fargo telephoned Kram and accepted the offer. Which of the following statements is correct under the statute of frauds?

A. No contract could be formed because Fargo's acceptance was oral.
B. No contract could be formed because Kram's letter was signed only by Kram.
C. A contract was formed and would be enforceable against both Kram and Fargo.
D. A contract was formed but would be enforceable only against Kram.

Answer (D) is correct.
REQUIRED: The true statement under the statute of frauds about oral acceptance of a written offer to sell real property.
DISCUSSION: An agreement to sell an interest in real property is within the statute of frauds. An agreement that meets the criteria for the formation of an oral contract (offer and acceptance, consideration, mutual assent, capacity of the parties, and legality) but is within the statute of frauds is enforceable only against a party who signs a written memorandum of the offer. Fargo's oral acceptance bound Kram but not Fargo.
Answer (A) is incorrect. A contract was formed, but it is enforceable only against the party who signed the writing. The statute of frauds addresses the enforceability of a contract, not its formation. **Answer (B) is incorrect.** The statute of frauds only requires the signature of the defendant. No writing needs to be signed by Fargo. **Answer (C) is incorrect.** Under the statute of frauds, a contract is generally not enforceable against a party who did not sign a writing.

18.8 Parol Evidence Rule

12. Morton Athletic Corporation contracted with Brandi Hart, a professional athlete, to be its primary spokesperson. During oral negotiations, Brandi agreed that she would represent Morton exclusively during the term of the contract. When Brandi appeared in an advertisement for Logan Athletic Wear, Morton sued Brandi for breach of contract. Brandi's best defense is that

A. Other evidence may be submitted to explain ambiguous terms in the contract.
B. The exclusivity term was not in a written contract intended to be complete.
C. A subsequent modification or rescission of the contract was made to include exclusivity.
D. A prior agreement exists that contains the items orally negotiated.

Answer (B) is correct.
REQUIRED: The best defense in a suit for breach of contract.
DISCUSSION: If the writing constitutes the entire and final agreement between the parties, Brandi is not bound by terms not in the contract. The parol evidence rule excludes any prior agreement or an oral agreement made at the time of the final writing that would tend to vary or contradict the terms of a written agreement intended to be complete. Most contracts contain a clause that states the writing constitutes the entire and final agreement between the parties. With certain exceptions, the parties must rely upon the wording in the document and cannot offer other evidence to determine the meaning of the contract.
Answer (A) is incorrect. Parol evidence is admissible to prove or explain the meaning of ambiguous terms in the contract explained or supplemented by course of performance or dealing or usage of trade. The facts do not indicate that admission of such evidence would constitute a defense. **Answer (C) is incorrect.** Parol evidence is admissible to prove or explain a subsequent modification or rescission of the contract. The facts given do not include such a modification or rescission. **Answer (D) is incorrect.** Any prior agreement or an oral agreement made at the time of the final writing that would tend to vary or contradict the terms of a written agreement intended to be complete is excluded by the parol evidence rule.

18.9 Performance, Discharge, and Breach

13. Dell owed Stark $9,000. As the result of an unrelated transaction, Stark owed Ball that same amount. The three parties signed an agreement that Dell would pay Ball instead of Stark, and Stark would be discharged from all liability. The agreement among the parties is

A. A novation.
B. An executed accord and satisfaction.
C. Voidable at Ball's option.
D. Unenforceable for lack of consideration.

Answer (A) is correct.
REQUIRED: The true statement about an agreement to discharge a debtor from liability.
DISCUSSION: A novation is a new contract that replaces and releases a party to the prior contract with another who was not originally a party. Replacing in the Stark-Ball contract the former promisor (Stark) with a new promisor (Dell) is a novation.
Answer (B) is incorrect. By an accord, a promisee agrees to accept a substituted performance by the promisor. Performance of the accord (execution of the contract) is the satisfaction. **Answer (C) is incorrect.** No basis for voidability is apparent. **Answer (D) is incorrect.** The promise by Dell to pay Stark's debt is consideration for Ball's discharge of Stark.

14. On May 25, Year 1, Smith contracted with Jackson to repair Smith's cabin cruiser. The work was to begin on May 31, Year 1. On May 26, Year 1, the boat, while docked at Smith's pier, was destroyed by arson. Which of the following statements is true with regard to the contract?

A. Smith would not be liable to Jackson because of mutual mistake.
B. Smith would be liable to Jackson for the profit Jackson would have made under the contract.
C. Jackson would not be liable to Smith because performance by the parties would be impossible.
D. Jackson would be liable to repair another boat owned by Smith.

Answer (C) is correct.
REQUIRED: The parties' liability when the subject matter of a contract is destroyed.
DISCUSSION: Nonperformance is excused when circumstances change so completely that performance is objectively impossible because no one could perform the duty. Impossibility discharges contractual obligations by operation of law. It occurs when the subject matter of, or an item or commodity essential to, the contract is destroyed. The impossibility must arise after and could not have been reasonably contemplated at contract formation.
Answer (A) is incorrect. Mutual mistake is present at, not after, contract formation. It would apply if, without the knowledge of the parties, the boat were destroyed before formation. **Answer (B) is incorrect.** To the extent the doctrine of impossibility applies, performance by both parties is excused, and the contract is canceled. **Answer (D) is incorrect.** Under the doctrine of impossibility, duties are discharged, not substituted. But performance of a promise to supply a commodity is not impossible when an alternative supply is available.

18.10 Remedies

15. In June, Mullin, a general contractor, contracted with a town to renovate the town square. The town council wanted the project done quickly, and the parties placed a clause in the contract that for each day the project extended beyond 90 working days, Mullin would forfeit $100 of the contract price. In August, Mullin took a 3-week vacation. The project was completed in October, 120 working days after it was begun. What type of damages may the town recover from Mullin?

A. Punitive damages because taking a vacation in the middle of the project was irresponsible.

B. Compensatory damages because of the delay in completing the project.

C. Liquidated damages because of the clause in the contract.

D. No damages because Mullin completed performance.

Answer (C) is correct.
REQUIRED: The damages, if any, that may be collected given a contract clause providing for penalties for late performance.
DISCUSSION: By a liquidated damages clause, the parties to a contract agree in advance to the damages to be paid in the event of a breach. A liquidated damages clause is enforceable if all of the following apply: (1) It is not intended as a penalty, (2) it reasonably forecasts the probable loss due to the breach, and (3) the loss is difficult to calculate.
Answer (A) is incorrect. Punitive damages are intended to punish a wrongdoer and to set an example for others. It is extremely rare for a court to award punitive damages in a contract suit. It might if a breach is malicious, willful, or physically injurious to the nonbreaching party, e.g., willful and malicious refusal to pay valid medical claims of an insured. **Answer (B) is incorrect.** Compensatory damages (also called actual damages or general damages) are damages incurred from the wrongful conduct of the breaching party. The usual measure of compensatory damages is the amount of money necessary to compensate the nonbreaching party for the breach. **Answer (D) is incorrect.** Mullin breached the clause in the contract requiring completion within 90 days.

16. Which of the following remedies is more likely to be available for a breach of a contract to sell real rather than personal property?

A. Rescission.
B. Specific performance.
C. Damages.
D. Replevin.

Answer (B) is correct.
REQUIRED: The remedy more likely to be available for a breach involving real rather than personal property.
DISCUSSION: The equitable remedy of specific performance will be granted when the legal remedy of damages is insufficient, for example, because the subject matter is unique. Each parcel of realty is considered unique, so contracts to sell real estate are specifically enforceable. Although contracts for the sale of antiques, heirlooms, and other rare items also are specifically enforceable, most contracts involving personal property are not.
Answer (A) is incorrect. The nonbreaching party may, if the breach is material, elect to rescind and not be bound by the contract. This remedy is customarily available for personal property. **Answer (C) is incorrect.** Damages is a typical remedy for breach of a contract involving personal property. **Answer (D) is incorrect.** Replevin is an action to recover personal property taken unlawfully.

18.11 Contract Beneficiaries

17. Ferco, Inc., claims to be a creditor beneficiary of a contract between Bell and Allied Industries, Inc. Allied is indebted to Ferco. The contract between Bell and Allied provides that Bell is to purchase certain goods from Allied and pay the purchase price directly to Ferco until Allied's obligation is satisfied. Without justification, Bell failed to pay Ferco and Ferco sued Bell. Ferco will

A. Not prevail, because Ferco lacked privity of contract with either Bell or Allied.
B. Not prevail, because Ferco did not give any consideration to Bell.
C. Prevail, because Ferco was an intended beneficiary of the contract.
D. Prevail, provided Ferco was aware of the contract between Bell and Allied at the time the contract was entered into.

Answer (C) is correct.
REQUIRED: The rights of a creditor who is a payee of a contract between the payor and the debtor.
DISCUSSION: A creditor beneficiary has standing to enforce a contract to which (s)he is a third party. Because the intent of the promisee (Allied) in entering into the contract with Bell was specifically to have return performance (payment) to discharge the debt to a third party (Ferco), the third party is a creditor beneficiary.
Answer (A) is incorrect. Ferco was an intended beneficiary of the contract between Bell and Allied. Also, Ferco is in privity of contract with Allied. **Answer (B) is incorrect.** An intended beneficiary may enforce a contract enforceable between the parties. An essential element of the contract was consideration, but not from Ferco. **Answer (D) is incorrect.** Creditor awareness is not sufficient. The parties to the contract must have intended direct benefit to the third party.

18. Rice contracted with Locke to build an oil refinery for Locke. The contract provided that Rice was to use United pipe fittings. Rice did not do so. United learned of the contract and, anticipating the order, manufactured additional fittings. United sued Locke and Rice. United is

A. Entitled to recover only from Rice because Rice breached the contract.
B. Entitled to recover from either Locke or Rice because it detrimentally relied on the contract.
C. Not entitled to recover because it is a donee beneficiary.
D. Not entitled to recover because it is an incidental beneficiary.

Answer (D) is correct.
REQUIRED: The status of a manufacturer regarding a construction contract stipulating the use of its product.
DISCUSSION: A person who is neither a primary contracting party nor an intended third-party beneficiary has no right to sue on a contract. United is a mere incidental beneficiary, a person who may have been indirectly affected by the agreement but was not intended to be directly benefited.
Answer (A) is incorrect. United was not an intended beneficiary. **Answer (B) is incorrect.** United's reliance is irrelevant. It is merely an incidental beneficiary. **Answer (C) is incorrect.** A person is a donee beneficiary if the promisor's performance was intended as a gift to that person.

18.12 Assignment and Delegation

19. Moss entered into a contract to purchase certain real property from Shinn. Which of the following statements is **false**?

A. If Shinn fails to perform the contract, Moss can obtain specific performance.
B. The contract is nonassignable as a matter of law.
C. The statute of frauds applies to the contract.
D. Any amendment to the contract must be agreed to by both Moss and Shinn.

Answer (B) is correct.
REQUIRED: The legal effect and assignability of a valid real estate contract.
DISCUSSION: Contracts are generally assignable. Assignment is ineffective if a risk or duty of a party to the contract is materially increased, or an exception otherwise applies.
Answer (A) is incorrect. Each parcel of real property is considered unique. Thus, monetary damages are deemed an inadequate remedy for the buyer. (S)he may seek specific performance. **Answer (C) is incorrect.** A contract for the purchase and sale of real property is within the statute of frauds. **Answer (D) is incorrect.** To be enforceable, a contract modification must be agreed to by both parties. But consideration may not be required.

20. One of the criteria for a valid assignment of a sales contract to a third party is that the assignment must

A. Be supported by adequate consideration from the assignee.
B. Be in writing and signed by the assignor.
C. Not materially increase the other party's risk or duty.
D. Not be revocable by the assignor.

Answer (C) is correct.
REQUIRED: The requirement for a valid assignment of a sales contract.
DISCUSSION: Unless agreed otherwise, most contract rights can be assigned. However, a contract right cannot be assigned if it would materially increase the risk or duty of the other party. If an assignment would materially increase the risk or duty sustained by the other party, the assignment is invalid.
Answer (A) is incorrect. Adequate consideration is not a required element of a valid assignment. Gratuitous assignments are permissible. **Answer (B) is incorrect.** Generally, no writing is required for an assignment of contract rights to be valid. However, the statute of frauds requires a writing in certain situations. **Answer (D) is incorrect.** A gratuitous assignment is generally revocable by the assignor.

Access the **Gleim CPA Premium Review System** featuring our SmartAdapt technology from your Gleim Personal Classroom to continue your studies. You will experience a personalized study environment with exam-emulating multiple-choice questions.

STUDY UNIT NINETEEN
AGENCY AND REGULATION

(21 pages of outline)

19.1	Agency Formation	532
19.2	Agent's Authority and Duties	535
19.3	Principal's Duties and Liabilities	539
19.4	Agency Termination	545
19.5	Employment Tax	547
19.6	Qualified Health Plans	549

The law of agency is a common law concept that allows one person to employ another to do his or her work. The American Law Institute's Restatement (Second) of the Law of Agency summarizes the common law. In 2006, the ALI published a new version, the Restatement of the Law Third, Agency. The law of agency relates to the rights and duties of the principal, the agent, and third parties. The emphasis on the CPA Exam will be

1) The formation and termination of an agency,
2) The duties of the agent to the principal and third parties,
3) The duties of the principal to the agent and third parties,
4) The agent's actual and apparent authority, and
5) The significance of whether the agency is disclosed.

The remainder of the study unit relates to employer compliance with the federal laws and regulations governing employment taxes and qualified health plans.

19.1 AGENCY FORMATION

1. **Overview**

    a. Agency describes an express or implied consensual relationship whereby two parties mutually agree that one party (the "agent") will act on behalf of the other party (the "principal") in dealing with third parties.

    1) The **agent** has authority to act on behalf of the principal and is subject to the principal's **control**.
    2) The **principal** must intend for the agent to act on the principal's behalf.
    3) Courts apply an objective standard, the "reasonable person standard," in determining whether parties have consented to an agency relationship.

    > **EXAMPLE 19-1   Agency Formation**
    >
    > Bud overheard Harold say, "I wish I had a boat." Bud went to Boatworld and told the salesperson that, acting as Harold's agent, he wanted to buy a boat. An agency was not formed because Harold never intended for Bud to act on his behalf.

    b. An agent must agree to act on the principal's behalf as a **fiduciary**.
    c. An agency must have a **legal purpose**.
        1) Agencies formed for an illegal purpose are terminated by operation of law.
    d. A **principal** must have legal **capacity** to perform an act assigned to the agent. Legal **incapacity** applies to individuals the law considers incapable of incurring any binding contractual obligations.
        1) A contract entered into with a third party by an agent on behalf of an incompetent principal is voidable by the principal. In this case, the agent is personally liable for the contract they entered into (presumably on behalf of the principal).
        2) An incompetent agent, such as a minor, can bind a competent principal because the agent's act is deemed to be the act of the principal.
    e. Personal acts, such as executing a will, may not be delegated.
    f. An agency relationship itself is not a contract. **The doctrine of consideration belongs exclusively to contracts.**
        1) Agents who act without receiving consideration are **gratuitous agents**. The rights and powers of gratuitous agents are the same as the rights and powers of agents who do receive consideration.
        2) If an agency relationship is formed through a contractual transaction, then the principal must provide consideration for the contract to be legally enforceable.

2. **Formation**
   a. The general rule is that conduct, by itself, is **sufficient** to form an agency relationship. An agency relationship can be formed by actions even if the parties do not orally or in writing express their consent.
      1) However, an agency must be in writing to comply with the **statute of frauds** if performance under the contract cannot be fulfilled within 1 year of contract formation.
      2) Some states require the agency to be in writing if the contract involves a sale of land.
      3) Some states apply the **equal-dignities rule**, which requires that the agency relationship be in writing if the agent is entering contractual transactions with third parties that must be in writing to be enforceable under the statute of frauds.
   b. An agency may be **implied in law** without intent to form the relationship.
      1) A person may be held liable as a principal for the act of another person regardless of whether the principal intended to grant any authority. For example, a court may determine that an agent acted properly outside of a delegated authority in an emergency when the principal was unavailable.
   c. **Agency by Estoppel**
      1) This condition may arise if
         a) A person presents himself or herself as an agent,
         b) The alleged principal knows (or should know) of the representation and fails to make an effective denial, and
         c) A third party detrimentally relies on the existence of this presumed agency.
      2) The principal is prevented from asserting the nonexistence of an agency after a third party has taken some action in reasonable reliance on its existence.
   d. A **power of attorney** is a formal written appointment of an agent signed by the principal. But it need not be for a definite period or signed by the agent.
      1) A **general power of attorney** authorizes the agent to do anything that may be necessary to transact the principal's legal affairs.
      2) A **special power of attorney** grants authority for only specific transactions.
      3) General and special powers of attorney ordinarily terminate upon incapacity of the principal. But any power of attorney may be exercised in good faith and with no knowledge of the principal's incapacity.
      4) A **durable power of attorney** remains in effect during a period of incapacity of the principal.
         a) This power of attorney must be expressly conferred in writing before the principal becomes incapacitated.
      5) All powers of attorney ordinarily terminate upon the **death** of the principal. But any power of attorney may be exercised in good faith and with no knowledge of the principal's death.
   e. An agency may be formed by **ratification** of another's acts.

3. **Types of Agents**

   a. **General agents** are authorized to perform all acts relevant to the purpose for which they are engaged.

   b. **Universal agents** are authorized to conduct all of the principal's business that the principal may legally delegate.

   c. **Special agents** are engaged for a particular transaction and are authorized to perform specific activities subject to specific instructions.

   d. A **del credere agent** acts not only as a salesperson or broker for the principal, but also as a guarantor of credit extended to the buyer. The del credere agent guarantees a third party's obligation to the principal.

      1) Because the primary purpose of the agent's guarantee is for the agent's benefit (to close the deal), it is not subject to the statute of frauds and, unlike other suretyship promises, it need not be in writing.

   e. Under the Third Restatement, a **power given as security** confers the ability to affect the legal relations of its creator. The power itself does **not** establish an agency or confer actual authority. However, it is created in the form of a manifestation of actual authority held for the benefit of the holder or a third party.

      1) For example, Debtor (the creator) and Creditor (the holder) agree in writing that, if Debtor defaults, Creditor will have Debtor's authority to transfer ownership of specified property to Creditor.

      2) The broad definition of a power given as security includes the traditional **agency coupled with an interest**. In this form of agency, the agent has a specific, current, beneficial interest in the subject matter of the agency.

         a) The principal does **not** have the right or power of termination.

         b) The agent's interest in the subject matter is **not** exercised for the benefit of the principal. An example is an agent-creditor's power to sell collateral if the debt is not paid.

EXAMPLE 19-2   **Agency Coupled with an Interest**

A stockbroker working on commission does not have an agency coupled with an interest. Receipt of a commission depends on whether the shareholder receives a benefit from the sale of the stock. The interest need not be an ownership or security interest in the stock itself.

STOP & REVIEW

You have completed the outline for this subunit.
Study multiple-choice questions 1 through 4 beginning on page 552.

19.2 AGENT'S AUTHORITY AND DUTIES

> **SUCCESS TIP**
>
> The CPA Exam has tested candidates' knowledge of an agent's actual and apparent authority. Candidates need to remember that the principal is liable on contracts made by an agent who has actual, apparent, or emergency authority.

1. **Authority**

   a. An agent has the authority to act on behalf of the principal under the principal's direction and control.

      1) The most important legal consequence of the agency relationship is the agent's power to bind the principal to third parties.
      2) In order to hold a principal liable for the acts of an agent, the agent must have **actual or apparent authority** to act on the principal's behalf.

   b. **Actual Authority**

      1) Actual authority is conveyed to the agent by the principal's words or conduct. The agent receives the right and power to bind the principal to third parties.

         a) **Express actual authority** results when the agent has been expressly told either by written or spoken words that (s)he may act on behalf of the principal.
         b) **Implied actual authority** is incidental authority the agent has inferred from words or conduct by the principal.
            i) It may be inferred from custom and usage of the business or by virtue of the agent's position relative to the purposes of the agency.
            ii) Express authority to achieve a result necessarily implies the authority to use reasonable means to accomplish the expressly authorized action.

   c. **Apparent Authority**

      1) Apparent authority results from the principal's words, conduct, or other facts and circumstances that would induce a reasonable person justifiably to conclude that the agent has actual authority.

         a) Apparent authority gives the agent the power, but not necessarily the right, to bind the principal to third parties.
         b) A third party's rights against the principal are **not** affected by secret limits placed on the agent's actual authority by the principal.
         c) The agent is liable to the principal for exceeding actual authority but **not** to the third party.

      2) Apparent authority is **not** based on the words or actions of the agent, and it cannot exist if the principal is **undisclosed** (the third party is unaware of any agency). It is based on justifiable reliance on the conduct of the principal.

         a) The agent has no apparent authority if the third party knows the agent lacks actual authority.

3) Apparent authority may continue after termination of the agency until the third party receives notice.
   a) Under the Second Restatement, apparent authority ends when the agency is automatically terminated by operation of law.
   b) Under the Third Restatement, apparent authority ends if it is unreasonable for third parties who deal with the agent to believe that (s)he has actual authority.

d. **Emergency Authority**
   1) A court may grant emergency authority when prompt action is needed.
   2) An agent's delegated authority may be extended if the public interest is served.

2. **Subagents**
   a. Generally, an agent is chosen because of his or her personal qualities. Thus, an agent does **not** have the power to **delegate** authority or to appoint a subagent unless the principal intends to grant it. But delegation that is not expressly authorized may be appropriate in an emergency.
   b. Evidence that the principal intends that the agent be permitted to delegate authority may include
      1) An express authorization,
      2) The character of the business,
      3) Usage or trade, or
      4) Prior conduct of the principal and agent.
   c. If the agent makes an unauthorized appointment of a subagent, the subagent is **not** able to bind the principal.
   d. If the agent is authorized to appoint a subagent, the subagent
      1) Is an agent of both the principal and the agent,
      2) Binds the principal as if (s)he were the agent, and
      3) Owes a fiduciary duty to the principal and the agent.

3. **Agent's Duties to the Principal**
   a. **Types of Duties**
      1) The principal and agent often enter into a contract stating the terms of their relationship, including specific duties.
      2) The agency relationship itself, however, is independent of any contract between the parties. This relationship is subject to the following five duties and obligations set forth under agency law:
         a) Loyalty
         b) Care
         c) Notification
         d) Obedience
         e) Accounting

b. **Duty of Loyalty**
1) The agency is a **fiduciary** relationship that imposes a **duty of loyalty** on the agent to act solely in the principal's interest with utmost loyalty and in good faith.
2) The agent's duty of loyalty encompasses specific duties of selflessness that serve to protect the principal's economic interest.
3) The agent is obligated to refrain from
   a) Competing with the principal;
   b) Purchasing goods from the agent for the principal without the principal's knowledge or permission;
   c) Accepting secret profits or transactions entered into on behalf of the principal;
   d) Representing the principal, if doing so creates a conflict of interest between parties;
   e) Misappropriating the principal's property; and
   f) Disclosing the principal's confidential information for the agent's own benefit or for the benefit of third parties.

c. **Duty of Care and Diligence**
1) The agent must use the care and skill of a reasonable person in like circumstances and with his or her special skills or knowledge in performing agency duties.
2) The agent must act prudently and cautiously to avoid injury to the interests of the principal.

d. **Duty of Notification (Duty of Disclosure)**
1) When an agent possesses information relating to the business that the principal may need or desire to know, the agent has **a duty to notify** the principal of all material facts.
2) The agent must make reasonable efforts to provide information to the principal that
   a) Is relevant to the subject matter of the agency, and
   b) The agent knows or should know will be imputed to the principal.
      i) An example is an agent's knowledge of dangerous conditions. The principal may be held liable to an injured third party to the same extent as if (s)he had actual knowledge of the dangerous condition.
3) A person receives notice by actual knowledge of a fact, having reason to know of its existence, or receiving formal notice.
   a) Thus, notice to an agent authorized to receive it is notice to the principal.
   b) Moreover, an agent's knowledge is assumed to be known by the principal if it is important to an authorized transaction.

EXAMPLE 19-3	Attribution of Agent's Knowledge to Principal

Allan is Peter's agent for the sale of art. Allan falsely and intentionally overstates the value of a painting to a buyer. Peter is assumed to have knowledge of the fraud.

- e. **Duty of Obedience**
    1) The agent must follow lawful, explicit instructions of the principal within the bounds of authority conferred.
    2) If the instructions are not clear, the agent must act in good faith and in a reasonable manner considering the circumstances.
    3) If an emergency arises and the agent cannot reach the principal, the agent may deviate from instructions to the extent that is appropriate.
- f. **Duty of Accounting**
    1) The agent must
        a) Account for money or property received or expended on behalf of the principal and
        b) **Not** commingle his or her money or property with that of the principal.

4. **Agent's Breach of Duty and Liability to Principal**
    a. The agent is liable to the principal for losses resulting from the agent's breach of a duty.
    b. Transactions between the principal and the agent may be voidable by the principal.
    c. A constructive trust in favor of the principal is imposed on profits obtained by the agent as a result of breaching the fiduciary duty.
        1) The agent, in effect, holds the profits in trust for the benefit of the principal.
        2) The principal recovers the profits by suing the agent.
    d. If the principal is sued for the agent's negligence or the agent ignores the principal's instructions, the principal has a right to indemnification from the agent.

5. **Agent's Contractual Liability to Third Parties**
    a. The agent may assume liability on any contract by
        1) Making the contract in his or her name,
        2) Being a party to the contract with the principal, or
        3) Guaranteeing the principal's performance.
    b. The agent is liable if the principal is undisclosed or partially disclosed.

6. **Agent's Tort Liability to Third Parties**
    a. A person is liable for his or her torts (e.g., negligence) even when acting as an agent of another.

STOP & REVIEW

You have completed the outline for this subunit.
Study multiple-choice questions 5 through 8 beginning on page 554.

19.3 PRINCIPAL'S DUTIES AND LIABILITIES

1. **Duties to the Agent -- Financial**
   a. If a contract exists between the agent and the principal, the principal has a duty to comply with the contractual terms. For example, if the duty to compensate is not expressly excluded, the principal should **compensate** the agent for services. This duty includes keeping accurate **records** of payments made to the agent.
      1) If compensation is **not** stated expressly, the reasonable value of the agent's services is implied.
      2) But if the agent agrees to act gratuitously, (s)he is **not** owed a duty of compensation.
   b. Whether the agency is gratuitous or contractual, the principal has a duty to **reimburse** the agent for authorized payments made or expenses incurred by the agent on behalf of the principal.
   c. Regardless of whether the agency is gratuitous or contractual, the principal has a duty to **indemnify** the agent. The indemnity is for losses suffered or expenses incurred while the agent acted
      1) As instructed in a legal transaction or
      2) In a transaction that the agent did not know to be wrongful.
   d. The principal does **not** owe a fiduciary duty to the agent.

2. **Duties to the Agent -- Occupational**
   a. The principal has a duty **not to impair** the agent's performance.
   b. The principal owes a **general duty of care** to the agent because a principal-agent relationship exists.
   c. The principal has a duty to **disclose known risks** involved in the task for which the agent is engaged and of which the agent is unaware.
   d. The principal has a duty to provide an agent who is an employee with reasonably **safe working conditions**.
   e. The principal does **not** owe a fiduciary duty to the agent.

3. **Agent's Remedies against Principal**
   a. The agent's remedies for a principal's breach of a duty include
      1) Withholding performance or terminating the agency relationship,
      2) Counterclaiming if the principal sues,
      3) Demanding an accounting, and
      4) Filing a civil action seeking tort and contract remedies.
         a) But certain contract remedies, e.g., specific performance, may not be available if the agency is not based on a contract.

4. **Contractual Liability to Third Parties**
   a. If the agent has actual or apparent authority, the principal generally will be held liable on contracts that the agent entered into with a third party.
   b. Whether the principal is disclosed, partially disclosed, or undisclosed determines the principal's and agent's contractual liability.
      1) **Disclosed principal.** If the third party knows the agent is acting for a principal and the identity of the principal, an agent who acts within actual or apparent authority ordinarily is not liable to the third party.
      2) **Partially disclosed principal.** The third party knows the agent is acting for a principal but does not know the identity of the principal.
         a) The liability of the agent and a partially disclosed principal is **joint and several liability**. The third party may sue either or both the principal and agent and collect any amount from either until the judgment is satisfied.
      3) **Undisclosed principal.** The third party is unaware of any agency and believes that (s)he is dealing directly with a principal, not an agent.
         a) The third party has no legal right to disclosure.
         b) **Actual** authority is unaffected. By definition, however, **apparent** authority does **not** exist.
         c) To enforce the contract, the third party may sue the agent of an undisclosed principal.
            i) The third party intended to deal only with the agent, and the agent is a party to the contract.
         d) The undisclosed principal generally may sue or be sued on the contract except when it would be unfair or unjust to the other party. But the undisclosed principal may not be able to enforce a contract that
            i) Requires that credit be extended by the third party,
            ii) Involves unique personal services of the agent,
            iii) Involves nondelegable duties, or
            iv) Is a negotiable instrument signed by the agent with no indication of his or her status.

> **EXAMPLE 19-4   Undisclosed Principal**
>
> If the agent issues a check to a third party on behalf of an undisclosed principal, the third party cannot enforce the check against the principal. The principal has not endorsed it.

         e) Under traditional rules, if the undisclosed principal is discovered, the third party must elect whether to hold the principal or the agent liable for performance. But the third party has no right to void an otherwise valid contract.
         f) If the agent does **not** have actual authority, the undisclosed principal generally is not liable to the third party.
         g) Whether the principal is disclosed does not affect the duties of the principal and agent to each other.

Contractual Liabilities					
Principal	Agent's Authority	Principal's Liability to Third Party	Principal's Duty to Reimburse Agent	Principal's Right to Indemnity from Agent	Agent Liable to Third Party
Disclosed	Actual	Yes	Yes	No	No
	Apparent	Yes	No*	Yes*	No
	No Authority	No	No	No	Yes
Partially Disclosed	Actual	Yes	Yes	No	Yes
	Apparent	Yes	No*	Yes*	Yes
	No Authority	No	No	No	Yes
Undisclosed	Actual	Yes	Yes	No	Yes
	Apparent	N/A	N/A	N/A	N/A
	No Authority	No	No	No	Yes

* The agent has exceeded actual authority, and the principal has not ratified the actions of the agent. If the principal ratifies the actions of the agent, the principal has a duty to reimburse the agent but not the right to indemnity.

5. **Ratification**

    a. Ratification is a voluntary election to treat as authorized an unauthorized act or contract purportedly done or entered into on the principal's behalf.

    1) Notice to a third party is not needed for ratification.
    2) Ratification is unnecessary if the agent's act is authorized.

    b. The principal must be aware of **all material facts** when assenting to the agent's act. The agent need not have performed his or her fiduciary duty or duty of due care.

    c. Ratification may be either express or implied. It may be inferred from the principal's words or conduct that reasonably indicates intent to ratify.

EXAMPLE 19-5	Ratification of an Unauthorized Act

Tony contracted to purchase 500 pounds of fish from Greg on behalf of Teresa's restaurant. Teresa did not know Tony or Greg and was unaware of the transaction. When the fish arrived, Teresa accepted the shipment. Her ratification of the transaction may be inferred.

    d. Ratification is all-or-nothing. The principal may not ratify part of a transaction.
    e. Ratification is irrevocable.
    f. Ratification relates back to the time of the act. The act is treated as if it had been authorized at the time it was performed.

g. An agent has no liability to the third party after ratification.
  1) The rights, duties, and remedies of the parties are the same as if the agent had actual authority.
  2) If a principal does not ratify, the agent also is liable to the third party for breach of the **implied warranty of authority**.
h. Under the Second Restatement, an undisclosed principal cannot ratify.
  1) Under the Third Restatement, an undisclosed principal may ratify if the unauthorized act was done on that person's behalf.
     a) An actual principal-agent relationship is not necessary.
     b) The person who performed the unauthorized act need not have purported to be an agent of another person.

EXAMPLE 19-6	Ratification by Undisclosed Principal

Tony agrees to sell 500 pounds of fish that belong to Greg to Teresa's restaurant. Tony claims to own the fish. When Greg learns of the transaction, he affirms. The ratification is effective under the Third Restatement because Tony acted on behalf of Greg.

i. Certain conditions terminate the power of ratification. Examples include
  1) The third party's withdrawal, death, or loss of capacity;
  2) Changes in circumstances; or
  3) Failure to ratify within a reasonable time.
j. The principal must have the capacity to contract at the time of the unauthorized act and at the time of ratification.

6. **Tort Liability**
   a. A principal may be liable in tort because of a personal act or the agent's wrongful act that results in harm to a third party.
      1) The principal's liability is greater when the agent is an employee rather than an independent contractor.
   b. **Direct liability** results from the principal's negligent or reckless action or failure to act in conducting business through agents. Examples include
      1) Negligently selecting an agent,
      2) Failing to give proper orders or make proper regulations,
      3) Failing to employ the proper person or machinery given risk of harm,
      4) Failing to supervise the agent, or
      5) Allowing wrongful conduct.

SU 19: Agency and Regulation 543

- c. **Vicarious liability** results from the actions of the agent for which the principal, whether or not disclosed, is liable. Thus, both the principal and the agent are liable.

    1) This type of liability is based upon the doctrine of **respondeat superior** (Latin for "let the master reply"). Vicarious liability holds employers liable for the tortious conduct of their employees.

    2) An employer may be held vicariously liable for the employee's conduct when the employee

        a) Commits a tort, whether negligently or intentionally;
        b) Was not authorized by the principal to perform the act; or
        c) Performs the act **within the scope of employment**.

            i) An act is within the scope of employment when it is work assigned by the employer or a course of conduct subject to the employer's control.

            ii) An act is **not** within the scope of employment when it is within an independent course of conduct not intended by the employee to serve a purpose of the employer.

    3) A principal may be vicariously liable for an agent's material **misrepresentation** regardless of whether the agent is an **employee** or an **independent contractor**.

        a) This misrepresentation must be within the scope of actual or apparent authority. It may constitute an innocent misrepresentation with all the elements of fraud except wrongful intent (scienter). It also may be a tort, for example,

            i) Fraud
            ii) Negligence
            iii) Defamation

> **EXAMPLE 19-7**   **Principal's Vicarious Liability for Misrepresentation**
>
> Mary Lou hired John, a real estate broker, as an independent contractor to market her 15-year-old home. John told Michelle that the home was only 5 years old. Michelle bought the home. Both Mary Lou and John are liable for any harm suffered by Michelle as a result of the fraudulent misrepresentation. Moreover, Mary Lou is entitled to be indemnified by John if she must pay damages to Michelle for John's misrepresentation.

- d. Any agreement between a principal and agent limiting the principal's liability has no effect on the liability of the principal to third parties.

7. **Criminal Liability**

    a. A principal is liable for his or her own criminal conduct.

    b. A principal is generally **not** liable for a crime committed by the agent but may be held criminally liable for a crime of the agent if

        1) The principal approves or directs the crime,
        2) The principal participates or assists in the crime, or
        3) Violation of a regulatory statute constituted the crime.

8. **Employee vs. Independent Contractor**
    a. An agent is either an employee or an independent contractor.
        1) A principal employer **controls** or has the right to control the manner and means of an employee's work.
        2) An employer **does not control** or have the right to control the manner and means of an independent contractor's work.

    NOTE: The Third Restatement does not use the term "independent contractor."

    b. Whether an agent is an employee depends on
        1) The parties' agreement about the degree of control by the principal;
        2) The extent of supervision by the principal;
        3) Whether the agent provides services exclusively for the principal;
        4) The relationship of the nature of the business and the work of the agent;
        5) The skills and specialization required for the task;
        6) How the agent is paid, whether at the end of all work or periodically per unit of time;
        7) Which party provides the agent's place of work, tools, and supplies; and
        8) The duration of the relationship.

    c. **Independent Contractors**
        1) The principal generally is not liable for the torts of the independent contractor.
        2) However, tort liability may result from a principal's own negligence, e.g., in the selection of the contractor.
        3) The principal also may be subject to **strict liability**.
            a) This liability of a principal is generally not vicarious.
            b) Some duties cannot be delegated as a matter of law or public policy, for example, an employer's duty to provide employees with a safe workplace.
            c) Persons engaging in ultrahazardous activity have strict liability. Contracting out ultrahazardous activities is not a shield against liability.
        4) The principal is liable for representations made on behalf of the principal by the independent contractor that are actually or apparently authorized or ratified by the principal.

You have completed the outline for this subunit.
Study multiple-choice questions 9 through 12 beginning on page 556.

STOP & REVIEW

19.4 AGENCY TERMINATION

1. **Termination by the Parties**
   a. An agency is based on the mutual consent of the parties. Thus, it may be terminated at will by either party or both even if the termination breaches a contract between principal and agent.
   b. A principal may revoke a grant of authority at any time.
      1) **Revocation** may be implicit or explicit.
   c. An agent may renounce the grant of authority by giving notice to the principal.
   d. If termination breaches a contract, the nonbreaching party has remedies provided by contract law.
   e. An agency for a specific period terminates when the period ends.

2. **Termination by Operation of Law**
   a. Under the Second Restatement, termination by operation of law terminates actual or apparent authority in the following cases:
      1) **Death** or **incapacity** of either the principal or the agent.
      2) The **illegality** of duties to be performed by an agent.

EXAMPLE 19-8	Illegality of the Agent's Duties

An agency has been formed in which the agent is expected to sell the principal's real estate. If the agent fails to obtain a real estate license, the agency is void. An unlicensed agent cannot legally sell real estate for the principal.

   a) A change of law that makes an authorized act illegal also terminates the agency.
      3) The principal's filing of a petition in **bankruptcy**.
      4) **Destruction** of the subject matter of the agency that makes fulfilling the purpose of the agency impossible.
      5) A **change in circumstances** (a change in business conditions or the value of a property) so significant that a reasonable person would infer that actual authority is terminated.
         a) The agency might be revived upon a return to the initial circumstances.
         b) If the agent knows that the principal is aware of the change and the principal does not give new directions, the agency may not terminate.
         c) If the agent has reasonable doubts as to how or whether the principal wants the agent to act, the agent may act reasonably. That is, the agency is not terminated.

b. The Third Restatement provides a broad rule. It states that an agent has actual authority when, at the time of performing an act that results in legal consequences for the principal, the agent reasonably believes that the principal wants the agent to perform the act. This belief should be based on the principal's manifestations to the agent.
 1) Accordingly, when changes have occurred so that the act on behalf of the principal is unreasonable, the agent has no actual authority.
 2) **Actual** authority is deemed to continue until the agent receives **notice**. Thus, the Third Restatement produces a different result in cases in which the Second Restatement automatically terminates actual authority, e.g., death, incapacity, or bankruptcy of the principal.
 3) The Third Restatement also provides that termination of actual authority does **not** end apparent authority.

3. **Agency Coupled with an Interest**
 a. An agency coupled with an interest may be terminated
  1) According to the terms of the agreement,
  2) By surrender of the authority by the agent, or
  3) Upon destruction of the subject matter of the agency.
 b. An agency coupled with an interest generally is **not** terminated by
  1) Revocation by the principal,
  2) Death of the principal, or
  3) Loss of legal capacity of the principal.

4. **Termination of Apparent Authority**
 a. Apparent authority of the agent continues to exist until the third party receives notice of the termination if the termination is by an act of the parties.
  1) **Actual** notice (an effective notification) to the third party is required if the third party has already dealt with the agent.
  2) **Constructive** notice generally suffices for other third parties.
   a) The requirement is satisfied by a message posted in a trade journal or in a paper of general circulation where the agent operated.
 b. According to the Third Restatement, terminations by operation of law may **not** end apparent authority.
  1) Apparent authority ends only when it is **unreasonable** for a third party to believe the agent has actual authority. For example, the death, incapacity, or bankruptcy of the principal does not automatically end apparent authority.
 c. If the authorization of the agent was in writing, the revocation of authorization also must be written.

STOP & REVIEW

You have completed the outline for this subunit.
Study multiple-choice questions 13 through 16 beginning on page 557.

19.5 EMPLOYMENT TAX

1. **Federal Insurance Contributions Act (FICA)**

    a. FICA provides programs for disabled employees and families of retired, disabled, and deceased workers including, in some cases, divorced spouses. Employers and employees contribute under this program.

    b. Employers must contribute (pay tax) based on the employee's pay.

    1) An employer subject to FICA taxes must file quarterly returns and generally deposit appropriate amounts on a monthly or semiweekly basis with an authorized depository institution.

        a) For example, a monthly depositor must deposit each month's taxes on or before the 15th day of the following month.

    2) Failure to deposit appropriate amounts results in penalties.

    3) Penalties also are imposed on persons who file returns and other documents without supplying taxpayer identification numbers.

    c. The employer must generally pay **6.20%** of the first **$142,800** of wages paid for 2021 plus **1.45%** of all wages for the Medicare portion. The employer generally must withhold the same amounts from the employee's wages. An employer that underwithholds and underpays is liable for the unpaid amount. But an employer that pays an employee's share has a right of reimbursement.

    1) Employers are responsible for withholding an additional 0.9% of an individual's wages paid in excess of $200,000 as Additional Medicare Tax ($250,000 married filing jointly or surviving spouse; $125,000 married filing separately).

    2) No employer match exists for Additional Medicare Tax.

    d. The CARES Act allows a refundable credit against employment taxes for eligible employers carrying on a trade or business during calendar year 2021 if

    1) The operation of the trade or business is fully or partially suspended by an appropriate governmental authority due to COVID-19 during any calendar quarter or

    2) The employer suffers a significant decline in gross receipts such that the gross receipts for the calendar quarter are less than 80% of gross receipts for the same calendar quarter in 2019.

        a) Employers that did not exist in 2019 can use the corresponding quarter in 2020 to measure the decline in their gross receipts.

    e. A **net investment income tax (NIIT)** of 3.8% is imposed. The tax applies to the lesser of (1) NII or (2) the excess of modified AGI over the applicable threshold amount. These amounts are used to calculate the Additional Medicare Tax.

    f. **Wages** are all forms of consideration paid for employment, including cash and the cash value of compensation in any medium other than cash. They include (1) wages and salaries, (2) commissions (including contingent fees), (3) bonuses, (4) productivity awards, (5) tips, (6) vacation and sick pay, (7) severance allowances, and (8) fringe benefits.

    1) Wages exclude

        a) Payments for moving expenses to the extent that it is reasonable to believe a corresponding deduction is allowable and

        b) Medical care reimbursements under a self-insured plan.

    2) Investment income is not subject to FICA tax except for the NIIT.

g. **Group term life insurance** payments for retirees are treated as wages to the extent they constitute gross income and are for periods during which retirees no longer have employee status.

h. The employer must **withhold FICA tax** from an employee's wages. The employee's contribution (tax) must be withheld upon each payment of wages, up to the maximum bases and at the same rates.

i. Contributions made by the employee are **not tax deductible** by the employee. Those made by the employer are deductible by the employer.

j. **Self-employed persons** are required to report their own taxable income and pay FICA taxes. FICA is calculated based on net income.

2. **Federal Unemployment Tax Act (FUTA)**

    a. FUTA provides for a system of temporary financial assistance for unemployed workers.

    b. FUTA tax is imposed on employers who

      1) Employ one or more covered individuals for some portion of a day in each of the 20 weeks in the current or preceding calendar year, or
      2) Pay actually or constructively $1,500 or more in wages in any calendar quarter of the current or preceding calendar year.

      NOTE: This general test does not apply to household employees or farmworkers.

    c. The FUTA tax is **6.0%** of the **first $7,000** of wages paid annually to each employee.

      1) The employee does not pay any part of the FUTA tax.
      2) The employer pays the FUTA tax to the IRS.

          a) FUTA tax is a deductible business expense of the employer.

    d. A credit against FUTA tax liability is provided to an employer for amounts paid into state unemployment funds.

      1) The credit cannot exceed 5.4% of the first $7,000 of wages.
      2) The amount paid to a state usually depends on the employer's past experience regarding the frequency and amount of unemployment claims.
      3) An employer is entitled to the maximum credit if they paid their state unemployment taxes in full, on time (or by the due date of Form 940), and on all the same wages as are subject to FUTA tax.

          a) The percentage used to determine the credit may be reduced if the employer pays unemployment taxes in a credit reduction state.

    e. **Benefits** are determined on a state-to-state basis. Thus, the state fixes the amount and duration of compensation. To collect unemployment compensation, the worker ordinarily must

      1) Have been employed and laid off without fault;
      2) Have filed a claim for the benefits; and
      3) Be able, available, and willing to work but not be able to find employment.

f. A state may refuse benefits to employees who

   1) Have voluntarily quit work without good cause,
   2) Have been discharged for good cause (misconduct), or
   3) Refuse to actively seek or accept suitable work.

STOP & REVIEW

You have completed the outline for this subunit.
Study multiple-choice questions 17 and 18 on page 559.

19.6 QUALIFIED HEALTH PLANS

1. **Means of Increasing Health Insurance Coverage**

   a. Qualified health plans are insurance plans that cover all of the required benefits of the Affordable Care Act.
   b. The goal of the Patient Protection and Affordable Care Act of 2010 (ACA) was to increase health insurance coverage by the following means:

      1) Expanding Medicaid

         a) However, the U.S. Supreme Court ruled that states cannot be compelled to participate in the Medicaid expansion.

      2) Requiring employers with at least 50 **full-time or full-time-equivalent employees** (FTEs) to offer **affordable minimum essential** health insurance coverage or pay a penalty
      3) Providing insurance premium subsidies for certain low- and middle-income individuals
      4) Requiring individuals without health insurance (e.g., employer coverage or Medicare) to purchase health insurance
      5) Creating insurance exchanges (markets in which individuals can buy health insurance)

         a) If a state does not set up an exchange, a federal exchange is established.

      6) Outlawing lifetime limits on or arbitrary cancellations of health insurance coverage
      7) Allowing a parent's policy to cover his or her nondependent children until age 26
      8) Requiring employers to disclose to employees

         a) The employer's coverage (or absence of coverage),
         b) Information about the use of exchanges,
         c) A **summary of benefits and coverage** (not a summary plan description) that facilitates comparison of health insurance plans, and
         d) The cost of coverage on W-2 forms (mandatory for employers that filed at least 250 W-2 forms the previous year).

2. **Grandfathered Plans**

    a. If an employer plan was in effect when the ACA was enacted on March 23, 2010, many of its elements may continue if, for example, the employer does not

       1) Reduce benefits,
       2) Change insurers, or
       3) Materially increase co-payments or deductibles.

3. **Employer Mandate**

    a. An employer with at least 50 FTEs must **pay** a penalty if it does not provide affordable essential coverage.

       1) If any employee receives a premium tax credit to buy coverage, the annual penalty for choosing not to provide coverage is determined as follows:

          $$\$2{,}700 \times (\text{Total FTEs} - \text{First 30 FTEs})$$

       2) An employer that offers coverage to FTEs still may be penalized. If the coverage (a) is unaffordable or (b) does not provide the minimum essential care or have the minimum actuarial value, the annual penalty is the lesser of the following:

          a) $\$2{,}700 \times$ (Total FTEs – First 30 FTEs)
          b) **$\$4{,}060 \times$ (FTEs who received a premium tax credit)**

    b. An employer offering coverage to full-time employees must include all employees who are regularly scheduled to work an average of 30 or more hours per week.

       1) The plan's waiting period for coverage cannot exceed 90 days.
       2) The employer also must determine the number of FTEs for

          a) Current employees who work variable hours and
          b) New employees whose hours are variable or have not yet been specified.

4. **Affordability**

    a. Affordability is based on the following factors:

       1) The lowest applicable wage paid by the employer
       2) The employer's lowest-cost eligible plan
       3) Employee-only coverage (excluding family or any other tier of coverage)
       4) The employee's premium contribution

    b. The cost of the employee's premium contribution should not exceed 9.83% of his or her household income. The affordability requirement, however, is also met if the monthly premium contribution is not greater than 9.83% of any of the following:

       1) The annual federal poverty level for a single person, divided by 12
       2) The employee's monthly income based on rate of pay and monthly hours worked
       3) The annual income reported in Form W-2, Box 1, divided by 12

5. **Essential Health Benefits**
    a. The insurance must cover the following medical services:
        1) Ambulatory patient services
        2) Emergency services
        3) Hospitalization
        4) Maternity and newborn care
        5) Mental health and substance use disorder services, including behavioral health treatment
        6) Prescription drugs
        7) Rehabilitative and habilitative services and devices
        8) Laboratory services
        9) Preventive and wellness services and chronic disease management
        10) Pediatric services, including oral and vision care

6. **Actuarial Value**
    a. Actuarial value is the expected percentage of covered expenses that the plan will pay. The following are the tiers of plans and expected reimbursement levels:

Tier	Reimbursement
Bronze	60% ± 2%
Silver	70% ± 2%
Gold	80% ± 2%
Platinum	90% ± 2%

    b. The **minimum** actuarial value allowed for an eligible employer plan is 60%. Thus, an employee should **not** pay more than 40% in deductibles, co-payments, and co-insurance (excluding the premium contribution).
        1) Employer contributions to health-savings accounts (HSAs) or health-reimbursement arrangements (HRAs) may increase the minimum actuarial value.

STOP & REVIEW

You have completed the outline for this subunit.
Study multiple-choice questions 19 through 22 beginning on page 559.

QUESTIONS

19.1 Agency Formation

1. Jim entered into an oral agency agreement with Sally in which he authorized Sally to sell his interest in a parcel of real estate, Blueacre. Within 7 days, Sally sold Blueacre to Dan, signing the real estate contract on behalf of Jim. Dan failed to record the real estate contract within a reasonable time. Which of the following most likely is true?

A. Dan may enforce the real estate contract against Jim because it satisfied the statute of frauds.
B. Dan may enforce the real estate contract against Jim because Sally signed the contract as Jim's agent.
C. The real estate contract is unenforceable against Jim because Sally's authority to sell Blueacre was oral.
D. The real estate contract is unenforceable against Jim because Dan failed to record the contract within a reasonable time.

Answer (C) is correct.
REQUIRED: The true statement about an oral agency to sell realty.
DISCUSSION: Oral agreement usually suffices to form an agency, but a contract involving a sale of land is required to be in writing in some states. Furthermore, the equal dignity rule applies in many states. In these states, the agency must be in writing if the authority granted to the agent is to enter into a contract required to be in writing. For example, an agreement to transfer an interest in land is subject to the statute of frauds and therefore must be in writing. The contract is therefore most likely to be voidable at Jim's option. It was required by the statute of frauds to be written, and Sally's agency was oral. In most other situations, the agent's authority may be oral.
Answer (A) is incorrect. The contract most likely operates only as an offer because the agency was oral. **Answer (B) is incorrect.** The contract most likely operates only as an offer because the agency was oral. **Answer (D) is incorrect.** If Jim and Dan had entered into a binding agreement, it would be effective without recording. Compliance with the recording statute is necessary to protect against parties not privy to the contract.

2. Forming an agency relationship requires that

A. The agreement between the principal and agent be supported by consideration.
B. The principal and agent not be minors.
C. Both the principal and agent consent to the agency.
D. The agent's authority be limited to the express grant of authority in the agency agreement.

Answer (C) is correct.
REQUIRED: The requirement to form an agency relationship.
DISCUSSION: Agency is an express or implied consensual relationship. Both the principal and agent must manifest consent to the grant of authority. The purpose and subject matter of the agency must be legal. The principal must have legal capacity to perform the act authorized.
Answer (A) is incorrect. Consideration is not required to form an agency. **Answer (B) is incorrect.** An agent need not have legal capacity to enter into a contract to be able to bind a principal on the contract. **Answer (D) is incorrect.** An agent's authority can extend to more than acts specifically expressed in the agreement. For example, a universal agent is authorized to conduct all business that the principal may legally delegate.

SU 19: Agency and Regulation

3. Noll gives Carr a written power of attorney. Which of the following statements is true regarding this power of attorney?

A. It must be signed by both Noll and Carr.
B. It must be for a definite period of time.
C. It may continue in existence after Noll's death.
D. It may limit Carr's authority to specific transactions.

Answer (D) is correct.
REQUIRED: The true statement about a power of attorney.
DISCUSSION: A power of attorney is a written authorization for the agent to act on behalf of the principal. It can be general, or it may be a special power of attorney that grants the agent restricted authority, such as for specific transactions.
Answer (A) is incorrect. A power of attorney is a delegation of authority and need only be signed by the principal. **Answer (B) is incorrect.** To be effective, a written power of attorney need not be for a definite period of time. **Answer (C) is incorrect.** In the absence of a special statute, the death of a principal terminates an agency relationship.

4. Which of the following actions requires an agent for a corporation to have a written agency agreement?

A. Purchasing office supplies for the principal's business.
B. Purchasing an interest in undeveloped land for the principal.
C. Hiring an independent general contractor to renovate the principal's office building.
D. Retaining an attorney to collect a business debt owed to the principal.

Answer (B) is correct.
REQUIRED: The action requiring a written agency agreement.
DISCUSSION: Oral agreement usually suffices to form an agency, but a contract involving a sale of land is required to be in writing in some states. Furthermore, the equal dignity rule applies in many states. In these states, the agency must be in writing if the authority granted to the agent is to enter into a contract required to be in writing. For example, an agreement to transfer an interest in land is subject to the statute of frauds and therefore must be in writing.
Answer (A) is incorrect. Purchasing office supplies does not require any formality and is not subject to the requirement of a writing unless the price of the goods is $500 or more. **Answer (C) is incorrect.** An independent contractor may be an agent, but the object of the agency, providing the service of office renovation, is not subject to the formality of a writing. **Answer (D) is incorrect.** A written agreement is not required. The object of the agency, collecting a debt, does not require a writing.

19.2 Agent's Authority and Duties

5. Ace engages Butler to manage Ace's retail business. Butler has **no** implied authority to

A. Purchase inventory for Ace's business.
B. Sell Ace's business fixtures.
C. Pay Ace's business debts.
D. Hire or discharge Ace's business employees.

Answer (B) is correct.
REQUIRED: The agent's implied authority.
DISCUSSION: An agent's actual authority is conveyed by communication to the agent from the principal. It is not feasible to state expressly each act an agent is authorized to perform. Thus, an agent may have express and implied actual authority. Implied actual authority is for acts reasonably necessary to execute express authority. Selling the business fixtures is not necessary to manage a retail business.
Answer (A) is incorrect. Buying inventory is an act necessary to execute the express authorization to manage the store. **Answer (C) is incorrect.** Paying business debts is an act necessary to execute the express authorization to manage the store. **Answer (D) is incorrect.** Hiring or discharging employees is an act necessary to execute the express authorization to manage the store.

6. Bo Borg is the vice president of purchasing for Crater Corp. He has authority to enter into purchase contracts on behalf of Crater, provided that the price under a contract does not exceed $2 million. Dent, who is the president of Crater, is required to approve any contract that exceeds $2 million. Borg entered into a $2.5 million purchase contract with Shady Corp. without Dent's approval. Shady was unaware that Borg exceeded his authority. Neither party substantially changed its position in reliance on the contract. What is the most likely result of this transaction?

A. Crater will be bound because of Borg's apparent authority.
B. Crater will not be bound because Borg exceeded his authority.
C. Crater will only be bound up to $2 million, the amount of Borg's authority.
D. Crater may avoid the contract because Shady has not relied on the contract to its detriment.

Answer (A) is correct.
REQUIRED: The most likely result when an agent exceeds his or her authority.
DISCUSSION: Apparent authority exists when a third party has reason to believe that an agent has the authority to enter into contracts of the nature involved based upon a principal's representations. Secret limitations placed on the agent's normal authority create apparent authority. In this case, it was reasonable for Shady to believe that Borg had the authority to enter into the contract, given Borg's position in the company as vice president of purchasing. That Dent secretly limited Borg's authority has no effect, and Crater Corp. can be held liable under the contract.
Answer (B) is incorrect. An agent with apparent authority has the power to bind a principal even if the agent exceeds his express authority. **Answer (C) is incorrect.** A principal is liable to the extent of an agent's apparent authority, not an agent's express authority. **Answer (D) is incorrect.** Reliance is irrelevant when the parties are bound to the contract.

7. North, Inc., hired Sutter as a purchasing agent. North gave Sutter written authorization to purchase, without limit, electronic appliances. Later, Sutter was told not to purchase more than 300 of each appliance. Sutter contracted with Orr Corp. to purchase 500 tape recorders. Orr had been shown Sutter's written authorization. Which of the following statements is true?

- A. Sutter will be liable to Orr because Sutter's actual authority was exceeded.
- B. Sutter will not be liable to reimburse North if North is liable to Orr.
- C. North will be liable to Orr because of Sutter's actual and apparent authority.
- D. North will not be liable to Orr because Sutter's actual authority was exceeded.

Answer (C) is correct.
REQUIRED: The true statement about liability for a contract beyond the agent's actual authority.
DISCUSSION: A principal is liable on contracts made by an agent who has actual or apparent authority. Sutter had apparent authority to make the contract because of the principal's communication (letter) shown to the third party. Moreover, the third party's rights against the principal are not affected by the secret limits placed on actual authority. Sutter had actual authority to buy up to 300 units and apparent authority to buy the rest.
Answer (A) is incorrect. The agent is not liable to the third party. The agent had apparent authority to buy all 500 tape recorders. **Answer (B) is incorrect.** The agent is liable to the principal for acting beyond actual authority. **Answer (D) is incorrect.** The principal is liable for acts of the agent within actual or apparent authority.

8. Chester Michaels appointed Regina Fairfax as his agent. The appointment was in writing and clearly indicated the scope of Regina Fairfax's authority and also that Fairfax was not to disclose that she was acting as an agent for Michaels. Under the circumstances,

- A. Fairfax is an agent coupled with an interest.
- B. Michaels must ratify any contracts made by Fairfax on behalf of Michaels.
- C. Fairfax's appointment had to be in writing to be enforceable.
- D. Fairfax has the implied authority of an agent but not apparent authority.

Answer (D) is correct.
REQUIRED: The true statement about a written agency with an undisclosed principal.
DISCUSSION: When an agent has express actual authority, (s)he also has implied actual authority to use reasonable means to accomplish the purposes of the express authority. However, apparent authority is granted to the agent by words or conduct directed by the principal to a third party. Thus, it does not exist when the principal is undisclosed.
Answer (A) is incorrect. An agent coupled with an interest has a legal interest in the property that is the subject matter of the agency, and Fairfax has no such interest. **Answer (B) is incorrect.** Fairfax was given actual authority by the appointment. No ratification is necessary. **Answer (C) is incorrect.** A writing is not necessary to create an agency relationship if the agreement cannot be performed within 1 year from its making.

19.3 Principal's Duties and Liabilities

9. Which of the following statements, if any, represent a principal's duty to an agent who works on a commission basis?

I. The principal is required to maintain pertinent records and pay the agent according to the terms of their agreement.

II. The principal is required to reimburse the agent for all authorized expenses incurred unless the agreement calls for the agent to pay expenses out of the commission.

A. I only.
B. II only.
C. Both I and II.
D. Neither I nor II.

Answer (C) is correct.
REQUIRED: The duties, if any, owed by a principal to an agent who works on commission.
DISCUSSION: Two implied fundamental duties of a principal to an agent are to compensate the agent for his or her services and to indemnify or reimburse the agent for authorized expenses incurred on behalf of the principal. Any renunciation of these duties requires an express agreement.

10. Neal, an employee of Jordan, was delivering merchandise to a customer. On the way, Neal's negligence caused a traffic accident that resulted in damages to a third party's automobile. Who is liable to the third party?

	Neal	Jordan
A.	No	No
B.	Yes	Yes
C.	Yes	No
D.	No	Yes

Answer (B) is correct.
REQUIRED: The liability of the employer and employee for the employee's negligence.
DISCUSSION: A principal is strictly liable for a tort committed by an agent within the scope of the agent's employment (vicarious liability). This liability is without regard to the fault of the principal. Vicarious liability does not apply when the agent is an independent contractor. A person is liable for his or her own negligent acts even if acting as an agent of another.
Answer (A) is incorrect. Agent status is not a shield to liability for one's own negligence, and an employer is vicariously liable for his or her employees' acts.
Answer (C) is incorrect. An employer is vicariously liable for employees' acts. This rule reflects the doctrine of respondeat superior. **Answer (D) is incorrect.** Agent status is not a shield to liability for a person's own negligence.

11. Generally, a disclosed principal will be liable to third parties for its agent's unauthorized misrepresentations if the agent is an

	Employee	Independent Contractor
A.	Yes	Yes
B.	Yes	No
C.	No	Yes
D.	No	No

Answer (A) is correct.
REQUIRED: The type(s) of agents, if any, for whose unauthorized misrepresentations the principal is liable.
DISCUSSION: The principal is liable for torts involving misrepresentations regardless of whether the agent is an employee or an independent contractor. The agent's misrepresentation must be (1) fraudulent, (2) negligent, or (3) innocent but material and with all of the elements of fraud except intent. A tort involving misrepresentation is an an example of vicarious liability. An example of tortious misrepresentation by an agent-independent contractor is the sale by a homeowner through a real estate broker who made a material misrepresentation to make the sale. But the principal generally is not liable for the tortious acts of an independent contractor that involve physical acts.

SU 19: Agency and Regulation

12. An agent will usually be liable under a contract made with a third party when the agent is acting on behalf of a

	Disclosed Principal	Undisclosed Principal
A.	Yes	Yes
B.	Yes	No
C.	No	Yes
D.	No	No

Answer (C) is correct.
REQUIRED: The liability of an agent to a third party when the principal is disclosed and undisclosed.
DISCUSSION: When a principal is undisclosed, the third party believes (s)he is dealing directly with the agent. Thus, under general contract law, an agent is liable to the third party because the third party intended to deal only with the agent. An agent who discloses the principal and acts within actual or apparent authority ordinarily binds only the principal.

19.4 Agency Termination

13. Under the Restatement (Second) of the Law of Agency, which of the following does **not** terminate an agency relationship?

A. Incapacity of the principal.
B. An agent's act of filing a bankruptcy petition.
C. Changing circumstances that make it unreasonable to believe the agent has actual authority.
D. Agent fails to obtain a required license.

Answer (B) is correct.
REQUIRED: The circumstance that does not terminate an agency relationship under the Second Restatement.
DISCUSSION: A principal's act of filing a voluntary petition in bankruptcy, not an agent's, terminates an existing agency.
Answer (A) is incorrect. Termination by operation of law terminates actual or apparent authority upon the death or incapacity of either the principal or the agent.
Answer (C) is incorrect. Termination by operation of law terminates actual or apparent authority upon a change in circumstances (a change in business conditions or the value of a property) so significant that a reasonable person would infer that actual authority is terminated.
Answer (D) is incorrect. The illegality of duties to be performed by the agent ends actual and apparent authority. Third parties have reason to know of the illegality.

14. Pell is the principal and Astor is the agent in an agency coupled with an interest. In the absence of a contractual provision relating to the duration of the agency, who has the right to terminate the agency before the interest has expired?

	Pell	Astor
A.	Yes	Yes
B.	No	Yes
C.	No	No
D.	Yes	No

Answer (B) is correct.
REQUIRED: The person with the right to terminate an agency coupled with an interest.
DISCUSSION: In an agency coupled with an interest, the agent has a specific, current, beneficial interest in property that is the subject matter of the agency. A principal does not have the right or power to terminate an agency coupled with an interest. In any agency, the agent may terminate at any time without liability if no specific period for the agency has been established.

15. Bolt Corp. dismissed Ace as its general sales agent and notified all of Ace's known customers by letter. Young Corp., a retail outlet located outside of Ace's previously assigned sales territory, had never dealt with Ace. Young knew of Ace as a result of various business contacts. After his dismissal, Ace sold Young goods to be delivered by Bolt and received from Young a cash deposit for 20% of the purchase price. It was not unusual for an agent in Ace's previous position to receive cash deposits. In an action by Young against Bolt on the sales contract, Young will

A. Lose because Ace lacked any implied authority to make the contract.
B. Lose because Ace lacked any express authority to make the contract.
C. Win because Bolt's notice was inadequate to terminate Ace's apparent authority.
D. Win because a principal is an insurer of an agent's acts.

Answer (C) is correct.
REQUIRED: The outcome of a suit by a third party against a principal whose agent had no actual authority.
DISCUSSION: When a principal discharges an agent, (s)he must give (1) actual notice of the discharge to those the agent had previously dealt with and (2) constructive notice to others who might have known of the agency. Ace continued to have apparent authority because of Bolt's failure to give constructive notice by publication in a newspaper of general circulation in the place where the agency activities occurred. Publication in trade journals of the termination would have provided such notice and effectively terminated Ace's apparent authority.
Answer (A) is incorrect. Young will win. Ace had apparent, although not actual (express or implied), authority. **Answer (B) is incorrect.** Ace's lack of express authority did not preclude the existence of apparent authority. **Answer (D) is incorrect.** A principal is not an insurer of an agent's acts. A principal is only liable when an agent acts with actual or apparent authority.

16. According to the (Second) Restatement of the Law of Agency, the apparent authority of a general agent for a disclosed principal will terminate without notice to third parties when the

A. Principal dismisses the agent.
B. Principal or agent dies.
C. Purpose of the agency relationship has been fulfilled.
D. Time period set forth in the agency agreement has expired.

Answer (B) is correct.
REQUIRED: The occurrence automatically terminating a general agent's apparent authority.
DISCUSSION: According to the (Second) Restatement of the Law of Agency, an agency and the agent's power to bind the principal terminate instantly upon the death of the principal because the principal must exist at the time the agent acts.
NOTE: According to the Restatement of the Law, Third, Agency, the principal's death does not automatically terminate actual or apparent authority. Continuation of actual and apparent authority protects from liability the agent and the parties who do business with the agent, respectively.
Answer (A) is incorrect. When an agent is dismissed, existing customers must be given actual notice. Other persons must be given constructive notice to terminate apparent authority. **Answer (C) is incorrect.** Fulfillment of the purpose of the agency does not terminate apparent authority. **Answer (D) is incorrect.** The expiration of the agency does not terminate apparent authority.

19.5 Employment Tax

17. Under the Federal Insurance Contributions Act (FICA), which of the following acts will cause an employer to be liable for penalties?

	Failure to Supply Taxpayer Identification Numbers	Failure to Make Timely FICA Deposits
A.	Yes	Yes
B.	Yes	No
C.	No	Yes
D.	No	No

Answer (A) is correct.
REQUIRED: The acts for which an employer is liable.
DISCUSSION: An employer subject to FICA taxes must file quarterly returns and deposit appropriate amounts on a monthly or semiweekly basis with an authorized depository institution. For example, a monthly depositor must deposit each month's taxes on or before the 15th day of the following month. Failure to deposit appropriate amounts results in penalties. Penalties are also imposed on persons who file returns and other documents without supplying taxpayer identification numbers.

18. Other than the net investment income (NII) tax, which of the following types of income is subject to taxation under the provisions of the Federal Insurance Contributions Act (FICA)?

A. Interest earned on municipal bonds.
B. Capital gains of $3,000.
C. Car received as a productivity award.
D. Dividends of $2,500.

Answer (C) is correct.
REQUIRED: The type of income to which Social Security tax applies.
DISCUSSION: The Social Security tax imposed by the FICA applies to virtually all compensation received for employment, including money or other forms of wages, bonuses, commissions, vacation pay, severance allowances, and tips. A car received as a productivity award is a form of compensation for employment. It is not excepted from application of FICA tax. Income derived from an investment, as opposed to compensation for employment, is not subject to FICA tax. But the NII tax applies to the lesser of (1) NII or (2) the excess of modified AGI over an applicable threshold amount.

19.6 Qualified Health Plans

19. The Affordable Care Act (ACA) requires an employer with at least 50 full-time or full-time-equivalent employees (FTEs) to offer them affordable essential health insurance coverage or pay a penalty. In which situation is the penalty **not** imposed?

A. An employer offers coverage to FTEs but the coverage is not affordable.
B. Any employee receives a tax credit to buy coverage and the employer does not provide affordable essential coverage.
C. An employer offers coverage to FTEs but the coverage does not provide the minimum essential care.
D. None of the answers are correct.

Answer (D) is correct.
REQUIRED: The circumstance in which the employer mandate of the ACA does not apply.
DISCUSSION: According to the ACA, an employer with at least 50 full-time employees or full-time-equivalent employees (FTEs) must offer them affordable essential health insurance coverage or pay a penalty. If any employee receives a tax credit to buy coverage, the annual penalty for choosing not to provide coverage is imposed. An employer offering coverage to FTEs also may be penalized if the coverage (1) is unaffordable or (2) does not meet minimum coverage or actuarial value standards.
Answer (A) is incorrect. The penalty is imposed when an employer offers coverage to FTEs but the coverage is not affordable. **Answer (B) is incorrect.** The penalty is imposed when any employee receives a tax credit to buy coverage but the employer does not provide affordable essential coverage. **Answer (C) is incorrect.** The penalty is imposed when an employer offers coverage to FTEs, but the coverage does not provide the minimum essential care.

20. The goal of the Patient Protection and Affordable Care Act of 2010 (ACA) was to increase health insurance coverage by all of the following means **except**

A. Allowing nondependent children up to age 21 to be covered by a parent's policy.
B. Expanding Medicaid.
C. Creating insurance exchanges and markets in which individuals can buy health insurance.
D. Providing insurance premium subsidies for individuals with low- or middle-incomes.

Answer (A) is correct.
REQUIRED: The means of increasing health insurance coverage under the ACA.
DISCUSSION: Among the primary ways by which the ACA increases health insurance coverage are (1) expanding Medicaid, (2) providing insurance premium subsidies for certain low- and middle-income individuals, (3) creating insurance exchanges, (4) allowing nondependent children up to age 26 to be covered by a parent's policy, and (5) mandating that certain employers provide coverage.
Answer (B) is incorrect. Expanding Medicaid is a means of increasing health insurance coverage. **Answer (C) is incorrect.** Creating insurance exchanges and markets in which individuals can buy health insurance is a means of increasing health insurance coverage. **Answer (D) is incorrect.** Providing insurance premium subsidies for individuals with low- or middle-incomes is a means of increasing health insurance coverage.

21. The Affordable Care Act (ACA) sets a 60% minimum actuarial value for an eligible employer plan. All of the following statements are true **except** that

A. Actuarial value indicates what percentage of covered expense the health plan will pay.
B. Employer contributions to health-savings accounts may decrease the minimum actuarial value.
C. An employee would not pay more than 40% of the covered expenses excluding the premium contribution.
D. The lowest tier of plan allowed by the ACA is bronze.

Answer (B) is correct.
REQUIRED: The true statement about the minimum actuarial value for an eligible employer plan.
DISCUSSION: According to the ACA, actuarial value is the expected percentage of covered expenses that the plan will pay. The minimum actuarial value allowed for an eligible employer plan is 60%. The minimum actuarial value is set by the ACA and will not be reduced by employer contributions.
Answer (A) is incorrect. The actuarial value is the expected percentage of covered expenses that the plan will pay. **Answer (C) is incorrect.** The minimum actuarial value allowed for an eligible employer plan is 60%. Thus, an employee should not pay more than 40% in deductibles, co-payments, and co-insurance (excluding the premium contribution). **Answer (D) is incorrect.** The four tiers of health plans, from highest to lowest, are platinum, gold, silver, and bronze.

22. Meen Co. has 40 full-time employees and 20 full-time-equivalent employees. Meen does not offer its employees affordable essential health insurance coverage. Furthermore, its employees received tax credits to buy coverage for this fiscal year. According to the Affordable Care Act (ACA), what amount must Meen pay as an annual penalty?

A. $0
B. $54,000
C. $81,000
D. $162,000

Answer (C) is correct.
REQUIRED: The penalty paid by an employer under mandate of the ACA.
DISCUSSION: If any employee receives a tax credit to buy coverage, the annual penalty paid by an employer with at least 50 full-time or full-time-equivalent employees (FTEs) is determined as follows:

Annual penalty = $2,700 × (Total FTEs − First 30 FTEs)

The employer has 60 FTEs and must pay a penalty for not providing coverage. Accordingly, the amount paid is $81,000 [$2,700 × (60 − 30)].
Answer (A) is incorrect. A penalty must be paid. **Answer (B) is incorrect.** To calculate the penalty, $2,700 should be multiplied by total FTEs in excess of 30, not by the number of full-time-equivalent employees. **Answer (D) is incorrect.** To calculate the penalty, $2,700 should not be multiplied by total FTEs.

STUDY UNIT TWENTY

SECURED TRANSACTIONS AND DEBTOR-CREDITOR RELATIONSHIPS

(25 pages of outline)

20.1	Security Interests and Attachment	561
20.2	Perfection of Security Interests	564
20.3	Priorities	568
20.4	Rights and Duties of Debtors, Creditors, and Third Parties	572
20.5	Bankruptcy Administration	575
20.6	Bankruptcy Liquidations	579
20.7	Reorganizations	583

This study unit covers issues related to debtor-creditor relationships. The first four subunits review the rights and duties of debtors and creditors under UCC Article 9, *Secured Transactions*. The remaining three subunits review federal bankruptcy law, including bankruptcy proceedings under Chapters 7 and 11 of the Bankruptcy Code.

20.1 SECURITY INTERESTS AND ATTACHMENT

1. **Security Agreements**

    a. A security agreement provides a seller (or lender) an interest in a specific asset that is pledged as collateral. If a debtor does not pay, the lender may proceed against the collateral.

        1) A **secured party** is the lender or seller who holds a security interest in the pledged asset.

    b. UCC **Article 9**, *Secured Transactions*, governs debtor-creditor transactions involving security interests.

    c. In commerce, parties often submit purchase orders and invoices to facilitate immediate transactions. The purchaser typically pays the seller on established payment terms, such as net 30. Before the purchaser pays, the seller often retains a security interest in the property sold.

    d. A security agreement may include an **after-acquired property** clause. Such a clause is important to a lender that finances inventory. It creates an interest in most types of personal property acquired by the debtor in the future.

        1) The clause provides for a **floating** lien that will attach (float) to specified property that the debtor acquires in the future.

        2) The security interest attaches in favor of the lender once the debtor has obtained an interest in (purchases) the property.

> **EXAMPLE 20-1**   **After-Acquired Property Clause**
>
> A typical after-acquired property clause created to protect a lender states that it applies to "all inventory now owned or hereafter acquired by the debtor."

    3) A security interest attaches to **consumer goods** under the clause only if the debtor acquires rights in the goods within 10 days after the secured party gives value.

2. **Security Interest**
    a. UCC Article 9 covers any transaction (regardless of form or name or, in most cases, whether title has passed) intended to create a security interest in personal property or fixtures, including consignments. A security interest secures payment or performance of an obligation.
        1) But mere identification of the goods to the contract or passage of title does **not** give any party a security interest. A security interest is a separate right that must be agreed to by the parties.
            a) An exception is a reservation of title by a **lessor** or **consignor**, which is intended to act as a security interest in the property.
        2) **Personal property** consists of all things movable and ownable.
            a) **Goods** are tangible personal property that is movable when the security interest attaches. The following are goods:
                i) **Consumer goods** are used for personal, family, or household purposes.
                ii) **Inventory** includes goods held for sale or lease or to be provided under a contract for service.

EXAMPLE 20-2	Classification of Goods

Wholesaler buys milk from farmers and sells it to restaurants. The milk is Wholesaler's inventory.

                iii) **Farm products** are crops, livestock, supplies, and unprocessed products of crops or livestock.

EXAMPLE 20-3	Classification of Goods

Milk in the possession of a dairy farmer is a farm product.

Sap that has been boiled into maple syrup is a farm product because boiling is so closely related to harvesting the sap. But once the syrup is bottled for resale, it becomes inventory.

                iv) **Equipment** consists of goods that are not consumer goods, inventory, or farm products. For example, a refrigerator purchased for use in a laboratory is equipment.
            b) **Fixtures** are goods that become part of real property (buildings or land) under state law. An example is a central heating system or built-in cabinets.

3. **Attachment**
    a. A security interest in collateral is not effective against the debtor or third parties until it attaches. Attachment must occur to be enforceable against the debtor, barring an explicit agreement stating otherwise. The debtor must agree to the security interest.
    b. The security interest attaches and becomes **enforceable** against the debtor when the following have occurred:
        1) The debtor has **authenticated** (signed manually or electronically) a security agreement (contract) that reasonably describes the collateral, or the secured party is in **possession** (or control) of the collateral.
        2) The secured party has given **value**.
            a) Contract consideration suffices and need not be new. An example is an agreement to take a security interest instead of enforcing a previously existing debt is considered value.
        3) The debtor
            a) Has **rights** in the collateral or
            b) Can transfer such rights (but not necessarily title).
    c. Attachment of a security interest in collateral gives the secured party rights to the proceeds of the collateral.

STOP & REVIEW

You have completed the outline for this subunit.
Study multiple-choice questions 1 and 2 on page 586.

20.2 PERFECTION OF SECURITY INTERESTS

1. **Overview**
   a. A secured party perfects its security interest to prioritize its claim over any other third party's interest in the collateral. Third parties include buyers from the debtor, creditors of the debtor, or a trustee in bankruptcy.
      1) Perfection gives priority over most unperfected interests and subsequent perfected secured interests.
      2) Perfection is **not** required to enforce the secured party's rights against the debtor.
   b. Perfection of a security interest occurs only after
      1) It has attached and
      2) Other requirements have been satisfied that relate to the particular collateral.
   c. Depending on the collateral, security interests are perfected in various ways:
      1) By filing a financing statement
      2) By possession or control of the collateral
      3) Automatically (but in certain cases for a brief period only)

2. **Perfection by Filing a Financing Statement**
   a. Filing a financing statement gives notice of the filer's security interest. It is not required for attachment. But it is required to perfect a security interest without a specific exception. The debtor's location controls the place of filing.
   b. The UCC requires the financing statement to contain
      1) The name of the debtor (but not a trade name only),
      2) The name of the secured party, and
      3) An indication (description) of the covered collateral.
         a) For example, a **fixture filing** must (1) indicate that it covers fixtures, (2) be filed in the **real property** records, and (3) describe the real property.

EXAMPLE 20-4 Perfection by Filing -- Name of the Debtor

Ralph Ortega is a sole proprietor of Small Business. Ortega borrowed money from Bank and gave a security interest in the equipment of Small Business. Bank should file the financing statement under Ortega.

EXAMPLE 20-5 Perfection by Filing -- Name of the Debtor

XYZ Partnership owns Dave's Plumbing. XYZ borrowed money from Bank and conveyed a security interest in its fleet of trucks. Bank should file the financing statement under XYZ Partnership, not Dave's Plumbing.

---

   c. A financing statement may be filed before a security agreement is reached or a security interest attaches. But filing is not a condition of attachment.
   d. A filed financing statement is effective for 5 years. A **continuation statement** extending perfection for another 5 years may be filed during the last 6 months of this period.
   e. If a debtor moves out of the jurisdiction where the security interest is perfected, it remains perfected until the earliest of
      1) Lapse of the original period of perfection,
      2) 4 months after the debtor changed location, or
      3) 1 year after transfer of the collateral to a debtor in another jurisdiction.

3. **Perfection by Possession**
    a. An example is a pawnbroker's loan of money and receipt of personal property as collateral. A security interest may be perfected by possession of the following:
        1) Goods
        2) Negotiable documents of title (e.g., warehouse receipts and bills of lading)
            a) A security interest in a negotiable document of title perfects a security interest in the goods it represents while the goods are held by the issuer of the document.
        3) Tangible chattel paper (e.g., writings reflecting an auto dealership's retention of title)
        4) Instruments
            a) Possession is optimal for negotiable instruments. A security interest not perfected by possession is defeated by a holder in due course.
                i) Also, perfection by possession is not limited to the 20-day automatic perfection period.
        5) Money
            a) Possession is the only way to perfect a security interest in money other than identifiable cash proceeds.
    b. If attachment occurs when the secured party takes possession of the collateral according to the security agreement, perfection and attachment are **simultaneous**.

EXAMPLE 20-6	Simultaneous Attachment

John arranged to borrow $10,000 from Julie for 30 days and to provide Julie a security interest in his boat on June 1. On June 2, John surrendered possession of the boat to Julie, and Julie gave John $10,000. Attachment occurred on June 2 because (1) John had rights in the collateral, (2) Julie had given value, and (3) Julie was in possession of the collateral. Perfection occurred simultaneously with attachment because Julie had possession of the boat when attachment occurred.

   1) Generally, the security interest becomes unperfected when possession ceases unless the secured party files a financing statement while in possession.

4. **Perfection by Control**

   a. Control perfects a security interest in investment property, electronic chattel paper, letter of credit rights, and deposit accounts. But a security interest in deposit accounts may be perfected only by control. Perfection ends when the secured party no longer has control.

      1) For example, a secured party has control over (a) a savings account if the secured party is the bank in which the account is maintained or (b) a certificated security delivered to the secured party.

5. **Automatic Perfection**

   a. A **purchase money security interest (PMSI)** results when

      1) A person obtains credit,
      2) The credit is used to acquire property, and
      3) That property is collateral for the debt.

EXAMPLE 20-7   PMSI

Debtor purchases an office copier. One week later, Debtor borrows $10,000 from Bank and gives Bank a security interest in all its office equipment. Bank's security interest in the copier is **not** a PMSI.

EXAMPLE 20-8   PMSI

Debtor borrows $10,000 from Bank to purchase office equipment. Debtor gives Bank a security interest in the equipment to be purchased. The next day, Debtor purchases a desk. Bank's security interest in the desk is a PMSI.

EXAMPLE 20-9   PMSI

Debtor purchased a computer on credit from Seller. Debtor also purchased in the same transaction additional software to install in the computer. Thus, Seller (the party that financed the purchase) has a PMSI in the computer and the software.

---

   b. The primary example of automatic perfection is a **PMSI in consumer goods**.

EXAMPLE 20-10   PMSI in Consumer Goods

Finance Co. lent Lori $1,000 to purchase a couch for use in her home and took a security interest in the couch. Lori used the $1,000 to purchase a couch. The security interest is a PMSI and is perfected without filing a financing statement or taking possession of the couch.

EXAMPLE 20-11   PMSI in Equipment

Finance Co. lent Factory, Inc., $1,000 to purchase a forklift and took a security interest in the forklift. Factory purchased a forklift with the $1,000. The PMSI is not automatically perfected because the forklift is equipment, not consumer goods.

c. The factoring of **accounts** (e.g., accounts receivable) is an outright sale that the UCC treats as a secured transaction. Perfection of a security interest in accounts ordinarily is created only by filing. A purchaser therefore must file to perfect its security interest in collections.

1) But if an insignificant amount of the assignor's accounts is transferred, perfection is by attachment.

d. With respect to security interests in **instruments, certificated securities, or negotiable documents**,

1) Perfection is automatic for the 20-day period after attachment to the extent that new value is given to obtain the security interest under an authenticated security agreement.

2) The security interest becomes unperfected at the end of 20 days unless the secured party perfects by other means.

6. **Proceeds**

   a. Proceeds include all items received upon disposition of collateral. Proceeds consist of any collateral that has changed in form.

EXAMPLE 20-12   Proceeds

A sheep rancher obtains credit and grants the creditor a security interest in the wool (goods in the form of a farm product). If the rancher exchanges the wool for a truck or cash, the truck or cash constitutes proceeds.

---

b. A security interest generally continues in collateral after its sale or other disposition. Moreover, a security interest attaches to **identifiable** proceeds.

1) The proceeds are perfected if the security interest in the collateral was perfected.

2) A perfected security interest in proceeds becomes unperfected on the 21st day after attachment. But perfection continues if the proceeds are identifiable amounts of cash or in certain other cases.

STOP & REVIEW

You have completed the outline for this subunit.
Study multiple-choice questions 3 and 4 on page 587.

20.3 PRIORITIES

1. **Overview**

    a. The protection provided by a security interest varies with its priority.

    1) One general rule is that a perfected security interest has priority over an unperfected security interest in the same collateral.
    2) A second general rule is that if unperfected security interests conflict, the first to attach or become effective has priority.
    3) A third general rule is that if continuously perfected security interests conflict, priority depends upon the order of filing or perfection with respect to the collateral.

2. **Priority of Unperfected Interests**

    a. An unperfected security interest is subordinate to, among others, the following:

    1) A perfected security interest in the same collateral.

EXAMPLE 20-13 **Perfected vs. Unperfected Security Interest**

On June 1, Bank lent Debtor $20,000 and took a security interest in Debtor's equipment. Bank did not file a financing statement or take possession of the equipment. On July 15, Finance Co. lent Debtor $30,000 and took a security interest in the same equipment. Finance Co. properly filed a financing statement. On August 1, Debtor filed for bankruptcy. Finance Co.'s security interest is perfected and has priority over Bank's unperfected security interest and over claims of Debtor's other unsecured creditors (to the extent of the value of the equipment).

---

   2) The rights of a **lien creditor**. Lien creditors include (a) a creditor who acquires a lien by judicial process, (b) an assignee for the benefit of creditors, or (c) a trustee in bankruptcy.

      a) The rights of lien creditors are subordinate to a prior perfected security interest.

EXAMPLE 20-14 **Bankruptcy Trustee vs. Unperfected Security Interest**

Bank has an unperfected security interest in Debtor's equipment as of June 1. Debtor files a petition in bankruptcy on August 1. The bankruptcy trustee has priority over Bank's security interest as of August 1. Knowledge of the unperfected claim by the trustee is not relevant to priority.

---

   3) A buyer of tangible chattel paper, documents, goods, instruments, or certificated securities who gives value, takes delivery, and has no knowledge of the security interest.

b. An unperfected security interest has priority over claims of the debtor's general creditors.

EXAMPLE 20-15	Unperfected Security Interest vs. General Creditors

Bank lends Debtor $15,000 and takes a security interest in Debtor's fleet of trucks. Bank fails to perfect the security interest by filing or taking possession of the collateral. Second Bank lends Debtor $20,000 but does not take a security interest in collateral. In a priority contest between Bank and Second Bank, Bank prevails.

3. **Priority of Perfected Interests**

    a. Priority usually dates from the time of filing or perfection, whichever is first.

EXAMPLE 20-16	Priority of Perfected Interests

Bank agreed to lend Debtor up to $50,000 as needed during the next year. On January 2, Year 1, Debtor executed a financing statement covering all owned or after-acquired equipment. The statement included a future advances clause. Bank filed the financing statement on January 3. Finance, Inc., lent Debtor $10,000 on March 1. Debtor executed a financing statement covering all owned or after-acquired equipment. Finance perfected its security interest by filing the financing statement on March 9. On July 1, Bank lent Debtor $30,000. On July 31, Debtor declared bankruptcy. Bank's security interest has priority over Finance's security interest because Bank filed before Finance filed or perfected. If Bank's financing statement had been filed on July 1, rather than on January 3, Finance's security interest would have priority over Bank's security interest. Finance's priority would date from March 9 and Bank's from July 1. Further, Bank's security interest would cover all $80,000 since it contained a future advances clause.

   b. Without filing or perfection in a subsequent period, priority no longer dates from the time of filing or perfection. Thus, the filing or perfection must be continuous.

EXAMPLE 20-17	Need for Perfection to Be Continuous

In Example 20-16, assuming no bankruptcy, Bank's filed financing statement lapses on January 3, Year 6. On January 4, Year 6, assuming no filing of a continuation statement, Finance has a perfected security interest and Bank has an unperfected security interest.

   c. If the security agreement contains a **future advances** clause, the perfected security interest ordinarily has the same priority for future advances as for the first advance.

       1) A future advances clause permits the secured party to advance additional funds to the borrower using the same collateral, for example, when the agreement is for a continuing line of credit.

EXAMPLE 20-18	Future Advances Clause

Bank lends David $50,000 to purchase equipment. David gives Bank a security interest in the equipment. A future advances clause provides that the liability for any funds lent by Bank to David in the future will be secured by the original equipment.

4. **Buyers of Goods**
   a. Generally, a perfected security interest in goods is effective against subsequent purchasers. However, certain third parties may acquire the collateral (goods) free of the security interest, even though the interest has been perfected.
      1) A buyer in the **ordinary course of business** (other than a buyer of farm products from a farmer) is not subject to any security interest given by the seller to another. The buyer's knowledge of the security interest is only relevant if the buyer knows that the purchase violates that interest.

EXAMPLE 20-19	Buyer in the Ordinary Course of Business

Family Grocery purchased frozen yogurt from Wholesaler. Wholesaler had given a security interest in its inventory to Freezers, Inc. Freezers had properly perfected the security interest. The president of Wholesaler disclosed the security interest to Family's president before selling the yogurt. If Wholesaler defaults on its obligation to Freezers, Freezers cannot exercise its rights as a secured party against Family.

      2) A buyer of **consumer goods from a consumer** is not subject to a security interest if the purchase is (a) made without knowledge of the security interest, (b) for value, (c) for consumer purposes, and (d) **prior to the secured party's filing**.

EXAMPLE 20-20	Buyer of Consumer Goods from a Consumer

Sam bought a dining table (a consumer good) from Tables, Inc., on credit. Tables took a purchase money security interest in the dining table that was automatically perfected. Several months later, Sam paid 50% of the purchase price to Tables. Sam then sold the table to Don. Don, unaware of Tables' security interest, paid $200 for the table and placed it in his dining room. Tables' security interest is unenforceable against Don. However, if Tables had filed a financing statement before Don purchased the table, Tables' security interest would be enforceable against Don.

5. **Purchase Money Security Interests (PMSIs)**
   a. A perfected PMSI in **goods (other than inventory)** has priority over a conflicting security interest in the goods if the PMSI is perfected when, or within 20 days after, the debtor takes possession. This priority is recognized even if the conflicting interest was perfected first. Moreover, it ordinarily extends to a perfected security interest in the identifiable proceeds of goods.
      1) Even in bankruptcy, a secured creditor with a perfected PMSI may seek its remedy against the specific collateral.

EXAMPLE 20-21	PMSI in Goods (Other than Inventory)

On January 2, Bank lent Debtor $50,000 and took a security interest in Debtor's currently owned and after-acquired equipment. On June 2, Equip Corp. sold Debtor equipment on credit and took a PMSI in the equipment. On June 19, Equip perfected the PMSI. Equip has priority over Bank.

b. A perfected PMSI in **inventory** has priority over a conflicting security interest if
   1) The PMSI is perfected when the debtor takes possession,
   2) An authenticated notice is sent to the other secured party,
   3) The notice is received within 5 years before the debtor takes possession, and
   4) The notice describes the collateral and states that the sender has or expects to have a PMSI in the debtor's inventory.

6. **Liens Arising by Operation of Law**
   a. The holder of the lien typically has provided services or materials with respect to the goods in the ordinary course of business and has possession of the goods.
      1) With possession, the lien has priority over a perfected security interest unless a state statute provides otherwise.
      2) Without possession, the lien is subordinate to a perfected security interest.
      3) A lienholder's knowledge of a security interest does not affect priority.

EXAMPLE 20-22	Lien of Provider of Services

Debtor borrows $5,000 from Bank to purchase a car and conveys a security interest in the car to Bank. Bank perfects the security interest. A week later Debtor takes the car to Best Body Shop for a new paint job. Best Body Shop knew of Bank's security interest. When Best Body finishes the job, Debtor cannot pay. Best retains possession of the car. Debtor defaults on payment to the bank. Bank sues Best, demanding delivery of the car. Best alleges its lien is a statutory artisan's lien on personal property that has priority (based on possession) over Bank's perfected security interest. The court holds that Best's lien has priority. Best's awareness of Bank's interest is irrelevant.

You have completed the outline for this subunit.
Study multiple-choice questions 5 and 6 on page 588.

STOP & REVIEW

20.4 RIGHTS AND DUTIES OF DEBTORS, CREDITORS, AND THIRD PARTIES

1. **Possession or Control of Collateral**
   a. The secured party in possession of collateral is a **bailee** who is **strictly liable** for unauthorized use or misdelivery. The obligations and rights of the secured party in possession are to
      1) Use reasonable care at all times to preserve the collateral, for example, in the case of instruments or chattel paper, by preserving rights against prior parties. Failure to use reasonable care is negligence, and the bailee may be liable for damages.
      2) Keep the collateral identifiable, although interchangeable collateral, such as grain, may be commingled.
      3) Bear the cost of reasonable expenses incurred for preservation, use, or custody of the collateral, e.g., insurance and taxes.
         a) This cost is chargeable to the debtor.
         b) The debtor has the risk of accidental loss or damage to the extent effective insurance coverage is deficient.
   b. A secured party with possession or control may either
      1) Keep proceeds from the collateral as security (excluding money or funds) or
      2) Create a security interest in the collateral.
   c. A secured party must file a **termination statement** of record within 1 month if (1) the collateral consists of consumer goods, (2) no obligation is secured by the collateral, and (3) no commitment to give value exists.
      1) The filing must be within 20 days after receipt of an authenticated demand from the debtor, if earlier.
      2) If the property is not consumer goods, a termination statement must be filed or sent to the debtor within 20 days after the debtor makes an authenticated demand given that no obligation is secured and no commitment to give value exists.

2. **Duty to Respond to Requests**
   a. A secured party generally must comply with a debtor's request for an accounting (e.g., the unpaid amount of the debt), a statement of account, or a list of collateral within 14 days.

3. **Default**
   a. The secured party has three options if the debtor defaults: (1) Sue the debtor for the amount due (reduce the claim to a judgment for the deficiency), (2) peaceably take possession and dispose of the collateral, or (3) accept (retain) the collateral.

4. **Repossession**
   a. Upon the debtor's default, the secured party may resort to self-help repossession or repossession by judicial action.
      1) Self-help repossession is without judicial action. It must be peaceable.
      2) Repossession by judicial action requires a court order or judgment against the debtor.

b. After repossession, the secured party may **dispose** of the collateral by **public or private** sale. The debtor cannot prevent sale.

1) Reasonable authenticated **notice** of the disposition must be given to the debtor. Notice of public disposition must include the time and place. Notice of a private disposition must include only the time after which disposition may occur.

   a) Other appropriate parties must be notified. For example, failure to notify another secured party may result in liability.
   b) Notice is reasonable if the debtor has adequate time to protect its interests.
   c) The debtor may waive notice.
   d) Notice to other secured parties is unnecessary if the collateral is consumer goods. The reason is that a purchase money security interest (PMSI) in consumer goods is perfected by attachment alone.

EXAMPLE 20-23	Notice of Disposition

Leo, with a loan from Local Bank, purchases a van and a boat. He signs, with respect to each purchase, a promissory note for half the loan amount and a security agreement. Leo thereby conveys to Bank a security interest in both the van and the boat, each securing payment when due of half the remaining amount on the loan. Leo defaults on payments to Bank. Bank takes lawful possession of both van and boat. Bank sends proper written notice to Leo that the van will be sold at auction 4 weeks after date of notice. The boat and van are sold at auction. Bank sues Leo for a deficiency in the net proceeds. With regard to the half of the amount secured by the van, the court awards a judgment for the deficiency. Because no reasonable notice was given regarding the sale of the boat, Bank is not entitled to a deficiency judgment for the part of the loan it secured.

2) Notice to the debtor is **not** required if the collateral is normally sold on a recognized market, perishable, or likely to decline quickly in value.

3) All aspects of the disposition must be commercially reasonable, including the time, place, manner, method, and terms.

4) A secured party's disposition of collateral

   a) Transfers to a **transferee for value** all of the debtor's rights,
   b) Discharges the security interest under which the disposition was made, and
   c) Discharges subordinate security interests or liens (unless a statute provides otherwise).

5) A transferee who acts in good faith is not subject to prior interests even if the secured party does not comply with applicable requirements.

6) The secured party may buy the collateral at any public disposition. If the collateral is customarily sold in a recognized market or is the subject of widely distributed price quotations, the secured party may buy it at private disposition.

7) The **proceeds** of collection or enforcement are applied in the following order:

   a) Payment of reasonable expenses of collection or enforcement
   b) Satisfaction of the debt owed to the secured party
   c) Satisfaction of the debts owed to subordinate secured parties
   d) Payment of any surplus to the debtor

8) If the disposition is commercially reasonable but the proceeds are insufficient, the debtor is liable for any deficiency.

5. **Acceptance of the Collateral**
    a. Acceptance of the collateral (strict foreclosure) may be an alternative to disposition.
    b. The secured party keeps the collateral in satisfaction of the debt.
    c. The secured party must send an authenticated notice to other claimants.
    d. The debtor must consent to the acceptance.
    e. Acceptance of collateral in partial satisfaction of the obligation is **not** permitted if the collateral is consumer goods.
    f. Disposition is required if the amount paid is at least (1) 60% of the cash price in the case of a PMSI in consumer goods or (2) 60% of the principal amount of the secured obligation in the case of a non-PMSI in consumer goods.
        1) The secured party must dispose of collateral within 90 days of taking possession. But the debtor and all secondary obligors may agree to a longer period in an authenticated agreement.
    g. Acceptance of collateral is not permitted if the debtor or any other party that is required to receive notice objects within 20 days of having received such notice. Then the secured party must dispose of the collateral.

6. **The Debtor's Remedies**
    a. The debtor may **redeem** his or her interest in the collateral at any time before
        1) The debt is satisfied by acceptance of the collateral,
        2) The collateral has been collected,
        3) The collateral is disposed of, or
        4) A contract for the disposition of the collateral is entered into.
    b. The secured party's failure to comply with Article 9 provides the debtor with a right to damages for any resulting losses from the disposition of collateral.

STOP & REVIEW

You have completed the outline for this subunit.
Study multiple-choice questions 7 and 8 on page 589.

20.5 BANKRUPTCY ADMINISTRATION

1. The **U.S. Constitution** (Article I) gives Congress the exclusive power to establish "uniform Laws on the subject of Bankruptcies throughout the United States." The federal statute is the Bankruptcy Reform Act of 1978.

2. **The Bankruptcy Code**

    a. The objectives are to ensure that (1) debtor assets are fairly distributed to creditors and (2) the debtor is given a fresh start.

    b. This outline covers the specific proceedings under the following chapters of the Code:

       1) Chapter 7: Liquidation
       2) Chapter 11: Reorganization

    c. The following summarizes the eligibility for filing under Chapters 7 and 11.

Types of Bankruptcy	Eligible	Ineligible
Chapter 7 Liquidation (voluntary or involuntary)	Individuals, including couples (subject to disqualification by a means test) Partnerships Corporations	Municipalities (eligible under Ch. 9) Railroads Insurers Banks Credit unions S&Ls
Chapter 11 Reorganization (voluntary or involuntary)	Railroads Most persons that may be debtors under Chapter 7	Shareholders Commodities and stockbrokers Insurers Banks Credit unions S&Ls

3. **Administration of Proceedings**

    a. Each federal judicial district has its own bankruptcy court. A judge hears the case after the moving party files a petition that identifies the applicable chapter.

       1) The result is an estate consisting of the debtor's property (a) at the time of filing or (b) that becomes subject to the proceeding. It is a separate legal entity.
       2) Insolvency or any prior filing is **not** a requirement for filing a petition.

    b. The filing of **any** petition operates as an **automatic stay** of most civil actions, including those by secured parties and judgment creditors, against the debtor or his or her property until the court acts. The filed petition, however, does not terminate security interests or liens. The following are activities **not** stayed:

       1) Alimony and child support collection
       2) Criminal proceedings
       3) Issuance of a notice of tax deficiency

4. **Termination of the Stay**
   a. A secured creditor may ask the court to recognize the priority of the existing security interest and allow foreclosure.
   b. The stay may be terminated because of serial filings suggestive of bad faith or abuse. If a Chapter 7 or 11 case is filed within a year after dismissal of another case, the stay generally terminates after 30 days. However, the stay continues in effect if the new filing is shown to be in good faith. After a third filing within 1 year, the stay will not go into effect unless good faith is shown.

5. **Voluntary Proceedings**
   a. Most petitions are voluntary. Any person eligible to be a **debtor** under a chapter may file under it. The debtor need **not** be insolvent, and no minimum debt or number of creditors is required.
      1) A voluntary petition results in an **automatic order for relief**. In the order, the court assumes exclusive authority over the case. The mandatory creditors' meeting is held within a reasonable time after the order.

6. **Involuntary Proceedings**
   a. An involuntary petition may be filed against an eligible debtor exclusively under **Chapter 7** or **Chapter 11**. The number or timing of involuntary petitions is not limited.
      1) An involuntary petition may **not** be filed against the following:
         a) Farmers
         b) Banks
         c) Insurers
         d) Nonprofit corporations
         e) Railroads
         f) Persons who owe less than $16,750
      2) If the debtor has **12 or more** different creditors, any **3 or more** who together hold unsecured claims of at least $16,750 may file an involuntary petition.
      3) If the debtor has **fewer than 12** creditors, any **1 or more** who alone or together have unsecured claims of at least $16,750 may file an involuntary petition.
         a) Any creditors who are the debtor's employees or are insiders, e.g., officers or directors of a corporation, relatives, or a partner, are **not** counted.
      4) Filing an involuntary petition results in an **automatic stay** but does **not** result in an automatic order for relief. If the debtor does **not** oppose the petition, however, the court will enter an order for relief.

5) If the debtor opposes the petition, the court must hold a hearing, and the petitioner must post a bond to compensate a debtor if the case is dismissed.
   a) The court orders relief on behalf of the creditors if it finds that either of two **statutory grounds** for involuntary bankruptcy exists:
      i) The debtor is not paying undisputed debts as they become due.
      ii) Within 120 days before the filing of the petition, a custodian, assignee, or general receiver took possession of all or most of the debtor's property.
   b) If the case is dismissed, the creditors may have to pay the debtor's costs, attorney's fees, and damages caused when the trustee took possession of the debtor's property.
      i) A petitioner who acted in bad faith may have to pay punitive damages for harm caused to the debtor's reputation.

7. **Debtor Rights and Duties**
   a. The debtor may continue to use, acquire, and dispose of his or her property until the court orders otherwise. The debtor also may incur new debts and operate a business. If necessary, the court may order the appointment of a **temporary** trustee to preserve the debtor's assets.

8. **Trustees**
   a. Within a reasonable time after the order for relief, which may be delayed in an involuntary case, the U.S. Trustee (an administrator for a federal district court) appoints an **interim trustee**. The interim trustee (1) represents the debtor's estate, (2) investigates the financial affairs of the debtor, and (3) holds the first meeting of creditors.
      1) A trustee is required in a Chapter 7 case. A trustee is **not** required in a Chapter 11 case, but the court may order the appointment of an interim trustee who then may be elected by the creditors as the permanent trustee.
      2) Under Chapter 7, the **permanent** trustee may be elected by qualified creditors at their required meeting. But the interim trustee may continue to serve.
      3) Under all other chapters, the trustee, if any, is appointed.
      4) **Creditor committees** may be required or permitted. The committee is responsible for facilitating communication among the debtor, the trustee, and the creditors.

b. The following are among the powers of the trustee:
   1) Collecting and accounting for property
      a) But a court may allow the debtor to file a bond and reacquire property from the trustee.
   2) Performing investigations
   3) Voiding preferential transfers
      a) A voidable preferential transfer is made (1) to or for the benefit of a creditor, (2) for or on account of an antecedent (preexisting) debt but not for new value, (3) during the debtor's insolvency, (4) within 90 days prior to filing the petition, and (5) to allow the creditor to receive a larger portion of its claim than from a distribution in bankruptcy.
   4) Voiding fraudulent transfers
      a) A property transfer is voidable if it was made within 2 years prior to filing with actual **intent** to hinder, delay, or defraud creditors.
   5) Assuming and performing an unperformed contract or unexpired lease, rejecting it, or assigning it to a third party with court approval
      a) But rejection is assumed unless the trustee acts within 60 days after the order for relief.
   6) Operating the debtor's business
   7) Selling, using, or leasing estate property
   8) Investing estate money
   9) Hiring professionals
      a) A qualified trustee may perform professional services for reasonable compensation with court approval.
      b) Service as a trustee impairs a CPA's independence regarding the debtor.
   10) Filing reports
   11) Objecting to creditor claims
   12) Objecting to a discharge in a proper case
   13) Distributing assets and closing the estate

   NOTE: The trustee cannot void a statutory lien (e.g., an artisan's lien) effective before filing.

SUCCESS TIP

Be prepared to answer bankruptcy questions. The AICPA tests this topic often. Exam questions have tested the details of bankruptcy law, such as the number of creditors and dollar amounts involved in filing an involuntary bankruptcy petition against a debtor.

STOP & REVIEW

You have completed the outline for this subunit.
Study multiple-choice questions 9 through 12 beginning on page 590.

20.6 BANKRUPTCY LIQUIDATIONS

1. **Chapter 7**

    a. Liquidation converts a debtor's nonexempt assets to cash distributed in conformity with the Code.

     1) An honest debtor then is discharged from the remaining debts and given a fresh start.

    b. Eligible parties are most debtors, including individuals, partnerships, and corporations.

2. **Debtor's Estate**

    a. The estate consists of all the debtor's **nonexempt** interests in property at the beginning of the case.

     1) The estate **excludes** the following:

        a) Earnings of the debtor for services after the beginning of a Chapter 7 case
        b) Contributions to employee retirement plans
        c) Contributions made more than 365 days prior to filing to educational retirement accounts and state tuition programs
        d) Most property acquired after the filing of the petition

     2) The estate **includes** the following:

        a) All **nonexempt** property currently held (wherever located)
        b) Interests in property to which the debtor becomes entitled within **180 days** after filing, such as

            i) Life insurance payments
            ii) Divorce settlements
            iii) Inheritances
            iv) Receipts from property in the estate
            v) Property acquired by the estate after the commencement of the case
            vi) Property recovered by the trustee under the avoidance powers

3. **Exempt Assets**
    a. Exempt assets are basic necessities for a fresh start. Only individual debtors are eligible.
    b. **States** are permitted to require their citizens to accept the exemptions of property defined by state law. If a state has not rejected the federal exemptions, the debtor has a choice.
    c. The following are among the **federal exemptions**:
        1) Up to $25,150 in equity in the debtor's residence
        2) An interest in a motor vehicle up to $4,000
        3) An interest up to $625 in items of household goods and furnishings, clothing, appliances, books, animals, crops, or musical instruments, with a total limited to $13,400
        4) An interest in jewelry up to a value of $1,700
        5) Any other property worth up to $1,325, plus any unused part of the $25,150 exemption in item 1) above, up to $12,575
        6) An interest in tools of the debtor's trade up to a total value of $2,525
        7) Any unmatured life insurance contract owned by the debtor
        8) The right to receive Social Security, certain welfare benefits, veterans' benefits, disability benefits, alimony and support, and certain pension benefits
        9) The right to receive certain personal injury and other awards up to $25,150
        10) Unemployment compensation
        11) Amounts in tax exempt retirement accounts (federal or state exemptions)

4. **Claims**
    a. The distribution process commences with creditors' filing of proofs of claim.
        1) A proof of claim must be filed within **90 days** after the first meeting of creditors but only by unsecured creditors.
        2) A timely claim is allowed unless disallowed by the court after objection.

5. **Rights of Creditors**
    a. The following is the order of priority of creditors:
        1) Secured creditors (who become general creditors to the extent collateral is deficient),
        2) Priority creditors (unsecured), and
        3) General creditors (other unsecured creditors).
    b. Members of a higher class of **priority creditors** are paid in full before members of a lower class receive anything. If the assets are insufficient to pay all claims in a given class, the claimants in the class share pro rata.
        1) The classes of priority claims listed in order of payment are as follows:
            a) Domestic support obligations
            b) Claims for estate expenses
            c) Claims of tradespeople (gap creditors) who extend unsecured credit in the ordinary course of business after the filing of an involuntary petition but before the earlier of the appointment of a trustee or the entry of the order for relief

- d) Wages (compensation) up to $13,650 owed to employees earned within 180 days prior to the earlier of (1) filing or (2) cessation of the debtor's business
- e) Certain contributions owed to the debtor's employee benefit plans resulting from employee services performed within 180 days prior to the earlier of (1) filing or (2) cessation of the debtor's business
- f) Claims of grain or fish producers up to $6,725 each for grain or fish deposited with the debtor but not paid for or returned
- g) Claims of consumers for the return of up to $3,025 each in deposits
- h) Certain income and other taxes owed to governmental entities
- i) Death and injury claims from operation of a motor vehicle by a legally intoxicated person

c. If any money remains after payments to secured creditors and priority creditors, the timely filed claims of **general creditors** are paid.

6. **Discharge**

    a. Individual debtors under Chapter 7 may receive a discharge from most debts that are unpaid after distribution of the debtor's estate, including the unsatisfied part of a secured debt.

    1) A discharge frees the debtor from further liability on certain debts.
    2) The court generally grants a discharge in a Chapter 7 proceeding.
    3) Corporations and partnerships cannot receive a Chapter 7 discharge.
    4) Most debtors are eligible for a discharge only once every 8 years.

    b. The following are grounds for **denial of a general discharge**:

    1) Fraudulently transferring or concealing (a) property within 1 year preceding the filing of the bankruptcy petition or (b) the property of the estate after filing
    2) Unjustifiably concealing or destroying business records or failing to keep adequate business records
    3) Making a false oath, a fraudulent account, or a false claim
    4) Failing to explain satisfactorily any loss or deficiency of assets
    5) Refusing to testify or to obey lawful orders of the court
    6) Filing a written waiver of discharge approved by the court
    7) Giving or receiving a bribe in connection with the case
    8) Committing within 1 year before filing any of these acts in a case involving an insider
    9) Being subject to a proceeding that may limit the homestead exemption
    10) Failing to complete a personal financial management course

---

EXAMPLE 20-24   Denial of General Discharge -- Fraudulent Transfer

On June 9, Amy Aker transferred property she owned to her son. The property was collateral for Aker's obligation to Simon. Aker transferred the property with the intent to defraud Simon. On July 7, Aker filed a voluntary bankruptcy petition. Because Aker transferred the property with the intent to defraud Simon within 1 year of filing the petition for relief, she will be denied a general discharge.

c. **Nondischargeable debts** include
   1) Most taxes, including federal income tax coming due within 3 years prior to bankruptcy
   2) Debts incurred on the basis of materially false financial statements if
      a) They were issued with the intent to deceive and
      b) The creditor reasonably relied on them.
   3) Unscheduled debts not included in required filings in time to permit a creditor without notice of the case to timely file a proof of claim
   4) Debts resulting from fraud (including securities fraud), misrepresentation, embezzlement, larceny, or breach of fiduciary duty but **not** negligence
   5) Debts resulting from alimony, maintenance, or child support awards
   6) Debts resulting from willful and malicious (but not unintentional) injury to another person or conversion of that person's property
   7) Debts resulting from certain educational loans made, funded, or guaranteed by a governmental unit
   8) Governmental fines and penalties, except those relating to dischargeable taxes
   9) Debts resulting from liability for operating a motor vehicle while legally intoxicated

7. **Dismissal**
   a. If a Chapter 7 case is dismissed, the debtor is not discharged.

8. **Revocation of a Discharge**
   a. A discharge previously granted may be revoked within 1 year if the trustee or a creditor proves that
      1) The discharge was obtained fraudulently,
      2) The debtor knowingly and fraudulently retained property of the estate, or
      3) The debtor failed to obey a court order.

STOP & REVIEW

You have completed the outline for this subunit.
Study multiple-choice questions 13 through 17 beginning on page 591.

20.7 REORGANIZATIONS

1. **Chapter 11 Plans**
   a. Partnerships, corporations, railroads, and debtors qualified for relief under Chapter 7 (except stock or commodity brokers) are eligible for a **reorganization**, not a liquidation. This procedure allows for
      1) A debtor (including an individual or a business) to restructure its finances,
      2) The business to continue, and
      3) The creditors to be paid.
   b. A case is commenced by filing a petition requesting an order for relief.
      1) Petitions may be **voluntary or involuntary**.
      2) A petition results in a suspension of creditors' actions.
      3) An involuntary petition must meet the Chapter 7 tests.
      4) Insolvency is not a condition precedent to a voluntary petition.
   c. An individual or company seeking protection under Chapter 11 generally is permitted to operate its own business as a **debtor-in-possession** with the rights and duties of a trustee.
      1) A court may appoint an examiner to investigate fraud, misconduct, or mismanagement if all of the following apply:
         a) Appointment is requested by an interested party.
         b) It is in the interests of creditors or equity security holders.
         c) The debtor's fixed, undisputed, unsecured debts exceed $5 million.
   d. A **committee of unsecured creditors** is appointed as soon as feasible after an order for relief has been granted. The committee generally consists of persons holding the seven largest unsecured claims.
   e. A **plan of reorganization** must be prepared and filed.
      1) The **debtor** has the exclusive right to file a plan during the 120 days after the order for relief and may file a plan at any time. If the creditors or shareholders do not approve the plan within 180 days, **any party** may file. Moreover, any party may file if a trustee has been appointed.
   f. A reorganization plan must (1) divide creditors' claims and shareholders' interests into classes, (2) state the treatment of each class and whether it is impaired, and (3) provide for payment. Members of each class must be treated equally unless they agree otherwise.
      1) A class is **impaired** unless the plan leaves its legal, equitable, and contractual rights unaltered.

g. The **court's confirmation** of the plan binds the debtor, creditors, equity security holders, and others. Confirmation may occur after acceptance or by cramdown.

   1) **Acceptance** by a **class** of claims requires the holders of more than 50% of the claims representing at least two-thirds of the dollar totals to approve the plan. A class of equity interests accepts the plan if the holders of at least two-thirds of the voting interests in dollar amount approve.

      a) To avoid a cramdown, the plan must be accepted by each class unless it is not adversely affected by the plan.
      b) The court may not confirm a plan not in the creditors' best interests.
      c) A spouse or child whose claims will not be paid in cash may block the plan.

   2) The bankruptcy court may confirm (approve and put into effect) the plan only if

      a) It is proposed in good faith,
      b) It provides for full payment of administrative expenses,
      c) Each class has accepted the plan or its interests are not impaired, and
      d) Each member of an impaired class has

         i) Accepted the plan or
         ii) Will receive at least the amount (s)he would have received under Chapter 7.

   3) Confirmation over the objection of one or more classes is a **cramdown**. The court may confirm if the other requirements are met and

      a) At least one impaired class (but not an insider) accepts the plan.
      b) The court finds that the plan is fair to the interests of the impaired class, e.g., secured creditors retain their security interests and payments equal the present value of the collateral.
      c) The court finds that the plan does not discriminate unfairly against any creditors.

h. After confirmation, the plan is implemented, and assets are distributed accordingly.

i. After the debtor has made all payments required under the plan, a debtor that is not an individual is **discharged** from debts incurred prior to confirmation of the plan except as provided in (1) the plan, (2) the confirmation order, or (3) the Bankruptcy Code.

SU 20: Secured Transactions and Debtor-Creditor Relationships 585

1) An individual's nondischargeable debts under Chapter 7 cannot be discharged under Chapter 11.

CHAPTER 11 REORGANIZATION

DEBTOR
↓
FILING OF PETITION
(voluntary or involuntary)
with
FEDERAL BANKRUPTCY COURT
↓
ORDER FOR RELIEF
↓
APPOINTMENT OF COMMITTEE
OF UNSECURED CREDITORS
↓
PLAN FILED ————→ Acceptance or Cramdown
↓
CONFIRMATION
BY COURT
↓
IF APPROPRIATE,
DEBTOR DISCHARGED

Figure 20-1

STOP & REVIEW

You have completed the outline for this subunit.
Study multiple-choice questions 18 through 20 beginning on page 593.

QUESTIONS

20.1 Security Interests and Attachment

1. Under the UCC Secured Transactions Article, for a security interest to attach, the

A. Debtor must agree to the creation of the security interest.
B. Creditor must properly file a financing statement.
C. Debtor must have title to the collateral.
D. Creditor must be in possession of part of the collateral.

Answer (A) is correct.
REQUIRED: The condition necessary for attachment.
DISCUSSION: Attachment occurs when the security interest is enforceable against the debtor with regard to the collateral. It is enforceable against the debtor and third parties when (1) the secured party has given value, (2) the debtor has rights in the collateral, and (3) the debtor has authenticated a security agreement describing the collateral or other evidence of authentication exists (e.g., the secured party has possession or control). Accordingly, a security agreement (a contract) must exist. It grants the secured party a security interest in described collateral, and the debtor must agree to the creation of a security interest.
Answer (B) is incorrect. Filing is not mandatory for attachment, but it may be necessary to perfect a security interest. **Answer (C) is incorrect.** The debtor must have rights in the collateral or the power to transfer those rights. However, the debtor need not have title to the collateral. **Answer (D) is incorrect.** Possession of the collateral in accordance with the security agreement is an alternative to the requirement that the security agreement be authenticated by the debtor.

2. Under the UCC Secured Transactions Article, which of the following after-acquired property may be covered by a debtor's security agreement with a secured lender?

	Inventory	Equipment
A.	Yes	Yes
B.	Yes	No
C.	No	Yes
D.	No	No

Answer (A) is correct.
REQUIRED: The scope of an after-acquired property clause.
DISCUSSION: A security agreement may provide for a security interest in after-acquired property. The security interest does not attach to consumer goods, unless the debtor acquires rights in them within 10 days after the secured party gives value. An after-acquired property clause can apply to both inventory and equipment.

20.2 Perfection of Security Interests

3. Perfection of a security interest permits the secured party to protect its rights by

A. Avoiding the need to file a financing statement.
B. Preventing another creditor from obtaining a security interest in the same collateral.
C. Establishing priority over the claims of most subsequent secured creditors.
D. Denying the debtor the right to possess the collateral.

Answer (C) is correct.
REQUIRED: The true statement about perfection of a security interest.
DISCUSSION: Unless perfection is by attachment, to establish priority over a previous unperfected creditor or a subsequent secured creditor, a secured party must give notice by perfecting its security interest. The methods of perfection include (1) filing a financing statement, (2) taking possession of the collateral, or (3) obtaining control of the collateral. The steps taken will depend upon the nature of the collateral.
Answer (A) is incorrect. Filing a financing statement is required to perfect an interest in certain types of collateral, such as the debtor's inventory not in the possession of the secured party. **Answer (B) is incorrect.** Perfection of a security interest does not bar other creditors from obtaining a security interest in the same collateral. **Answer (D) is incorrect.** Possession is one means of perfecting a security interest, but the parties ordinarily expect the debtor to maintain possession.

4. Burn Manufacturing borrowed $500,000 from Howard Finance Co., secured by Burn's current and future inventory, accounts receivable, and its proceeds. Burn's representative authenticated a sufficient security agreement that described the collateral. The security agreement was filed in the appropriate state office. Burn subsequently defaulted on the repayment of the loan, and Howard attempted to enforce its security interest. Burn contended that Howard's security interest was unenforceable. In addition, Green, who subsequently gave credit to Burn without knowledge of Howard's security interest and filed a financing statement but did not have a purchase money security interest (PMSI) in inventory, is also attempting to defeat Howard's alleged security interest. The security interest in question is valid with respect to

A. Both Burn and Green.
B. Neither Burn nor Green.
C. Burn but not Green.
D. Green but not Burn.

Answer (A) is correct.
REQUIRED: The true statement about the validity of a security interest in inventory, both current and after-acquired, and accounts receivable.
DISCUSSION: Before attachment of the security interest, the creditor gave value, the debtor had rights in the collateral, and the debtor authenticated a sufficient security agreement. Thus, attachment has occurred, and the security interest is enforceable between the debtor (Burn) and the secured party (Howard). Because Howard's security interest was perfected by filing a financing statement, Green is assumed to have notice of Howard's security interest. Howard's claim has priority over Green's because Howard filed and perfected before Green. However, if Green had perfected a PMSI in inventory and met the notice requirements, Green would have priority.

20.3 Priorities

5. On June 15, Harper purchased equipment for $100,000 from Imperial Corp. for use in its manufacturing process. Harper paid for the equipment with funds borrowed from Eastern Bank. Harper gave Eastern an authenticated security agreement covering Harper's existing and after-acquired equipment. On June 21, Harper was petitioned involuntarily into bankruptcy under Chapter 7 of the Federal Bankruptcy Code. A bankruptcy trustee was appointed. On June 23, Eastern duly filed a sufficient financing statement. Which of the parties will have a superior security interest in the equipment?

A. The trustee in bankruptcy, because the filing of the financing statement after the commencement of the bankruptcy case would be deemed a preferential transfer.

B. The trustee in bankruptcy, because the trustee became a lien creditor before Eastern perfected its security interest.

C. Eastern, because it had a perfected purchase money security interest without having to file a financing statement.

D. Eastern, because it perfected its security interest within the permissible time limits.

Answer (D) is correct.
REQUIRED: The party with a superior security interest in equipment after bankruptcy.
DISCUSSION: The equipment is purchase money collateral that secures the purchase money obligation arising from the lender's giving value to permit the debtor to obtain rights in the collateral. Thus, Eastern Bank has a purchase money security interest (PMSI). A PMSI in goods other than inventory or livestock has priority over a perfected conflicting security interest in the same collateral if it is perfected at the time the debtor receives possession of the collateral or within 20 days thereafter. Even in bankruptcy proceedings, a secured creditor with a perfected security interest may pursue its remedy against the particular property. Thus, Eastern Bank's perfected PMSI in the equipment is superior (it is not inventory). However, the trustee in bankruptcy has the status of a hypothetical lien creditor and can defeat a nonperfected security interest in the equipment.
Answer (A) is incorrect. Filing is not a transfer. It perfects the PMSI. **Answer (B) is incorrect.** Eastern could perfect its PMSI and retain its priority in the equipment by filing for up to 20 days after the debtor received possession. **Answer (C) is incorrect.** Filing was required for perfection, even though it could be done up to 20 days after the debtor received possession of the collateral.

6. Under the UCC Secured Transactions Article, what is the order of priority for the following security interests in store equipment?

I. Security interest perfected by filing on April 15.

II. Security interest attached on April 1.

III. Purchase money security interest attached April 11 and perfected by filing on April 20.

A. I, III, II.
B. II, I, III.
C. III, I, II.
D. III, II, I.

Answer (C) is correct.
REQUIRED: The order of priority for the security interests in equipment.
DISCUSSION: The basic rule is that conflicting security interests in the same collateral will rank in priority according to the time of filing or perfection. If a purchase money security interest (PMSI) in goods (e.g., equipment) other than inventory or livestock is perfected when the debtor receives possession of the collateral, or within 20 days afterward, the PMSI has priority over a conflicting security interest even if it was perfected first. The reasonable assumption is that the debtor took possession between April 11 (when the security interest attached) and April 20 (when perfection occurred). Furthermore, a perfected security interest generally has priority over a security interest that has attached but is not perfected.

20.4 Rights and Duties of Debtors, Creditors, and Third Parties

7. Under the UCC Secured Transactions Article, if a debtor is in default under a payment obligation secured by goods, the secured party has the right to

	Reduce the Claim to a Judgment	Sell the Goods and Apply the Proceeds toward the Obligations Secured	Peacefully Repossess the Goods without Judicial Process
A.	Yes	Yes	No
B.	Yes	No	Yes
C.	No	Yes	Yes
D.	Yes	Yes	Yes

Answer (D) is correct.
REQUIRED: The rights of a secured party when a debtor defaults on a payment obligation.
DISCUSSION: After default by a debtor, a secured party essentially may choose among three remedies. The secured party may (1) sue the debtor for the amount owed (reduce the claim to judgment); (2) peaceably take possession of (foreclose on) the collateral, with or without judicial process, and dispose of it in a commercially reasonable manner that includes applying the proceeds to the costs of disposition and to the obligations secured; and (3) accept (retain) the collateral in full or partial satisfaction of the obligations secured if certain conditions, for example, consent of the debtor, are met. These remedies are cumulative and allow the creditor, if unsuccessful by one method, to pursue another remedy. They also may be exercised simultaneously.

8. Under the UCC Secured Transactions Article, which of the following statements is most likely true concerning the disposition of collateral by a secured creditor after a debtor's default?

A. A good-faith transferee for value and without knowledge of any defects in the sale takes free of any subordinate liens or security interests.

B. The debtor may not redeem the collateral after the default.

C. Secured creditors with subordinate claims retain the right to redeem the collateral after the collateral is sold to a third party.

D. The collateral may only be disposed of at a public sale.

Answer (A) is correct.
REQUIRED: The statement most likely to be true about disposition of collateral.
DISCUSSION: When a secured party disposes of collateral after default, (1) the transferee for value receives all of the debtor's rights in the collateral, (2) the security interest under which the disposition occurs is discharged, and (3) subordinate security interests or liens are discharged unless a specific statute provides for a lien that is not dischargeable in this manner. As long as the transferee acts in good faith, (s)he will receive the property free of the foregoing interests even if the secured party does not comply with the requirements for the sale under Article 9 or any judicial proceeding.
Answer (B) is incorrect. The debtor always may redeem his or her interest in the collateral after default and before the secured party (1) collects the collateral (e.g., from account debtors); (2) disposes of, or enters into a contract for disposition of, the collateral; or (3) accepts collateral in full or partial satisfaction of the obligations secured. **Answer (C) is incorrect.** A good-faith transferee for value takes the property free of any subordinate security interests or liens unless a specific statute provides for a lien that is not dischargeable in this manner. **Answer (D) is incorrect.** Disposition sales may be either public or private.

20.5 Bankruptcy Administration

9. Green owes the following amounts to unsecured creditors: Rice, $5,700; Zwick, $5,200; Young, $16,800; and Zinc, $5,900. Green has not paid any creditor since January 1, Year 1. On March 15, Year 1, Green's sole asset, a cabin cruiser, was seized by Xeno Marine Co., the holder of a perfected security interest in the boat. On July 1, Year 1, Rice, Zwick, and Zinc involuntarily petitioned Green into bankruptcy under Chapter 7 of the Federal Bankruptcy Code. If Green opposes the involuntary petition, the petition will be

A. Upheld because the three filing creditors are owed more than $16,750.
B. Upheld because one creditor is owed more than $16,750.
C. Dismissed because there are fewer than 12 creditors.
D. Dismissed because the boat was seized more than 90 days before the filing.

Answer (A) is correct.
REQUIRED: The status of an involuntary petition under Chapter 7.
DISCUSSION: If the debtor has fewer than 12 creditors, any 1 or more creditors who alone or together have unsecured claims of $16,750 or more can file an involuntary petition under Chapter 7 or Chapter 11. If the debtor has 12 or more creditors, any 3 or more who together hold unsecured claims of at least $16,750 can file an involuntary petition. The three filers are owed $16,800 ($5,700 + $5,200 + $5,900).
Answer (B) is incorrect. Young did not join in filing the petition. **Answer (C) is incorrect.** A debtor with fewer than 12 creditors may be involuntarily petitioned into bankruptcy by one or more creditors who alone or together are owed more than $16,750. **Answer (D) is incorrect.** A challenged involuntary petition is not dismissed if the debtor is generally not paying his or her bills as they become due or, within 120 days before filing, a custodian or receiver took possession of all or most of the debtor's property to enforce a lien against the property.

10. To file for bankruptcy under Chapter 7 of the Federal Bankruptcy Code, an individual must

A. Have debts of any amount.
B. Be insolvent.
C. Be indebted to more than three creditors.
D. Have debts in excess of $16,750.

Answer (A) is correct.
REQUIRED: The requirement to file for protection under Chapter 7 of the Bankruptcy Code.
DISCUSSION: Under Chapter 7, generally, a debtor's nonexempt assets are converted into cash, the cash is distributed among creditors, and the debtor is discharged from most remaining obligations. Any person eligible to be a debtor under Chapter 7 may file a petition.
Answer (B) is incorrect. Insolvency is not required to file a voluntary petition. It is only necessary that the person be under Chapter 7. **Answer (C) is incorrect.** Number-of-creditors thresholds apply only to involuntary petitions filed by creditors. **Answer (D) is incorrect.** Amount-of-debt thresholds apply only to involuntary petitions.

11. A party involuntarily petitioned into bankruptcy under Chapter 7 of the Federal Bankruptcy Code who succeeds in having the petition dismissed could recover

	Court Costs and Attorney's Fees	Compensatory Damages	Punitive Damages
A.	Yes	Yes	Yes
B.	Yes	Yes	No
C.	No	Yes	Yes
D.	Yes	No	No

Answer (A) is correct.
REQUIRED: The recovery allowed a debtor whose involuntary bankruptcy was dismissed.
DISCUSSION: A debtor who successfully contests an involuntary bankruptcy petition could recover his or her costs, including reasonable attorney's fees. The court may require the petitioner to pay damages if (s)he is found to have acted in bad faith. A petitioner whose conduct is malicious or otherwise egregious also may be required to pay punitive damages.

SU 20: Secured Transactions and Debtor-Creditor Relationships

12. Which of the following statements is true with respect to a voluntary bankruptcy proceeding under the liquidation provisions of the Bankruptcy Code?

A. The debtor must be insolvent.
B. The liabilities of the debtor must total $16,750 or more.
C. It may be properly commenced and maintained by any person who is insolvent.
D. The filing of the bankruptcy petition constitutes an order for relief.

Answer (D) is correct.
REQUIRED: The true statement about a voluntary bankruptcy proceeding.
DISCUSSION: The voluntary bankruptcy petition is a formal request by the debtor to the court for an order for relief. Under the liquidation provisions, an order for relief is automatically given to the debtor upon the filing of the petition.
Answer (A) is incorrect. Insolvency is not required. A statement that the debtor has debts is all that is needed. **Answer (B) is incorrect.** A voluntary bankruptcy proceeding requires no minimum amount of debtor liabilities. **Answer (C) is incorrect.** The courts have discretion not to grant relief that would constitute a substantial abuse of the bankruptcy laws. Also, certain entities, e.g., banks, are not eligible for voluntary bankruptcy.

20.6 Bankruptcy Liquidations

13. Which asset is included in a debtor's bankruptcy estate in a liquidation proceeding?

A. Proceeds from a life insurance policy received 90 days after the petition was filed.
B. An inheritance received 270 days after the petition was filed.
C. Property from a divorce settlement received 365 days after the petition was filed.
D. Wages earned by the debtor after the petition was filed.

Answer (A) is correct.
REQUIRED: The asset included in a debtor's bankruptcy estate.
DISCUSSION: Most assets in which the debtor has a legal or equitable interest at the date Chapter 7 proceedings began are included in the estate. Other property may be added to the estate. For example, it includes property acquired by the debtor within 180 days after filing the petition if the property was acquired (1) by inheritance, (2) as proceeds of a life insurance policy, or (3) from a property settlement in a divorce case.

14. A person who voluntarily filed for bankruptcy and received a discharge under Chapter 7 of the Federal Bankruptcy Code

A. May obtain another voluntary discharge in bankruptcy under Chapter 7 after 5 years have elapsed from the date of the prior filing.
B. Will receive a discharge of all debts owed.
C. Is precluded from owning or operating a similar business for 2 years.
D. Must surrender for distribution to the creditors any amount received as an inheritance within 180 days after filing the petition.

Answer (D) is correct.
REQUIRED: The true statement about a discharge under Chapter 7.
DISCUSSION: The bankruptcy estate available for distribution to creditors includes all the debtor's nonexempt legal and equitable interests in property on the date of filing. It includes proceeds and profits from that estate. Certain property acquired after filing is also included: inheritances, property settlements (divorce), and life insurance proceeds to which the debtor becomes entitled within 180 days after filing.
Answer (A) is incorrect. Discharge is barred if there was a Chapter 7 discharge within the 8 years preceding filing the petition. **Answer (B) is incorrect.** Certain debts are nondischargeable. **Answer (C) is incorrect.** A debtor who receives a Chapter 7 discharge may own or operate a similar business without a time restriction.

15. Which of the following transfers by a debtor, within 90 days of filing for bankruptcy, could be set aside as a preferential payment?

A. Making a gift to charity.
B. Paying a business utility bill.
C. Borrowing money from a bank secured by giving a mortgage on business property.
D. Prepaying an installment loan on inventory.

Answer (D) is correct.
REQUIRED: The transfer that is preferential.
DISCUSSION: A preferential transfer is made for the benefit of a creditor within 90 days prior to filing the petition and on account of an antecedent (preexisting) debt. The transfer must have (1) been made when the debtor was insolvent and (2) resulted in the creditor's receipt of a larger portion of its claim than it otherwise would have received as a distribution in bankruptcy. A prepayment is on account of an existing debt and is therefore a voidable preference.
Answer (A) is incorrect. A gift to a charity is not on account of an antecedent (preexisting) debt. Answer (B) is incorrect. Payment of accounts payable in the ordinary course of the debtor's business is not a voidable preference. Answer (C) is incorrect. A contemporaneous exchange between the debtor and another, even a creditor, for new value may not be set aside. The transfer of a security interest enables the debtor to acquire the new property.

16. Which of the following claims will be paid first in the distribution of a bankruptcy estate under the liquidation provisions of Chapter 7 of the Bankruptcy Code if the petition was filed July 15, Year 1?

A. A secured debt properly perfected on March 20, Year 1.
B. Inventory purchased and delivered August 1, Year 1.
C. Employee wages due April 30, Year 1.
D. A federal tax lien filed June 30, Year 1.

Answer (A) is correct.
REQUIRED: The claim paid first.
DISCUSSION: The Bankruptcy Code classifies creditors into several categories according to the priority of their claims against the debtor. It states that secured creditors' claims will be satisfied in full to the extent of the value of the security before unsecured creditors' claims will be considered. To the extent the security is insufficient, the secured creditor becomes an unsecured creditor. The tax lien, even if a security interest, would have lower priority than the secured debt perfected earlier.
Answer (B) is incorrect. A secured claim has priority over the inventory purchase before unsecured claims are satisfied. Answer (C) is incorrect. The secured claim has priority over employee wages. Answer (D) is incorrect. Even if the federal tax lien is a secured claim, the first perfected of two security interests has priority.

17. Debtor's business was not paying its undisputed debts as they became due. Intending to protect the assets, Debtor transferred them to a corporation controlled by a sibling. The understanding was that Debtor would receive stock after resolution of the financial problems. Five months later, Debtor filed for bankruptcy. Will a trustee who has discovered the transfer be able to recover the assets?

A. The trustee cannot recover the assets because the transfer was more than 90 days before the petition was filed in bankruptcy.
B. The assets can be recovered as a fraudulent conveyance.
C. The assets can be recovered as a preferential transfer.
D. The assets cannot be recovered because the corporation is a separate legal entity.

Answer (B) is correct.
REQUIRED: The true statement about recovery of assets transferred by a debtor prior to bankruptcy.
DISCUSSION: A fraudulent conveyance is one made with actual intent to hinder, delay, or defraud creditors. A conveyance is also fraudulent if it results in insolvency or if the debtor receives less than a reasonable value while (s)he is insolvent. Fraudulent conveyances are voidable if the transfers are made within 2 years before the petition is filed. Thus, without regard to whether the new corporation had knowledge of the fraud or insolvency, the trustee can recover the assets because they were transferred with the intent to defraud creditors within 2 years of bankruptcy.
Answer (A) is incorrect. The trustee can recover the assets. They were fraudulently transferred within 2 years prior to the bankruptcy. **Answer (C) is incorrect.** The transfer was not a preferential transfer but a fraudulent conveyance. A preferential transfer is made when one creditor is preferred over another. **Answer (D) is incorrect.** A fraudulent conveyance is voidable no matter to whom the transfer was made.

20.7 Reorganizations

18. Under Chapter 11 of the Federal Bankruptcy Code, which of the following would **not** be eligible for reorganization?

A. Retail sole proprietorship.
B. Advertising partnership.
C. CPA professional corporation.
D. Savings and loan association.

Answer (D) is correct.
REQUIRED: The entity ineligible for Chapter 11 reorganization.
DISCUSSION: Reorganization under Chapter 11 of the Bankruptcy Code is available only for eligible debtors. These include partnerships and corporations, railroads, and any person that may be a debtor under Chapter 7 (but not stock or commodity brokers). Ineligible debtors under Chapter 7 include municipalities, insurance companies, banks, credit unions, and savings and loan associations.

19. Under Chapter 11 of the Federal Bankruptcy Code, which of the following actions is necessary before the court may confirm a reorganization plan?

A. Provision for full payment of administration expenses.
B. Acceptance of the plan by all classes of claimants.
C. Preparation of a contingent plan of liquidation.
D. Appointment of a trustee.

Answer (A) is correct.
REQUIRED: The prerequisite to court confirmation of a reorganization plan.
DISCUSSION: The debtor generally has the exclusive right to file a reorganization plan during the 120 days after the order of relief. To be effective, the plan must be confirmed by the bankruptcy court. The plan must provide for full payment of administration expenses.
Answer (B) is incorrect. A plan that is fair and equitable may be confirmed without approval of all classes of creditors (a cramdown plan). **Answer (C) is incorrect.** Chapter 11 enables restructuring instead of liquidation. A contingent plan of liquidation is not required. **Answer (D) is incorrect.** The court has discretion to appoint a trustee given evidence of dishonesty or mismanagement or if such action is in the best interests of the parties. But the debtor normally remains in possession of his or her assets and continues to operate the business.

20. Under the reorganization provisions of Chapter 11 of the Federal Bankruptcy Code, after a reorganization plan is confirmed and a final decree closing the proceedings entered, which of the following events usually occurs?

A. A reorganized corporate debtor will be liquidated.
B. A reorganized corporate debtor will be discharged from all debts except as otherwise provided in the plan and applicable law.
C. A trustee will continue to operate the debtor's business.
D. A reorganized individual debtor will not be allowed to continue in the same business.

Answer (B) is correct.
REQUIRED: The status of a debtor after completing a Chapter 11 reorganization.
DISCUSSION: At the conclusion of Chapter 11 proceedings, a corporate debtor is discharged from most debts of the business. Exceptions include debts that are provided for in the plan of reorganization approved by the creditors and certain nondischargeable debts.
Answer (A) is incorrect. A Chapter 11 reorganization allows the debtor's finances to be restructured, not liquidated. **Answer (C) is incorrect.** A trustee is usually not appointed to run the debtor's business. The court may, however, order the appointment of a trustee for cause or if such action is in the best interests of the parties. **Answer (D) is incorrect.** A reorganized individual debtor may continue in the same business without any restrictions.

Access the **Gleim CPA Premium Review System** featuring our SmartAdapt technology from your Gleim Personal Classroom to continue your studies. You will experience a personalized study environment with exam-emulating multiple-choice questions.

APPENDIX A
OPTIMIZING YOUR SCORE ON
THE TASK-BASED SIMULATIONS (TBSs)

Each section of the CPA Exam contains multiple testlets of Task-Based Simulations. The number of TBS testlets and the number of TBSs in each testlet are the same for each exam section except BEC.

TBSs per Exam Section

	Testlet 3	Testlet 4	Testlet 5	Total
AUD	2	3	3	8
BEC	2	2	N/A*	4
FAR	2	3	3	8
REG	2	3	3	8

*Testlet 5 of BEC is Written Communications.

Task-Based Simulations are constructive response questions with information presented either with the question or in separate exhibits. Question responses may be in the form of entering amounts into a spreadsheet, choosing the correct answer from a list in a pop-up box, or reviewing and completing or correcting a draft of a document. In the AUD, FAR, and REG exam sections, you will also have to complete a Research task, which requires you to research the relevant authoritative literature and cite the appropriate guidance as indicated. You will not have to complete a Research task in BEC.

It is not productive to practice TBSs on paper. Instead, you should use your online Gleim CPA Review Course to complete truly interactive TBSs that emulate exactly how TBSs are tested on the CPA Exam. As a CPA candidate, you must become an expert on how to approach TBSs, how to budget your time in the TBS testlets, and the different types of TBSs. This appendix covers all of these topics for you and includes examples of typical TBSs. Use this appendix only as an introduction to TBSs, and then practice hundreds of exam-emulating TBSs in your Gleim CPA Review Course.

Task-Based Simulations -- Toolbar Icons and Operations

The following information and toolbar icons are located at the top of the testlet screen of each TBS. All screenshots are taken from the AICPA Sample Test (www.aicpa.org). The examples that follow are taken from our online course. The CPA Exam, the Sample Test, and all screenshots are Copyright 2021 by the AICPA with All Rights Reserved. The AICPA requires all candidates to review the Sample Tests and Tutorials before sitting for the CPA Exam.

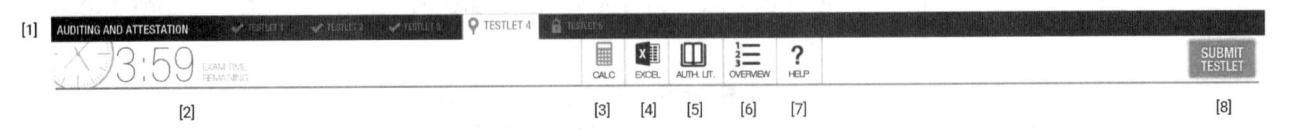

1. **Exam Section and Testlet Number:** The testlet number will be 3, 4, or 5 for the simulations.
2. **Time Remaining:** This information box displays how much time you have remaining in the entire exam. Consistently check the amount of time remaining to stay on schedule.
3. **Calculator:** The calculator icon launches a basic tool for simple computations. It is similar to calculators used in common software programs. The calculator tape is saved and accessible throughout the entire testlet; it does not clear until a new testlet is entered or the "Clear Tape" function is employed. Numbers (but not text) can be copied and pasted between the calculator, any exhibits, the question content and answer fields, and Excel.

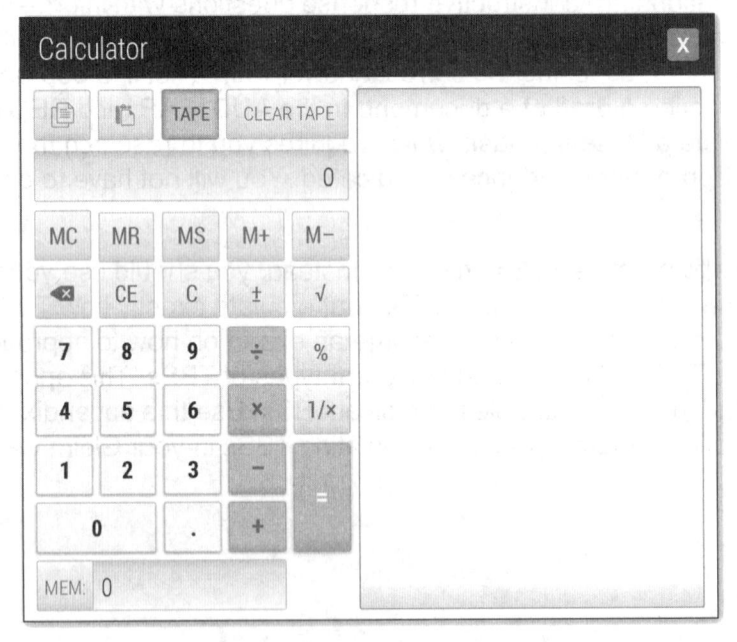

4. **Excel:** Instead of the proprietary spreadsheet used previously, candidates will now have access to the desktop version of Excel, which launches by clicking the spreadsheet icon found in the top toolbar.
    - The exam spreadsheet will perform the same essential functions as a regular desktop Excel spreadsheet.
    - Candidates can easily transfer data out of and into Excel, for example, by copying from Excel and pasting to the answer fields of a simulation or into the calculator, and vice versa. Excel will retain all of the information entered while in a testlet, even if Excel is closed and/or when navigating between simulations. Excel will only clear when beginning a new testlet. There is also an option to manually save any work.
    - Work done and calculations performed within Excel will not be graded. Many of Excel's less relevant features and some functions of Excel that may threaten user security will not work.

5. **Authoritative Literature:** The Authoritative Literature for AUD, FAR, and REG is available in every TBS testlet. You can use either the table of contents or the search function to locate the correct guidance. The table of contents will not populate until a source has been selected.
    - An extremely useful feature is that candidates can bookmark a document by clicking the bookmark icon next to the document title. All bookmarked documents will be listed in a section that appears above the table of contents, and hovering over the bookmarked items reveals the full title in a pop-up box.
    - The Advanced Search options have been altered to include the following:
        - "All of these words:" multiple words at a time, in no particular order
        - "This exact phrase:" exact words in an exact order
        - "Any of these words:" one or more of the entered words in no particular order
        - "None of these words:" none of the words entered
    - Clicking the "Search within:" box next to the search bar allows candidates to limit their search to a specific folder or sub-folder. Within the Advanced Search field, candidates must once again click the "Search within:" box in order to limit their search to a designated sub-folder, even if the "Search within:" box is activated for the basic search.
    - The search function of the Authoritative Literature tool can be used at a basic level to find words or numbers. A search can be enhanced with an asterisk, which searches for anything starting with the word, or with a question mark in place of a character, which indicates that any character can appear in that specific position in the search term. Up to three question marks can be used.

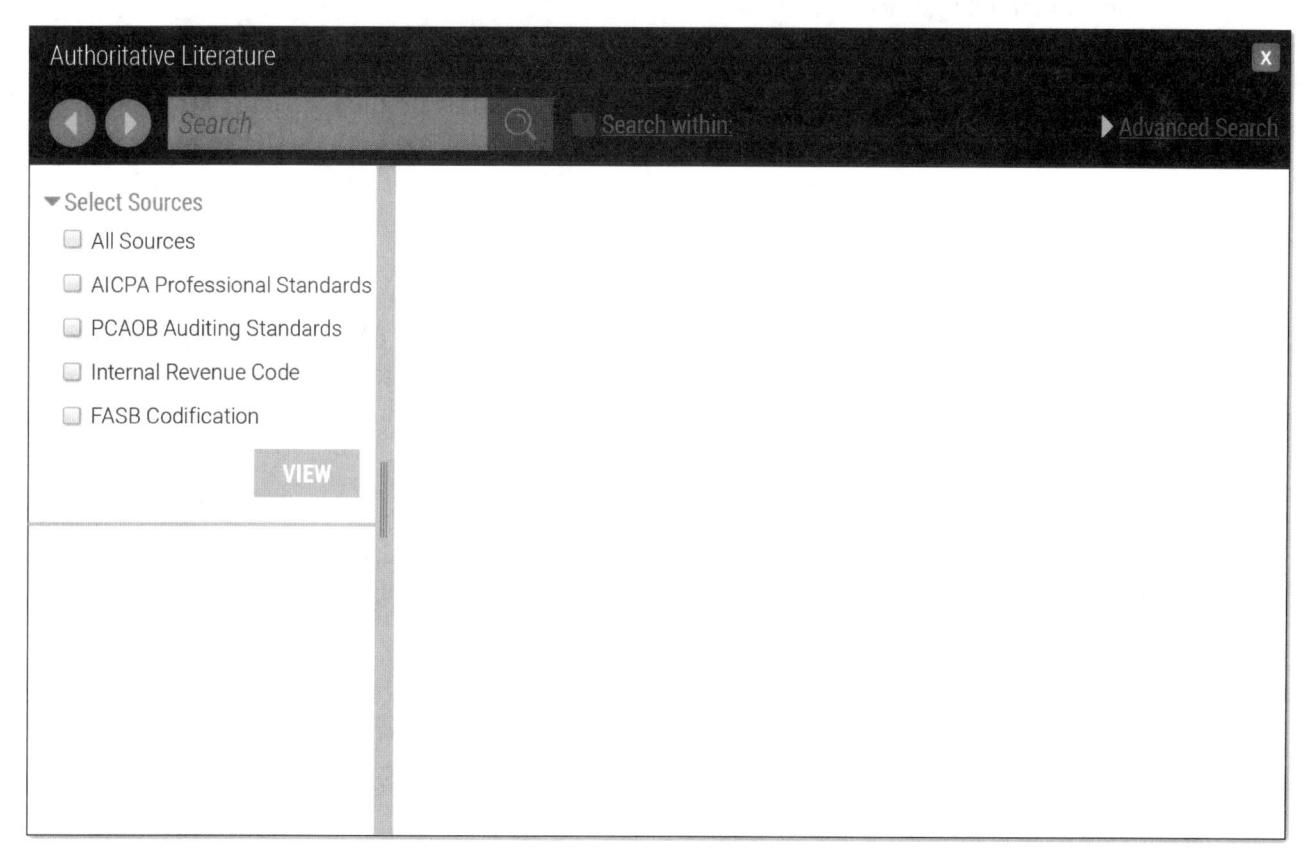

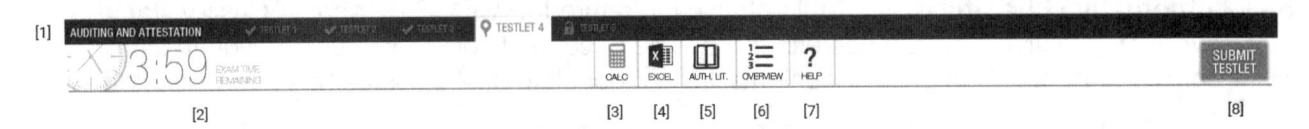

598   Appendix A: Optimizing Your Score on the Task-Based Simulations (TBSs)

[Toolbar image with labels: [1] AUDITING AND ATTESTATION, TESTLET 1, TESTLET 2, TESTLET 3, TESTLET 4, TESTLET 5; [2] 3:59 EXAM TIME REMAINING; [3] CALC; [4] EXCEL; [5] AUTH. LIT.; [6] OVERVIEW; [7] HELP; [8] SUBMIT TESTLET]

6. **Overview:** The overview lets you review and navigate the questions within a testlet. You can also use it to view, add, and remove bookmarks.

7. **Help:** The help icon provides important information about certain functions and tool buttons specific to the type of task you are working in. It also provides directions and general information but does not include information related specifically to the test content. It can be navigated via either the table of contents or the search bar.

8. **Submit Testlet:** There are two options when you choose this icon from the toolbar.

    - In any of the first four testlets, you will be asked to select either Return to Testlet or Submit Testlet. Return to Testlet allows you to review and change your answers in the current testlet. Submit Testlet takes you to the next testlet. After submitting your testlet, you will receive a prompt that allows for an optional break.

    - In the final testlet, you will be asked to select either Return to Testlet or Quit Exam. Choose Quit Exam if you wish to complete the exam. You will not be able to return to any testlet, and you will not receive credit for any unanswered questions. To prevent accidentally ending your exam, you will be asked to verify your selection, or you can choose Go Back. Upon verifying you wish to End Exam, you will be required to leave the test center with no re-admittance.

Navigation between simulations within a testlet is done using the number and arrow buttons directly beneath the toolbar or the arrow buttons at the bottom of the simulation. You can navigate between simulations within a testlet at any time before you submit the testlet.

[Navigation buttons: 1 2 at top; ◀ 1▪ ▶ at bottom]

Clicking on a number will take you to the corresponding simulation. Clicking on the bookmark icon beside the number on the left will flag the simulation to remind you to return to it before submitting the testlet.

Appendix A: Optimizing Your Score on the Task-Based Simulations (TBSs) 599

Workspace: TBSs have a designated workspace where all of the exam tools and exhibits open.

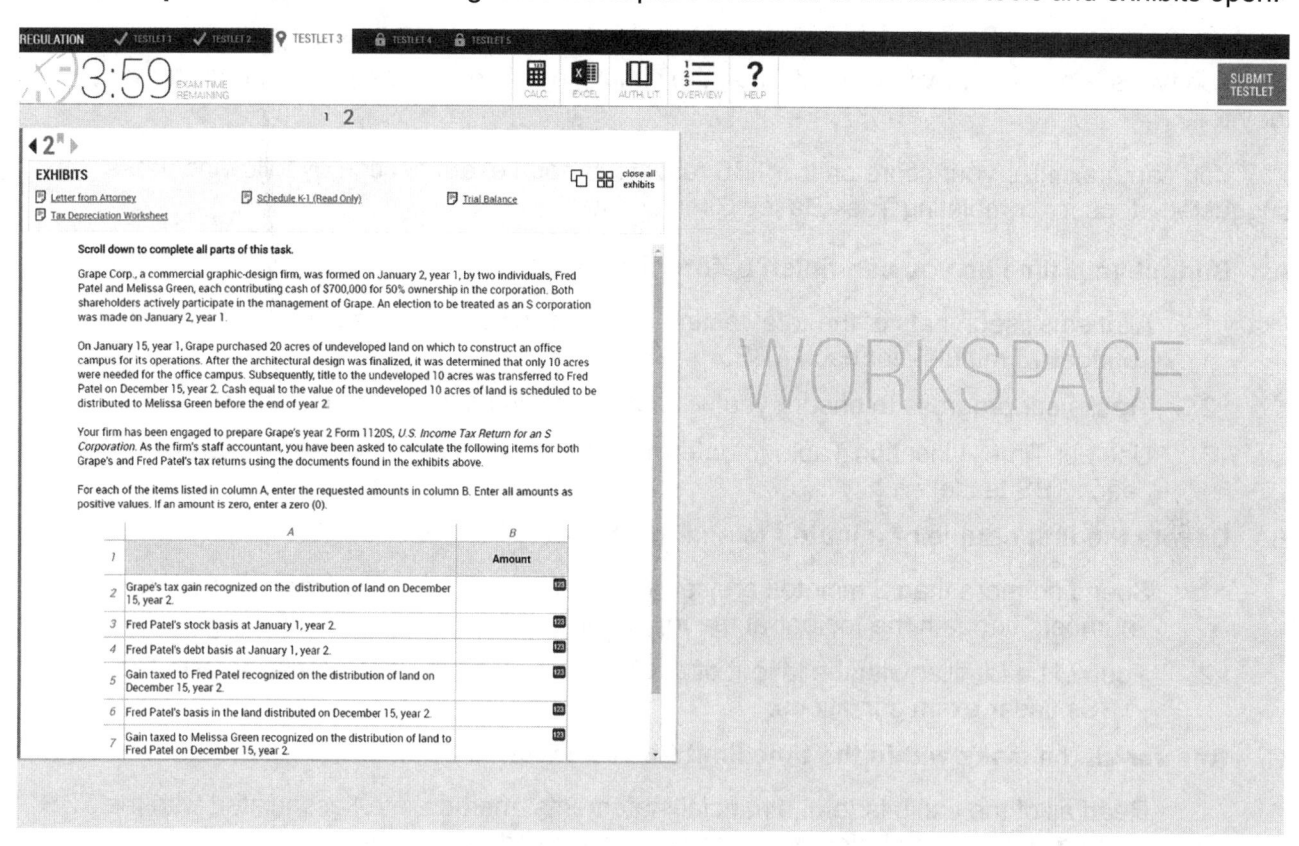

You can have multiple exam tools and exhibits open simultaneously, and you are able to freely resize and move each window.

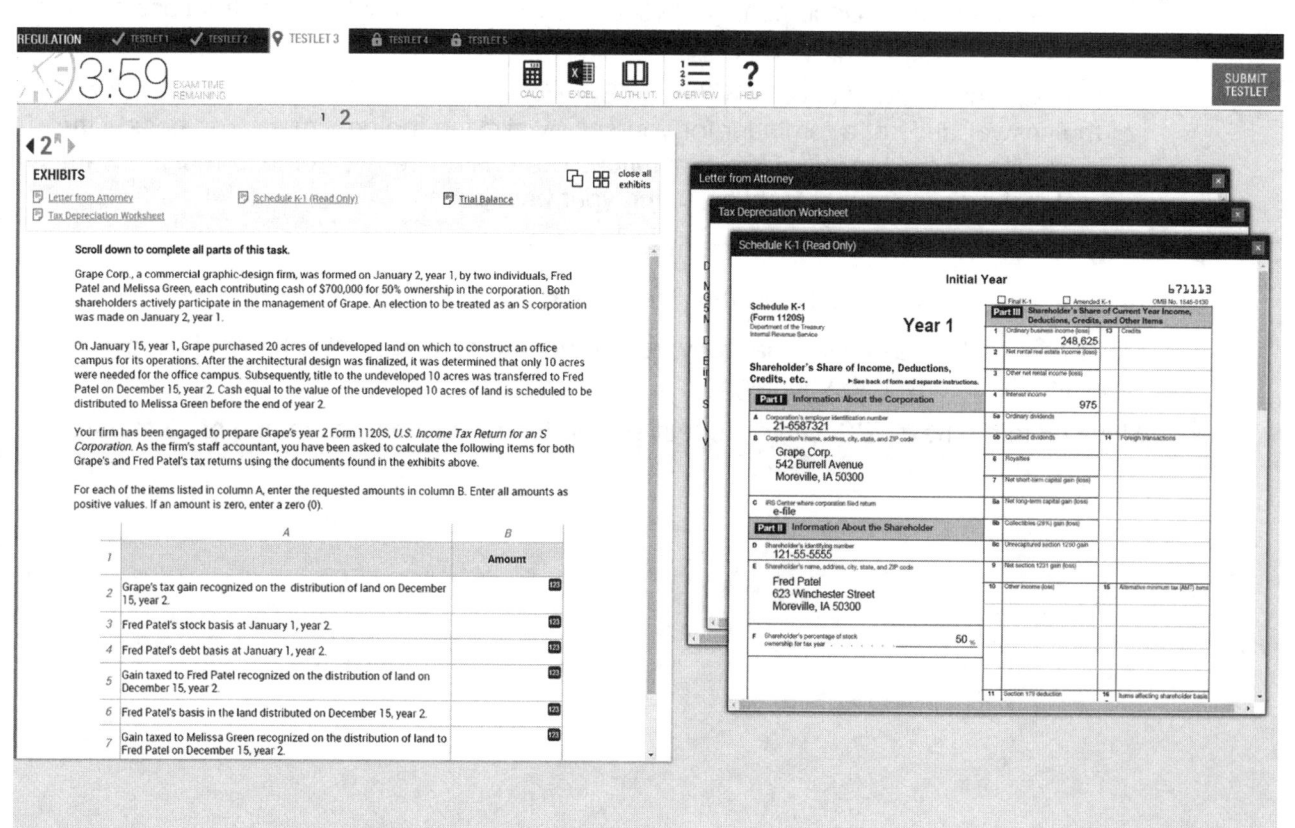

Answering Task-Based Simulations

Do not be intimidated by TBSs. Just learn the material and practice answering the different question types. Knowing **how** to work through the simulations is nearly as important as knowing what they test.

You can maximize your score on the TBS testlets of each exam section by following these suggested steps for completing Task-Based Simulations.

A. **Budget your time so you can finish before time expires.**
   1. Allot small segments of the total testing time to each specific task. We recommend you budget 18 minutes for each TBS.
   2. Track your progress to ensure you will have enough time to complete all the tasks.
   3. Use our Time Allocation Table to determine the time at which you need to start and finish each TBS testlet.

B. **Devote the first couple of minutes to scanning each TBS.**
   1. Spend no more than 2 minutes previewing the TBSs you received by clicking through the numbers beneath the toolbar at the top of the screen.
   2. You will be familiar with the layout of the TBSs if you have been practicing with Gleim TBSs under exam conditions.

C. **Answer all the tasks within the time limit for each testlet.**
   1. Read all of the exhibits (e.g., financial statements, memos, etc.) associated with the TBS you are working on before you attempt to answer the simulation.
      a. We have included detailed directions on using exhibits as source documents in the next section on Document Review Simulations. Much of those instructions can also be used when answering regular TBSs that contain exhibits.
   2. Do not skip any of the questions within a TBS. Make an educated guess if you are unsure of the answer and set a reminder for yourself by clicking the bookmark icon beside the TBS number at the top left of the simulation. There is no penalty for incorrect answers, so do not move on without at least selecting your best guess.

D. **Spend any remaining time wisely to maximize your points.**
   1. Ask yourself where you will earn the most points.
   2. Move from task to task systematically, reviewing and completing each one. Focus specifically on any TBS you flagged.
   3. Move on to the next TBS within the testlet or to the next testlet at the end of 18 minutes.

Appendix A: Optimizing Your Score on the Task-Based Simulations (TBSs) 601

DOCUMENT REVIEW SIMULATIONS

Within the Task-Based Simulation testlets included in each CPA Exam section, you may find a Document Review Simulation (DRS). You are required to review various exhibits to determine the best phrasing of a particular document. The document will contain underlined words, phrases, sentences, or paragraphs that may or may not be correct. You then must select answer choices that indicate which (if any) changes you believe should be made in the underlined words, phrases, sentences, or paragraphs.

The DRSs always include the actual document you must review and correct and one or more exhibits. Exhibits vary from one DRS to the next because they contain the information to be used as sources for your conclusions. For example, these exhibits may be financial statements, emails, letters, invoices, memoranda, or minutes from meetings. You must read each DRS exhibit so that you are always aware of the resources available.

Answering Document Review Simulations

A. **Familiarize yourself with every part of the DRS.**

   Review each exhibit so you know what information is available. If your subject-matter preparation has been thorough, you should be able to identify quickly the most relevant information in each part of the DRS.

B. **Address every underlined portion of text in the DRS.**

   You must make an answer selection for every modifiable section of a DRS because each counts as a separate question. You will know an answer has been selected when you see that the white outline in the blue icon has changed to a white checkmark.

C. **Read the underlined section and answer choices carefully and completely.**

   Each underlined portion of text may have four to seven answer choices that may include the options to revise the text, retain the original text, or delete the text. Verify that each word or amount is correct in your choice before making your final selection.

D. **Clearly understand the information in the exhibits.**

   Quickly survey the various items; then analyze the most relevant facts specifically and refer to them to reduce the possible answer choices. Keep in mind that the relevant information may be presented or worded differently than the document you are revising.

E. **Double-check that you have officially responded to each underlined portion of text.**

   If you have time, go through the entire DRS once more to confirm that every underlined section has a white checkmark next to it.

MANAGING TIME ON THE TBSs

Managing your time well during the CPA Exam is critical to success, so you must develop and practice your time management plan before your test date. The only help you will receive during your actual CPA Exam is a countdown of the hours and minutes remaining. When there are less than 2 minutes left in an exam section, the exam clock will begin to include the seconds and turn red, but you should be doing your final review by that point.

Each of the testlets on the exam is independent, and there are no time limits on individual testlets. Therefore, you must budget your time effectively to complete all five testlets in the allotted 4 hours.

The key to success is to become proficient in answering all types of questions in an average amount of time. When you follow our system, you'll have 2-17 minutes of total extra time (depending on the section) that you will be able to allocate as needed.

Each exam will begin with three introductory screens that you must complete in 10 minutes. Time spent in the introductory screens does not count against the 240 minutes you get for the exam itself. Then you will have two MCQ testlets. Each testlet contains half the total number of MCQs for that section (36/testlet for AUD, 31/testlet for BEC, 33/testlet for FAR, and 38/testlet for REG). Based on the total time of the exam and the amount of time needed for the other testlets, you should average 1.25 minutes per MCQ.

The final three testlets in AUD, FAR, and REG will have eight TBSs each: two in Testlet #3, three in Testlet #4, and three in Testlet #5. BEC will have four TBSs in two testlets, then a final testlet of three Written Communications (WCs). We suggest you allocate approximately 18 minutes to answering each TBS. On BEC, budget 25 minutes for each of the three WCs (20 minutes to answer, 5 minutes to review and perfect your response).**

To make the most of your testing time during the CPA Exam, you will need to develop a time management system and commit to spending a designated amount of time on each question. To assist you, please refer to the Gleim Time Management System.

The table below shows how many minutes you should expect to spend on each testlet for each section. Remember, you cannot begin a new testlet until you have submitted a current testlet, and once you have submitted a testlet, you can no longer go back to it.

Time Allocation per Testlet (in minutes)

Testlet	Format	AUD	BEC	FAR	REG
1	MCQ	45	38*	41*	47*
2	MCQ	45	38*	41*	47*
3	TBS	36	36	36	36
15-Minute Break					
4	TBS	54	36	54	54
5	TBS/WC	54	75	54	54
Total		234	223	226	238
Extra Time		6	17	14	2
Total Time Allowed		240	240	240	240

*Rounded down

**BEC candidates may prefer to allocate more time to the TBSs and reduce the 17 minutes of extra review time after the WCs. In this case, we suggest 20 minutes per TBS, for a total time of 40 minutes in Testlet 3 and 40 minutes in Testlet 4, leaving 9 minutes of final review after the WCs.

Appendix A: Optimizing Your Score on the Task-Based Simulations (TBSs)

The exam screen will show hours:minutes remaining. Focus on how much time you have, NOT the time on your watch. Using the times on the previous page, you would start each testlet with the following hours:minutes displayed on-screen:

Completion Times and Time Remaining

	AUD	BEC**	FAR	REG
Start	4 hours 0 minutes	4 hours 0 minutes	4 hours 0 minutes	4 hours 0 minutes
After Testlet 1	3 hours 15 minutes	3 hours 22 minutes	3 hours 19 minutes	3 hours 13 minutes
After Testlet 2	2 hours 30 minutes	2 hours 44 minutes	2 hours 38 minutes	2 hours 26 minutes
After Testlet 3	1 hour 54 minutes	2 hours 8 minutes	2 hours 2 minutes	1 hour 50 minutes
15-Minute Break			
After Testlet 4	1 hour 0 minutes	1 hour 32 minutes	1 hour 8 minutes	0 hours 56 minutes
After Testlet 5	0 hours 6 minutes	0 hours 17 minutes	0 hours 14 minutes	0 hours 2 minutes

Next, develop a shorthand for hours:minutes. This makes it easier to write down the times on the noteboard you will receive at the exam center.

	AUD	BEC**	FAR	REG
Start	4:00	4:00	4:00	4:00
After Testlet 1	3:15	3:22	3:19	3:13
After Testlet 2	2:30	2:44	2:38	2:26
After Testlet 3	1:54	2:08	2:02	1:50
15-Minute Break			
After Testlet 4	1:00	1:32	1:08	0:56
After Testlet 5	0:06	0:17	0:14	0:02

The following pages of this appendix contain five example TBSs. We have included a variety of TBS types, including Research, Numeric Entry, Option List, Global Response Grid, and DRS, along with suggestions on how to approach each type. The answer key and our unique answer explanations for each TBS appear at the end of this appendix.

Again, do not substitute answering TBSs in your Gleim CPA Review Course with answering the TBSs presented here. Refer to these TBSs only for guidance on how to answer this difficult element of the exam. It is vital that you practice answering TBSs in the digital environment of our online course so that you are comfortable with such an environment during your CPA Exam.

**BEC candidates may prefer to allocate more time to the TBSs and reduce the 17 minutes of extra review time after the WCs. In this case, we suggest 20 minutes per TBS, for a total time of 40 minutes in Testlet 3 and 40 minutes in Testlet 4, leaving 9 minutes of final review after the WCs.

RESEARCH

This type of TBS requires that you research within the Authoritative Literature, which is accessible at the top of the TBS toolbar (shown below), to find the best supporting guidance for the presented scenario. Although there is only one question to answer in the Research TBS, it counts as much as a TBS with multiple questions, so you must treat it with the same gravity as any other TBS. Our suggested steps on how to answer this task type follow:

1. Read through the given scenario to identify the question being asked and, within that, the key terms to search for in the literature. In this example, the question is asking for the penalties assessed to a return preparer for failing to sign a return, so the key terms are preparer, penalty, and sign.
2. Select the source(s) relevant to the question being asked; then click "View." For this question, we want to look within the Internal Revenue Code.
3. Type the key term(s) into the search box and click the magnifying glass.
4. Review the first 10 results. Use your knowledge of the topic to decide whether the search results fit the question you are researching. Often, the first search will not yield the correct answer, and it is necessary to narrow your scope.
5. Restrict your search to only the most relevant section of the literature by using the "Search within" function. To do so, choose the subtitle of the literature from the table of contents that is most likely to contain the related section. Click on that subtitle, type your term into the search box, select the "Search within" checkbox, and click the magnifying glass. This will populate the results with only matches from that specific subtitle. For example, this Research question refers to penalties assessed to a return preparer. Therefore, Subtitle F, Procedure and Administration, is the subtitle to search within.
6. From these streamlined results, select the exact paragraph that corresponds to the given scenario and enter your response using the on-screen formatting prompts.

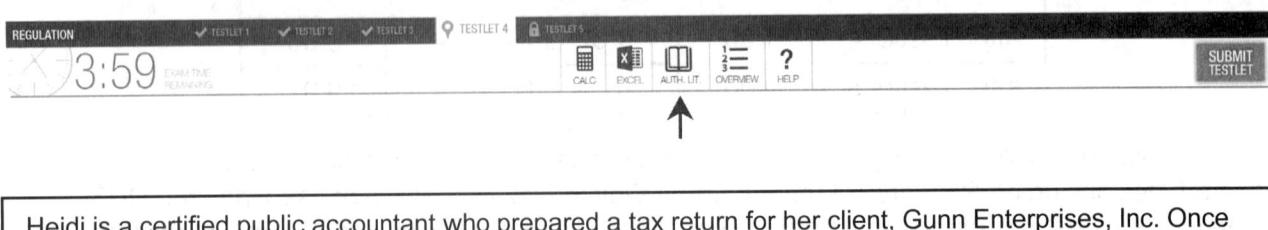

Heidi is a certified public accountant who prepared a tax return for her client, Gunn Enterprises, Inc. Once complete, the tax return was reviewed and then mailed to the client. However, because Gunn had a balance due on its account, Heidi refused to sign the completed tax return. The client mailed the unsigned tax return to the IRS and received a refund shortly after.

Research and cite the appropriate IRC section that addresses the penalty for a return preparer's failure to sign a return.

Enter your response in the answer fields below.

IRC § [   ] ([   ])

LIQUIDATION: NUMERIC ENTRY

> This type of TBS requires that you calculate and then respond with some kind of number, e.g., an amount of currency, a ratio, etc. After clicking a cell, a field will appear that will automatically format your response. Be sure to review the formatted response before finalizing your answer. There are also options to cancel an entry or reset the cell to blank. Some Numeric Entry TBSs (like this one) may require you to review additional documentation in the form of exhibits to gather all of the information you need to answer the questions.

Son, Inc., and Clef, Inc., are both taxable domestic C corporations.

Using the information in the exhibits below and on the next page, enter either the correct amount or holding period (in number of months) for each item below.

For each item, enter the appropriate amounts in the shaded cells below. If the amount is zero, enter a zero (0).

Item	Answer
1. Loss recognized by Clef, Inc., on the distribution of the computer	
2. Gain recognized by Clef, Inc., on the distribution of the concert piano	
3. Son, Inc.'s basis in the building	
4. Son, Inc.'s basis in the computer	
5. Dawn's gain or loss recognized on the distribution of the piano, keyboard, and cash	
6. Dawn's holding period for the piano on December 31, 2021	
7. Dawn's holding period for the keyboard on December 31, 2021	

LIQUIDATION: EXHIBITS

Fair Market Value as of August 31, 2021, immediately before the distribution

Asset	Fair Market Value
Building	$550,000
Computer	25,000
Piano	15,000
Keyboard	3,000

Adjusted Basis as of August 31, 2021, immediately before the distribution

Asset	Clef's Adjusted Basis	Date of Purchase
Building*	$250,000	August 31, 2017
Computer	30,000	August 31, 2017
Piano	10,000	August 31, 2017
Keyboard	4,000	August 31, 2017

*Subject to a $175,000 mortgage. Clef has claimed allowable depreciation on the building using the straight-line method.

The following balances are as of January 1, 2021.

Party	# of Clef Shares Owned	Basis in Clef Shares	Accumulated Earnings and Profits
Son, Inc.	800	$200,000	—
Dawn*	200	$50,000	—
Clef, Inc.	—	—	$10,000

*Dawn owned none of the outstanding shares of Son.

August 31, 2021

Dear Shareholders,

It is with sadness that I announce that we will have finished the complete liquidation of Clef, Inc., later today. After sustaining unexpected hardships over the past few months, we were finally able to pay all of our liabilities to our third party creditors on July 4 earlier this year. Today, the continued unexpected adversity has officially won the war, and we will be locking our doors for the last time this evening.

The details of the liquidation have been finalized, and the following distributions will occur before the end of today:

- Son will receive a building and a computer.
- Dawn will receive a concert grand piano, an electronic keyboard, and $82,000 in cash.

After these distributions have been made, Clef will have no other assets other than an amount reserved for taxes.

Thank you both for your dedication and perseverance to Clef; we could not have operated for this long if it was not for the two of you. The rest of us here at Clef wish you nothing but the best in both of your respective future endeavors.

Sincerely,
George Casio, CEO

BASES FOR LIABILITY: OPTION LIST

> This TBS is an example of an Option List, which is in essence a series of multiple-choice questions. This type of task requires that you select a response from a list of choices. Some Option List TBSs may also require Numeric Entry type responses.

The CPA firm of Martinson, Brinks, & Sutherland, a partnership, was the auditor for Masco Corporation, a medium-sized wholesaler. Masco leased warehouse facilities and sought financing for leasehold improvements to these facilities. Masco assured its bank that the leasehold improvements would result in a more efficient and profitable operation. Based on these assurances, the bank granted Masco a line of credit.

The loan agreement required annual audited financial statements. Masco submitted its audited financial statements to the bank. They showed an operating profit of $75,000, leasehold improvements of $250,000, and net worth of $350,000. In reliance on the statements, the bank lent Masco $200,000. The audit report that accompanied the financial statements disclaimed an opinion because the cost of the leasehold improvements could not be determined from the company's records. The part of the audit report applicable to leasehold improvements reads as follows:

> Additions to fixed assets for the year were found to include principally warehouse improvements. Most of this work was done by company employees, and the costs of materials and overhead were paid by Masco. Unfortunately, complete, detailed cost records were not kept of these leasehold improvements, and no exact determination could be made of the actual cost of the improvements. The total amount capitalized is set forth in note 4.

Late in the following year, Masco went out of business, at which time it was learned that the claimed leasehold improvements were totally fictitious. The labor expenses charged as leasehold improvements proved to be operating expenses. No item of building material cost had been recorded. No independent investigation of the existence of the leasehold improvements was made by the auditors.

If the $250,000 had not been capitalized, the income statement would have reflected a substantial loss from operations, and the net worth would have been correspondingly decreased.

The bank has sustained a loss on its loan to Masco of $200,000 and now seeks to recover damages from the CPA firm.

Items 1 through 8 are questions regarding CPA liability. Select the correct answer from the option list provided. Each choice may be used once, more than once, or not at all.

Question	Answer
1. What basis for liability does not apply to an accountant?	
2. What basis for liability applies to Martinson, Brinks, & Sutherland?	
3. What is the class of persons to which the bank belongs for the purpose of determining the accountant's liability for negligence?	
4. What element of fraud is not included in negligent misrepresentation?	
5. Intent is an element of fraud. What may be substituted for intent?	
6. What type of causation is an element of negligence?	
7. One characteristic of a primary beneficiary is that the accountant is retained principally for its benefit. What is another characteristic, if any, of a primary beneficiary?	
8. What is the class of persons to which a defendant is liable for fraud?	

Option List

A) Negligence	I) Primary beneficiaries
B) Gross negligence	J) Privity of contract
C) Fraud	K) Proximate cause
D) Relationship to a specific transaction	L) Identification of the third party
E) Strict liability in tort	M) Duty to discover fraud
F) Foreseen third parties	N) Supervening cause
G) Reasonably foreseeable users	O) Scienter
H) Implied cause	P) None of the answer choices

GAINS AND LOSSES: GLOBAL RESPONSE GRID

> In Global Response Grid simulations, each distinct question has its own response table. This TBS is a type of Global Response Grid that uses both Numeric Entry and Option List questions.

For each of the following transactions, determine the amount and character of the gain or loss. For each item, enter the appropriate amount in the associated cell in the amount column. If the amount is zero, enter a zero (0). Then, select from the option list provided the character of the gain or loss. Each choice may be used once, more than once, or not at all.

1. Sale of 1,000 shares of XYZ common stock purchased on 10/15/20 for $20,000 and sold on 2/15/21 for $23,000.

Amount	Character

2. Sale of 2,000 shares of ABC common stock purchased on 3/23/21 for $125,000 and sold on 12/31/21 for $139,000.

Amount	Character

3. Sale of van purchased on 1/25/20 for $10,000 and sold on 6/03/21 for $9,000.

Amount	Character

4. Sale of land purchased on 06/30/04 for $110,000 and sold on 7/04/21 for $169,000.

Amount	Character

5. $45,000 of insurance recovery received from a 5-year-old building that was destroyed in a fire. The building was used in a business, had a FMV of $65,000, and an adjusted basis of $50,000.

Amount	Character

Option List
A) Ordinary income
B) Ordinary loss
C) Short-term capital gain
D) Long-term capital gain
E) Short-term capital loss
F) Long-term capital loss

Appendix A: Optimizing Your Score on the Task-Based Simulations (TBSs) 609

DOCUMENT REVIEW SIMULATION (DRS)

This type of TBS requires that you analyze certain words or phrases in a document to decide whether to (1) keep the current text, (2) replace the current text with different text, or (3) delete the text. You must review various exhibits (e.g., financial statements, emails, invoices, etc.) presented with the original document in order to find the information necessary for each response.

EXHIBITS close all exhibits

- Warning Letter
- Wildcat Complaint
- Martha Jones Complaint
- Notice of Action/Change
- OSHA Form 300a
- Distributor Agreement
- Installation Agreement
- OSHA Form 301

During the audit of Jayhawk Corporation, your audit manager has instructed you to meet with Bob Smith, Jayhawk's director of internal auditing, to obtain information on the two pending civil claims against the company and on the sole workers' compensation claim. After meeting with Bob Smith and reviewing the relevant support, you drafted the below memorandum for your audit manager's review.

Use the information from the exhibits presented on the following pages. To revise the document, review each segment of underlined text below and select the needed correction, if any, from the list provided. If the underlined text is already correct in the context of the document, select *[Original Text]* from the list. If removal of the underlined text is the best revision to the document, select *[Delete Text]* from the list if available.

To: Manager
From: You
Re: Information provided by Bob Smith, Jayhawk Corp.'s director of internal auditing

Bob Smith is concerned that Jayhawk Corp. needs to disclose a potential liability in a slip-and-fall lawsuit. <u>Jayhawk is potentially liable because California Distributor, LLC, is Jayhawk's agent as of the date of the alleged slip-and-fall incident.</u>

- [A] *[Original Text]* Jayhawk is potentially liable because California Distributor, LLC, is Jayhawk's agent as of the date of the alleged slip-and-fall incident.
- [B] Jayhawk may be liable, but California Distributor, LLC, will indemnify Jayhawk for any losses.
- [C] Jayhawk is not liable because California Distributor, LLC, is an independent contractor.
- [D] Jayhawk is not liable because California Distributor, LLC, is not an agent as of the date of the alleged slip-and-fall incident.
- [E] Jayhawk is not liable because the agency was for an illegal purpose.

-- Continued on next page --

Jayhawk Corp. and Wildcat, Inc., entered into a contract on December 7, 20X0, by which Jayhawk agreed to sell a Jayhawk Widget to Wildcat. The agreement also provided for installation of a Jayhawk Widget at Wildcat's premises. This equipment was essential to the functioning of Wildcat's production facility. Jayhawk then hired Ace Installer, LLC, to perform the installation, which was completed on December 10, 20X0. When the defective Jayhawk Widget malfunctioned, Ace Installer made repairs and agreed to pay damages to Wildcat. Ace Installer made this agreement because of its obligation to indemnify Jayhawk. But Ace Installer failed to pay, and Wildcat sued Jayhawk for $750,000 of lost revenue. <u>Jayhawk is not liable to Wildcat because of Ace Installer's indemnification agreement.</u>

- [A] *[Original Text]* Jayhawk is not liable to Wildcat because of Ace Installer's indemnification agreement.
- [B] Jayhawk is not liable to Wildcat because Ace Installer is an independent contractor.
- [C] Jayhawk is liable to Wildcat because it materially breached its contract with Wildcat.
- [D] Jayhawk is liable only for the price paid by Wildcat for the Jayhawk Widget and its installation.

Jayhawk South is the southeastern distributor of widgets manufactured by Jayhawk Corp. of Fort Scott, Kansas. On January 11, 20X0, one of its employees sustained a work-related injury resulting in a workers' compensation claim. Jayhawk South also reports to the Occupational Safety and Health Administration (OSHA). <u>Jayhawk South must recognize a liability for potential fines from OSHA due to employee safety issues.</u>

- [A] *[Original Text]* Jayhawk South must recognize a liability for potential fines from OSHA due to employee safety issues.
- [B] *[Delete Text]*
- [C] Jayhawk South must recognize in its financial statements the workers' compensation settlement.
- [D] Jayhawk South must recognize a contingent liability for damages exceeding the workers' compensation settlement.
- [E] Jayhawk South's insurer need not pay the claim if the employee was contributorily negligent.

Appendix A: Optimizing Your Score on the Task-Based Simulations (TBSs) 611

DRS: EXHIBITS

OSHA's Form 301
Injury and Illness Incident Report

U.S. Department of Labor
Occupational Safety and Health Administration

Form approved OMB no. 1218-0176

Attention: This form contains information relating to employee health and must be used in a manner that protects the confidentiality of employees to the extent possible while the information is being used for occupational safety and health purposes.

This *Injury and Illness Incident Report* is one of the first forms you must fill out when a recordable work-related injury or illness has occurred. Together with the *Log of Work-Related Injuries and Illnesses* and the accompanying *Summary*, these forms help the employer and OSHA develop a picture of the extent and severity of work-related incidents.

Within 7 calendar days after you receive information that a recordable work-related injury or illness has occurred, you must fill out this form or an equivalent. Some state workers' compensation, insurance, or other reports may be acceptable substitutes. To be considered an equivalent form, any substitute must contain all the information asked for on this form.

According to Public Law 91-596 and 29 CFR 1904, OSHA's recordkeeping rule, you must keep this form on file for 5 years following the year to which it pertains.

If you need additional copies of this form, you may photocopy and use as many as you need.

Information about the employee

1) Full name __Robert Dean__

2) Street __200 Longfellow Dr.__
   City __Gainesville__ State __FL__ ZIP __32608__

3) Date of birth __10 / 30 / 1960__

4) Date hired __5 / 24 / 2008__

5) ☒ Male ☐ Female

Information about the physician or other health care professional

6) Name of physician or other health care professional __Dr. Williams__

7) If treatment was given away from the worksite, where was it given?
   Facility __Stoneridge Medical Center__
   Street __Stoneridge Drive__
   City __Gainesville__ State __FL__ ZIP __32606__

8) Was employee treated in an emergency room?
   ☒ Yes
   ☐ No

9) Was employee hospitalized overnight as an in-patient?
   ☐ Yes
   ☒ No

Information about the case

10) Case number from the *Log* __02__ *(Transfer the case number from the Log after you record the case.)*

11) Date of injury or illness __1 / 11 / X0__

12) Time employee began work __8:00__ ☒ AM ☐ PM

13) Time of event __8:30__ ☒ AM ☐ PM ☐ Check if time cannot be determined

14) **What was the employee doing just before the incident occurred?** Describe the activity, as well as the tools, equipment, or material the employee was using. Be specific. *Examples:* "climbing a ladder while carrying roofing materials"; "spraying chlorine from hand sprayer"; "daily computer key-entry."
    __Employee was working on building a fence around Jayhawk South's building. A bee flew out of the building materials and stung employee on upper left thigh.__

15) **What happened?** Tell us how the injury occurred. *Examples:* "When ladder slipped on wet floor, worker fell 20 feet"; "Worker was sprayed with chlorine when gasket broke during replacement"; "Worker developed soreness in wrist over time."
    __Lifted building materials and bee flew out from under them.__

16) **What was the injury or illness?** Tell us the part of the body that was affected and how it was affected; be more specific than "hurt," "pain," or sore." *Examples:* "strained back"; "chemical burn, hand"; "carpal tunnel syndrome."
    __Upper left thigh was stung. It became red, swollen, and achy because of an allergic reaction.__

17) **What object or substance directly harmed the employee?** *Examples:* "concrete floor"; "chlorine"; "radial arm saw." *If this question does not apply to the incident, leave it blank.*
    __Bee__

18) **If the employee died, when did death occur?** Date of death __N/A / /__

Completed by __Peggy Prince__
Title __Operations Officer__
Phone (__555__) __555__ - __5555__ Date __5 / 15 / X0__

Public reporting burden for this collection of information is estimated to average 22 minutes per response, including time for reviewing instructions, searching existing data sources, gathering and maintaining the data needed, and completing and reviewing the collection of information. Persons are not required to respond to the collection of information unless it displays a current valid OMB control number. If you have any comments about this estimate or any other aspects of this data collection, including suggestions for reducing this burden, contact: US Department of Labor, OSHA Office of Statistical Analysis, Room N-3644, 200 Constitution Avenue, NW, Washington, DC 20210. Do not send the completed forms to this office.

NOTICE OF ACTION/CHANGE
DIVISION OF WORKERS' COMPENSATION
Attention: Information Management
200 East Gaines Street
Tallahassee, FL 32399-4226
For assistance call 1-800-342-1741 or contact your local EAO Office
COMPLETE ALL APPLICABLE SECTIONS BEFORE FILING WITH THE DIVISION

SENT TO DIVISION DATE	DIVISION RECEIVED DATE
2/29/20X0	

PLEASE PRINT OR TYPE

SOCIAL SECURITY NUMBER	EMPLOYEE NAME (First, Middle, Last)	DATE OF ACCIDENT (Month-Day-Year)
222-44-6666	Robert Dean	1/11/20X0

INDICATE ONLY ACTION OR CHANGE - PLEASE REFER TO KEY FOR DWC-4 TYPES/CODES ON REVERSE SIDE

ALL INDEMNITY SUSPENDED: _____ EFFECTIVE DATE __-__-__ REASON CODE: _____
INDEMNITY REINSTATED AFTER SUSPENSION: _____ EFFECTIVE DATE __-__-__ DISABILITY TYPE: _____

RELEASED TO RETURN TO WORK DATE: __-__-__ RESTRICTIONS?: ☐ YES ☐ NO
ACTUAL RETURN TO WORK DATE: __-__-__ RESTRICTIONS?: ☐ YES ☐ NO
DATE FINAL SETTLEMENT ORDER MAILED: __-__-__
OVERALL MMI DATE: __-__-__ PI RATING: ____ % BAW DATE OF DEATH __-__-__

PERMANENT IMPAIRMENT BENEFITS (D/A'S PRIOR TO 01/01/94): DATE PAID: __-__-__
IMPAIRMENT INCOME BENEFITS (D/A'S ON OR AFTER 01/01/94): START DATE: 1 - 11 - X0 WEEKLY RATE: $ 391.83
TOTAL NUMBER OF WEEKS OF ENTITLEMENT: 1

PERMANENT TOTAL:
DATE ACCEPTED/ADJUDICATED __-__-__
WEEKLY PT SUPPLEMENTAL RATE $ _____
WEEKLY PT SUPP EFFECTIVE DATE __-__-__

AVERAGE WEEKLY WAGE AND/OR COMPENSATION RATE AMENDMENTS:
PREVIOUS AWW: $ 527.12
PREVIOUS COMP RATE: $ 351.43
AMENDED AWW: $ 587.74
AMENDED COMP RATE: $ 391.83
RETROACTIVE TO D/A: ☑ YES ☐ NO
IF NO, GIVE EFFECTIVE DATE: __-__-__

BENEFIT ADJUSTMENTS

BENEFIT ADJUSTMENT CODE _____ BENEFIT ADJUSTMENT CODE _____
DISABILITY TYPE ADJUSTED _____ DISABILITY TYPE ADJUSTED _____
WEEKLY ADJ AMOUNT $ _____ WEEKLY ADJ AMOUNT $ _____
EFFECTIVE DATE _____ EFFECTIVE DATE _____
ADJUSTMENT END DATE _____ ADJUSTMENT END DATE _____

CORRECTIONS OF:
☐ SOCIAL SECURITY NUMBER/CORRECT #: _____
☐ DATE OF ACCIDENT/CORRECT DATE: __-__-__
☐ EMPLOYEE'S NAME/CORRECT NAME: _____
☐ CLAIMS-HANDLING ENTITY: _____

CLASS CODE
NAICS CODE

REMARKS: A change has been made to the Average Weekly Wage and/or Compensation Rate.

CC:
Hopper Tax Consultants
5562 Wellington Lane
Briston, FL 34418

INSURER NAME
Plymouth Insurance Company

INSURER CODE #	DATE PREPARED: (Month-Day-Year)	CLAIMS-HANDLING ENTITY NAME, ADDRESS & TELEPHONE
2233	04 - 30 - 20X0	4292 Main Street Barstow, FL 36614
SERVICE CO/TPA CODE #	CLAIMS-HANDLING ENTITY FILE # 3399	

Any person who, knowingly and with intent to injure, defraud, or deceive any employer or employee, insurance company, or self-insured program, files a statement of claim containing any false or misleading information commits insurance fraud, punishable as provided in s. 817.234. Section 440.105(7), F.S.
Form DFS-F2-DWC-4 (03/2009) Rule 69L-3.025, F.A.C.

Department of Health and Human Services

Public Health Service
Food and Drug Administration
College Park, MD 20740

SEP 28 20X0

WARNING LETTER

CERTIFIED MAIL
RETURN RECEIPT REQUESTED

Jayhawk Corporation
Fort Scott, Kansas

Re: CFS-AA-03-0X

Dear Sir or Madam:

This is to advise you that the Food and Drug Administration (FDA) obtained a sample packet of your Special Health Remedies product and promotional literature at the American Society of Pharmacognosy (ASP) conference in Portland, Maine, during the week of June 14, 20X0. The FDA has reviewed the labeling for Special Health Remedies on your website, as well as the label of the sample packet we collected. This review found serious violations of the Federal Food, Drug, and Cosmetic Act (the Act). You can find the Act and its implementing regulations on FDA's website at http://www.fda.gov.

New Drug

Furthermore, the therapeutic claims in your labeling indicate that the product is intended for the diagnosis, cure, mitigation, treatment, or prevention of disease in man. Similar claims and testimonials also appear on your website.

These claims are evidence that your product is intended for use as a drug within the meaning of section 201(g)(1)(B) of the Act [21 U.S.C. § 321(g)(1)(B)]. Your product is also a new drug under section 201(p) of the Act [21 U.S.C. § 321(p)] because this product is not generally recognized as safe and effective for its intended uses. New drugs may not be legally marketed in the U.S. without prior approval from FDA as described in section 505(a) of the Act [21 U.S.C. § 355(a)].

The above violations are not meant to be an all-inclusive list of deficiencies in your product and its labeling. It is your responsibility to ensure that products marketed by your firm comply with the Act and its implementing regulations.

The Act authorizes the seizure of illegal products and injunctions against manufacturers and distributors of those products. You should take prompt action to correct these deviations and prevent their future recurrence. Failure to do so may result in enforcement action without further notice. Federal agencies are advised of the issuance of all Warning Letters about drug products so that they may take this information into account when considering the award of contracts.

Please notify this office, in writing, within fifteen (15) working days of the receipt of this letter, as to the specific steps you have taken to correct the violations noted above and to assure that similar violations do not occur. Include any documentation necessary to show that correction has been achieved. If corrective actions cannot be completed within fifteen working days, state the reason for the delay and the time within which the corrections will be completed.

Your response should be directed to Compliance Officer, Food and Drug Administration, Center for Food Safety and Applied Nutrition, Office of Compliance, Division of Enforcement, 5100 Paint Branch Parkway (HFS-608), College Park, Maryland 20740.

Sincerely,

Office of Compliance
Center for Food Safety and Applied Nutrition

IN THE SIXTH JUDICIAL DISTRICT
DISTRICT COURT OF BOURBON COUNTY, KANSAS

WILDCAT, INC.,)
)
        Plaintiff,)
)
        v.)   Case No. 23 BR 195 RT
)
JAYHAWK CORP.,)
)
        Defendant.)
)

COMPLAINT

COMES NOW Plaintiff, Wildcat, Inc., by and through its undersigned attorney, and sues the Defendant, Jayhawk Corp., and alleges:

1. This is an action for damages that do not exceed $750,000.

2. On 12/7/20X0, Plaintiff purchased a Jayhawk Widget and the installation of a Jayhawk Widget at Wildcat, Inc.'s premises.

3. On 12/10/20X0, Jayhawk notified Wildcat, Inc., that the Jayhawk Widget was installed, operational, and ready for use.

4. On 12/27/20X0, the Jayhawk Widget malfunctioned, causing Wildcat, Inc.'s production facility to cease all operations.

5. On 12/27/20X0, subsequent to the malfunction, Plaintiff notified Defendant of the failure of the Jayhawk Widget.

6. On 1/14/20X1, Ace Installer repaired the Jayhawk Widget and certified it to be operational and ready for use.

7. Between 12/27/20X0 and 1/14/20X1, Plaintiff's loss of revenue was $750,000. Plaintiff then negotiated a settlement with Ace Installer, which agreed to pay Plaintiff $750,000. But Generic Bank did not pay Plaintiff the sum it was legally and contractually required to receive due to insufficient funds in Ace Installer's account.

Wherefore Plaintiff demands judgment against Defendant for damages, interest, court costs, and attorney's fees.

Harkon Davis

Harkon Davis, #92367
Attorney For Plaintiff
101 S.W. Litigation Drive
Fort Scott, KS 66701

AGREEMENT FOR THE INSTALLATION
OF ONE (1) JAYHAWK CORPORATION WIDGET

This Agreement is made this [___7th___] day of [_____December 20X0_____] by and between **JAYHAWK CORPORATION** ("JAYHAWK"), a company incorporated in Fort Scott, Kansas, company registration no. 63947XX62G and ACE INSTALLER, LLC ("the Contractor").

WHEREBY IT IS AGREED BETWEEN THE CONTRACTOR AND JAYHAWK as follows:

1   QUANTITY AND PRICE OF WORK

1.1   The Contractor shall, subject to the terms and conditions of this agreement, install one (1) Jayhawk Widget and all the components and accessories as specified in Annex A attached hereto (collectively "the Equipment") for the aggregate price of five hundred thousand U.S. dollars ($500,000.00) ("the price"). The installation will be at the premises of WILDCAT, INC., in Fort Scott, Kansas. Annex A hereto shall be read together with and form an integral part of this agreement.

1.2   The Contractor shall be responsible for the furnishing of all designs, labor, and tools for the installation of the Equipment.

2   WARRANTY AND MAINTENANCE

2.1   The Contractor **HEREBY WARRANTS** that the Equipment shall be free from installation defect for a period of not less than twelve (12) calendar months from the date of commencement of warranty as specified in the Certificate of Acceptance issued by JAYHAWK. The Contractor also **HEREBY WARRANTS** that the Equipment has no design flaws or defects for a period of not less than five (5) years from such date of commencement of warranty.

2.2   Any fault due to material, workmanship, or structural faults or design flaws or defects that may be observed during the relevant warranty period specified in Clause 2.1 shall be made good by the Contractor at its own expense, which shall include the cost of labor and replacement of parts.

3   INSURANCE AND INDEMNITY

3.1   The Contractor shall also insure against any damage, loss, death, or injury that may occur to any person or property whatsoever in carrying out or omitting to carry out its duties under this agreement and shall **INDEMNIFY** and **keep JAYHAWK and its related and associate companies INDEMNIFIED** in respect of all claims, costs, and other expenses arising out of such damage, loss, death, or injury.

3.2   The Contractor **INDEMNIFIES JAYHAWK and its related or associated companies** in full from and against all actions, proceedings, liability, loss, damage, costs, and expenses whatsoever (including without limitation legal costs and expenses on a full indemnity basis, and any fines, penalties, levies, and charges) that may be brought against any of them or that any of them may suffer or incur.

IN WITNESS WHEREOF, the parties hereto have hereunto set their hands on the day and the year first above written.

SIGNED BY: _____*Caleb Green*_____
                        (Name)
for and on behalf of:
JAYHAWK CORPORATION

SIGNED BY: _____*Jean Taylor*_____
                        (Name)
for and on behalf of:
ACE INSTALLER, LLC

OSHA's Form 300A (Rev. 01/2004)
Summary of Work-Related Injuries and Illnesses

Year 20 X0

U.S. Department of Labor
Occupational Safety and Health Administration
Form approved OMB no. 1218-0176

All establishments covered by Part 1904 must complete this Summary page, even if no work-related injuries or illnesses occurred during the year. Remember to review the Log to verify that the entries are complete and accurate before completing this summary.

Using the Log, count the individual entries you made for each category. Then write the totals below, making sure you've added the entries from every page of the Log. If you had no cases, write "0."

Employees, former employees, and their representatives have the right to review the OSHA Form 300 in its entirety. They also have limited access to the OSHA Form 301 or its equivalent. See 29 CFR Part 1904.35, in OSHA's recordkeeping rule, for further details on the access provisions for these forms.

Number of Cases

Total number of deaths	Total number of cases with days away from work	Total number of cases with job transfer or restriction	Total number of other recordable cases
0 (G)	1 (H)	0 (I)	0 (J)

Number of Days

Total number of days away from work	Total number of days of job transfer or restriction
5 (K)	0 (L)

Injury and Illness Types

Total number of . . . (M)

(1) Injuries ___1___
(2) Skin disorders _____
(3) Respiratory conditions _____
(4) Poisonings _____
(5) Hearing loss _____
(6) All other illnesses _____

Establishment information

Your establishment name __Jayhawk South__

Street __1 Bill Self Dr.__

City __Gainesville__ State __FL__ ZIP __32601__

Industry description (e.g., Manufacture of motor truck trailers)
__Widget distribution__

Standard Industrial Classification (SIC), if known (e.g., 3715)
__ __ __ __

OR

North American Industrial Classification (NAICS), if known (e.g., 336212)
__5__ __1__ __1__ __1__ __9__

Employment information (If you don't have these figures, see the Worksheet on the back of this page to estimate.)

Annual average number of employees __25__

Total hours worked by all employees last year __48,300__

Sign here

Knowingly falsifying this document may result in a fine.

I certify that I have examined this document and that to the best of my knowledge the entries are true, accurate, and complete.

__Tricia Testament__ __HR Manager__
Company executive   Title

(__555__) __555__ - __5555__   __1/30/X0__
Phone   Date

Post this Summary page from February 1 to April 30 of the year following the year covered by the form.

Public reporting burden for this collection of information is estimated to average 50 minutes per response, including time to review the instructions, search and gather the data needed, and complete and review the collection of information. Persons are not required to respond to the collection of information unless it displays a currently valid OMB control number. If you have any comments about these estimates or any other aspects of this data collection, contact: US Department of Labor, OSHA Office of Statistical Analysis, Room N-3644, 200 Constitution Avenue, NW, Washington, DC 20210. Do not send the completed forms to this office.

DISTRIBUTOR AGREEMENT

THIS AGREEMENT is made this 6th day of July, 20X0, by and between Jayhawk Corporation, with its principal place of business located in Fort Scott, Kansas (the "Company"), and California Distributor, LLC, located in Berkeley, California (the "Distributor").

NOW, THEREFORE, in consideration of the promises hereinafter made by the parties hereto, it is agreed as follows:

ARTICLE I
APPOINTMENT OF DISTRIBUTORSHIP

1. <u>Distribution Right</u>. The Company hereby appoints and grants Distributor the exclusive and non-assignable right to sell **ONLY** the special health remedies of the Company ("Remedy") listed in the then current "Price List" (Exhibit "A" attached hereto). The distribution right shall be limited to customers who have places of business in, and will initially use the Company's products in, the geographic area in California.

2. <u>Prices</u>. All prices stated are FOB the Company's offices in Fort Scott, Kansas. Prices do not include transportation costs which shall be borne by Distributor.

3. <u>Terms</u>. Terms are net cash upon delivery, except where satisfactory credit is established in which case terms are net thirty (30) days from date of delivery.

ARTICLE II
DELIVERY

1. <u>Purchase Orders</u>. Distributor shall order Remedy by written notice to Company. Each order shall specify the number of units to be shipped, the type of units to be shipped, and the desired method of shipment and the installation site.

2. <u>Shipment</u>. All shipments of Remedy shall be made FOB Company's plant.

ARTICLE III
DURATION OF AGREEMENT

1. <u>Term</u>. The term of this Agreement shall be for five (5) years from the date hereof, unless sooner terminated. Termination shall not relieve either party of obligations incurred prior thereto.

2. <u>Termination</u>. This Agreement may be terminated only:

   (a) By either party for substantial breach of any material provision of this Agreement by the other.
   (b) Upon termination of this Agreement all further rights and obligations of the parties shall cease.

ARTICLE IV
GENERAL PROVISIONS

1. <u>Relationship of Parties</u>. The agency relationship between the parties established by this Agreement shall be solely that of Company and Distributor and all rights and powers not expressly granted to the Distributor are expressly reserved to the Company.

2. <u>Assignment</u>. This Agreement constitutes a personal contract and Distributor shall not transfer or assign same or any part thereof without the advance written consent of Company.

3. <u>Entire Agreement</u>. The entire Agreement between the Company and the Distributor covering the Remedy is set forth herein and any amendment or modification shall be in writing.

IN WITNESS WHEREOF, the parties have caused this Agreement to be executed by their duly authorized officers as of the date and year indicated above.

COMPANY   DISTRIBUTOR

By: _____*Herm Cooper*_____   By: _____*Lucienne Tanaguil*_____
(Authorized Officer)   (Authorized Officer)

Belinda Holiday, State Bar #923697
10 N.W. Main Street
Berkeley, CA 94704

Attorney for: Plaintiff Martha Jones

SUPERIOR COURT OF CALIFORNIA

ALAMEDA COUNTY

MARTHA JONES,   )   Case No.: A03-19576
)
      Plaintiff,)
)
      vs.   )
)
CALIFORNIA DISTRIBUTOR, LLC, and)
JAYHAWK CORP.,   )
)
      Defendants.)

COMPLAINT

COMES NOW Plaintiff, Martha Jones, by and through her undersigned attorney, and sues the Defendants, California Distributor, LLC, and Jayhawk Corp., and alleges:

1. This is an action for damages that do not exceed $1,250,000.00.

2. On 9/1/20X0, Plaintiff visited California Distributor on its premises in Berkeley, California.

3. California Distributor is Jayhawk Corp.'s agent in California.

4. Defendants were grossly negligent by allowing a pool of water to form on their recently polished marble flooring.

5. As Plaintiff walked into California Distributor's office, she did not notice the water, slipped, and fell onto her back.

6. An ambulance took Plaintiff to Mercy Hospital where she was diagnosed with a broken back.

7. Plaintiff is no longer able to walk normally and is unable to be employed.

8. Plaintiff is suing for pain, suffering, and permanent disability.

9. Plaintiff requests a trial by jury.

Wherefore Plaintiff demands judgment against the Defendants, jointly and severally, for damages, interest, court costs, and attorney's fees.

Belinda Holiday

Belinda Holiday
Attorney For Plaintiff

ANSWERS 1 OF 4

1. Research (1 Gradable Item)

Answer: IRC § 6695(b)

§ 6695. Other assessable penalties with respect to the preparation of tax returns for other persons

(b) Failure to sign return

Any person who is a tax return preparer with respect to any return or claim for refund, who is required by regulations prescribed by the Secretary to sign such return or claim, and who fails to comply with such regulations with respect to such return or claim shall pay a penalty of $50 for such failure, unless it is shown that such failure is due to reasonable cause and not due to willful neglect. The maximum penalty imposed under this subsection on any person with respect to documents filed during any calendar year shall not exceed $25,000.

2. Liquidation (7 Gradable Items)

1. **$0.** A corporation recognizes no loss in a complete liquidation on a distribution of appreciated property to a parent corporation (one that owns 80% or more of the voting power and the total value of the stock of the liquidating subsidiary).

2. **$5,000.** When an 80%-or-more-owned subsidiary is liquidated, the rules generally applicable to complete liquidations apply to distributions to shareholders other than the parent corporation. Thus, the liquidating corporation recognizes the $5,000 gain realized on the piano as if it were sold to Dawn at its FMV.

3. **$250,000.** A parent corporation's basis in property received in a distribution in complete liquidation of its 80%-or-more-owned subsidiary is the subsidiary corporation's basis in the property immediately before the distribution.

4. **$30,000.** A parent corporation's basis in property received in a distribution in complete liquidation of its 80%-or-more-owned subsidiary is the subsidiary corporation's basis in the property immediately before the distribution.

5. **$50,000.** When an 80%-or-more-owned subsidiary is completely liquidated, the rules generally applicable to complete liquidations apply to distributions to shareholders other than the parent corporation. Thus, Dawn treats the amounts distributed (the cash and the FMV of the other property) as realized in exchange for her stock. She realizes and recognizes a gain of $50,000 [$82,000 (cash) + $15,000 (piano) + $3,000 (keyboard) – $50,000 basis in her stock].

6. **4 months.** Dawn's basis in the piano was not determined by reference to Clef's basis in it. Thus, her holding period began the day after she acquired the piano (September 1).

7. **4 months.** Dawn's basis in the keyboard was not determined by reference to Clef's basis in it. Thus, her holding period began the day after she acquired the keyboard (September 1).

ANSWERS 2 OF 4

3. Bases for Liability (8 Gradable Items)

1. <u>Strict liability in tort.</u> Liability without fault is not a basis for recovery from an accountant.
2. <u>Negligence.</u> The auditors failed to exercise reasonable care and diligence. Omitting an investigation of the leasehold improvements was negligent. The accountant breached a legal duty, and the breach actually and proximately caused the defendant's damages. The auditors were not grossly negligent because the facts do not indicate that they failed to use even slight care.
3. <u>Foreseen third parties.</u> The majority rule is that the accountant is liable to foreseen (but not necessarily individually identified) third parties (foreseen users and users within a foreseen class of users). Foreseen third parties are those to whom the accountant intends to supply the information or knows the client intends to supply the information. They also include persons who use the information in a way the accountant knows it will be used. Financial statements are commonly distributed to lenders.
4. <u>Scienter.</u> Negligent misrepresentation includes all elements of fraud except scienter. Scienter is actual or implied knowledge of fraud.
5. <u>Gross negligence.</u> Gross negligence is failure to use even slight care. The element of intent required to prove fraud is satisfied by gross negligence.
6. <u>Proximate cause.</u> The plaintiff must prove that (a) the defendant breached a legal duty to the plaintiff and (b) the breach actually and proximately caused the plaintiff's damages. The concept of proximate cause limits liability to damages that are reasonably foreseeable.
7. <u>Identification of the third party.</u> A third party is considered to be a primary beneficiary if (a) the accountant is retained principally to benefit the third party, (b) the third party is identified, and (c) the benefit pertains to a specific transaction.
8. <u>Reasonably foreseeable users.</u> Liability for fraud extends to all reasonably foreseeable users of the accountant's work product.

4. Gains and Losses (10 Gradable Items)

1. <u>$3,000; Short-term capital gain.</u> Taxpayer realized $23,000 on the sale when he had a $20,000 cost basis in the stock. Thus, he realized and recognized a gain of $3,000. The stock was a capital asset. Gain from the sale or exchange of a capital asset held for less than 1 year is short-term capital gain.
2. <u>$14,000; Short-term capital gain.</u> Taxpayer realized $139,000 on the sale when he had a $125,000 cost basis in the stock. Thus, he realized and recognized a gain of $14,000. The stock was a capital asset. Gain from the sale or exchange of a capital asset held for less than 1 year is short-term capital gain.
3. <u>$1,000; Long-term capital loss.</u> Taxpayer realized $9,000 on the sale when he had a $10,000 cost basis in the van. Thus, he realized a loss of $1,000. The van was personal-use property, not depreciable. Thus, it was a capital asset. Loss from the sale or exchange of a capital asset held for more than 1 year is long-term capital loss.
4. <u>$59,000; Long-term capital gain.</u> The amount realized was $169,000. Vacant land is not depreciable, so its basis was the $110,000 cost. Thus, there is a $59,000 gain ($169,000 – $110,000). The vacant land is personal-use property held as a capital asset. Since the property was held for over 12 months and sold after May 5, 2003, it is included in the 15% bracket.
5. <u>$5,000; Ordinary loss.</u> Section 1033 nonrecognition does not apply to losses. The amount of the casualty loss is the adjusted basis, net of amounts recovered, e.g., insurance proceeds. Thus, taxpayer recognizes a loss of $5,000 ($50,000 adjusted basis – $45,000 recovery). Section 1231 property is depreciable or real property used in a trade or business and held for more than 1 year, and nonpersonal capital assets held for more than 1 year and involuntarily converted. If there is a net loss for the year from involuntary conversion of property, including by fire, used in the trade or business or capital assets held long-term for investment or in connection with a trade or business, the loss is treated as an ordinary loss. If so, even if the involuntarily converted properties are otherwise Sec. 1231 property, the gains and losses are not included further in Sec. 1231 computations.

ANSWERS 3 OF 4

5. Document Review (3 Gradable Items)

1. A. *[Original Text]* <u>Jayhawk is potentially liable because California Distributor, LLC, is Jayhawk's agent as of the date of the alleged slip-and-fall incident.</u> A principal generally is not liable for a tort (e.g., negligence committed by an independent contractor).

    B. <u>Jayhawk may be liable, but California Distributor, LLC, will indemnify Jayhawk for any losses.</u> The agreement between Jayhawk and California Distributor does not address indemnification. Moreover, the duty to reimburse or indemnify generally extends from the principal to the agent.

    C. **Correct:** <u>Jayhawk is not liable because California Distributor, LLC, is an independent contractor.</u> An agent ordinarily is either an employee or an independent contractor. A principal-employer has an actual right of control over the physical efforts of an employee. But an independent contractor is responsible only for a result. Based on the facts given, the principal has no physical control over the agent's sales efforts or the maintenance of its premises. Accordingly, the agent is an independent contractor. A principal generally is not responsible for the torts (e.g., negligence) of an independent contractor unless the principal has itself committed a tort (e.g., negligent hiring of the independent contractor).

    NOTE: Jayhawk may argue that no agency existed because an agency for an illegal purpose is terminated by operation of law. However, although the FDA has determined that the product is an illegal drug, the plaintiff will argue that an agency by estoppel was created. This condition results when (1) a person presents himself or herself as an agent, (2) the alleged principal knows (or should know) of the representation and fails to make an effective denial, and (3) a third party detrimentally relies on the existence of this presumed agency. Consequently, Jayhawk's best argument is that California Distributor is an independent contractor.

    D. <u>Jayhawk is not liable because California Distributor, LLC, is not an agent as of the date of the alleged slip-and-fall incident.</u> The accident occurred on September 1, 20X0. But the term of the agency was for 5 years from July 6, 20X0.

    E. <u>Jayhawk is not liable because the agency was for an illegal purpose.</u> Plaintiff can argue persuasively that an agency by estoppel was created.

2. A. *[Original Text]* <u>Jayhawk is not liable to Wildcat because of Ace Installer's indemnification agreement.</u> Jayhawk has a direct contractual obligation to Wildcat that is unaffected by Jayhawk's contract with Ace Installer.

    B. <u>Jayhawk is not liable to Wildcat because Ace Installer is an independent contractor.</u> Jayhawk's liability is based on its sale of a defective product, not by a defective installation.

    C. **Correct:** <u>Jayhawk is liable to Wildcat because it materially breached its contract with Wildcat.</u> An implied warranty of merchantability arises in every sale by a merchant who deals in goods of the kind sold. The issue is whether the goods are fit for the ordinary purposes for which such goods are used. Accordingly, the buyer may recover damages because the goods were not as warranted. The measure of damages appropriately includes consequential damages for lost revenue. These damages are awarded if they are foreseeable to a reasonable person at the time of contracting.

    D. <u>Jayhawk is liable only for the price paid by Wildcat for the Jayhawk Widget and its installation.</u> It was reasonably foreseeable that the failure of the Jayhawk Widget, equipment essential to the production facility's operations, would result in lost revenue.

ANSWERS 4 OF 4

3. A. *[Original Text]* Jayhawk South must recognize a liability for potential fines from OSHA due to employee safety issues. The entity's minimal amount of work-related injuries and illnesses does not justify imposition of fines. Employers are required to provide a workplace free of recognized hazards, not a risk-free workplace.

   B. **Correct:** *[Delete Text]* The entity's minimal amount of work-related injuries and illnesses does not justify imposition of fines. Employers are required to provide a workplace free of recognized hazards, not a risk-free workplace.

   C. Jayhawk South must recognize in its financial statements the workers' compensation settlement. The employer's insurer pays the claim. Thus, the employer recognizes only insurance expense.

   D. Jayhawk South must recognize a contingent liability for damages exceeding the workers' compensation settlement. Recovery under the state workers' compensation statute is the employee's exclusive remedy against the employer.

   E. Jayhawk South's insurer need not pay the claim if the employee was contributorily negligent. Neither contributory negligence nor comparative negligence of the worker is a defense of the employer. Assumption of the risk also is not a permissible defense.

APPENDIX B
AICPA UNIFORM CPA EXAMINATION
REG BLUEPRINT WITH GLEIM CROSS-REFERENCES

The AICPA has indicated that the Blueprints have several purposes, including to

- *Document the minimum level of knowledge and skills necessary for initial licensure.*
- *Assist candidates in preparing for the Exam by outlining the knowledge and skills that may be tested.*
- *Apprise educators about the knowledge and skills candidates will need to function as newly licensed CPAs.*
- *Guide the development of Exam questions.*

For your convenience, we have reproduced the AICPA's Regulation Blueprint. We also have provided cross-references to the study units in this book that correspond to the Blueprint's coverage.

Appendix B: AICPA Uniform CPA Examination REG Blueprint with Gleim Cross-References

Area I – Ethics, Professional Responsibilities and Federal Tax Procedures (10-20%)

Gleim Study Unit	Content group/topic	Skill: Remembering and Understanding	Skill: Application	Skill: Analysis	Skill: Evaluation	Representative task
	A. Ethics and responsibilities in tax practice					
SU 1	1. Regulations governing practice before the Internal Revenue Service	✓				Recall the regulations governing practice before the Internal Revenue Service.
			✓			Apply the regulations governing practice before the Internal Revenue Service given a specific scenario.
	2. Internal Revenue Code and Regulations related to tax return preparers	✓				Recall who is a tax return preparer.
		✓				Recall situations that would result in federal tax return preparer penalties.
			✓			Apply potential federal tax return preparer penalties given a specific scenario.
SU 2	**B. Licensing and disciplinary systems**	✓				Understand and explain the role and authority of state boards of accountancy.
	C. Federal tax procedures					
SU 3	1. Audits, appeals and judicial process	✓				Explain the audit and appeals process as it relates to federal tax matters.
		✓				Explain the different levels of the judicial process as they relate to federal tax matters.
			✓			Identify options available to a taxpayer within the audit and appeals process given a specific scenario.
			✓			Identify options available to a taxpayer within the judicial process given a specific scenario.

Appendix B: AICPA Uniform CPA Examination REG Blueprint with Gleim Cross-References 625

Area I – Ethics, Professional Responsibilities and Federal Tax Procedures (10-20%) (continued)

Gleim Study Unit	Content group/topic	Remembering and Understanding	Application	Analysis	Evaluation	Representative task
	C. Federal tax procedures (continued)					
SU 1, SU 3	2. Substantiation and disclosure of tax positions	✓				Summarize the requirements for the appropriate disclosure of a federal tax return position.
			✓			Identify situations in which disclosure of federal tax return positions is required.
			✓			Identify whether substantiation is sufficient given a specific scenario.
SU 3	3. Taxpayer penalties	✓				Recall situations that would result in taxpayer penalties relating to federal tax returns.
			✓			Calculate taxpayer penalties relating to federal tax returns.
SU 3	4. Authoritative hierarchy	✓				Recall the appropriate hierarchy of authority for federal tax purposes.
	D. Legal duties and responsibilities					
SU 2	1. Common law duties and liabilities to clients and third parties	✓				Summarize the tax return preparer's common law duties and liabilities to clients and third parties.
			✓			Identify situations which result in violations of the tax return preparer's common law duties and liabilities to clients and third parties.
SU 1, SU 2	2. Privileged communications, confidentiality and privacy acts	✓				Summarize the rules regarding privileged communications as they relate to tax practice.
			✓			Identify situations in which communications regarding tax practice are considered privileged.

Appendix B: AICPA Uniform CPA Examination REG Blueprint with Gleim Cross-References

Area II – Business Law (10–20%)

Gleim Study Unit	Content group/topic	Skill: Remembering and Understanding	Skill: Application	Skill: Analysis	Skill: Evaluation	Representative task
SU 19	**A. Agency**					
	1. Authority of agents and principals	✓				Recall the types of agent authority.
			✓			Identify whether an agency relationship exists given a specific scenario.
	2. Duties and liabilities of agents and principals	✓				Explain the various duties and liabilities of agents and principals.
			✓			Identify the duty or liability of an agent or principal given a specific scenario.
SU 18	**B. Contracts**					
	1. Formation	✓				Summarize the elements of contract formation between parties.
			✓			Identify whether a valid contract was formed given a specific scenario.
			✓			Identify different types of contracts (e.g., written, verbal, unilateral, express and implied) given a specific scenario.
	2. Performance	✓				Explain the rules related to the fulfillment of performance obligations necessary for an executed contract.
			✓			Identify whether both parties to a contract have fulfilled their performance obligation given a specific scenario.

Appendix B: AICPA Uniform CPA Examination REG Blueprint with Gleim Cross-References 627

Area II – Business Law (10-20%) (continued)

Gleim Study Unit	Content group/topic	Skill				Representative task
		Remembering and Understanding	Application	Analysis	Evaluation	
	B. Contracts (continued)					
	3. Discharge, breach and remedies	✓				Explain the different ways in which a contract can be discharged (e.g., performance, agreement and operation of the law).
		✓				Summarize the different remedies available to a party for breach of contract.
			✓			Identify situations involving breach of contract.
			✓			Identify whether a contract has been discharged given a specific scenario.
			✓			Identify the remedy available to a party for breach of contract given a specific scenario.
SU 20	**C. Debtor-creditor relationships**					
		✓				Explain the rights, duties and liabilities of debtors, creditors and guarantors.
		✓				Recall basic bankruptcy concepts, for example, types of bankruptcies, rights of debtors and creditors and discharge of indebtedness.
		✓				Explain the difference between a secured and unsecured creditor and the requirements needed to perfect a security interest.
			✓			Identify rights, duties or liabilities of debtors, creditors or guarantors given a specific scenario.

Area II – Business Law (10-20%) (continued)

Gleim Study Unit	Content group/topic	Skill: Remembering and Understanding	Skill: Application	Skill: Analysis	Skill: Evaluation	Representative task
SU 19	D. Federal laws and regulations (e.g., employment tax, qualified health plans and worker classification)					
		✓				Summarize federal laws and regulations, for example, employment tax, qualified health plans and worker classification federal laws and regulations.
			✓			Identify violations of federal laws and regulations, for example, employment tax, qualified health plans and worker classification federal laws and regulations.
SU 17	E. Business structure					
	1. Selection and formation of business entity and related operation and termination	✓				Summarize the processes for formation and termination of various business entities.
		✓				Summarize the non-tax operational features for various business entities.
			✓			Identify the type of business entity that is best described by a given set of nontax-related characteristics.
	2. Rights, duties, legal obligations and authority of owners and management	✓				Summarize the rights, duties, legal obligations and authority of owners and management.
			✓			Identify the rights, duties, legal obligations or authorities of owners or management given a specific scenario.

Appendix B: AICPA Uniform CPA Examination REG Blueprint with Gleim Cross-References 629

Area III – Federal Taxation of Property Transactions (12-22%)

A. Acquisition and disposition of assets

Gleim Study Unit	Content group/topic	Remembering and Understanding	Application	Analysis	Evaluation	Representative task
SU 9	1. Basis and holding period of assets		✓			Calculate the tax basis of an asset.
			✓			Determine the holding period of a disposed asset for classification of tax gain or loss.
SU 9, SU 10	2. Taxable and nontaxable dispositions		✓			Calculate the realized and recognized gain or loss on the disposition of assets for federal income tax purposes.
			✓			Calculate the realized gain, recognized gain and deferred gain on like-kind property exchange transactions for federal income tax purposes.
				✓		Analyze asset sale and exchange transactions to determine whether they are taxable or nontaxable.
SU 9, SU 10	3. Amount and character of gains and losses, and netting process (including installment sales)		✓			Calculate the amount of capital gain or loss for federal income tax purposes.
			✓			Calculate the amount of ordinary income and loss for federal income tax purposes.
			✓			Calculate the amount of gain on an installment sale for federal income tax purposes.
				✓		Review asset transactions to determine the character (capital vs. ordinary) of the gain or loss for federal income tax purposes.
				✓		Analyze an agreement of sale of an asset to determine whether it qualifies for installment sale treatment for federal income tax purposes.

Area III – Federal Taxation of Property Transactions (12-22%) (continued)

Gleim Study Unit	Content group/topic	Remembering and Understanding	Application	Analysis	Evaluation	Representative task
	A. Acquisition and disposition of assets (continued)					
SU 10	4. Related party transactions (including imputed interest)	✓				Recall related parties for federal income tax purposes.
		✓				Recall the impact of related party ownership percentages on acquisition and disposition transactions of property for federal income tax purposes.
			✓			Calculate the direct and indirect ownership percentages of corporation stock or partnership interests to determine whether there are related parties for federal income tax purposes.
			✓			Calculate a taxpayer's basis in an asset that was disposed of at a loss to the taxpayer by a related party.
			✓			Calculate a taxpayer's gain or loss on a subsequent disposition of an asset to an unrelated third party that was previously disposed of at a loss to the taxpayer by a related party.
			✓			Calculate the impact of imputed interest on related party transactions for federal tax purposes.
	B. Cost recovery (depreciation, depletion and amortization)					
SU 9			✓			Calculate tax depreciation for tangible business property and tax amortization of intangible assets.
			✓			Calculate depletion for federal income tax purposes.
				✓		Compare the tax benefits of the different expensing options for tax depreciation for federal income tax purposes.
				✓		Reconcile the activity in the beginning and ending accumulated tax depreciation account.

Area III – Federal Taxation of Property Transactions (12-22%) (continued)

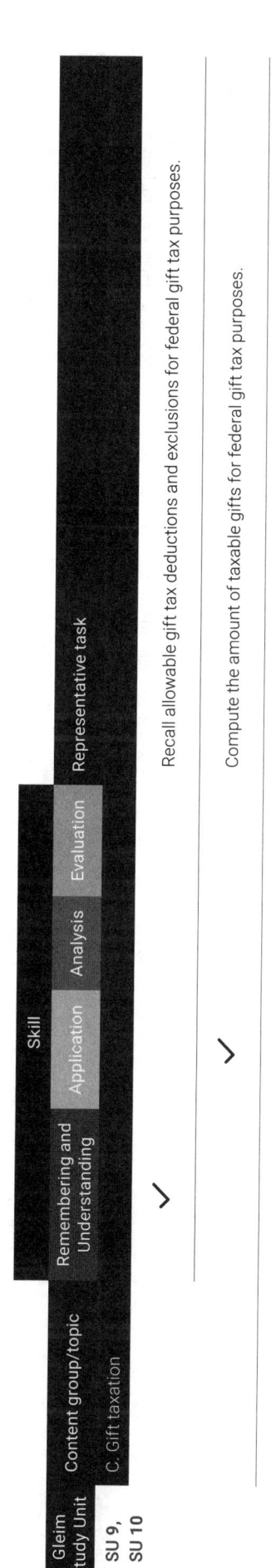

Gleim Study Unit	Content group/topic	Skill: Remembering and Understanding	Skill: Application	Skill: Analysis	Skill: Evaluation	Representative task
SU 9, SU 10	C. Gift taxation	✓				Recall allowable gift tax deductions and exclusions for federal gift tax purposes.
			✓			Compute the amount of taxable gifts for federal gift tax purposes.

Area IV – Federal Taxation of Individuals (including tax preparation and planning strategies) (15-25%)

Gleim Study Unit	Content group/topic	Skill: Remembering and Understanding	Skill: Application	Skill: Analysis	Skill: Evaluation	Representative task
SU 4, SU 6	A. Gross income (inclusions and exclusions)		✓			Calculate the amounts that should be included in, or excluded from, an individual's gross income as reported on federal Form 1040 – *U.S. Individual Income Tax Return*.
				✓		Analyze projected income for use in tax planning in future years.
				✓		Analyze client-provided documentation to determine the appropriate amount of gross income to be reported on federal Form 1040 – *U.S. Individual Income Tax Return*.
SU 4	B. Reporting of items from pass-through entities		✓			Prepare federal Form 1040 – *U.S. Individual Income Tax Return* based on the information provided on Schedule K-1.
SU 6, SU 7	C. Adjustments and deductions to arrive at adjusted gross income and taxable income		✓			Calculate the amount of adjustments and deductions to arrive at adjusted gross income and taxable income on federal Form 1040 – *U.S. Individual Income Tax Return*.
			✓			Calculate the qualifying business income (QBI) deduction for federal income tax purposes.
				✓		Analyze client-provided documentation to determine the validity of the deductions taken to arrive at adjusted gross income or taxable income on federal Form 1040 – *U.S. Individual Income Tax Return*.
SU 8	D. Passive activity losses (excluding foreign tax credit implications)	✓				Recall passive activities for federal income tax purposes.
			✓			Calculate net passive activity gains and losses for federal income tax purposes.
			✓			Prepare a loss carryforward schedule for passive activities for federal income tax purposes.
			✓			Calculate utilization of suspended losses on the disposition of a passive activity for federal income tax purposes.

Appendix B: AICPA Uniform CPA Examination REG Blueprint with Gleim Cross-References 633

Area IV – Federal Taxation of Individuals (including tax preparation and planning strategies) (15-25%) (continued)

Gleim Study Unit	Content group/topic	Remembering and Understanding	Application	Analysis	Evaluation	Representative task
SU 8	E. Loss limitations		✓			Calculate loss limitations for federal income tax purposes for an individual taxpayer.
				✓		Analyze projections to effectively minimize loss limitations for federal income tax purposes for an individual taxpayer.
				✓		Determine the basis and the potential application of at-risk rules that can apply to activities for federal income tax purposes.
SU 3	F. Filing status	✓				Recall taxpayer filing status for federal income tax purposes.
		✓				Recall relationships meeting the definition of dependent for purposes of determining taxpayer filing status.
			✓			Identify taxpayer filing status for federal income tax purposes given a specific scenario.
SU 8	G. Computation of tax and credits	✓				Recall and define minimum requirements for individual federal estimated tax payments to avoid penalties.
			✓			Calculate the tax liability based on an individual's taxable income for federal income tax purposes.
			✓			Calculate the impact of the tax deductions and tax credits and their effect on federal Form 1040 – *U.S. Individual Income Tax Return*.

Area V – Federal Taxation of Entities (including tax preparation and planning strategies) (28-38%)

Gleim Study Unit	Content group/topic	Skill: Remembering and Understanding	Skill: Application	Skill: Analysis	Skill: Evaluation	Representative task
SU 11, SU 13, SU 14, SU 15, SU 16	A. Tax treatment of formation and liquidation of business entities		>			Calculate the realized and recognized gain for the owner and entity upon the formation and liquidation of business entities for federal income tax purposes.
				>		Compare the tax implications of liquidating distributions from different business entities.
				>		Analyze the tax advantages and disadvantages in the formation of a new business entity.
SU 16	B. Differences between book and tax income (loss)		>			Identify permanent vs. temporary differences to be reported on Schedule M-1 and/or M-3.
			>			Calculate the book/tax differences to be reported on a Schedule M-1 or M-3.
			>			Prepare a Schedule M-1 or M-3 for a business entity.
				>		Reconcile the differences between book and taxable income (loss) of a business entity.
	C. C corporations					
SU 4, SU 11, SU 12	1. Computations of taxable income, tax liability and allowable credits		>			Calculate taxable income and tax liability for a C corporation.
			>			Calculate the credits allowable as a reduction of tax for a C corporation.

Appendix B: AICPA Uniform CPA Examination REG Blueprint with Gleim Cross-References 635

Area V – Federal Taxation of Entities (including tax preparation and planning strategies) (28-38%) (continued)

Gleim Study Unit	Content group/topic	Remembering and Understanding	Application	Analysis	Evaluation	Representative task
	C. C corporations (continued)					
SU 11	2. Net operating losses and capital loss limitations		✓			Calculate the current-year net operating or capital loss of a C corporation.
			✓			Prepare a net operating and/or capital loss carryforward schedule for a C corporation.
SU 12, SU 13	3. Entity/owner transactions, including contributions, loans and distributions		✓			Calculate an entity owner's basis in C corporation stock for federal income tax purposes.
			✓			Calculate the tax gain (loss) realized and recognized by both the shareholders and the corporation on a contribution or on a distribution in complete liquidation of a C corporation for federal income tax purposes.
			✓			Calculate the tax gain (loss) realized and recognized on a nonliquidating distribution by both a C corporation and its shareholders for federal income tax purposes.
			✓			Calculate the amount of the cash distributions to shareholders of a C corporation that represents a dividend, return of capital or capital gain for federal income tax purposes.
				✓		Reconcile an owner's beginning and ending basis in C corporation stock for federal income tax purposes.
SU 12	4. Consolidated tax returns	✓				Recall the requirements for filing a consolidated federal Form 1120 – *U.S. Corporation Income Tax Return*.
			✓			Prepare a consolidated federal Form 1120 – *U.S. Corporation Income Tax Return*.
			✓			Calculate federal taxable income for a consolidated federal Form 1120 – *U.S. Corporation Income Tax Return*.

Area V – Federal Taxation of Entities (including tax preparation and planning strategies) (28-38%) (continued)

C. C corporations (continued)

Gleim Study Unit	Content group/topic	Skill: Remembering and Understanding	Skill: Application	Skill: Analysis	Skill: Evaluation	Representative task
SU 13	5. Multijurisdictional tax issues (including consideration of local, state and international tax issues)	✓				Define the general concept and rationale of nexus with respect to multijurisdictional transactions.
		✓				Define the general concept and rationale of apportionment and allocation with respect to state and local taxation.
		✓				Explain the difference between a foreign branch and foreign subsidiary with respect to federal income taxation to a U.S. company.
		✓				Explain how different types of foreign income are sourced in calculating the foreign tax credit for federal income tax purposes.
		✓				Recall payment sources to determine federal tax withholding requirements.
		✓				Identify situations where the base erosion and anti-abuse tax (BEAT) would apply.
		✓				Identify factors that would qualify income as Foreign Derived Intangible Income (FDII).
		✓				Define the components of Global Intangible Low-Taxed Income (GILTI).
			✓			Identify situations that would create nexus for multijurisdictional transactions.
			✓			Identify the federal filing requirements of cross border business investments.
			✓			Calculate the apportionment percentage used in determining state taxable income.

Area V – Federal Taxation of Entities (including tax preparation and planning strategies) (28-38%) (continued)

Gleim Study Unit: SU 14

Content group/topic	Remembering and Understanding	Application	Analysis	Evaluation	Representative task
D. S corporations					
1. Eligibility and election	✓				Recall eligible shareholders for an S corporation for federal income tax purposes.
	✓				Recall S corporation eligibility requirements for federal income tax purposes.
	✓				Explain the procedures to make a valid S corporation election for federal income tax purposes.
		✓			Identify situations in which S corporation status would be revoked or terminated for federal income tax purposes.
2. Determination of ordinary business income (loss) and separately stated items		✓			Calculate ordinary business income (loss) and separately stated items for an S corporation for federal income tax purposes.
			✓		Analyze both the accumulated adjustment account and the other adjustments account of an S corporation for federal income tax purposes.
			✓		Analyze the accumulated earnings and profits account of an S corporation that has been converted from a C corporation.
			✓		Analyze components of S corporation income/deductions to determine classification as ordinary business income (loss) or separately stated items on federal Form 1120S – U.S. Income Tax Return for an S Corporation.
3. Basis of shareholder's interest		✓			Calculate the shareholder's basis in S corporation stock for federal income tax purposes.
			✓		Analyze shareholder transactions with an S corporation to determine the impact on the shareholder's basis for federal income tax purposes.

Area V – Federal Taxation of Entities (including tax preparation and planning strategies) (28-38%) (continued)

Gleim Study Unit	Content group/topic	Skill: Remembering and Understanding	Skill: Application	Skill: Analysis	Skill: Evaluation	Representative task
	D. S corporations (continued)					
	4. Entity/owner transactions (including contributions, loans and distributions)		✓			Calculate the realized and recognized gain or loss to the shareholder of property contribution to an S corporation.
			✓			Calculate the allocation of S corporation income (loss) after the sale of a shareholder's share in the S corporation for federal income tax purposes.
				✓		Analyze the shareholder's impact of an S corporation's loss in excess of the shareholder's basis for federal income tax purposes.
				✓		Analyze the federal income tax implication to the shareholders and the S corporation resulting from shareholder contributions and loans as well as S corporation distributions and loans to shareholders.
	5. Built-in gains tax	✓				Recall factors that cause a built-in gains tax to apply for federal income tax purposes.
	E. Partnerships					
SU 15	1. Determination of ordinary business income (loss) and separately stated items		✓			Calculate ordinary business income (loss) and separately stated items for a partnership for federal income tax purposes.
				✓		Analyze components of partnership income/deductions to determine classification as ordinary business income (loss) or separately stated items on federal Form 1065 – U.S Return of Partnership Income.
SU 15	2. Basis of partner's interest and basis of assets contributed to the partnership		✓			Calculate the partner's basis in the partnership for federal income tax purposes.
			✓			Calculate the partnership's basis in assets contributed by the partner for federal income tax purposes.
				✓		Analyze partner contributions to the partnership to determine the impact on the partner's basis for federal income tax purposes.

Appendix B: AICPA Uniform CPA Examination REG Blueprint with Gleim Cross-References 639

Area V – Federal Taxation of Entities (including tax preparation and planning strategies) (28-38%) (continued)

E. Partnerships (continued)

Gleim Study Unit	Content group/topic	Remembering and Understanding	Application	Analysis	Evaluation	Representative task
SU 15	3. Partnership and partner elections	✓				Recall partner elections applicable to a partnership for federal income tax purposes.
SU 16	4. Transactions between a partner and the partnership (including services performed by a partner and loans)		✓			Calculate the tax implications of certain transactions between a partner and partnership (such as services performed by a partner or loans) for federal income tax purposes.
				✓		Analyze the tax implications of a partner transaction with the partnership (such as services performed by a partner or loans) to determine the impact on the partner's tax basis for federal income tax purposes.
SU 16	5. Impact of partnership liabilities on a partner's interest in a partnership		✓			Calculate the impact of increases and decreases of partnership liabilities on a partner's basis for federal income tax purposes.
				✓		Analyze the impact of partnership liabilities as they relate to the general partners and limited partners for federal income tax purposes.
SU 16	6. Distribution of partnership assets		✓			Calculate the realized and recognized gains (losses) by the partnership and partners of liquidating distributions from the partnership for federal income tax purposes.
			✓			Calculate the realized and recognized gains (losses) by the partnership and partners of nonliquidating distributions from the partnership for federal income tax purposes.
			✓			Calculate the partner's basis of partnership assets received in a liquidating distribution for federal income tax purposes.
			✓			Calculate the partner's basis of partnership assets received in a nonliquidating distribution for federal income tax purposes.

Appendix B: AICPA Uniform CPA Examination REG Blueprint with Gleim Cross-References

Area V – Federal Taxation of Entities (including tax preparation and planning strategies) (28-38%) (continued)

Gleim Study Unit	Content group/topic	Skill: Remembering and Understanding	Skill: Application	Skill: Analysis	Skill: Evaluation	Representative task
SU 15, SU 16	E. Partnerships (continued) 7. Ownership changes	>				Recall the situations in which a partnership would be terminated for federal income tax purposes.
			>			Calculate the allocation of partnership income (loss) after the sale of a partner's share in the partnership for federal income tax purposes.
			>			Calculate the revised basis of partnership assets due to a transfer of a partnership interest for federal income tax purposes.
SU 17	F. Limited liability companies	>				Recall the tax classification options for a limited liability company for federal income tax purposes.
SU 5	G. Trusts	>				Recall and explain the differences between simple and complex trusts for federal income tax purposes.
SU 5	H. Tax-exempt organizations 1. Types of organizations	>				Recall the different types of tax-exempt organizations for federal tax purposes.
	2. Unrelated business income	>				Recall the different types of unrelated business income for tax-exempt organizations for federal tax purposes.

INDEX

150% declining balance. 233

200% declining balance. 233
2021 individual income tax rates. 159

Abetting or aiding. 19
Above-the-line deductions. 160
Accelerated cost recovery (ACR). 233
Acceptance. 502, 584
   Of collateral. 574
Accident and health plans. 148, 398
Accord and satisfaction. 513
Accountant-client privilege. 35
Accountant's duties. 31
Accounting method. 109, 110, 298, 330, 392
Accounts receivable. 244
Accrual method. 113
Accumulated adjustments account (AAA). 402
Act
   Affordable Care. 549
   Bankruptcy Reform, of 1978. 575
   Federal
      Insurance Contributions (FICA). 144, 547
      Unemployment Tax (FUTA). 146, 548
   Revised
      Model Business Corporation. 479
   Uniform
      Limited Partnership. 474
      Partnership. 467
   Uniform Div. of Income for Tax Purp. (UDITPA). 371
Actual authority. 470, 535
   Express. 535
   Implied. 535
Ad valorem taxes. 169
Adaptation. 225
Additional Child Tax Credit. 204
Adjusted basis. 230
Adjustments. 425, 583
Administration, S corporations. 393
Administrative
   Law. 49
   Proceedings. 30
Adoption
   By corporation. 480
   Credit. 201
Advertising. 14
   Fees. 14
Affiliated group. 330
Affordable Care Act. 549
After-acquired property clause. 561
Agency. 531
   By estoppel. 533
   Coupled with an interest. 534, 546

Agent. 470, 484
   Authority. 535
   Breach of duty. 538
   Del credere. 534
   Duties to. 539
      Principal. 536
   Enrolled. 12
   General. 534
   Legal status. 544
   Special. 534
   Sub-. 536
   Types. 534
   Universal. 534
Agreements. 510
   Operating. 476
   Preincorporation subscription. 480
   Stock subscription. 480
Aiding or abetting. 19
Alimony. 162
   And separate maintenance payments. 85
Allocable cost. 227
Allocation. 397
Alternative depreciation system. 234
American Opportunity Credit. 204
Amortizable items. 397
Amortization. 241
Annual exclusion. 284
Annuity. 88, 95
Apparent authority. 470, 535, 546
Apportionment, UDITPA. 372
Articles of
   Incorporation. 480, 481
   Organization. 476
Assessment of deficiency. 59
Asset
   Depreciation range (ADR). 233
   Distributions of partnership. 445
   Exempt. 580
   Lump-sum. 227
Assignee rights. 520
Assignment. 519
   Of
      Income. 63
      Rights. 518
Assignor's warranties. 520
At-risk rules. 210, 400, 426
Attachment. 563
Attorney. 12
Authentication. 563
Authority of the board. 484
Automatic
   Order for relief. 576
   Perfection. 566
   Stay. 575
Automobile expenses. 138
Awards. 91, 96

Bad debts. 112, 139, 311

Bankruptcy. 575
   Code. 575
   Liquidations. 576
   Reform Act. 575
   Reorganization. 367
   Voluntary and involuntary. 576
Bargained-for exchange. 504
Bartered services or goods. 86
Basis. 224, 364
   Adjusted. 230
   Boot. 300
   Distributed property. 342
   Distributee. 449
   Gift. 284
   Like-kind exchanges. 268
   Partner's. 416
   Partnership's. 418
   Shareholder. 300
Beneficiary
   Donee. 517
   Incidental. 518
Best practices for tax advisors. 14
Betterment. 225
Bilateral contracts. 500, 504
Blueprints, AICPA. 623
Board of directors. 480, 482, 484
Bond. 111
   Market discount. 251
   Premium treatment. 251
   Repurchase. 303, 312
Bonus depreciation. 240
Boot. 267, 299, 365
Branch. 369
Breach. 515
Brother-sister. 333
Building rehabilitation. 232
Built-in gains (BIG) tax. 406
Business
   Expense. 135, 142
   Gifts. 140
   Income. 85, 135
   Judgment rule. 486
   Organizations. 467
   Property. 275
Buyers of goods. 570
Bylaws. 480

C corporation. 479
Cafeteria plans. 150
Capacity. 506
Capital
   Assets. 244
   Contributions. 302
   Cost recovery. 233
   Expenditures. 142
   Gains and losses. 208, 316, 372
   Recovery, corporate distribution. 341
   Return of. 94
Capitalization. 468, 476
Capitalized costs. 225
Carryovers. 329, 361, 397
Cash method. 110
Casualty losses. 177, 206, 232, 251, 313
Censure. 15

Certificate of
   Authority. 479
   Limited partnership. 474
Certified public accountant (CPA). 12
Chapter
   7 liquidation. 579
   11 reorganizations. 583
Character. 365, 397, 424, 442
Charging order. 469
Charitable
   Contributions. 173, 305
   Deductions. 121, 285
Check-the-box regulations. 296
Child
   And
      Dependent Care Credit. 196
      Other Dependents Tax Credit. 198
   Support. 85
Circular 230. 15
Claim-of-right doctrine. 111
Claims for refund. 58
Class action suit. 484
Client
   Compliance. 13
   Confidential information. 36
   Funds. 13
   Records. 14
   Responsibilities to. 36
Closed cases. 61
Clothing. 173
Collateral. 574
Commercial impracticability. 514
Committee
   Of unsecured creditors. 583
   Reports. 48
Compensation. 136, 308
   Injury or sickness. 98
Compensatory damages. 516
Complete liquidation. 361
Completed-contract. 116
Complex trusts. 122
Composition with creditors. 513
Conditional acceptance. 502
Conduct of practice. 13, 15
Confidentiality. 36
   Privilege. 20
Confirmation. 584
Conflict of interest. 13
Conflicting
   Interest transactions. 485
   Tax authority. 48
Consensual relationship. 532
Consent to disclosure. 20
Consequential damages. 516
Consideration. 504
   Legal sufficiency. 504
   Past. 504
   Substitutes for. 505
Consolidated returns. 330
Consolidation. 331, 366, 487
Constant yield method. 311
Constitutional rights. 488
Constructive
   Fraud. 34
   Ownership. 334, 360
   Receipt. 110

Index

Contraction of corporation. 363
Contracts. 499, 508
    Annuity. 88, 95
    Assignment. 518
    Beneficiaries. 517
    Breach. 515
        Mitigation. 516
    Capacity. 506
    Conditions. 515
    Duties of parties. 515
    Employment. 507
    Express and implied. 499
    Legality. 507
    Long-term. 116
    Part performance. 511
    Preincorporation. 479
    Price. 117
    Remedies, discharges. 515
    Restraint of trade. 507
    Substituted. 514
    Suretyship. 510
    Third-party. 517
    Unilateral and bilateral. 500
    Valid, unenforceable, voidable, void. 500
Contractual
    Defenses. 32
    Liability. 31, 538, 541
Contributed property. 416
Contributors and reviewers. iv
Control. 299, 364, 566, 572
    Of collateral. 572
Controlled
    Foreign corporation (CFC). 93, 375
    Group. 333
Convention, mid-
    Month. 235
    Year. 235
Conversion of income. 64
Copy of tax return. 18
Copyrights. 244, 372
Corporate
    Basis in property. 300
    Credits, disallowed. 328
    Distributee. 363
    Distribution gain. 339
    Distributor. 363
    Gains. 361
    Level items. 397
    Opportunity. 485
    Powers. 481
    Tax. 357
        Computations. 327
    Taxable income. 295
Corporations. 467
    Advantages. 488
    Books and records. 483
    Deductions. 303
    Disadvantages. 489
    Financial structure. 482
    Formation. 479
    Income tax formula. 298
    Inspection rights. 483
    Operation. 481
    Professional. 479
    Termination. 488
Corpus. 122

Cost
    Allocable. 227
    Basis. 224
Counteroffer. 502
Court system. 50
Covenant not to compete. 507
Coverdell Education Savings Accounts (CESA). . . 165
CPAs. 12
Cramdown. 584
Creditor. 472
    Committees. 577
    -Debtor relationships. 561
    Rights. 572, 580
Credits. 195
    General Business. 200
    Nonrefundable personal. 195
    Refundable. 202
Criminal liability. 543
Current
    Distributions. 446
    -Year receipts. 118
Customary partner services. 440

Damages. 516
De minimis
    Expense. 227
    Fringe benefits. 147
Death. 545
    Benefits. 148
Debt
    Basis. 399
    Discharge. 232
    Nondischargeable. 582
Debtor
    -Creditor relationships. 561
    -In-possession. 583
    Remedies. 574
    Rights and duties. 572, 577
Deductible charitable contributions. 121
Deductions. 112, 160, 166
    Dividends-received. 306
    Education. 164
    Health savings account. 160
    Itemized. 167
    Of a corporation. 303
    Other miscellaneous. 178
Default. 572
Defenses
    Contractual. 32
    Fraud. 35
Deferred like-kind exchanges. 267
Delegation of performance. 521
Dental expenses. 168
Depletion. 243
Depreciable
    Basis. 229
    Property. 244, 278
Depreciated property distribution. 358
Derivative suit. 484
Diligence. 13
Direct
    Liability. 542
    Suit. 484
Directors, board of. 480, 482, 484

Index

Disaffirm. 506
Disallowed corporate credits. 328
Disaster areas. 207
Disbarment. 15
Discharge. 515, 581
    Agreement. 513
    By operation of law. 514
    Indebtedness. 92
    Of debt. 302
    Revocation. 582
Disciplinary mechanisms
    AICPA. 29
    IRS. 30
    SEC. 30
Disclosed principal. 540
Disclosure of
    Tax positions. 56
    Taxpayer information. 19
Dismissal. 582
Display racks. 369
Disposition. 264
    Of installment obligations. 266
Disproportionate distributions. 448
Dissenters (appraisal) rights. 484
Dissociation. 471
Dissolution. 472, 475, 488
Distributions. 339, 402, 445, 468, 476, 482
    Amount. 339
    Bankruptcy. 580
    In kind. 472
    Money. 446
    Property. 403, 446
    Shareholder treatment of. 403
    Taxable stock. 344
Dividends. 331, 340, 372, 482
    Not essentially equivalent to. 360
    -Received deduction (DRD). 306
    Stock. 98
Due
    Dates. 55
    Partnership return. 429
Duress. 509
Duties of partners. 470
Duty
    Of loyalty. 485
    To
        Disclose facts. 508
        Respond to requests 572

Earned Income Credit (EIC). 202
Earnings and profits (E&P). 338
Economic benefit. 111
Education
    Deductions. 164
    Expenses. 309
    Tuition and fees. 284
Educator expenses. 160
Elderly or Disabled Credit. 198
Election. 330, 420
    S corporations. 391
Eligibility, S corporations. 390
Eligible parties. 579
Emergency authority. 536

Employee. 544
    Achievement awards. 140
    Benefits. 147
        S corporation. 398
    Discounts. 147
    Expenditures. 82
    -Owners. 398
Employer
    Mandate. 550
    -Provided
        Educational assistance. 147
        Life insurance. 148
Employment tax. 139, 547
Engagement letter. 31
Enrolled agent. 12
Entertainment expenses. 138, 309
Equity insolvency test. 482
Essential health benefits. 551
Estate. 360, 579
Estimated tax payments. 52, 336
Estoppel promissory. 505
Exchange. 244
Exclusions. 94
Exempt
    Organizations. 109, 119
    Status. 119
Exemption. 109
Express
    Authority. 485
    Condition. 515
    Contracts. 499
Extension. 55, 60
    Automatic 6-month. 55
Extraordinary dividend, corporate. 342

Failure to file. 60
Family partnership. 428
FBAR. 379
Federal
    Insurance Contributions Act (FICA). 144, 547
    Unemployment Tax Act (FUTA). 146, 548
Feeder organizations. 120
Fees. 13
    That may be advertised. 14
Fiduciary. 532
    Duty. 470, 485, 537
    Relationship. 485
FIFO. 116
Filing. 564
    Of a petition. 575
    Requirements. 54
    Status. 65
Financing statement. 564
Fines, corporate taxable income. 310
Fiscal year. 420
Fixed amount stated. 440
Foreign
    Corporation. 479
    -Earned income exclusion. 99
    Financial assets. 380
    Tax Credit (FTC). 196, 328
        Limit. 329
    Travel expense. 138
Foreseeable user. 34

Foreseen third parties. 33
Form
   966. 362
   990-T. 121
   1023. 120
   1040. 247
   1065. . . . . 429, 469
   1099-DIV. 339, 362, 405
   8938. 380
   FinCEN Report 114. 379
Formation. 298, 416, 476
   Agency. 532
Foster care. 99
Fraud. 19, 60, 65, 508
   Defenses. 35
   Elements. 508
   In the
      Execution. 508
      Inducement. 508
   Liability. 34
   Statute of. 510
Fringe benefits. 147, 398
   De minimis. 147
   Employee discounts. 147
   Qualified transportation. 147
Frivolous
   Submission. 18
   Tax return. 18
Frustration of purpose. 514
Full
   Disclosure. 485
   -Time equivalent employees (FTEs). 549

Gain. 341
   Capital. 316
   Long-term capital. 245
   Net capital. 245
   On sale of principal residence. 98
   Partnership's. 418
   Realized. 357
   Recognized. 245, 264, 416
      Corporate. 339
Gambling winnings/losses. 91
General
   Business Credit. 200
      Recapture. 406
   Creditors. 581
   Partner. 474
Genuine assent. 508
Gift. 96, 229
   Amount. 283
   Business. 140
   Corporate taxable income. 307
   Partnership interest. 427
   Property. 280
   Tax. 261, 283
Gleim, Irvin N. iii
Good faith. 470, 513
Government publications. 244
Grantor trust. 122

Gross
   Income. 79, 80
      Corporation. 302
   Negligence. 34
   Profit. 117
      Percentage. 118, 265
Group term life insurance. 548
Guaranteed payment. 440

Head of household. 66
Health
   Plans. 148
   Savings Account. 160
Holding period. 245, 418
Homeowners' associations. 120
Household items. 173
Hybrid methods. 118

Illegal activities. 91
Illegality. 502, 514, 545
Implied
   Authority. 485
   Condition. 515
   Contracts. 499
   In
      Fact. 499, 515
      Law. 515, 533
Impossibility. 514
Improper purpose. 483
Imputed interest. 83, 284
Incentive stock options. 149
Incidental damages. 516
Includible corporations. 330
Income. 122
   Business. 85, 135
   Corporate taxable. 295
   Estate or trust. 87
   Foreign-earned, exclusion. 99
   Gross. 79, 80
      Corporation. 302
   In respect of a decedent (IRD). 87
   Individual tax formula. 79
   Investment. 87, 171
   Multiple assets. 280
   Ordinary. 268
   Other gross. 91
   Partner's, taxable. 421
   Partnership. 87, 421
   Passive investment tax. 405
   Rent. 86
   Royalties. 87
   S corporations. 87
   Sec.
      1245 ordinary. 278
      1250 ordinary. 278
   Self-employment. 135
   Sinking-fund. 303
   Tax. 122, 139, 170
      -Exempt. 142
      Formula, corporation. 298
   Unrealized. 94
Incompetence. 502
Incorporation. 480

Indemnify.	486
Independent contractors.	544
Individual income tax	
Formula.	79
Rates.	159
Inducements.	91
Information request.	13
Inherent authority.	485
Inheritance.	428
Inherited property.	230, 280
Injunction.	517
Innocent misrepresentation.	509
Insolvency.	575
Installment	
Method.	117
Sales.	264, 280
Insurance.	169, 310
Expense.	139
Payments for living expenses.	99
Intangible.	142, 241
Inter vivos gifts.	284
Intercompany transactions.	332
Interest.	372
Distributional.	477
Expense.	171, 312
On	
A loan.	112
Government obligations.	97
Transferability of.	488
Intergroup transactions.	335
Internal revenue	
Bulletin (IRB).	50
Code (IRC) of 1986.	48
Service (IRS)	
Disciplinary mechanisms.	30
Practicing before.	11
Disbarment.	15
Suspension.	15
Publications.	50
Inventory.	115, 244, 427, 571
Produced.	115
Purchased.	115
Investment	
Income.	87, 171
Interest expense.	171
Involuntary	
Conversions.	271
Proceedings.	576
IRAs.	162
IRS reallocation.	397
Issuing stock.	487
Itemized deductions.	167
Joint	
And several liability.	471
Ethics enforcement program (JEEP).	29
Ventures.	473
Judicial	
Determination.	477
Law.	50
Jury duty pay.	165

Kiddie Tax.	54, 63
Land.	244
Lease	
Cost of acquiring.	241
Improvements.	99
Of land.	278
Least aggregate deferral tax year.	419
Legality.	504, 507
Legislative law.	48
Letter, 30-day.	59
Liabilities, like-kind exchanges.	268
Liability.	299, 364, 416
After delegation.	521
Contractual.	31, 538, 540
Criminal.	543
Direct.	542
Fraud.	34
Joint and several.	471
Limited.	488
Nonrecourse.	444
Of	
Members and managers.	477
Partners.	471
Personal.	486
Principal's.	539
Recourse.	443
Relief.	427
Shareholder property contribution.	299
Subsidiary liquidation.	364
To third parties.	31
Tort.	542
Treatment of partnership.	443
Unlimited personal.	468
Vicarious.	543
Licensing.	29
Statutes.	507
Lien	
Arising by operation of law.	571
Artisan's.	571
Life insurance proceeds.	94, 148, 302
Lifetime Learning Credit.	197
LIFO.	116
Recapture.	406
Like-kind exchanges.	267
Limited	
Liability.	488
Company (LLC).	296, 476
Manager-managed.	477
Termination.	477
Partnerships (LLPs).	473
Partner.	474
Partnership.	474
Liquidated damages.	516
Liquidating distributions.	448
Liquidation.	363
Bankruptcy.	576
Corporate.	361
Loans.	94, 140, 441
Lodging.	137, 149
Long-term contracts.	116

Loss 331, 448
   Capital 208, 316
   Casualty and theft 177, 206, 232, 313
   Corporate
      Liquidation 361
      Unrecognized 339
   Disaster areas 207
   Limits 426, 442
   Long-term capital 245
   Net operating 208, 316
   Passive activity limitation rules 211, 317
   Recognition 358
   Recognized 245
Losses 468, 476
Lump-sum assets 227

Mailbox rule 503
Main purpose rule 510
Majority interest tax year 419
Management 477
Marital deduction 285
Market discount bonds 251
Married filing
   Joint return 65
   Separate return 65
Meals and lodging 136, 149, 309
Mediating 369
Medical
   Expenses 168, 284
   Reimbursement plans 142
Merger 366, 450, 487
Minimum rental and personal use 143
Minority shareholders, subsidiary liquidation 364
Minors, contracts 506
Mirror image rule 502
Missionary sales 369
Mistake 509
   Mutual 509
   Unilateral 509
Mitigation 61
Modification 513
Modified Accelerated Cost Recovery System
   (MACRS) 234
Moment of dispatch 503
Money damages 486
Moving expenses 161
Multinational transactions 374
Multiple jurisdictions, taxes 368
Multistate Tax Commission 369
Mutual assent 501

Natural business year 420
Negligence 18, 32, 486
Negligent misrepresentation 32, 508
Net
   Earnings from self-employment 145
   Investment income tax (NIIT) 145
   Operating loss (NOL) 208, 316
   Rents and royalties 372
   Unearned income of dependent 54
Nexus 368, 369
Nonbusiness bad debt 249

Noncorporate
   Business entities 478
   Shareholder 363
Nonpartner capacity 441
Nonrecognition 364, 366
   Requirements 367
   Transactions 267
Nonrefundable personal credits 195
Non-U.S. taxpayer 328
Notes receivable 244
Notice of
   Assignment 520
   Deficiency (ND) 59
   Disbarment 15
   Suspension 15
Novation 480, 514

Occupational license tax 138
Offer 501
Office, in-home 369
Officers 485
Operating
   Agreement 476
   Days method 233
Operation 474
Operations, S corporations 394
Ordinary income 268
Organizational expense 304
Organizations
   50-percent limit 175
   Exempt 119
Original issue discount (OID) 311
Other adjustments account (OAA) 402

Parent-subsidiary 333
Parol evidence 512
   Rule 512
Partial
   Liquidation 360, 363
   Transfer 519
Partially disclosed principal 540
Partner
   Capital accounts 418
   Distributive share 424
   General 474
   Liabilities 474
   Limited 474, 475
   Partnership dealings 440
   Purchased interest 418
   Rights 474
Partners
   Duties of 470
   Powers of 470
   Rights of 469
Partnership
   Admission and withdrawal 471
   By estoppel 468
   Income 87
   Limited 474
      Liability 473
   Representative 429
   Return due 429
   Statement of authority 470

Index

Partnerships. 415, 439, 467
    Capital. 428
    General. 467
    Ordinary income. 423
    Services. 428
    Spouses. 428
Pass-through entities. 328
Passive
    Activity loss (PAL). 426
        Limitation rules. 211, 317, 401
    Investment income (PII). 391, 405
Patent. 372
Patient Protection and Affordable Care Act of
    2010 (ACA). 549
Payment, third party. 85
Payroll factor. 372
Penalty. 18, 162, 401, 429
    Accuracy-related. 57
    For disclosure. 20
    IRA. 163, 164
    Tax. 337
Percentage-of-completion. 117
Perfection of security interests. 564, 569
Performance. 515
Perpetual life. 488
Personal
    Interest expense. 172
    Property. 236
    Service corporation (PSC). 297
Persons
    Intoxicated. 506
    Lacking mental capacity. 506
Physical compulsion. 509
Piercing the corporate veil. 481
Plan of reorganization. 583
Points paid. 171
Political contributions. 142, 285
Possession of collateral. 565, 572
Power of attorney. 533
Powers of partners. 470
Practice
    Conduct of. 13
    Rules of. 11
    Who may. 12
Precontribution
    Gain. 424
    Loss. 361, 424
Preemptive rights. 483
Preferred shareholder. 482
Preincorporation
    Contracts. 479
    Subscription agreement. 480
Premature withdrawal penalties. 162
Prepaid income. 113
Principal. 122, 470, 532, 540
    Duties to. 536
Priority. 568
Private
    Activity bonds. 97
    Foundations. 120
    Letter rulings (PLR). 49
Privileged communication and confidentiality. 35
Privity. 33
Prizes. 91, 96
Pro rata distributions. 363
Procedural requirements of tax return preparers. . . . 18

Proceeds. 567
Professional
    Associations. 297
    Corporations. 479
    Ethics Division. 29
    Standards. 32
Profits and losses. 468, 476
Prohibited transactions. 119
Promise to pay. 112
Promissory estoppel. 505
Promoter. 479
Proof of claim. 580
Proper purpose. 483
Property. 441
    Contributed. 416
    Factor. 372
    For services. 228
    Tax. 138, 169
    Transactions. 223, 261
Proportionate distribution. 343
Protected in-state activities. 369
Public
    Law 86-272. 369
    Policy. 142
Punitive damages. 516
Purchase money security interest (PMSI). 566

Qualified
    Dependent. 69
    Exchange accommodation arrangement or
        agreement. 269
    Foreign taxes. 328
    Residence interest. 170
    Transportation fringe benefits. 147
Qualifying
    Child. 198
    Person. 66
    Relative. 198
    Widow(er). 68
Quasi-contract. 505

R&E expenditures. 310
Ratification. 506, 541
Real property. 236, 244, 278
Realized gain. 357
Reasonable
    Basis. 18
    Belief. 18
    Care. 32
    Person. 532
Recapitalization. 367
Recapture. 277
Receipt by an agent. 111
Recognized gain. 264, 416
Recordkeeping. 57
Records request. 13
Recovery
    Of tax benefit. 91
        Item. 98
    Tax benefits. 178
Recruiting. 369

Index

Redemption. 574
    Stock. 357
    U.S. Savings Bonds. 97
Reformation. 516
Refund. 58, 303, 337
Refundable credits. 202
Regulations, Treasury. 49
Reimbursement
    Employee expenses. 82
    Moving expenses. 82
Reincorporation. 367
Rejection. 502
Related party sales. 262
Release. 514
Reliance on others. 485
Remedies. 515, 516
Rent. 86, 136
    Prepaid. 86, 111
Rental
    Income. 86
    Property. 143
    Real estate. 212
    Value of parsonage. 99
Reorganizations. 365, 583
    Types. 366
Replevin. 516
Reportable transactions. 17
    Listed. 17
Reporting
    Corporate liquidation. 362
    Requirements. 429
Repossession. 265, 572
Required writing. 510, 511
Res. 122
Rescission. 516
    Mutual. 513
Research Credit. 201
Respondeat superior. 481, 543
Restitution. 517
Restoration. 225
Restraint of trade. 507
Retirement Savings Contribution Credit. 197
Return preparer. 16
Revenue
    Procedure. 49
    Ruling. 49
Reviewers and contributors. iv
Revised
    Model Business Corporation Act (RMBCA). . . . 479
    Uniform
        Limited Partnership Act (RULPA). 474
        Partnership Act (RUPA). 467
        Principal and Income Act. 122
Revocability of assignments. 520
Revocation. 502, 545
Right
    Assignable. 519
    To
        Assign. 519
        Sublease. 519
Rights of partners. 469
Roth IRA. 163
Royalties. 87
Rule, main purpose. 510

Rules
    And regulations, disregard of. 57
    Of practice. 11

S corporation. 307, 389, 479
    Income. 87
    Reported items. 394
    Stock basis. 398
Safe harbor. 363
Sale. 244
    Installment. 264, 280
    Of principal residence. 273
    Partnership interest. 426
    Related party. 262
    Treatment. 358
Sales factor. 372
Samples. 369
Sanctions for violations. 15
Schedule
    D. 247
    K. 429
Scholarships/fellowships. 82, 96
Scienter. 508
Sec.
    179 expense. 238
    351 exchange for stock. 280, 299
    444 election. 420
    1202 Qualified Small Business Stock. 274
    1231 property. 276
    1245 ordinary income. 268, 278
    1250 ordinary income. 268, 278
Secured transactions. 561
    Third party rights. 572
Securities
    And Exchange Commission (SEC). 30
    Debt. 482
    Equity. 482
Security
    Agreement. 561
    Interest. 562, 563, 566
        Perfection. 564
Self-
    Dealing. 485
    Employed
        Health insurance payments. 161
        Individuals contributions. 161
    Employment
        Income. 135
        Net earnings. 145
        Tax. 145, 161
    Tender. 487
Separately stated items. 421
    S corporations. 395
Services. 417, 440, 441
    Intra-family. 94
Shareholder. 479, 482
    Property contribution. 299
    Reorganizations. 365
    Rights of. 483
    Suit. 484
    Treatment. 340, 358, 362, 403
Shifting of income. 62

Short
- Sales. 250
- Tax year. 110
- -Term capital. 245

Signature. 18, 429
Simple trust. 122
Single, tax status. 65
Sinking-fund income. 303
Small business stock. 249
SmartAdapt. 2
Social Security
- Benefits. 89
- Tax. 144

Solely for stock. 299
Soliciting orders. 369
Specific
- Performance. 516
- Transaction. 620

Split. 450
- Stock. 344, 482

Spousal support. 285
Standard deduction. 166
Start-up costs. 141, 249
State boards of accountancy. 29
Stated minimum amount. 440
Statement of
- Dissociation. 471
- Dissolution. 472

Statute of
- Frauds. 467, 510
- Limitations. 60, 515

Statutory violations. 507
Stock. 309
- Distributions. 343
- Dividends. 98, 482
- In trade. 244
- Loss. 249
- Reacquisition. 358
- Redemptions. 311, 357
- Rights. 343
- Split. 344, 482
- Subscription agreement. 480

Straight-line depreciation. 233
Strict
- Foreclosure. 574
- Liability in tort. 33
- Performance. 513

Student loan interest deduction. 164
Subchapter C E&P. 404
Sublease. 519
Submission, frivolous. 18
Subpart F income. 375
Subsidiary. 369
- Liquidation. 364

Substantial
- Performance. 513
- Understatement. 57

Substantially
- All of a return. 11
- Disproportionate. 359

Supreme Court. 51
Suretyship. 510
Suspension. 15

Tax. 138, 169, 313
- Ad valorem. 169
- Advisors, best practices. 14
- Attributes. 364
- Authority. 48
- Avoidance. 64
- Brackets. 328
- Built-in gains. 406
- Corporate. 357
- Computations. 327
- Court. 51
- Credits. 195
- Employment. 139
- Estimated payments. 336
- Evasion. 19, 64
- -Exempt income. 142
- Gift. 283, 285
- Income. 139, 170
- Unrelated business. 121
- Kiddie. 54
- Liability. 54
- Understatement of. 19
- Limit on benefits. 334
- Matters partner (TMP). 429
- Medicare. 144
- Multiple jurisdictions. 368
- Occupational license. 138
- Partnership year. 419
- Passive investment income (PII). 405
- Payments, estimated. 52
- Planning. 62
- Procedures. 52
- Property. 138, 169
- Rates. 123
- Regular income. 328
- Return. 55
- Positions. 16
- Preparers. 16
- Not subject. 16
- Procedural requirements of. 18
- Sales. 138
- Self-employment. 145, 161
- Social Security. 144
- Unemployment. 146
- Withholding. 380
- Year. 110, 297, 330, 392, 416

Taxable income. 166
Taxation. 246, 469, 477
Taxpayer
- Consent to disclosure. 20
- Copy of return. 18
- Information, disclosure of. 19

Tender offers. 487
Termination. 471
- By the parties. 545
- Corporations. 488
- Of
- Offer. 502
- Partnership. 450
- Operation of law. 545
- Redemptions. 359
- S corporations. 391

Time value of money. 62
Timing of income recognition. 62
Tips. 111

Tort. 32
    Liability. 542
Trade
    Expense. 135
    Restraints, Contracts. 507
Training. 369
Transactions, fraudulent. 19
Transfer
    Corporation. 365
    Partial. 519
    Pricing. 375
Transferable interest, partner's. 469
Travel
    Expenses. 137, 309
    Lodging. 137
Treasure trove. 91
Treasury stock. 302
Trustee. 484, 577
    Powers. 578
Trusts. 109, 122

U.S.
    Supreme Court. 51
    Tax Court. 59
UCC Article 9. 561
Ultra vires. 481
Ultrahazardous activity. 544
Understatement of tax liability. 19
Undisclosed principal. 540
Undue influence. 510
Unearned income, net. 54
Unemployment. 548
    Benefits. 88
    Tax. 146
Unenforceable contracts. 500
Uniform
    Capitalization rules. 226
    Div. of Income for Tax Purp. Act (UDITPA). . . . 371
Unilateral contracts. 500
Unit of production method. 233
Unrealized
    Income. 94
    Receivables (URs). 427
Unrelated business income tax. 121
Unrestrained claim. 303
Use of capital. 440

Vacant land. 142
Valid contracts. 500
Vicarious liability. 543
Violations, sanctions for. 15
Void contracts. 500
Voidable contracts. 500, 508
Voting rights. 483

Wages. 547
Warranties. 520
Wash sales. 248
Willful evasion of tax liability. 19
Winding up. 472, 475
Withholding. 52

Work Opportunity Tax Credit. 201
Working papers. 36
Worthless securities. 311
Writing requirement. 510, 511